Warman's®

COUNTRY
ANTIQUES PRICE GUIDE

Don & Elizabeth
JOHNSON

Published by

700 E. State Street • Iola, WI 54990-0001
Telephone: 715/445-2214

www.krause.com

Please, call or write us for our free catalog of publications.
Our toll-free number to place an order or obtain a free catalog is 800-258-0929
or please use our regular business telephone, 715-445-2214.

Library of Congress Catalog Number: 2001088101
ISBN: 0-87349-219-6

Printed in the United States of America

DEDICATIONS

To my parents, who instilled in me a love of the simple things in life—the wonder of newborn chicks, the taste of a pear fresh off the tree in the side yard, the uncomplicated joy of bouncing a ball off the side of Grandma and Grandpa Burley's barn. More importantly, I treasure the moral and spiritual values you instilled in our family. You are a gift from God, and I love you.

To my Lord and Savior, who calmed the rough waters under a boat filled with faithless disciples, and who stilled my soul when I stepped out of my selfishness and invited Him into my life. You are the best gift from God, and I worship you.

Don Johnson

To Carrie and Hope, who admirably cope with the upheaval that ensues when we are on deadline, even if it does mean eating an entire bag of Hershey's Kisses for breakfast and then playing firefighter in your underwear and workboots while brandishing butterfly nets! I love you.

Mama

ACKNOWLEDGMENTS

To Kris Manty, our editor—The projects just keep getting smoother. Thanks for another fine job from your end in Iola. Someday we may actually make a deadline!

To Ellen Schroy, author of numerous *Warman's* titles and the backbone of Krause Publication's line of antiques and collectibles books—We've said it before; we'll say it again. You're the best! Your advice is unfailing. Your friendship is treasured. Now, if we could just keep you away from those slippery steps.

To a very special friend—You kept both the coffee and the encouragement flowing and provided a quiet haven to escape to during those times when the mountain of work seemed insurmountable.

We would also like to thank the following, who were instrumental in submitting catalogs and providing assistance with illustrations for this book. We cannot adequately express our appreciation. Without your help, this project would not have been possible. Thank you!

Alderfer's
501 Fairgrounds Rd.
Hatfield, PA 19440
(215) 393-3000
www.alderfercompany.com

Buffalo Bay Auction Co.
5244 Quam Circle
Rogers, MN 55374
(763) 428-8480
www.buffalobayauction.com

Carr Auction & Real Estate
West Highway 156, P.O. Box 300
909 Auction Ave.
Larned, KS 67550
(316) 285-3148
www.carrauction.com

Barry and Barbara Carter
Knightstown Antique Mall
136 W. Carey St.
Knightstown, IN 46148
(765) 356-5665

Collectors Auction Services
RR 2, Box 431 Oakwood Rd.
Oil City, PA 16301
(814) 677-6070
www.caswel.com

Cyr Auction Co.
P.O. Box 1238
100 Lewiston Rd.
Gray, ME 04039
(207) 657-5253
www.cyrauction.com

C. Wesley Cowan
747 Park Ave.
Terrace Park, OH 45174
(513) 248-8122
www.historicamericana.com

Doug Davies Auctions
P.O. Box 5542
Lafayette, IN 47903
(765) 449-4515
www.daviesauctions.com

Fricker Auctions
P.O. Box 852
Bloomington, IL 61702
(309) 663-5828
www.frickerauctions.com

Garth's Auctions, Inc.
2690 Stratford Road
P.O. Box 369
Delaware, OH 43015
(740) 362-4771
www.garths.com

Gary Metz's Muddy River Trading
Company
P.O. Box 1430
Salem, VA 24153
(540) 387-5070

Green Valley Auctions, Inc.
2259 Green Valley Lane
Mt. Crawford, VA 22841
(540) 434-4260
www.greenvalleyauctions.com

John Hathaway (fruit jars)
3 Mills Road
Bryant Pond ME 04219-6320
(207) 665-2124
www.megalink.net/~meidea

Horst Auctioneers
50 Durlach Dr.
Ephrata, PA 17522
(717) 859-1331

Jackson's Auctioneers & Appraisers
2229 Lincoln St.
Cedar Falls, IA 50613
(319) 277-2256
www.jacksonauctions.com

Dave Kessler Auctioneers
510 Greenbriar Dr.
Richmond, IN 47374
(765) 965-1492
www.kesslerauctions.com

Wm Morford
RD#2
Cazenovia, NY 13035
(315) 662-7625
www.morfauction.com

Sandy Rosnick Auctions
15 Front Street
Salem, MA 01970
(978) 741-1130

Skinner, Inc.
The Heritage on the Garden
63 Park Plaza
Boston, MA 02116
(617) 350-5400
www.skinnerinc.com

Skinner, Inc.
357 Main St.
Bolton, MA 01740
(978) 779-6241
www.skinnerinc.com

SoldUSA
6415 Idlewild Rd.
Suite 207
Charlotte, NC 28212
(704) 364-2900
www.SoldUSA.com

Southern Folk Pottery Collectors
Society
220 Washington St.
Bennett, NC 27208
(336) 581-4246

Bruce and Vicki Waasdorp
P.O. Box 434
10931 Main St.
Clarence, NY 14031
(761) 759-2361
www.antiques-stoneware.com

Andrew Walther and Shane Hawkins
Walther & Hawkins
218 W. Main St.
Centerville, IN 47330

INTRODUCTION

In the early 1970s, when my mother bought a high-back dry sink at auction for $150, my Grandma Burley just shook her head. Grandma looked at the dry sink, adorned in a dirty coat of white paint, and figured her daughter belonged in an asylum. In her mind, $150 was a ridiculous amount of money to spend on any piece of furniture, much less something that had already been used in another person's home. (Of course, this was the woman who, if she needed a piece of furniture, would slip on an apron, go to her workshop, and make it herself.)

Once refinished, that poplar dry sink was a part of my parents' dining room for years. Today, however, it has a place of honor in my living room. I lured it away from my mother by dangling a rather large carrot in front of her—an unusual dry sink with wainscoting sides and pressed-wood panels of sheaths of wheat flanking the wide single door. I had picked up the wainscoted dry sink at a farm auction while living in southern Indian. Of course, "picked up" is a relative term. With its expansive top, it nearly filled the bed of my truck. The easy part was getting it home from the auction. Moving it into the house was another matter entirely, not just because it equaled the combined weight of the defensive line of any given NFL team, but because it nearly took the Corps of Engineers and a guy named Bubba to figure out a way to force it through the widest doorway in the house without resorting to the use of a small nuclear device to clear a path. As much as I loved that dry sink, and as much as I hated the thought of having to coerce the thing back through the doorway, I jumped at the chance to swap it for the high-back example that, regardless of how remote, had family ties.

In the years since I've owned that high-back dry sink, it has displayed and stored a variety of things, from stoneware to compact disks. But nothing is more valuable than what's found there now—numerous family photographs. It's a fitting combination. After all, no category of antiques seems more deeply rooted in the concept of family than country. When I think of country, my mind races barefoot through the grass to my grandparents' farm. It's there I hold special memories of my childhood, from crawling inside a barrel and rolling down the slope beside the bank barn to grabbing a splint basket to help gather eggs. My grandparents, like that barn and the earthen embankment that leaned against it, are gone now. But memories of them and that place remain vivid in my mind.

But, don't fool yourself into thinking that country antiques are all related to the farm.

Can you define that?

What's country? When it comes to antiques, you can ask that question to 12 people and get a dozen different answers. Some immediately think of farm items, such as milking stools and weather vanes. Those fit. For others, the term country conjures up thoughts of primitives, such as pie safes and stoneware. There's nothing wrong with that. Yet others envision early items, such as mocha ware and Windsor chairs. That's okay, too.

Actually, everyone is right. However, to truly understand what country is, you have to go where it's being sold. There's no better place to refine your definition than Nashville, Tenn., the site of Heart of Country Antiques Show. The leading country-themed show in the United States, Heart of Country, along with several other country-related antique shows that run simultaneously, is held twice a year. As a biannual barometer, Heart of Country indicates that most collectors have only a limited interest in items that are strictly farm-

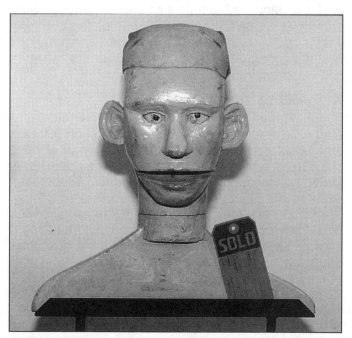

Today's country market isn't just about pie safes and stoneware. Items with a folk-art quality, such as this carved-wooden puppet head, fit in perfectly with more traditional wares.

related. Instead, today's marketplace for all things country has become more refined.

Country is now synonymous with Americana. The country movement in the 21st century emphasizes the decorative aspect. In their search for just the right item to hang on a wall, place on a shelf, or display in the corner of a den, collectors increasingly turn two directions. First, they're returning to the roots of the country genre—early American furniture and accessories. When it comes to country, "Made in the U.S.A." carries more clout than any union label ever could. Second, collectors are paying particular attention to vintage items with a folkish look.

Shoppers are also demanding strength in what they buy, wanting bang for their buck. A Windsor fan-back side chair isn't good enough if they can afford one with bold bulbous turnings. They aren't satisfied any more with a simple red-and-black game board; they want one in green and yellow with gallery ends.

Consider one Parcheesi board that sold at auction by Skinner, Inc., in 2000. Wooden with a multicolor design in original paint, it was estimated to bring $2,000 to $3,000. Bidders thought otherwise, taking the piece to an astounding $17,250. The folkish character of the board certainly boosted the bidding, particularly when the market for folk art is as strong as ever. Bright original paint was also instrumental in determining the final price. Collectors are willing to pay a premium for items in original condition. Whether it's the brightly painted surface of a dower chest or the fine patina of a tiger maple corner cupboard in untouched finish, buyers will dig deep into their bank accounts when it comes to originality.

King of the mountain

Regardless of the category, whether it's Gaudy ironstone or seed boxes, condition remains the most important factor in determining the value of an item in today's marketplace. Auctioneer Gary Metz, who specializes in antique advertising, explains it this way: "Condition rules the roost."

Buyers are putting faith in the sage advice offered by countless dealers and collectors over the years: Buy the best you can afford. Most collectors purchase out of passion rather than for investment potential alone. Yet, wise buyers know that an item in excellent condition is much more likely to increase in value than the same piece in lesser shape. The marketplace is full of tattered quilts, but find one in pristine condition and, despite how ordinary the pattern might be, a collector will take a second look and probably start reaching for her

checkbook. It's in searching for those top-notch examples that the hunt really begins.

Rarity still plays an important role in today's country marketplace. Nonetheless, most buyers will closely scrutinize even the rarest item for condition problems. A unique Shaker basket would no doubt draw strong interest from the ever-competitive community of Shaker collectors. But if that item has been spray-painted and nibbled on by mice, interest in that rarity will dwindle. After all, who wants a basket that's a basket case?

Points for originality

Most collectors are purists when it comes to country items—they understand the need for restoration, but they prefer pieces in great original condition. Sometimes, however, the line between original and altered can be blurred. That's especially true when considering painted items.

Anyone who collected during the 1970s probably recalls the mistakes of our past. There was a time when people looked at original paint and reached for a can of stripper. The true value of an item was quickly diminished because we mistakenly thought a pie safe's original red paint was second-rate in comparison to the potential beauty of varnished wood.

Today, collectors recognize the character and value inherent in original surfaces. Painted furniture and accessories are among the most sought-after of all country items. Unfortunately, competition translates into higher prices, which has encouraged unscrupulous sellers to fake "original paint."

How do you distinguish good paint from bad? That can be a problem. In the late 1980s, I visited a shop run from an old barn in central Penn-

Some of the most popular country antiques have been reproduced. Is this toleware coffeepot a 19th-century original or a cleverly crafted 20th-century copy?

sylvania. As I examined a cupboard in what I perceived to be beautiful old paint, the dealer informed me that the cupboard was old, but the paint job was new. I was amazed. "My boy does a good job," she said of the man she hired to create the look of an old painted surface. Good was definitely an understatement. The man was a Rembrandt when it came to faking painted surfaces. The scary thing was that an entire section of the barn was filled with his handiwork.

The cupboard's paint showed wear in all the appropriate places, and I think it would have fooled most people. Although the dealer was honest with her customers, telling them the paint on some of her furniture wasn't original, subsequent sellers might not be as generous with that information. As for that cupboard I examined nearly 15 years ago, I can only image how much more natural it must look today, having been in use in someone's home since that time.

Since some newly painted items on today's market are good enough to fool even long-time dealers and collectors, what's a buyer to do to keep from getting taken?

First, know your dealer. The best antique dealers understand that their business is only as good as their reputation. As such, they are honest and fair with their customers. I can think of countless dealers I wouldn't hesitate to buy from, whether I was spending $20 or $20,000. While I know that I need to do my own homework before buying an item, I also know that I can trust what they tell me about a piece. And, most importantly, I know they will honestly describe any defects or restoration.

Second, don't spend a large sum of money without getting a money-back guarantee that describes in detail the item you are buying, including its age and any defects or restoration. Many reputable dealers and most major auction houses have such a policy in place. However, don't expect to get that same peace of mind from antique malls or smaller auction companies. In those venues, the rule is still *caveat emptor*—let the buyer beware. Their policy can be summed up in three words: All sales final.

Especially in those cases where you're on your own to determine the legitimacy of an item, use common sense to judge the item's authenticity. Examine all the surfaces. Does the paint or patina look right? Is there wear in the appropriate places? If an item is painted, is the paint more vivid in corners and other areas where it would have been less likely to fade from exposure to light? Feel the surface. Are there rough edges that might indicate newly cut

pieces of wood? Smell it. That may sound strange, but you'd be surprised what you can learn when you close your eyes and conduct an examination with your nose. The smell of fresh paint or varnish should immediately send up a red flag warning you that the finish isn't original. The scent of sawdust might indicate additions or new construction.

The most important thing you can do to keep from being fooled is to walk into a shop, show, or auction with a brain oozing with knowledge gained from practical experience. Find a dealer or collector who is willing to mentor you. Hands-on learning is still the best education you can get. Handle as many authentic items as possible. After you've held enough pieces of decorated stoneware, it's much easier to tell when a piece has been faked. It will look wrong. When you pick it up, it will most likely feel wrong. Most professional auctioneers and dealers understand the importance of spending time educating collectors.

Four troublemakers

Just as Mary couldn't seem to shake that pesky little lamb of hers, the antiques and collectibles industry has four tagalongs of its own: reproductions, fakes, forgeries, and fantasy items.

Of the four, the reproductions category is the only one that isn't always considered something akin to the Black Death. When properly marked and dated, reproductions serve as a valuable tool to help fill holes in collections. A well-made reproduction silhouette is an inexpensive alternative when an original is either unavailable or unaffordable. Reproductions that are clearly marked remove the question of whether a collector is getting the real thing or is being stuck with an imposter.

Not all reproductions are a bad thing, provided they're clearly marked. This new hooked rug makes a great addition to a country home at a fraction of the cost of an original.

Fakes, forgeries, and fantasy items have always had a negative connotation on the antiques market. Whether handled by unwitting dealers or unscrupulous sellers, these pieces have caused much wailing and gnashing of teeth on the part of collectors who later learned they had spent good money for bad merchandise.

What's a collector to do? Study. Subscribe to newsletters. Talk to other dealers and collectors. As much as possible, handle legitimate merchandise, as well as the reproductions, fakes, forgeries, and fantasy items. Hands-on experience is still the best teacher.

The ever-shrinking world

Just as the definition of country antiques has changed over the years, so has the marketplace for those objects. Finding the best items used to mean making a cross-country trip to one of the better antique shows or visiting the shop of a well-known dealer. Now, fantastic merchandise is as close as the nearest computer connected to the Internet.

The World Wide Web hasn't completely altered the face of the country market, but it does provide people with another place to buy and sell. And don't be fooled into thinking that smalls are the only things offered online. One dealer recently told us his family frequently ships large pieces of furniture cross-country to customers. The cost to ship a step-back cupboard 2,000 miles is often no more than the buyer would have paid in sales tax had he purchased the piece locally.

The biggest complaint we hear (and sometimes make ourselves) is that sellers on the Internet aren't honest about the condition of items. Internet auctions can be especially brutal when it comes to

The Internet allows buyers to shop from the comfort of their own home. It only takes a few clicks of the mouse to buy everything from spatterware to corner cupboards.

unknowledgeable or unscrupulous sellers misrepresenting merchandise, especially when dealing with condition. Nothing can take the place of personally examining an antique that catches your fancy. When that's not a possibility, potential buyers shouldn't hesitate to ask questions. Never buy from a seller who doesn't or won't fully answer your questions.

We strongly recommend that anyone buying on the Internet deal only with sellers who have a written policy guaranteeing customer satisfaction. Reputable online dealers, as well as those who work from traditional brick-and-mortar storefronts, won't hesitate to refund your money if you're unhappy with a purchase.

Cyberspace is a wonderful tool that many dealers and auctioneers have used to expand their business, and it's been the number-one factor in erasing the gap between regional pricing differences. A collector stuck in East Calf's Tongue, Neb., in the dead of winter is no longer isolated from the rest of the antiquing world if he has a computer and Internet access. Suddenly, he is a viable buyer in the world marketplace.

The concept of selling to people who don't have direct access to an item has long been the driving force behind mail-order sales and absentee auctions, thanks to catalogs for each. The Internet has simply expanded on the premise that you can buy great antiques without leaving the comfort of your home.

Although the Internet has leveled the playing field as far as prices are concerned, there's no guarantee that those prices will rise as a result. As with any other commodity, antiques sold on the Internet are subject to the laws of supply and demand. Common items generally attract little or no interest. Try selling an ordinary aqua quart Ball Perfect Mason fruit jar on eBay, and you'll be lucky to get a bid. However, rare and desirable items offered through online auctions usually sell for top-dollar. List a Hamilton No. 3 Glass Works fruit jar and watch as the bidding soars.

Treasures lost

There is, of course, life beyond the Internet. While that venue provides collectors with an excellent source for country antiques, many people still enjoy the adrenaline rush that accompanies walking into a mom-and-pop back-roads antique shop that has early Currier and Ives prints hanging next to vintage cherry corner cupboards filled with Historical Staffordshire. Nothing can beat the thrill of the hunt. Although those shops seemed plentiful 15 years ago, they're few and far between today. Two things

This painted sign has a great country look. It was found at an estate auction.

As those old-time shops closed, the antiques business lost many of its great treasures. Gone was the opportunity to rummage through a shop, but, more importantly, collectors lost personal contact with knowledgeable dealers who were often eager to answer questions and pass along information about the items they sold.

Fortunately, not all antique shops have gone the way of the 5-cent Coke. Many fine businesses, big and small, still exist, and collectors still have some options when it comes to finding country items. Antique malls continue to play a large role in the marketplace, as do antique shows and auctions. While many of those markets specialize in country furniture and accessories, their reputations generally draw a strong contingent of collectors. A larger pool of interested buyers often translates into fewer bargain prices. However, we frequently hear from collectors who have made wonderful buys—both in terms of desirability and price—in other arenas. One of our favorite purchases in recent years, a painted wooden sign promoting a cure, was bought at an advertising auction. We've also made good finds at flea markets, antique malls, and estate auctions.

Parting words

Everything we've written to this point is worthless if you don't remember two simple words: Have fun. Collecting should be a hobby. Enjoy it. Share it with your friends and family members. Revel in the opportunity to hunt for great merchandise. Rejoice in a wonderful find. And, if the passion for collecting ever becomes an aggravating, obsessive search that leaves you kicking the cat and mad at the world, it's time to sell your frakturs and yellowware and take up bonsai.

Collecting should be fun. We hope it always remains so. Enjoy the hunt!

Don Johnson

caused their demise. First, many were run by older dealers who have since retired or died. Second, the proliferation of antique malls, combined with the popularity of the Internet, gave those dealers other outlets through which to sell their merchandise. They no longer had to pay the overhead to keep a shop when they could rent a booth in a mall or offer their merchandise to a worldwide market online.

ABOUT THE BOOK

Put that in writing

After much study and research, and with a newly refined definition of country, we set out to create a price guide that would accurately reflect the changes that have occurred in that market. You won't find art pottery in *Warman's Country*, but there are numerous listings for blue-and-white pottery. Search all you want at the best country-related antique shows; you'll be hard pressed to find a piece of Depression glass. That's why we've not included it here. But, we do include bride's bottles and early flasks.

Remember when spinning wheels were a popular logo on the business cards of antique dealers? Once an icon of the country movement, spinning wheels are no longer fiercely contested when offered at auction. They're also seldom seen at today's country antique shows. Almost no one wants them. However, painted boxes, which are easy to display and always functional, generate fierce competition whenever they come onto the market. In response to these trends, our listings emphasize the boxes, while giving minimal attention to spinning wheels.

More than just values

As part of Warman's Encyclopedia of Antiques and Collectibles, this book goes beyond merely providing values for the items listed. Additional information sure to be of value to readers includes:

Background: If you like something enough to look it up in a price guide, chances are good you want to know a little bit more about it. We include background information for each category.

References: Due to the seemingly infinite number of books covering the antiques and collectibles industry, we limited reference works to titles we believe provide the most useful historical information as well as accurate prices. Most of the titles listed are readily available from booksellers. Some out-of-print books are also listed, but these can be located on the Internet or by contacting a specialty bookseller.

Periodicals: The advantage to periodicals comes in their ability to keep abreast of a changing marketplace. Newsletters are great sources of insider information. Weekly and monthly trade papers and magazines can help you understand and follow the market. We have included those publications we consider helpful.

Collectors' Clubs: It's hard to keep a good thing to yourself. Collectors love to share their enthusiasm with others, and collectors' clubs offer the perfect avenue for that. We've included many clubs, but there may be others we are not aware of. Use our suggestions as a starting point, but don't hesitate to ask fellow collectors and dealers about other clubs they may know of.

Museums: The best way to acquaint yourself with a specific field is to study as many examples as possible. For this reason, we have listed museums that maintain significant collections in specific areas. Of course, you can never go wrong by making a trip to the Smithsonian Institution in Washington, D.C.

Reproduction Alerts: Reproductions remain a problem throughout the antiques and collectibles trade. When we were aware of reproductions within a specific category, we used this alert to call your attention to them.

Collecting Hints: In many categories, we've included tidbits of information that provide further insight into a category or that help to put the marketplace in perspective.

About those listings

We've tried to provide listings that are more detailed than those found in most other price guides. Vague or incomplete listings have always been the wobbly leg of the antiques industry. If a

This booth typifies the country motif. The market for country antiques is as much about an overall look as it is about individual items.

price guide simply states "ABC plate" without any further description, then the value given is useless. Those pieces of educational dinnerware were made from a variety of materials, from porcelain to tin, and their designs and colors are tremendously important when determining value. The same holds true for most other country items, from chests of drawers to hooked rugs.

With more than 6,000 listings, we've included detailed descriptions whenever possibly. Our intent is to provide readers with a visual image of the object, noting variations, colors, sizes, etc. When comparing an actual item to a listing in this book, we hope it will be readily apparent whether or not you're looking at the same thing that we have described here.

And just how did we determine the values listed in this book? We consulted the experts. The vast majority of the listings were derived from prices paid during cataloged sales conducted by major American auction houses. The advantage to this is that you know someone actually paid that price for the item listed. Why is that important? Consider the couple that took a doll to an antique show to get an idea of what it was worth. The verbal estimates they received ranged from $200 to $20,000. We find auction prices to be a more reliable indicator of the market.

The prices we have included are as current as possible, with most of the items having sold within the past year. Prices realized for game boards offered at auction three years ago would not accurately reflect the current market, particularly in light of the present infatuation with those pieces.

Because we worked extensively from auction catalogs, we were at the mercy of the auctioneers who provided the descriptions for their merchandise. Keep in mind that the process of describing any item is not an exact science. That's especially true when considering condition. Fortunately, the auctioneers we worked with created detailed catalogs. Unfortunately, there was not always agreement as to which terminology to use.

For the most part, our listings reflect their usage of terms and descriptions. In addition, we relied on their measurements, which are generally accurate to within one-quarter of an inch.

Not all of the items included in this book are in pristine condition. In a perfect world, every piece of spatterware would be chip-free, every blanket chest would have its original feet, and every highboy would be festooned with original hardware. But such is not the case. Items are damaged and hardware needs to be replaced. We've intentionally listed items in as-found condition in order to more appropriately represent the true market.

We've limited the number of abbreviations in the descriptions in order to reduce the need to search for a key to explain those truncated words. Since price guides generally sound as if Tonto wrote them, we've also tried to make our descriptions less stilted.

Closing words

We hope you like what you see and that you find this book useful. If you would like to share any information you might have regarding reference material, clubs, museums, etc., we would love to hear from you. Auctioneers who conduct cataloged sales specializing in country-related items and Americana are encouraged to submit catalogs and prices realized for inclusion in the future editions.

We're always glad to hear what readers think. You can contact us at:

Don and Elizabeth Johnson
5110 S. Greensboro Pike
Knightstown, IN 46148
djohnson@spitfire.net

"Do not store up for yourselves treasures on earth, where moth and rust destroy, and where thieves break in and steal. But store up for yourselves treasures in heaven, where moth and rust do not destroy, and where thieves do not break in and steal. For where your treasure is, there your heart will be also. —Matthew 6:19-21

ABBREVIATIONS

c. = circa
C. = century
cond. = condition
d = deep
decor = decorated
dia = diameter
ed.= edition
EXC = excellent
gal = gallon(s)
ground = background
h = high
illus = illustrated
l = long
litho = lithographed
NM = near mint
mkd = marked
orig = original
oz = ounces
pc = piece(s)
pr = pair
pt = pint
qt = quart
sq = square
unmkd = unmarked
vol. = volume(s)
w = wide

ABC Plates

Background: Most ABC plates were imported to the United States from England. They were highly popular between 1780 and 1860, when literacy rates were low. Originally available for only a few cents, they served a practical purpose on the table while also affording an inexpensive education.

References: Susan and Al Bagdade, *Warman's English & Continental Porcelain*, 3rd ed., Krause Publications, 1998; Irene and Ralph Lindsay, *ABC Plates & Mugs*, Collector Books, 1998; Margaret and Kenn Whitmyer, *Collector's Encyclopedia of Children's Dishes*, Collector Books, 1993.

Collectors' Club: ABC Plate & Mug Collectors, 67 Stevens Ave., Old Bridge, NJ 08857.

Collecting Hint: Condition problems such as chips, cracks, and knife marks quickly reduce the value of an item.

Also See: Staffordshire Transferwares.

Ironstone, plate
  Child on daybed with angels hovering above, black transfer, accents in red, blue, yellow and green, J.&G. Meakin, 5-1/4" dia 200.00
  "Crusoe Rescues Friday," brown transfer, green and blue accents, 7-1/4" dia 190.00
  "Crusoe Viewing the Island," brown transfer, yellow and blue accents, 8-1/4" dia 200.00
  Donkey's head surrounded by holly, thistles and birds in flight, black transfer, A. Meir & Son, discoloring, 8-1/2" dia 95.00
  Farmer and cattle, black transfer, accents in red, green, yellow and blue, J.&G. Meakin, 4-1/2" dia 180.00

Staffordshire ABC plate, scene of Rugby players, 6-3/4" dia, $150.

Hay wagon, black transfer, accents in yellow, red, blue and black, J.&G. Meakin, 4-1/2" dia ... 150.00
"Little Boys at Marbles Play on the Summer Holiday," black transfer, accented in green, red and blue, Elsmore & Forster, 5-1/2" dia 170.00
Man in Colonial dress with soldier tipping his hat to black man, pink transfer, hairline, minor discoloring, 5" dia 90.00
"A Sioux Indian Chief," Indian on horseback, brown transfer, nick, glaze wear, 8-1/4" dia 120.00
"The Soldiers," boy and dog dressed as soldiers, pink transfer, discoloring, 7" dia 160.00
"Swallow," bird on left half, ABCs on right, brown transfer, accents in red, blue and green, discoloring, 7-3/8" dia 90.00
"Titmouse," bird on left half, ABCs on right, brown transfer, accents in red, blue green and yellow, discoloring, 8-1/4" dia 110.00
Pearlware, plate, "Christmas Day," child eating, black transfer, black stripe, molded scroll design band, F.&B. Godwin, New Wharf, 7" dia 340.00
Porcelain, plate
  "Chairs to Mend," man carrying chairs, 8-1/2" dia 220.00
  "For My Nephew" and "JLK," boys at play, pink transfer, Staffordshire, 5-5/8" dia 150.00
  "Franklin's Proverb" and "Keep Thy Shop and Thy Shop Will Keep Thee," black transfer, accents in green, blue, yellow and red, two glaze flakes, 6-1/8" dia 150.00
  "Nightingale," brown transfer, polychrome decor, E.M. & Co., imperfections, 6-1/4" dia 110.00
  "The New Pony," black transfer, accents in red, green and blue, discolored, 5-1/8" dia.........110.00
  Scottish hunters with dogs behind rocks, brown transfer, minor discoloring, 6-7/8" dia 80.00
  "Trap Bat & Ball" and "GHI," children playing with ball and bat, pink transfer, Charles Allerton & Sons, crack, 5-7/8" dia 130.00
  "The Walk," rider on horse, black transfer, accents in red, yellow and green, minor discoloring, 6" dia 170.00
Tin, mug
  "A Good Girl," black letters, yellow ground, 2-1/4" h, 3" dia 325.00
  Band of flowers, 1-7/8" h, 2-3/4" dia 175.00
Tin, plate
  "God Save the Union Now and Forever," four pinholes, 6-3/4" dia... 70.00
  "Liberty," boy and girl reading from newspaper, 5-5/8" dia 60.00
  Plain, ABCs border, minor rust, 6-1/4" dia 120.00
  Two cats playing with yarn, red border, yellow and black letters, Ohio Art Co., 4-1/4" dia 100.00
  "Washington," bust of George Washington, 13 stars in arch, rust, significant dents, three pinholes, 5-5/8" dia 70.00
  "Who Killed Cock Robin?" embossed, 7-3/4" dia 121.00

Advertising

Background: Advertisers of the 19th and early 20th centuries understood the necessity of catching the attention of potential customers. Colorful graphics were an important feature of mass-produced advertising items beginning in the late 1800s. Not only did bright, creative packaging attract attention, it also helped customers identify and locate a particular brand during an era in which many people could not read. Those same colorful designs serve as head-turners for today's collectors, just as they did for buyers of a bygone era.

References: Bob and Sharon Huxford, *Huxford's Collectible Advertising*, 4th ed., Collector Books, 1999; Don and Elizabeth Johnson, *Warman's Advertising*, Krause Publications, 2000; Robert Reed, *Advertising Postcards*, Schiffer Publishing, 2001.

Periodical: *Advertising Collectors Express Newsletter*, P.O. Box 221, Mayview, MO 64071.

Collectors' Clubs: Advertising Cup & Mug Collectors of America, P.O. Box 680, Solon, IA 52333; Antique Advertising Assoc. of America, P.O. Box 1121, Morton Grove, IL 60053, www.pastime.org; Farm Machinery Advertising Collectors, 10108 Tamarack Dr., Vienna, VA 22182; The National Assoc. of Paper & Advertising Collectors, P.O. Box 500, Mount Joy, PA 17552; Porcelain Advertising Collectors Club, P.O. Box 381, Marshfield Hills, MA 02151-0381.

Collecting Hint: Painted wood continues to gain strength on the country market, and rising prices reflect increased interest. In the field of advertising items, signs and crates of painted-wood are especially popular.

Reproduction Alert: Watch for newer signs made to resemble antique versions. For painted-wood signs, a close examination of both the paint and the wood should reveal telltale signs of authenticity—dirt, wear, and aging. Also, be aware that contemporary manufacturers have created an overabundance of reproduction signs made of paper and tin.

Bill Hook
- Arctic Brand Evaporated Milk, shows can with polar bear, heavy wire hanger, celluloid disk 1-3/4" dia 168.00
- Ceresota Flour, cardboard back showing boy slicing bread, heavy wire hook at bottom, minor edge roughness, cond. 8-, 5-1/2" h, 3" w 217.00

Bin
- "C.F. Blanke & Co. Roasted Coffee, Drink Blanke's Exposition Brand Roasted Coffee," wood, black stencil, paint loss, cracks to wood, 33" h, 22" w, 16" d 770.00

McLaughlin's Coffee, litho tin, roll top pictures cup and saucer, front with leaves and flowers, green ground, red sides, wear, scuffing, cond. 7, 22-1/2" h, 18" w, 12" d 660.00

Box, Stickney and Poor's Mustard, paper labels outside and under lid, 4" h, 15" w, 8" d 82.50

Calendar, De Laval, 1916, paper, boy in bib overalls on floor with flowers, girl sitting on shipping crate, separator in background, one corner replaced, cond. 8.5+, 23-3/4" h, 11-7/8" w 715.00

Display, cast aluminum, standing pig box with handle, hinged back opening to reveal skeleton and internal organs "Property of Moorman Manufacturing Co., Quincy, Ill.," 15" l 1,300.00

Globe, milk glass
- "Auto Hotel," etched, 1-pc, cond. 7, 16" dia... 385.00
- "Barber Shop," fired-on design, triangular, text in black, red and blue stripes at edges, cond. VG, 12" h, 9-1/2" w 825.00

Match holder
- Ceresota Flour, embossed die-cut tin, hanging, boy slicing bread, cond. 8+, 5-1/2" h 440.00
- Columbia Flour, embossed die-cut tin, hanging, Miss Liberty dressed in American flag, bag of flower on basket, cond. 8, 5-1/2" h 1,155.00
- De Laval, tin, hanging, die-cut, miniature separator, "1,750,000 In Use" variation, cond. NM, torn orig box with missing flap, 6-1/4" h 632.50
- Garland Stoves and Ranges, litho tin, hanging, name in medallion over rectangular holder flanked by floral motif, die-cut back with shaped top, cond. 8+, 7" h, 4" w 672.00
- Sharples, tin, hanging, "Tubular Cream Separators, The Sharples Separator Co." on basket, shows cows in field over woman working separator, cond. 8+, 6-3/4" h 440.00

Mug, Round Oak Stoves and Ranges, pottery, trademark image of Indian, c. 1907, 5" h 170.00

Pail
- "Mammy's Favorite Brand Coffee, C.D. Kenny Co., Buffalo, N.Y.," litho tin, shows mammy holding tray, floral border, orange ground, dents, scratches, cond. 8-, 4 lb., 10-5/8" h, 6" dia 467.50
- "Pure Canadian Honey," metal, yellow beehive and 2 bees under yellow "Honey," blue ground, rust to lid and bottom, 8 lb, 6-1/2" h, 6-1/4" dia 115.50

Pocket mirror, celluloid
- ""Dr. Lesure's Remedies, Prove their worth by the results they accomplish, Free Private Treatment of Domestic Animals, Send for Free Booklet," shows doctor, cow, horse and sheep, cond. 8.5+, 2-1/8" dia 632.50
- "Finck's 'Detroit Special' Overalls, 'Wear Like a Pig's Nose,' Sold By All Wide Awake Dealers," shows pig on cobalt ground, oval, 1-3/4" h, 2-3/4" w 385.00

Poster, Winchester shells, "Shoot them and avoid trouble," shows skunk coming out of hollow log and spraying black man and dog, cropped, framed, 18-3/4" h, 27" w 330.00

D.M. Ferry & Co. Flower Seeds box, three children in flower garden, 6-3/4" h, 11-1/2" w, $440.

Pot scraper, litho tin, "Mt. Penn Stove Co., Reading, Penna.," shows green clover, mint cond. 132.00

Scoop, Harrison's St. Nichol's Coffee, shows coffee can, red lettering, white ground, litho tin, wear, cond. 7, 4" h, 1-3/4" w 250.00

Seed box

D.M. Ferry & Co., "Choice Flower Seeds From D.M. Ferry & Co., Detroit, Mich.," shows 3 children in flower garden, oak, litho paper label under lid, cond. 8.5, 6-3/4" h, 11-1/2" w, 9-3/4" d 440.00

"D.M. Ferry & Co., Choice Flower Seeds," under-lid litho paper label of children gardening, refinished case 110.00

"Seeds from Rush Park Seed Co." on front decal with considerable wear, "Rush Park Seed Co., Independence Iowa, Celebrated & Reliable Seed, Grown From Selected And Choice Seed Stock, Are Absolutely Fresh and Can Be Depended to Give Entire Satisfaction, Iowa Grown Seed Are The Best Try Them" on inside decal with edge chipping, wood with litho paper decals, 5-1/2" h, 28" w, 13-1/2" 176.00

Shaker Seed Co., Mt. Lebanon, N.Y., paper labels, divided interior, fruit label on top, traces of old labels along edges, cracks, 3-1/2" h, 23-1/2" w, 12" d 192.50

Sioux City Nursery & Seed Co., "Reliable Seeds, From the Sioux City Nursery & Seed Co. Sioux City, Iowa," wood, machine dovetails, paper labels on front and inside lid, chipping to labels 187.00

Sign, painted metal

"Let Us Furnish Your Home, F.L. Grant, The Furniture Man, Salamanca," diamond ring motif at top over man and woman, cond. 8.5+, 36-1/2" h, 12" w... 360.00

"Tractors With Lugs Prohibited," embossed, black text, yellow ground, cond. 8, 8" h, 12" w....... 66.00

Sign, painted wood

Bear River T House, black bear over "River T House" lettering in green paint, raised green border, white ground, 34" h, 22" w................ 1,540.00

"Daniel Spangler Cigar Manufacturer," black lettering on green ground, "A.M. Wright, Signs, Red Lion, Pa.," in small lettering at bottom, 14" h, 30-3/4" w 805.00

"Eggs," black letters with yellow trim, white ground, 6" h, 30" w 275.00

"Germania Cave," gold letters and flourishes, black ground, arched lettering with arched cutout at bottom, 45" h, 82" w 990.00

"Meat Market," brown letters and border, yellow highlights, white ground, 13" h, 98" w......... 440.00

"Wall Papers," old black alligatored paint, gray lettering, applied molding, 7-3/4" h, 40-1/4" w........330.00

"We Do Razor Honeing & Concaveing," black letters, red-and-white diagonal stripes, 9-1/2" h, 62" l 1,100.00

"White Mt. Grange," arrow shape, white letters, black ground, 101" l................................... 220.00

Sign, paper

"Corn King Manure Spreaders, International Harvester Company of America," oval images of brook and horse-drawn manure spreader in field, two panels show two different models, ©1908, archival backing, cond. G, 25-1/2" h, 20" w................550.00

"Success, The Horse's Friend, E.L. McClain Mfg. Co., Greenfield, O.," shows horse writing testimonial letter, includes 1889 calendar, cond. 8+, 24" h, 19" w... 1,210.00

Sign, porcelain

"5¢," oval, white text, red ground, edge nicks, cond. 9-9.25, 7" h, 5-1/2" w 165.00

"Barber Shop," flange sign, white on cobalt panel, red, white and blue diagonals slant toward center, cond. EXC, 12" h, 24" w 258.50

"Ice Cold Water," 2-sided, black ice-capped text on white ground, c. 1950s-1960s, cond. 9.25-9.5, 20" h, 10" w.. 121.00

"Pony Express Trail, 1860 1861," silhouette of rider on horseback, minor chips to edges, minor water stain, 14" dia.. 830.50

Advertising crate, "White Fawn Biscuit, The Geo. Young Bakery, Utica, N.Y.," lithographed paper on wood, $190.

Sign, reverse-painting on glass
 "Entrance," gold-colored tin backing, white text, rust spotting, paint running on some text, 3-3/4" h, 18" w 22.00
 "Spectacles, Eye Glasses & Artificial Eyes," chipping to gold, black ground, framed, restored, 8" h, 20" w 412.50
 "Spectacles Properly Fitted," two eyes over white text, black ground, framed, paint chips, 17-3/4" h, 33-3/4" w 275.00
Sign, tin
 "Dr. Hess Stock & Poultry Preparations Sold Here," flange sign, litho tin, banner shape, shows farm animals on yellow and blue ground, cond. 7-8, 11" h, 18-1/4" w 880.00
 "Kreso Dip No. 1 For All Livestock and Poultry, Parke Davis & Co.," round vignettes of sheep, cow, horse and pig, also shows chickens, collie and turkeys, nail holes, minor bend, scattered scratches, 18" h, 28" w 1,485.00
Thermometer, painted wood
 "Dr. A.C. Daniels' Famous Veterinary Medicines, Home Treatment For Horses and Cattle, Dog Remedies," with advertising for New York merchant, cond. 7, 20-3/4" h, 5" w 385.00
 "Dr. A.C. Daniels' Warranted Horse Remedies/Horse Medicines," lists various horse cures, cond. 7, 21" h, 4-7/8" w, ... 385.00
 "International Stock Food and Veterinary Preparations, Guaranteed," shows harness horse, rounded top, cond. 8+, 24" h, 6" w 935.00

"Stoneware, The Best Food Container" advertising sign, tin over cardboard, 19" h, 13" w, $1,650.

Thermometer, porcelain
 "Chew Mail Pouch Tobacco, Treat Yourself To The Best," white and yellow text, blue ground, orig wooden frame, no tube, 1920s-1930s, cond. 8.25, 74" h, 19" w 632.50
 "Treat Yourself To The Best, Chew Mail Pouch Tobacco," white and yellow text, cobalt ground, white border, minor scratches, chips, 38-1/2" h, 8" w 231.00
Tin
 "Compliments of Santa Claus, Wishing You Merry Christmas and Happy New Year," colorful St. Nick in holly wreath, back shows Santa in sleigh and church scene in sepia colors, turn of the century, cond. 8.5, 3-1/2" h, 3-1/2" dia 907.50
 Dan Patch Gall Salve, litho tin, horse head in oval medallion, International Stock Food Co., c. 1909, cond. 8, 2-1/2" dia 38.50
 "Dr. Daniels' Hoof Food, Perfection Hoof Dressing," litho tin, hand-soldered, Dr. Daniels on front, hooves in various states of health on back, cork top, cond. 7, 4-3/4" h, 3-1/8" dia 305.00
 "Tiger Bright Chewing Tobacco," litho tin, hinged, round image of tiger's head, red and gold checkered ground, cond. 8+, 2-1/8" h, 6" w, 4" d 220.00
Tip tray, litho tin
 "Dr. A.C. Daniels' Horse & Cattle Medicines," shows heads of three white horses, scalloped edge, cond. NM, 4-1/4" dia 1,705.00
 "Hubig's Famous Pies, A Guarantee Against Cellar Made Pies" on rim, center shows factory with horse-drawn delivery wagon and "Fall Festival 1906," cond. 8, 3-5/8" dia 264.00

Amish

Background: The Amish take their name from Jacob Ammon (or Amen), who founded the sect in Switzerland and southern Germany in 1698. The group followed a strict interpretation of Mennonite principles. Many members migrated to Pennsylvania around 1730 to 1740, and later spread to Ohio and Indiana, among other states.

Collecting Hint: Typically, Amish quilts are crafted of plain, dark fabrics arranged in simple geometric designs.

Reference: Patricia T. Herr, *Amish Arts of Lancaster County*, Schiffer Publishing, 1998.

Bucket bench, red repaint, pine, scrolled ends dovetailed into top, attributed to Indiana, 19" h, 24" w, 10-1/2" d 550.00
Chair cushion, floral design, red and pink flowers, black ground, geometric border, stuffed, Lancaster County, Pa., early 20th C., 17" sq 30.00
Cupboard, two-pc, walnut, butternut and oak, two glass doors over pie shelf over three drawers over two paneled doors, shaped bracket feet, cove-molded cornice, old varnish, found in Walnut Creek, Ohio, 80-1/2" h, 51-3/4" w, 19-1/4" d 1,320.00

Doll

8-3/4" h, hand-sewn, stuffed cotton body and head, light-blue dress, light-blue apron, black bonnet, clothing machine-sewn, early 20th C., replaced bonnet ties, soiling, stains 85.00

11-1/2" h, hand-sewn, stuffed cotton body and head, medium-brown cotton dress, black bonnet, early 20th C., wear, soiling 120.00

13-3/4" h, machine-sewn, stuffed white oilcloth body, orange dress, white apron, black bonnet, light-blue knit booties, early 20th C., wear, soiling 110.00

14-3/4" h, hand-sewn, stuffed cotton and denim body, purple machine-sewn dress, white cotton apron and bonnet, early 20th C., soiling, minor stains 80.00

16" h, coarsely woven white cloth body, light-blue long-sleeve dress and gray sleeveless dress, blue wool cape with buttons, black bonnet 192.50

17-1/2" h, stuffed fabric, purple hand-sewn head and body, blue arms and legs, gray dress, white cap, Centre County Pa., early 20th C 175.00

19" h, stuffed fabric, blue body with white head, white arms and legs pinned with safety pins, blue dress, white apron and cap, Centre County, Pa., early to mid-20th C., soiling 95.00

Kas, one-pc, grain-painted, orange-brown over tan graining, poplar, two doors, shaped bracket feet, paneled ends, beveled cornice, 93-1/4" h, 64" w, 20-1/4" d 990.00

Amish grain-painted kas, $990. (Photo courtesy of Garth's Auctions, Delaware, Ohio)

Pillow, floral design, two-sided, wool punch work on velvet, stuffed, Lancaster County, Pa., early 20th C., 16-1/4" sq 30.00

Pincushion, geometric design in yellow, green and brown, edged in silk ribbon, wool cross-stitching on canvas, Lancaster County, Pa., early 20th C., wear, 5" sq, pair 75.00

Quilt

Bars pattern, alternating stripes of yellow and blue, 84" x 94" 825.00

Crib quilt, pieced, black, magenta, burgundy and mauve, 17-1/2" x 18-1/4" 27.50

Doll quilt, Tumbling Blocks, red and green on purple ground, blue border, lavender squares in all four corners, black fabric back, early/mid 20th C., 17-1/4" x 17-1/2" 85.00

Flying Geese, red wool triangles pieced in a diamond grid on green-black squares, c. 1880 .... 522.00

Four Patch, red and blue squares, yellow ground, sawtooth border in blue and yellow, blue and red outer borders, Pennsylvania, 80" x 82" 660.00

Nine Square, cotton, squares of 9 small multicolor blocks of print fabric alternated with purple squares having a quilted basket design, wide purple border, Centre County Pa., early 20th C., 72" x 90" 275.00

Rug, hooked, floral pattern, gray center surrounded by blue geometric border with four large red and pink flowers with green leaves, Lancaster County, Pa., early 20th C., rectangular, wear, 23" x 39" 250.00

Stand, one drawer, oak, turned legs, scalloped front apron, one-board top slightly warped, old varnish, found in Winesburg, Ohio, 27-1/2" h, top 19-1/2" x 20-1/4" 935.00

Wood bin, old blue repaint, bracket feet, scalloped sides, shelf at top, square nails, screws added, wear, 44-1/2" h, 32" w, 20" d 1,045.00

Apothecary Cabinets

Background: These cabinets take their name from the apothecary, an early druggist. Having multiple rows of small drawers, the cabinets were originally used to store drugs and other items handled by a pharmacist. The size of the cabinet and the number of drawers it contained varied greatly from example to example.

Collecting Hint: Apothecary cabinets are especially hot on today's market, where they are being offered in larger numbers. The fact that their country look is supplemented by generous storage space is convincing many shoppers to buy.

11 drawers, curly maple drawer fronts with bold figure, poplar case, orig white porcelain and brass pulls, old green paint on back, refinished, 8-1/4" h, 41-1/2" w, 7-1/4" d 770.00

19 drawers, poplar, old finish, square nails, some damage to backboards, 24-1/2" h, 21" w, 7" d 1,045.00

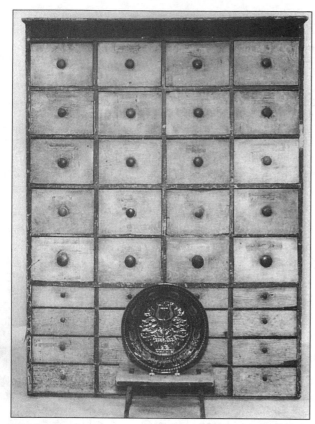

Thirty-six-drawer apothecary in brown and tan grained repaint, 66" h, 48-1/4" w, $3,520. (Photo courtesy of Garth's Auctions, Delaware, Ohio)

20 drawers (four rows of five) stepped over two-door cupboard base, blue paint, 64" h, 34" w, 22" d.. 7,150.00

29 drawers, weathered yellow paint, three drawers over 18 drawers (three rows of six) over five drawers over three drawers, unfinished sides, 45" h, 40" w, 19" d........ 880.00

36 drawers (nine rows of four), pine, old worn brown and tan grained repaint, flat base, top 20 drawers 4" deeper than lower 16 drawers, short compartment across full width of the top, some brass and wood knobs replaced, 66" h, 48-1/4" w, 15-1/2" d.................................. 3,520.00

48 drawers (eight rows of six), pine, bottom two rows with deeper drawers, 36" h, 38" w, 6" d 385.00

50 drawers (seven rows of seven, over one long drawer), pine, orig bluish-gray paint, high-back shelf, bootjack feet, most drawers with old penciled or ink labels, orig brass pulls, 57-1/2" h, 37-3/4" w, 9" d 24,200.00

Apple Parers & Slicers

Background: It's possible that even children in the early 19th century preferred their apples without the peel. Using a knife to complete the chore was the only method available until Moses Coates invented a mechanical apple parer in 1803. However, it wasn't until 1873 that the first patent for a mechanical apple parer and corer was issued to Landers, Frary & Clark of Boston.

Reference: Don Thornton, *Apple Parers*, Off Beat Books, 1997.

Collectors' Club: International Society for Apple Parer Enthusiasts, 735 Cedarwood Terr., Apt. 735B, Rochester, NY 14609.

Collecting Hint: Common apple parers are of little interest to collectors. Instead, look for unusual machines, including complex cast-iron variations and early wooden examples.

Reproduction Alert: Cast-iron apple parers are still available from hardware stores and specialty catalogs.

Cast iron
- Baldwin 72 .... 75.00
- Goodell Bonanza, 16" h, 23" l........................ 170.00
- Goodell Eureka 88, 1874 patent date, 16-1/2" h, 21" l 2,185.00
- Goodell Turntable '98, 11" h 40.00
- Reading Hardware Co., 1878 patent date 75.00
- Sinclair Scott Co., 8-3/4" h.............................. 60.00
- Unmarked, clamps parallel to tabletop, semi-circular shape, turned wood handle, Oct. 6, 1863 patent date 182.50

Wooden, rectangular base
- Scrolled end fitted with later leather strap to secure in place, turned post supports wrought-iron peeler, opposite end with iron crank with double prongs 425.00
- Threaded clamp attaches to the table, wooden crank on one side with iron prong to hold apple opposite the crank, hand-held wooden paddle-shaped peeler with iron blade, 6" h (with clamp), 14" l, 8" w.. 300.00

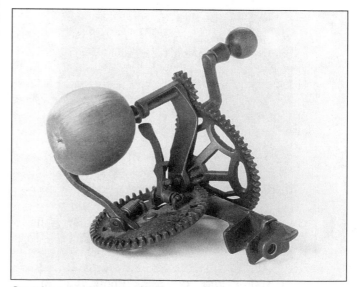

Cast-iron apple parer, $150.

Band Boxes

Background: The name band box derives from the lightweight, utilitarian pasteboard boxes used by the English to hold neckbands and lacebands. Popular in America from 1820 to 1850, they were available in a variety of sizes and were generally covered with decorative wallpaper having floral or geometric patterns. Boxes covered with paper depicting historical scenes are especially prized, as are those with a maker's label and those which are part of a matched set.

Reference: Arene Burgess, *19th Century Wooden Boxes*, Schiffer Publishing, 1997.

Collecting Hint: A maker's label can double the value of a band box.

Hannah Davis, oval
    10-1/2" l, 5-1/2" h, light yellow (darkened) wallpaper with white, pink and brown floral designs, newspaper-lined interior, "Warranted Nailed Band Boxes, made by Hannah Davis, Jaffrey (N.H.)," wear 1,485.00
    14-3/4" l, worn orig floral paper in green, white and beige on wooden base, lined with old newspaper and labeled "Band Boxes made by Hannah Davis, Jaffrey, N.H." 715.00
    19" l, Napoleon pattern paper in shades of green and white with touches of gilt, yellow ground, paper label, with booklet about Hannah Davis, imperfections 402.50
Oblong
    7" l, 5-1/4" w, 3-1/8" h, colorful paper in green, yellow, white and brown diamonds, lines and foliage scrolls, wear 440.00
    17" l, 10" w, 10" h, blue wallpaper, floral and landscape decor, wear, soiling 192.50
Oval
    6" l, 3-1/2" w, 3" h, basket-weave pattern in blue, dark blue and white, tan band with burgundy dots around lid, partial newspaper lining, minor edge wear, small flakes 687.50
    7-1/8" l, 4" w, 3" h, mustard, green and tan leaves around base, roses on lid, red and black band, pencil inscription, small hole in lid, minor flaking 605.00
    8" l, 5-1/4" w, 4-1/4" h, base and lid covered with tan paper with green and brown scroll print, small edge flakes 495.00
    9-1/4" l, 6-3/4" w, 4-3/4" h, poplar, brown, white and cream design, lined with early advertisements for medicines, stains, edge wear to lid............. 137.50
    12-1/4" l, 10-1/4" w, 7-1/4" h, blue with white lines and stars, pink and white flowers, green leaves, overall wear, insect damage on bottom 385.00

Barrels, Kegs, and Canteens

Background: Wooden barrels served as storage containers for everything from nails to flour and were made by coopers. Kegs and other smaller staved pieces were the specialty of the "white cooper." Kegs were used to hold and dispense all manner of liquids, as well as gunpowder. Early kegs were closed by using a mallet to drive a wooden plug into the bunghole; later examples featured a threaded plug. Canteens resembled kegs and could be equipped with straps and flung over the shoulder for carrying.

Care: These wooden items should not be exposed to high heat or low humidity as both conditions promote cracking. For a few days several times a year, items originally designed to hold liquids should be filled. This will allow the joints to swell and will help maintain the soundness of the piece.

Barrel, wooden, tapered shape, stave and metal bands, finger-lapped cover, red paint, wear, loose rims, 21-1/2" h 1,150.00
Canteen, wooden, painted, carved with date 1812 .... 275.00
Canteen, wooden, stave-constructed
    Barrel shape, 6 lapped staves, old natural finish, carved "D.P., 1815," 8-1/4" l 346.50
    Old blue-green repaint, iron bands, bail handle, embossed initials, warped sides, 8-1/2" dia ...302.50
    Worn blue repaint, flat base, arched sides, cracks in 1 stave, 8-1/4" h, 9" w, 6-1/2" d 440.00

Wooden barrel with finger-lapped cover, red paint, 21-1/2" h, $1,150. (Photo courtesy of Skinner Auctioneers & Appraisers of Antiques & Fine Arts, Boston and Bolton, Mass.)

Keg
    Coopered and paint-decor by Joseph L. Lehn, Lancaster County, Pa., rounded sides surrounded by four wide iron bands, orange with thin yellow stripes flanking metal bands, iron arched handle, 12-1/4" h, 6-7/8" dia 525.00
    Painted, red, 6" h 275.00
Rundlet, wooden, turned barrel form, painted light red over gray, 19th C., cracks, wear, 5" h 115.00
Water keg, stave construction, worn orig red paint, old stopper, 8-3/4" dia 275.00

Baskets

Background: The appearance and construction of baskets has changed little in 5,000 years. Always utilitarian but sometimes with a decorative look, most are made of wood splint, willow rods, or various grasses. However, offbeat materials such as matchbook covers and bottle caps have also been used. Basket styles can vary widely, as can their values.

Reference: Don and Carol Raycraft, *Collector's Guide to Country Baskets*, Collector Books, 1985 (1994 value update).

Museums: Heard Museum, Phoenix, AZ; Old Salem, Inc., Winston-Salem, NC.

Reproduction Alert: Modern reproductions and contemporary examples are plentiful.

Collecting Hint: Save your money for baskets that are in very good condition. Damaged examples tend to be poor investments, even at low prices.

Berry, woven splint, large "AP" on sides in black paint, square with flat bottom, sides flare to rounded rim, iron tacks, Shaker, 4" h, 3-3/4" dia 75.00
Buttocks, woven splint
    14 ribs, 2-1/2" h (including handle), 3" l 440.00
    18 ribs, 3-1/2" h (including handle) 165.00

Double-lid basket with hickory handle, 11" x 6", $220.

Bushel basket with double bentwood handles, $125.

20 ribs, 6" h (excluding handle), 12-3/4" x 19-1/2" 192.50
23 ribs, 3" h (excluding handle), 6" l 137.50
24 ribs, 3-1/4" h (excluding handle), 5" x 7", twisted handle with diamond at ends 148.50
24 ribs, 8" h (excluding handle), 14" x 16" 220.00
26 ribs, 4-1/2" h (including handle) 330.00
26 ribs, splint breaks, 9" h (excluding handle), 13" w, 15" d 110.00
28 ribs, tightly woven, anchored handle, late stained finish, 8-1/4" h... 220.00
34 ribs, minor damage, 7" h (excluding handle), 14" w, 12" d 192.50
36 ribs, minor breaks, 10" h (excluding handle), 15" x 19" 220.00
54 ribs, minor damage at handle, 5-1/4" h (including handle) 577.50
Cheese
    11" dia, 4" h, round top, six-sided bottom, woven splint.. 137.50
    22-1/2" dia, 7-1/2" h, round top, hexagonal base, woven splint, few breaks, one repair 269.50
    23" dia, Shaker, woven splint......................... 247.50
    24" dia, woven splint..................................... 440.00
Goose feather
    Rye straw, 18" h.. 137.50
    Woven splint, old red paint, domed lid, round, 18" h, 15" dia 715.00
Half buttocks basket, woven splint
    8 ribs, bentwood handle, minor damage, 7" h....137.50
    9 ribs, bentwood handle, dark finish, minor damage, 7-1/4" h 137.50
    16 ribs, bentwood handle, minor wear, 9" h... 275.00
    28 ribs, minor breaks, 12-1/2" h (excluding handle), 12-3/4" w 247.50
Indian
    Mic Mac, hanging, 13" h, 10" w, 7" d 220.00
    Passamaquoddy, woven splint with lid, red and blue designs, ring handles, 19" dia, 17" h 71.50
    Woodland, woven splint, natural, red blue and green woven design, handles wrapped in splint, 14-1/2" w 137.50

Woodland, woven splint, buttocks, 28 ribs, two-tone brown and natural, 6" h (excluding woven handle), 11" x 12-1/2" 522.50

Melon, woven splint
    18 ribs, flat base, bentwood handle, 7-1/4" h..... 165.00
    28 ribs, five dark stained bands, 5-1/4" h (excluding bentwood handle), 11" w 522.50

Nantucket
    4-1/8" dia, 3-3/8" h, woven, round, wooden bottom painted green, rounded bottom with straight sides, bentwood rim painted green, arched handle...2,000.00
    9" dia, 8-1/4" h, woven, round wooden bottom, wrapped rim, swivel bentwood handle, minor rim break.. 715.00
    9-1/2" dia, 6" h, round, woven, wooden bottom, bentwood swing handle, pieced repair at handle post.. 1,485.00
    10-1/4" dia, 9" h, round, turned wooden base, carved wing handle................................... 2,070.00
    13-1/4" dia, 5" h, woven cane/splint, round, turned wooden base, swivel bentwood handle with brass ears, breaks on rim and edge of base, rim wrap incomplete 110.00
    Basket purse, turned ivory fittings and two flying gulls on lid, mkd "Wm. & J. Reis, 1973 Nantucket Island," swivel handle, 7-1/2" h, oval 7-1/2" x 10" 825.00
    Basket purse with cover, oval, cherry plaque and base, ivory seagull signed "C.F. Sayle," 20th C., 5-3/4" h, 9-1/2" l, 6-1/2" d 575.00

Picnic, splint, hinged wood lid, oblong, metal reinforcement/straps, sheet-iron arched handle, open rectangular woven-in handles, 9" h (excluding handle), 21" w, 11-1/8" d.. 120.00

Rye straw
    3-3/4" h, 8-7/8" dia, coiled, round, flat bottom, single coil rye straw foot, rounded sides, bound with splint, some wear on foot, some loss of splint 60.00
    4-5/8" h, 12" dia, coiled, round, bread basket, bound with splint, flat bottom................................. 150.00
    5-1/4" h, 11-3/4" dia, coiled, round, woven-in arched handles on top rim, round coiled foot 225.00
    Gathering, coiled, bound with splint, round with flat bottom, coiled round foot, sides slightly rounded and are fitted with arched bentwood handles attached with woven splint, Centre County, Pa., 19th C., 8-3/4" h (excluding handles), 13-3/4" dia 2,800.00
    Storage, swollen oval form, probably Pa. origin, losses, 18" h 316.25

Splint, kettle shape
    Old black paint, 6" h, 9" dia............................ 825.00
    Worn yellow paint, minor damage, 8" h, 13-1/2" dia 550.00

Splint, low
    4" sq, 2" h, potato-stamp decor 770.00
    13" dia, 5" h, old dark-green paint, round 550.00

Splint, melon
    12 radiating ribs, coarsely woven, small breaks, 6-1/2" h 71.50
    16 flat bentwood staves, arched handle, two short sections of splint missing, 13-1/2" h 176.00
    20 flat ribs, tightly woven, two blue-green stained lines along the bottom, small breaks, 6-1/2" h 82.50
    22 ribs, tightly woven, decorative stacked weaving where handle meets basket, minor breaks, 13-1/2" h 82.50
    26 ribs, tightly woven, damaged bottom, 17" h 220.00
    Tightly woven, designs beneath arched handle, 8-1/8" h, 9-1/4" dia.................................... 82.50

Splint, miniature, 4" h, 6" dia, 2 handles 385.00

Splint, oval
    Cross-weave design bentwood top and bottom, natural finish, edge wear, 19-3/4" x 14-1/2", 9" h 99.00
    Oval top, square base, oval rim, 7" l, 4-1/8" h, old green paint over red, bentwood handle...... 467.50
    Oval top, square base, 20" w, 20" d, 16" h, tightly woven, pierced handles, carved hickory feet, scrubbed.. 192.50

Splint, rectangular
    11-1/2" w, 12-1/4" d, 4-1/2" h, dark-green paint, square design, narrow splints, minor breaks, paint wear.. 357.50
    12-3/4" w, 11-1/4" d, 6-1/4" h, tightly woven wide splint base, loosely woven narrow splints on top, breaks..110.00
    13" l, watercolor designs in red, blue and yellow 247.50

Splint, round
    5" dia, 4" h, blue and red geometric potato stamp decor, square base, round top, few breaks on lid... 935.00
    10" dia, 6-3/4" h, swing handle 467.50

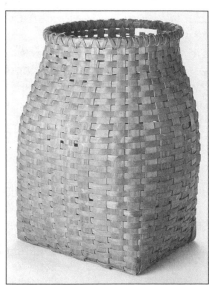

Pack basket, white oak splint, $150.

12-1/2" dia, 7-1/2" h, orig blue paint, 2 wide splints at top, finely woven splints taper at bottom, minor breaks... 247.50

14-1/2" dia, double handles, minor edge chips on splints, one handle cracked 110.00

18-1/2" dia, 14-3/4" h, green paint around center band, other bands in reddish cast, damage 110.00

Round top, square base, 4-1/2" sq, 4-1/4" h (excluding handle), swing handle with looped and pierced ends... 275.00

Round top, square base, 8-3/4" h, bentwood handle... 275.00

Round top, square base, 9" h, arched bentwood handle... 82.50

Round top, square base, canted sides, 13-3/4" h, natural with stained salmon and black weaving, geometric loops around center, arched handle, few splint breaks... 357.50

Splint, square, handled, 12-1/2" h, 11" sq 60.50

Beds

Background: Beds have traditionally served as places of rest and privacy. In many cases, they were valued as important heirlooms, symbolizing the continuity of the family line.

References: Eileen and Richard Dubrow, *Styles of American Furniture 1860-1960*, Schiffer Publishing, 1997; Tim Forrest, *Bulfinch Anatomy of Antique Furniture*, Bulfinch Press, 1996; John T. Kirk, *American Furniture: Understanding Styles, Construction, and Quality*, Harry N. Abrams Publishers, 2000; Milo M. Naeve, *Identifying American Furniture*, W.W. Norton, 1998; Ellen T. Schroy, *Warman's American Furniture*, Krause Publications, 2001; Robert W. and Harriet Swedberg, *Collector's Encyclopedia of American Furniture*, Vol. 1 (1990, 1996 value update), Vol. 2 (1992, 1999 value update), Vol. 3 (1998), Collector Books; —, *Encyclopedia of American Oak Furniture*, Krause Publications, 2000.

Collecting Hint: Rope beds are one of the sleepers on today's furniture market. Buyers often shy away from vintage examples because early beds are too short and/or too narrow to accommodate modern mattresses. However, specialty mattresses can be ordered, and bed rails can be extended.

Canopy, Federal, tall post

Maple, carved and ribbed posts with acanthus leaves, inverted and carved bell on foot posts, period posts, added headboard, orig (extended) side rails, attributed to New York, 69-1/2" h, 55" w.. 1,650.00

Tapering pencil headposts, arched headboard, reeded vase, cup-and-ring turned footposts, on casters, arched tester, old refinish, New England,

Low post bed, grain-painted, probably northern New England, c. 1825-35, 46-1/2" h, 52" w, 79" l, $1,495. (Photo courtesy of Skinner Auctioneers & Appraisers of Antiques & Fine Arts, Boston and Bolton, Mass.)

19th C., 61" h, 53-1/2" w, 75" l, tester 78-1/4" h.. 1,380.00

Jenny Lind, walnut, peaked head and footboards with cutout design and spool trim over spool-turned spindles, spool-turned posts and legs, 52" w 121.00

Low post

Classical, mahogany, carved, New England, c. 1820, pineapple-carved finials on leaf spiral and ring-carved posts, vase-and-ring turned legs with brass cuffs and casters, scrolled and shaped headboard, old refinish, imperfections, 60" h, 49-1/4" w, 72" l.. 2,875.00

Tiger maple, New England, 2nd quarter 19th C., ball tops, ring-turned posts, shaped headboard, similar ring-turned legs on casters, side rails with angle irons, old surface, minor height loss, 50-1/4" h, 49" w, 75-1/2" l.. 1,610.00

Pencil post, hardwood and poplar, old red finish, age but not period, canopy frame with old worn crewel trim, 84" h, 51" w, rails 72" l 220.00

Rope

Cherry, cleaned down to old finish, turned posts, ball finials, scrolled headboard, turned crest, found in Ashland County, Ohio, 59-3/4" h, 51" w, orig rails 76-1/4" l 1,210.00

Cherry and poplar, old varnish finish, turned posts, tapered feet, urn finials, headboard and footboard with identical scrolled boards, rails missing, 52" w... 330.00

Curly maple, refinished, well-turned feet and posts, acorn finials, scalloped and turned footboard, shaped headboard, good figure, replaced rails, 53" h, rails 76" l.. 1,045.00

Four post, country style, poplar, simple tapered posts in red wash, shaped headboard, orig rails and canopy, 60-1/2" h, 46-1/2" w............. 1,045.00

Grain-decor, old black over red graining, poplar, high post, tapered legs, ball and turned finials on posts and headboard, orig rails, rope pegs removed, 53" w, rails 68" l 522.50

Tall post bed, New England, old refinish, 61" h, 53-1/2" w, 75" l, tester 78-1/4" h, $1,380. (Photo courtesy of Skinner Auctioneers & Appraisers of Antiques & Fine Arts, Boston and Bolton, Mass.)

Hardwood, old red wash, posts with bun finials, turned legs, vase feet, replaced pine headboard, edge wear, stains, 39-1/4" h, 51" w, rails 61" l 275.00

Maple, tightly figured, old worn finish, tapered legs and posts, turned trumpet finials, cutout ends on headboard, turned blanket rail footboard, orig rails, glued repair to one finial, 47-1/2" w, rails 69" l 495.00

Maple, turned posts, scroll-cut headboard and footboard, light cherry color, 56" h, 51-1/2" w, orig rails 69-1/4" l 143.00

Poplar, red finish, turned posts, bell finials, orig round screw-in rails, added castors, 54" h, 52" w, rails 10-1/2" l 137.50

Poplar, turned feet, ring-turned posts, low scrolled headboard, refinished, small chip on post, 33" h, 50" w, orig rails 71" l 110.00

Rope, cannonball
Cherry, rolled crest and smaller balls on ends of headboard, 10 turned spindles, blanket roll with vase turnings, turned cylinder feet, minor edge damage, 42" h, 53" w, rails 75-1/4" l 275.00

Curly maple and cherry, refinished, traces of old red, turned posts, scalloped headboard, replaced rails, 54-1/2" w, rails 75-3/4" l 1,650.00

Curly maple and maple, good figure, old worn finish, turned legs, turned posts and ball finials, headboard with cutout ends and shaped corners, footboard with blanket bar, orig rails, 51-1/2" h, rails 69" l 770.00

Rope, painted
Old black over earlier red, turned legs, molded cross pieces, pegged, headboard and footboard with peaked tops, mushroom finials, Pennsylvania origin, 33-1/2" h, 52" w, rails 74" l 577.50

Old red, poplar and pine, turned legs, high turned feet, suppressed ball finials, orig rails, 37" h, 47-1/2" w, 71" l 357.50

Old red (thin), poplar, round legs, turned posts and ball finials, scrolled headboard missing its crest, no rails, 48" w 55.00

Old red, posts turned and chamfered with rounded finials, pegged, orig rails, 31" h, 42" w, rails 72" l 275.00

Sheraton
Country style, tall posts, maple and poplar, turned feet, ring-turned posts, acorn finials, flat tester top, refinished, 84" h, 51-1/2" w, orig rails 73" l 1,650.00

Tiger maple, early to mid 19th C., baluster-turned posts, urn finials surmounted by small balls, ball feet, headboard with horizontal panel with out-rounded ends below round ring-turned rail, footboard with ring-turned blanket rail, replaced side rails, refinished 300.00

Tall post
Cherry, probably New England, early 19th C., octagonal tapering pencil posts continuing to square tapering feet, flat tester frame, shaped headboard, old finish, imperfections, 81-3/4" h, 40-1/2" w, 70-1/2" l 1,840.00

Federal, mahogany, carved, probably Southern states, early 19th C., square tapering birch posts, arched pine headboard, reeded tapering footposts with tobacco-leaf carving, reeded legs, turned feet, with rails and flat tester, restoration, patches, 83-1/2" h, 56-3/4" w 4,025.00

Federal, mahogany, shaped headboard, reeded and leaf-carved column posts with line inlay, tester top, rails converted to queen size, 90" h 1,265.00

Federal, maple and birch, red-stained, Mass. or N.Y., c. 1815, vase- and ring-turned reeded and swelled foot posts, tapering pencil head posts, shaped pine headboard, arched tester frame, later urn finials, imperfections, 69-1/2" h, 51-1/2" w, 71" l 1,725.00

Bedwarmers

Background: Popular during the 19th century, bedwarmers were large metal pans with a hinged, perforated lid. Situated on the end of a long handle, the pan was filled with hot coals and then slid under the covers of a bed to warm it before its owners retired for the evening. Copper and brass are the most commonly found examples, typically with a turned wooden handle.

FYI: Bedwarmers are also known as warming pans.

Brass pan
Engraved copper lid, turned wooden handle, found in Conn., 38" l 275.00

Engraved flower, turned wooden handle, lid stuck, pan battered, handle worn 55.00

Engraved rosette, scrolls and rope design on lid, turned wooden handle, old refinishing, traces of orig paint, small split near hinge, 44-3/4" l .. 275.00

Pierced lid, turned wooden handle, English, 43" l 275.00

Tooled lid, turned wooden handle, 40" l 253.00

Copper pan
  Engraved flowers and foliage on brass lid, turned handle with paint decor, broken hinge, 40" l 192.50
  Sunburst design on tooled brass lid, turned wooden handle with worn orig graining, 42" l 275.00

Bellows

Background: Bellows existed as early as the 15th century. Generally made of wood and leather with metal fittings, they are used to force a concentrated stream of air to assist in combustion of a fire. Turtle-back bellows are those with a rounded surface.

Collecting Hint: Collectors look for decorated examples. Designs other than flowers and fruit are especially prized. Condition plays an important role in determining value.

Decorated
  Cornucopia of fruit, gilt, green, brown and black, red ground, brass tip and tack decor, restored leather, 18" l 517.50
  Cornucopia, fruit and foliage design, orig red paint, freehand and stenciled design in black, gold, green and yellow, brass nozzle, old leather worn, 17" l 1,100.00

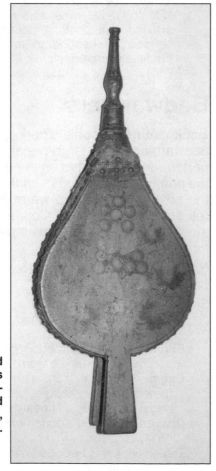

Bellows, red ground with stenciled flowers and fruit, brass nozzle, worn paint and leather, 17-1/2" l, $137.50.

Floral decor, orig yellow paint, green and black striping and stenciling, freehand detail in red, green, gold and black, brass nozzle, professionally releathered, minor wear, 16-1/2" l 302.50
Floral decor, orig rosewood graining (worn), worn leather, brass nozzle, 15" l 82.50
Fruit and foliage decor in gold, bronze and black, red ground, black striping, orig paper label for "Eckstein and Richardson, No. 36 North Third Street, Philadelphia," extreme leather wear 275.00
Fruit and foliage decor, orig yellow paint, stenciled and freehand design in red, green, brown and black, brass nozzle, old worn releathering, wear, 17-1/2" l 605.00
Fruit and foliage, orig yellow paint, stenciled and freehand design in red, green, brown and black, brass nozzle, very worn old leather, wear .. 275.00
Fruit and foliage decor, yellow paint, green banding, 18" l 330.00
Leaf and flourish, old dark-red repaint, gold stencil, worn simulated leather, 18-3/4" l 49.50

Decorated, turtle back
  Basket of flowers in gold and green stencil and freehand, red ground, stenciled gold borders, old releathering, brass nozzle, wear, flaking, 17-3/8" l 110.00
  Bird and berries, old black paint, multicolor design, brass nozzle, worn old releathering, wear, 17-1/2" l 660.00
  Fruit, mustard ground, brass nozzle, old repaint, wear, 16-1/2" l 192.50
  Fruit in compote, orig green paint, tan border, yellow stencil, brass nozzle, old releathering, minor wear, 17" l 935.00

Benches

Background: Benches evolved from medieval times, when they were the primary form of seating. Oblong narrow seats designed to accommodate several people, benches can be made with or without backs. Most benches on today's market are made of pine.

Cobbler's, pine, old refinish, three drawers, four compartments, high tapered legs, with shoe pattern cut out of 1829 newspaper, 20" h, 36" w, 14" d 1,815.00
Kneeling, orig grain-decor, pine, arched cutouts on legs, square nails, possibly Shaker, "#35" on base with "— Field," worn paint, 7-1/2" h, 45-1/2" w, 6-1/4" d 302.50
Courting or tête-à-tête bench, maple, traces of old paint, turned/tapered feet with ring-turned posts, woven cane seat, curved arms, shaped backrest, refinished, 31-5/8" h, 23" w, 43" l 1,210.00
Curly maple, old varnish, bold curl, arched cutouts on feet, short aprons, age cracks, wear, braces added, found in Holmes County, Ohio, 17-1/2" h, 50-1/4" w, 12" d 220.00
Grain-decor, old brown graining over mustard repaint, green showing beneath, pine, shaped legs mortised through the top, braces screwed into legs and top, age

Prayer bench, early gray paint over original light-gray, pine, c. 1880, 66" l, $500.

cracks, edge wear, water damage to legs, 17-1/4" h,
72" w, 11-1/2" d 247.50
Painted
Orig electric-blue paint, worn, pine, mortised, curved
bootjack legs, age cracks, 18" h, 10' w,
11" d... 220.00
Worn gray, pine, cutout legs mortised through top,
two diagonal braces, age cracks, edge damage,
20" h, 89" w, 14-1/2" d 247.50
Green repaint, scrubbed top, poplar, mortised, bootjack ends, beaded apron, age cracks, 18-1/2" h,
13-1/2" w, 39" l.. 357.50
Old light-green repaint, pine, bootjack ends, age
cracks in top, 11" h, 8-3/4" w, 24" l 275.00
Old red, pine, mortised, bootjack ends, square nails,
embossed name on end, 8" h, 9" w,
31-1/2" l... 495.00
Pine, refinished, scalloped ends, shaped legs mortised
through the seat, made of old wood, minor insect damage, 19-1/2" h, 59" w, 13" d............................. 330.00
Poplar, country style, stained finish, bootjack ends, 3-
board top, square nails and screws, late, 19" h, 34" w,
11" d 110.00

Bennington & Bennington-Type Pottery

(see Rockingham)

Background: Captain John Norton established
Norton Pottery of Bennington, Vt., in 1793. Initially,
the factory produced earthenware kitchen items
and bricks, but by 1815, gray stoneware had been
added to the company's output. The impressed
mark was usually highlighted with cobalt. Numerous family members joined the operation through
the years, and several changes were made to the
mark, but the Norton name was always included.

Considered one of the greatest potters of his
time, Christopher Webber Fenton began producing stoneware in Bennington around 1835, after
leasing part of the Norton Pottery. It was he who
introduced the famous Rockingham glaze to
America. Developed in England, the brown glaze
was named for the Marquis of Rockingham. In

1849, Fenton patented a flint enamel glaze that
added flecks and streaks of color to the Rockingham glaze. The blues, greens, yellows, and
oranges of "Fenton's Enamel" were perfect com-
plements for the rich, chocolate brown glaze. In
spite of tremendous variety and large output, Fenton's factory closed in 1858, due to financial con-
cerns and poor marketing.

Reference: Richard Carter Barret, *Bennington Pottery and Porcelain*, Crown, 1958; John Spargo, *The
Potters & Potteries of Bennington*, Dover, 1972.

Museum: The Bennington Museum, Bennington,
VT; East Liverpool Museum of Ceramics, East Liverpool, OH; National Museum of American History,
Smithsonian Institution, Washington, DC; Shelburne Museum, VT; Wadsworth Atheneum, Hartford, CT.

FYI: Hound-handled pitchers with mottled Rockingham glaze were distinctive Bennington products.
Proving that imitation is indeed the sincerest form
of flattery, at least 55 variations of the hound-handled pitcher were made by more than 30 potteries.

Note: Confusion and crossover abound between
Bennington and Rockingham-glazed wares. Since
so much of what Bennington produced featured a
Rockingham-type glaze, we have chosen to list all
of these items in the Rockingham category.

Bible Boxes

Background: The Bible was an important piece of
family history, containing records of births, deaths,
and marriages. Because Bibles were treasured and
handed down from generation to generation, small
chests were constructed for storing them. Bible
boxes were either plain or enhanced with carving,
and the hinged lids were either flat or affixed on a
slant so that the piece could also serve as a small
desk or a reading stand.

Oak, carved roses and leaves tied with ribbon, 2-1/2" h,
11" w, 7-1/2" d 190.00

Paint-decorated slide-lid Bible box, decorated with a potted plant and floral corners, 10" high, 13-1/2" wide, 4" deep, $1,400.

Walnut, dovetailed case, lid with breadboard ends, cast-iron bail handles on case, split on applied base trim, 21" l 357.50

Walnut and tiger maple, walnut case with diamond motif along sides, tiger maple edge molding and raised center panel on lid, hingeless lid recessed over base, square-nail construction, from a Masonic lodge, 4-1/4" h, 11-1/2" w, 8-1/2" d 250.00

Blanket Chests

Background: Chests are commonly defined as containers with flat, hinged lids, usually having feet but no handles. Mainly used for storage, they held everything from textiles to musical instruments, but because they were primarily used as a receptacle for blankets, they are commonly referred to as blanket chests. Many were fitted with a till, a small compartment for valuables.

FYI: In the Pennsylvania-Dutch communities, blanket chests were often presented to young boys and girls to be used for storing their belongings. Because these chests were kept for a lifetime, they were often subject to several moves. Since the feet were often detached during transportation, it is not uncommon to find examples with replaced feet.

Chippendale
Poplar, country style, old brown varnish stain over earlier yellow, bracket feet, dovetailed case, molded-edge lid, interior till with lid, old nailed repairs to hinge rail, 23-1/2" h, 48-1/2" w, 21-1/2" d 357.50
Poplar and pine, old dark-red repaint, ogee feet, molded base, dovetailed case, 2-board top with molded edge, chip on 1 foot, hinges and lock replaced, drill holes, 26-1/2" h, 50-1/2" w, 22" d 770.00
Decorated
Orig blue grain-decor, Conn., late 18th C., six-board construction, molded top edge, molded base, shaped bracket feet, minor paint wear, 23-1/2" h, 42" w, 17" d... 2,070.00
Brown and tan grain-decor, simulated knots, Vermont origin, 25" h, 42" w, 17" d................ 2,475.00

18TH CENTURY UNICORNS

Have you ever seen a unicorn?

Take a look at these mythical beasts on this paint-decorated blanket chest dated 1797. Probably from Berks County, Pa., this gem has an arched center panel with black rampant facing unicorns on a cream ground flanking a tulip-like flower emerging from a handled cup in orange and green, surmounted by an orange and green eight-point star in a circle. Two tombstone-shaped panels each have a cream ground with a small, black-handled urn flanked by orange and green facing parrots. The urn is surmounted by an orange, green, and black pinwheel-like flower, with two large yellow, orange, and green tulips and a small carnation-like flower on each side. The chest's lid was painted to match the front, but had substantial wear. The ends have tombstone-shaped panels each with a cream ground having a black handled urn holding a tall green stem surmounted by a large orange, green, and black pinwheel-like flower flanked by two yellow, orange and green tulips and a small carnation-like flower. In addition to wear, the chest had some damage to the feet. It measured 23-1/2" h, 50-1/2" w, 12-3/8" d.

Unicorn-decorated blanket chest dated 1797, $77,000. (Photo courtesy of Horst Auctioneers, Ephrata, Pa.)

Orig brown over salmon sponging, pine, "James Mortlane, 1850" script signature within decor, black bracket feet, applied base molding, dovetailed, till, wear, two feet repaired, hinges replaced, 22-3/4" h, 38" w, 17-1/2" d 715.00
Orig burnt sienna graining and inlay simulation, yellow ground, six-board construction, arched feet, lidded till, New England, early 19th C., paint wear, restored molding, 22-1/4" h, 38" w, 17" d 10,350.00
Green and yellow, smoke-grained, black ball feet, 25" h, 48" w, 22" d 1,375.00
Mustard and brown, vinegar-grained, New England, early 19th C., six-board construction, iron carrying

handles on side, 13-1/4" h, 29" w,
15-3/4" d 1,840.00
Red and yellow grain-decor, black bracket base, 25"
h, 48" w, 22" d.. 1,375.00
Scratch-decor, pine, Marshfield or South Scituate,
late 17th C., molded lift top on pintle hinges, front
decor with geometric patterns and initials "A.S.,"
sides with cutwork feet, refinished, repairs, 21" h,
38-3/4" w, 16" d 8,050.00
White panel, initials "J.T.K." in blue stenciled floral
border, poplar, six-board construction, molded top,
cutout bracket feet, possibly Schoharie County,
N.Y., early 19th C., restorations, 21-3/4" h, 36" w,
18-3/4" d 2,990.00
Flame birch, one drawer, bat-wing pulls and escutch-
eons, 32" h, 43" w, 17" d 880.00

Grain-decorated

Orig black flame graining, red ground, yellow initials
on lid, inside of lid mkd "Susan Slater 1826," pine,
cutout feet, beveled-edge lid, till, minor wear,
22-1/2" h, 43" w, 16-1/2" d 1,650.00
Orig brown flame graining, pine, six-board construction, cutout end feet, shaped front bracket, one
drawer, applied molding on lid, old brasses (one
missing ring), one front foot split and nailed, edge
damage, 33-1/4" h, 49" w, 19-1/2" d 550.00
Orig red over yellow flame graining, poplar, turned
feet, molded base, dovetailed case, one-board top
and sides, wrought-iron strap hinges, large interior
till, bear-trap lock with key, attributed to Sonnenburg Mennonite Community, 27" h, 52-3/4" w, 22-
3/4" d 2,310.00
Orig vinegar graining faded to olive and mustard-yel-
low, black bracket feet and lid edge-molding, orig
unfaded red visible in places, pine, dovetailed
case, till, wrought-iron strap hinges, bear-trap lock
with key, pencil inscription, 22-3/4" h, 40" w,
18" d 3,300.00

New England grain-decorated blanket chest in original
burnt sienna on yellow, early 19th C., 22-1/4" h, 38" w,
$10,350. (Photo courtesy of Skinner Auctioneers &
Appraisers of Antiques & Fine Arts, Boston and Bolton, Mass.)

Miniature

Chippendale, grain-decor, old gray paint with black-
daubed graining, pine, ogee feet, dovetailed case,
2 dovetailed drawers, molded-edge lid, till, old
repair to hinge rail of lid, 11" h, 16" w,
9-3/4" d 24,200.00
Grain-decor, pine, reddish-brown flame graining,
yellow ground, red showing at points of wear, well-
shaped bracket feet, applied lid molding, Pennsylvania origin, 10" h, 15-3/8" w, 7-3/4" d .. 22,550.00
Painted, old blue, pine, dovetailed case, molded-
edge lid and base, dovetailed bracket feet, old
repaired crack in rear foot, 15-1/2" h, 21" w,
12" d 8,800.00
Walnut, old finish, turned feet, dovetailed case,
molded bottom edge, edge-molding applied to lip,
till, nailed repair to lid hinge rail, 14-3/4" h, 20-1/2"
w, 12-3/4" d... 550.00

Miniature, decorated

Diamond and initials in yellow, old green over black
paint, bracket feet, dovetailed case, lid with
applied edge molding, interior divider missing,
repaired break in lid at hinge rail, 7-1/2" h, 12-3/4"
w, 7-1/4" d.. 1,210.00
Flowers stenciled in black and white, old olive paint,
all over red ground, pine, removable bracket-foot
base added, lid replaced, 14-1/2" h, 30-1/4" w,
13" d 605.00
Swag design, orig green and black paint, poplar and
pine, side boards extend to form runner feet,
applied molding at base, lid molding replaced,
found in Maine, 7" h, 15" w, 7" d................. 605.00

Miniature, painted

Orig green, pine, tapered square legs, molded base,
dovetailed case, interior lock, one-board top,
molded edge, minor wear, 9-1/2" h, 15-5/8" w,
9-3/8" d 770.00
Old dark-green over lighter-green, pine, high boot-
jack feet, applied base moldings, molded-edge lid,
worn paint, 10" h, 14" w, 6-1/2" d 605.00
Old red, pine, crazed over-varnish, dovetailed,
tapered feet, molding around base and lid, till, fitted lock, 10-3/4" h, 18" w, 8-1/2" d 660.00
Old red, worn white initials, pine, bracket feet, dovetailed case, molded-edge lid, wire hinges,
wrought-iron hasp, 9-3/8" h, 17" w,
8-3/4" d 1,760.00
Old dark red, pine, bracket feet, rosehead nails, lid
initialed "T.R." in white, molded edge, till missing
its lid, feet repaired, 11-1/4" h, 18-1/2" w,
11" d 715.00
Orig yellow, black turned feet, pine, dovetailed case,
molded bottom edge, applied edge-molding on
beveled lid, Pa. origin, 9-1/2" h, 15-1/4" w,
7-1/2" d 5,225.00

Painted

Orig black over red, poplar, bracket feet, elaborate
scalloped apron, 1-board top, applied beveled
trim, till, glued break in one rear foot, Ohio origin,
23" h, 37-3/4" w, 19" d 1,925.00

Blanket chest in old red paint, New England, 19th C., 48" h, 36" w, $5,750. (Photo courtesy of Skinner Auctioneers & Appraisers of Antiques & Fine Arts, Boston and Bolton, Mass.)

New York blanket chest with simulated burlwood panels, grain-painted surrounds, early 19th C., 24" h, 42" w, $747.50. (Photo courtesy of Skinner Auctioneers & Appraisers of Antiques & Fine Arts, Boston and Bolton, Mass.)

Blue sides and bracket base, natural top, wear, 20" h, 36" w, 18" d.. 1,265.00

Orig dark-blue, pine, molded trim around base, six-board construction, dovetailed case, interior till with dovetailed drawer beneath, wrought-iron strap hinges, wrought-iron handles on sides, missing molded trim around top, some renailing, edge and surface wear, 18" h, 38-3/4" w, 17-1/2" d 165.00

Orig dark-blue, pine, wide boards, applied trim at base and on lid, till lid missing, age cracks, 19" h, 41" w, 19-1/2" d 770.00

Old electric blue, worn, small turned front and tapered rear feet, molded base, inset panels on sides, one-board top with molded surround, edge damage, hinges replaced, 22" h, 40" w, 18" d 660.00

Old blue-green, pine, dovetailed case, till, wood handles on side, feet are runners, lid worn, edge damage, split at replaced hinges, 17-1/8" h, 43-1/2" w, 17-1/2" d 412.50

Old brown over brownish-green repaint, pine, dark-red turned feet, dovetailed, molded base, till, two-board lid with step-down molding, rear feet replaced, 23-1/2" h, 37" w, 20-1/4" d 440.00

Brown-red, 1 drawer, bootjack ends, 34" h, 41" w, 16-1/2" d.. 880.00

Gray, simple construction, 20" h, 41" w, 17" d ... 192.50

Dark-red brushed decor over earlier salmon, pine, black turned and tapered feet, molded base, dovetailed case, one-board top with applied molding, wrought-iron strap hinges, one hinge replaced, corner chips on lid, old replacement lock, 23-1/2" h, 43" w, 20-1/2" d 550.00

Red, bootjack ends, wear, some loss to wood, 18" h, 31" l, 13" d 165.00

Red, shoe-foot, 22" h, 33" w, 15" d 935.00

Red finish, pine, six-board construction, scalloped feet on ends, molding around base and top,

wrought-iron hinges, rosehead nails, later square nails added, age cracks, 24-1/2" h, 49-1/2" w, 19" d 220.00

Orig red, six-board construction, high bootjack ends, molded-edge top, staple hinges, interior till with shelf beneath, one foot repaired, missing till lid, 24-3/4" h, 47-1/4" w, 17-3/4" d.................... 770.00

Orig red, pine, six-board construction, flat base, molded-edge top, internal lock, 16" h, 34-3/4" w, 15" d 440.00

Orig red, poplar, turned and tapered feet, molded base, dovetailed case, one-board top with molded trim, lock and till lid missing, feet chipped .. 577.50

Orig red, walnut, bracket feet, dovetailed case, ivory diamond-shaped escutcheon, till over dovetailed drawer, 1-board top with applied molded edge, one foot replaced, missing till lid, 21-3/4" h, 43-3/4" w, 18-1/2" d 825.00

Orig dark-red wavy lines over lighter red, poplar, scalloped bracket feet, beveled apron, dovetailed case, brass key escutcheon, two-board top, applied trim, round nails, 21-1/4" h, 37" w, 19-1/4" d 715.00

Old salmon repaint, turned ball feet, one-board top with molded edge, dovetailed, feet replaced, 19-1/2" h, 37-1/2" w, 15-1/2" d.................... 330.00

Pennsylvania, grain-decorated

Orig brown on yellow ground, pine and poplar, black turned feet, edge-molding on base and lid, dovetailed case, till, 20-3/4" h, 37-3/4" w, 18-1/4" d 1,265.00

Faded red graining over bright yellow, poplar, turned feet, dovetailed case, molded-edge lid, till with lid, back signed "Elimna Beecher 1848," 26" h, 37-1/4" w, 19-1/2" d 990.00

Orig red flame graining, poplar, turned feet, dovetailed case, edge-molding on base and lid, till, damaged lid lip, lock missing, wear, 23" h, 37" w, 18-1/4" d 660.00

Orig red and green panels, brown-grained yellow stiles and rails resembling curly maple, pine, lid and bracket feet red with green trim, four panels with applied finger-carved rectangles, till, minor edge damage, one front foot facing damaged, found in Johnstown area, 25" h, 48-1/2" w, 21" d 4,400.00

Orig vinegar grained sponging, brown on white ground, black turned feet, pine, dovetailed case, edge-molding on base and lid, wrought-iron bear-trap lock and key, till missing except for lid, wear, edge damage, 25" h, 47-1/2" w, 22" d 550.00

Orig brown vinegar graining on salmon ground, black turned feet, poplar, dovetailed case with applied moldings, two dovetailed overlapping drawers, molded-edge lid, interior till with lid, old replacement glass drawer pulls, some wear, 28" h, 43-3/4" w, 20-1/2" d 660.00

Pennsylvania, paint-decorated

Worn dark-blue and red with three painted panels with polychrome flowers, bracket feet, dovetailed case, one-board lid with mortise and tenon breadboard ends and molded edge, till with two drawers, lock missing, old repaints, age cracks, edge damage, 24-1/4" h, 49" w, 18-3/4" w 1,375.00

Orig black, red trim, "Regina Jaeckelin 1805" in white, poplar, ogee feet, dovetailed case, two dovetailed overlapping drawers, wrought-iron strap hinges, bear-trap lock with key, till and three secret drawers, orig brasses, replaced escutcheons, attributed to Lehigh County, Pa., 26-3/4" h, 51-1/4" w, 23" d 7,480.00

Dark red early repaint with yellow compass stars on drawers, hearts and oval fan above, black turned feet, inset panel above each of three drawers, two-board top with beveled edge-molding, cracked corner post, three small holes drilled through lid, 30-1/2" h, 47-1/2" w, 23-1/2" d. 660.00

Orig reddish-brown over orange, poplar, turned feet, molded base, dovetailed case, one-board top with beveled molding, till lock missing, minor wear, restoration along hinge rail 770.00

Robin's-egg blue, pine, dovetailed case, dovetailed bracket feet, wear, age cracks, repairs to hinge rail, 19-3/4" h, 42-1/4" w, 17-1/4" d 632.50

Orig decor with old repaint on lid and base molding, pine, two arched panels on front in dark blue with pots of tulips and large red flowers, dark-blue pillars at either end of front panel, double hearts in the corners, red turned feet, wrought-iron strap hinges, bear-trap lock and till, attributed to Lebanon County, Pa., 25-3/4" h, 52-1/2" w, 22-1/2" d 1,870.00

Sponge-decor, orange and yellow, black turned feet, molded base and lid, 24" h, 44" w, 20" d . 2,750.00

Sheraton

Painted, country style, early red repaint, pegged, turned feet, inset panels on ends, two panels on front, till, two-board top with beveled molding,

small dents, wear on one corner of lid, 24-1/2" h, 39" w, 20" d... 550.00

Painted, country style, stenciled gold flowers, cherries and strawberries surrounded by green leaves, old red paint over earlier blue-green, pine, turned feet, one dovetailed drawer, wrought-iron strap hinges, till, one-board top, molded surround, replaced oval brasses, 28-1/4" h, 36-1/4" w, 18" d 1,127.50

Soap Hollow, decor, poplar, orig red paint, black and yellow trim, gold stenciled foliage, flowers and "Jeremias Wever, 1859, Mf. by C.C.B.," bracket feet, dovetailed case, applied moldings, two dovetailed drawers, divided by cutout wooden panel with heart and circles in black over yellow, old glass pulls, replaced inlaid escutcheons, minor feet repairs, some edge damage and wear, 28-1/2" h, 49-1/2" w, 22-3/4" d......11,000.00

Sonnenberg, poplar, orig dark-red paint with yellow striping, polychrome floral decor on front panel, compass star in red and yellow on lid, bracket feet, dovetailed case, molded-edge lid, interior till, 23-1/4" h, 37-5/8" w, 19-3/8" d 10,450.00

Walnut, old finish, ogee feet, two overlapping dovetailed drawers in base, dovetailed case, molded-edge lid, wrought-iron strap hinges, till with lid and two secret drawers, orig brasses, lock missing, small repairs to feet, 28" h, 51-1/2" w, 23-1/2" d 7,260.00

Blue & White Pottery and Stoneware

Background: Although termed blue and white, this category also includes blue and gray pottery and stoneware. Widely produced from the late 19th century through the 1930s, these items were originally marketed as inexpensive wares for everyday household use. Butter crocks, pitchers, and salt boxes are among the most commonly found pieces. Many examples feature a white or gray body with an embossed geometric, floral, or fruit pattern. The piece was then highlighted with bands and splashes of blue to accentuate the molded pattern.

Reference: Kathryn McNerney, *Blue & White Stoneware*, Collector Books, 1995; Terry Taylor and Terry & Kay Lowrance, *Collector's Encyclopedia of Salt Glaze Stoneware*, Collector Books, 1997.

Collectors' Club: Blue & White Pottery Club, 224 12th St., N.W., Cedar Rapids, IA 52405.

Also See: Spongeware

Batter jar

Wildflower, glaze flaw, 4 chips on lid.............. 385.00

Bowl

Apricot pattern, milk bowl, 4" h, 9-1/2" dia 80.00

Blue banded, 14-3/4" dia 125.00

Colonial, base crack, 12" dia 300.00

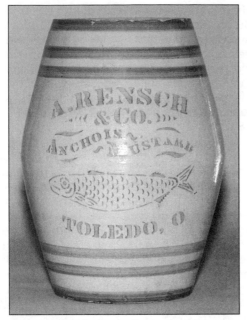

Ovoid jar, "A. Rensch & Co., Anchois (sic), Mustard, Toledo, O.," base marked "Burley, Winter & Co., Crooksville, O.," no lid, $1,200.

Diffused, 2-3/4" h, 7" dia 140.00
Diffused, chips, base cracked, 6" h, 12" dia 85.00
Flying Birds, berry bowl 125.00
Flying Birds, milk bowl, 2 chips, 3-3/4" h,
    9-1/2" dia 525.00
Butter crock
    Basketweave, base/rim/lid chips.................. 150.00
    "Butter" in oval, blue sponging, 9" dia............ 275.00
    Colonial, with lid, 4-1/4" h 375.00
    Colonial, tall form, new lid.......................... 300.00
    Cows, minor base flakes, lid missing large
        piece 225.00
    Daisy, unusual scrollwork pattern, no lid........ 150.00
    Daisy & Trellis, with lid, minor glaze flake at
        bail 80.00
    Diffused, advertising "Rockwell City, Iowa," mint
        cond.. 160.00
    Eagle, with lid.. 1,080.00
    Indian & Deer, with lid................................ 2,225.00
    Lovebird, with lid 541.50
    Peacock, chipped lid................................. 300.00
Canister
    "Cake," blue bands, damaged lid.................. 140.00
    "Cereal," Basketweave, no lid...................... 383.00
    "Coffee," Basketweave, inner rim chips,
        mended lid... 75.00
    "Cookies," two glaze flakes/chip, damaged
        lid 175.00
    "Raisins," Basketweave, with lid, mint cond... 350.00
    "Sugar," Basketweave, hairline on jar, mismatched
        lid 60.00
    "Sugar," Wildflower, with lid, chipped............ 185.00
    "Tobacco," Basketweave, with lid.................. 780.00

Chamber pot, Wildflower, hairline 150.00
Coffeepot, Peacock, no lid 2,225.00
Cooler, "Maxwell House Ice Tea," small lid chip,
    hairline 300.00
Grease jar, Flying Birds, with lid........................ 1,100.00
Jardiniere, Tulip.. 525.00
Lid
    Apple Blossom, salt lid................................ 135.00
    Apricot, salt lid 140.00
    Basketweave "Tobacco" canister lid 295.00
    Flying Birds, 9" dia.................................... 355.00
    Wildflower, salt lid 55.00
Match holder, Flemish 85.00
Meat tenderizer
    Wildflower, crazed, replaced handle.............. 375.00
    Windmill 80.00
Miniature, canteen, G.A.R., Davenport, Iowa, 1914
    .... 275.00
Mug
    Basketweave, gold trim................................ 85.00
    Cattail, Western Stoneware, three flakes 150.00
    Dainty Fruit 600.00
    Wildflower 91.00
Pie plate, rim chips... 125.00
Pitcher
    American Beauty Rose 440.00
    Arches & Columns 565.00
    Avenue of Trees.. 275.00
    Basketweave, water pitcher.......................... 125.00
    Beaded Swirl.. 1,172.00
    Cattail, small flake on base, 7" h 130.00
    Cattails and Rushes, mint cond., 10" h.......... 200.00

Cherry Cluster and Basketweave pitcher, 6-1/4" h, $200.

Cherry Band, plain, two hairlines, 6" h............ 128.00
Cherry Band, "A.E. Laidley, Pandora, Iowa," spider hairline in base, repaired chips on spout, 8-1/2" h 375.00
Cherry Band, "Merry Christmas, Andrew Westin & Co.," 8-1/2" h 382.00
Cherry Band, oval advertising "T.L. Jones & Co., 1916, Arnold, Neb.," 9-1/2" h 2,826.00
Cows, two inner rim chips, tight hairlines....... 170.00
Dainty Fruit 400.00
Daisy.. 785.00
Dutch Boy & Girl 125.00
Dutch Farm Scene, tall variation.................... 175.00
Eagle.. 300.00
Flying Birds, two small lip flakes, hairline 450.00
Garden Rose 315.00
George & Martha Washington, White Hall, mint cond.. 375.00
Indian Boy & Girl, hairline, crazing................. 200.00
Leaping Deer 347.50
Old House & Trees (castle), chips, 8" h......... 200.00
Peacock, minor base flakes......................... 1,330.00
Rose & Fishscale, repaired spout, hairline, 9" h 120.00
Swan 485.00
Tulip 344.50
Wildflower 150.00
Windmill, tight hairline................................... 100.00
Rolling pin
  Colonial... 1,215.00
  Wildflower 247.50
  Wildflower, advertises "Compliments of C.N. Allen, Jr.," 8" l 435.00

Wildflower nutmeg spice container with lid, 4-1/4" h, $225.

Salt crock
  Apple Blossom, replaced lid, burst glaze bubble.. 75.00
  Butterfly, with lid.. 280.00
  Colonial, hanging, lid cracked/glued............. 210.00
  Eagle, with lid.. 685.00
  Good Luck, hanging, missing lid..................... 85.00
  Peacock, missing lid, chips...........................110.00
Slop jar, with lid 786.00
Soap Dish
  Cat 100.00
  Scroll, back advertises "Capitol City Stoneware Co., Indianapolis," mint cond. 350.00
  Wildflower 157.50
Spittoon, spongeware, blue bands, imperfections, 5" h, 7-1/2" dia... 99.00
Wash pitcher & bowl
  Basketweave, gold trim, mint cond. 300.00
  Bowknot, spider hairline in bowl 325.00
  Bowknot & Rose, stenciled design 175.00
  Scroll, pitcher only, large size 150.00
Water cooler
  Apple Blossom, four-gal, with lid, mint cond.. 1,500.00
  Cupid, four-gal, replaced lid, interior repainted at spigot 500.00
  Cupid, five-gal, lid damage, chips, glaze flaw on front 300.00
  Polar Bear & Elk, four-gal, one large and one small chip on lid, manufacturer's flaw on base 550.00
  Rebecca at the Well, six-gal, cracks.............. 325.00

Bootjacks and Boot Scrapers

Background: Designed to ease the removal of boots, bootjacks were primarily made of cast iron or wood. The heel of a boot is placed in the U- or V-shaped opening at the front of the jack, the other foot is placed on the rear of the jack, and the boot is pried off the front foot. In 1852, the United States Patent Office awarded its first patent for a bootjack to Saris Thomson of Hartsville, Mass. Examples range from crude, one-of-a-kind versions to elaborate, artistic castings and carvings.

Boot scrapers are metal devices used for cleaning mud and other unsavory farm by-products from the soles of work boots and shoes. Generally located outside the main residence, they were an important fixture of life in early rural America.

Reproduction Alert: The Cricket and Naughty Nellie designs are among the most reproduced bootjacks. Handle any examples being considered for purchase. Reproduction castings are generally lighter weight and of poor quality.

Bootjacks

Lyre-shaped, cast iron, painted black, minor rust, 3-1/8" h, 11-1/4" l, 5" w....................................... 45.00

Naughty Nellie, cast iron, brown paint, 10" l........... 25.00
Naughty Nellie, cast iron, unusual gilt polychrome decor
   lingerie, paint loss, 11-1/2" l 373.75

Boot Scrapers

Cast iron, octagonal pan base, flared rim with relief
   designs, double dolphin supports, shell center, pitted,
   10" h, 12-1/2" w, 15-1/2" d 192.50
Cast iron, scalloped oval base, decorative cast bail top
   with black shoeshine boy finial, brush attachment
   missing, 13" h.. 137.50
Cast iron, scalloped pan base, brushes mounted in
   brackets on either side, black boy finial, black
   repaint 247.50
Wrought iron, side-wall type scraper, twisted supporting
   braces, 18th C., 12-1/2" h, 10" l 230.00

Bottles

Background: This is one of those broad categories that needs an entire book of its own in order to
do the topic justice. Some of the more highly collected types of bottles are listed here.

References: Ralph & Terry Kovel, *Kovels' Bottles
Price List*, 11th ed., Three Rivers Press, 1999; John
Odell, *Digger Odell's Official Antique Bottle and
Glass Collector Magazine Price Guide Series*, Vols.
1 through 8, self-published (1910 Shawhan Rd.,
Morrow, OH 45152), 1995; Jeff Wichmann, *Antique
Western Bitter Bottles*, Pacific Glass Books, 1999;
—, *The Best of the West Antique Western Bitters
Bottles*, Pacific Glass Books, 1999.

Periodicals: *Antique Bottle and Glass Collector*,
P.O. Box 187, East Greenville, PA 18041; *Canadian Bottle and Stoneware Collector*, 179D Woo-
dridge Crescent, Nepean, Ontario K2B 7T2
Canada.

Collectors' Clubs: Federation of Historical Bottle
Collectors, 88 Sweetbriar Branch, Longwood, FL
32750; Midwest Antique Fruit Jar and Bottle Club,
P.O. Box 38, Flat Rock, IN 47234.

Museum: The National Bottle Museum, Ballston
Spa, NY.

Also See: Flasks.

Amber, globular, 24 ribs swirled to the left, Zanesville,
   Ohio, minor scratches, tiny broken blister,
   8-1/2" h... 495.00
Bitters
   Burdock Blood Bitters, Buffalo NY, aqua, partial
      label, 8-1/2" h 28.00
   "Digestine Bitters, P.J. Bowlin & Son, Sole Propri-
      etors, St. Paul, Minn.," amber, overall design,
      8-1/4" h 300.00
   "S.B. Rothenburg, Sole Agent, U.S.," embossed
      horseshoe, milk glass, 9-1/8" h 140.00

Bride's bottle, etched
tulip design, 11" h, $100.

Bride's bottles
Note: All bride's bottles listings are polychrome enamel
decor, unless otherwise noted.
   Clear, flowers on all sides, orig pewter collar minus
      threads, 5-1/4" h, 2-5/8" w, 2" d 169.50
   Clear, flowers on all sides, orig pewter collar, light
      residue, 6-1/2" h, 3-1/2" w, 2-1/2" d 310.75
   Clear, flowers on all sides, orig pewter collar and
      screw cap, minor paint loss, minor light residue,
      5-3/4" h, 2-1/2" w, 1-7/8" d........................ 169.50
   Clear, flowers on all sides, orig pewter collar with
      threads, 6-1/4" h, 2-3/4" w, 2-1/4" d 310.75
   Clear, flowers on all sides, orig pewter collar with
      threads, minor paint loss, 5-3/4" h, 2-1/2" w,
      1-7/8" d 169.50
   Clear, 2 green lovebirds on yellow heart on front,
      yellow urn and blue flowers on back, flowers and
      vines on sides and corners, orig pewter collar with
      threads, minor paint loss, light residue, 5-3/4" h,
      2-7/8" w, 2-1/4" d 423.75
   Clear, peddler on front, flowers on back, orig pewter
      collar, some paint loss, 5-1/4" h, 2-3/4" w,
      2" d 310.75
   Clear, standing lady in blue dress, "Love me as I
      love you" German inscription on back, flaring lip,
      4-5/8" h, 2-5/8" w, 2" d 423.75
   Clear, standing man in red coat holding cup on front,
      flowers on sides and back, minor wear, light resi-
      due, 6" h, 3" w, 2-5/8" d 621.50
   Clear, white dove on branch, flowers on sides, orig
      pewter collar with threads, heavy interior stain,
      minor paint loss, 5" h, 2-5/8" w, 2-1/4" d 56.50

Clear, white hare in yellow oval on front, floral decor on sides and back, orig pewter collar with threads, two minor paint flakes, 6-3/4" h, 3" w, 2-1/2" d 508.50

Fiery opalescent, two blue lovebirds on red heart on front, floral decor on sides and back, flaring lip, minor paint loss, 5" h, 2-5/8" w, 2-1/2" d..... 395.50

Opaque blue (pale), flowers on all sides, pewter collar with protruding threads, minor paint loss, 5-1/2" h, 3-1/8" w, 2-5/8" d 423.75

Opaque white, flowers on all sides, orig pewter collar and screw-on cap, paint loss to one bloom, 4-3/8" h, 2-1/4" w, 1-3/4" d........................... 310.75

Opaque white, standing lady on front, tulip decor on sides and back, orig pewter collar and corked pewter stopper, lip flake, light wear to decor, 5" h, 2-1/4" w, 1-3/4" d 508.50

Opaque white, tulips on all sides, flaring lip, 5-1/4" h, 3" w, 2-1/2" d 254.25

Opaque white, yellow bird on branch above flowers on front, floral decor on sides and back, pewter collar, 5" h, 2-3/4" w, 2" d........................... 423.75

Opaque white, two yellow lovebirds on red heart on front, floral decor on sides and back, orig pewter collar and screw-on cap, 4-7/8" h, 2-5/8" w, 2-1/4" d.. 480.25

Sapphire blue, two white lovebirds on a green heart, floral decor, retains part of orig pewter collar, 5-1/2" h, 2-3/4" w, 2-1/4" d...................... 1,017.00

Sapphire blue, flowers on all sides, plain lip, 6-1/2" h, 3-1/4" w, 2-5/8" d 621.50

Figural

Acrobat, clear, probably Italian, female circus acrobat upside-down on ball, early 20th C., 16-1/2" h 50.00

Black bear, deep olive-green, European, late 19th C., 11" h 125.00

Cabin, "St. Darkes 1860 Plantation X Bitters, Patented 1862," dark amber, c. 1870, 10" h 165.00

George Washington bust, yellow-green, bitters, mid/late 20th C., reproduction, 10" h 45.00

Revolver, golden-amber to yellow-amber, 8" l . 95.00

Gin

Olive, blown, American, late 18th or early 19th C., wear, 15-1/2" h, 7-1/2" sq 977.50

Olive-amber, American, early 19th C., flared rim, tapered body, 13-1/2" h 316.25

Ludlow

Bottle green, blown, bubble-filled glass, applied lip, 5-1/8" and 5-3/4" h, pr 330.00

Olive-amber, blown, applied lip, minor wear, 8-1/4" h 220.00

Medicine

"Dr. Liebig's German Invigorator, 400 Geary St., S.F.," light yellow-amber, lip flake, 8-1/2" h... 80.00

"Dr. Pierce Extract of Smart-Weed, R.V. Pierce, M.D., Buffalo, N.Y.," aqua, 5" h 20.00

"The Great South American Nervine Tonic, Stomach & Liver Cure," clear, shaped like a Warner's Safe Cure bottle, weak embossing, 9-3/4" h....... 100.00

"Hall's Pulmonary Balsam, J.R. Gates & Co., Proprietors S.F.," rectangular, aqua, 6-1/2" h 55.00

"Indian Cough Syrup, Warm Springs, Oregon," rectangular, clear, 7-7/8" h................................ 50.00

"Owl Drug Co.," rectangular, one-wing owl, amber, 4-1/2" h 75.00

"Owl Drug Co.," square, one-wing owl, milk glass, 5" h 65.00

"Wm. H. Gregg M.D., New York, Constitution, Life Syrup," plain back for label, gothic arches, aqua, 8-5/8" h 55.00

"Wm. Radams Microbe Killer, Cures All Diseases," shows man hitting skeleton with bat, amber, 10-1/2" sq 225.00

Poison

"Melvin & Badger, Apothecaries, Boston, Mass.," irregular hexagon, cobalt, content stain, 5" h..70.00

"H.K. Mulford Co., Chemists, Philadelphia," skull/crossbones embossed above "Poison," rectangular with diamond ribbing on all four edges, cobalt, 3-1/4" h 120.00

"Owl Drug Co.," two-wing owl on pedestal embossed "T.O.D. Co.," "Poison" on left panel, light cobalt, 6-1/4" h 325.00

"Poison" on three panels, irregular hexagon shape, moss green, 5-1/2" h 200.00

Bowls

Background: These utilitarian vessels have been made from a variety of materials, including wood, ceramics, and glass. The focus here is on wooden examples, primarily from the 19th century. Whether carved by hand or turned on a lathe, wooden bowls were often painted to add a touch of color to the otherwise mundane kitchen of the 1800s.

Reference: Linda Campbell Franklin, *300 Years of Kitchen Collectibles*, 4th ed., Krause Publications, 1997.

Burl

2" dia, 7/8" h, turned foot 247.50

5" dia, 3-1/4" h, dark patina interior, worn patina exterior, age hairline 181.50

5" dia, 1-5/8" h, dark patina, turned foot and ring at rim, natural imperfections in rim 385.00

5-1/4" dia, 3" h, footed, 19th C........................ 316.25

5-3/4" dia, 4-1/2" h, ash, good figure, turned foot, turned ring around the side, domed lid with finial, exterior crack in bottom 1,650.00

7-1/4" dia, 2-1/2" h, ash, good patina, thinly turned with raised rim and turned foot, rim crack... 385.00

7-3/4" dia, 2-1/2" h, good figure, decorative rings.. 660.00

7-3/4" dia, 3" h, good figure, turned foot and rim, worn interior, natural imperfections, scorch mark 605.00

9" dia, good figure, old dark finish, sides slightly canted, raised ring around center of body, shallow... 715.00

11-3/8" dia, 3-1/2" h, good figure, old nut-brown finish, turned foot, incised line on body, shallow spiral-carved grooves around rim................. 1,430.00

13-3/4" dia, 4-1/2" h, ash, good figure, scrubbed finish, turned foot, raised ring around rim, tight 3" age crack... 1,595.00

14" dia, 4-1/2" h, ash, old patina................. 1,430.00

14" dia, 6" h, ash, refinished, wide band near foot, raised molding on rim............................ 1,650.00

14" w, 12-1/8" d, 5" h, ash, old refinish, hewn irregular oval shape 220.00

14-1/4" dia, 5-1/2" h, ash, excellent figure, turned foot, raised ring on rim, refinished, small putty repair, hairline.. 1,265.00

15" dia, 6" h, ash, good figure, raised ring around rim, light refinish, rim crack...................... 2,420.00

15" w, 12" d, 4-1/4" h, oval, good figure, old dry surface, hewn 2,090.00

15-3/4" dia, 5" h, ash, good figure, old scrubbed finish, age cracks, some putty in-fill............. 1,100.00

16" dia, 5" h 2,310.00

16-1/2" x 19-1/2" (out of round), 7-3/4" h, ash, sloping sides, small rim split, two carved rectangular handles, one handle glued 7,700.00

16-3/4" dia, 5" h, old scrubbed surface, tapered sides, raised ring around rim, early rim chips 715.00

17" dia, 6-1/4" h, ash, good figure, old worn patina, pieced repair in bottom............................ 1,100.00

17-1/2" dia, 4-3/4" h, ash, good figure, nut-brown refinish, turned foot, raised ring around rim, putty repairs.. 1,430.00

18" dia, 5-1/2" h, ash, good figure, traces of red paint, detailed foot and rolled rim, minor age cracks and edge wear 1,980.00

20" dia, 8" h, elliptical shape, cutout handles, 18th C., minor age cracks................................ 2,760.00

21" dia, 8-1/2" h, ash, scrubbed finish, two age cracks with old putty repair, worn 1,650.00

Miscellaneous

Almond shape, dark patina, leather thong hanger, attributed to Zoar, 12-5/8" x 20-1/4", 4-1/2" h 495.00

Dough, hewn, shaped double handles, refinished with small insect holes, oblong, 30" w, 21-1/2" d... 275.00

Rectangular, 20" l, 11" w, 4" h, gray paint...... 165.00

Rectangular, 21" l, 14" w, 5" d, green paint.... 192.50

Rectangular, 21" l, 16-1/2" w, 7" d, red paint . 247.50

Rectangular, 23-1/2" l, 17" w, 7" h, gray paint.... 660.00

Stave-constructed, two heart cut-out handles on extended staves, old red and green paint, steel bands, 9-1/4" dia 302.50

Wooden, turned

4" dia, taupe.. 385.00

5" dia, 2" h, sage-green paint 660.00

Turned wooden bowl in old orange paint, 10" dia, $175.

7" dia, old red painted exterior, varnished interior 55.00

10-1/4" dia, green paint 137.50

11" dia, 4" h, fruitwood, shiny varnish, "1# 6oz" carved on bottom, filled-in age crack.......... 247.50

12" dia, green paint...................................... 330.00

12" dia, 3" h, green paint 165.00

12" dia, 3" h, putty paint................................ 495.00

12-7/8" dia, curly maple, good figure, slightly out of round, refinished................................... 275.00

12-7/8" dia, 3-3/8" h, light mustard painted exterior, interior in worn traces of dark red with green stripes, wear... 412.50

13" dia, red paint.. 137.50

13" dia, 4-1/2" h, natural finish...................... 385.00

13-1/2" dia, gray paint.................................. 165.00

13-5/8" dia, 4-1/8" h, old dark-red painted exterior, dark patina interior, interior worn from use . 605.00

14" dia, 3-7/8" h, old green paint, out of round, minor wear, hole for hanging, ... 330.00

15" dia, green paint...................................... 110.00

15-1/2" dia, 4-1/2" h, blue paint 357.50

15-3/4" x 14-3/4", 5" h, curly maple, varnished, slightly oval.. 247.50

16" dia, mustard paint, old stitch repair 110.00

18" dia, blue paint... 550.00

18" dia, pumpkin paint, metal patches.......... 192.50

19" dia, mustard paint.................................. 165.00

19-1/2" dia, 6-3/8" h, bird's-eye maple, worn varnish finish, raised rim, light stains 467.50

22" dia, mustard paint.................................. 440.00

24" dia, red paint, staple repair...................... 110.00

Boxes

Background: Box is a generic term used to denote a variety of storage containers. Although typically made of wood, they were also produced in a number of other mediums. This category examines a variety of types. Some forms, such as candle boxes and cutlery boxes, are covered in separate categories elsewhere in this book.

Reference: Arene Burgess, *19th Century Wooden Boxes*, Schiffer Publishing, 1997.

Collecting Hint: Decorated examples are highly sought by collectors. Look for examples in original paint with strong colors and unusual designs. Early dated examples also attract added attention.

Bentwood, oval
>Decor, hearts in olive-gold stencil, black ground, one nailed finger, with lid, alligatored on top, 1-3/4" h, 5-1/2" w, 3-3/4" d 247.50
>Decor, foliage flourishes in green, yellow and black, salmon-red ground, pine, seven-finger laced construction, wrought-iron handle, cracked lid, 5-3/8" h, 14-1/2" w, 9" d 770.00
>Decor, floral design in red, green, yellow and gray on black ground, wear, 10" l 3,080.00
>Grain-decor, orig black graining with varnish, Hersey-type finger, iron tacks, lid glued, 5-1/2" l 192.50
>Painted, blue, 1-1/2" h, 3-3/4" l, 2-1/4" w 467.50
>Painted, old green, 1-finger construction, steel tacks, 4" l 357.50
>Painted, old worn green, lapped seams, lid with some traces of black, some old filled chips, 13" l 605.00
>Varnish finish worn, 1-finger construction, steel tacks, 6" l 99.00

Bentwood, round
>6-1/4" dia, star design in black on lid, old olive-gray ground, lapped seams, iron tacks 412.50
>8" dia, old dark green paint, one finger 495.00
>8-3/4" dia, 3-3/4" h, medium green paint worn at edges, overlapping seams, some edge damage on base 275.00
>9" dia, hardwood and pine, old patina, lapped seams, chip carvings, piercings include compass star and heart, steel and copper tacks, few breaks, age cracks 770.00
>10" dia, old light-green repaint, lapped seams, some wear 143.00
>10" dia, pine and beech, old dark finish, lapped seams, steel tacks, lid with primitive inscription "Jew Denmnia, S J C," edge damage 247.50
>11-1/2" dia, 8-1/4" h, donut box, black graining on dark-red ground, faint stenciled flowers on side within beaded frames with inverted corners, round lid with carved handle, two splits in body, edge damage to lid, attributed to Ohio 385.00
>12" dia, 6-1/2" h, revarnished oak, wire nails, bentwood handle attached with wooden pegs, edge damage 82.50
>15" dia, 7" h, old patina, lapped seams, copper tacks, lid, swivel handle 467.50
>18-1/4" dia, 13-1/4" h, old dark finish, lapped seams on base, finger on lid, square nails, lid decorated with nine square brass tacks 220.00

Birch bark, oval, wooden ends, birch bark on lid, sawtooth edges, cutout triangle designs, edge wear, 4-1/2" h, 6-1/8" l 137.50

Decorated
>Basket of flowers on lid, orig green ground, swags and tassels in red, gray and black on front and sides, yellow, black, red and white border, green interior, lock and till, 5" h, 10-1/2" w, 5-3/4" d 10,175.00
>Baskets of fruit, tulips and shells, pine, tulips on ends, two baskets of fruit on front panel, four shells on lid, decor in gold, red and white, black ground, gold borders, inset panels, ball feet, ring pull, lock with brass escutcheon, Massachusetts, 5-1/2" h, 10" w, 6-3/4" d 7,700.00
>Bird, old mustard ground, blue long-tailed bird on lid, green swags and tassels with white flowers on panels, black band accents on corners, interior in cream-white paint with simple floral decor on lid, initials "M.P.D," dovetailed case, hinged lid, iron bail handle, paint wear, edge damage, 7-1/4" h, 7-3/8" w, 5-5/8" d 935.00
>Eagle, chip-carved decor, light/dark geometric inlay designs, "V.L. Quinn" on lid, walnut, edge damage, age crack, glued repairs, 13-1/2" l 357.50
>Eagle and banner, pheasants, orig red paint, eagle and banner and "Hannah Miller" on lid, pheasants and cornucopia on front, birds kissing on one end and apart on the other, decor in yellow, green, gold and black, interior lined in worn orange paper, ball feet, small areas of touchup on lid, found in Vermont, 4-3/4" h, 9" w, 4-5/8" d 12,100.00
>Floral decor, old green and brown scrolled repaint, brick-red ground, three divided interior compartments, 4th compartment in lid, crazing, 8-1/4" h, 13" w, 7" d 357.50
>Floral decor, red and yellow flowers with green leaves on lid, black ground, pine, 5" h, 15" w, 10" d 495.00
>Floral decor, orig reddish-orange paint, over-varnished natural wood panels with polychrome floral decor, European, beech, 4-3/4" h, 12-3/4" w, 8" d 412.50
>Floral and geometric decor, pine, black paint, white, red yellow and red decor, dovetailed case, wire hinges, pencil inscription "Douglas 1822, Massachusetts" inside, 6-1/4" h, 15-3/4" w, 7-3/4" d 2,750.00
>Grain-decor, orig black and red graining, ogee sides, dovetailed case, square feet, molded-edge lid, brass bail handle on top 550.00
>Grain-decor, old brown graining, yellow ground, poplar, orig brass bail handle, 6-1/4" h, 14" w, 8-3/4" d 495.00
>Grain-decor, orig brown graining over green ground with gesso beneath, dovetailed, wrought-iron handles on ends, initials worked into decor on front panel, paper label "Jon-- Aldrick, Brattleboro," one bail missing, edge wear, 12-1/2" h, 32" w, 13" d 440.00

Box with decoration of a basket of flowers, swags and tassels, green ground, 5" h, 10-1/2" w, $10,175. (Photo courtesy of Garth's Auctions, Delaware, Ohio)

Grain-decor, old brown and black graining, yellow line borders, bracket feet, arched apron, dovetailed case, ivory diamond-shaped escutcheon, molded-edge lid, lift-out tray, four styles of graining inside, tray and interior old blue, 6" h, 10-1/2" w, 7" d 715.00

Grain-decor, orig brownish-red flame graining, dovetailed, minor damage at hinges, 7" h, 12" w, 7" d 247.50

Grain-decor, green vinegar graining, 10" h, 24" w, 12" d 935.00

Grain-decor, green vinegar graining, metal lock, wear, 15" h, 32" w, 15" d............................. 275.00

Grain-decor, orig red and black graining, pine, dovetailed, brass lock and hasp, brass bail, embossed oval escutcheon, wire hinges, some wear, 5" h, 10" w, 5-1/2" d 330.00

Grain-decor, worn orig reddish-brown vinegar graining over yellow ground, partial early wallpaper lining, dovetailed, pine, bail handle missing from lid, 7" h, 14-5/8" w, 7-1/4" d............................. 330.00

Grain-decor, rust and black, ochre ground, zigzag striped sides, bottom decor with spotted dog in a landscape surrounded by zigzag border, white interior, minor paint loss, 4" h, 12" w, 6-1/2" d... 1,955.00

Grapes and leaves decor, old red repaint, stencil design on front, yellow borders, poplar, embossed brass escutcheon, replaced ring pull on lid, 5" h, 11" w, 6-1/2" d... 247.50

House and tree decor in orig paint on sides and top in red, blue, green, salmon, black and brown, pine, wooden-peg construction, minor wear and age crack, 6" h, 9-7/8" w, 7-3/8" d 660.00

Incised decor, pinwheel on lid, red paint, 2" h, 4" w, 3" d 495.00

Painted, pine, orig black paint, stripes in red, olive and yellow, divided interior in old powdery blue, dovetailed, 4-1/2" h, 10" w, 5-1/2" d............ 990.00

Painted, pine, orig dark brown, green and yellow, dovetailed case, lined with period wallpaper, orig brass ring handle, 6" h, 14" w, 10-1/2" d 550.00

Painted, pine, orig brownish-red paint, molded bracket feet with cutouts, dovetailed case, domed top, 8-3/4" h, 13-1/4" w, 8-3/4" d............. 1,100.00

Painted, poplar, orig green paint, black and yellow striping, brass knob, 4" h, 9" w, 5" d 1,760.00

Painted, poplar, orig red paint, yellow border, dovetailed case, chamfered-edge top, replaced ivory escutcheon, floral wallpaper on interior of lid, 4-1/2" h, 8" w, 5" d 1,265.00

Painted, poplar, orig yellow paint, black and red stripes, gold monogram on lid, dovetailed case, two dovetailed drawers, interior and drawers lined in red paper, landscape lithograph under lid, orig embossed brass hardware with ring handles, 5" h, 11-3/4" w, 7-3/4" d 3,850.00

Painted, orig yellow, leaves stenciled on black border, dovetailed, wire hinges, hasp lock, 5-1/4" h, 10-1/2" w, 6-1/4" d 2,310.00

Rose decor, old repaint, raised-panel sliding lid with yellow, green and blue rose mulled decor and geometric border in white, blue and green, sponged reddish-brown decor on base with blue trim and white initials "M.H.D. 1866," pine, 6-1/2" h, 19" w, 12-1/4" d.. 550.00

Sponge-decor, black and brown sponge ground over earlier red, green and yellow border, initials on top, maple, brass lock, 4" h, 12-1/4" w, 7-1/2" d....412.50

Sprigs in blue, light-green ground, red line detail, blue border, poplar, till, lock and key, attributed to Dauphin County, Pa., worn edges, 5" h, 9-1/2" w, 6" d 770.00

Star decor, pine and poplar, orig red paint, black, red, green, yellow and white star ornaments on lid, front, side and ends, vine decor on base trim, till with secret drawer, homemade wire and tin hinges, found in New York state, 7" h, 16" w, 8" d 4,400.00

Star flowers and linear in alligatored yellow and red, old dark-green ground not orig, pine, dovetailed, lift-lid, lock, minor wear, 1 hinge repaired, 4-3/4" h, 8-5/8" w, 4-1/2" d 1,100.00

Woman decor, early repaint, panel on lid shows lady in green dress seated with her arm on a table, red corners, gold striping, matching borders on front and sides, interior painted blue-gray, poplar, edge wear, 4-5/8" h, 13-7/8" w, 9-5/8" d 1,650.00

Dome-top, decorated

Orig black paint, blue edge striping, stenciled decor in red and silver, freehand red and yellow flowers on lid, pine, brass bail handle and lock with hasp, New England, possibly Massachusetts, minor edge wear, 5" h, 10" w, 6-1/2" d 5,225.00

Old black repaint with yellow striping over earlier red, pine, found in Maine, orig brass bail on lid, bails added on ends, 9" h, 18" w, 9" d 495.00

Brown and green grained ground, yellow lines, lid with two green ground circles with red initials "MB," pine, nailed, paint worn, staple hinges broken, hasp gone, 11" h, 22-3/4" w, 12-3/4" d 137.50

Old green repaint over red, strawberries and "Friendship's Token" stenciled on lid in gold and red, pine, wallpaper-lined interior, porcelain knob, minor edge wear, 4" h, 8" w, 6" d 137.50

Birds, urn and flowers on lid, birds and flowers on front, bright flowers on sides, old blue-green decor, wrought-iron nails, broken wire pull on lid, minor insect damage, 12-1/2" h, 19" w, 13" d 660.00

Floral design in white with yellow dividers, orig red ground, poplar, square nails, interior with partial 1839 New York newspaper, stains, age cracks, 8-1/2" h, 22" w, 9" d 2,530.00

Floral design with birds, baskets and swag in old white, red, blue and green, edge wear, age cracks, hasp missing, 12-1/4" h, 19-1/4" w, 13-1/4" d 715.00

Orig floral design, red and white flowers, dark-green foliage, tan ground, birds and large urn on lid, rosehead nails, wire bail handle, minor insect damage, replaced hinge 687.50

Flowering plants on top, front and sides in red, green, white and yellow, old deep-blue repaint, large bird perched on branch on lid, yellow line borders, iron hasp lock, wire bail on lid, wear, 8-7/8" h, 14-1/8" w, 9-1/8" d 440.00

Initials ML in large red octagonal border on lid, same border around top and sides, mustard ground, tacked leather trim, metal lock and hasp, from Conn., 7-1/4" h, 14-1/2" w, 6-1/2" d 5,225.00

Tulips, white and red with green leaves, dark-blue ground, yellow edging, tin lock and hasp, wire hinges, bail handle, wear, 4-5/8" h, 8-1/8" w, 3-7/8" d 302.50

Tulips and other flowers, red, white and green, dark over-varnish, early T-head nails, ornate hasp lock, age cracks, 10" h, 15-3/4" w, 9-1/8" d 275.00

Dome-top, grain-decorated

Orig black graining, red ground, dovetailed, minor age cracks in lid, hasp missing, found in Cape Cod, 13" h, 28-1/2" w, 14" d 935.00

Old brown sponged graining, poplar, dovetailed, wrought-iron lock (hasp incomplete), brass bail handle, interior lined with worn printed paper, late fraktur glued inside lid, 11-3/4" l 220.00

Orig brown flame graining, poplar, dovetailed case, wrought-iron lock with hasp, end handles, age crack in lid, 12" h, 24" w, 12" d 770.00

Orig brown vinegar graining, poplar, dovetailed, iron and brass lock, missing hasp, 13" h, 30" w, 14-1/2" d 165.00

Orig brown vinegar graining, poplar, dovetailed, wrought-iron lock, missing hasp, 11-5/8" h, 23" w, 12" d 137.50

Ochre, mustard and brown, vinegar graining, swirled design, found in Albany Plantation, Maine, 12-1/2" h, 24" w, 13" d......... 4,125.00

Grained red repaint, yellow- and red-lined borders, painted fans in corners, gold "A.H." on lid, poplar, fitted lock, minor age cracks, 5" h, 10-1/2" w, 6-1/2" d 715.00

Red and black, 11" h, 27" w, 14" d 660.00

Red and black graining, green banding, yellow striping, matching set of three ranging from 8" h, 17-1/2" w, 9" d to 15" h, 36" w, 17" d 3,850.00

Orig vinegar graining, pine, incomplete orig wrought-iron handles and hasp, age crack in top, 16-1/2" h, 32-1/2" w, 13-1/4" d 357.50

Dome-top, leather-covered, brass tacks

Pine, floral scroll paper interior, brass bail handle, embossed escutcheon, square nails, replaced brass lock and hasp, hinges removed, some tacks missing, wear, 4-3/4" h, 10" w, 6" d 110.00

Rosehead nails, lined with early newspaper and cut-out from Maine Militia enrollment certificate dated 1835, old green paint on inside edge of lid and base, wrought-iron lock, 5" h, 10" w, 6" d ... 550.00

Dome-top, painted

Old green, pine, wire end handles, staple hinges, age crack in lid, 4-3/4" h, 10-1/2" w, 5-3/4" d 302.50

Old green, pine, wooden pegs, applied base molding, wire hinges, found in Kingston, Mass., 6" h, 10-1/2" w, 7" d 550.00

Old green, black line detail, faint fans on lid, pine, dovetailed, orig brass bail pulls on ends, hasp lock, wear, found in Maine, 9" h, 22" w, 10-1/2" d 357.50

Old green, yellow striping, initials in oval and 1828 date, 15" h, 29" w, 15" d 412.50

Old red, poplar, brass lock and hasp, brass bail handle on top, 5" h, 10" w, 5" d 660.00

Dome-top, sponged, orig red decor, pine, dovetailed, orig brass bail handle on top, brass lock with hasp, 6" h, 14" w, 9" d 990.00

Donut, decor, orig gold floral stenciling, mustard ground, with lid, wear, age cracks, 6-3/4" h, 9-1/2" dia .. 522.50

Dresser, decor, early 19th C., orig green paint, lid stenciled in gold with fruit, stag and star on sides, domed top with leather hinge, rectangular box with rounded sides, bracket-shaped feet, minor wear, 5-3/8" h, 8" w, 4" d......... 575.00

Hanging

Indian, birch bark, two pockets, 11" h, 9" w ... 440.00

Painted "Mail" below tombstone-shaped top, two pockets mkd "Received" and "To Go" 660.00

Painted, brown, two open slant-front compartments, shaped sides, lollipop hanger, 19th C., wear, scratches, 24" h, 9-3/8" w, 5-1/2" d 2,070.00

Painted, brown, lollipop top, one pocket, 11" h 247.50

Painted, dark red, pine, slanted hinged lid on upper compartment, open lower compartment, early 19th C., minor split, wear, 13-3/4" h, 6-3/4" w 488.75

Painted, orig red, black line borders, slant lid with beveled edges, arched crest with half-moon-shaped cutout, dovetailed, wooden pegs, old damage at corner on lid, glued hairline on crest, 16" h, 12-1/2" w, 10" d 550.00

Pine, orig dark finish, slant lid, beveled base, orig surface-mounted brass hinges, lollipop-shaped crest with hole in center, dovetailed, 17" h, 11-5/8" w, 11" d 990.00

Harvard

5" l, 3-1/2" w, 1-1/2" h, oval, grained.............. 385.00

5-1/4" l, 4" w, 2-1/4" h, oval, dark-green paint.... 330.00

6-1/2" l, 5-1/4" w, 2-3/4" h, oval, black paint .. 302.50

Set of three nested boxes, red paint, "B.Sprague" on lids, largest is 2-3/4" h, 6-1/2" w, 5" d 6,050.00

Hat

Bentwood, oval, refinished, steel nails and wooden pegs, pine base and lid, few pegs missing, 10" h, 14-1/4" w, 11-1/4" d 192.50

Wallpaper-covered top hat box, green wallpaper, brown, gold and green floral pattern, 19th C., scattered losses, stains, wear, 8-3/4" h.......... 1,495.00

Inlaid, walnut with figured maple and other woods, diamond and triangular inlaid designs, old worn finish, base and lid edge molding, interior till, found in Ohio, 13-3/4" l.. 440.00

Miscellaneous

Apple or berry box, wooden, old worn salmon red paint, laced panels in side and bottom, one pc of lace missing, 3-1/4" h, 7-1/2" sq 275.00

Apple or bread box, oval stave construction, old dark red, green and gold paint, cutouts including hearts in handles, damage and repair, attributed to Pa., 11" l... 302.50

Farrier's, blue paint, stenciled horse decor, 14" h, 18" w, 15" d.. 275.00

Hanging scrub box, pine, 38" h........................ 55.00

Hanging wall box, pine, old brown paint, scalloped end panels, three beaded crosspieces on front, arched back, age crack on back panel, 14" h, 18" w, 4-3/4" d.. 165.00

Hanging wall box, poplar, old dark varnish, slant lid with divided interior, lower drawer with beveled edges and divided interior, brass pull, dovetailed case, 11" h, 15" w, 9-1/4" d........................ 302.50

Vinegar-grained box in ochre, mustard and brown, 12-1/2" h, 24" w, $4,125. (Photo courtesy of Cyr Auction Company, Gray, Maine)

Hanging wall box, poplar, refinished, traces of green, three stepped compartments, square nails, age crack in one side, 20-3/4" h, 10-1/4" w, 5-3/4" d.. 302.50

Marbled paper, applied engraving of a woman, 1-1/2" h, 4" w, 5" d....................................... 605.00

Painted, old blue, square nails, hand plane marks, removable lid, 9-1/8" h, 9-1/2" w, 8-5/8" d .. 220.00

Taper box made like a pipe box, mahogany, old finish, wire nails, 10" h................................... 302.50

Utility box, cherry and poplar, red repaint, dovetailed, base molding, one drawer, divided compartments, top has three compartments (one with lid), 7-1/2" h, 16" w, 8-1/2" d............................. 825.00

Walnut, old alligatored finish, dovetailed base and lid, till, two interior drawers with mahogany veneer fronts, brass key hole and hinges, glued repair, 5" h, 11-1/2" w, 5-5/8" d 247.50

Walnut, old varnish finish, molded-edge base, lid with additional applied moldings, lock and key, 5-1/4" h, 11" w, 5-1/2" d 247.50

Offering, decor, house-shaped, iron with old paint, German lettering on one end, door on one side tabbed for lock, painted doors and windows on all sides, minor wear, welded repairs, 8" h, 7" w, 5-1/2" d.......... 275.00

Pencil

Rectangular, children at North Pole litho, green paint, minor wear, 7-7/8" l............................ 71.50

Rectangular, Mother Goose litho, worn varnish, stains, minor wear, 7-7/8" l 27.50

Sled-shaped, children sledding litho, minor wear, 1" h, 8-1/4" l, pr.. 247.50

Scouring, hanging

Rectangular with peaked top, back tapers toward bottom, sides with arched tops, scalloped front, back with traces of blue paint, New England, late 18th/early 19th C., 2" pc of wood missing from one side, 12-1/4" h, 5-1/4" w, 3-1/4" d 90.00

Softwood, large circular top, back flares toward base, applied molding across top and down sides, rectangular bottom with beveled edges, refinished, 22-1/4" h, 8-1/2" w, 3-1/2" d 150.00

Slide Lid

Brown finish, dovetailed case, slide lid with carved thumbhole and beveled edges, old nail holes, restoration to edge of lid, 6" h, 15-1/2" w, 12" d 275.00

Decor, elaborate stylized floral design in gold, black, red and yellow on blue ground, small area of touchup on rim, minor age crack, attributed to Pa., 3-1/2" h, 7-1/4" w, 4-1/4" d....................... 8,525.00

Decor, tulips in red, yellow and green, salmon ground with black dots, decor probably orig, pine, wood pegs, minor edge wear, 5" h, 12" w, 6-1/2" d... 1,375.00

Grain-decor, orig red vinegar graining on sides, old electric-blue repaint on lid and base, pine, dovetailed, chamfered lid, dovetail chips, small hole in lid, 3-3/4" h, 13-3/4" w, 9-5/8" d 440.00

Painted, orig gray, "Lissie" in script on lid, pencil inscription under lid "Hawes 186-," square-nail construction, chamfered lid, crack along lid track, two nails added, 7-5/8" h, 11-1/4" w, 10-1/2" d 247.50

Snuff

Burl, round, double incised lines on top and bottom, 2-3/8" dia 137.50

Burl, round, good figure, 2-7/8" dia 220.00

Burl, round, hinged lift lid with inset mirror, 2-3/8" dia 247.50

Burl with tortoise shell liner, round, lid with glass lens over brass repousse portrait medallion of George Washington, age crack, liner damaged, 2" dia 165.00

Coin silver, oval, hinged lid, maker's mark, possibly American, 3-1/2" l 605.00

Horn, oval, two-pc, carved initials and 1779, fleur-de-lis decor, 3" x 2-1/4" 467.50

Leather, shoe form, 19th C., wear, loss, 2-1/8" h, 4" l 115.00

Papier-mâché, double lid, painted, top lid on round box depicts hunter, attendant and dog, inner lid shows erotic couple, 19th C., minor wear, 7/8" h, 3-3/8" dia 172.50

Storage

Leather-covered, wooden, black leather, brass tack border decor, brass tag inscribed "Wm. S. Lincoln," interior covered with printed fabric depicting presidents Washington through Andrew Jackson and a Worcester, Mass., manufacturer's label, wear, losses to leather, 6-1/2" h, 17" w, 13" d 431.25

Painted, old gray-blue, pine, possibly Ohio, early 19th C., dovetailed tapering box, rectangular slant-lid top opens to shallow and deep compart-

Storage box in old gray-blue paint, 46-1/2" h, 47-3/4" w, $3,450. (Photo courtesy of Skinner Auctioneers & Appraisers of Antiques & Fine Arts, Boston and Bolton, Mass.)ca

ments, bracket feet, 46-1/2" h, 47-3/4" w, 22" d 3,450.00

Round, wooden, worn orig yellow paint, polychrome stenciled birds and flowers, matching lid with handle, wear, decor faded, age cracks, 7-3/4" h, 11-1/2" dia 1,760.00

Bride's Boxes (see Dower Chests)

Bucket Benches

Background: Also known as water benches, these items traditionally had a closed cupboard below a single shelf raised above the cupboard top. The shelf often had a gallery around it. Used prior to indoor plumbing, the cupboard top held a wash basin and pails of fresh water. Additional containers of water and other items could be stored in the base. Evolving from this form were examples without the closed bottom—having one or more exposed shelves for holding buckets of water. Pine was most often used to make bucket benches, which almost always date to the 19th century.

Cupboard-base, painted

Dark-brown, softwood, 7-1/2" deep shelf across top at back, cyma-shaped sides extending down to top of cupboard base, one small drawer centered over two paneled doors, plank sides with arched cutouts at base, 44-7/8" h, 44-3/4" w, 16-1/2" d 1,900.00

Early gray, splashboard around all four sides tapers from 9" in back to 2-5/8" in front, two paneled doors, plank ends with arched cutout feet, scrubbed top, 34-1/2" h, 49" w, 18" d 4,400.00

Painted

Red, pine, two shelves, arched cutout feet on end boards, 35" h, 40" w, 12" d 880.00

Red (old), bootjack ends, two deep shelves in base, scalloped side panels, two shallow shelves at top, arched gallery, square nails, 51-1/2" h, 43-3/4" w, base 12-3/4" d 2,200.00

Red (old), pine, square-nail construction, one-board ends, bootjack cutouts, one-board shelf at bottom, two-board top with rounded front corners, minor damage to finish on feet, 27-1/2" h, 48" w, 16" d 660.00

Red repaint, pine, scrolled ends dovetailed into top, attributed to Indiana Amish, 19" h, 24" w, 10-1/2" d 550.00

Red wash, dovetailed case, three mortised shelves, incised molded ends on case and shelves, bootjack feet, two-board back, 49-1/2" h, 42" w, 12-1/2" d 605.00

Yellow, two shelves, bootjack feet, backboard behind lower shelf, 40" h, 40" w 825.00

Yellow repaint (old) over earlier colors, cutout ends and feet, two paneled doors in base, three dovetailed drawers in top shelf and gallery top, cast-

Bucket bench with traces of old red paint, 40" h, 55-1/2" w, $4,025. (Photo courtesy of Skinner Auctioneers & Appraisers of Antiques & Fine Arts, Boston and Bolton, Mass.)

Wooden bucket in red paint, 4-1/2" h, $225.

iron pulls and latches over-painted, Pennsylvania origin, 48" h, 42" w, 17-1/4" d 4,400.00

Pine, refinished, three graduated stepped shelves, truncated sides, top shelf enclosed on the back, top with added boards, 44" h, 35-1/2" w, 4-1/2" d to 14-3/4" d... 495.00

Poplar, traces of various colors, bootjack ends, beaded cross stretcher, scalloped side supports, 33-1/4" h, 37" w, 8-1/2" d top shelf, 15-1/2" d center shelf ... 1,155.00

Buckets

Background: Buckets were a necessity in rural America, and many specialized bucket forms evolved over the years. Buckets were used to collect, store, and transport all manner of liquids, including milk, water, and sap. Many sugar buckets, the form most people are familiar with, found their way into homes where they were used as sewing baskets or storage containers.

Examples which retain their period paint or which have a manufacturer's mark command premium prices.

Bentwood staves and handle, dark patina, 10-1/4" h, 12" dia 247.50

Bentwood staves completely cover exterior, swing handle, interior and base in worn red paint, exterior cleaned down to surface, 5-3/8" h, 7-3/4" dia ... 220.00

Graniteware

Black/white swirl 265.00

Blue/white, straight sides flare to top, bail handle, 7-7/8" h, 10-1/2" dia..................................... 85.00

Blue/white swirl, black rim, bail handle, minor dents, some loss to graniteware finish, about two gal 195.00

Emerald Ware, green/white swirl exterior, white interior, black rim, bail handle, about two gal ... 275.00

Miniature

Tin, green with yellow stencil, "Linwood Park," bottom embossed with battleship and "Remember the Maine," wire bail, black wooden handle, wear, dents, three small rim splits, 4" h, 6" dia......115.50

Wooden, painted, orig orangish-red, wear and fading, brass bands, turned lid, wire bail handle, minor age cracks, 4" h............................... 220.00

Painted

Blue, pinned handle, 17" h............................ 440.00

Blue-green, stave and lapped wooden bands, curved swing handle, pegged joinery, 14-1/4" h... 1,150.00

Mustard with black stencil "Armours Veribest Mince Meat," stave construction, metal bands, wire bail with wooden handle, top stuck, 11" h, 11-3/8" dia 220.00

Light gray, bentwood staves and handle, age crack in bottom, 7-1/2" h, 11" dia 550.00

Yellow, berry bucket..................................... 220.00

Yellow, metal bands, 11-1/2" h........................ 55.00

Stave constructed, old black repaint, gold line borders, three wide bands with pegged bentwood handle, minor wear and chips, 13-3/4" h, 11-1/4" dia 577.50

Burl

Background: A burl is a type of growth or knot on some trees that results in a twisting and turning of the grain, producing exceptionally strong wood with a particularly beautiful pattern or design. Burl items will not easily crack or warp.

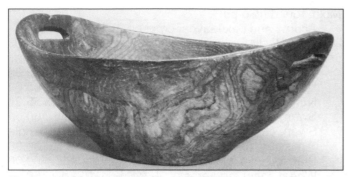

Burl bowl with cutout handles, 20" dia, 8" h, minor age cracks, $2,760. (Photo courtesy of Skinner Auctioneers & Appraisers of Antiques & Fine Arts, Boston and Bolton, Mass.)

Box
>   Book-shaped, sliding lid, 5-1/4" h, 2-1/2" w,
>   1-3/4" d 357.50
>   Carved, old varnish finish, made from 1 pc of wood,
>   hinged lid, brass closure, relief rococo border on
>   lid with "S.K." and shells, front has incised lines
>   with relief border, sides have Greek key design,
>   bottom initialed "F.G.S.R.," 1-5/8" h, 3-7/8" w,
>   2-1/2" d 330.00
>   Round, turned base and lid, ivory finial, interior
>   carved into separate compartments, replaced foot,
>   2-1/4" h, 5-1/8" dia 192.50

Butter paddle
>   Bird-head handle (stylized), 11-1/8" l 715.00
>   Circle carved at end of handle, wide bowl,
>   9" l 2,035.00
>   Scrolled handle, carved fluting, dark patina, scorch
>   marks, 7-3/4" l 2,530.00

Ladle, hand-hewn, bowl-shaped with ring decor, flared
>   handle with incised line and star decor, refinished,
>   filled knot holes, 11-1/2" l 440.00

Mallet
>   Burl head, 15-1/2" circum, 11" l 33.00

Mortar, old finish, turned detail, edge damage, age
>   crack, 6-1/2" h 60.50

Soap dish, rectangular, canted sides, 1-5/8" h, 5" w,
>   3-7/8" d 550.00

Urn with cover, 10" h 192.50

Butter Churns

Background: Homemakers have long used churns to create butter. Skim the cream off of fresh milk, put the cream into a container, create sufficient agitation, and butter is produced. Wooden churns were primarily used during the 1800s, although stoneware examples became popular during the second half of the 19th century. Both types involved a wooden dasher or "stomper" with a perforated flat head that was moved up and down in the container. Other variations included box- and barrel-shaped churns with a crank handle. Glass churns were primarily used during the 20th century.

Reference: Linda Campbell Franklin, *300 Years of Kitchen Collectibles*, 4th ed., Krause Publications, 1997.

Also See: Stoneware.

Glass, Dazey
>   1 qt., beveled edge 2,500.00
>   1 qt., round label 2,100.00
>   2 qt., bullseye 325.00
>   3 qt., bullseye 325.00
>   4 qt., bullseye 140.00
>   6 qt., sloped shoulder 200.00
>   8 qt., sloped shoulder 300.00

Glass, unmarked, 2 qt. 95.00

Wooden
>   Grain-decor, poplar and ash, black circle graining on
>   red ground, white striping, stenciled "E.H. Funks,
>   Champion Churn, Sturgis, Mich.," 1868 patent,
>   missing dasher, 24" h, 14-1/2" w, 13-3/8" d ...770.00
>   Miniature, natural finish, tapering sides, raised
>   medallion handle on rim, with lid/dasher, mkd
>   "Fearing, Hingham," 9-3/4" h 605.00
>   Natural finish, wooden staves, piggin handle 192.50

Wooden, painted
>   Gray-green, with dasher and lid, wear, minor paint
>   loss, 47-1/4" h 431.25
>   Old green, pine, two lapped hickory bands, one iron
>   band, wooden dasher, oak lid, base warped and
>   loose, 16-3/4" h 165.00
>   Mustard, metal staves 302.50
>   Red, carved locking staves, 42" h 440.00
>   Old red, four lapped staves (one missing), rosehead
>   nails, old mismatched lid, wear, 20-1/2" h 82.50
>   Orig red, tapered design, three iron staves, minor
>   age crack in bottom, 24" h 220.00
>   Red exterior, yellow interior, stave-constructed, steel
>   bands mkd "John Bradley & Co Stourbridge," with
>   lid/dasher, 18-1/2" h 440.00

One-gal. churn with graphic design, Western Stoneware Co., Monmouth, Ill., $1,500.

Butter Molds and Stamps

Background: Two-piece butter molds and one-piece butter stamps are popular with collectors of kitchen items, as well as with those interested in items exhibiting a folk art flair. Molds were used to both shape and stamp the butter, and they are primarily found in rounded-cup form and rectangular-box form; stamps are usually round with a knob handle protruding from the back, although rare lollipop versions do exist. Many were factory made; however, some quite obviously were chiseled by hand. Sheaves of wheat, flowers, and pineapples are among the more common designs; Germanic tulips and animal patterns are more difficult to find.

References: Linda Campbell Franklin, *300 Years of Kitchen Collectibles*, 4th ed., Krause Publications, 1997; Paul E. Kindig, *Butter Prints and Molds*, Schiffer Publishing, 1986.

Collectors' Clubs: Butter Pat Collectors International, 38 Acton St., Maynard, MA 01754; Butter Pat Patter Assoc., 265 Eagle Bend Dr., Bigfork, MT 59911.

Reproduction Alert: Reproduction butter molds and stamps were made as early as the 1940s, so age does not necessarily guarantee authenticity.

Note: Butter molds and butter stamps could both be used to print a design on butter. That is why these items are often referred to as butter prints.

Lollipop stamp, one-sided
   Compass flower, hexagonal design, chamfered handle, Pennsylvania, small age split, 4-7/8" dia, 9-3/8" l 770.00
   Crane-like bird flanked by flower and foliage, cracked oval handle, 2-3/4" dia, 6" l 325.00
   Large carved tulip flanked by small leaves and small 6-pointed stars, chip-carved design around rim, round tapered stick handle, plain back, 4" dia, 8-1/4" l 550.00
Lollipop stamp, two-sided, bunch of grapes on one side, cornucopia of flowers on other, flattened oval handle, several rim cracks, 3-1/2" dia 150.00
Mold, rectangular (two-pc)
   Eight individual carved designs including strawberries, acorns, varnish finish, 11" h, 5-1/2" w . 137.50
   Cow, ornamental designs along outer edge, surface worn from use, minor age crack, 3-1/2" x 4-7/8" 192.50
   Fish, dark patina, lollipop handle, scratches, 3-1/4" x 8-1/4" 192.50
   Geometric, radial designs flanked by crescent shapes, carved five-point star in circle flanked in corners by fan motifs, walnut, 4-1/2" x 7-3/4" 130.00
   Grapevine with leaves and cluster of grapes, 4-1/2" x 6-1/4" 85.00

Mold, round (two-pc)
   Acorns and oak leaves, cracked, 5-1/8" h, 4-3/4" dia 80.00
   Floral and foliage, notch-carved band around rim, 4-3/8" dia 40.00
   Leaf, 4" dia 60.00
   Nut and leaf, 3-3/4" dia 55.00
   Swan, outer mold with two cracks, 4-3/4" dia .. 80.00
   Swan, chip-carved border, threaded wooden handle missing, 5-3/8" dia 230.00
   Star, top with two age cracks, 4-1/2" dia 50.00
   Wheat sheaf, age cracks, 4-1/4" h, 4-1/2" dia . 50.00
Stamp, single (one-pc)
   Acorn flanked by oak leaves, chip-carved border, early replaced handle, insect damage, 4" dia 85.00
   Cow feeding from trough, small floral design above, flanked by cluster of four small diamonds, spool-shaped handle, 4" dia 350.00
   Cow with tree at right, 3-5/8" dia 170.00
   Eagle, 3-5/8" dia 550.00
   Eagle, sawtooth border, 3-3/4" dia 230.00
   Eagle flanked by floral design, eight-point star at left, chip-carved border, crack, 4-1/8" dia 300.00
   Eagle surrounded by stars, cross-hatched feathers, minor age crack, 4-1/4" dia 770.00
   Eagle with shield, good patina, 2-5/8" dia 220.00
   Flower, chip-carved detail, scratched numbers on back, 3-3/4" dia 192.50
   Flower, compass flower below, chip-carved detail, small age cracks, 4-1/4" dia 220.00
   Flower, star-shaped flower flanked by leaves, 3-5/8" dia 55.00
   Flower and foliage, minor wood loss to edges, 4-3/8" dia 170.00
   Flower flanked by scrolled leaves, surrounded by concentric lines, round knob-shaped handle, rim wear, 3-1/4" dia 75.00
   Flower surrounded by leaves, minor edge damage, 4-3/8" dia 110.00
   Fruit with small leaves surrounded by concentric line border, 2-7/8" dia 40.00
   Heart, four small hearts surrounding cluster of four small rosettes, chip-carved border, significant wood loss to edges, later replaced handle, 4-1/4" dia 400.00
   Leaf, scrolled foliate design at side, 2-7/8" dia 45.00
   Mum-like flowers, small hole, worm holes, 4-1/4" dia 550.00
   Pomegranate and two curled leaves, notch-carved border, 3" h, 4-1/2" dia 100.00
   Six-pointed star, concentric circular lines and swirled outer band, slightly round back, wear, 1-3/4" h, 3-5/8" dia 180.00
   Thistle, with knob-shaped handle, 3-3/4" dia ... 75.00
   Thistle and rose, chip-carved detail, 3-5/8" dia 130.00
   Thistle and leaves, three light age lines, 3-1/2" dia 370.00
   Tulip-like flower and small bird flanked by flora and sprigs, chips, 2" h, 3-1/8" dia 120.00

Tulip-like floral sprig with incised leaves, slightly rounded back, age crack, 3-3/8" h, 3-1/2" dia 150.00

Wheat sheaf, half-round, 3-7/8" h, 6-3/8" w ... 522.50

Wheat sheaf, round, chip-carved border, 3-5/8" dia 120.00

Stamp, double (one-pc)

Bird on branch on one print, tulip and four rosettes on other, connected by tapered center shaft-like handle, chip-carved borders, 3-1/8" dia...... 375.00

Bird with small sun above bird's back on one print, tulip with stem flanked by two small rosettes and two small petaled florets on other, connected by tapered center shaft-like handle, slight crack, 3-1/4" dia and 2-5/8" dia 270.00

Butter Paddles

Background: These wooden utensils could be used to work a small amount of butter and to move butter from one container to another.

FYI: Strictly utilitarian, butter paddles were seldom decorated except for the possible addition of a design at the end of the handle. However, decorative woods such as tiger maple were sometimes used.

Reference: Linda Campbell Franklin, *300 Years of Kitchen Collectibles*, 4th ed., Krause Publications, 1997.

Bird's-eye maple, age cracks, 9-1/8" l 55.00

Burl

Bird-head handle (stylized), 11-1/8" l 715.00

Circle carved at end of handle, wide bowl, 9" l 2,035.00

Scrolled handle, carved fluting, dark patina, scorch marks, 7-3/4" l 2,530.00

Paddle with butter print handle, floral on one side, floral medallion on other, worm holes, 11-7/8" l 247.50

Softwood, spade-shaped blade with carved heart and leaf design, tapered flattened handle with incised line design ending in rounded end, 9-1/4" l 250.00

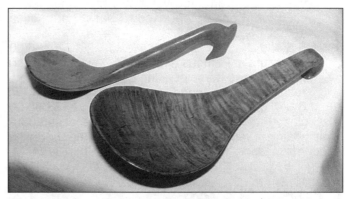

Butter paddles: Bird-handle example (left), $175; 11" tiger maple paddle, $550.

Cabinets

Background: A cabinet is a piece of case furniture having drawers, shelves, or compartments.

Dental

Oak, open area over eleven drawers over one drawer over one paneled door, scrolled sides at top, scalloped bonnet, 60" h, 27" w, 17" d 1,375.00

Walnut, two paneled doors over eleven drawers, molded base and cornice, 38" h, 31" w, 13" d 440.00

Veterinary

"Dr. Lesure's Warranted Veterinary Medicines" stenciled on bonnet top, wood, glass front, circa 1890s, cond. 8+, 28-1/2" h, 15-3/4" w, 5-3/4" d 1,485.00

"Dr. Lesure's Famous Remedies," wood, litho tin panel, shows horse peeking through oval opening, refinished case, cond. 8+, 26-7/8" h, 20-3/4" w, 6-3/4" d 5,060.00

Wall, glazed arched door with two lower recessed panels, painted, embossed metal tag "Peter J. Blackledge" on door, wear, splitting, 21-1/2" h, 13-3/4" w, 6-3/4" d.. 345.00

Candle Boxes

Background: A candle box is a hanging wall box in which candles were kept. Originally made of wood, the candle box was introduced in England during the 17th century. The form eventually evolved into tabletop examples, as well as boxes made of other material, such as tin.

Collecting Hint: Most examples were purely functional, and thus the form tends to be rather plain. Look for boxes with unusual designs, such as heart-shaped cutouts. Fancier woods, such as tiger maple, and original painted surfaces also boost value.

Slide-lid candle box in old red paint, "ALAD 1843," 4-1/2" h, 14" w, $1,650. (Photo courtesy of Garth's Auctions, Delaware, Ohio)

Slant-lid candle box with heart cutout handle, old red paint, 10" h, 11-1/2" w, $600.

Hanging

One-drawer, mahogany, old dark finish, slant-lid top, scalloped crest with arched top, one dovetailed drawer with beaded-edge top, molded base, porcelain pull, brass hinges, one end of drawer repaired, 17-3/4" h, 10-5/8" w, 5-3/4" d 605.00

Mahogany, old finish, slanted hinged lid, scalloped crest, dovetailed case, age cracks, base damaged, 8-1/2" h, 9-1/2" w, 6-3/8" d............... 165.00

Mahogany, old reddish-brown finish, dovetailed, arched back crest, 7" h, 11-7/8" w, 5-3/4" d 165.00

Pine, old red paint, three lollipop finials on crest, dovetailed case, chip-carved circle designs and trim across the front, molded base, rose head nails, split backboard, empty nail holes from missing brace, 15" h, 15-3/4" w, 7" d 6,600.00

Stenciled, silver and black roses on orig dark-green, yellow line detail, walnut, arched back with sides tapering down to the front panel, traces of red overpaint, chip on right side, square nails, 7-3/4" h, 14" w, 6" d... 330.00

Tabletop

Pine, refinished, one-board sides, chamfered slide lid, square nails, slight damage along lid channels, 7-5/8" h, 20" w, 10-1/2" d.......................... 220.00

Tin, cylinder, scalloped crest, raised decor lines, worn brown japanning, 5-1/2" h, 11-1/4" l 165.00

Walnut, orig dark finish, sliding lid, dovetailed, divided interior with 1 partition missing, chips, age cracks on lid, 6" h, 18" w, 6-3/4" d 192.50

Tabletop, wooden, decorated

Orig brown sponging and bands of green leaves, poplar, dovetailed, molded edge on rim, sliding lid with raised panel, found in Ohio, minor edge damage, 4" h, 10-1/2" w, 6" d 5,775.00

Orig brown ground with flowering tulip in red, white and light blue with stars and buds beneath, freehand "Rarkus Anna 1869" in red on side, pine, dovetailed, minor edge wear, 6" h, 13" w, 9" d 935.00

Orig dark-red paint, lid mkd "ALAD 1843" in white relief-carved panel, dovetailed, sliding lid, molded edge around base, pegged, later interior pencil inscription, 4-1/2" h, 14" w, 6-1/2" d......... 1,650.00

"PMG" and "1874" painted on end, red ground, softwood, nailed, slide lid with three carved finger notches, wear, 8" h, 13-3/8" w, 11-1/8" d 250.00

Tabletop, wooden, painted

Old black worn paint over blue, hardwood, molded lid, replaced knob and end molding on lid, 4" h, 10-1/4" w, 6" d.. 385.00

Green, slide lid, 3" h, 12" w, 4" d.................... 192.50

Old red, pine, sliding lid, tab handle, worn, 8" l (excluding handle) 412.50

Candle Molds

Background: During the 19th century, candle molds made it possible for families to make inexpensive candles at home. Tin molds were the most affordable, with examples having from one to 50 tubes. Candle molds were also made of iron, pewter, and redware. The latter are often found in wooden holders and tend to be more valuable.

Reproduction Alert: New tin candle molds have been made for years.

Tin

Three-tube, round top and base, 6-1/4" h 220.00

Four-tube, two rows of two, 11" h 100.00

Six-tube, two rows of three, oblong, rust, seam break, 10-1/8" h... 65.00

Eight-tube, two rows of four, curved feet, ear handle, 11" h 385.00

Twelve-tube, unusual placement, four conical feet, 10-3/4" h 357.50

Twelve-tube, two rows of six, rectangular, significant rust, 10-3/4" h..110.00

Twelve-tube, round, two ear handles, some rust, 11-1/2" h, 9" dia 550.00

Sixteen-tube, four rows of four, rectangular, wear, dents, rust, 10-5/8" h 140.00

Twenty-four-tube, four rows of six, oblong, 10-3/4" h... 290.00

Twenty-four-tube, four rows of six, rectangular, dents, significant rust, 10-3/4" h 150.00

Wooden frame

Twelve-tube, three rows of four, pine frame, pewter tubes, old refinish, high feet, scalloped ends, age cracks, 17-1/4" h, 15" w, 8-5/8" d 687.50

Thirty-six-tube, four rows of nine, walnut frame, tin tubes, old finish, bootjack ends, square nails, 12-3/4" h, 16" w, 7-3/4" d........................... 825.00

Thirty-six-tube candle mold in red-painted frame stenciled "J. Walker, E. Bloomfield," $2,300. (Photo courtesy of Garth's Auctions, Delaware, Ohio)

Tin candle mold with twelve widely spaced tubes, $150.

Candle Stands

Background: A slender stand having a small top designed to support a candlestick is referred to as a candle stand. Used to augment the lighting arrangement in a room, many candle stands consisted of a small circular top, a turned shaft, and a tripod base. The majority of the tripod candle stands found in America were made in the Chippendale style during the last half of the 18th century.

References: Eileen and Richard Dubrow, *Styles of American Furniture 1860-1960*, Schiffer Publishing, 1997; Tim Forrest, *Bulfinch Anatomy of Antique Furniture*, Bulfinch Press, 1996; John T. Kirk, *American Furniture: Understanding Styles, Construction, and Quality*, Harry N. Abrams Publishers, 2000; Milo M. Naeve, *Identifying American Furniture*, W.W. Norton, 1998; Ellen T. Schroy, *Warman's American Furniture*, Krause Publications, 2001; Robert W. and Harriet Swedberg, *Collector's Encyclopedia of American Furniture*, Vol. 1 (1990, 1996 value update), Vol. 2 (1992, 1999 value update), Vol. 3 (1998), Collector Books; —, *Encyclopedia of American Oak Furniture*, Krause Publications, 2000.

Adjustable
  Chestnut, good patina, early turned and threaded post and adjustable candle bar, two sockets, the base a later replacement, 40-1/2" h 1,485.00
  Hard and softwood, old patina, oval chip-carved base, three turned legs, turned column, rectangular top with gallery edge, threaded shaft with adjustable candle arm, two tin sockets, branded "A. Mattes," made from old parts, probably constructed in the late 19th C., 38" h 275.00
  Painted black, turned finial atop screw shaft, two-candle arm with tin holders and drip cups, stepped tripod base, minor wear, 17" h 575.00
  Tin, two-socket, adjustable rectangular candle tray, sand-blasted conical tin base, c. 1840, 26-3/4" h 920.00
  Windsor-style, painted, dark green over earlier red, tripod base, bamboo-turned column, round center shelf, threaded wood column at top with shaped adjustable cross-piece with candle sockets at each end, 20th C., chips at one candle socket and on threads, 41-3/4" h 495.00
Chippendale
  Birch, orig red paint, old refinishing on square top, tripod base, snake feet, turned column, ovolo corners, age crack in top, 25-1/2" h, top 15-3/4" x 16" 1,980.00
  Cherry, probably Conn. River Valley, c. 1770-90, top with ovolo corners and serpentine sides, vase-and-ring turned post, cabriole legs, pad feet, refinished, 27-1/2" h, top 18-3/4" x 19" 1,035.00
  Cherry, old dark finish, high tripod base, snake feet, urn turned column, square one-board top, applied edge, dovetailed drawer with brass pull, 26-3/4" h, 17-1/4" w, 17" d 4,125.00

Adjustable candle stand in maple, oak and ash, traces of salmon-orange paint, New England, late 18th/early 19th C., 44" h, $1,995. (Photo courtesy of Skinner Auctioneers & Appraisers of Antiques & Fine Arts, Boston and Bolton, Mass.)

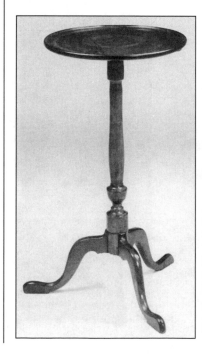

Chippendale candle stand, Massachusetts, 18th C., old refinish, 27-3/4" h, $2,070. (Photo courtesy of Skinner Auctioneers & Appraisers of Antiques & Fine Arts, Boston and Bolton, Mass.)

Chippendale tilt-top birch candle stand, New England, c. 1780, $1,725. (Photo courtesy of Skinner Auctioneers & Appraisers of Antiques & Fine Arts, Boston and Bolton, Mass.)

Cherry, old dark finish, tripod base, snake feet, turned column, two-board round top, 25-1/2" h, 18" dia 4,070.00

Cherry, old finish, tripod base, snake feet, turned column threaded to screw into cleat, two-board round top, old nailed repair at base, 27-3/8" h, top 17-3/8" dia 1,375.00

Cherry, old finish, tripod base, snake feet, slender turned and tapered column, two-board top, scalloped edge, added screws, restoration at base of column, 28" h, top 16-1/2" x 17" 1,540.00

Cherry, old finish, tripod base, snake feet, turned column, urn and rings, round one-board top with repaired split, 26-1/8" h, 18" dia 990.00

Cherry, old refinishing, tripod base, snake feet, turned column well-shaped scalloped top, column repaired, 27-1/4" h, top 15" x 16" 1,650.00

Mahogany, old dark finish, tripod base, reeded knees tapering to padded snake feet, one-board round top, wrought-iron brace, one leg cracked, 26-1/4" h, 17-5/8" dia 2,460.00

Mahogany, old refinish, tripod base, snake feet with pads, turned column, birdcage with turned posts, one-board dish-turned top, age but not period, edge repairs to top, 29" h, 19" dia 770.00

Maple, old dry red surface, figured square top, tripod base, snake feet, well-shaped turned column, old base repair, screw and brace added, short split in top, 23-1/2" h, top 14-5/8" x 15-1/8" 3,300.00

Painted, country style, cherry, old red with black brushed graining, tripod base, snake feet, turned column, one-board top, old nailed repair to legs at column, minor age crack in top, 25" h, top 15" x 16" 825.00

Painted, old red repaint, green detail on rings of turned column, checkerboard square top, tripod base, repairs to base and leg, 25-1/2" h, top 13-1/2" x 13-3/4" 3,575.00

Tilt-top, Chippendale style, cherry and curly maple, old finish, tripod base, turned column, dish top, birdcage support, hand-made, early 20th C., 28" h, 18" dia 385.00

Tilt-top, country style, birch, orig red paint, tripod base, snake feet, turned column, oval top, column base repaired, 27-3/4" h, top 14" x 19".... 5,280.00

Walnut, old alligatored varnish finish, tripod base, snake feet, turned column, round one-board top, column base cracked, one leg braced, nail added to center of top, 25-1/2" h, 16" dia 660.00

Classical

Tiger maple, New England, c. 1825, rectangular top, canted corners, vase-and-ring turned post, tripod scrolled legs, old finish, 28-1/2" h, top 16-3/4" x 21-3/4" 1,380.00

Tiger maple, New England, c. 1825, shaped top, vase-and-ring turned support, tripod scrolled legs on ball feet, old refinish, imperfections, 28-1/2" h, top 19" x 16-1/4" 920.00

Classical tiger maple candle stand, New England, c. 1825, 28-1/2" h, $1,380. (Photo courtesy of Skinner Auctioneers & Appraisers of Antiques & Fine Arts, Boston and Bolton, Mass.)

Tilt-top, bird's-eye maple and tiger maple, New England, c. 1820, top with canted corners, ring- and urn-form pedestal, tripod scrolling legs, old refinish, 28-1/2" h, top 20-3/4" x 17-1/2" 1,092.50

Decorated

Birch, old red wash, yellow striping, tripod base, high snake feet, tapered turned column, square top, base restoration, cracked cleat, new screws, 26-3/4" h, 13-1/2" w, 14" d 1,430.00

Cherry, grain-decor to resemble rosewood, possibly Conn., late 18th C., circular top, boldly turned post, tripod cabriole legs, pad feet, 27" h, 15-3/4" dia 2,645.00

Sponge-decor in gray, New England, c. 1820, dia- mond-shaped top, black-banded border, brown- and black-painted ring-turned post, acorn pen- dant, three curving legs, 26-1/8" h, top 16-1/8" x 24" 2,185.00

Federal

Cherry and birch, New England, c. 1810-20, rectan- gular top, vase-and-ring turned post, three shaped tapering legs, old refinish, imperfections, 26-3/4" h, top 14-3/4" x 16" 575.00

Maple, New England, c. 1780, octagonal top, vase- and-ring turned support, spider legs, refinished, imperfections 575.00

Federal, tilt-top

Birch, red paint, Mass., c. 1810, octagonal top, vase-and-ring turned post, tripod spider scratch- beaded legs, spade feet, 30" h, top 16" x 23" 4,025.00

Cherry, old alligatored finish, tripod base, well- shaped saber legs, carved acanthus leaf column, one-board octagonal top with cross-banded inlay, molded edge, 28-1/4" h, top 17-1/4" x 22-3/4" 467.50

Federal tilt-top cherry candle stand with inlaid stringing, New England, early 19th C., refinished, 26-1/8" h, $1,725. (Photo courtesy of Skinner Auctioneers & Apprais- ers of Antiques & Fine Arts, Boston and Bol- ton, Mass.)

Cherry, New England, early 19th C., hexagonal top, ring-turned pedestal, spider legs, earlier red stained surface, repairs, 28" h, top 23-1/4" x 14-3/4" 488.75

Cherry, New England, early 19th C., octagonal top, ring-turned pedestal, spider legs, old refinish, imperfections, 29-1/2" h, top 20-5/8" x 13" . 805.00

Cherry, inlaid, New England, early 19th C., octago- nal top, inlaid banded edge, vase-and-ring turned post, spider legs inlaid with stringing, refinished, minor imperfections, 26-1/8" h, top 21-3/4" x 13-1/2" 1,725.00

Cherry and birch, New England, c. 1800-10, oval top, vase-and-ring turned post, tripod cabriole legs, arris pad feet, refinished, minor imperfec- tions, 28-3/4" h, top 15-1/2" x 27" 805.00

Hepplewhite

Birch, ring-turned urn column, spider legs, spade feet, Maine origin, 28" h, top 15" sq 275.00

Birch, turned column, spider legs, 15" sq top with notched corners 660.00

Cherry, country style, tripod base, snake feet, urn- turned column, two-board top with shaped cor- ners, refinished, restorations with cleat damage, loose top, 25-3/4" h, 17" sq 522.50

Cherry, old finish, tripod base, snake feet, turned birch column, one-board top with applied gallery, column repaired, top reattached, 25-1/4" h, 19-1/8" w, 16-3/8" d 770.00

Cherry, old finish, tripod base, spider legs, boldly turned column rectangular top, scalloped edge, glued repair to one leg, 27-1/2" h, top 16-1/4" x 19-1/2" 935.00

Cherry, old worn reddish-brown finish, tripod base, high spider legs, turned detail on column, octago- nal top, restoration to base and one leg, 26-1/4" h, 17-1/2" w, 19" d 660.00

Mahogany, tripod base, spade feet, turned and pan- eled column, octagonal one-board top and cleat are old replacements, two feet ended out, 29" h, 21" w, 16" d 440.00

Mahogany, tripod base, spider legs, turned column, rectangular top with cut corners, worn finish, repairs to base, tilt top fastened with screws, 28" h, 16-1/4" w, 22-1/4" d 412.50

Hepplewhite, tilt-top

Birch, high tapered spider base, ring-turned urn col- umn, bone turnbuckle, one-board octagonal top probably an old replacement, refinished, 27-1/4" h, 18" w, 22" d 275.00

Cherry, old dark finish, high tripod spider legs, scal- loping around bottom of column, one-board oval top, hairline in one leg, 25-3/4" h, top 15-5/8" x 21 .... 1,375.00

Walnut, high spider legs, urn-turned column, one- board top with figure, shaped corners, refinished, restorations, 29-3/4" h, top 20-1/4" x 18-3/4" 330.00

Miscellaneous

Birch, New England, early 19th C., square top, vase-and-ring turned pedestal, cabriole legs, refinished, imperfections, 26" h, top 16-1/2" sq............. 632.50

Cherry, impressed "A. Shove" (Abraham Shove was a Windsor chair maker who worked in Bristol County, Mass. in the early 19th C.), square top with scratch-beaded edge, swelled ring-turned pedestal, cabriole leg base, pad feet, old refinish, one leg replaced, 27" h, top 15-1/4" x 14-7/8" 1,495.00

Cherry, painted, possibly Conn. River Valley, c. 1760-80, circular dish top, vase-and-ring turned post, cabriole legs, pad feet, 27-1/2" h, top 16-1/2" dia... 2,070.00

Country style, cherry and maple, old refinishing, tripod base, turned legs fitted into round tapered platform, column with stacked ring turnings, reset dished top with repairs and age cracks, cleat and legs replaced, found in Montgomery County, Pa., 26-3/4" h, top 14-1/4" dia........................... 385.00

Country style, painted, poplar, old green repaint over black, tripod base, snake feet, turned column, round one-board top, 25" h, 19" dia............ 935.00

Country style, pine and oak, refinished, X-shaped base with tapered ends, square column with beveled edges, one-board square top, reconstruction, 24-3/4" h, top 14-7/8" w, 15-7/8" d................ 55.00

Drop-leaf, country style, old black repaint, traces of striping (probably Victorian), four spider legs, turned column, dovetailed drawer, pine top with D-shaped leaves, minor insect damage, restoration, attributed to New York state, 25-3/4" h, 12-1/2" w, 17" d, 5" leaves...................................... 2,200.00

Dunlap N.H., black paint, urn-turned column, snake legs, octagonal top, 23" h, top 13-1/2" w 10,450.00

Painted, old black, probably Norwich, Conn., late 18th C., circular molded top with scalloped lower edge, vase-and-ring turned post, tripod cabriole legs, pad feet, imperfections, 27-1/2" h, 13-3/4" dia.. 9,775.00

Tilt-top, cherry, Conn. River Valley, snake legs, turned column, top with rounded ends, 28" h, top 22" x 19" 275.00

Tilt-top, maple, top with diamond-shaped protruding corners, urn column, snake feet, 19" h, top 28" x 19" 660.00

Queen Anne

Cherry, Norwich Conn. area, late 18th C., circular molded top with scalloped carved lower edge, vase-and-ring turned post, cabriole legs, pad feet, refinished, 28-1/2" h, 13-1/2" dia 6,900.00

Old finish, urn-turned column, snake feet, square top, 27" h, top 17-1/2" sq........................... 990.00

Maple, probably New England, c. 1740-60, round top, vase-and-ring turned post, tripod cabriole legs, pad feet, old refinish, 27-1/2" h, 14" dia 1,725.00

Transitional, painted, hardwood, old black repaint over early red, yellow striping, tripod base, snake feet, urn-turned column, one-board oblong eight-sided top, age cracks in top, 26-1/2" h, top 15-3/4" x 22".........1,320.00

Candlesticks

Background: A small movable stand or support for holding a candle is referred to as a candlestick. These hand-held devices have been made of glass, wood, metal, and pottery.

References: Veronika Baur, *Metal Candlesticks*, Schiffer Publishing, 1996; Ronald F. Michaels, *Old Domestic Base-Metal Candlesticks*, Antique Collectors' Club, 1999.

Brass

Capstan base, top flange repaired, 5-1/4" h.. 715.00

Chamberstick, side pushup, saucer handle, English, dents, 4-1/2" h 88.00

Chamberstick, wide socket lip, pushup, 4-3/4" h 275.00

Dutch, mid-drip, minor battering, 7-1/2" h, pr. 385.00

French, domed base with scalloped edge, paneled baluster stem and socket, resoldered stem, 8-3/4" h 220.00

French, domed base with scalloped edge, paneled baluster stem, 9" h, pr 935.00

French, domed base with scalloped edge, paneled stem, removable scalloped-edge bobeche, 9-5/8" h, pr.. 1,650.00

Mid-drip, domed ring-turned base and center column turned from solid stock, slightly dished mid-drip pan, minor dents, 7-3/8" h 1,100.00

Neoclassical, tapered square base, turned stem, pushup, polished, 4-1/2" h, pr...................... 82.50

Neoclassical, side push up, minor dents, English... 137.50

Iron wedding band hogscraper candlestick marked "Dowler," 9-3/4" h, $525.

Platform base, primitive paw feet, raised rim, incised ring turnings, stem turned from single piece, 9" h 247.50

Queen of Diamonds, pushup, 11-1/2" h, pr.... 275.00

Ring-turned, stepped base, baluster stem, polished, 8-1/2"' h 247.50

Saucer base, side pushup, English, 6-3/4" h . 385.00

Spanish, round domed base, unusual baluster stem, 8-3/4" h 550.00

Spanish, mid-drip, round domed base battered, lip damage, 9-3/4" h 137.50

Square base, 4 short feet, baluster stem, 5" h 330.00

Traveling, wide saucer base, mkd "N25" also "SB" and crown, dents, short rim splits, 3-1/4" h, 4-1/2" dia, pr 60.50

Victorian, beehive, pushup, mkd England, 6" h, pr 165.00

Brass, Queen Anne

Domed base with eight scallops, baluster stem, socket, scalloped lip, English, 6-3/4" h, pr 440.00

Domed foot with six large and six small scallops, paneled stem and lip, side pushup, English, 7-1/2" h, pr 1,980.00

Domed petal base, scalloped rim, pushup, 8-1/8" h 275.00

Octagonal base, bold ring-turned column, diamond facets at center, pushup, mkd "The King of Diamonds," 12-1/2" h, pr 495.00

Petal base and socket, baluster stem, minor corrosion, repaired split at petal lip, 7-3/4" h 330.00

Rockingham candlestick, in-the-making imperfection on socket, 8-1/2" h, $632.50. (Photo courtesy of Garth's Auctions, Delaware, Ohio)

Ring-turned base, boldly turned column, orig pushup, 12" h, pr 275.00

Scalloped base, baluster stem, 7-3/8" h 467.50

Scalloped base, baluster stem, resoldered repair on lip, English, 6-1/4" h 302.50

Scalloped base, English, 7-1/2" h, pr 1,870.00

Scalloped base, paneled baluster stem, scalloped lip, English, 9-1/2" h, pr 2,530.00

Scalloped base, paneled baluster stem, scalloped top, English, 7-3/8" h 605.00

Scalloped base, slender stem, paneled baluster, scalloped lip, 8-1/4" h, pr 2,860.00

Scalloped base, turned column, resoldered break above base, slightly canted, 8-1/8" h 165.00

Scrolled foot, baluster stem, scalloped lip, English, 7-3/4" h, pr 440.00

Square base with scalloped corners, engraved initials, dated 1772, light pitting, 6-1/4" h, pr 770.00

Scalloped base, turned column, pushups missing, 19th C., 6-7/8" h, pr 220.00

Glass, clambroth, square stepped base, fluted column, petal socket, minor flakes, heat check in socket, 9-1/4" h 247.50

Hogscraper

Sheet iron, round base, tubular shaft, ejector mechanism on side, ejector knob stamped "HYD," minor rust, 6-1/2" h, 3-3/4" dia 190.00

Sheet iron, round base, tubular shaft secured by nut and bolt, ejector intact, illegible mark, flared drip catcher, minor rust, 7" h, 3-7/8" dia 130.00

Sheet iron, round base, tubular shaft secured by nut and bolt, ejector mechanism intact and mkd "Bill," flared drip catcher, minor dents, rim somewhat rough, 5-1/4" h, 3-3/4" dia 110.00

Tin, conical, base weighted with sand, three candle sockets, sand leaking, 6-1/2" h, pr 247.50

Tin and iron, round base with rounded rim, tubular shaft with ejector mechanism intact, iron ejector knob stamped "Patented 1853," flared drip catcher with hook on side, wear, 3-7/8" h, 3-3/4" dia 190.00

Jamb-spike candleholder, wrought iron, late 18th/early 19th C., minor rust, 12" l 175.00

Toleware, pushup type, domed square base, orig yellow on worn brown japanning, 6" h 165.00

Canes

Background: During the 18th and 19th centuries, canes and walking sticks were integral parts of a gentleman's wardrobe. Although utilitarian in nature, many were carved or otherwise embellished to serve as decorative accessories as well. However, glass canes and glass walking sticks were glassmaker's whimsies and were purely ornamental rather than functional.

References: Catherine Dike, *Canes in the United States*, Cane Curiosa Press, 1995; Ulrich Klever,

Walkingsticks, Schiffer Publishing, 1996; George H. Meyer, *American Folk Art Canes,* Sandringham Press, 1992.

Collectors' Club: Cane Collectors Club of America, 2 Horizon Rd., Suite G18, Fort Lee, NJ 07024.

Museums: Essex Institute, Salem, MA; Valley Forge Historical Society, Valley Forge, PA.

Collecting Hint: Intricately carved and detailed canes are collected as pieces of American folk art, and competition for them is fierce.

A PATRIOTIC SNAKE?

What makes a great folk art cane? Subject matter is important, as is the quality of the craftsmanship. This example had the best of both worlds.

Dating to shortly after the Spanish-American War, it was made from a curled root. The handle was carved in the form of a snake biting the shaft. The entire length of the shaft has carved patriotic slogans and names, including "Bunker Hill Monument," "Don't Tread on Me," "First in War and First in Peace," "First in the Hearts of His Countrymen," "Give Me Civil and Religious Liberty or Give Me Death," and "The Union Must and Shall Be Preserved."

Carved scenes and figures include American flags, a hand holding a dagger, an American eagle in a patriotic shield, a sword and scale of justice, monuments, and a group of stacked guns. Text covers nearly all of the free space on the shaft and includes "Let us stick to the Constitution as the shipwrecked mariner clings to his last plank when night and the storm closes up on him."

Folk art cane, 34" l, $2,300. (Photo courtesy of Cowan's Historic Americana, Terrace Park, Ohio)

Carved ivory
  Bulldog head, glass eyes, Malacca shaft, gold-plated repousse band 522.50
  Cockatiel head, walrus ivory, thorn wood shaft, three shrinkage cracks in head, c. 1870s 220.00
  Dog head walking stick, knob shaped like wrinkled fabric with three different dogs sticking out their heads, tapering walnut shaft, head 2" dia 412.50
  Fist clenching snake, walrus ivory, c. 1860, rosewood shaft, several hairlines, thumb chipped 550.00
  Greyhound with glass eyes, second pc of ivory carved to form collar and tree trunk, tapered wood shaft, gold-plated collar engraved "Henry Dec. 25/69" 357.50
  Hand holding a biscuit, swirling sleeve, walrus ivory 770.00
  Horse head, two-part ivory handle, gold mounts, engraved "Augustus Oskamp in memory of my father died Sept. 11, 1845," minor wear, 37-3/4" l 357.50
  Horse hoof with horseshoe, wooden shaft 715.00
  Japanese faces, nine interlocking frowning faces carved into 1-1/2" dia ball, Malacca shaft, sterling band, c. 1890 .... 1,045.00
  Man's face, wearing tall hat, relief-carved, engraved gold band, possibly American Indian, age cracks 165.00
  Mongoose attacking a snake, ebony shaft, silver collar, c. 1900 .... 605.00
  Pinwheel, ball with primitive pinwheel and diamond carving, bone collar, tapered wood shaft, ferrule missing, moderate checking to ivory, some discoloration 176.00
  Turkish knot, neck ends in raised carved-diamond band, wooden shaft 550.00
Carved wood
  Alligator, its tail turned down, mounted on tapered wood shaft in imitation bamboo 110.00
  B.C. engraved initials, twisted curly maple, glued break 220.00
  Bird, carved and attached bird handle, plain shaft, minor edge damage to handle, small putty repair, 35-1/2" l 55.00
  Chip-carved art stick, orig finish, round knob end, handmade brass ferrule, 19th C. 143.00
  Civil War veteran's walking stick, heavily carved with U.S. flag inscriptions such as "We Stand by the Flag" and "In God We Trust," presentation inscription "To Jackson Vermilyer By An Old Vet Edwin H. Smith, July 4th 1888" on a ribbon around the shaft (both served as privates in Co. B of the 9th N.Y. Heavy Artillery) 1,045.00
  "Devil's Den," natural stick shaft with burned panel and decor, bark handle, Gettysburg souvenir, typical of canes carved from wood collected at battlefield sites and sold at reunions and as souvenirs 192.50

Dog handle, dark-brown paint, root-carved, worn... 165.00

Goat and snake, comical goat-head handle, 3-D snake wraps around the shaft 357.50

Golf, handle resembles putter, metal and wood inlaid dots on putter head, c. 1920...................... 220.00

Hand holding skull, hand is flesh-colored, bark extends into handle at top end 522.50

Indian chief, carved and painted full-figure Indian with war bonnet, vest and loin cloth, cow-horn handle.. 385.00

Indian motif, bent flattened handle, shallow-carved bust of an Indian in a full headdress and "Mt. Clemens Mich. 1903," two freestanding vines spiral down the tapering shaft, made from one pc of hickory 247.50

Lion, head of a male African lion, knobby kelp-covered shaft, kelp dry and flaking near base.. 357.50

Lion's head, glass eyes, gold metal band with presentation engraving dated 1924, Malacca shaft, horn ferrule 467.50

Man's face and monkey's face (double headed), inlaid eyes, man with beard and collar, 38-1/4" l 660.00

Man's head, wearing skull cap, single pc of burl, probably German...................................... 247.50

Parakeet's head and wings, glass eyes, stepped cane shaft.. 192.50

Relief-carved, bamboo cane with images of couples kissing, children, horseshoe with clover, woman's portrait and alligator, American, c. 1880.. 385.00

Sea serpent, open mouth with teeth and tongue, lower shaft turned in imitation of bamboo, single pc of hardwood 165.00

Shoe, upside-down, some incised lines......... 330.00

Snake, one spiraling snake, black bead eyes, salmon repair, mushroom cap handle, 31-1/2" l 357.50

Snake, two spiraling snakes, inlaid mother of pearl disk on top of handle, brass cap, iron tip, worn varnish, 34" l 302.50

Stag's hoof and leg, walrus ivory, Malacca shaft, split in ivory base 165.00

Tiger, snarling face with glass eyes, dark-stained stripes, mounted on knobby tapered shaft in old green stain, two teeth missing.................... 121.00

War of 1812 relic cane, oak shaft with 1-3/4" octagonal shaped gold head with domed top, three side panels on head engraved "Wood of the Flag Ship Lawrence," "I would rather be right than to be President H. Clay" and "Perry's Victory Lake Erie Sept 10th 1813," a relic from wood from the Lawrence, (crippled by the British in the Battle of Lake Erie) 1,870.00

Woman's leg handle, burl walnut, shamrock-carved oak shaft with inscriptions............................ 99.00

Zouave, carved head of man, natural burl, bark-covered shaft with small patches missing........ 605.00

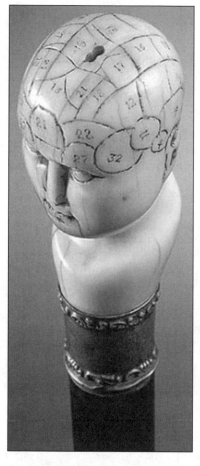

Phrenology cane, walrus tusk carved in the shape of a human head, the skull divided into sections numbered according to phrenology doctrine, c. 1850, $1,320. (Photo courtesy of Cowan's Historic Americana, Terrace Park, Ohio)

Glass, blown

Amber, twisted handle and end, possibly Zanesville, flake on end, 37-1/4" l................................. 27.50

Clear, red, blue and light-green spiral stripes, open end with roughness, 73" l 247.50

Clear, white spiral stripes, open end, 61-1/2" l 247.50

Metal

Dog's head on end of crook, silver pointer hound, wooden shaft... 330.00

Fishing motif, white metal handle decor with twisted brass wire with a fishhook and hooked trout, wood shaft.. 220.00

G.A.R. handle, white metal crook handle with initials for Grand Army of the Republic, eagle over flag and crossed bayonets, ebony colored wooden shaft.. 275.00

Goose head, white metal with glass eyes, rattan shaft.. 220.00

Knights of Pythias, plated white metal head with fraternal symbols, painted red shaft 275.00

Loyal Order of Moose, pewter-colored metal head with moose on top, four sets of shamrocks cascade down the handle, wooden shaft........ 275.00

Odd Fellows, copper-plated white metal handle with the three rings of the International Order of the Odd Fellows, wooden shaft, handle dented in two places 192.50

Skull, pewter-colored metal, natural rustic shaft, patches of bark missing 330.00
Whalebone and ivory, decor with five baleen bands at top of shaft, America, 19th C., age cracks, 34-1/2" l 1,265.00

Canteens

(see Barrels, Kegs, and Canteens)

Cast Iron

Background: Cast iron was first made in the 18th century. As a result of its high carbon content, it is more apt to break under stress than is wrought iron. Articles formed from cast iron are made in molds and don't require the laborious, time-intensive effort that goes into producing wrought iron.

Collectors' Clubs: Cast Iron Seat Collectors Assoc., RR 2, Box 38, Le Center, MN 56057; Cast Iron Collectors, Southern Chapter, P.O. Box 355, Swainsboro, GA 30401; Cast Iron Toy Collectors of America, 1340 Market St., Long Beach, CA 90805; Griswold & Cast Iron Cookware Assoc., P.O. Drawer B, Perrysburg, NY 14129-0301.

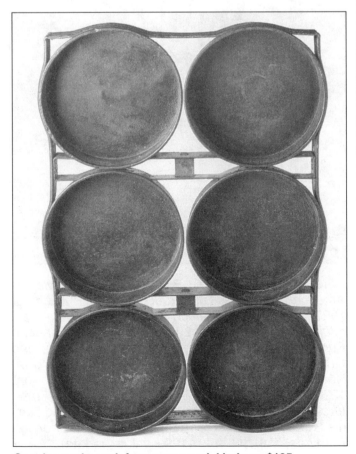

Cast-iron cake rack from commercial bakery, $125.

Architectural ornament, clasped hands, bird and banner with "LOTM," flat relief casting, weathered red, black and silver paint, worn, 6" h 302.50
Eagle, cast in two sections with hollow body, detailed feathers with wings spread and perched on a rock, late green paint, two mounting brackets on base, 13-1/2" h, 30-1/4" w, 10" d 330.00
Eagle finial, spread wings, gold repaint, 9" h, 15-1/4" w 165.00
Grill, Horace Greeley, Campbell Foundry Co., Harrison N.J., 19th C., fan-shaped grill with grease reservoir, three legs, 3-1/4" h, 25" w, 16-3/4" l 230.00
Muffin tin, hearts motif (eight) 110.00
Pitcher pump, "The Deming Co., Salem, Ohio," drive rod missing, 18" h 45.00
Stove plate, Friedensburg, Bucks County, Pa., made by Shearwell Furnace, Dietrich Welker, design of man on horse and handled urn with flowers, framed by plain arches and twisted columns, 19" x 22" 605.00
Teakettle, S.S. Sheppard & Co., Philadelphia, flared sides, rounded shoulder curved spout, arched handle, late 19th C., mkd "6 Qt," wear, rust, 7-1/4" h, 8" dia 135.00
Umbrella holder, platform base, removable pan, ornate backplate with openwork columns and scrolling, relief squirrel on center medallion, dark-green repaint, 33-1/2" h, 18-1/2" w 467.50
Vegetable dish, open, oval, slightly flared sides, minor rust, 2-3/8" h, 11" w, 8-1/4" d, pr 110.00

Chair Tables

Background: The chair table is truly a dual-purpose piece of furniture. A chair designed with a large circular or rectangular back, it became a table when the back was pivoted and pulled down to rest on the arms. The form first appeared in the 17th century, but most examples on today's market are from the 1800s. Other names for chair tables include hutch table and table chair.

Round top
   Grain-decor, pine and maple, New England, c. 1800, circular overhanging top, square legs, box stretchers, scrubbed top, base in red and brown graining, some imperfections, 27-3/4" h, 42" dia 4,312.50
   Maple and pine, circular overhanging top, block-vase-and-ring turned supports and legs, turned stretchers, traces of old red paint, late 18th or early 19th C., imperfections, 28" h, 54" dia 13,800.00
   Painted, black, square legs, arms, 28-1/2" h, 46" dia 440.00
   Painted, early red, top attached with dowels, chair with shaped arms, plank seat, shoe feet, New England, 18th C., minor losses, top reshaped, 27-1/2" h, 54-1/4" w, 48-3/4" d 6,900.00

Chair table in old red paint, 27" h, 46" dia, $6,600. (Photo courtesy of Cyr Auction Company, Gray, Maine)

Painted, old red, square legs taper to arms, drawer under seat, box stretcher, 27" h, 46" dia 6,600.00
Pyrography, floral and other decor, sides with 2 large oval cutouts, 47" h 495.00
Square top, painted, red base, scrubbed top, square legs and arms, 26" h, top 40" x 39" 1,375.00

Chairs

Background: The best-known type of country chair is the Windsor, made in both comb-back and bow-back (or hoop-back) styles. The comb-back has a horizontal top rail. The bow-back is characterized by a horizontal bar that has been steamed and bent into a semi-circle to form the arms and middle support for the back spindles. Both versions feature a solid saddle seat and turned or rounded spindles and legs.

The ladder-back chair also epitomizes the phrase country furniture. Alternately referred to as a slat-back, the name is derived from the characteristic series of horizontal arched slats that forms the back of the chair. Some examples have as many as six slats, and most have quarter-woven rush or splint seats.

A WINDSOR WONDER

Sherlock Holmes called it "elementary." This fan-back Windsor armchair certainly has the right elements—form, carved details, and original paint—to catch the eye of anyone who appreciates early furniture. The piece was probably made in Connecticut around 1790 to 1800. In original green paint, it features a serpentine crest with scroll-carved ears, carved scrolled knuckled handholds, vase-and-ring turned supports, a carved incised saddle seat, splayed vase-and-ring turned legs and turned swelled stretchers. Standing 42" high with a seat 17-1/2" high, it sold for $51,700 at a Skinner auction.

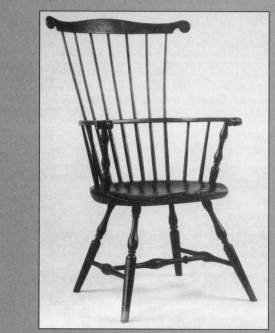

Fan-back Windsor armchair, $51,700. (Photo courtesy of Skinner Auctioneers & Appraisers of Antiques & Fine Arts, Boston and Bolton, Mass.)

References: Eileen and Richard Dubrow, *Styles of American Furniture 1860-1960*, Schiffer Publishing, 1997; Tim Forrest, *Bulfinch Anatomy of Antique Furniture*, Bulfinch Press, 1996; John T. Kirk, *American Furniture: Understanding Styles, Construction, and Quality*, Harry N. Abrams Publishers, 2000; Milo M. Naeve, *Identifying American Furniture*, W.W. Norton, 1998; Ellen T. Schroy, *Warman's American Furniture*, Krause Publications, 2001; Robert W. and Harriet Swedberg, *Collector's Encyclopedia of American Furniture*, Vol. 1 (1990, 1996 value update), Vol. 2 (1992, 1999 value update), Vol. 3 (1998), Collector

Books; —, *Encyclopedia of American Oak Furniture*, Krause Publications, 2000.

Arrowback

Decor, side chair, red paint, yellow and green foliage on crest, shield-shaped seat, bamboo-turned legs, 35" h, set of four 2,970.00

Decor, side chair, orig black graining, red ground, green border detail, stepdown crest with restoration, wear, 34" h 385.00

Banister-back, armchair

Hardwood, dark finish, old reproduction, one foot damaged, joints loose, 45" h 165.00

Maple and ash, arched crest, four molded banisters, vase-and-ring turned stiles, ball finials, shaped arms with scrolled terminals, trapezoidal rush seat, cylinder and ring-turned legs, swelled vase-and-ring turned double stretchers, old refinish, New England, mid-18th C., 47-1/2" h 8,050.00

Painted, old black, Conn., c. 1725-75, double arched and scalloped crest rail, vase-and-ring turned stiles, serpentine arms, ring-turned front legs with turned feet, imperfections, 49" h 6,900.00

Painted, old black, stretcher base, turned feet, sausage-turned front posts, shaped arms with scrolled hand rests, four vertical ribbed slats, turned posts and finials, restorations, feet ended out, replaced arms and woven splint seat, 46-1/2" h 687.50

Banister-back armchair, old black paint, Connecticut, c. 1725-75, $6,900. (Photo courtesy of Skinner Auctioneers & Appraisers of Antiques & Fine Arts, Boston and Bolton, Mass.)

Painted, traces of old black, well-turned posts, legs and finials with half-turned slats, old woven splint seat, feet ended out, 45-1/2" h 1,265.00

Banister-back, side chair

Grain-painted, old brown grained repaint, bulbous-turned front stretcher, three turned half-spindles in back, scalloped crest, old rush seat with damage, chips on turnings, 42" h 550.00

Hardwood, old refinishing, sausage-turned legs, turned front stretcher, three turned half-spindles, turned posts, scalloped crest, replaced splint seat, feet ended out, 41" h 357.50

Hardwood, turned feet/legs, turned posts, three-molded slats, yoke crest, rush seat, 19th C., old refinishing, 43" h... 165.00

Old black repaint, gold striping, carved Spanish feet, turned stretchers and front legs, turned posts and finials, four turned half-spindles, scalloped crest, replaced rush seat, 41-1/4" h 935.00

Old black repaint, gold striping, sausage-turned legs, ball feet, four turned half-spindles, arched and scalloped crest, turned finials, replaced rush seat, 43-1/2" h 495.00

Old black repaint, traces of earlier red, turned legs and posts, boldly turned front stretcher, three slats, shaped crest, turned finials, splits to old paper rush seat painted yellow, insect damage to one rung, 42" h 990.00

Old green repaint, three turned half-spindles, bulbous-turned front stretcher, replaced rush seat, 41" h 495.00

Buggy seat, maple and ash, New England, late 18th C., six arched slats, three turned tapering stiles, turned arms and supports, tapered legs, double stretchers, old refinish, 35-3/4" h 1,495.00

Chippendale

Armchair, English, country style, oak, square legs, mortised and pinned stretcher base, slip seat, shaped knuckle arms, pierced splat, shaped crest with carved ears, refinished, wear, repairs, crest probably replaced, some height loss to feet, 40" h..522.50

Armchair, English, mahogany, old worn/alligatored surface, cabriole legs, ball-and-claw feet, acanthus-carved knees, upholstered seat, scrolled arms, pierced/carved back with intricate twined design and initial "L," 19th C., 43" h 1,045.00

Easy chair, upholstered, New England, late 18th C., arched crest, shaped wings, out-scrolled arms, down-sweeping supports, trapezoidal cushioned seat, Marlborough front legs, raked and chamfered rear legs, square stretchers, 44-1/4" h 2,760.00

Ribbon-back, side chair, birch, old dark reddish-brown finish, pegged, square legs with molded corners, front stretcher, splayed rear posts, replaced paper rush seat, height loss, 37" h 110.00

Ribbon-back side chair, mahogany, northern New England, c. 1760-80, serpentine incised crest rail with pierced bow, over three similar horizontal splats, incised shaped stiles, over-upholstered seat, square beaded front legs, shaped back legs, square stretchers, old refinish, imperfections 1,035.00

Ribbon-back side chair, rush seat, pumpkin repaint with green trim, 39" h, pr 1,210.00

Chippendale, side chair

Country style, maple, old worn dark finish, square legs, stretcher base, rush seat, tapered rear posts, pierced vase splat, yoke crest with carved ears, feet ended out, restorations, 39" h 110.00

Mahogany, carved, Boston, c. 1760-80, serpentine crest rail ending in raked molded terminals, chip-carved and diamond-interlaced splat with C-scrolls, molded trapezoidal seat frame, cabriole front legs, arris knees, scratch-carved high pad feet, early surface, orig cond., minor imperfections, 36-1/2" h 10,925.00

Mahogany, carved, Boston, c. 1760-80, serpentine crest with low relief-carved leafage, molded stiles, interlaced pierced Gothic splat, molded slip seat, square straight legs and H stretchers, inside of seat rail impressed "E. Iohonnot," old dark surface, 37-1/2" h 13,800.00

Mahogany, carved, Boston or North Shore, Mass., c. 1790, shaped and carved crest rail ending in scrolled terminals, pierced splat, outward flaring stiles, trapezoidal slip seat, straight bracketed beaded front legs, raked rear legs, beaded square stretchers, one turned rear stretcher, old finish 3,737.50

Mahogany, carved, Boston or Salem, Mass., c. 1770, shaped carved crest rail ending in scrolled terminals, pierced and carved splat, outward flaring stiles, trapezoidal seat, front cabriole legs with pad feet on platforms, rear chamfered raked legs, block-and- ring turned stretchers, old finish, minor imperfections, 37-3/4" h........................... 7,475.00

Mahogany, carved, Philadelphia, c. 1760-80, serpentine crest, two central C-scrolls above two trefoils and interlaced Gothic strapwork on a molded shoe, trapezoidal molded seat frame, pierced front brackets, straight front legs with beaded edges, rear raking legs, old surface, 37-1/2" h 3,737.50

Square molded legs and seat frame, slip seat in late upholstery, pierced back splat, scalloped crest, early 20th C., restoration, refinished, three cherry, one mahogany, 37" h, set of four............. 1,375.00

Walnut, Mass., c. 1760-80, serpentine crest, carved terminals above chamfered raking stiles, vasiform splat, trapezoidal slip seat, front cabriole legs with pad feet on platforms, turned stretchers, refinished, minor imperfections, pr 6,325.00

Walnut, Newbury, Mass., c. 1760-1780, serpentine crest rail, heart-pierced vasiform splat, trapezoidal slip seat, front cabriole legs ending in pad feet on platforms, refinished, 37-1/2" h................. 1,955.00

Walnut, Philadelphia, c. 1755-70, serpentine crest, beaded edges, raked ears, central carved shell above reverse-carved pierced splat with C-scrolls, trapezoidal seat frame, central carved shell over front cabriole legs, claw-and-ball feet, rear rounded legs, old refinish, 42-1/2" h........ 6,900.00

Walnut, square legs with stop fluting, "H" stretcher, pierced splat, carved crest, reupholstered slip seat, old repairs and replacements, 38" h .. 330.00

Commode chair, armchair, red and black paint, yellow striping, gold and silver stenciled cornucopia and floral motif on crest, paint restoration, 42" h 110.00

Corner

Chippendale, probably Conn., c. 1770-80, shaped crest, outscrolled arms, vase-and-ring turned supports, 2 pierced vasiform splats, rush slip seat, valance frame, square legs, box stretchers, refinished, 32" h... 5,175.00

Painted, maple, New England, c. 1780, pillow back crest, scrolled terminals, three vase-and-ring turned supports, splint seat, double stretchers, old black paint, gold accents, imperfections, 30" h 345.00

Queen Anne, maple, refinished, front duck foot, turned rear feet, turned posts, arched slats, curved arms, old replacement seat, tops of posts ended out, 31" h 192.50

Queen Anne, maple, scrolled arms, cabriole front leg and three turned back legs, reupholstered slip seat, restoration, 30-1/8" h 1,430.00

Queen Anne, two pierced splats, Spanish front foot, turned posts, bulbous turned front stretchers, rush seat, 31-1/2" h 2,750.00

Decorated

Armchair, grain-decor, orig black over red, light stenciling on crest, yellow line detail, tapered legs, shaped seat, turned arm supports, spindles and rear posts, scrolled arms, five-spindle back with medallion crest, Ohio origin, minor wear, restoration to arm, 32-1/4" h 412.50

Child's, armchair, stretcher base, turned posts, woven cord seat, tapered rear posts with finials, three arched slats, shaped arms notched underneath, refinished, height loss, 22" h 412.50

Decorated, side chair

Floral decor in red and green, yellow ground, pillow-back, three half spindles, plank seat, turned legs, pr 660.00

Old light-brown ground, polychrome floral decor, yellow bordered by black, gold striping, shaped crest, pierced vasiform splats, plank seat with rolled front rails, ring-turned legs and stretcher, Pa., c. 1840, minor surface imperfections, 33-5/8" h, set of six 3,335.00

Orig black over red graining, gold highlights, stenciled cornucopia on crest, scroll-cut back, rabbit ears, old rush seat, one section trim missing, 33-3/4" h, pr... 605.00

Pennsylvania decorated side chairs, old light-brown ground, polychrome floral decoration with yellow, black and gold accents, c. 1840, set of six, $3,335. (Photo courtesy of Skinner Auctioneers & Appraisers of Antiques & Fine Arts, Boston and Bolton, Mass.)

Fiddle-back armchair, maple, Hudson River Valley area or Connecticut, 18th C., refinished, $2,530. (Photo courtesy of Skinner Auctioneers & Appraisers of Antiques & Fine Arts, Boston and Bolton, Mass.)

Painted, old but not orig, red and black graining, yellow striping, stenciled bird and foliage in red, green and gold, 31-1/2" h 55.00

Probably Maine, early 19th C., orig cream paint, dark-green highlights, gilt and green shell and leaf decor on crest, 7 raked tapered spindles, incised seat, splayed incised legs, turned stretcher, 36-1/2" h, set of five 16,100.00

Federal

Easy chair, circular, mahogany, New England, c. 1815-20, arched crest, curving back, out-scrolling arms, vase-and-ring turned front legs, square raked and tapering rear legs, on casters, 42" h 3,450.00

Side chair, mahogany, New England, c. 1790, arched molded crest rail, shaped stiles, pierced carved splats, trapezoidal slip seat, square beaded tapering front legs, raked rear legs, square stretcher, refinished, minor imperfections, 37-1/4" h, pr 2,990.00

Fiddle-back, side chair

Conn., late 18th C., yoke crests, vasiform splats, column vase-and-reel turned posts topped by capped urn finials, trapezoidal rush seat, column-and-ring turned legs, turned feet, double stretcher, assembled set of four, one black with gold floral decor, one with red wash, one with old refinish, one refinished, 38-3/4" h, set 2,300.00

New Haven Colony, Conn., area, c. 1790-1810, old red paint, yoked crest, vasiform splat, ring-turned front legs, double stretcher, replaced splint seat, imperfections, pr 632.50

Hitchcock, old black over red grained paint, stenciled gold foliage, turned legs, ring-turned front stretcher, paper rush seat, backsplat with pierced design, ring-turned crest with medallion in center, one splat restored, one foot chipped, 33-3/4" h, set of six 825.00

Ladderback

Armchair, "Lyndonville" (Vt.), three slats, turned arms/legs/stretchers, caned seats of different ages, 35" h, set of four 462.00

Armchair, orig worn red paint, stretcher base with sausage-turned front legs, ring-turned arm supports, scroll arms, four arched slats, turned posts with old replacement finials, replaced paper rush seat, some height loss to base, 39-1/2" h 495.00

Armchair, red paint over earlier gray, turned legs, stretcher base, scrolled arms, turned supports run through the seat rail to side stretchers, 4 arched slats with sausage-turned posts and turned finials, replaced rush seat, 44-1/2" h 935.00

Side chair, county style, curly maple turned posts and front stretcher, oak or ash arched slats and side stretchers, splint seat, old refinish, 39-1/2" h 495.00

Side chair, country style, maple with oak slats, brown with traces of old red at turnings, reeded seat an early replacement, 37-1/2" h 137.50

Side chair, country style, maple with oak stretchers and shaped splats, natural matte finish, 39-1/2" h 110.00

Side chair, old black paint, button feet on front legs, well-turned stretcher, posts with sausage-turnings, large finials, replaced rush seat, 43" h 825.00

Side chair, painted, old black repaint, worn splint seat, tapered posts, turned finials, 38-1/4" h 247.50

Wagon seat, orig green paint, slat back, shaped arms, replaced rush seat, back feet ended out, found in Brewster, Mass., 30-3/4" h, 34-1/2" w, 19" d 935.00

Weaver's chair, natural finish, turned feet and stretchers, splint seat, two arched slats on back, belonged to Indiana coverlet weaver David Isaac

Graves, purchased in 1901 near the Graves farm in Middleboro, Ind., joints need regluing, 38" h 770.00

Miscellaneous

Double seat, maple and hickory, mushroom arms, three tapered rear posts with finials, two slats per side, woven splint seat, pegged construction, old refinish, some foot loss, 29-3/4" h 550.00

High-back plank child's chair, walnut, J-curve and ear carving on sides, nailed, replaced seat, age cracks, edge damage, 35" h 247.50

Painted side chair, old black, gilt highlights, maple, Portsmouth, N.H., c. 1735-1750, carved yoke crest on vasiform splat flanked by molded raked stiles above over-upholstered seat, medial stretcher with ball-and-reel turnings flanked by block-and-baluster turned front legs, Spanish carved feet joined to rear raking legs by square stretchers, 40" h 3,737.50

Plank seat, three turned half spindles on back, old green repaint, black and gold detail, fruit decor on crests and front of seats, areas of wear, 31" h, set of four 308.00

Plank seat, five-spindle back, tapered legs, stretcher base, shaped seat, mkd "T. Oldham" (Wooster, Ohio), refinished, 33-1/2" h........................... 71.50

Weaver's armchair, old black repaint over earlier red, stretcher base with double rungs, turned front posts, replaced woven canvas tape seat, three arched slats on back, tapered rear posts, 33-1/2" h.. 165.00

Queen Anne, armchair

Country style, old black repaint, yellow striping, relief-carved crest, stiles with beaded edges, arms with scrolled hand rests, found in Portland, Maine, feet ended out, contemporary rush seat, restorations, 43-3/4" h 1,540.00

Old refinish, Spanish feet, well-turned front stretcher and arm posts, rush seat, molded arms with well-developed scrolls, molded and curved back, urn-shaped splat, relief-carved scallops on crest, pegged construction, some age, small chips on foot, 43-1/2" h 1,430.00

Walnut, Philadelphia, c. 1740-60, serpentine crest with incised beading, scrolled ears, vasiform splat, shaped arms, scrolled and carved knuckles, intricate carved arm supports, slip seat, shaped rails, cabriole front legs with paneled trifid feet, raked round back legs, refinished, 38-1/4" h.. 5,175.00

Queen Anne armchair, walnut, Philadelphia, c. 1740-60, refinished, $5,175. (Photo courtesy of Skinner Auctioneers & Appraisers of Antiques & Fine Arts, Boston and Bolton, Mass.)

NO ORDINARY SEAT

Some people might have a difficult time feeling at ease in this easy chair. At least, they would once they knew what it is and what it's worth.

This Queen Anne wingback was made in Philadelphia during the mid-18th century, and it even has some of its original fabric. The legs are walnut, with the front cabriole legs ending in slipper feet. The piece was sold by Horst Auctioneers for $450,000.

Queen Anne wingback, $450,000. (Photo courtesy of Horst Auctioneers, Ephrata, Pa.)

Queen Anne, side chair

Banister, country-style, turned front legs and stretcher, woven splint seat, turned rear posts, 3 half-turned posts on back with faint incised compass stars, heart crest with finials, some height loss, 40-3/4" h 440.00

Cherry and maple, old finish, Spanish feet, turned front posts and stretchers, old worn rush seat, tapered rear posts, molded bottom slat, vase splat, yoke crest, feet ended out, insect damage, 40" h 220.00

Country style, alligatored finish, boldly turned posts and front stretcher, old worn rush seat, attributed to Samuel Durand, 40-1/2" h 550.00

Country style, old dark alligatored finish, banister back, urn-shaped splat, button feet, bulbous turned front stretcher, 39" h, pr 1,650.00

Country style, maple, painted, old dry red, contoured back, shaped crest, urn splat, splint seat in old light-green paint, 42-1/4" h 1,045.00

Country style, maple, painted, old red paint, turned posts and stretchers, vase-formed splat, ram's-horn shaped crest, damaged splint seat possibly orig, 40" h 385.00

Fiddle-back, Dominy Workshop, East Hampton, L.I., c. 1770-1800, yoked crest rail, vase-and-ring turned stiles and tapering legs, vasiform splat, trapezoidal rush seat, boldly turned medial stretcher, pad feet, old black paint, minor imperfections, 39" h 3,910.00

Maple, fiddle splat, turned stretchers, 42" h 1,650.00

Maple, Mass., c. 1740-60, yoked crest rail, vasiform splat, molded shoe, raked and chamfered stiles, over-upholstered balloon seat, front cabriole legs, pad feet, rear shaped and raked legs, vase-and-ring turned stretchers, old refinish, minor restoration 4,312.50

Maple, Mass., c. 1740-60, yoked crest rail, vasiform splat, molded shoe, raked and chamfered stiles, trapezoidal slip seat, front cabriole legs with pad feet, rear chamfered raked legs, block vase-and-ring turned stretchers, old refinish, 41" h 4,312.50

Maple, ring-turned front legs, turned front stretchers, varnished paper rush seat, tapered turned rear posts, urn-shaped splat, refinished, feet shortened, replaced seat, 38-3/4" h 275.00

Painted, black repaint, gold line detail probably Victorian, cabriole legs, boldly turned front stretcher, vase-shaped splat, worn rush seat with traces of black paint, attributed to John or Samuel Durand, Milford, Conn., 41" h 660.00

Painted, old black repaint, gold decor probably Victorian, cabriole front legs, urn-shaped splat, well-turned posts, replaced rush seat, 39-7/8" h 715.00

Side chair, painted, old black repaint, yellow striping probably Victorian, cabriole front legs, boldly turned front stretcher, urn-shaped splat, rush seat in worn cream repaint, 39-1/4" h 990.00

Painted, old alligatored red over black repaint, cabriole front legs with bold turnings, urn-shaped splat, replaced rush seat, attributed to Samuel Durand, Milford, Conn., 40-3/4" h 880.00

Sheraton

Armchair, country style, bamboo turnings, shaped seat, half-spindle back, rabbit-ear posts with two slats, green repaint, possible repairs, 34" h, 17-1/2" seat 192.50

Faux bamboo armchair, three prs of two turned slats with ball dividers between prs, double slat also repeated under arms and as front stretcher, woven seat, 34" h, pr 1,650.00

Hitchcock type, worn orig red and black graining, yellow striping, stenciled decor, cutout slats, wear, touchup and over-varnish, replaced paper rush seats, six side chairs, two armchairs with scrolled arms, 33" h, set of eight 3,080.00

Side chair, curly maple and bird's-eye maple, flared ring-turned legs, turned rungs and front stretcher, woven-paper rush seat, one-slat back, reattached rolled crest, 33-3/4" h, pr 550.00

Side chair, grain-decor, old worn red and black graining, yellow striping, gold floral design on crest, refinished seat with added yellow striping, 34-1/2" h, set of 4 .... 990.00

Slat-back

Delaware Valley, c. 1760, three arched slats, cylinder-and-ring turned stiles with ball finials, trapezoidal rush seat, turned posts, double turned stretchers, four chairs with old red-brown wash, four with brown finish, 36-1/2" h, set of eight 1,725.00

Slat-back armchair, maple, Delaware River Valley, 18th C., old refinish, $9,200. (Photo courtesy of Skinner Auctioneers & Appraisers of Antiques & Fine Arts, Boston and Bolton, Mass.)

Painted, old black, New England, 18th C., turned finials, arched slats, down-turned scrolled hand-holds, vase-and-ring turned legs, rush seat, pieced feet, 45-1/2" h 1,035.00

Pine and ash, Scituate or Marshfield, Mass., area, early 18th C., deeply incised finials, four graduated arched slats, incised turned arms with mushroom caps, turned double stretchers, remnants of old red paint, imperfections, height loss, 43-3/4" h 2,875.00

T-back, oak, slightly shaped wooden seat, 38" h, set of five 165.00

Wagon

Bench, old dark-brown repaint, two sections, turned and tapered legs, turned rungs, woven splint seat, arched slats, curved arms with medallion hand rests, one arm replaced, short turned finials, age cracks 550.00

Seat, New England, mid-19th C., old red paint, square crest, tapering spindles, stay rail, early splint seat, turned legs, imperfections, 34-1/2" h 460.00

Windsor

Arrow-back armchair, old worn mustard paint, bamboo-turned legs and stretchers, well-shaped round seat, incised rain gutters around front and back, arrow-shaped arm supports, 32" h 275.00

Arrow-back, Mass., c. 1815-25, inscribed in chalk "A. Wills" (for Abethus Williams, Raynham, Mass.) on the underside, curving crest, four arrow-back spindles, balloon-shaped incised seat, shaped medial stretcher, ring-turned legs

Wagon seat, old red paint, New England, mid-19th C., $460. (Photo courtesy of Skinner Auctioneers & Appraisers of Antiques & Fine Arts, Boston and Bolton, Mass.)

and stretchers, old dark-red ground, indistinct yellow and green stencil decor on crest and stiles, old surface, 34" h, set of seven (six side chairs, one armchair) 2,645.00

Bamboo armchair, five-spindle, old brown paint, mustard decor on crest, shaped seat, flared sides, 34-1/2" h 275.00

Bamboo armchair, seven-spindle, hardwood, worn finish, H stretcher, one back post replaced, 34-1/4" h 275.00

Bamboo side chairs, six-spindle, stretcher base, shaped seat, small domed finial on posts, refinished, 36" h, set of six 715.00

Bamboo side chair, seven-spindle, old black repaint over earlier red, shield-shaped seat, birdcage crest, one spindle split, 34-1/2" h, similar pr... 962.50

Bamboo side chair, seven-spindle, black repaint, embossed "Wilder," shield-shaped seat, rain gutter, arched crest, early wrought-iron brace, 34" h 192.50

Bamboo side chair, seven-spindle back, old refinish, some curl in the legs, H stretcher base, D-shaped seat, early pieced repair in seat, glue break, 35-1/2" h.. 220.00

Bamboo side chairs, seven-spindle, old yellow repaint over earlier black, well-shaped seats with incised detail, restorations including few replaced spindles, areas of touchup, 34" h, set of four 990.00

Birdcage armchair, seven-spindle, refinished, stretcher base, round seat, three spindles through crest, restored crack in seat, some height loss, 34-1/2" h.. 192.50

Birdcage child's side chair, five-spindle, red paint, 25-1/2" h 412.50

Birdcage side chair, seven-spindle, Mass., c. 1810, old putty green, red pinstriping, concave crest rail, shaped seat, splayed legs, H stretcher, 35" h, pr.. 3,565.00

Birdcage side chair, seven-spindle, old reddish-brown finish, bamboo legs, stretcher base, well-shaped shield seat, restoration, 32-1/2" h.. 247.50

Birdcage side chair, seven-spindle, old white paint with traces of salmon, bamboo-turned legs and posts, shaped seat, 34" h 275.00

Birdcage side chair, seven-spindle, old worn brown paint, yellow striping, bamboo turnings, shaped seat, repairs, 33-1/4" h, set of four 990.00

Birdcage, youth size, five-spindle, bamboo turned legs and stretchers, shield-shaped seat, old black repaint with gold striping, repairs, 25" h 192.50

Bow-back armchair, seven-spindle, alligatored black paint over earlier colors, stretcher base with bamboo turnings, round seat, molded bow, scrolled arms, repaired crack in seat with bowties underneath, unreadable signature, Pa. origin, 36" h 935.00

Bow-back armchair, seven-spindle, refinished, splayed base, shield-shaped seat with rain gutter, scrolled arms with incised line borders, arms mortised through the molded bow, 37-1/4" h 495.00

Bow-back armchair, nine-spindle, black repaint over earlier red finish, bamboo turnings, H stretcher, well-shaped seat, rain gutter, tenoned arms with carved scrolls and shaped supports, cross stretcher replaced, 34" h 330.00

Bow-back armchair, nine-spindle, black repaint, yellow striping, splayed base, bulbous turned legs and "H" stretcher, shield-shaped seat with rain gutter, molded bow, scrolled arms, one spindle broken below bow, age cracks in seat, some height loss, minor repairs, 37-1/2" h 550.00

Bow-back side chair, seven-spindle, apple-green paint, 37-1/2" h 1,045.00

Bow-back side chair, seven-spindle, apple-green paint over red, 37" h, set of four 2,420.00

Bow-back side chair, seven-spindle, old light-green paint over earlier white, Conn., c. 1790, shaped saddle seat, splayed bulbous vase-and-ring turned legs, ring-turned swelled stretchers, 36-1/4" h 460.00

Bow-back side chair, seven-spindle, old red paint over black, bamboo-turned legs and H-stretcher, splayed base, saddle seat, molded bow, 38" h 330.00

Bow-back side chair, seven-spindle, old red repaint over white, bamboo turnings, saddle seat, molded edge, attributed to Boston area, 38" h, pr 1,430.00

Bow-back side chair, seven-spindle, worn dark-green paint, bamboo turnings, H-stretcher base, shield-shaped seat, 37" h, set of six 1,375.00

Bow-back side chair, nine-spindle, 38" h 770.00

Bow-back side chair, nine-spindle, black paint, early 20th-C. repro with good detail, 36-1/2" h 440.00

Bow-back side chair, nine-spindle, black over red paint, yellow detail, intentional wear, vase-and-ring turned legs, stretcher base, shield-shaped seat, "David T. Smith, Morrow, Ohio" reproduction, 38-1/4" h 1,650.00

Bow-back side chair, nine-spindle, branded "E. Tracy" (Ebenezer Tracy, Lisbon, Conn., 1764-1803), bamboo-turned legs, H stretcher, shaped seat, hoop-shaped bow, old dark finish, well-executed repairs, 35-1/2" h 880.00

Brace-back armchair, blue-black repaint, splayed base, turned legs, H stretcher, shaped seat, turned spindles, turned arm supports, scrolled mahogany arms, beaded edge bow, one arm braced, tail piece replaced, attributed to R.I., 36" h 715.00

Brace-back continuous-arm armchair, painted, dark green, reproduction by "D.R. Dimes" (no longer made) in Tracy style, one with cracked seat, 37" h, set of ten 3,850.00

Brace-back continuous-arm armchair, stamped "EB Tracy" (Lisbon, Conn.), bowed crest with beaded edge, tapering spindles, tail piece, shaped seat, splayed bulbous-turned legs, swelled stretchers, late 18th C., imperfections, 37" h, pr 4,025.00

Brace-back bow-back side chair, seven-spindle, black paint, R.I., 38" h 550.00

Brace-back bow-back side chair, seven-spindle, red/brown paint, 39" h 1,980.00

Brace-back bow-back side chair, seven-spindle, old refinish, splayed base, bulbous-turned leg and H stretcher, shield-shaped seat, molded bow, minor age cracks, chip in one brace, old repair in one seat, 34-3/4" h and 35-1/2" h, set of three 1,815.00

Brace-back bow-back side chair, seven-spindle, stained hickory, maple and pine, R.I., c. 1795, incised bowed crestrail, ring-turned spindles, applied scrolled mahogany arms, vase-and-ring turned legs, turned swelled stretchers, old dark refinish, 39" h... 7,475.00

Brace-back bow-back side chair, eight-spindle, Windsor-style, vase-and-ring turned legs, stretcher base, "Wallace Nutting" paper and impressed label, 37-1/2" h.......................... 440.00

Brace-back bow-back side chair, nine-spindle, green paint, turned legs and H stretcher, 36-1/2" h 1,100.00

Brace-back fanback, splayed base, bulbous turned legs and H stretcher, saddle seat, turned back posts, back spindles, shaped and curved crest, old black repaint, old repairs and replacements, 36-1/2" h 220.00

Comb-back armchair, seven-spindle, bamboo turnings, H stretcher, shaped seat and arms, refinished, restorations, 45" h......................... 1,100.00

Comb-back, armchair, nine-spindle old refinishing, H stretcher, vase-and-ring turned legs, D-shaped seat, rain gutter, scrolled knuckle arms, bowed arm rail, arched crest, scrolled ears, restorations, 43-3/4" h.. 1,045.00

Comb-back writing armchair, black over red paint, mustard vinegar graining on seat, blunt arrow feet, D-shaped seat, drawer under seat and writing platform, scrolled ears, intentional wear, "David T. Smith, Morrow, Ohio" repro, 47" h 935.00

Continuous-arm, maple and hickory, N.Y., late 18th C., beaded arched crest, shaped handholds, bulbous-turned arm supports, incised shaped seat, splayed bulbous ring-turned legs, swelled H stretcher, old refinish, imperfections, 37" h 2,070.00

Continuous-arm, old brown finish, splayed base, distinctive turned detail and H stretcher, oval seat, turned arm posts, bamboo spindles, shaped arms, beaded-edge bow, attributed to Conn., descended in the family of Col. Thomas Knowlton, 37" and 39-3/4" h, pr... 5,225.00

Continuous-arm, old dark finish with traces of paint, brace backs and faint signature "A.D. Allen," splayed base, turned legs and H stretcher, shield-shaped seat, shaped arms, turned posts, repair at bow in arm, age cracks in seat, 38-1/2" h, pr 4,620.00

Fan-back armchair, five-spindle, painted white, turned legs and H stretcher, 40" h 880.00

Fan-back armchair, seven-spindle, turned legs and H stretcher, carved ears, 47" h 1,650.00

Fan-back side chair, five-spindle, southern N.H. or northern Mass., c. 1790, orig green paint, serpentine crest above tapering spindles, shaped plank seat with pommel, bulbous-turned splayed legs, swelled H stretcher, 35-1/4" h 2,070.00

Fan-back side chair, seven-spindle, old dark refinishing, splayed base, bulbous-turned legs and H stretcher, saddle seat, replaced stretcher, repaired crack in seat and crest needs reglued, 38" h 247.50

Fan-back side chair, seven-spindle, painted, old worn black, traces of earlier red, vase-and-ring turned legs, H stretcher, shield seat, rain gutter, turned rear posts, shaped crest, attributed to R.I. or Conn., age crack in seat, 33-1/4" h 1,980.00

Fan-back side chair, seven-spindle, painted black, turned legs and H stretcher, 37" h, pr 1,430.00

Fan-back side chair, seven-spindle, refinished, turned stretcher base, shield seat, turned rear posts, shaped crest, found in Pembroke, Maine, legs ended out, 35-1/2" h, pr 825.00

Fan-back side chair, seven-spindle, turned legs and H stretcher, carved ears, 35" h 330.00

Fan-back side chair, seven-spindle, vase-and-ring turned legs, H stretcher base, shield seat with incised rain gutter at back, curved back with turned posts, shaped crest, refinished, restoration, 35-3/8" h 715.00

Fan-back Windsor side chair, original green paint, southern New Hampshire or northern Massachusetts, c. 1790, $2,070. (Photo courtesy of Skinner Auctioneers & Appraisers of Antiques & Fine Arts, Boston and Bolton, Mass.)

Fan-back side chair, eight-spindle, old refinish, splayed base, bulbous turned legs, H stretcher, saddle seat, turned posts, curved yoke crest, pieced repair on crest, seat repairs, 1 cross stretcher replaced, 36-3/4" h 275.00

Fan-back side chair, nine-spindle, orig green paint, probably Pa., c. 1800, shaped crest, scrolled ears, saddle seat, splayed vase-and-ring turned legs, swelled ring-turned stretchers, inscribed "Mary 1799," 37" h 2,530.00

Fan-back side chair, nine-spindle, shaped crest with carved ears, shaped seat, stretcher base with nice splay, refinished surface retains warm brown color, restoration, 35-3/4" h 357.50

Fan-back side chair, nine-spindle, X-stretcher, bamboo-turned legs, 26-1/2" h 825.00

High-back armchair, ash, maple and pine, possibly southwestern R.I., c. 1790-1800, seven-spindle, serpentine crest, shaped handholds, vase-and-ring turned supports and legs, saddle seat with pommel, turned swelled stretchers, old refinish, minor imperfections, 38-1/2" h 2,415.00

Plank seat, stencil and paint decor, red and black grained paint, yellow edge striping, stenciled fruit and foliage motif to crest rails, paint worn, 30" h, set of four 467.50

Rod-back side chair, seven-spindle, New England, c. 1800, bamboo-turned crest rail and stiles enclosing three spindles, shaped seat, splayed bamboo-turned legs and stretchers, old brown paint, mkd "N. Tuck" in chalk (there were Tuck family Windsor chair makers in Boston, 1790-1805), 34" h, set of six 6,325.00

Sack-back armchair, seven-spindle, black over vestiges of old green paint, maple and ash, New England, c. 1780-90, shaped arms on baluster-and-ring turned supports, saddle seat, splayed baluster-and-ring turned legs, bulbous H stretcher, 36-1/2" h 2,070.00

Sack-back armchair, seven-spindle, old black paint, Conn., c. 1780-1800, knuckled armholds, ring-turned and swelled arm supports, shaped seat with pommel, splayed bulbous ring-turned legs, swelled H stretcher, repairs, 36" h 977.50

Sack-back armchair, seven-spindle, old black paint, gilt striping, attributed to Amos D. Allen, Windham, Conn., c. 1780, shaped arms, saddle seat, vase-and-ring turned supports and legs, bulbous stretchers, 35" h 4,025.00

Sack-back armchair, seven-spindle, old refinishing, splayed base, turned legs and H stretcher, shaped seat, turned arm supports, shaped arms, bowed crest rail, seat cut for a potty and plugged, other old repairs, 37-1/2" h 440.00

Sack-back armchair, seven-spindle, old refinishing, splayed base, turned vase-and-ring legs and H stretcher, oval seat with rain gutter, arm supports match legs, shaped arms, base restoration with replacements, 37-3/4" h 467.50

Sack-back armchair, seven-spindle, old worn black over green paint, New England, c. 1790, shaped arms with vase-and-ring turned supports, shaped seat, splayed vase-and-ring turned legs, swelled H stretcher, 39" h 14,950.00

Sack-back armchair, seven-spindle, orig finish, turned legs and H stretcher, 38" h 6,875.00

Sack-back armchair, seven-spindle, refinished, splayed base, turned legs and H stretcher, turned arm supports, shaped seat, restoration with replacements, 37-1/2" h 385.00

Sack-back armchair, nine-spindle, black over red paint, yellow detail, intentional wear, "David T. Smith, Morrow, Ohio" reproduction, 33-1/2" h, pr 1,210.00

Sack-back side chair, seven-spindle, old brown paint, New England, c. 1815-20, bamboo-turned crest rail, turned stiles with finials, splayed legs, turned stretchers, imperfections, 35" h, set of four 2,415.00

Side chair, seven-spindle, orig dark-red paint, black striping, incised "W. Miller," Delaware River Valley, early 19th C., stepped crests, bamboo-turned stiles, shield-shaped seat, splayed legs, 34" h, set of six 4,025.00

Step-down child's side chair, old paint, 20" h 192.50

Step-down, seven-spindle, refinished, bamboo-turned legs, shield-shaped seat, most with rain gutters, few rungs replaced, one with pieced repairs on crest, 34" h, assembled set of six 1,155.00

Chalkware, Vintage

Background: Chalkware, a substance used by sculptors to imitate marble and also to harden plaster of Paris, was developed by English inventor William Hutchinson in 1848. Vendors sold the early chalkware items, which were inexpensive and colorful and which were often copies of popular Staffordshire pieces.

Collecting Hint: Don't confuse 19th-century examples with 20th-century chalkware that often served as carnival prizes.

Bank, roly-poly form, man with hands behind his back, nose chip, 8" h 165.00

Bird on plinth, worn orig black and goldenrod paint, 6-1/2" h.. 880.00

Canary on square pedestal base with ball top, yellow with red, black and brown accenting, worn paint, broken/glued, 6-1/8" h.. 210.00

Cat, seated, worn orig red, black and yellow paint, wear and edge damage, 5-1/8" h.............................. 385.00

Cat bank, reclining, with mouse in mouth, green polychrome body, red bow, brown highlights, base chips, 6" h, 7-3/4" w.. 220.00

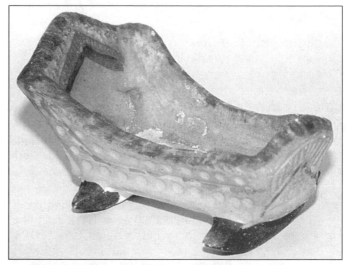

Chalkware miniature cradle, 6" l, $275.

Deer, reclining, red, ochre, brown and black paint, 19th C., repair, paint wear, 5-3/4" h, 10" w, pr........... 488.75

Dove, traces of paint on eyes, cast-pewter feet, one with beak worn down, one with two toes broken off, 5-3/4" h, 8-1/4" l, pr 300.00

Dog

    Painted collar, mouth, nose and accents, 10" h 522.50

    Seated, molded detail, worn orig red, black and yellow paint, wear and base chips, hole between the legs, 5-3/4" h 385.00

    Standing pug, painted collar and details, 10" l 357.50

Flowers and fruit in vase, and fruit arrangement in an urn, yellow, red, green and tan paint, minor paint loss, 12" h, pr 1,840.00

Fruit

    In footed urn, mantle ornament, red, yellow, green and tan paint, repair, 16" h 2,185.00

    In urn, mantle ornament, orange, green, red, black and yellow, minor touchups, chips, 8" and 11-1/4" h, pr... 1,495.00

Girl, white pantaloons, yellow dress with red stripes, matching hat, 9-1/2" h................................... 1,155.00

Lovebirds, kissing pr on pedestal, yellow bodies, red breasts, green wings, wear, one wing repaired, 5-1/4" h 165.00

Parrot on plinth, very worn yellow, green, black and red paint, stains on base, 7-1/8" h 49.50

Poodle, old black repaint, red base and tail, roughness around base, 7-5/8" h, 5-3/4" w 302.50

Rabbit, seated, worn orig red, yellow and black paint, 5-1/4" h.. 577.50

Rooster

    Red, green and black orig paint, worn 5-1/2" h 357.50

    Red, mustard, black and green paint, worn.. 920.00

Squirrel, chewing on nut in front paws, gray wash, tail with red details, 7-1/8" h 412.50

Cheese Items

Background: The making of cheese occurred two or three times a week in early American homes. Cheese baskets were used to hold the curds while they were being drained through cheesecloth. The crudest drainers have just a perforated board for a bottom, while later, more elaborate examples were woven of splint. Specialty items developed to assist in the process included sieves, tubs, boards, paddles, knives, presses, and molds.

Drainer
    Windsor style, wooden, mortised and pegged base, natural finish, attached basket with 12 spindles, one crosspiece missing, insect holes, 8-7/8" h, 24" w, 11-1/2" d 192.50
    Windsor style, wooden, round top, square bottom 605.00
Ladder, wooden, H-shaped, slightly tapered rounded sides, mortised dowels, holds strainer, 17-5/8" l, 5-3/4" h... 65.00
Mold, pierced tin
    Diamond, pierced floral design on bottom, four round feet, wire ring on side, 2-5/8" h, 5-5/8" x 8-3/8" 325.00
    Heart, pierced floral design on bottom, three triangular feet, arched handle on side of heart, 3-5/8" h, 4-5/8" w, 5-3/8" l 400.00
    Heart, pierced floral design on bottom, three triangular feet, arched handle on side of heart, 3" h, 4-3/8" w, 5-1/8" l 310.00

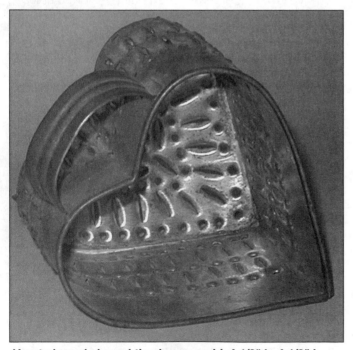

Heart-shaped pierced-tin cheese mold, 4-1/2" h, 4-1/2" l, $350.

Heart, pierced radial design, three tapered conical feet, wire ring on side, 3-7/8" h, 5-3/4" x 6-3/4" 360.00
Round, rounded bottom, applied round gallery-like foot, arched handle on side of top rim, 4-1/8" h (excluding handle), 5" dia 100.00
Round, rounded bottom, three ring-shaped feet, two arched side handles, 4-1/4" h, 4-1/2" dia 60.00

Chest of Drawers

Background: Chests of drawers were developed as adaptations of the early chest form, with a series of drawers being added to provide ready access to the items stored therein. Also referred to as a bureau in America, the chest of drawers was used as a receptacle for clothing and was popular during the last quarter of the 18th century.

References: Eileen and Richard Dubrow, *Styles of American Furniture 1860-1960*, Schiffer Publishing, 1997; Tim Forrest, *Bulfinch Anatomy of Antique Furniture*, Bulfinch Press, 1996; John T. Kirk, *American Furniture: Understanding Styles, Construction, and Quality*, Harry N. Abrams Publishers, 2000; Milo M. Naeve, *Identifying American Furniture*, W.W. Norton, 1998; Ellen T. Schroy, *Warman's American Furniture*, Krause Publications, 2001; Robert W. and Harriet Swedberg, *Collector's Encyclopedia of American Furniture*, Vol. 1 (1990, 1996 value update), Vol. 2 (1992, 1999 value update), Vol. 3 (1998), Collector Books; —, *Encyclopedia of American Oak Furniture*, Krause Publications, 2000.

Bowfront, cherry, New England, early 19th C., four drawers, top with inlaid edge over case of cockbeaded graduated drawers, cyma-curved veneered skirt, high French feet, old refinish, old replaced brasses, 39" h, 38-1/2" w, 23" d.. 4,600.00
Chippendale
    Birch, four drawers, bracket feet, dovetailed overlapping drawers, one-board top with molded edge, refinished, one foot repaired, replaced back supports and glue blocks, edge damage, replaced brasses, 32-1/2" h, 40-1/2" w, 19-1/2" d 550.00
    Birch, four graduated drawers, ogee feet, full reeded columns, brass bat-wing pulls and escutcheons, 34" h, 36" w 1,375.00
    Cherry, four drawers, ogee feet, drawers with beaded trim, reeded quarter columns, 2-board top with molded edge, replaced feet, reset top, replaced brasses, 36-1/2" h, 42" w, 23-1/4" d 3,575.00
    Cherry, refinished, scalloped bracket feet, four drawers with molded edges, replaced two-board scal-

Chippendale painted birch chest, old Spanish brown, Massachusetts or New Hampshire, late-18th C., 36" h, 36" w, $2,645. (Photo courtesy of Skinner Auctioneers & Appraisers of Antiques & Fine Arts, Boston and Bolton, Mass.)

loped top, replaced brasses, repairs to feet and drawer edges, 39" h, 43" w, 25" d............ 1,100.00

Curly maple and pine, orig red flame graining, one-board ends, cutout feet, three dovetailed overlapping drawers (deep top drawer has two drawer fronts), molded-edge top, backboard mkd "L.L. 1807" and "P.P.H.G--1847," replaced brass bails, 42-1/2" h, 39-1/4" w, 22" d...................... 6,050.00

Mahogany, four drawers, figured one-board top with applied molding and 1-1/4" rear overhang, case with fluted quarter columns, padded ogee feet, graduated and dovetailed drawers with figured fronts with applied beading and 3/4 dust shelves, attributed to Philadelphia, mellow refinish, feet repairs, 33-1/2" h, 40-1/2" w, 22" d.......... 4,125.00

Mahogany, four drawers, overhanging top with serpentine front and sides, conforming cockbeaded case with graduated drawers, molded base, carved claw-and-ball feet, Boston, c. 1760-80, replaced brasses, old finish, 32-1/4" h, 36" w, 20" d.. 34,500.00

Mahogany and mahogany veneer, ogee feet, scalloped returns, one-board sides, four dovetailed drawers with beaded borders, embossed deer brasses, molded-edge top, refinished, replaced feet, 33-3/4" h, 42" w, 22" d...................... 2,310.00

Maple, New England, c. 1800, rectangular top, cockbeaded case of four drawers, bracket feet, refinished, replaced brasses, imperfections, 36-1/2" h, 39" w, 18-3/4" d 1,495.00

Maple, probably Mass., c. 1800, rectangular overhanging top with molded lower edge, cockbeaded case of 4 graduated drawers, bracket feet, replaced brasses, old refinish, minor imperfections, 36-1/4" h, 37-5/8" w, 18" d 2,070.00

Oxbow, mahogany, probably Boston, c. 1760-80, molded overhanging top, shaped front and square corners, cockbeaded case of four reverse-serpentine drawers with blocked ends, conforming bracket feet, orig brasses, back stenciled "H.A. Hancock," old refinish, minor restoration, 31" h, 32-1/2" w, 22" d 58,600.00

Serpentine, mahogany, Mass., c. 1760-80, shaped molded top, four graduated cockbeaded drawers, molded base, carved claw-and-ball feet, one drawer mkd "Basle Williams" in chalk, old replaced brasses, old refinish, minor restorations, 33-3/4" h, 39-3/4" w, 20" d 16,100.00

Tiger maple, southern New England, c. 1781, four thumb-molded graduated drawers, dovetailed bracket feet, molded-edge top, replaced brasses, old refinish, minor imperfections, 38-1/2" h... 2,990.00

Walnut, country style, four drawers, refinished, replaced bracket feet, old brasses but not period, 40" h, 37" w, 10-1/2" d 990.00

Country style

Cherry, old finish, bracket feet with shaped front apron, four dovetailed drawers with beaded edges, poplar/pine secondary woods, replaced wooden pulls, pieced repairs, replaced apron, 40-3/4" h, 43-1/2" w, 19-1/2" d...................... 1,017.50

Curly maple, old reddish-brown finish, cut-out feet, scrolled apron, one-board ends and top, four dovetailed drawers, old repairs, 42-3/4" h, 42" w, 17-1/4" d.. 2,145.00

Pine, orig black over reddish-brown flame decor, tapered and turned feet, one-board sides and top, two short over four long graduated dovetailed drawers, turned wooden pulls, high scalloped backsplash, replaced feet, some paint touchup, 52" h, 44" w, 19-7/8" d............................ 1,265.00

Empire

Cherry, six drawers (two short drawers over one long stepped over three long), paneled ends, turned and applied half columns, turned feet, refinished, 51-3/4" h, 44" w, 21" d 715.00

Cherry and walnut, four drawers (one stepped over three), high turned feet, paneled ends, molded base, full turned and carved pilasters below relief-carved panels, replaced glass pulls, small cracks in base molding, 51-3/4" h, 45" w, 26" d 880.00

Cherry and walnut with curly maple veneer, four drawers (one deep stepped over three), turned feet, half-turned pilasters, clear-cut glass knobs, paneled ends, one-board top, baseboards replaced, minor drawer restoration, 51-3/4" h, 44" w, 22" d.. 1,760.00

Curly maple and cherry, four drawers, turned feet and posts with rope-carved pilasters, curly inlaid panels on either side of top drawer, beaded-edge

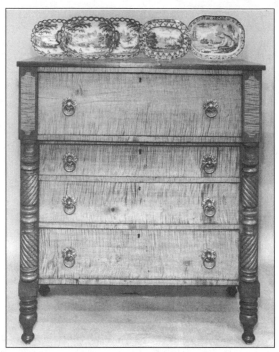

Empire chest of drawers, curly maple and cherry, marked "Jacob Kinney--Weston Ohio," refinished, replaced brasses, 49-7/8" h, $1,375. (Photo courtesy of Garth's Auctions, Delaware, Ohio)

drawers, signed "Jacob Kinney--Weston Ohio" on backboard, refinished, age cracks, replaced brasses, Ohio origin, 49-7/8" h, 43-3/4" w, 21-3/4" d 1,375.00

Grain-decor, red and black decor case, vinegar-grained drawer fronts, two small drawers on top and one long stepped over three long, shaped backsplash, 48" h, 42" w, 21" d 715.00

Mahogany, four drawers, country style, Maine origin, turned legs, scrolled crest, replaced brasses, old refinish, 46-1/2" h, 39-1/4" w, 18-1/4" d 770.00

Federal

Bowfront, mahogany and mahogany veneer, inlaid, probably Mass., c. 1800, six drawers (three short over three long), bow-front top with reeded edge, conforming case, inlaid stringing, cutout feet, shaped skirt, orig oval brass pulls, old refinish, minor imperfections, 38-1/2" h, 39-1/2" w, 24" d... 4,312.50

Bowfront, mahogany and tiger maple veneer, probably Portsmouth N.H., c. 1805-15, bowed top with double string inlaid edge, four cockbeaded drawers each with maple veneer panels outlined with stringing and mahogany cross-banding, string inlaid base, shaped cut-out feet, old finish, orig brasses, imperfections, 34" h, 39-3/4" w, 21-1/4" d 18,400.00

Bowfront, tiger maple, birch and tiger maple veneer, Mass., c. 1810-20, top with elliptical front and

Federal chest of drawers, $18,400. (Photo courtesy of Skinner Auctioneers & Appraisers of Antiques & Fine Arts, Boston and Bolton, Mass.)

ovolo corners, case of four cockbeaded graduated drawers, quarter ring-turned columns, vase-and-ring turned legs, ball feet, replaced brasses, restored, 38-1/2" h, 39" w, 21-1/2" d........ 5,980.00

Cherry and bird's-eye maple veneer, Hubbardton Vt., c. 1810-20, attributed to Asahel Jones (1766-1822), cherry top with veneered edge, case of four cockbeaded drawers of bird's-eye maple veneer with mahogany cross-banded veneer surrounds, cyma-curved veneered skirt, replaced brasses, old refinish, 36-1/4" h, 40" w, 18-1/2" d 4,312.50

Cherry and bird's-eye maple veneer, possibly Vt., c. 1820, rectangular top with reeded edge, case of four cockbeaded graduated drawers, flanked by reeded panels above vase-and-ring turned feet, replaced brass pulls, old refinish, 39-1/2" h, 39-1/2" w, 19" d 2,415.00

Cherry and mahogany veneer, N.H., c. 1810, top with inlaid edge, four graduated scratch-beaded

Federal chest of drawers, bird's-eye maple veneer, possibly Vermont, c. 1820, replaced pulls, old refinish, 39-1/2" h, $2,415. (Photo courtesy of Skinner Auctioneers & Appraisers of Antiques & Fine Arts, Boston and Bolton, Mass.)

drawers, cyma-curved veneered skirt with central panel bordered by cross-banded maple veneer, replaced brasses, old refinish, imperfections, 37-1/2" h, 42" w, 21-1/2" d 2,300.00

Poplar, orig red graining on yellow ground, ebonized detail, attributed to North Jackson, Ohio, high turned feet, half-column pilasters, 4 dovetailed drawers, scroll crest, replaced hardware, 53-1/2" h, 41-3/4" w, 20-1/2" d 7,150.00

Mahogany and figured maple, seven drawers (three short stepped over one long stepped over three long), spiraling acanthus-carved columns, turned feet, broken-arch backsplash, glass pulls, 53" h, 43" w, 20" d 1,705.00

Walnut, probably Va., c. 1800, four cockbeaded graduated drawers, overhanging rectangular top, flaring French feet, replaced oval brasses, refinished, restorations, 38-1/4" h, 37" w, 21-1/2" d 4,312.50

Hepplewhite

Birch, four drawers, 39" h, 38" w, 18" d 1,100.00

Birch, red paint, four drawers, high feet, bowed apron, 36-1/2" h, 40" w, 17" d 3,300.00

Birch and figured mahogany veneer with inlay, high shaped feet, scalloped aprons, banded inlay across the front, four dovetailed drawers with figured veneer fronts and band inlay, orig brass pulls and escutcheon plates, two-board top with rounded edge, veneer damage, 40-3/4" h, 40" w, 18-3/4" d 3,190.00

Bowfront, New England, mahogany veneer and birch with inlay, four dovetailed drawers, high French feet, scalloped apron, stringing on top edge, inlaid band around base, quarter circles on feet, refinished, replaced brasses, minor veneer repairs, 36" h, 39" w, 21" d 2,200.00

Bowfront, red wash, four drawers, mahogany drawer fronts, scalloped apron, ring pulls, 39" h, 39" w, 20" d 2,475.00

Cherry with inlay, four drawers, old finish, high cut-out feet, scrolled apron, drawers with cockbeading, banding and medallion inlay on apron, banding on drawer fronts, replaced brasses, edge and veneer damage, 43-1/2" h, 45-1/4" w, 25-1/4" d 4,840.00

Cherry with inlay, four drawers, refinished, French feet, scalloped apron, chamfered corner posts with three-line inlay, banded walnut inlay around base, drawers with stringing, orig brasses, minor edge repairs, feet replaced, 38-1/4" h, 42-1/2" w, 21" d 2,860.00

Mahogany, old dark refinish, four graduated dovetailed drawers, French feet, scalloped apron, string inlay around base/top, beaded edges, one-board sides/top, well-done base restoration, replaced oval eagle brasses, 40-1/2" h, 41-3/8" w, 19" d 3,025.00

Mahogany, refinished, four drawers, high French feet, scalloped apron, beaded edges, orig brass pulls, one-board sides, top with reeded molding, age cracks, restorations, 37-3/4" h, 41-3/4" w, 20-3/8" d 1,375.00

Mahogany, satinwood banding, four drawers, French feet, shaped apron, brass pulls/escutcheons, 41" h, 40" w, 18" d 1,925.00

Mahogany and figured mahogany veneer, four drawers, French feet, shaped apron, band inlay, replaced eagle brasses, restorations, 39-1/4" h, 44-1/2" w, 20-1/2" d 1,182.50

Maple and birch with some curl, country style, five dovetailed overlapping drawers with orig brasses, bracket feet, scrolled apron, dovetailed case, key escutcheon plates are period replacements, minor repairs, 42-3/4" h, 39-1/4" w, 19-1/4" d 6,600.00

Walnut, country style, four dovetailed drawers, high French feet, shaped front/side aprons, band inlay across front of base and two lines around top, poplar secondary wood, one-board top with age cracks, old replaced thistle brasses, replaced runners, 41-1/4" h, 42-5/8" w, 18-1/2" d 1,760.00

Walnut with some figure, old finish, four dovetailed overlapping drawers, French feet, dovetailed case, full dust shelves, orig oval brasses, two-board top with beaded edge, attributed to Ohio, some insect damage, repairs to feet, 40-1/4" h, 38-1/2" w, 20-1/2" d 3,300.00

Walnut (figured), inlaid, old finish, four dovetailed drawers, French feet with pads, shaped apron, applied beading, full dust shelves, period brasses, string inlay on drawers and top edge, banding around base, minor repairs, three locks missing, 38-3/4" h, 38-3/4" w, 21-1/2" d 2,750.00

Miniature

Cherry, four graduated drawers, inlaid designs including vine and geometric shapes beside drawers, inlaid fan on scalloped apron, brass pulls, wear, 23" h, 20" w 10,450.00

Eastlake, walnut, three drawers, old dark finish, drawers and crest with incised carving with black and gold detail, scalloped top section with mirror and candle shelves, 22-3/4" h, 12-1/2" w, 6" d 247.50

Empire, walnut, four drawers, old varnish, scrolled feet, shaped pilasters, orig turned wood pulls, one-board top, 11-5/8" h, 12-1/4" w, 8" d 467.50

Hepplewhite, figured mahogany veneer, four drawers, old dark finish, French feet, molded base and case, chamfered corners, drawers with beaded edges, white porcelain knobs, molded top, 20th C., 15" h, 10-3/4" w, 7" d 550.00

Hepplewhite, mahogany, four drawers, refinished, French feet, turned wooden knobs, English, repairs, feet replaced, 14-1/4" h, 13" w, 9-1/4" d 660.00

Mahogany, four drawers, applied molding around base, brass pulls, applied tapered round columns on front edges, small backsplash with scalloped corners, wire and finishing nails, refinished, velvet linings added, 13" h, 12" w, 8-5/8" d 467.50

Mahogany and mahogany veneer, three drawers, old finish, turned front feet, tapered rear feet, old brass pulls, applied and turned half columns, minor veneer chips, one pull replaced, 15" h, 14-1/8" w, 9-3/8" d 1,540.00

Mahogany veneer on pine, three drawers, button feet, mismatched wooden pulls, minor repairs, 7-1/2" h, 9-3/4" w, 6-1/4" d......................... 192.50

Painted, orig red wash, yellow line detail, four drawers, scalloped bracket base, molded edge, one-board top, wire nails, replaced brasses, 17-3/4" h, 11-1/4" w, 7-1/2" d 852.50

Miniature Empire chest of drawers, mahogany, 17-1/2" h, 18" w, $1,540.

Pine, four graduated drawers, molded top, carved backsplash, shaped bracket base, 19th C., imperfections, 20" h, 9-1/2" w, 6-1/4" d 575.00

Sheraton, cherry and cherry flame veneer, refinished, turned feet, half-turned pilasters, ivory teardrop escutcheons, beaded edges, turned pulls, reeded molding on top, minor repairs, 22-1/2" h, 19" w, 12-1/2" d 2,310.00

Sheraton, cherry and walnut, scalloped apron with paneled sides, dovetailed drawers, turned wooden pulls, replaced feet, refinished, 17" h, 14" w, 7-1/4" d 1,100.00

Sheraton style, curly maple, three drawers, turned feet, scalloped apron, wooden pulls, incised trim on top edge, 16" h, 16" w, 9-3/4" w 715.00

Walnut (figured), three drawers, attributed to Medina County, Ohio, scalloped base and side panels, wooden pulls, refinished, glued repair to one end panel, 8-1/4" h, 8-1/8" w, 4-3/4" d 302.50

Other

Cherry, six drawers (three short over three long), top center drawer with round line inlay, other drawers with oblong line inlay, reeded half columns, turned feet, shaped apron, 43" h, 40" w 4,400.00

Cherry and bird's-eye maple veneer, four drawers (one with bird's-eye veneer stepped over three with cherry fronts), Ohio origin, old finish, turned front feet, paneled ends, half-turned pilasters, knobs replaced, 45-1/2" h, 43" w, 21" d 495.00

Cottage, walnut, six drawers (three short over three long), refinished, scalloped feet, one-board top, arched backsplash, turned wooden pulls, front returns replaced, age cracks in side panels, 39-3/4" h, 41-1/2" w, 18-1/2" d.................... 687.50

Curly maple with good figure and walnut, Ohio, old refinishing, dovetailed bracket feet, molded base, one-board ends, two short over three long dovetailed overlapping drawers, two-board walnut top, age cracks, replaced brasses, small repairs, 39-1/2" h, 37-1/2" w, 20-1/4" d................. 1,760.00

Grain-decor, old black and brown grained decor over earlier red, maple and birch, four drawers, high bracket feet, old replaced brass pulls, minor age cracks, 34-1/2" h, 37" w, 17-1/2" d 1,980.00

Grain-decor, old red flame graining, maple and poplar, turned feet with black paint, three dovetailed drawers, top drawer with divided interior, orig wooden pulls, two-board top with round molded edge, 29-1/2" h, 26-1/2" w, 19-1/4" d........ 4950.00

Grain-decor, orig brown flame grain over red, areas of black repaint, black sides and tapered feet, pine, six drawers (two short over four long), drop aprons, inset panels on ends, molded trim around top, stenciled "D. Miller, 1882" and "Mfg. by P.D. Mishler" on one drawer, small areas of touchup, edge chips, knot hole out of top, age cracks, 51-1/2" h, 40" w, 20" d 1,100.00

Grain-decor, orig red flame graining, four drawers, poplar scalloped aprons, turned wood pulls, inset panels on sides, one-board top with molded edge, backsplash missing, age cracks in corner posts, 38" h, 39-1/2" w, 16-1/2" d 1,155.00

Painted, early, old red, four drawers with beaded edges, high scalloped bracket feet, molded base, one-board ends, applied rounded molding below molded trim around top, rosehead nails, old replaced brass pulls and oval lock escutcheons, feet restoration, 43" h, 39" w, 19-1/4" d 2,860.00

Painted, red, five drawers, simple box form, Bennington knobs, 49" h, 27" w, 22" d 2,035.00

Queen Anne

Country style, cherry, cleaned down to old red, high bracket feet with apron drop, four dovetailed overlapping drawers, molded-edge top, attributed to Pa., one foot ended out, edge damage, minor repair to drawer lip, two backboards replaced, red enhanced, 44" h, 38" w, 17-3/4" d 2,255.00

Four-drawer, old dark-brown stain, New England, mid-18th C., overhanging top, high arched feet, turned wooden pulls, imperfections, 40-1/2" h, 38" w, 16-1/4" d 2,990.00

Red-stained birch and butternut, Conn., 18th C., five drawers (two short over three long), molded cornice, bracket base, old red surface, replaced pulls minor losses, 40-1/4" h, 36-3/4" w, 18-3/4" d 2,645.00

Queen Anne chest of drawers, red-stained birch, Connecticut, 19th C., replaced pulls, 40-1/4" h, 36-3/4" w, $2,645. (Photo courtesy of Skinner Auctioneers & Appraisers of Antiques & Fine Arts, Boston and Bolton, Mass.)

Sheraton

Birch, flame-grain drawer fronts, four drawers, incised beading, ring-turned feet, walnut pulls, one-board top with reeded front edge, refinished, minor damage to rear foot, 34-3/4" h, 41-1/4" w, 18-3/4" d 1,320.00

Bowfront, four drawers, mahogany, cookie-corner, reeded and ring-turned columns, shaped apron and backsplash, 40" h, 42" w, 18" d 2,200.00

Bowfront, four drawers, mahogany, cookie-corner, twisted and ring-turned columns, 39-1/2" h, 38" w, 16" d 1,265.00

Bowfront, six drawers (two short stepped over four long), brass pulls/escutcheons, shaped backsplash, turned feet, rope-twist columns, 43" h, 36" w... 3,300.00

Cherry, country style, old finish, four dovetailed drawers with edge beading, banded inlay around base and top edge, turned feet, scrolled apron, solid ends, diamond inlaid escutcheons, replaced brasses, attributed to Stark County, Ohio, 45-3/4" h, 41" w, 19-1/4" d 3,575.00

Cherry with some curl, country style, seven dovetailed drawers (upper row of two stacked narrow drawers flanked by two deep drawers over three long drawers), applied beading, rounded-edge top, scrolled apron, posts with reeded columns, refinished, edge damage and repairs, locks removed, keyholes filled, feet ended out, 45-1/2" h, 44" w, 22-1/2" d 990.00

Curly maple and cherry, country style, two short over three long graduated dovetailed drawers, escutcheon inlays, two-board top, old clear swirled-rib glass knobs, turned feet, scalloped front apron, refinished, one front foot ended out, side of one drawer repaired, found in Orrville, Ohio, 45-1/2" h, 39-1/8" w, 20-1/2" d 1,045.00

Flame birch, four drawers (one stepped over three), short scalloped apron, ring-turned pilasters over turned feet, 40" h, 40" w, 18" d 880.00

Painted, red, four drawers (one stepped over three), shaped backsplash, turned feet, turned half columns, 45" h, 43" w, 19" d 1,650.00

Poplar, country style, cleaned down to old green finish, high turned legs, raised-panel sides, three dovetailed drawers, replaced wooden pulls, 30-1/4" h, 19-1/4" w, 19" d 1,100.00

Soap Hollow, dark-brown paint, yellow striping, softwood, double-scrolled splashboard across back, three small drawers with rounded fronts and Quaker locks over one long cockbeaded drawer stepped over three long graduated cockbeaded drawers, black-stenciled foliage surrounding inlaid diamond-shaped keyhole surrounds, lower three drawers flanked by half-round pilasters, front and side edges of top faced with half-round molding having ring turnings, side panels and round feet painted black, signed "SM" and dated 1851 inside of case, wear and significant paint blistering, 54-1/2" h, 40-1/2" w, 22-1/4" d 1,350.00

Chest on Chest

Background: A chest on chest is a tall chest of drawers mounted on a similar, yet slightly larger chest of drawers. These imposing pieces of furniture are also referred to as double chests of drawers or, simply, tallboys. They were widely used in America during the second half of the 18th century.

References: Eileen and Richard Dubrow, *Styles of American Furniture 1860-1960*, Schiffer Publishing, 1997; Tim Forrest, *Bulfinch Anatomy of Antique Furniture*, Bulfinch Press, 1996; John T. Kirk, *American Furniture: Understanding Styles, Construction, and Quality*, Harry N. Abrams Publishers, 2000; Milo M. Naeve, *Identifying American Furniture*, W.W. Norton, 1998; Ellen T. Schroy, *Warman's American Furniture*, Krause Publications, 2001; Robert W. and Harriet Swedberg, *Collector's Encyclopedia of American Furniture*, Vol. 1 (1990, 1996 value update), Vol. 2 (1992, 1999 value update), Vol. 3 (1998), Collector Books; *Encyclopedia of American Oak Furniture*, Krause Publications, 2000.

Chippendale

Cherry, Conn., 18th C., scrolled molded top flanks central plinth above three small drawers, the central drawer with carved pinwheel, over three long drawers flanked by fluted quarter columns, base with four thumb-molded drawers, shaped bracket base, old refinish, replaced brasses, imperfections, 84" h, 34" w, 18-1/2" d 13,800.00

Cherry, Delaware River Valley, c. 1770-90, 2-pc, 11 drawers, upper section with three short over two short over three graduated long drawers, lower section with three graduated long drawers, all flanked by fluted quarter columns, molded base with ogee bracket feet, molded cornice, replaced brasses, restoration, imperfections, 78-3/4" h, 40" w, 20-1/2" d.. 12,650.00

Hepplewhite

Mahogany veneer over pine, eight drawers, old finish, high bracket feet, shaped aprons, dovetailed drawers with beaded borders (two short over three long in the top, three long in the base), orig turned pulls with engraved mother of pearl inserts, ivory escutcheon plates (one missing), sides of dovetailed case with orig painted decor, line inlay on borders of top, stepped and cove-molded cornice, some waist molding missing, veneer chips, puttied repairs, 80" h, 44" w, 24" d 3,740.00

IT'S IN THE WILL

As if this Chippendale cherry carved chest on chest isn't good enough by itself, it's accompanied by interesting provenance.

The chest was made by Peter Newcomb, in Lebanon, Conn., in 1788. It featured carved rosettes on the scrolled molded cornice, and the center drawer at the top had a carved sunburst. Other features included fluted quarter columns with lamb's tongues, a molded base with a pierced central drop, shaped ogee bracket feet ending in platforms, and an early surface. The brass pulls had been replaced. The piece measured 91" h, 40-1/2" w, 17-1/2" d.

Newcomb's will, proved in 1799, included the following, "I give to my 2nd daughter Jemima the bead (sic) she now lies on with the furniture thear (sic) to belonging and also one case with draws (sic) and two plain chests." The case with drawers was this high chest, which was sold at Skinner for $37,950.

Chippendale chest on chest, $37,950. (Photo courtesy of Skinner Auctioneers & Appraisers of Antiques & Fine Arts, Boston and Bolton, Mass.)

Hepplewhite, mahogany veneer over pine, 8 drawers, old finish, minor damage and repairs, 80" h, 44" w, $3,740. (Photo courtesy of Garth's Auctions, Delaware, Ohio)

Chest over Drawers

Background: The lift top, which opens into a well resembling a deep blanket chest, is the feature that distinguishes this furniture form from a chest of drawers. The front of the case has at least one drawer at the bottom, although many examples also have one or more false drawers, so the piece appears to be a traditional chest of drawers. The form dates from 1680 to around 1840 and is sometimes called a mule chest.

References: Eileen and Richard Dubrow, *Styles of American Furniture 1860-1960*, Schiffer Publishing, 1997; Tim Forrest, *Bulfinch Anatomy of Antique Furniture*, Bulfinch Press, 1996; John T. Kirk, *American Furniture: Understanding Styles, Construction, and Quality*, Harry N. Abrams Publishers, 2000; Milo M. Naeve, *Identifying American Furniture*, W.W. Norton, 1998; Ellen T. Schroy, *Warman's American Furniture*, Krause Publications, 2001; Robert W. and Harriet Swedberg, *Collector's Encyclopedia of American Furniture*, Vol. 1 (1990, 1996 value update), Vol. 2 (1992, 1999 value update), Vol. 3 (1998), Collector Books; *Encyclopedia of American Oak Furniture*, Krause Publications, 2000.

Grain-decorated chest over drawers, original red, green and yellow paint, northern New England, replaced brasses, 36-1/2" h, 38" w, $16,100. (Photo courtesy of Skinner Auctioneers & Appraisers of Antiques & Fine Arts, Boston and Bolton, Mass.)

Empire, grain-decor, orig reddish-brown graining in imitation of flame-figured wood with line inlay, black turned feet, pine, two false drawers over two dovetailed drawers, turned pulls, molded-edge lid, minor edge damage, found near Hampton, N.H., 40" h, 40" w, 18-3/4" d 1,650.00

Grain-decor
   Grayish-blue vinegar graining (orig), grayish-olive ground, black and yellow edge striping, pine, bottom mkd "Daniel," attributed to Essex, Mass., high cutout feet, scrolled apron, two false drawers over two dovetailed drawers, lift lid with applied molding, 41-3/4" h, 42-3/4" w, 19-3/8" d 7,700.00
   Red flame graining, pine, two false drawers over three drawers, bracket feet 3,300.00
   Red flame-graining (orig), pine, attributed to New York State, two drawers, turned feet, one-board top/sides, turned mahogany pulls, internal locks, one lock missing, minor age crack, 40-1/2" h, 43-1/2" w, 18" d 1,320.00
   Red and black paint simulating rosewood, top, sides and skirt with facade is putty- and sponge-painted in shades of gold, green and red, Mass., c. 1825-35, 2 drawers, cyma-curved skirt, high French feet, orig brasses and surface, minor imperfections, 37" h, 42-3/4" w, 18-5/8" d 63,000.00
   Red paint and sponged black graining (old), pine, six-board, high cutout feet, two drawers, hinged lid, mismatched Rockingham knobs with chips, old replaced hinges, 42-3/4" h, 38-1/4" w, 17-1/4" d 2,090.00

Red, green and yellow paint (orig), northern New England, molded top, two drawers, shaped bracket feet, replaced brasses, 36-1/2" h, 38" w, 17-5/8" d 16,100.00
Red and yellow vinegar graining (orig), New England, early 19th C., one drawer, bracket feet, shaped sides, replaced brasses, 31" h, 36-5/8" w, 18-1/4" d 7,475.00

Painted
   Blue, pine top, one drawer, shaped front bracket feet, bootjack ends, New England, early 19th C., 29" h, 36" w, 17" d 1,840.00
   Dark-green, two drawers, 44" h, 39" w, 18" d 825.00
   Red, one drawer, scalloped apron, 35" h, 39" w, 17" d 2,640.00
   Red, one drawer, pine, probably Mass., late 18th C., cutout ends, imperfections, 31-1/2" h, 36-3/4" w, 18-1/4" d 1,495.00
   Red, three fake drawers over two working drawers, Mass., early 18th C., half-round moldings, molded bracket base, old replaced bat-wing engraved pulls, small repairs, 39-1/4" h, 35-1/2" w, 17" d 2,070.00
   Red repaint (old), pine, high bracket feet, scalloped apron on front and sides, two drawers with cock-beaded edges, replaced oval brasses, interior fitted with iron lock and hinges, molded lid with battens beneath either end, minor age cracks, 35-1/4" h, 36" w, 17-1/2" d 2,585.00

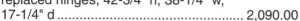

Red with white trim (orig), pine, country style, six-board construction, cutout feet, scrolled front foot bracket, two dovetailed drawers, molded-edge lift lid, 42-1/2" h, 43" w, 18-1/2" d 3,410.00

Pine, cleaned down to traces of orig red, high bracket feet, one-board sides, bootjack ends, two false drawers over two drawers, turned wooden pulls, one-board top with molded trim, replaced hinges, edge chips, damage to drawer lips, pieced repair on lower drawer, 42" h, 40-1/4" w, 17" d.................... 770.00

Tiger maple, Long Island, N.Y., second half of the 19th C., molded lift top, two recessed panels over two short drawers over one long drawer, bracket feet, centered shaped pendant, replaced brasses, old refinish, imperfections, 43-1/2" h, 42" w, 16-1/2" d 6,900.00

Christmas Collectibles

Background: Christmas has been celebrated for years, and the mid-19th century saw a sharp increase in the number of items manufactured for use as decorations in homes, offices, or businesses during the Christmas season. But, it wasn't until 1891 that Christmas actually became a national holiday.

References: Robert Brenner, *Christmas Past*, 3rd ed., Schiffer Publishing, 1996; —, *Christmas Revisited*, Schiffer Publishing, 1986; —, *Christmas Through the Decades*, Schiffer Publishing, 1993; Jill Gallina, *Christmas Pins Past and Present*, Collector Books, 1996; George Johnson, *Christmas Ornaments, Lights and Decorations*, Vol. 1 (1987, 1998 value update), Vol. 2 (1996), Vol. 3 (1996), Margaret and Kenn Whitmyer, *Christmas Collectibles*, 2nd ed., Collector Books, 1994 (1996 value update).

Collectors' Club: Golden Glow of Christmas Past, 6401 Winsdale St., Golden Valley, MN 55427.

Belsnickle

6" h, composition, wide-eyed, pink robe, mica flecks, multicolor base, black boots, green feather tree 192.50

7-3/4" h, composition, yellow robe, applied beads, black boots and base, wire left from feather tree, wear............................ 357.50

8" h, composition, orange robe, gold glitter, black base and boots, green feather tree 330.00

8-1/2" h, composition, white robe with silver glitter, red and pink trim, brown base, black boots, green feather tree, mkd "Germany," stain, base repaired 110.00

9-1/8" h, composition, white robe and base, mica flecks, green glitter, red pipe-cleaner trim, black boots, green feather tree, minor edge damage............................ 660.00

11-1/4" h, composition, white robe, mica flecks, black boots and base, red pipe-cleaner trim, remnants of green feather tree, wear on base............................ 825.00

"Merry Christmas" pink luster mug showing St. Nick, $60.

13" h, yellow coat with gold glitter, white base with silver glitter, black boots, green feather tree, wear, splits, old repair 990.00

Box, "Santa Claus Electric Candles," slide-lid, late dovetailing, chromolithographs of Santa in sled pulled by reindeer, ends have children decorating a tree, edge wear, some litho damage, 6-1/4" h, 13" w, 6" d.................... 137.50

Feather tree, 54" h, old white and green decor, turned wooden base, areas of feather loss, base damage............................ 275.00

Fence (tree fence)

Cast iron, diamonds and scallops with fans on top rail, ball finials, green and gold paint, seven sections and two-part gate, incomplete, wear, minor edge damage, largest section 4-3/4" h, 12" l 242.00

Wooden, spindle picket fence, dark-green repaint over lighter green, wear, 5-1/2" h, 16-1/2" x 16-1/2" 302.50

Ornament

Angel, pink wax, fur dress, fiber wings, blonde wig, brass horn, 4-1/2" l 27.50

Animals, blown glass, silver deer, rooster, horse (worn), blue penguin, striped horse, 2-1/2 to 3-1/2" l, set of 6.................... 137.50

Cluster-type, berries, walnuts and pinecones in silver, gold, red, blue and yellow, 1-1/2" to 2-3/4" h, set of 15.................... 110.00

Doll head, silver bonnet, red trim, 1 glass eye missing, 2-3/4" h 49.50

Fruit, pears and peaches, paint, wire and mica flecks, 1-3/4" to 3" h, set of 6.................... 126.50

Grapes, cobalt glass, stamped brass cap, German, 19th C., 4-1/2" h 325.00

Grapes, silver glass, stamped brass cap, German, 19th C., minor wear, 5-1/2" h.................... 225.00

Kugel, ovoid shape, gold glass, stamped brass cap, German, 19th C., some wear, 6" h, 4-1/4" dia 150.00

Girl candy container, $500.

Kugel, round, cobalt blown glass, embossed brass hanger, slight discoloration, 4-3/8" dia........ 137.50

Kugel, round, silver, brass hanger reattached, minor flakes, 7" dia 121.00

Parrot, clip-on, white with frosted dots, fiber tail, 3-3/4" l (excluding tail) 27.50

Pinecone, silver, gold, orange, red and multicolor, 2-1/2" to 3-3/4" h, set of 8 .... 104.50

Santa Claus figurines

Papier-mâché, painted face, black base, white mica-flecked robe, holds worn feather tree, wear, 10" h 550.00

Papier-mâché, red felt coat, white wool trim, rabbit fur beard, blue felt pants, black painted boots, probably held feather tree, 13-3/4" h 825.00

Papier-mâché, sitting on polar bear, white with red trim, minor damage, 9-3/4" h, 8-1/2" l 132.00

Plaster, painted face and legs, hooded felt robe, holds feather tree, mkd "Made in Western Germany," minor wear, paint flaking, 8-3/4" h 137.50

Tin windup, Santa with feather tree, red, white, green and yellow paint, Santa turns in circle, music box needs work, base damage, wear, 7-1/2" h 385.00

Tree stand, cast iron

Base is brown tree stump and green pine boughs, tree holder is red and white Santa with a wicker basket on his back, 6-1/2" h, 9-1/2" sq 330.00

Openwork stars and plumes, two scenes of St. Nicholas leading a horse and knocking on windows, German verses, green paint, 4-7/8" h, 10" dia 55.00

Tree topper, Santa Claus on ball, red silvered glass Santa with a tree, painted face, gold glitter, rough end, 9-1/4" h 55.00

Cigar Cutters and Cigar Lighters

Background: Cigar cutters and lighters, used to snip off one end and light the other, were common fixtures in many 19th-century general stores, cigar shops, and taverns. Businesses found these cast-iron items were a good way to advertise their products, and examples featuring advertising are especially sought by collectors.

Cigar cutter

Bell Telephone symbol cast on top, "Public Station Local And Long Distance Telephone" on top with hole for cutting, lever and thumb rest on side, mounted at slanting angle in fluted base with cast rope at bottom, all mounted on stepped wood block, worn nickel plate with match striker, oval, 4-1/2" x 3" 605.00

"Smoke Geo. W. Childs Cigars" lighter with oil lamp, metal, $7,500.

"Betsy Ross 5 Cent Cigar," oval portrait of Ross with U.S. flag in her hand, mounted in shield-shaped frame above cutting mechanism, ornate scrollwork base with match strikers on sides, some rust, 7-1/2" h, 8-1/4" l, 6" w 770.00

"The V Cutter," painted cast-iron, base embossed "K B & B, New York," two holes for screwing to counter, wear and tarnish to finish on front plate, 6-1/2" h 231.00

Cigar lighter, countertop

Advertises "Geo. W. Childs, Cigar, Harburger Maker, Homan Co., New York," cast white metal, four paw feet, desk at back and man sitting on desk chair, cornucopia at left of desk spilling coins on floor, basket-shaped lamp at left with brass burner and shade ring holding a white milk glass ball-shaped shade, lighters at front corners, painted gold with red accents, mkd "M.E. Moore," shade with some roughness, paint wear, 10-1/2" h, 9-1/8" w 3,800.00

Wireless No. 12, Eldred Mfg. Co., Chicago, wooden and metal, brass tank for lighter fluid, used four dry cell batteries, restored, 5-1/4" x 7-3/4" x 9-3/4" 660.00

Clocks

Background: The earliest domestic clocks were driven by weights and were of the hanging variety in order to provide enough room beneath the mechanism for the fall of the weights. Clocks driven by springs were perfected around 1525 and resulted in a much more compact piece. With the introduction of the pendulum as a regulator in the mid-17th century, the tall case clock was created. Originally, the tall case clock was designed to protect the weights from outside interference, but it quickly gained importance as a decorative piece of furniture as well. Ultimately, shelf and mantel clocks became popular because they were less expensive and more convenient to display.

Reference: Robert W.D. Ball, *American Shelf & Wall Clocks*, 2nd ed., Schiffer Publishing, 1999.

Banjo, mahogany case, brass trim and facade, old gold repaint, brass works, painted steel face mkd "A. Willard Jr., Boston," old replacement reverse-painted glass panels, bottom pan shows ship with American flag, eagle finial, with weight and pendulum, case has damage and loose seams, 33" h 1,100.00

Grandfather's

Cherry with figured mahogany veneer cross-banding, mellow finish, cutout feet, scrolled apron, chamfered corners, cove molding between sections, bonnet with freestanding columns, arched pediment with goose necks, turned finials, brass works stamped "J.E. Stretcher" (John Stretcher, worked 1828-1829, Cincinnati and Hillsboro, Ohio), second hand, calendar movement, painted

Calumet Baking Powder advertising clock, refinished oak frame, $750.

metal face with polychrome flowers in crest, shells in spandrels, with pendulum, weights and keys, touchups to face, 94" h 6,050.00

Cherry, old finish, signed "Read & Watson," scalloped base, high feet, molded waist, tombstone door with beaded trim, dovetailed hood with freestanding pillars and broken-arch top, wooden works, orig painted Masonic decor on face, with weights and pendulum, restorations to works and bonnet, 90-1/2" h 2,475.00

Decor, pine, orig reddish-brown vinegar grained paint, face in orig painted decor with gilded spandrels and crest with red swag in the arch, signed "L. Watson, Cincinnati," cutout feet, scalloped apron, molded waist, reeded quarter columns with brass trim, bonnet with free-standing reeded columns, molded and curved cornice with fretwork, three brass finials, few areas of touchup, one finial replaced, Ohio, 91" h............................ 27,500.00

Decor, walnut, old dark transparent graining, ebonized moldings, gilded detail and date "1781," period case, painted detail probably Centennial, engraved "Adam Brant, New Hanover" (Montgomery County, Pa., died 1804), ogee feet, fluted quarter columns, moldings between sections, tombstone detail on door, dovetailed bonnet with freestanding columns and arched door, molded cornice with high goosenecks and turned gilded ornaments in crest and spandrels, calendar movement, second hand, phases of the moon dial, minor repairs, old replaced feet, finial missing, 94-1/2" h 15,940.00

Hardwood with some figure, country style, bracket feet, overlapping door with tombstone arch, bonnet with freestanding front columns, arched cornice, brass works, engraved face with old repaint, mkd "Edward Spalding, Providence" (R.I.), face mismatched with works, replaced feet, replaced finials, refinished, 84" h 3,025.00

Walnut, dark orig finish, "Wilson" engraved signature on the back of works (possibly William Wilson, Newton, Pa.), ogee feet, inset panel in base, cove moldings between sections, overlapping door with scalloped top corners, dovetailed bonnet, freestanding turned columns, arched door and molded cornice with gooseneck pediment with brass rosettes and turned flame finial, brass works with second hand and calendar movement, painted iron face with pheasant crest and rose spandrels, with weights and pendulum, minor restorations, 97" h 7,150.00

Pillar and scroll

Ephraim Downes, mahogany veneer, old finish, wooden works, painted wooden face, paper label "Ephraim Downes for George Mitchell, Bristol, Conn.," reverse painting on bottom glass probably an old replacement with some flaking and old touchup repair, with weights and pendulum, minor repairs, replaced finials, 31-1/4" h 2,200.00

Mark Leavenworth, mahogany veneer, old finish, wooden works, painted wooden face, paper label "Improved Clocks Made and Sold by Mark Leavenworth, Waterbury, Connecticut," with weights and pendulum, repairs to case, replaced feet, very worn reverse painting, mismatched finials, 30-1/2" h 880.00

Eli Terry & Sons, mahogany veneer, refinished, high bracket feet, scalloped apron, orig paper label, worn reverse-painting on lower part of door, freestanding pillars, arched crest, orig paint on dial,

with weights, key and pendulum, replaced brass finials, worn, professional restorations, 32" h, 16-1/2" w 1,430.00

Shelf

Eli Terry, Plymouth Conn., c. 1817-19, mahogany, flat cornice above glazed door enclosing painted and gilt wooden dial and 30-hour wooden weight-driven movement with outside escapement, flanking freestanding columns, lower section with farmstead painting, flat molded base, engraved label, old finish, imperfections, 20-3/4" h, 16" w 4,255.00

Empire, triple-decker, Seth Thomas, bottom door with eagle in scroll surround, top door with reverse-painted flowers, rosewood and walnut veneer case, applied gilt pilasters, stepped cornice, 32-1/2" h, 18" w, 6" d 495.00

Tall case

Isaac Blasdel, Chester, N.H. (1738-1791), curly maple, hood with flat molded cornice above tombstone arch and glazed door flanked by full standing columns, brass dial, engraved "Isaac Blasdel, Chester," cast-pewter spandrels framing the engraved chapter ring and calendar aperture, pull-up posted frame single-weight movement, waist with thumb-molded tombstone door with glazed opening, on molded stepped base, refinished, minor imperfections, 85" h..................... 23,000.00

William Cummens (1768-1834), Boston or Roxbury, Mass., Federal, mahogany, inlaid, the hood with pierced fretwork joined by three inlaid plinths and brass finials above the arched cornice molding, inlaid tombstone glazed door with brass beaded liner framing the white-painted iron dial with polychrome and gilt floral decor, second and calendar aperture inscribed "Warranted by Wm. Cummens," all flanked by reeded brass stop-fluted columns, the waist with inlaid molded rectangular door flanked by reeded brass stop-fluted quarter columns on the string-inlaid base, ogee bracket feet, orig finials, old refinish, minor imperfections, 96-1/2" h.. 34,500.00

Daniel Dole, Hallowell, mahogany case, painted wooden dial, brass works, 86" h.............11,000.00

John Field, Cumberland, R.I., (worked 1760-80), cherry, molded hood with carved rosettes and spiral-carved finials mounted on fluted plinths above glazed door with arched top opening to engraved brass dial with silvered engraved arch inscribed "Soon Man's Hour is Up and We Are Gone" over a Father Time figure moving against a painted landscape above a silvered chapter ring with numbers for date, hour and seconds, silvered plate engraved "John Field Cumberland No. 2," eight-day brass weight-driven movement, flanked by fluted free-standing columns above thumb-molded shell-carved blocked waist door on blocked and shell-carved base, ogee bracket feet, old surface, imperfections, 95" h.............. 61,900.00

Cherry and curly maple tall case clock, refinished, Ohio provenance, 96" h, $5,775. (Photo courtesy of Garth's Auctions, Delaware, Ohio)

Jacob Gorgas, Ephrate, Pa., c. 1790, Chippendale, eight-day works, calendar and second dial, floral-painted face, gilt ornamentation, walnut case, broken-arch pediment, flame finials, arched door with heart-shaped escutcheon, reeded quarter columns, side lights, over a conforming case, base with applied turtle, ogee feet, minor loss, 96" h 17,050.00

John Gorgas, inlaid, c. 1810-15, veneered case front, beehive scrolled top, shield-shaped side lights, hand-painted face with Arabic and Roman chapter rings, sweep second hand, fruit-decor spandrels, ship dial, colonettes, waisted case with chamfered corners, paneled base, finials missing, 93" h 4,950.00

Silas Hoadley, painted pine case, wood works, flat top, simple design 1,375.00

Emanuel Meily, Lebanon, Pa., Federal, cherry, inlaid, eight-day key-wound brass movement, hour strike with moon dial, calendar, sweep second hand, iron plate behind face stamped "Osborne," face and moon dial, steel and brass hands, roses in face corners, Arabic numerals, bonnet with broken-arch top, plain scrolls flank center plinth surmounted by urn-shaped finial, small square plinths on top corners with urn-shaped finials, tombstone-shaped door, stringing and diamond inlay, waist with carved shell drawer, inlaid stringing and fans, front of base with 8-point inlaid star in oval and fans in corners, French feet, 93" h, 18" w 14,000.00

Michael Striby, walnut case, flat top, flat fluted columns, face with Arabic and Roman numerals, second hand, date, floral spandrels, moon-phase dial, over waisted case with fluted quarter columns, on base with conforming columns, ogee bracket feet, 87" h 6,050.00

Cherry and curly maple, refinished, high bracket feet, scalloped apron, chamfered case corners, inset panels on base and door with applied burl band inlay, dovetailed hood with turned pilasters, bonnet top, wag-on-the-wall works with key and pendulum, repair to one gooseneck, 96" h, (pen-and-ink note inside door: clock purchased from Frank Boutelle near Goshen, Ohio, in 1889, signed by Frank G. Fisher, Milford, Ohio, 1925) 5,775.00

Country style, pine, refinished, "E. Edwards, Ashby" painted face added, moldings between sections, one-board door, bonnet with free-standing columns, broken-arch pediment, turned center finial, replaced spring-wind works from a shelf clock, restorations, 81-1/4" h 687.50

Country style, poplar, old red finish, bracket feet, scalloped aprons, molded waist, narrow door, early embossed lion pull, flat hood, cove-molded cornice, brass works, orig painted face including gilt, scroll-work spandrels and urn top with areas of repaint, two painted paper coverings for empty holes, signed "Turner," hood restorations, base board replaced, 82-1/2" h, 15" w, 9" d 2,530.00

Federal, mahogany, inlaid, N.Y. or N.J., c. 1800, scrolled pediment with brass rosettes above frieze with central inlaid keystone and edge inlays over polychrome painted iron dial with second hand and calendar aperture, eight-day movement, hood flanked by free-standing inlaid columns, over shaped waist door flanked by inlaid quarter columns, above base with cyma-curved skirt and bracket feet, case with neoclassical stringing and banding, also patterned and pictorial inlays, inlaid carved circles and rectangles, old refinish, veneer loss, glass cracked, 93-1/2" h 13,800.00

Federal, mahogany, inlaid, N.Y. or N.J., c. 1800-10, hood with scrolling crest, cast-brass rosettes, plinth of contrasting stringing on keystone, frieze with inlaid fluting at the corners above the free-standing fluted columns flanking the glazed door, floral-painted arched dial, calendar aperture, second hand, eight-day brass weight-driven movement, waist with three bands of inlaid fluting at the top, fluted quarter columns at the corners, door with elliptical inlay within a rectangle at the bottom, base with cove molding at the top, circular inlay in the front and bracket feet, old refinish, replaced feet, 92" h 7,475.00

Mahogany and mahogany veneer, possibly N.Y. or N.J., c. 1815-20, hood with molded swan's neck cresting, glazed tombstone door flanked by reeded columns, painted iron dial with polychrome and gilt designs of an urn in the arch and shield spandrels, second hand, calendar aperture, eight-day brass weight driven movement, waist with shaped door flanked by reeded quarter columns, base with cutout feet, old finish, minor imperfections 6,900.00

Transitional, Chippendale to Hepplewhite, figured mahogany and mahogany veneer, cut bracket feet, molded waist, chamfered corners, door with shaped top, hood with freestanding columns, broken-arch top, refinished, pieced repairs on goose-necks and feet, replaced finials, wag-on-the-wall works cut to fit, repainted decor, with weight and pendulum, 91" h 2,475.00

L. Watson, Cincinnati signed face, cherry and burl veneer, bracket feet, band inlay around base, inset panel on front, cove-molded waist with chamfered corners, door fitted with light burl band of inlay on edge and dark burl oval at center with scalloped top, dovetailed hood, broken-arch top, free-standing columns, brass finials, orig painted floral detail on face, wooden works, with pendulum and weights, refinished, replaced hands, 92-1/2" h 8,745.00

Walnut, old dark varnish finish, bracket feet, line inlay on case with oval on door and circle on base, flower inlay at center, chamfered corners, cove-molded waist, broken-arch top with arched door, freestanding columns, orig painted face includes birds and flowers, calendar dial removed, plate added, 91" h 3,575.00

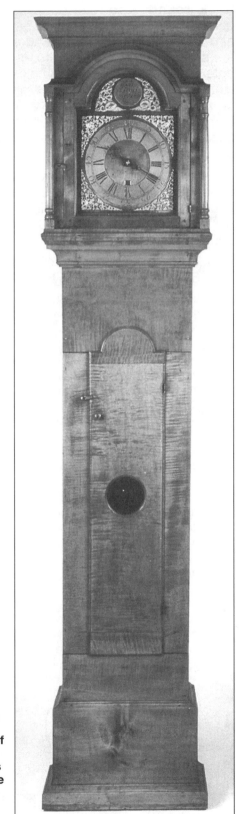

Isaac Blasdel, Chester, N.H., tall case clock, curly maple, refinished, 85" h, $23,000. (Photo courtesy of Skinner Auctioneers & Appraisers of Antiques & Fine Arts, Boston and Bolton, Mass.)

Coffee Grinders

Background: Also referred to as coffee mills, the golden age of coffee grinders began around 1870 and lasted for approximately 50 years. Large commercial grinders for use in stores, restaurants, and hotels were the earliest examples. Coffee grinders small enough for home use weren't introduced until around 1890. The advent of electricity, coupled with technological advances in coffee grinding and packaging, ultimately spelled the demise of small coffee mills.

References: Edward C. Kvetko and Douglas Congdon-Martin, *Coffee Antiques*, Schiffer Publishing, 2000; Joseph Edward MacMillan, *MacMillan Index of Antique Coffee Mills*, Cherokee Publishing, 1995.

Collectors' Club: Assoc. of Coffee Mill Enthusiasts, 5941 Wilkerson Rd., Rex, GA 30273.

Advertising, American Beauty, litho tin top, cast-iron grinder, wooden handle, orig tin cup, cond. 8+, 12" h... 825.00

Double wheel

13" h, Enterprise, cast iron, old red and blue repaint, yellow details, finial replaced 357.50

24" h, Enterprise, cast iron, worn red paint, floral decals, one drawer, 1873 patent date, replaced nickel-plated eagle finial, minor edge damage.. 770.00

24-3/4" h, Enterprise, cast iron, worn orig red paint, yellow and black line decor, decals, walnut base, glued break on lid, eagle finial replaced 385.00

Hotel, mahogany, old finish, molded base, dovetailed storage compartment, front peg locks the lift-off top and bottom, stepdown molding around top edge, brass crank and hopper, 12-3/4" h, 10-1/2" sq 632.50

Tabletop, marked

Enterprise, No. 0, C-shaped clamp base attaches to table or counter, bowl-shaped top, iron crank with turned elongated knob-shaped handle, orig black paint, decals, some wear, 13-3/4" h 130.00

Landers, Frary & Clark, wood and cast iron, square base, tin drawer, ornate scroll design in cast-iron top, hinged half-lid, iron crank with turned wooden handle, 8-1/4" h, 5-7/8" sq 100.00

Tabletop, unmarked

Wooden and brass, cherry case, orig dark finish, dovetailed, molded base with half-round end panels, drawer, orig brass pull, brass hopper, serpentine handle with turned wooden finial, drawer chipped, base cracks, 10-1/8" h 220.00

Wooden and cast iron, arm mkd "Adams," ceramic knob, drawer, square nails, 5-7/8" h, 6-5/8" sq 82.50

Wooden and iron, pine case, old dark-brown alligatored finish, molded base, turned wooden pull,

Enterprise coffee grinder, cast iron, 1873 patent date, replaced finial, 24" h, $770. (Photo courtesy of Garth's Auctions, Delaware, Ohio)

fluted iron hopper, wrought-iron crank, minor age cracks, 9-1/2" h, 7" sq................................. 165.00

Wooden and pewter, cherry case, old dark finish, beveled base and top, drawer with turned pull, pewter hopper, cast-iron crank, rim splits in hopper, 9-1/4" h 137.50

Wooden and tin, fruitwood, tin hopper, wrought-iron crank, crack in top board, 10-1/2" h............ 275.00

Comforters

Background: These bedcoverings resemble quilts but are less refined. Typically found in patchwork designs, they lack the fine quilting which stitches the top of the comforter to its backing. Instead, the two sides are generally secured with yarn.

Also See: Quilts

Multicolor, c. 1940s, 72" x 88" 40.00

Patchwork, 2-1/2" squares of solid and plaid wool and cotton in various colors, blue binding, wool backing, 66" sq.. 160.00

Patchwork, made from wool suiting, patches in blue, grays, browns, blacks and red, red binding, minor wear, 72" sq 375.00

Patchwork, oblong patches of assorted colored wool suiting material, 64" x 82 .... 35.00

Conestoga-Related

Background: This famous icon of early American life takes its name from Conestoga, Pa., in Lancaster County, where Conestoga wagons were made. The wagons were known for traveling on soft soil and for crossing the prairies. Any item associated with the Conestoga is valued for its historical nature, as well as for the craftsmanship evidenced by much of the metalwork on the wagons and their accessories.

Hounds band, wrought iron, oval with wide flared flange dated "1825" three times, illegible signature, minor rust, 4-1/8" h, 7-1/2" x 4" 375.00

Housings, tooled leather, worn around a horse's neck to protect it from rain and dust, provenance of Michael Shreiner family (see related sidebar), matching set of four, with period early leather saddle worn by lead horse 700.00

Tar bucket, wooden, oval top with conforming lid, late leather handle, 5" section of side rim of lid broken/ missing, 9-1/2" h, top 8-3/4" x 5" 180.00

Toolbox hardware, wrought iron, mounted on wooden board, four pcs comprise a pr of 8-1/4" l hinges with tulip-shaped base and diamond end, large pierced inverted heart-shaped hasp, initials "IM" in large lettering flanking a six-lobed cutout radial design surrounded by a border of incised scallops and small oval cutout, a long hasp extends from bottom of heart with flared scrolled ends, 13-3/8" l, 6-1/2" w 1,750.00

Wagon jack, wooden and wrought iron
    Dated 1772, signed "John Gorner," trace of orig orange paint, large pc of wood missing from back, 23" h (unextended) 450.00
    Dated 1776, incised diamond/dot design, wear, rust, 22" h 150.00

A LANDIS WAGON

It's not every day that you get the opportunity to buy a Conestoga wagon. However, bidders received just such a treat in January 2000 when Horst Auctioneers in Ephrata, Pa., sold a full-size Conestoga wagon that had descended through the Michael Shreiner family of Lancaster County.

The wagon had come from the family's farm, located along the Oregon Pike, half a mile from the Landis Valley Farm Museum, where blacksmith John Landis originally resided. Landis built the wagon in the late 18th century.

Among the wagon's original accessories were a toolbox with ornate iron hardware, feed box, axe holder, wooden bentwood hoops, tar bucket, and chains. Having a curved bed and paneled sides, the wagon sold for $52,000.

Cookie Boards

Background: Generally made of wood with a carved motif, these boards were used to create cookies with a sculpted look, after imprinting the design in the dough. Cake boards, marzipan boards, and springerle molds also fall into this category. Made in both Europe and the United States during the 19th century, they are often prized for the folk art nature of their designs.

Reference: Linda Campbell Franklin, *300 Years of Kitchen Collectibles*, 4th ed., Krause Publications, 1997.

Reproduction Alert: A variety of designs have been reproduced.

Cast iron
    12 segments, birds, animals, buildings, etc., rectangular, 7-3/4" h, 5-1/4" w 220.00
    Acorn and oak leaves, oblong, 5-3/4" l 192.50
    Basket of flowers, oval, 5-1/2" l 137.50
    Bird on branch, almond shape, 5-1/4" l 165.00
Wooden, one-sided
    Animal, round, European, 12-1/2" dia 93.50
    Dog sitting in basket, scrubbed finish, minor insect damage on back, 3-3/4" h, 4" w 60.50
    Eagle with banner and "E. Pluribus Unum," Washington, Lady Liberty, harvest goddess, cornucopia and stars, carved mahogany, 11-7/8" h, 8" w... 4,625.00

Patriotic cookie board, including eagle, Washington and Lady Liberty, carved mahogany, 11-7/8" h, $4,625. (Photo courtesy of Garth's Auctions, Delaware, Ohio)

Heart having three carved roses with vine border, dark refinish, age cracks, minor insect damage, putty filler, 7-3/4" h, 6-3/4"w 440.00

Man in kilt and woman in long dress (William of Orange and Mary Stewart), 18" h, 6-1/2" w.... 440.00

Round, pine, old patina, two-board with inset cleats and handle, 24" h, 19-1/2" dia 192.50

Tree-like motif flanked by two elf figures, sailing ship at bottom, initialed "HM" on one side, 6-3/8" x 16-1/4" 85.00

Wooden, two-sided

Eagle and shield in almond on one side, basket of flowers in circle and cornucopia in an almond on other side, mahogany, old dark worn patina, Conger quality, unmarked, 7-3/8" h, 15" w 4,840.00

Man, woman in fancy dress, age cracks, worm holes, 13-3/4" h, 5-1/8" w 110.00

Man holding chicken by its feet on one side, woman with chicken in a basket on her back on other, age cracks in ends, iron staple hanger added, 15" h, 7-1/2" w 165.00

Various designs, six carved images per side, animals, windmills, fish, ship, etc., 25" h, 3-1/2" w 192.50

Cookie Cutters

Background: Naive in design and humble in origin, tin cookie cutters were often constructed from scraps left over after traveling tinsmiths finished their hired work. Some were even made from the flattened remnants of tin canisters. Most of the cookie cutters on today's market are tin examples from the 19th and 20th centuries. Age and design are both important. Collectors look for early examples with unusual motifs, especially those pieces that cross into the realm of folk art.

Reference: Linda Campbell Franklin, *300 Years of Kitchen Collectibles*, 4th ed., Krause Publications, 1997.

Periodical: *Cookies*, 9610 Greenview Ln., Manassas, VA 20109.

Collectors' Clubs: Cookie Cutter Collectors Club, 1167 Teal Rd. SW, Dellroy, OH 44620; National Cookie Cutters Collectors Club, 2763 310th St., Cannon Falls, MN 55009.

Reproduction Alert: A variety of cookie cutters have been reproduced.

Tin

Christmas motif, oval with multiple images including tree, Santa, angels, deer and hearts, 7-1/2" h, 11-1/4" w 192.50

Dutch man and woman, 6-7/8" h, pr 126.50

Eagle, wings at side, minor wear/rust, 4-3/4" h, 4-1/8" w 400.00

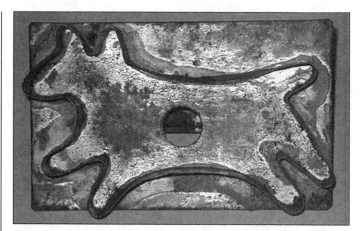

Running dog cookie cutter, 5-1/4" l, $85.

Heart cookie cutter, 2-1/2" h, $40.

Eagle, wings spread, round piece inset to define legs, 4-7/8" h, 5-1/2" w 375.00

Heart, applied handle, 8-1/4" l 49.50

Man wearing hat, 7-7/8" h and 9-1/2" h, pr 49.50

Man wearing hat, dancing, 10" h 22.00

Rabbit, running, applied handle, 7-1/4" l 49.50

Reindeer, minor rust, 5-3/4" h, 5-1/4" w 350.00

Santa, full figure, mkd "Cake Art, Germany," soldered seam loose, 11-1/2" h, 4-1/2" w 137.50

Soldier on horseback, plumed helmet, rust, loose seam, 10" h, 9" l 935.00

Copper

Background: Copper articles such as bed warmers, kettles, and measures played important roles in 19th-century households.

References: Mary Frank Gaston, *Antique Brass & Copper*, Collector Books, 1992 (1994 value update); Henry J. Kaufmann, *Early American Copper, Tin & Brass*, Astragal Press, 1995.

Reproduction Alert: Many modern reproductions exist.

FYI: To prevent poisoning, copper culinary items were lined with a thin protective coating of tin. The items were relined when necessary.

Chestnut roaster, pierced lid, engraved tulip, well-turned handle, dents on base, 36" l 357.50

Containers, ear handles, dovetailed, 4-1/2" h with one handle, 6" high with two handles, pr 302.50

Eagle figure, gilt, spread-wing, perched on ball, 19th C., dents, repairs, 14-1/2" h................................. 1,495.00

Funnel, rounded bottom, tapered spout, C-shaped handle, dents to spout, polished, 7-1/4" h, 5-/8" dia 25.00

Jug, hammered, dovetailed, scrolled strap handle, 9-1/2" h... 550.00

Ladle, 6" dia copper bowl with rounded bottom, wrought-iron handle having 4" rounded section with a tapered flattened section at the top, round end, 20-3/8" l... 45.00

Measure

    Haystack form, pouring spout, 1/2 gal, polished, dents, 7-1/4" h 335.00

    Round with flat bottom, straight sides, broad flared tapering spout, C-shaped handle, wear, dents, 10" h, 6-5/8" dia 25.00

Pan, hammered, dovetailed seams, flat lid with wrought-iron handle initialed "LCC," found in Pa. 275.00

Copper teakettle, unmarked, $200.

Pitcher, haystack form, dovetailed seams, riveted strap handle, lid shaped to cover spout, scrolled finial, 10-1/4" h 357.50

Strap handle, from old still in Dover, Ohio, 6" and 9-1/4" h, pr... 330.00

Teakettle, marked

    "C.A. Bayard," dovetailed, gooseneck spout with flap, domed lid with scrolled finial, swivel handle, 7" h 220.00

    "G. Shuman," dovetailed, rounded sides and shoulder, curved gooseneck spout, applied mounts on kettle's shoulder, large arched hinged handle, rounded lid with cast-brass knob finial, 7" h (excluding handle), 8-1/2" dia................. 1,550.00

    "Wrought Iron Range Co., St. Louis," straight sides, stamped bands, wear, small pinhole, 7-1/2" h, 9-1/4" dia 35.00

Teakettle, unmarked

    Dovetailed, brass trim on finial and handle, dents, old repair, 9-3/4" h 77.00

    Dovetailed, cylinder-type handle, acorn finial, pitting, holes, 12" h... 55.00

    Dovetailed, hinged cover on spout, scrolled finial, stamped initials, 10" h 165.00

    Dovetailed and hammered, domed lid, ring finial, large arched handle finished with beveled edges, dents, 10-3/4" h 165.00

Coverlets

Background: These woven bedcoverings were made as early as the 18th century; however, all coverlets woven before 1817 feature geometric patterns. Those coverlets, referred to as overshot, became second-rate after the introduction of the Jacquard loom attachment, which allowed professional weavers to create complex designs, including text. Jacquard coverlets, often personalized with the maker's name or motif in one or more corners, were widely made until the time of the Civil War, when less-expensive machine-woven blankets destroyed the market for coverlets. Some coverlets were made after the war, but by then their demise was certain.

Most coverlets were made in two colors, blue and white. Coverlets with more than two colors tend to be more valuable, as are those with unusual designs, including political and railroad motifs.

References: Gail C. Andrews and Donald R. Walters, eds., *A Checklist of American Coverlet Weavers*, The Colonial Williamsburg Foundation, 1978; Clarita S. Anderson, *Weaving a Legacy: The Don and Jean Stuck Coverlet Collection*, Columbus Museum of Art and Harry N. Abrams, 1995.

Collecting Hint: Most collectors search for coverlets from a particular region. Many coverlets that aren't signed by the maker can be identified by the cornerblock design.

Jacquard

"1839" and two flower buds in corner blocks, two-color, navy blue and white, rose medallions, flowering branch borders, minor wear, 72" x 90" 275.00

A WOMAN WEAVER

Men's work! Such was the business of professional coverlet weaving during the 19th century. A woman's place was in the home, not behind a Jacquard loom.

To every rule, of course, there's usually an exception. When it comes to weaving, that exception was Sarah LaTourette. Born in 1822, she was one of 14 children of weaver John LaTourette, who settled in Fountain County, Ind., in 1828 and set up shop. Sarah and her brother Henry (noted for being the only coverlet weaver born in Indiana) eventually joined the family business. Following John's death in 1849, Sarah and Henry carried on the work of coverlet weaving. The last known LaTourette coverlet was woven by Henry in 1871.

The LaTourettes' coverlets are easily identified by their cabbage-like floral design above the date in the corner block. The word "YEAR" was added to the coverlet block after John's death, helping to set apart the later work of his children. Unfortunately, there's no way to tell Sarah's coverlets from Henry's, but collectors don't care. For them, simply owning an example associated with the only female professional coverlet weaver is reward enough.

LaTourette coverlet, blue and white, $1,500.

"A.C. 1859," two-color, navy blue and white, flowering plants on central ground, double snowflake corner blocks, double urn of flowers border, 1 pc, minor stains, 73" x 86" 412.50

"Agriculture and Manufacturers are the Foundation of Our Independence," two-color, navy blue and white, border includes eagle, monkeys and people 770.00

"Henry Adolf, Hamilton County, Indiana, 1851," large floral medallion, borders of birds by flowering trees and pots of flowers by trees, single weave, wear across the top, 70" x 88" 275.00

"Philip Allabach" in border, two-color, navy blue and white, floral medallion, eagle corners, zigzag border, 66" x 82" 440.00

"Martin B. Brenemen, Washington Twp., York Co., Pa. 1838," four-color, brick red, light blue, navy blue, natural white, stars and four rose medallions, eagle and tree border, minor moth damage and stains, 88" x 76" 550.00

"C.F.N.Y. 1848," two-color, navy blue and white, snowflakes, diamonds and pinwheels on central ground, buildings border 715.00

"Daniel Fisher, South Bend, H. Hepler, 1854," four-color, navy blue, red, amber and white, rose and floral medallions, borders with bird, feather and Maltese cross, wear, fringe loss, 72" x 86" 275.00

"Made by John S. Goodman, Black Creek, Luzerne Co. For Susan Gardner, Penn 1850," two-color, blue and white, starburst medallions, borders of birds and double roses, 84" x 94" 605.00

"Made by P.H. For Mary S. Hixson, U.M.T., Beth 1841," two-color, navy blue and white, floral medallions, bird and tree border, fringe on end only, two-pc, minor stains, wear, 76" x 86" 660.00

"Anna M. Hasbrouck, N.Y. 1838," two-color, blue wool and natural cotton, Lilies of France in a central medallion, crooked eagle border, 73" x 91" 935.00

"S. Hausman, Trexlertown, 1842," four-color, red, green, mustard and white, 24 leaf and flower panels, tulip border, stains, moth damage, 74" x 98" 247.50

"Sebastian Hipp, 1854" (Richland County, Ohio), four-color, salmon, green, white and navy blue, tulips and foliage design, basket of flowers border with small houses and stars, two holes, light stains, loss to bottom edge, 74" x 80" 247.50

"Samuel Hippart, Mount Joy, LC, PA 1833," four-color, navy blue, tomato red, green and white, stars and rose medallions, eagle and tree borders, summer/winter weave, wear, fringe loss, 78" x 96" 330.00

"E.K." and "1845" star corner blocks, four-color, green, gold, navy blue and tomato red, 20 divided panels with four flowers each, flowering plant borders, single weave, one pc, wear, stains, 82" x 96" 302.50

Mathias Klein coverlet, 1840, 5-color, red, dark-blue, light-blue, olive green and white, $1,000.

"Philip Krebs 1855 D.A. Shark," four-color, dark-blue, red, olive-green and cream, starburst center with stylized tulips, border of floral urns and scrolled leaves, minor stains, 94" x 88" 635.00

"C. Lochman, Hamburg, Berks County, 1835," two-color, tomato red and white, star and floral medallions, bird and flowering tree border, few stains, stitched repair, hole, 80" x 98" 412.50

"J.H. March, 1841" (John Henry March, Salona, Pa.) and American eagle clutching a thunderbolt and olive branch, 4-color, green, red, dark-blue and natural, floral and star design, floral border, fringed sides and bottom, minor moth damage, 78" x 96" 850.00

"Elizabeth Mittower, Benton, N.Y., 1832," two-color, navy blue and white, eagles and roses motif.. 1,045.00

John Muir floral corner block dated 1834, two-color, navy blue and white, circular and floral medallions, floral border, wear, damage, 74" x 98"......... 110.00

Muir family (John, Robert, Thomas and William, Ind., 1850-1892), dated 1850, two-color, navy and white, floral medallions with leaf scroll, thistle border, double weave, wear, stains, repairs, dime-size hole, 74" x 80" 247.50

"Made by D.L. Myers, Bethel Township, for James Chambers, 1839," five-color, pink, red, black, navy blue and white, floral medallions, bird and flowering tree border, wear, edge damage, edges turned under, 72" x 96" 220.00

"Ohio 1836" and "Ohio 1839" cornerblocks, attributed to Abram Allen, Wilmington, Ohio, two-color, navy blue and white, floral design, bird and cherries border, double weave, one-pc, minor wear, stains, 78" x 78" each, pr........................ 2,475.00

"Charlotte M. Palmer, Jacob Impson 1838," two-color, black and cream, snowflake and floral motif, 82" x 88" 770.00

"Gabriel Rausher, Delaware County, Ohio, 1845," four colors, navy blue, light blue, red and white, floral and starflower medallions, bird and rose tree

borders, single weave, wear, stains, repair, 72" x 83" 385.00

"Sarah E. Savage 1852," two-color, blue and white, floral medallion, border of urns and classical column, minor stains, losses, small repair, 86" x 75" 172.50

"M. Sharp, W.C.N.J., L.M.T. Bethel Phila, RD. 1835," two-color, blue and white, floral medallions, eagle and tree borders, double weave, wear, minor edge damage, worn fringe, 78" x 88" 770.00

"Sidney, Shelby County, Ohio," four-color, navy blue, tomato red, dark grayish blue and white, geometric floral medallions, bird borders and building borders, minor stains, 68" x 92"........................ 935.00

Harry Tyler, Jefferson Co., New York (attributed), lion corner blocks with "1842," border shows eagle with shield and trees, "Clarissa Carter" along bottom edge, single weave, stains, minor damage, half only, 34" x 84" 220.00

"Peter Uhl, Portage County, Ohio, 1852," three-color, olive green, red and white, urns of flowers design, rose and buildings borders, wear, fringe loss, 66" x 83".. 357.50

"P. Vincent, New York, 1835," two-color, blue and white, floral medallions (16), eagle and trees border, 80" sq 715.00

"Washington, Hail, 1869," two-color, red and white, floral medallion corners show bust of Washington, eagle, horses and steamboats, border shows capitol building and birds, one-pc, stains, 74-1/2" sq 522.50

"E. Willse 1831," two-color, navy blue and white, four-rose design, side border with two rows of flowers, eagle with two animals on end borders, very worn, repaired, replaced fringe, 69" x 83" 660.00

Jacquard, unmarked
Floral medallions and border, two-color, tomato red and white, single weave, minor wear, 77" x 93" 385.00

"J.R. Gebhart, Maytown, Lancaster Co., 1842, S. Filby" coverlet, blue and white, $650.

Floral medallions surrounded by vintage, flowers and long-tailed birds, floral and chain link borders, dated 1851, two-color, navy blue and white, edge wear, some repair, 79" x 88"...................... 247.50

Flower corner blocks, Christian and heathen border, pattern of stars, flowers and leaves, four-color, navy blue, mustard, salmon and white, edge wear, 70-1/2" x 88" 110.00

Grapevine border with leaf and heart medallions in red, medium blue, white and navy blue, light stains, 69" x 86"... 192.50

Hemfield railroad, corner blocks with male bust, double border of trains, two-color, deep rusty red and indigo.. 4,400.00

Lion corner blocks, medallion design, tree borders, two-color, blue and white, 80" x 90"............ 550.00

Peacocks feeding their young and urns of flowers, two-color, navy blue and white, building borders, palm tree corner blocks, fringe on one side, double weave, stain, minor wear, 76" x 84"...... 385.00

Pheasants (flying) corner blocks, nine geometric medallions, double borders of pots of flowers, single border with flowers and foliage, two-color, tomato red and white, two-pc, 90" sq 715.00

Rose medallions, twelve plates each with four roses, surrounded by men's faces and chain link, double borders of baskets of flowers, two-color, navy blue and white, edge wear, stains, some puckering, 69-3/4" x 73" 192.50

Snowflake or flower corner blocks, sixteen leaf panels surrounded by flowers, intricate double foliage borders with "1834," two color, navy blue and white, stains, wear, small holes, 72" x 89" 440.00

Sun corner block, dated 1857, center floral medallion surrounded by spread eagles and banners, deer, birds and domed buildings, border of vining flowers, two-color, navy blue and white, one-pc double weave, 70" x 86" 715.00

Urn corner blocks, foliage medallions in grid pattern, floral borders, two-color, navy blue and white, stains, edge wear, 82" x 88" 220.00

Urns, birds and flowering vines repeated three times, three-color, brown, red and white, cotton chintz, whole cloth, 90-3/4" x 79"............. 2,070.00

Overshot

Geometric pattern, three-color, tomato red, brown and white, wear, stains, 69" w, 91" l 110.00

Optical pattern, two-color, navy blue and natural, fringe on three sides, 74" x 88"....................110.00

Optical pattern, two-color, navy blue and white, fringe on one end, two-pc, minor wear, 70" x 86" 192.50

Optical pattern, three-color, navy blue, red and white, 78" x 92".. 302.50

Snowflake, three-color, tomato red, dark navy blue and white, summer and winter, top edge with tattered brown print binding, 80" x 100"......... 220.00

Summer and Winter, two-color, navy blue and white, some wear, no fringe, 72" x 88"....................110.00

Summer and Winter, three-color, navy blue, red and white, Nine Patch and Snowball design, pine tree borders, minor wear, fringe damage, 64" x 90" 605.00

Wool, tomato red, two colors of green and gray, fringed border, minor holes, 76" x 80" 55.00

Cradles and Cribs

Background: A cradle is defined as a baby's small crib or bed that is mounted on rockers, although the term has also been used for cribs that swing as well as those that neither swing nor rock. Cribs are defined as baby beds on tall legs, typically of turned construction.

"Henry Audolf, Wayne Co., Indiana, 1840" coverlet, four-color, dark-blue, red, olive-green and white, $850.

Cherry crib in a red stain, Connecticut, early 19th C., 44" l, $517.50. (Photo courtesy of Skinner Auctioneers & Appraisers of Antiques & Fine Arts, Boston and Bolton, Mass.)

Cradles

Baby

Cherry, old worn finish, square corner posts, turned acorn finials, shaped sides and ends with heart cutouts, shaped rockers, primitive, some edge damage, 20" h, 35" w, 16" d 275.00

Hooded, mahogany, old dark finish, mortised rockers with scrolled ends, shaped footboard, top board of hood has flame veneer, Chippendale-style brasses on ends, veneer repair, found in Hillsdale, Mich., 26-1/2" h, 40" w, 18" d 330.00

Painted, old dark-brown, softwood, flaring sides, ends with rounded top with crescent-shaped cutouts, 3 small iron knobs on each side, broad cheese-cutter rockers with scrolled ends, 22" h, 44" w, 18" d 125.00

Doll

Grain-painted, orig black over red, poplar, chamfered rockers, turned legs and finials, scalloped head and foot boards, finial chip, edge wear, 11" h, 16-1/2" l 220.00

Hooded, poplar and hickory, old reddish-brown finish, dovetailed, cutout rockers, bentwood had age cracks, 19" l 110.00

Painted, old red finish, gold stripes, poplar, scalloped head/foot boards, scrolled sides, incised leaf detail, repainted birch rockers, glued crack in headboard, 13-5/8" h, 18-3/4" l 110.00

Painted, red, yellow stripes, softwood, horizontal dowel rods and vertical spindles, turned corner posts/legs mortised into rockers, 11-3/4" h, 19-1/2" l 50.00

Painted, red, yellow stripes, red and cream scrolled floral design, straight flared sides, head and footboards with arched tops, scrolled cutouts, curved rockers with scrolled ends, 10-5/8" h, 21-3/4" l 150.00

Cribs

Cherry, red stain, Conn., early 19th C., turned finials, ring-turned tapering swelled supports and legs, ball feet, one hinged side, orig linen mattress support and webbing, orig surface, minor imperfections, 43-1/2" h, 28" w, 44" l 517.50

Decor, New England, early 19th C., scrolled head and footboards, side rails with vasiform spindles, ring-turned legs and feet, orig yellow and black paint, stenciled floral and fruit designs on head and footboards, imperfections, 33" h, 25-1/2" w, 52" l 431.25

Crock Stands

Background: Also known as crock benches because of their shape, these 19th-century utilitarian items were used to hold stoneware. Sometimes painted, they were seldom decorated. Crock stands often had more than one tier.

Folding, poplar, worn red paint, turned back legs, three shelves, decorative brackets, 49-1/2" h, 41" w, 32" d 1,210.00

Painted, old mustard, three-tier, semicircular, stepped shelves, found in Pa., wear, age splits, 36" h, 49-1/2" w, 25-1/2" d 660.00

Pine, green overpaint, shaped ends, stepped shelves, weathered, 22" h, 40" w, 11-1/4" d 324.50

Cupboards

Background: The term cupboard is used to describe a number of pieces of furniture that are generally enclosed with doors and have shelves or space for storing dishes, linens, food, and clothes. Originally, the name referred to an open structure designed specifically to hold cups, hence the name.

References: Eileen and Richard Dubrow, *Styles of American Furniture 1860-1960*, Schiffer Publishing, 1997; Tim Forrest, *Bulfinch Anatomy of Antique Furniture*, Bulfinch Press, 1996; John T. Kirk, *American Furniture: Understanding Styles, Construction, and Quality*, Harry N. Abrams Publishers, 2000; Milo M. Naeve, *Identifying American Furniture*, W.W. Norton, 1998; Ellen T. Schroy, *Warman's American Furniture*, Krause Publications, 2001; Robert W. and Harriet Swedberg, *Collector's Encyclopedia of American Furniture*, Vol. 1 (1990, 1996 value update), Vol. 2 (1992, 1999 value update), Vol. 3 (1998), Collector Books; *Encyclopedia of American Oak Furniture*, Krause Publications, 2000.

Chimney, pine, paneled door, 60" h, 13" w, 9" d 715.00

China, curved glass, oak, claw feet, 3 shelves, refinished, 57" h, 37" w 385.00

Corner

Architectural, cherry, 16-pane door (upper three panes with arched tops) over two drawers over two paneled doors, turned feet, broken-arch pediment with rosettes, three urn finials, 93" h, 21" d 14,300.00

Architectural, cherry, one-pc, two six-pane doors over two drawers over two paneled doors, elaborate cornice, cutout feet, scalloped apron, pilasters with applied moldings, replaced brasses, repair to one top door, reset hinge, 88-3/4" h, 62" w 4,675.00

Architectural, poplar, refinished, two-pc, arched door with 15 panes over two drawers over two paneled doors, half-turned pilasters, raised/scalloped bracket feet, molded base, butterfly shelves with spoon cutouts, broken-arch pediment, finials and drawer pulls replaced, minor restoration, Pa. origin, 90-1/2" h, 44-1/2" w, 24" d 5,610.00

Cherry, probably Mid-Atlantic states, 12-pane door over two recessed panel doors, molded base, flaring cornice, replaced hardware, refinished, height loss, other repairs, 85-3/4" h, 44" w, 28-1/4" d 4,312.50

Cherry, one-pc, high cutout feet, scalloped apron, 12-pane door with orig glass and brass ring pull, base with two raised-panel doors, molded trim on waist, three butterfly shelves, stepped-down cornice, old dark finish, some plate rails missing or replaced, 91-3/4" h, 46" w, 22-1/2" d 6,600.00

Cherry, one-pc, old finish, cove-molded cornice, two eight-pane doors (some orig glass) over two doors with inset panels, scroll-cut apron, bracket feet, hardware replaced, 82-1/4" h, 51" w 3,520.00

Cherry, one-pc, old varnish finish, scalloped apron, shaped feet, two four-pane doors with molded mullions over two paneled doors, orig cornice with repair at one corner, bottom interior painted tan, 79-3/4" h, 49" w, 22" d 3,850.00

Cherry, one-pc, shaped bracket feet, apron, molded base and waist, two eight-pane doors of old wavy glass, two beaded doors with inset panels, reeded side panels, elaborate cornice, old finish, Ohio origin, cracked back feet, some dentil molding missing, 90-1/2" h, 57" w, 21" d 8,250.00

Cherry, country-style, one-pc, shaped bracket feet, two eight-pane doors with flat mullions over two paneled doors, sliding brass latch, beveled cornice, 83-1/2" h, 53" w, 18-1/2" d 3,300.00

Child-size, orig brown paint, poplar and pine, two doors with inset panels, shaped bracket feet, stepped cornice, found in Ohio, 36-1/4" h, 28" w,14-1/2" d... 770.00

Chippendale, two-pc, cherry, ogee feet, molded apron and waist, two doors in top section, each with eight panes of old wavy glass and arched top panels, base with two dovetailed drawers with early oval brasses over two doors with beaded edges and inset panels with molded surround, elaborate stepdown molding on cornice, refinished, 83-1/2" h, 51-3/4" w, 24-1/2" d 13,200

Curly maple, two-pc, reproduction by "David T. Smith, Morrow, Ohio," high scalloped base, 12-pane door over two raised-panel doors, molded waist and cornice, good figure, 90" h, 43" w, 18" d 1,540.00

Hepplewhite, two-pc, cherry, high bracket feet, scallops on apron, one door in top with 12 panes of old glass, molded mullions, arched top panels, round molding at waist, two dovetailed drawers over two paneled doors in base, brass pulls, brass turnbuckle, beaded backboards with square nails, refinished, 89-1/4" h, 47" w, 23" d........... 7,425.00

Hepplewhite, walnut with inlay, refinished, French feet, scalloped apron, 12-pane door over one drawer over paneled door, molded cornice, replaced feet and bottom door hinges, repairs, inlay a later addition, 96-1/4" h, 42" w, 23" d 2,860.00

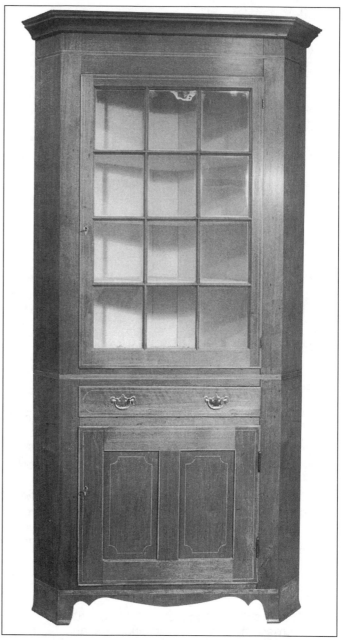

Hepplewhite corner cupboard, walnut, inlay a later addition, refinished, repairs, 96-1/4" h, 42" w, $2,860. (Photo courtesy of Garth's Auctions, Delaware, Ohio)

Open top, red paint, blue interior, lollipop shelves, 86" h, 47" w 1,650.00

Painted, blue, two-pc, 15-pane door over two paneled doors, cove-molded cornice, 90" h, 43" w, 29" d 5,225.00

Painted, old red paint, one-pc, country style, pine, flat base, mortise and tenon, wide raised-panel single door at top and bottom, alterations, small pieced repair, areas of repaint, possibly Georgia origin, 75-3/4" h, 37" w, 23" d 2,090.00

Painted, two-pc, pine, old worn dark-blue repaint over earlier cream color, bracket feet, dovetailed case, reeded stiles, two paneled doors over dove-tailed drawer over two paneled doors, geometric relief design band at frieze, molded cornice, serpentine shelves with cutouts for spoons and red finish in upper section, possibly Hackensack, N.J, 84-3/4" h, 45" w 15,400.00

Pine, one-pc, Conn., c. 1730, dentil and cove-molded cornice, arched open cupboard with step-molded surround and two red-washed shaped shelves, door with three raised panels, domed plaster and lath back, lacks finish, minor imperfections, 77-1/4" h, 52" w............................. 4,140.00

Pine, one-pc, painted, old green repaint, tall and narrow construction, scalloped apron, paneled bottom door, top door with geometric arrangement of 13 panes of glass, red interior, green backboards, repairs, replaced perimeter molding, 87-1/2" h, 27" w 1,155.00

Pine, one-pc, old dark varnished finish, bracket feet, molded trim, single nine-pane door over two inset-paneled doors, applied molding around top door, stepped-out cornice and dentil molding, rosehead nails, hinges and back foot replaced, pads added on front feet, 81" h, 50" w, 27" d 5,500.00

Pine, one-pc, orig red finish, bracket feet, arched apron, picture-frame molding on front of case, two upper doors each with one short over one long pc of glass, early brass latch, ring pulls, two paneled doors in base with replaced wooden pulls, stepped cornice, Pa. origin, two small sections of molding replaced, 78" h, 47-1/2" w, 23-1/2" d.. 3,300.00

Poplar, country style, one-pc, old dark cherry finish, cutout feet, paneled doors (one over one), wide stiles, molded cornice, 74" h, 45-1/2" w 1,210.00

Southern stepback, walnut, two eight-pane doors over two blind doors, shaped bracket feet, picture frame molding around case, step-down cornice with scrolled crest and applied rosettes, yellow pine secondary wood, 94" h, 56-1/2" w 5,500.00

Walnut, country style, two-pc, 12-pane door over three dovetailed drawers over two paneled doors, bracket feet, poplar secondary wood, refinished, replaced cove-molding cornice, originally one pc, 89-1/2" h, 43-1/2" w................................. 3,300.00

Walnut, old brown grained repaint, scalloped bracket feet with molded apron, two paneled doors in base, one upper door with nine panes of old glass, cove-molded cornice, orig brass knob on bottom doors, replaced glass knob on upper door, 79" h, 48-1/4" w, 25-3/4" d 4,675.00

Walnut, old finish, one-pc dovetailed case, attributed to James Gheen (worked 1778-1796), Piedmont, N.C., rosehead-nail construction, reeded chamfered corners with lamb's tongue, bracket feet, raised-panel doors with rectangular panel in bottom door and tombstone panel in top door, molded cornice, wrought-iron surface-mount hinges, feet

ended out, front bracket replaced, some edge damage, 83" h, 41" w, 18-5/8" d 9,625.00

Walnut, country style, old refinish, one-pc, scalloped bracket feet, upper door with nine panes of old glass with carved mullions, lower door with two inset panels, bottom door varies from top, cove-molded cornice, repaired breaks in feet, replaced rear foot, pieced repairs on both doors, cupboard originally two-pc and has been reconstructed and bottom door replaced, 84" h, 44-1/4" w 3,190.00

Walnut, high feet, scalloped apron, banded inlay on base, two upper doors each with eight panes over a false drawer with two turned pulls over two doors with line inlay and inset panels, arched top with rosettes and urn finial, line inlay on crest, teardrop inlay on pilasters, Southern, chip on crest, rear foot has lost height, alterations to doors and height, 81-1/4" h, 37" w, 19-1/2" d.. 2,475.00

Corner, hanging
Grain-decor, red and yellow, one door, 23" h, 22" w, 12" d 220.00

Painted, old green repaint, paneled door, mortised, finish stains, wear, attributed to Morrow County, Ohio, 30-3/4" h, 34-1/4" w, 20-1/2" d 467.50

Painted, old worn blue repaint, pine, raised arched-panel door in beaded frame, scalloped shelves, base and cornice molding, replaced lock and "HL" hinges, false bottom added, ends of cornice replaced, 35" h, 29" w............................. 2,200.00

Old reddish-brown finish, one paneled door, molded base and top, pegged, two small sections of base molding missing, 39-1/4" h, 33-1/2" w, 19-1/2" d 1,210.00

Hanging
Cherry and walnut with mahogany veneer, country style, old dark finish, dovetailed case with picture-frame molding, door has mullions with four panes of old wavy glass, two interior shelves with remnants of wallpaper covering, 26" h, 24" w, 9-3/4" d 550.00

Grain-decor, reddish paint, two doors each with two raised panels, molded cornice, 32" h, 25" w, 10" d 990.00

Painted, dark-brown, pine, scalloped base with one drawer, one door with old glass insert, beveled edges, molded top with scalloped crest, glued sliver on one side, 32" h, 21" w, 8" d 192.50

Painted, dark green over lighter green decor, pine, raised-panel door, wrought-iron snipe hinges, molded base, stepped cornice, reproduction, hand-made with older wood, signed "Loose," 23-1/4" h, 21-1/4" w, 11-3/4" d 220.00

Painted, gray repaint, pine, dovetailed case, chamfered corners, molded base, raised-panel door, two shelves and one drawer inside, age cracks, 31" h, 25" w, 9-1/2" d 880.00

Painted, old crackled salmon and red repaint over earlier grained paint, pine and poplar, peaked shape, two-pc, two paneled doors over four drawers (two rows of two), six interior compartments, pigeonholes under peaked top, square nails, molded base, peaked section missing its door, lower side molding missing, 45-1/2" h, 35-1/2" w, 11" d.. 1,265.00

Painted, old mustard repaint, cherry and ash, dovetailed case, small open shelf on bottom, shaped sides, one door with two raised panels, beaded trim, cove-molded cornice with edge damage, small glued repair on back, 42" h, 25" w, 11-1/4" d 990.00

Painted, old putty repaint over earlier red, molded base with scalloped compartment, four dovetailed drawers (two short over two long), molded cornice, replaced brass pulls, 23-1/4" h, 16-3/4" w, 12" d 1,320.00

Painted, old reddish-brown finish, pine, door with two panels, divided interior, dovetailed case with picture-frame molding, 12" h, 19-3/4" sq 495.00

Painted, orig dark-red, poplar, molded base, stepped cornice, paneled door over one drawer, interior with vertical pigeonholes, dovetailed case, latch missing, 26" h, 23" w, 12" d............... 880.00

Painted, orig red paint and floral decor, pine and chestnut, mortised/pegged door with four inset panels having tulips, side panels have vines and flowers, one-board back, two shelves, replaced pull, 29" h, 19-1/4" w, 9" d 3,575.00

Pine, raised-panel door, rattail hinges, 24" h, 27" w, 19" d 1,375.00

Walnut, old dark finish, two paneled doors, molded trim around base, white porcelain pulls, pegged, stepped cornice with applied decor on each side, minor chip, 33-1/2" h, 34" w, 12-1/4" d 330.00

Walnut, old finish, dovetailed case, paneled door with beaded frame, molded cornice with dentil trim, some edge damage and repairs, Ohio origin, 25-3/4" h, 20-1/2" w, 13-3/4" d................. 1,760.00

Walnut, old finish, tombstone case, one-board door, applied molding to case and door, white porcelain knob, two pcs of trim replaced, 31" h, 23" w, 12" d 385.00

Jelly

Cherry, refinished, scalloped base, paneled ends, two door with inset panels in bottom and added punched tins at top, dovetailed gallery with shaped ends, 51" h, 41-1/4" w, 20-1/4" d 880.00

Cherry and poplar, refinished, shaped feet, one-board ends, two drawers with flame veneer over two paneled doors, drawer pulls removed and holes filled, slight warp, 59" h, 46-3/4" w, 18-1/2" d 1,485.00

Grain decor, pine, orig reddish-brown graining, bracket feet, molded base and cornice in worn black paint, two doors with inset panels having crosshatch decor as do side panels, mortised joints on door, back constructed with "T" and rosehead nails, one shelf missing, glued repairs to feet, some edge damage, 66" h, 45" w, 17" d 5,390.00

Grain-decorated jelly cupboard in original reddish-brown, some damage and repairs, 66" h, 45" w, $5,390. (Photo courtesy of Garth's Auctions, Delaware, Ohio)

Grain decor, pine and poplar, old yellow graining over red, one-board ends, cutout feet, two dovetailed drawers over two paneled doors, high gallery back, old replaced wooden pulls, old brass latches on doors, found in Smoketown, Pa., 47-1/2" h, 40" w, 13" d 3,960.00

Grain decor, poplar, yellow grained decor over earlier red and black, bracket feet, elaborate scalloped front apron, two dovetailed doors over two paneled doors, dovetailed gallery top with shaped corners, square-nail construction, white porcelain knobs, minor edge wear, 51" h, 42-1/2" w, 19" d 1,540.00

Grain decor, poplar and pine, old comb graining, turned and tapered feet, applied molding around the base, two stepped-out dovetailed drawers with chamfered borders over two doors with inset panels, high peaked backsplash, replaced latches and porcelain knobs, 55-3/4" h, 45" w, 21" d...................................... 1,430.00

Painted, old green, two doors (each with three panels), rattail hinges, molded cornice, 69" h, 53" w, 21" d 1,980.00

Yellow pine, old refinish, partial built-in (one corner rounded, one square), chipped baseboard and cornice, raised-panel door, adjustable shelves, edge damage, Southern origin, 56-3/4" h, 42" w, 11" d.. 275.00

Milk, painted, robin's-egg blue with white inserts, one door with floating panel, cutout bracket feet, 63" h, 32" w, 12" d 550.00

Miscellaneous

Miniature, cherry and poplar, cleaned down to old red paint, shaped feet, square nails, mortised door with two inset panels, wrought-iron lock, two interior shelves, top scrubbed, one foot ended out, 26-1/4" h, 21" w, 8" d 605.00

Miniature, grain-decor, orig brown over tan graining, scalloped base on front and sides, one door with inset arched panels, old turned wooden pull, top in old red repaint, 12-1/2" h, 14-3/8" w, 9" d 247.50

Painted, old gray, red and blue showing at points of wear, pine, one-board ends, cutout feet, cutout front foot bracket, single raised-panel upper and lower doors over dovetailed drawer, molded cornice, replaced brass H hinges and bails, doors show signs of having had H hinges and being turned and rehinged, interior with modern paint, found in R.I., 73" h, 38-1/2" w, 21-1/2" d 5,775.00

Painted, worn orig red, pine, one door, one-board back and sides, square nails, replaced turned wood pull, mouse hole in base, 36" h, 18-3/4" w, 11-1/4" d 440.00

Small, country style, one door, gray repaint, mixed woods, cut bracket feet, one-board ends and door, cast-iron latch, square nails, age cracks, 24" h, 19-1/2" w, 10-1/2" d 550.00

Zoar, Ohio, cherry, dovetailed case, molded base and cornice, one dovetailed drawer, door with raised panel and diamond design, wrought-iron rattail hinges with leaf finials, old refinish, missing feet, small base chip, lip damage on drawer, 36" h, 26-3/4" w, 14-1/4" d 3,575.00

Pewter (all one-pc stepback unless noted)

Pine, old refinishing, ends have cutout feet, beaded board front with 1 door, spoon cutouts on right half of middle shelf of top section, cut down, restorations, old alterations, 63-1/8" h, 53" w, 18" d 1,320.00

Pine, refinished, old nut-brown color, two doors in base with inset panels, shallow top section with three removable shelves and molded plate bar across the bottom with spoon cutouts, reconstruction with additions, 76" h, 48" w, 20-3/4" d, top 6-5/8" d 1,265.00

Pine, refinished, paneled door, truncated top with two shelves, perimeter molding, red interior, paneled back is off, reconstruction, small size, 66" h, 34-1/2" w, 16-1/2" d 605.00

Poplar, country style, old red, attributed to Ohio, cutout feet, simple apron detail, door with four raised

Pewter cupboard, refinished pine, reconstruction with additions, 76" h, 48" w, $1,265. (Photo courtesy of Garth's Auctions, Delaware, Ohio)

panels, three shelves at top, beaded-edge stiles, replaced molded cornice, 79" h, 39-1/4" w, 14" d 3,960.00

Walnut, old finish, scalloped front apron, high feet, bootjack ends, two paneled doors in base, three shelves in top, molded cornice, 76" h, 40-1/4" w, 11-1/2" d 1,760.00

Stepback

Miniature, country style, old dark-red repaint, poplar, two paneled doors over pie shelf over two paneled doors, picture-frame molding around case and doors, turned wood pulls, square and round nails, end sections of cornice replaced, 24" h, 12-1/2" w, 8-5/8" d 880.00

Miniature, painted, old worn dark-brown repaint over original red, poplar, end panels with scalloped bases, three small shelves at top, stepped-down cornice, backboard missing, 31-3/4" h, 17-1/2" w 660.00

Miniature, pine, short bracket feet with arched cutouts on sides of base, arched front apron, compartment in the base with slant lid, two shelves in top with arched opening, cove-molded cornice, wire nail construction, refinished, short crack in arch with small pc missing, 21-3/4" h, 16-2/3" w, 9-1/2" d 440.00

Miniature, walnut, old finish, short saber legs, bin in base with lift lid and interior mirror, 1-drawer top with turned pull, early brass key escutcheons, some wire nails, brown ink label for maker and family, 11-1/2" h, 12-1/2" w, 8-1/2" d 577.50

Painted, dark-red repaint, poplar, two-pc, two two-pane doors over one drawer over two paneled doors, shaped bracket feet, beveled cornice, 81-1/2" h, 39-1/2" w, 17-3/4" d 1,540.00

Stepback cupboard in old blue paint, two-piece, New England, early 19th C., 80-1/2" h, 36-1/2" w, $7,475. (Photo courtesy of Skinner Auctioneers & Appraisers of Antiques & Fine Arts, Boston and Bolton, Mass.)

Painted, light blue, pine, New England, early 19th C., cornice over two doors over three open compartments and stepped-out surface over two doors, red interior, surface losses, repairs 2,990.00

Painted, old blue, New England, early 19th C., two pc, two raised-panel doors with four-shelf interior over pie shelf, stepped-out lower case with two raised-panel doors, 80-1/2" h, 36-1/2" w, 17" d 7,475.00

Painted, red exterior, gray interior, two plank doors over two plank doors, simple cornice, 71" h, 45" w, 18" d 1,375.00

Open, one-pc, poplar, old gray finish, one-board sides, bootjack ends, two one-board doors, two shelves in top with plate rests, scalloped crest, square nails, some later nails added, 67-3/4" h, 32-3/4" w, 17-1/2" d 495.00

Pine, two-pc, old refinish, cutout feet, two short over two long paneled doors, molded cornice, 75" h, 48-1/2" w, 17-1/2" d 1,089.00

Wall

Grain-decor, brown over tan vinegar graining, green detail, Chippendale-style, two-pc, ogee feet, molded base, top with two doors with raised panels over high pie shelf, base with three drawers over two paneled doors, cove-molded cornice, 83" h, 51" w, 18-1/4" d 1,760.00

Grain-decor, brown vinegar graining over tan, gray detail, Chippendale-style, two-pc, top with two raised-panel doors over high pie shelf, base with three drawers over two raised-panel doors, ogee feet with scalloped returns, molded base, cove-molded cornice, 82" h, 51" w, 18-1/2" d... 1,045.00

Grain-decor, old black over brown grained decor, two pc, pine, molded base with one drawer over two arched panel doors, narrower top with two arched glass doors, paneled sides, step-down cornice, edge wear, one pane cracked, 71-1/4" h, 35-1/2" w, 17-3/4" d 1,100.00

Grain-decor, old red and grained surface, poplar, probably N.Y., 19th C., one door opens to single shelf and closet, incised cutout feet, base reshaped, 76-1/4" h, 37" w, 17-1/4" d......... 920.00

Grain-decor, reddish-brown over tan grained repaint, two pc, walnut, bracket feet, scalloped apron, top with three three-pane doors over high pie shelf, base with two drawers over two paneled doors, stepped cornice, 85-1/4" h, 49" w, 18-1/2" d.. 1,925.00

Pine, Hackensack, N.J., c. 1800-10, upper section with two six-pane doors opening to stepped shelves, flanked by reeded pilasters, lower projecting section with central long drawer flanked by short drawers above two recessed paneled doors with flanking recessed panels, all with applied moldings, molded base, cutout feet, overhanging stepped molded and reeded cornice, old refinish, 84" h, 51" w 6,900.00

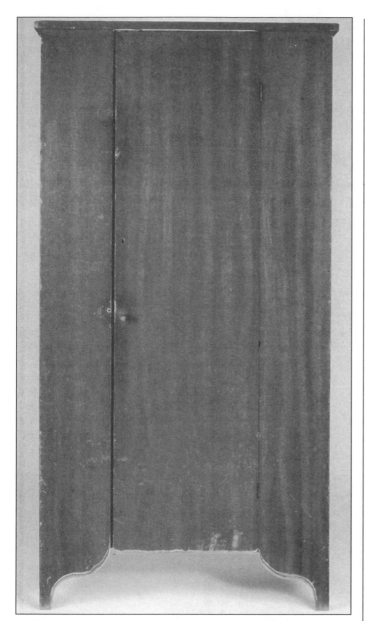

Wall cupboard in old red and grained surface, base reshaped, 76-1/4" h, 37" w, $920. (Photo courtesy of Skinner Auctioneers & Appraisers of Antiques & Fine Arts, Boston and Bolton, Mass.)

Oak wall cupboard, pressed design on drawers and lower doors, $400.

Pine, reeded pilasters, two upper doors fitted with decorative geometric mullions, two lower doors with inset panels, interior fitted with reeded columns matching outside and having arched top, old refinishing, base molding replaced, some height loss and restoration, scratches on one side, two panes cracked 76" h, 42-1/2" w, 15" d 2,750.00

Walnut, two-pc, mellow refinish, bracket feet, shaped cutouts on bottom of end panels, two paneled doors over pie shelf in top, two short drawers over two paneled doors in base, molded cornice, cast-iron latches with porcelain pulls, one door swollen and won't close properly, 85-1/2" h, 45" w, 18" d 2,090.00

Walnut, two-pc, old refinish, tapered bracket feet, bootjack ends, top with two paneled doors over pie shelf, base with two dovetailed drawers over two paneled doors, beveled cornice, chip on rear foot, one end of cornice replaced, 85-3/4" h, 45" w, 19" d 1,870.00

Cutlery Boxes and Trays

Background: Cutlery boxes have lids while cutlery trays feature open tops. Both typically have a center divider with a cutout handhold. Most of the examples on today's market date to the 19th century.

Collecting Hint: Don't confuse cutlery boxes with knife boxes, which generally have a slanted top with slots for inserting knives, handle up.

Box

    Painted, black, elaborate scrolls and silhouette cut-out, 7" h, 11" w, 7" d.................................... 825.00

    Painted, worn green, yew or oak, arched divider with cutout handle, English, 7" h, 12-1/2" w, 8-3/4" d.. 165.00

    Walnut, double lift lids, canted top, shaped crest with cutout handle, old finish, age cracks, 9" h, 14" w, 12-3/4" d.. 440.00

Bentwood maple cutlery tray, $150.

    Walnut, double lids, dovetailed, beveled edge on base, canted sides, incised carved panels, raised divider at center, cutout handle, old dark finish, minor age cracks, 8" h, 12-3/4" w, 8-1/2" d.. 302.50

    Walnut, double lids, oblong, straight sides, center divider with arched handle and oval cutout, iron locks, dovetailed, stained, wear, missing splinter of wood, 7-1/4" h, 18-1/2" w, 11-5/8" d 350.00

Tray

    Cherry, old mellow finish, canted sides, dovetailed, two compartments, arched center board, cutout for handle flanked with small scrolls, one scroll with old break on tip, 5-5/8" h, 14-3/4" w, 8-7/8" d.. 302.50

    Curly maple, open, oblong, flared straight sides, center divider with arched top, oval cutout handle, dovetailed, small repairs, 5-1/2" h, 15-1/4" w, 8-1/4" d.. 190.00

    Grain-decor, orig brown, pine, canted sides, pierced opening for handle, square-nail construction, worn, 5-1/2" h, 12" w, 8" d 247.50

    Painted, green, canted sides, turned handle on center divider.. 137.50

    Painted, putty, canted sides, shaped ends, divider with opening for handle, 5" h, 14" w, 8" d... 440.00

    Painted, yellow, heart cutout handle in center divider.. 126.50

    Smoke-decor, canted sides, 9" l 825.00

    Softwood, flared sides, center divider with oval cut-out, refinished, 3-1/2" h, 13-1/2" w, 9-1/4" d.. 55.00

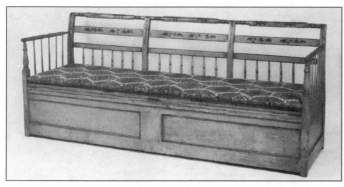

Windsor daybed, New England, early 19th C., 84" I, $4,025. (Photo courtesy of Skinner Auctioneers & Appraisers of Antiques & Fine Arts, Boston and Bolton, Mass.)

Daybeds

Background: This form began as a couch with six or eight legs and a sloped end supporting the head and back. However, the term is often used to refer to a small, narrow couch that can also double as a bed.

Softwood, square legs taper upward and flair out to form arm posts that are connected by two splats, scalloped design to top of each end, 1 end slightly higher, dark stain, 31-3/4" h, 72" w, 23-3/4" d 800.00

William and Mary, maple, old refinish, turned stretcher base, eight legs, adjustable headboard with urn splat and scalloped crest with fixed chains, turned and canted posts, old replaced rush bottom, well-executed replaced headboard, top posts ended out, 38-1/2" h, 68" w, 22" d 2,200.00

Windsor, painted and decor, New England, early 19th C., triple-section back above hinged fold-out bed, bamboo-turned arms and tapered spindles, orig yellow ground with orig brown leaf and berry stencil decor and striping, replaced seat with 20th C. textile cover, minor surface imperfections, 36-1/2" h, 84" I, 26" d................. 4,025.00

Decoys

Background: Designed to coax waterfowl into target range, decoys have been made of wood, papier-mâché, canvas, and even metal. These hand-carved and even machine-made decoys have been recognized as an indigenous American art form.

References: Bob and Sharon Huxford, *The Collector's Guide to Decoys*, Vol. I (1990), Vol. II (1992), Collector Books; Carl F. Luckey, *Collecting Antique Bird Decoys and Duck Calls*, 2nd ed., Books Americana, 1992; Donald J. Petersen, *Folk Art Fish Decoys*, Schiffer Publishing, 1996.

Collectors' Clubs: Midwest Decoy Collectors Assoc., P.O. Box 4110, St. Charles, IL 60174; Minnesota Decoy Collectors Assoc., P.O. Box 130084, St. Paul, MN 55113; Ohio Decoy Collectors and Carvers Assoc., P.O. Box 499, Richfield, OH 44286.

EYE-OPENER

The record price for a decoy sold at auction is $684,500 paid for a sleeping Canada goose made by A. Elmer Crowell. It sold in January 2000 by Guyette anSd Schmidt, Inc., West Farmington, Maine, in conjunction with Sotheby's.

Museums: Havre de Grace Decoy Museum, Havre de Grace, MD; Ward Museum of Wildfowl Art, Salisbury, MD.

Specialty Auctions: Decoys Unlimited, 2320 Main St., West Barnstable, MA 02668; Gary Guyette & Frank Schmidt, Inc., P.O. Box 522, West Farmington, ME 04992, phone 207-778-6256.

Blue jay, orig paint, carved wood, mounted on carved maple leaves, handwritten signature "A.E. Crowell Cape Cod," A. Elmer Crowell (1862-1952), East Harwich, Mass., 5-1/2" h, 7-1/2" I 2,645.00

Brandt Goose, wooden, old paint, glass eyes, wear, age crack in block, damage to bill, 17-1/2" I 247.50

Canada Goose

Tin, painted, silhouette-type, 8" h, 30" I 302.50

Waxed canvas-covered hollow body, carved neck and head, old paint, glass eyes, 15-1/2" h 220.00

Waxed canvas-covered hollow body in black and white paint, carved neck and head, glass eyes, 15-1/2" h 302.50

Wooden, preening, old gray, black and white paint, 8" h, 20-1/2" w 247.50

Wooden, preening, on large iron nail legs, painted with feather outlines, tack eyes, age cracks, 15-3/4" h, 24" I... 550.00

Swan decoy, carved and painted, two-piece hollow body, $4,887.50 (Photo courtesy of Skinner Auctioneers & Appraisers of Antiques & Fine Arts, Boston and Bolton, Mass.)

Wooden, preening, contemporary, orig distressed finish, attributed to Walker family of Salisbury, 21" l 880.00

Wooden, swimmer, dark brown and white paint, black head, unsigned, 11-1/2" h, 31" w 165.00

Wooden, swimmer, old brown, white and black paint, 26-1/2" l 137.50

Wooden, swimmer, orig paint, oval Crowell brand, A. Elmer Crowell, (1862-1952), East Harwich, Mass., repairs, age split, 11" h, 23-1/2" l 3,450.00

Wooden, extended neck, large iron nail legs, painted with feather outlines, tack eyes, hole drilled in base for stand, 25-1/2" h, 24" l 660.00

Wooden, extended neck, old worn repaint, age cracks, square-nail repair, 21-1/2" h, 29" w.. 550.00

Wooden, unsigned, glass eyes, old worn and weathered black-and-white paint, 14-1/2" h, 22-1/2" l 220.00

Coot, Gus Wilson, carved wood, black, 17" l 880.00

Crow, balsa wood, worn black paint, wear, damage, 16" h.. 192.50

Duck

Black duck, carved wood, orig paint, oval Crowell brand, A. Elmer Crowell (1862-1952), East Harwich, Mass., minor paint loss, repairs, 6-1/2" h, 17-1/2" l 1,380.00

Bluebill, wood/cork, worn repaint, glass eyes, old label attributes to Jim Foote, Pte Mouille, Mich., 14" l 165.00

Brandt, wooden, swimming position, hollow body, old repaint, 19" l.. 385.00

Canvasback, wooden, signed "R. Madison Mitchell, 1945," female with cracked neck, well-done repaint, 16" and 16-1/2" l, pr...................... 825.00

Canvasback, wooden, unsigned, orig paint, replaced glass eyes, minor age cracks, 17-1/4" l 110.00

Canvasback drake, hollow body, old black, red and white paint, attributed to Clifford Moody Lind, Freemont, Wis., cracks in head, minor edge wear, 18-1/2" l 220.00

Mallard, wooden, painted feather details, glass eyes, two-part, early 20th C., 17-1/2" l 605.00

Mallard drake, wooden, old factory decoy, glass eyes, old repaint, edge damage, age cracks, 16" l.. 115.50

Mallard hen, wooden, sleeper, orig paint, possibly a Maryland marker, chip on tail, 14-1/2" l 385.00

Mason, black duck, glass eyes, 17" l, pr....... 2,200.00

Mason, bluebill, orig black, white and gray paint, glass eyes, minor wear, professional repair to tip of tail, neck puttied, 13-3/4" l 247.50

Mason, golden eye, 13" l 220.00

Mason, mallard drake, early repainted finish, light- and dark-gray body with brown, green, black and white, dark-green head, glass eyes, orange bill, small chip on bill, thin pc of neck missing, 15-1/2" l........ 220.00

Mason, mallard drake, wooden, worn repaint, tack eyes, some damage, 15-1/2" l 247.50

Mason, teal, glass eyes 715.00

Turtle decoy, traces of black and yellow paint, 30" l, $797.50.

Merganser, painted, orig plumes, wear, 17" l, pr 880.00

Merganser, worn old working repaint, glass eyes, age cracks, old puttied repair, 14-3/4" l 220.00

Merganser drake, red-breasted, orig paint, oval Crowell brand, A. Elmer Crowell (1862-1952), East Harwich, Mass., age split, minor paint loss, 5-1/2" h, 19-1/2" l 8,625.00

Pintail, wooden, painted, early 20th C., 20-1/2" l 220.00

Red head drake, wooden, old repaint, glass eyes, loose head, 14-1/2" l................................. 302.50

Fish

4-3/4" l, carved wood, blue back, white belly, red and black dots, rusted metal fins 27.50

9" l, carved wood, striped, gold, black and white paint, red head, metal fins, tack eyes 192.50

11" l, carved wood, silver repaint, brown dots, metal fins.. 110.00

14" l, 7-1/2" h, carved, four-color, applied tin fins, incised gills and mouth, tack eyes, signed "S.W.," contemporary, on stand 55.00

Goose, wooden, old blue-green paint, black sponging, white head and tail, tack eyes, age cracks, chip on bill, 18" l.. 330.00

Little blue heron, miniature, carved wood, orig paint, mounted on carved wooden "rock," rectangular Crowell stamp, A. Elmer Crowell (1862-1952), East Harwich, Mass., 7" h, 6-1/2" l 4,025.00

Pheasant, carved wood, painted, early 20th C., minor paint loss, 4-1/2" h, 13-1/2" l 172.50

Sandpiper, miniature, carved wood, orig paint, mounted on carved clam shell, oval Crowell stamp, A. Elmer Crowell (1862-1952), East Harwich, Mass., 5-1/2" h, 6" l... 4,600.00

Shore bird

Curlew, old paint, bead eyes, on base, tip of beak damaged, 15" h, 14" l 467.50

Plover, good age, old paint, wooden button eyes, inserted beak, some damage, beak split, 9" l 192.50

Yellow leg, old paint, tack eyes, on base, 11-3/4" h, 15-1/4" l 165.00

Yellow leg, wooden, old paint, tack eyes, on base, 13-3/4" h, 15" l 192.50

Unidentified, flying, some age with old paint, copper tack eyes, 15-1/4" h, 15" wingspan 385.00

Unidentified, contemporary, carved and painted, 14-3/4" h 231.00

Unidentified, contemporary, carved and painted, on stand, 12" h 412.50

Unidentified, primitive, good age, old crusty paint, bead eyes, hole in tail, modern replacement for broken beak, 16" h, 11" l 165.00

Unidentified, primitive, good age, old paint, tack eyes, shot scars, square-nail beak an old replacement, hole in tail, 10-3/4" h, 10-3/4" l 137.50

Swan

Carved and painted, flattened full body, white with black and yellow features, mounted on carved oblong base painted blue and white, crackles, small losses on wings, American, 19th C., 13" h, 16-3/4" w 14,950.00

Carved and painted, two-pc hollow body, solid neck and head, late 19th C., wood loss, early repair, paint loss 4,887.50

Wilson's snipe, carved wood, orig paint, mounted on carved clam shell, rectangular Crowell stamp and paper label, A. Elmer Crowell (1862-1952), East Harwich, Mass., 6-1/2" h, 9" l 6,325.00

Desks

Background: Desk styles have varied greatly over the years, from the simplicity of a desk on frame to more elaborate slant-lid desks with carvings and fitted interiors. Regardless of the style, the purpose was the same, to afford the user a place to sit and work, with one or more compartments for storing writing material and paperwork.

References: Eileen and Richard Dubrow, *Styles of American Furniture 1860-1960*, Schiffer Publishing, 1997; Tim Forrest, *Bulfinch Anatomy of Antique Furniture*, Bulfinch Press, 1996; John T. Kirk, *American Furniture: Understanding Styles, Construction, and Quality*, Harry N. Abrams Publishers, 2000; Milo M. Naeve, *Identifying American Furniture*, W.W. Norton, 1998; Robert W. and Harriet Swedberg, *Collector's Encyclopedia of American Furniture*, Vol. 1 (1990, 1996 value update), Vol. 2 (1992, 1999 value update), Vol. 3 (1998), Collector Books; *Encyclopedia of American Oak Furniture*, Krause Publications, 2000.

Also See: Secretaries

Chippendale

Oxbow slant-front, cherry, Concord, Mass., area, c. 1800, four scratch-beaded reverse serpentine drawers, top drawer arced, interior of small drawers above valance compartments, molded base, four shaped ogee feet, replaced brasses, old surface, repairs, surface imperfections, 43-1/2" h, 40" w, 21-1/4" d 10,350.00

Chippendale slant-front desk, birch, northern New England, mid/late 18th C., refinished, replaced brasses, 43" h, 39" w, $3,105. (Photo courtesy of Skinner Auctioneers & Appraisers of Antiques & Fine Arts, Boston and Bolton, Mass.)

Reverse serpentine, slant-front, Boston, c. 1760-80, arched top drawer over three graduated drawers, ogee bracket feet, interior of one short drawer flanked by two long drawers over five short drawers and ten valanced compartments, old replaced brasses, old refinish, repairs to lid, 43-1/2" h, 41-1/2" w, 22" d 6,900.00

Chippendale, slant-front

Birch, northern New England, mid/late 18th C., four drawers with cockbeaded surrounds, molded base, shaped bracket feet, two-stepped interior with open valanced compartments above small drawers and central opening, refinished, replaced brasses, imperfections, 43" h, 39" w, 18" d 3,105.00

Birch, old refinish, dovetailed case, bracket feet, four dovetailed drawers with cockbeading, fitted interior of eight drawers and pigeonholes, replaced brasses, feet damage, old nailed repair, 41-1/2" h, 39-3/4" w, 17-1/2" d 2,475.00

Birch, good figure, scalloped bracket feet, molded base, four dovetailed drawers, beaded edges, dovetailed case, interior with six drawers (one with shell carving) and pigeonholes, refinished, replaced bat-wing brasses, feet restored, 41-1/2" h, 39" w, 20" d 2,860.00

Birch, R.I., c. 1780, four graduated drawers, ogee bracket feet, interior with concave shell-carved prospect door flanked by eight compartments, orig stained finish, old replaced brasses, restoration, 42" h, 37-3/4" w, 19-1/2" d 11,500.00

Birch and cherry, refinished, scalloped bracket feet, molded base, four drawers, dovetailed case, beaded trim around drawer holes, seven interior drawers and seven pigeonholes with scalloping, replaced base and brasses, reconstruction on interior, 40-1/2" h, 40" w, 19-1/4" d 1,540.00

Cherry, line/tulip inlay, French feet, scalloped aprons, banded inlay across base, two-board sides, four dovetailed drawers, replaced oval brasses, elaborate interior, refinished, 46" h, 41-3/4" w, 21" d 7,150.00

Curly maple, old finish, bracket feet, dovetailed case, fitted interior with four dovetailed drawers/ center door, chestnut/pine/poplar secondary woods, replaced brasses, 40-1/2" h, 39" w, 17-3/4" d 3,410.00

Mahogany, line inlay, scalloped ogee feet, molded base, four dovetailed drawers, dovetailed case with chamfered corners, interior with seven drawers, one door and six pigeonholes, refinished, replaced eagle brasses, restoration, 43-1/2" h, 43-1/2" w, 21-5/8" d 2,090.00

Mahogany, New York, claw-and-ball front feet, ogee rear feet, dovetailed case, gadrooned apron, four dovetailed overlapping drawers, fitted interior with eight pigeonholes over six small drawers, burned area on writing surface, old replaced brasses, edge repair to lid, front feet replaced, 42" h, 48" w, 20-1/4" d 2,200.00

Mahogany and birch, claw-and-ball feet, molded apron, four dovetailed drawers in base, old batwing brasses, interior with 15 drawers with seven carved shells, some blocked fronts, small door at center with glass inset, dovetailed case, attributed to Salem or Ispwich, Mass., refinished, restorations, 43" h, 42-1/4" w, 20-1/4" d 3,630.00

Maple, dovetailed case, bracket feet, scalloped aprons, molded base, four dovetailed drawers with beaded edges, old brasses, fitted interior with six drawers and pigeonholes and relief-carved fan at center, back painted black, refinished, replaced hinges, loose lid due to breaks at hinge rail, drawer sides stained, 41-1/4" h, 37-3/4" w, 20" d 2,860.00

Maple, four drawers, bracket base, 42" h, 35-1/2" w, 17" d 7,150.00

Maple, New England, 18th C., four graduated thumb-molded drawers, shaped bracket feet, interior of valanced compartments with scrolled dividers, orig brasses, refinished, imperfections, 41-1/2" h, 35-1/4" w, 17-5/8" d 6,325.00

Painted, maple and pine, old red paint, bracket feet, dovetailed case, four dovetailed drawers, simple interior with five drawers and two compartments, replaced brasses, 41-3/4" h, 37" w, 18-1/2" d 12,100.00

Federal, lady's desk
Mahogany, bird's-eye maple and rosewood veneer, Gilman Clifford, Gilmanton, N.H. area, c. 1810, inlaid three-panel frieze above two veneered doors flanked by inlaid simulated columns over a foldout felt-lined writing surface, over a case of three cockbeaded drawers outlined in bird's-eye maple inlay flanked by bird's-eye veneered panels, ring-turned tapering legs, early surface, replaced brasses, some veneer loss, 57-1/2" h, 41-3/8" w, 20" d 9,775.00

Mahogany and mahogany veneer, Mass., c. 1810, flat molded cornice, upper section of two beaded and veneered doors, lower projecting section with foldout writing surface over case of three cockbeaded and veneered drawers, ring-turned legs, shaped skirt, old glass pulls, interior of three shaped document drawers flanked by two short drawers above three valanced compartments, old refinish, imperfections, 53" h, 39-1/2" w 3,220.00

Federal, slant-front
Cherry, New England, c. 1800, four cockbeaded graduated drawers, flaring French feet, cutout skirt, interior with central prospect door in front of two concave carved drawers flanked by three valanced compartments and two drawers, old replaced brasses, old finish, imperfections, 42-3/4" h, 40-3/4" w 3,450.00

Cherry and bird's-eye maple, New England, c. 1815-25, case of four cockbeaded graduated drawers with bird's-eye maple veneer, interior of three drawers and five compartments, scrolled cutout base, replaced wooden pulls, old refinish, imperfections, 40-1/2" h, 38" w 2,415.00

Federal slant-front desk, cherry and bird's-eye maple, New England, c. 1815-25, old refinish, 40-1/2" h, 38" w, $2,415. (Photo courtesy of Skinner Auctioneers & Appraisers of Antiques & Fine Arts, Boston and Bolton, Mass.)

Mahogany and mahogany veneer, New England, c. 1790, four graduated veneered drawers with inlaid edge, inlaid bracket feet, interior with seven drawers and seven valanced compartments, old replaced brasses, old refinish, imperfections, 43-1/2" h, 39-3/4" w, 19" d 2,875.00

Hepplewhite, slant-front
> Birch, high bracket feet, dovetailed case, four dovetailed drawers, fitted interior with four drawers/eight pigeonholes, replaced apron and brasses, repairs at later hinges, 42-3/4" h, 39-3/4" w, 19-1/2" d 1,320.00
>
> Cherry, dovetailed case, bracket feet, scalloped apron, banded inlay across base, four dovetailed drawers with line inlay, fitted interior with 10 drawers and door in curly maple veneer, replaced brasses, repairs, 46-1/4" h, 41" w, 19-3/4" d 1,650.00

Lady's
> Oak, drop-front over one drawer, cabriole legs, 40" h, 28" w, 16" d 302.50
>
> Oak, drop-front over one drawer over simple applied carvings, short gallery top, cabriole legs, 41" h, 27" w, 14" d 192.50

Lap, walnut, orig finish, Ohio, slant lid, velvet insert, smaller hinged door at front lifts to reveal 3 compartments, old floral decals on top, 3-1/4" h, 12-1/8" w, 8-3/4" d 82.50

Miniature
> Chippendale, slant-lid, three drawers, bracket base, 27" h 3,080.00
>
> Slant-front, two drawers, arched front and side skirt, brown paint, leather hinges, wear, loose top, loss to drawer edge and knob, 10" h, 7-5/8" w, 6-3/4" d 575.00

Painted, old red, pine, New England, 19th C., rectangular top above interior of 16 drawers and flaring shaped sides, pullout writing surface over case of three graduated drawers, tag notes used by "North Family, Mt. Lebanon, NY," imperfections, 48" h, 36" w, 19" d 5,750.00

Queen Anne, slant-front, maple, coastal southern New England, c. 1750-60, case of four graduated drawers, bracket feet, fishtail drop pendant, interior prospect door with two concave arched panels flanked by five shaped compartments above flanking short drawers and blocked drawer, old replaced brasses, old refinish, minor imperfections, 39-1/4" h, 17" w, 35" l 6,900.00

Rolltop, mahogany, C roll, single pedestal, 45" h, 42" w, 32" d 330.00

Schoolmaster's
> Desk on frame, poplar, orig red wash, stretcher base, turned legs, one drawer, slant-lid top, 10 interior pigeonholes, dovetailed gallery, wobbly base, 47-1/2" h, 39" w, 26-1/2" d 660.00
>
> Fall-front with breadboard ends, lid supported by two slides that flank a drawer in the desk's apron, fitted interior, turned legs with ball feet, later red paint, worn, 37-1/2" h, 37-1/2" w, 22" d 850.00
>
> Slant-front with lift lid, painted black over earlier light blue, softwood, one drawer in skirt, tapered square legs, interior in old red paint with three tiers of drawers with blue drawer fronts and orange surrounds, paint wear, 36" h, 31-3/8" w, 21-3/4" d 750.00

Desk in old red paint, New England, 19th C., 48" h, 36" w, $5,750. (Photo courtesy of Skinner Auctioneers & Appraisers of Antiques & Fine Arts, Boston and Bolton, Mass.)

Stand-up desk in old red stain, pine, New England, early 19th C., 44" h, 30" w, $1,380. (Photo courtesy of Skinner Auctioneers & Appraisers of Antiques & Fine Arts, Boston and Bolton, Mass.)

Slant-front

Cherry, rope-twist and ring-turned legs, mortised construction, four interior dovetailed drawers and hidden compartment, inlaid diamond-shaped escutcheon plate, refinished, replaced hinges, 35-1/2" h, 32-3/4" w, 23-3/4" d..................... 825.00

Cherry and curly maple, orig dark finish, turned legs, four drawers over slant lid, one drawer below, 12 interior drawers, gallery top with turned spindles, found near Zanesville, Ohio, minor veneer restoration, one leg cracked, 60-1/2" h, 41-3/4" w, 30" d 6,050.00

Grain-decor, yellow and cream color, one drawer, square tapering legs, simple gallery, 36" h, 20" w, 22" d 7,425.00

Walnut, slant-front over two paneled doors, compartmented interior, applied molded base, 43" h, 37" w, 17-1/2" d................................... 275.00

Tabletop, slant-lid, burl, chestnut bottom, old finish, dovetailed, repairs, 9-1/2" h, 21-1/2" w, 15-1/2" d.................................... 1,320.00

Tambour, mahogany, sliding doors over fold-over writing surface over three drawers, oval brass pulls, square tapering legs 5,500.00

Desks and Bookcases

(see Secretaries)

Display Cases

Background: General stores and other 19th-century businesses used display cases that are often sought by collectors today. Some advertise a product, while others are plain. The framework can be wood or metal.

Glass with tin edges and bottom, sloping hinged lid, decorative tin scrollwork on lid corners, 4-1/4" h, 9-1/2" w, 7-1/4" d... 330.00

Softwood and glass, rectangular with sloping front, molded top, molded base on four feet, rear door hinges down, old red paint with gray panel on top and sides in stained finish, wear, 11" h, 21-1/4" w, 8-3/4" d... 230.00

Universal, countertop, wood and glass, decal on all four sides, refinished, glass shelves missing, 29-1/2" h, 20-1/2" sq.. 368.50

Zeno Gum, countertop, glass and oak, slant front, mirrored back door with spool-turned trim, shaped bonnet pressed "Zeno" in wood, mirror silvering worn, cond. 9.25, 17" h, 10" w, 8" d...................................... 907.50

Document Boxes

Background: Eighteenth-century desks typically had a small vertical drawer for storing important papers. This form evolved into a small box used for the same purpose. Wood and tin were the two primary types of boxes used, and both were often decorated.

Collecting Hint: The market for decorated boxes has exploded in recent years, with painted-wood examples in elaborate decorations bringing high prices.

Basswood, mustard and red decor on finger-swirled vinegar background, orig brass bail on lid, age crack on lid, minor wear, 6" h, 15" w, 17-1/2" d 990.00

Decorated

Orig black over red to simulate rosewood, gold and black line details on borders, pine, dovetailed, brass hinges, internal lock, minor wear, 7" h, 11-5/8" w, 6-1/2" d 302.50

Orig floral decor on a green ground, yellow and black striping, poplar, dovetailed with molded base and lid, till, lock with key, wear and fading, age cracks in till, 6-3/4" h, 16" w, 8-1/4" d 687.50

Floral panels on front and lid, sponge-decor ends, orig red, blue, yellow and black, pine, minor hairlines, 6-1/2" h, 13" w, 7-1/4" d 357.50

Flowers handpainted on sides, urn of flowers, bees and swags across domed lid, mustard ground an old repaint, red interior with lock, key missing, 4-5/8" h, 10-1/2" w, 7-1/2" d..................... 220.00

Foliage in red and green on top and front, old darkgreen over lighter-green ground, basswood, dovetailed, orig brass bail handle on top, iron hasp lock, wire hinges, 6-1/2" h, 18" w, 8-1/2" d 1,320.00

Geometric design in orig orange and black, red ground, poplar, minor edge wear, 6-1/2" h, 10-7/8" w, 6-1/2" d.. 165.00

Leaves and fruit in gold stencil, orig red paint, black border, pine, dovetailed, orig brass bail on lid, wrought-iron hasp lock, pencil sig "L.B. Lawrence 2-19-08" inside, 5-1/2" h, 12" w, 6" d 3,850.00

Grain-decorated

Old reddish-brown flame-grained repaint, poplar, dovetailed, brass lock with swinging keyhole cover having embossed eagle, pencil signature for "Geo. Quinby 1853," hasp missing, 7" h, 20-1/2" w, 10" d 247.50

Orig graining imitates rosewood, stenciled gold decor on lid, yellow striping, poplar, brass lock, orig brass bail on lid, 1910 pencil inscription in lid, 7" h, 19" w, 8-1/2" d 880.00

Mahogany and mahogany veneer, old finish, ebony line and trim inlay, beaded drawer front with ivory pulls, brass lion ring pulls on sides, diamond-shaped escutcheon inlay missing, edge chips, old replaced brass ball feet, English, 8-1/8" h, 11-1/2" w, 8" d 220.00

Mahogany veneer, string inlay, variegated diamonds, boxes and large star, inlay lifting in spots, 3-1/2" h, 12" w, 8" d 467.50

Pine, old refinishing, six-board, dovetailed, incised molding around top/bottom, interior lock missing its catch, wear, restorations, 10-1/2" h, 15-1/2" w, 10" d.................99.00

Poplar, molded base and trim around lid, nail construction, brass hinges, refinished, minor damage to interior lock, 6-1/2" h, 14" w, 7-5/8" d 247.50

Rosewood veneer, ebonized edges, brass escutcheon and lid medallion, edge damage, 8" l.................. 93.50

Dolls and Accessories

Background: Made from a wide variety of materials, dolls have always been favorite playthings of the young and the young at heart. Their enduring popularity convinced makers to design entire lines of miniature accessories, complete wardrobes, and a plethora of houses for them.

References: Maryanne Dolan, *The World of Dolls*, Krause Publications, 1998; Jan Foulke, *Insider's Guide to China Doll Collecting*, Hobby House Press, 1995; —, *14th Blue Book Dolls & Values*, Hobby House Press, 1999; Dawn Herlocher, *Doll Makers and Marks*, Antique Trader Books, 1999; R. Lane Herron, *Warman's Dolls*, Krause Publications, 1998; Constance King, *Collecting Dolls Reference and Price Guide*, Antique Collectors' Club, 1999; Patsy Moyer, *Doll Values, Antique to Modern*, 3rd ed., Collector Books, 1999; John Darcy Noble, *Rare & Lovely Dolls of Two Centuries*, Hobby House Press, 2000; Lydia Richter, *China, Parian, and Bisque German Dolls*, Hobby House Press, 1993.

Collectors' Clubs: Annalee Doll Society, P.O. Box 1137, Meredith, NH 03253, www.annalee.com; Delightful Doll Club, 4515 Rita St., La Mesa, CA 91941; Doll Collector International, P.O. Box 2761, Oshkosh, WI 54903; Doll Family Collectors' Club, 1301 Washington Blvd., Belpre, OH 45714; Madame Alexander Doll Club, P.O. Box 330, Mundelein, IL 60060.

Museums: Aunt Len's Doll House, New York, NY; Children's Museum, Detroit, MI; Doll Castle Doll Museum, Washington, NJ; Doll Museum, Newport, RI; Toy and Miniature Museum of Kansas City, MO; Gay Nineties Button and Doll Museum, Eureka Springs, AR; Margaret Woodbury Strong Museum, Rochester, NY; Mary Merritt Doll Museum, Douglassville, PA; Mary Miller Doll Museum, Brunswick, GA; Washington Dolls' House and Toy Museum, Washington, DC.

Specialty Auctions: McMasters Doll Auctions, P.O. Box 1755, Cambridge, OH 43725, phone 614-432-4419; Skinner, Inc., Bolton Gallery, 357 Main St., Bolton, MA 01740, phone 508-779-6241; Theriault's Auction, P.O. Box 151, Annapolis, MD 21404.

Miniature doll with pottery head and feet, cobalt-painted hair, 1-1/4" l, $75

DOLLS

Who's the winner in the Battle of the Sects? When it comes to Amish and Mennonite dolls, the Amish generally come out on top in both quantity offered and prices realized. Here are some examples from several well-known auction houses:

Amish doll

   8-3/4" h, hand sewn, stuffed cotton body and head, light-blue dress, light-blue apron, black bonnet, clothing machine-sewn, early 20th C., replaced bonnet ties, soiling, stains.........85.00

   11-1/2" h, hand sewn, stuffed cotton body and head, medium-brown cotton dress, black bonnet, early 20th C., wear, soiling.............120.00

   13-3/4" h, machine-sewn stuffed white oilcloth body, orange dress, white apron, black bonnet, light-blue knit booties, early 20th C., wear, soiling.......................110.00

   14-3/4" h, hand sewn, stuffed cotton and denim body, purple machine-sewn dress, white cotton apron and bonnet, early 20th C., soiling, minor stains.......................80.00

   16" h, coarsely woven white cloth body, light-blue long-sleeve dress and gray sleeveless dress, blue wool cape with buttons, black bonnet 192.50

   17-1/2" h, stuffed fabric, purple hand-sewn head and body, blue arms and legs, gray dress, white cap, Centre County, Pa., early 20th C..... 175.00

   19" h, stuffed fabric, blue body with white head, white arms and legs pinned with safety pins, blue dress, white apron and cap, Centre County, Pa., early to mid 20th C., soiling .95.00

Mennonite doll

   Female, white and brown polyester body, green long sleeve dress, 16" h...........................60.50

   Male, white fabric body, yellow cotton shirt, green pants, black suspenders, Jefferson County, Pa., early 20th C. 180.00

Doll Accessories

Doll Buggies

Wood, red paint, mustard stencil, wooden-spoke wheels with white line details, turned handle, seat upholstery replaced, minor wear, touchups, 27-1/4" h 247.50

Wood and metal, orig yellow and orange paint with blue, white and red striping, folding sunscreen with worn leatherized cloth covering, wooden spoke wheels with metal rims, 26" h, 34" l 330.00

Plate, tin, ABC

Boy and girl rolling hoops, minor rust, 2-7/8" dia 50.00

Man on horseback, minor rust, 2-5/8" dia 160.00

Star motif in center, 3" dia 60.00

Shoes, high-top, black leather, black glass buttons, fringed tassels, 4-1/2" h 130.00

Sled, doll-size, poinsettia in red and yellow, dark-green paint over earlier blue, yellow stripe, pine, curved metal runners, three small holes, minor paint wear, light rust, 17" l 550.00

Dolls

Advertising, Miss Flaked Rice, printed cloth, fitted with handmade cotton dress in blue print, wear, a few holes, 23-1/2" h 247.50

Bisque head

German, Ernest Heubach, jointed kid body, sleep eyes, open mouth, black wig, white cotton dress, straw hat, late 19th C., soiling, 21-1/2" h 250.00

Papier-mâché gentleman doll, 27" h, $3,125. (Photo courtesy of Cyr Auction Company, Gray, Maine)

German, Schoenau and Hoffmeister, ball-jointed composition body, stationary glass eyes, open mouth, black wig, red dress, black shoes, early 20th C., one finger restored, soiling, 26-1/2" h 140.00

German, Simon and Halbig, ball-jointed composition body, sleep eyes, open mouth, pierced ears, mkd "SH-719-12," fair wig, white cotton dress, black leather shoes, mid/late 19th C., cracked head, restoration, 22" h 200.00

German, Simon and Halbig, jointed composition body, sleep eyes, open mouth, pierced ears, mkd "SH1079, 3, DEP," fair wig, white cotton dress, black shoes, late 19th C., legs restored, 11-1/4" h 180.00

German, Adolf Wislizenus, ball-jointed composition body, sleep eyes, open mouth, pierced ears, fair wig, white cotton dress, late 19th C., 23" l 310.00

German, stuffed jointed kid leather body and legs, sleep eyes, open mouth, mkd "dep 154, 8-1/2," brown wig, leather arms, white cotton dress, knit stockings, late vinyl tie shoes, late 19th C., 20-1/2" l 400.00

Black, cloth, hand and machine stitched island lady, multi-color long dress, broad striped sash, embossed brass earrings, matching turban, flat woven hat beginning to unravel, 15-3/4" h 192.50

Papier-mâché gentleman, orig paint and clothes, 27" h 3,125.00

Papier-mâché head, excelsior-filled oilcloth-like body, stationary glass eyes, painted closed mouth, fair wig, composition arms, white cotton dress, leather button shoes, mid-19th C., hands damaged, lower legs partially detached, 31" h 150.00

Penny doll, molded composition head, carved wooden arms and legs, kid body, painted features, black hair, blue eyes, red shoes, white dress, neck and feet repaired, two loose limbs, 8-1/2" h 275.00

Shrunken apple head, black women, orig clothes, set of three 88.00

Stocking doll, black, stuffed cloth body, head with pearl buttons for eyes, stitched nose and mouth, dressed in red/white polka-dot bandana and green floral print dress with white shawl and apron, early/mid 20th C., soiling, 13-1/2" h 110.00

Tin head, German, stuffed cloth body, painted fair hair, blue eyes, bisque hands with chips on fingers, orig plaid cotton dress soiled, paint flakes, 14" h 70.00

Tin head, stuffed rag body, old worn repaint, one eye damaged, Amish-made dress, 19" h 192.50

Wax head, stuffed cloth body, glass eyes, fair wig, jointed composition arms and legs, blue high-top shoes, dress in early fabric, 10-1/2" h 200.00

Wooden, carved and turned, pegged and articulated limbs, crudely carved body with stained finish, painted head and facial features, old hand-stitched dress, undergarments and cloak, 13" h 385.00

Wood-jointed, Mason and Taylor, composition head with crudely molded features, painted eyes, molded hair painted brown, bottom of legs painted white with blue shoes, redressed, 11-1/2" h 500.00

Doll Furniture

Background: Rufus Bliss, of R. Bliss Manufacturing Co. in Pawtucket, R.I., was a well-known dolls' furniture maker. In addition to his painted tin furniture, he produced a popular line of "cottage furniture," which consisted of wooden bedroom furniture decorated with lithographed paper. Cast-iron dolls' house furniture worthy of note was manufactured by J.&E. Stevens Co. of Cromwell, Conn.

References: Nora Earnshaw, *Collecting Dolls' Houses and Miniatures*, Pincushion Press, 1993; Dian Fillner with Patty Cooper, *Furnished Dollhouses 1880s-1980s*, Schiffer Publishing, 2001; Dian Fillner and Patty Cooper, *Antique and Collectible Dollhouses and their Furnishings*, 1998; Herbert F. Schiffer and Peter B. Schiffer, *Miniature Antique Furniture: Doll House and Children's Furniture from the United States and Europe*, Schiffer Publishing, 1995; Margaret Towner, *Dollhouse Furniture*, Running Press, 1993.

Museums: Mineral Point Toy Museum, WI; Washington Dolls' House and Toy Museum, Washington, DC.

Bed

    Rope, cannonball, cherry, refinished, scalloped headboard, arched footboard, 22" l, 13-3/4" w 192.50

    Rope, pine, spool-turned posts, turned footboard, peaked headboard, 15-1/4" h, 14-1/2" w, 21-1/2" l 77.00

Chair, four-spindle, plank seat, old green paint with strawberries and foliage on seat and crest, wear, some edge damage, 9-1/4" h............................. 605.00

Chest of drawers with mirror top, cast iron, three drawers, overall pierced diamond and hearts design, painted yellow, red and gray, one mirror bracket broken, 6-3/8" h, 4-3/4" w....................................... 360.00

Doll-size twig rocking chair in old blue paint, 6-1/4" h, $175.

Cradle

    Birch, northern New England, c. 1820, two-panel hood, pieced scrolled dovetailed cradle with canted sides, cornice with inlaid oval panel, old finish, 11-1/2" h, 21" l, 8" w 2,185.00

    Painted orange, dark-green trim and decor, curved sides and headboard, wear, 11-1/4" h, 14" w, 18" l 345.00

    Softwood, straight dovetailed sides, arched foot and headboard, broad curved rockers with tapered rounded ends, wear, one rocker tip broken off, 8-1/2" h, 17-1/4" l... 110.00

Dresser, tramp art, three drawers, old white repaint, gold trim, worn, age cracks, 21-1/2" h, 15-1/2" w, 8-3/4" d 357.50

Dry sink, old brown over tan comb-graining, pine, cut bracket feet, two doors in base, surface-mounted iron hinges, white porcelain pulls, small drawer at left below flat work surface, trim molding across backsplash, 13-1/4" h, 13-1/2" w, 8" d 825.00

Doll Houses

Background: Early doll houses were reserved for the wealthy and were designed primarily as display cabinets for collections of valuable miniatures rather than as playthings for children. The first American doll houses were made in the late 18th century, but it wasn't until 1860, with the development of chromolithography, that they were mass-produced.

References: Nora Earnshaw, *Collecting Dolls' Houses and Miniatures*, Pincushion Press, 1993; Dian Fillner with Patty Cooper, *Furnished Dollhouses 1880s-1980s*, Schiffer Publishing, 2001; Dian Fillner and Patty Cooper, *Antique and Collectible Dollhouses and their Furnishings*, 1998; Constance Eileen King, *Dolls and Dolls' Houses*, Hamlyn, 1989.

Museums: Mineral Point Toy Museum, WI; Washington Dolls' House and Toy Museum, Washington, DC.

Colonial Revival style, white siding, porch with columns, mansard roof with wooden shingles in old black paint, two brick painted chimneys, windows trimmed in red, removable sides reveal rooms, roof removes to reveal attic with stairs, 40" h, 40" w, 30" d 330.00

Wooden, two-story brick design, printed paper covering imitating red brick and gray slate, glass windows, rag curtains, gray interior, open at back and roof, two chimneys, paper worn, 25-1/4" h, 26" w, 14" d............385.00

Doorstops

Background: Popular during the late 19th century, doorstops could be either flat-backed or three-dimensional. American toy manufacturer Hubley, well-known its for cast-iron vehicles, also carved out a niche producing metal doorstops.

Reference: Jeanne Bertoia, *Doorstops*, Collector Books, 1985 (1996 value update).

Collectors' Club: Doorstop Collectors of America, 2413 Madison Ave., Vineland, NJ 08630.

Reproduction Alert: Reproductions abound as prices for original examples continue to escalate.

Note: All listings are cast iron.

Bulldog, Hubley, facing right, orig brown/white body, black/red facial features paint wear, 9-3/4" h,
9" l 160.00

Cat, reclining
    Full-bodied, mkd Hubley, orig gray paint with polychrome, wear, light rust, 11" l 275.00
    Half body, gold repaint, wear, 3-3/4" h,
    7-1/2" w 275.00
    Mkd Hubley, old white paint, pink ears, green and black eyes, wear, 5-3/4" h, 10-1/2" w 412.50

Cat, sitting
    Full-bodied, worn orig paint, unmarked Hubley,
    8-1/2" h 302.50
    Orig paint, unmkd, 12-1/2" h 330.00

Cat, standing, arched back, raised tail, full-bodied worn black paint, green eyes, 10-5/8" h, 7-1/2" l 330.00

Gnome warrior, orig paint, mkd 7795, Bradley & Hubbard, 13-1/4" h 550.00

Lion, recumbent, full-bodied, glass eyes,
7-1/2" l 517.50

Mammy, Hubley, full-figure, hands on hips, red polka-dot bandana, black dress, white apron, paint loss, rust,
12" h 1,265.00

Owl, orig paint, mkd 7797, Bradley & Hubbard,
16" h 1,100.00

Punch, old green repaint, 12-1/2" h 82.50

Punch and Judy cast-iron doorstop, original paint, 12" h, $1,725. (Photo courtesy of Skinner Auctioneers & Appraisers of Antiques & Fine Arts, Boston and Bolton, Mass.)

Punch and Judy, red, blue, black and white paint, 19th C., paint loss, 12" h 1,725.00

Rabbit, sitting
    Full-bodied, mkd "The Kramer Bros Fdy Co., Dayton, OH," old white repaint, light rust,
    10-1/4" h 357.50
    Hubley, unpainted, 11-1/2" h 190.00

Rooster, cast iron, full bodied, traces of polychrome paint, 6-1/2" h 247.50

Spaniel, standing, painted black with red collar, white, brown and black eyes, minor wear, 11" h,
6-5/8" l 350.00

Squirrel, sitting upright on log with nut in front paws, old gray repaint, traces of yellow, 11-1/2" h 907.50

Stagecoach with two horses, mkd Hubley, orig polychrome paint, 5-3/4" h, 11" w 110.00

Dough Boxes

Background: Dough boxes are simple wooden troughs for storing rising bread dough. From the 18th and 19th centuries, they generally had canted sides and an overhanging lid. Examples on stands had splayed legs, with the added height allowing the top of the box to be used as a work surface.

No stand
    Painted, blue-green, cover with carved handle, 10" h, 23" w, 14" d 275.00
    Painted, old dark-green repaint over earlier light-green, chamfered edge on base, tapered sides, wooden handles, shaped bar handle on lid, glued repairs on ends, 7" h, 23" w, 11-1/2" d 302.50
    Painted, old mustard over earlier red, poplar and pine, one top cleat repositioned, some side molding missing, Pa. origin, 12-1/2" h, 34" w,
    16-1/4" d 330.00
    Red wash, softwood, open top, applied notched utensil brackets across top and bottom of back side, side with small suppressed heart-shaped cutout handles, dovetailed, wear, 8-3/8" h, 17-1/2" w, 10-1/4" d 475.00

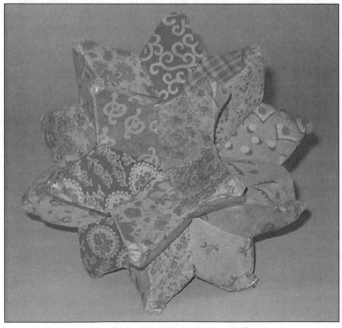

Fabric doorstop, weighted center, 6" h, $150.

Dough box on stand, drawer in base, old brown paint over red wash, Lancaster County, Pennsylvania, $3,500.

Vinegar-grained, red and black, 6" h, 16" w, 10" d 165.00

Walnut, dark patina, beveled edge on baseboard, tapering sides, double handles, one-board top, 10" h, 23-1/2" w, 12-1/2" d 385.00

On stand

Poplar and pine, refinished, high turned legs, dovetailed bin, top with breadboard ends, pieced restoration, 30" h, 55" w, 29-1/2" d 770.00

Sheraton, country style, poplar, dark refinishing, ring-turned splayed legs, beveled molding beneath dovetailed bin, scrubbed interior, two-board top, age crack, 30" h, 38-3/4" w, 20" d 385.00

Softwood, dovetailed case, splayed-leg base, cutout apron, 29-1/2" h, 40-1/2" w, 18" d 550.00

Dower Chests

Background: Also known as marriage chests or hope chests, dower chests were used to store linens and other similar articles taken by the bride to her new home. They were quite common in rural Pennsylvania and generally date to 1760-1830. Usually made of pine or poplar by local carpenters, they were decorated by self-taught artists who incorporated designs and symbols of significance to the owners.

Attributed to Christian Selzer (1789-1831), Lebanon County, Pa., late 18th C., white pine top with molded edge and strap hinges, heavy molded base and bracket feet, dovetailed pine case, front shows three arched floral-painted panels on white ground outlined in red containing a blue vase with red, blue and yellow flowers with brown leaves, orig paint, height loss, other imperfections, 23" h, 51-1/2" w, 22-1/4" d........................ 6,325.00

Buildings, orig decor includes yellow, white and tan buildings on lid with trees in background, white, red, salmon and yellow flowers and foliage around sides of

Dower chest attributed to Christian Selzer (1789-1831), Lebanon County, Pennsylvania, 23" h, 51-1/2" w, $6,325. (Photo courtesy of Skinner Auctioneers & Appraisers of Antiques & Fine Arts, Boston and Bolton, Mass.)

lid and base, bentwood, laced seams, edge wear, 8" h, 18" w, 12" d 2,200.00

Courting couple on lid, man in red coat and stockings, woman in white dress with orange bodice and bustle, sides with white and red tulips with yellow and green, edge loss on sides of lid, seams relaced with leather, overlapping seams on base and lid, 6-3/8" h, 18" l.. 1,100.00

Courting couple and landscape with trees on top, orig salmon ground (faded from orig orange that shows under overlap of lid), blue borders, yellow and white stripes, base with white, green and blue flowers, German inscription, bentwood, laced seams, wear, edge damage, base missing laces and bottom, oval, 7" h, 18-3/4" w, 12-1/4" d.. 797.50

Floral decor, orig paint with brown bands and black reserves, polychrome floral decor on sides, full-length figure of woman on lid, pine, oval bentwood with laced seams, wear and damage, minor age cracks, insect damage, 17-1/2" l.. 1,320.00

Floral decor, orig red, yellow and orange flowers, salmon ground, laced seams, wooden pegs, lid darkened, few nails added, 4-1/2" h, 12-1/4" w, 7-1/2" d 605.00

Man with flowers, orig red paint, polychrome tulips on sides, white lid with full-length figure of man flanked by flowers and bordered by German inscription, pine, wear and damage, reinforcing staves added to inside of base, relaced seams, 17-1/2" l 1,045.00

Rose on lid, tulips around sides of lid and base, old blue repaint, bentwood, laced seams, 4-3/4" h, 12" w, 7-3/8" d 550.00

Tulips, orig decor in white, red and orange, natural ground, pine, bentwood with laced seams, wear, colors faded, some damage, age cracks, 15-1/4" l... 935.00

Dry Sinks

Background: Made almost exclusively during the 19th century, dry sinks consist of a shallow well over a low closed cupboard. Variations include examples with high backs and shelves, and some with cupboard tops. The wells were usually lined with zinc.

Dry sink in old apple-green paint, $2,000; stoneware $200 to $300 each.

Reproduction Alert: Dry sinks are among the most commonly faked and altered pieces of country furniture. Reproductions also exist, but most are obvious.

Cupboard-top, two-pc, decor, old dark-brown paint, brown feathering over yellow on raised door panels, poplar and chestnut, bracket feet, top with two raised-panel doors, base with one silver drawer over two raised-panel doors, well lining missing, two pieced repairs, attributed to Ohio Amish, 68" h, 44-1/2" w, top 11-1/2" d, base 19-1/4" d.............................. 2,200.00

High-back
    Chestnut, silver drawer and two paneled doors, top with three shallow open compartments and shaped back, 50" h, 42" w, 16" d................. 605.00
    Grain-decor, worn combed decor, poplar and pine, high bracket feet, two-door base with inset panels and beaded sides, stepback top with shaped side panels, two nailed drawers flank open compartment at center, 50-1/2" h, 48" w, 18-3/4" d................................ 2,090.00
    Painted, old gray, walnut and ash, scalloped front feet and end panels, two paneled doors in base, shaped scallops on either end of the well and stepback top, three upper drawers below shelf, scalloped crest, chips on drawer lips, glued repair, 68" h, 48" w, 17-3/4" d............................ 5,775.00

Painted
    Black paint, traces of dark-blue and red on backsplash, walnut, one-board top and sides with cutout feet, two doors in base with double raised panels flanking dovetailed drawer over stationary raised panel, cracked drawer front, 33" h, 54-1/4" w, 22-1/4" d................................. 3,300.00
    Orig dark brown, one-board ends, scalloped aprons, two drawers over two doors with inset panels, sur-

face wear, one foot ended out, found in Ohio, 33-1/2" h, 42" w, 17-1/2" d.......................... 990.00
    Old red, pine, New England, early 19th C., rectangular well, projecting splashboard, two doors, cutout feet, imperfections, 30" h, 42" w, 17-1/2" d 632.50
    Old red, pine and poplar, turned feet, two paneled doors in base, one dovetailed silver drawer at left, well at right with lift lid, backsplash with scalloped ends, some paint touchup, door pulls and turnbuckles replaced, minor repair to 1 foot, 36-1/2" h, 49" w, 21-1/2" d 1,210.00
    Old red, walnut and poplar, cut bracket feet, two paneled doors, silver drawer beside well, worn finish, back foot chipped, 32-1/2" h, 43" w, 18-3/4" d... 1,760.00
    Red, primitive, square legs, small size, 33" h 330.00
    Traces of early red, softwood, scalloped backboard, small drawer centered over two paneled doors, one-board ends with bootjack cutouts, scrubbed surface, 42-1/2" h, 48-5/8" w, 19-3/4" d......................850.00
    Yellow milk paint, two doors, zinc-lined top, 30-1/2" h, 37" w, 19-1/2" d 440.00

Walnut and maple, refinished, two doors with inset panels, silver drawer with rounded front in upper right, low shaped backboard, short tapered feet, 34" h, 54-1/4" w, 20" d 825.00

Drying Racks

Background: Most commonly used to dry herbs or clothes, these racks were utilitarian and generally of plain construction, often little more than horizontal bars on vertical supports. Some were painted, but they were generally not decorated.

Herb drying rack, folding, pine, white finish, two-section, mortised, age cracks, glued repair, 38" h, 58-1/2" w... 60.50

Painted, late cream-colored, softwood, two-sections with two vertical posts connected by three horizontal splats, each section 41-3/4" h, 23-1/8" w.......... 180.00

Pine, old patina, two sections, each with three bars, 30" h, 23" w 192.50

Pine, old reddish-brown finish, arched and mortised shoe feet, two cross pieces, 30-1/4" h, 26" w 330.00

Pine, vertical posts connected by three horizontal splats mortised into posts, rectangular plank feet, natural unfinished wood, 66" h, 43-3/8" w, feet 13-1/2" d 275.00

Poplar, dry white finish, three-section, replaced hinges, 60" h, 95" w... 55.00

Dye Cabinets

Background: From the countertops of country stores, these cabinets have divided interiors that held

Diamond Dyes cabinet, oak with lithographed tin panel, $825.

packages of dye. Varieties with wooden cabinets and lithographed-tin inserts are the most valuable.

Collecting Hint: Oak examples are the most common. Walnut is seen less often and is more valuable.

Diamond Dyes

"Best Results, Diamond Dyes for Dyeing or Tinting, The Blue Package is for Silk or Wool Only..., Easy to Use, Diamond Dyes for Dyeing or Tinting, The White Package Dyes or Tints Any Goods...," white diamond logo on doors, red/yellow diamond logo on side, tin, two doors, holder on side, dents, scratches, rust, 15-5/8" h, 18-1/2" w........... 121.00

Children at play with house in background, embossed litho tin, oak cabinet, some rust on panel, 24-5/8" h, 15-1/4" w, 8-7/8" d........... 825.00

"The Diamond Dyes, Domestic Fancy Dying," child in diamond-shaped frame surrounded by flowers and feathers, wooden with litho tin panel, cond. 8+, 20-1/4" h, 16-1/2" w, 9-1/4" d............. 3,630.00

"Diamond Dyes, Easy to Use, Perfect Results," red and white text on dark ground, litho tin, cond. 8+, 16" h, 18-1/2" w, 6-1/2" d............................. 88.00

"Diamond Dyes, The Standard Package Dyes of the World," five children playing near steps, house in background, blue and yellow text, wooden with litho tin panel, opens from front and back, cond. G, 24-5/8" h, 14-3/4" w, 8-1/8" d................... 1,072.50

"It's Easy To Dye With Diamond Dyes," washer woman motif, wooden with litho tin panel, refinished case, cond. 7, 29-3/4" h, 22-1/4" w, 9-3/4" d.. 1,375.00

"It's Easy to Dye With Diamond Dyes," woman and girl with ribbon, other children with ball, wooden with litho tin panel, chips, scratches, worn finish, 30" h, 23" w, 10" d 880.00

Rainbow Dyes, "Rainbow Dyes Beautifully Brilliant, One Dye For All Fabrics," countertop model, wood, paper decals, front edge of base missing, scratches, stains, orig contents, 16-3/4" h, 6" w, 12-1/2" d............ 825.00

Rit

"Never say 'dye' say Rit" on top, front shows woman with product and dyed garment over "Cake or Flake 10¢," round medallions of Rit/Flaked Rit boxes, woodgrain ground, tin, peaked top, six drawers in back, labels loose, three handles missing, minor stains, 16-1/4" h, 10" w 148.50

"New Improved Rit, Guaranteed To Fast Dye Or Tint, Washes as it Dyes," blue and yellow text, woodgrain ground, slant-front, three drawers in back, cond. G, 8-1/4" h, 11-1/4" w, 14" d 88.00

Tintex, "Tints and Dyes Anything Any Color, Tintex, Tints As You Rinse," shows woman dying blouse, color chips behind her and packages of product, countertop display, litho tin, 35 compartments in back, cond. 8+, 23-3/8" h, 21-3/4" w, 7-1/2" d 550.00

Egg-Related

Background: More than 1,000 patents were awarded for items designed to beat eggs, and most of them were issued prior to the 1900s.

Reference: Don Thornton, *Beat This: The Eggbeater Chronicles*, Off Beat Books, 1994.

Collectors' Club: Eggcup Collectors' Corner, 67 Stevens Ave., Old Bridge, NJ 08857.

Basket, wire
    5" h (excluding handle), squat form 30.00
    6-1/2" h (excluding handles), squat shape, fold-down top 45.00
    7-1/2" h (excluding handles), pear shape 110.00
Carrier, wooden
    One dozen, Star, missing lid 27.50
    Two dozen, slat construction, wire latch and wire spring holder.. 33.00
    Three dozen, Badger, unpainted, restoration, 12" sq 38.50
    "J.J. Bryan, Springfield, Ore.," black letters, mustard paint, made by Quincy Egg Carrier Co., worn, minor damage, lid missing............................ 95.00
Sign, painted wood
    "Eggs," black letters with yellow trim on white ground, 6" h, 30" w 275.00

Egg crate in old blue paint, "C.L. Major & Co., The Leaders, Vicksburg, Mich.," $250.

    "Eggs For Sale," pewter-blue letters, white ground, sawtooth ends, pine, 10" h, 24" w 265.00
    "Fresh Eggs," dangling wooden eggs, wear, 8-1/4" h, 18" w.. 150.00

Family record, ink and watercolor on paper, Decost family, 13" x 15-3/4", $2,300. (Photo courtesy of Skinner Auctioneers & Appraisers of Antiques & Fine Arts, Boston and Bolton, Mass.)

Family Registers and Records

Background: During the 19th century, genealogy records were sometimes created in the form of decorative charts or needlework pictures.

Ink and watercolor on paper, Decost family, floral decor, heart at top center, eight circles with other information, grained frame, creases, toning, 13" h, 15-3/4" w 2,300.00

Needlework

"A Family Registry," alphabet, family names and dates, 1824 last date, vining floral border, moss green, cream, brown and blue, on homespun, framed, minor stains, 18" h, 19-1/4" w 385.00

"Wrought by Betsey J. Brown 1826," chart of family names and dates above pictorial panel of house with trees and outbuilding, geometric floral border, stains, 17" h, 17-1/4" w 2,415.00

"Wrought by Julia Stoddard Aged Eleven Years AD 1828," family record, alphabets and family of Ebenezer Stoddard and Lydia Williams, cross stitch with border of vining flowers and flower basket, holes, light stains, 21-1/2" h, 18-1/4" w 1,540.00

Watercolor on paper, Stevens/Smith family, Dover, N.H., 1823-29, vining floral decor, heart at top center, seven circles with other information, creases, tears, stains, 13-1/2" h, 16-1/2" w 1,610.00

Farm-Related

Background: The words "farm" and "country" are synonymous. This category includes a selection of items related to farm life.

Reference: C. H. Wendel, *Encyclopedia of American Farm Implements & Antiques*, Krause Publications, 1997.

Collectors' Clubs: Farm Machinery Advertising Collectors, 10108 Tamarack Dr., Vienna, VA 22182; The Feedsack Club, 25 S. Starr Ave., Apt. 16, Pittsburgh, PA 15202-3424; International Harvester Collectibles, 310 Busse Hwy., Suite 250, Park Ridge, IL 60068-3251.

Museum: Landis Valley Farm Museum, Lancaster, PA.

Advertising

Flour sack, printed paper, "Harvest Queen Improved Roller Flour, Red Mills," shows woman in bonnet, Centre Hill, Pa., framed, soiled, stains, 20" h, 14" w 50.00

Flour sack, printed paper, "Snow Flake, Pine Creek Mills, 48 lbs.," shows snow scene of a mill, framed, soiled, stains, 20" h, 14" w 80.00

Sign, paper, "Buckeye, Our New Low Down Drills, They Are Endorsed And Demanded," central scene of man driving two-horse team pulling drill, four smaller images of different horse-drawn equipment, 30" h, 21-1/4" w 715.00

Sign, paper, "Compliments of Ohio Rake Co., Dayton, O.," Statue of Liberty in center, images of ship at sea, Civil War battle, farmer using horse-drawn rake, framed, cond. 8+, 28-1/2" h, 34-1/2" w 2,310.00

Sign, paper, "Deere Vehicles Are All Right," shows stag pulling buckboard, orig frame, light stains, small pinhole spots of litho loss, 23-1/2" h, 31-1/2" w 1,771.00

Bridal rosette, heart shape 38.50

Cider press, oak and other hardwoods, old refinish, mortised and pegged, base with four legs, threaded wooden shaft missing its handle, 44" h, 26" w, 15" d 220.00

Feed chest, smoke-decor on off-white ground with black smoke, slant-lid, three interior compartments, turned legs with ball feet, wear, mouse holes, 35-1/2" h, 53-1/4" w, 24" d... 375.00

Grain bin

Blue paint, New England, 19th C., overhanging lift top, cutout feet, 30-1/2" h, 31-1/4" w, 21" d............977.50

Brown orig paint, poplar, wide boards, shaped bracket base, applied molding, slant front, large iron hinges, feet cracked, 39" h, 49-1/2" w, 22" d 412.50

Hatchel

Folk-decorated, hardwood, scratch-carved compass designs highlighted in old red and black, some tooth loss to round nest of deteriorating spikes, 30" l 330.00

Wood and iron, round hole at each end with sheet-iron diamond-shape sheaths, center of base sheathed with tin having "1814" and punched floral design on one side and "Abr Brenm" on other, top side with 11 rows of steel spikes, wooden cover with slightly flared sides, 4-3/8" h, 12-1/2" l, 4-3/4" d 55.00

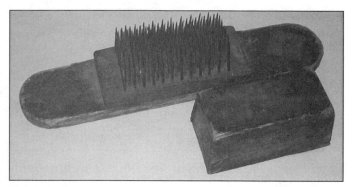

Hatchel with cover, original green paint, 18" l, $180.

Hay fork, wooden, four-prong, three wooden prongs on front with fourth mounted on handle with iron bracket, 84" l 60.00

Incubator, salesman's sample, "Successful, Des Moines Incubator Co.," wooden, orig decals, turned legs, glass doors, brass trim, cond. 8+, 12-1/2" h, 15-1/2" w, 11-1/2" d 2,640.00

Milking stool, wooden, crescent-shaped seat, three round splayed stake legs, primitive, refinished, 8" h, 17" w, 7" d 35.00

Sleigh bells, set of six, graduated, on leather hame strap, 24" l 137.50

Firearms & Related

Background: The 15th-century Matchlock Arquebus was the forerunner of the modern firearm. The Germans refined the wheelock firing mechanism during the 16th and 17th centuries. English settlers arrived in America with the smoothbore musket; German settlers had rifled arms. Both used the new flintlock firing mechanism.

A major advance was achieved when Whitney introduced interchangeable parts into the manufacturing of rifles. Continued refinements in firearms continued in the 19th century. The percussion ignition system was developed by the 1840s. Minie, a French military officer, produced a viable projectile. By the end of the 19th century cartridge weapons dominated the field.

References: Robert W.D. Ball, *Springfield Armory Shoulder Weapons 1795-1968*, Antique Trader Books, 1997; Ralf Coykendall Jr., *Coykendall's Complete Guide to Sporting Collectibles*, Wallace-Homestead, 1996; Jim Dresslar, *Folk Art of Early America: The Engraved Powder Horn*, Dresslar Publishing, 1996; Norman Flayderman, *Flayderman's Guide to Antique American Firearms and their Values*, 7th ed., Krause Publications, 1998; Herbert G. Houze, *Colt Rifles and Muskets From 1847-1870*, Krause Publications, 1996; John Ogle, *Colt Memorabilia Price Guide*, Krause Publications, 1998; Nick Stroebel, *Old Gunsights 1850-1965*, Krause Publications, 1999.

Periodicals: *Gun List*, 700 E. State St., Iola, WI 54990; *Historic Weapons & Relics*, 2650 Palmyra Rd., Palmyra, TN 37142; *Military Trader*, P.O. Box 1050, Dubuque, IA 52004.

Collectors' Clubs: American Society of Military History, Los Angeles Patriotic Hall, 1816 S. Figuerora, Los Angeles, CA 90015; Winchester Arms Collectors Assoc., P.O. Box 6754, Great Falls, MT 59406.

Museums: Battlefield Military Museum, Gettysburg, PA; Fort Ticonderoga Museum, Ticonderoga, NY; Museum of Weapons & Early American History, Saint Augustine, FL 32084; National Firearms Museum, Washington, DC; Remington Gun Museum, Ilion, NY; Springfield Armory National Historic Site, Springfield, MA.

Reproduction Alert: Reproduction and fake powder horns are plentiful.

Specialty Auctions: Sanford Alderfer Auction Co., 501 Fairgrounds Rd., Hatfield, PA 19440, phone 215-393-3000, www.alderfercompany.com; James D. Julia, Inc., P.O. Box 830, Fairfield, ME 04937, phone 207-453-7125.

Advertising
  DuPont Black Sporting Powders poster, paper, 1909, winter scene with two children hunting, cond. 8-, 20-1/4" h, 14-1/2" w 687.50
  DuPont Sporting Powders poster, paper, 1919, winter scene with old man and boy on log by guns, dog listening, metal strips intact, cond. 8-, 25-3/8" h, 17" w 935.00

Flask, brass, pear-shape, American eagle with wings partially spread on both sides, brass and steel spring mechanism at top, 4-3/8" l, 2" w 130.00

Long rifle, flintlock
  "M. Fordney" (Melchior Fordney, Lancaster, Pa.), Kentucky rifle, raise-carved walnut stock in old refinish, nine silver and brass inlays, carvings include C scrolls on buttstock and around cheek piece and tang, checkered wrist and relief scrolling ahead of lock and side plate, reconversion to flint, patch box and trigger guard replaced, shortened slightly, 55-1/2" l 6,050.00
  "A. Schweitzer" (Abraham Schweitzer, Lancaster and Chambersburg, Pa.), curly maple in old dark finish,

"H.&W.T. Carey, Xenia, O." muzzleloader, octagonal barrel, old repairs, 45-3/4" l, $210.

raise-carvings include C scrolls behind the cheek piece and detailing around the tang, engraved horse-head patch box with silver star and thumb piece inlay, Dreppert lock an old replacement, stock professionally ended out, 47-3/4" octagon to round smooth bore barrel, 63" l 8,525.00

"D. Sheets," mark uncertain, curly maple in varnished-over old dark finish, simple raise carving around cheek piece and comb, brass hardware with bird's-head patch box, engraved eagle cheek piece inlay, old repair at tang, lock is reconverted, 62-3/4" l 3,025.00

Unsigned, curly maple in old dark finish and over-varnish, full stock, brass hardware including four-pc patch box, Golcher lock with double-throated hammer, some characteristics similar to William or Peter Young, 39-1/4" octagon barrel, 54-1/2" l 2,640.00

Unsigned, curly maple with good figure, brass hardware, engraved and pierced patch box, engraved silver cheek piece inlay and oval thumb piece, expertly restocked using old parts, brass repair near lock, with a few accessories, 56-1/2" l 1,430.00

Long rifle, percussion, "J. Yeager" in block stamping, curly maple with good figure and patina, brass hardware including engraved patch box and toe plate signed "S. McClain," eagle inlay over cheek piece, some wear ahead of lock, 51-1/4" l 1,320.00

Pistol, flintlock, Johnson, model of 1836, 8-1/2" barrel 2,420.00

Pistol, pepperbox, Remington-Elliot, .32 caliber, rubber grips, 5" l 192.50

Pistol, percussion
Aston model 1842, 8-1/2" barrel 935.00
Lock with abbreviated stamp for Middletown, Conn., and dated 1847, walnut stock with age cracks, brass hardware, 8-1/2" round barrel, probably by Aston or Johnson, missing ramrod attachment, 14" l 440.00

Powder flask
Cow horn, incised "Lancaster" and with landscape scene, 17-1/2" l.. 315.00
Deer head, fox and oak leaf pattern, Hawksley, brass top, three-slot charger, spring not working, 7-3/4" h 120.00
Eagle, embossed, copper, 3-1/2" h................. 115.00
Fluted pattern, American Flask & Cap Co., brass, two plugs on bottom, 4-1/2" h.................... 375.00
Hanging Game pattern, copper 420.00
Ivy pattern, J.M. Hawksley, minor corrosion, dent, 9" h, 4-1/2" w 120.00
Lyre pattern, French, copper and brass, 5-1/2" h, 2-1/2" w 420.00

Powder horn
Cow horn, screw tip, curved, wooden butt, stopper missing, crack, 11" l 325.00
Horn, wooden butt, cast brass knob, stopper and U-shaped piece of horn missing, 11" l 110.00

Revolver
Colt new Line 32, serial #13010, 6" l 165.00
Marlin XX Standard 1873, .22 caliber, brass frame, 6-3/4" l 82.50

Remington-Beals Navy, .36 caliber, hairline on grip, 13-1/2" l 632.50

Rifle
Remington Model 1841, .58-caliber, 33" barrel 2,090.00
Remington Zouve, Model of 1863, .58-caliber, with bayonet/sheath, 33" barrel 3,300.00
Springfield Model 1861, .58-caliber, with bayonet, 40" barrel 3,630.00

Firefighting

Background: Volunteer fire companies have played a vital role in the protection and social growth of many towns and rural areas. Paid professional firemen usually are found only in large metropolitan areas.

References: Andrew G. Gurka, *Hot Stuff! Firefighting Collectibles*, L-W Book Sales, 1994; James Piatti, *Firehouse Memorabilia*, Avon Books, 1994.

Periodicals: *Fire Apparatus Journal*, P.O. Box 141295, Staten Island, NY 10314, http://fireapparatusjournal.com; *Vintage Vehicle & Fire Engine Magazine*, Rt. 3, Box 425, Jasper, FL 32052, www.vintagevehicle.com/MASTOF97.htm.

Collectors' Clubs: Antique Fire Apparatus Club of America, 5420 S. Kedvale Ave., Chicago, IL 60632; Fire Collectors Club, P.O. Box 992, Milwaukee, WI 53201; Fire Mark Circle of the Americas, 2859 Marlin Dr., Chamblee, GA 30341; Great Lakes International Antique Fire Apparatus Assoc., P.O. Box 2519, Detroit, MI 48231.

Museums: American Museum of Fire Fighting, Hudson, NY, www.firemumsumnetwork.org; Fire

Fire buckets painted "Semper Paratus L.T. Jackson," 15-1/2" h, pair, $7,475. (Photo courtesy of Skinner Auctioneers & Appraisers of Antiques & Fine Arts, Boston and Bolton, Mass.)

Museum of Maryland, Lutherville, MD; Hall of Flame, Phoenix, AZ, www.halloflame.org; New England Fire & History Museum, Brewster, MA; New York City Fire Museum, NY, www.nyfd.com/museum.htlm; Smokey's Fire Museum, Chamblee, GA.

Bucket, leather, painted
    Black ground, bell-shaped, 9" h 385.00
    Black ground with red letters, 12" h 330.00
    "Constitution" banner in black, red and gold, old yellow ground, black trim, brass stud trim, 8-1/2" h 385.00
    "Protector 17" (?) in gilt and black lettering, red ground, gilt and black bands, lettering obscured, handle replaced, 13-3/4" h 373.75
    "Semper Paratus L.T. Jackson" in gilt in a leafy scrolled decor black cartouche, red ground, black bands, 15-1/2" h, pr 7,475.00
Fire hose box, painted wood, from early fire hose wagon, long rectangular box with hinged lid, chamfered front panel with painted scene of a ship near a rocky shore, top and sides painted red with yellow decor trim, 19th C., paint wear, 10-1/4" h, 39-1/4" l, 10" d 230.00
Helmet, leather, brass eagle, painted leather shield with "10, LFD," worn old added brass gimbal lamp, 14" l 302.50

Fireplace Equipment

Background: In the Colonial home, the fireplace was the gathering point for heat, meals, and social interaction. It maintained its dominant position until the introduction of central heating in the mid-19th century. In rural areas, however, farmhouses retained their working fireplaces as sources of heat well into the 20th century.

Reference: John Campbell, *Fire & Light in the Home Pre-1820*, Antique Collectors' Club, 1999.

Reproduction Alert: Because fireplaces have retained their appeal and often serve as decorative focal points, modern blacksmiths have begun reproducing many of the old implements.

Broiler
    Rotating, wrought iron, round, seven parallel flattened bars across top, three squared legs, rectangular feet, tapered/flattened handle extends from one leg and has loop end, 19th C., rust, 3-3/8" h, 15-5/8" dia, 24-1/2" l 190.00
    Rotating, wrought iron, round, nine parallel flattened bars across top, Y-shaped base, three rectangular legs, bottom of Y curved up to form tapered flattened handle with pod end, 19th C., rust, 2-5/8" h, 12" dia 210.00
    Rotating, wrought iron, round, pinwheel design, Y-shaped base, three rectangular legs, square feet, tail of Y forms long flattened handle, loop end with scrolled tip, rust, 4-1/2" h, 12-1/2" dia, 30-5/8" l 400.00

Broom
    Orig red paint, black, yellow and gold striping, stenciled freehand floral decor in bronze powder and black, horsehair bristles, wear, flaking, 28" l 247.50
    Wooden handle, 49-1/4" l 35.00

Crane, wrought iron
    12-1/4" h, 36" l, vertical bar, horizontal arm with large scrolled hook, substantial rusting 120.00
    19-1/2" h, 39-1/2" l, vertical bar, horizontal arm, both with square pegs on back for fitting into wall brackets, small hook end, some pitting 70.00
    46" h, 50-1/2" l, vertical bar, horizontal arm with small hook, slightly curved diagonal brace, bottom of vertical post with wall mount attached, substantial rust 170.00
    57-1/4" h, 45-3/4" l, vertical bar, horizontal arm, diagonal brace, substantial rust 50.00

Fender
    Brass top rim, scroll decor in vertical wirework, American or English, late 18th or early 19th C., 10" h, 59-1/2" w, 15" d 2,875.00
    Brass and wire, flattened base rim, American or English, early 19th C., wire breaks, dents, 27" h, 40" l, 15-1/2" d 220.00
    Wire, curved sides, spiral design, brass trim, 12" h, 44" l 632.50

Fireback, cast iron, figures in relief, floral garland border, floral basket cartouche flanked by sphinx, dated 1663, cracked, 26" x 16-1/2" 110.00

Fireplace inset, Federal, cast iron, mkd "Wyer & Noble," bowfront base, scalloped side panels with relief fans and faces, biscuit corners on top with circular and oval fans, orig seamed brass finials, feet missing, back plate cracked, 28" h, 32-1/4" w, 22-3/4" d 330.00

Fire screen, mahogany with old finish, tripod base, snake feet, urn-turned column and pole, urn finial, oval frame with figured mahogany veneer, watercolor on silk scene of bird and flowers, 19th C., stains on silk, repairs to base of column, 54" h 1,760.00

Frying pan, sheet iron, round with long flattened wrought-iron handle, flared sides, 19th C., 10" brace attached to side of pan, pitting, black paint 55.00

Gridiron
    Wrought iron, seven round parallel rods for square top, arched legs, slightly curved feet, flattened diagonal handle extends up from front leg and has round end, rust, 2-1/4" h, 8-7/8" w, 14" l 140.00
    Wrought iron, nine flattened rods form square top, square legs, slightly curved tapering/flattened handle extends from front set of legs, pod-shaped end, 19th C., bottom of both front feet broken off, 4" h, 9-1/2" w, 20-3/4" w 140.00
    Wrought iron, nine iron rods form top, squared legs, scrolled feet, handle extends from front legs and bends up, 19th C., significant rust, 2-5/8" h, 17-1/2" l, top 9-3/4" x 11" 75.00

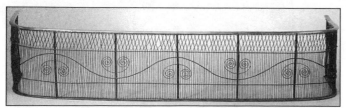

Fireplace fender, iron with brass rim, 10" h, 59-1/2" w, $2,875. (Photo courtesy of Skinner Auctioneers & Appraisers of Antiques & Fine Arts, Boston and Bolton, Mass.)

Kettle tilter, wrought iron, flattened bar with two large scrolled hooks to hold kettle, curves upward forming handle that is round and ends in mushroom-like finial, small iron bracket on top of bar with swiveling loop for hanging on trammel, minor rust, 10-3/8" h, 19-1/2" l 410.00

Kick toaster, wrought iron, T-shaped tripod base, rectangular frame having two rods on either side, one above the other, forming rack for holding toast, handle extends outward and curves up slightly, ends in pod with hole for hanging, minor rust, 5" h, 13-1/8" w, 17-5/8" l 220.00

Log fork, wrought iron, long round handle, cast-brass ovoid finial, some rust, 44" l 25.00

Set

 Four pcs, brass andirons with turned column, urn finial and ball feet, matching tongs and shovel, early 19th C. 577.50

 Four pcs, brass ball-top andirons with ring-turned and faceted plinths on scrolled legs with ball feet, shovel and tongs with brass ring-turned and ribbed finials, minor dents, wear.................. 747.50

 Five pcs, ribbed ring-turned andirons, similar tongs and shovel, jamb hook with urn finials, 19th C., minor wear... 747.50

Shovel and tongs, wrought iron, brass finials, 30" l, pr... 55.00

Trammel, wrought iron

 Top, slide bar and catch with scalloped finials, engraved detail with cross and "1809," adjusts from 43" to 60"... 495.00

 Bar with 8 holes and swivel loop at top, separate rod hooks into holes of bar and has large hook with scrolled tip at its base, 19th C., substantial rust, 25-1/2" l 160.00

 Round bar with loop having 3-3/4" dia ring, flattened bar with ratchet device, rust, 46-1/2" l 100.00

 Round bar with plain hook, wide flattened sawtooth bar with ratchet device, large hook at bottom of flat bar, substantial rust, 42-1/4" l 65.00

Trivet, rotating, wrought iron, round top with straight center bar flanked by double-arched bars, mounted to tripod base with two cabriole-style legs and one round vertical, tapered flattened handle with large loop end, minor damage on top, 18-1/2" l, 9-1/2" dia 450.00

Waffle iron, cast iron

 Four rectangular compartments with geometric designs, long round double handles, 19th C., significant pitting, some rust, 8-1/4" x 6-1/4", 27-1/2" l 75.00

 Double, rectangular with star-like designs, 4-1/4" x 7-1/8", 26" l... 82.50

 Round, heart design, rod handles with ring ends, 8-1/2" dia, 22-3/4" l 165.00

 Round, interior with graduated rows of rectangles, tapered handle, late 19th C., rust, 8-3/4" dia, 23" l 40.00

Firkins

Background: Small wooden containers used for butter or lard, many firkins were painted.

Painted firkins in mustard, red and sage-green, $325 to $450.

Collecting Hint: The color, condition and originality of the paint are usually the biggest factors in determining the value of a firkin.

Reproduction Alert: Beware of reproductions as well as vintage examples that have been repainted.

6-1/2" h, green paint... 330.00
7" h, blue paint... 357.50
8" h, red paint,... 137.50
9" h, white paint... 165.00
9-1/2" h, blue paint,.. 605.00
10" h, black paint,... 165.00
10" h, blue paint 357.50
10" h, red paint 165.00
10" h, yellow paint,... 165.00
11" h, blue paint.. 82.50
11-3/4" h, gray paint.. 495.00
12" h, mustard paint.. 82.50
13" h, blue paint 165.00
13-3/4" h, blue body, black trim 137.50
14" h, blue paint 660.00
14" h, gray paint 165.00

Flags

Background: The Americana aspect of flags makes them a natural with collectors, and age and rarity play major roles in determining value. Condition is especially important when considering flags that are more readily available.

Collectors' Club: North American Vexillological Assoc., 1977 N. Olden Ave., Suite 225, Trenton, NJ 08618.

American

 Thirteen-star, mid-19th C., hand-sewn wool, double appliquéd cotton stars, from the family of a Mass. Civil War veteran, soiled, fabric loss, 60" x 100" 2,185.00

Fifteen-star, wool, soiled, fading, fabric loss, three rows of five stars, 30" x 66" 2,990.00

Sixteen-star, homespun cotton, hand-sewn, c. 1800, four rows of four stars, fading, 37" x 66" 4,600.00

Twenty-star, cotton, hand-sewn, early 19th C., minor stains, small tears, 38-1/2" x 53-1/2" 4,312.50

Twenty-five-star, muslin, machine and hand-sewn, five rows of five stars, probably a naval ensign, probably pre-Civil War, scattered browning, 80" x 142" 1,045.00

Thirty-five-star, Great Star flag, printed muslin, center star larger and bordered with blue then white border, two outer rings of stars and one star in each corner, c. 1863, slight discolor and wear, 19-1/4" x 28" 1,540.00

Thirty-nine-star, silk, six rows of stars in a 6-7-7-6-7-6 pattern, 11-1/2" x 17-3/4" 165.00

Forty-eight-star, lopsided stars, c. 1920, attributed to Marie Miller 1,210.00

Confederate

U.V.C. (United Veterans of the Confederacy) battle flag, Army of Northern Virginia pattern, pieced silk, 1" hoist, three brass grommets, red ground, purple bars, white stars, machine- and hand-sewn, gold fringe border, uppercase "A" at top, probably for Company A, 34" sq..................................... 357.50

U.V.C. battle flag, Army of Northern Virginia pattern, printed cotton, on wood staff with spear-point finial, toning, repaired tear, 12" sq.................. 176.00

U.V.C. flag, hand-sewn wool, red over white over red stripes, faded blue canton with circular pattern of five stars, mounted on wood staff, late 19th C., short tear, 10" x 18" 935.00

Nullification flag, sixteen-star Northern Abolitionist "exclusion" flag, c. 1851-58, hand-sewn cotton, 23 red/white stripes, blue canton with four rows of four stars, moderate stains, small holes, minor edge tears, 45" x 47"..3,850.00

Thirteen-star American flag, fabric loss, 60" x 100", $2,185. (Photo courtesy of Skinner Auctioneers & Appraisers of Antiques & Fine Arts, Boston and Bolton, Mass.)

Flasks

Background: A flask is a bottle with a narrow neck and a broad, flat body. Flasks were made in an assortment of sizes and colors, and they often featured portraits of famous individuals, early American presidents, inscriptions, and decorative designs.

References: Gary Baker et al., *Wheeling Glass 1829-1939*, Oglebay Institute, 1994; Ralph and Terry Kovel, *Kovels' Bottles Price List*, 11th ed., Three Rivers Press, 1999; Kenneth Wilson, *American Glass 1760-1939*, 2 vols., Hudson Hills Press, 1994.

Periodical: *Antique Bottle & Glass Collector*, P.O. Box 187, East Greenville, PA 18041.

Collectors' Club: The National Early American Glass Club, P.O. Box 8489, Silver Spring, MD 20907.

Ceramic

Book form, Rockingham-type, repaired corner, 6" h, one-pint 316.25

Pig, white clay, Albany slip, anatomically correct, incised "Bardolph Pottery," open nose flakes, 6-1/2" l 660.00

Potato, white clay, brown Rockingham-like glaze, 5-1/4" h 275.00

Pretzel, pottery, mkd "Patent applied for 1908," cap missing, 3-1/2" h, 5-1/2" w...................... 330.00

Glass

Sixteen vertical ribs swirl on neck, aqua, multiple tiny blisters, pot stones, attributed to Mantua, Ohio, 5-1/8" h 137.50

American Eagle, "Westford Glass Co., Westford Conn.," olive-green, half pint, 6-1/2" h........ 192.50

American Eagle and Cornucopia, GII-73, olive amber, sickness, some residue and wear, half pint, 6-3/4" h 71.50

Bull's-eye disk, amber, attributed to Conn., 9-1/2" h 357.50

Cabin and "Hard Cider," GX-22, aqua, wear, minor stain, damage, pint, 6-1/2" h...................... 935.00

Chestnut, aqua, sixteen ribs broken swirl, attributed to Mantua, Ohio, 5-1/8" h 357.50

Chestnut, deep violet blue, sixteen ribs broken swirl, wear, short neck, rough lip, has grinding, 4-1/2" h 495.00

Double Eagle, GII-119, aqua, half pint, 6-3/8" h 137.50

Double Eagle, GII-24, aqua, interior stain, rough lip, pint, 6-5/8" h 82.50

Duck with "Will you take a drink...," GXIII-30, aqua, worn, scratched, stain, half-pint, 6" h 220.00

Eagle with "Continental," reverse shows Indian with "Cunninghams Pittsburgh, Pa.," GII-142, aqua, minor residue, wear, 9-1/4" h..................... 165.00

"Father of his Country/Taylor Never Surrenders," Washington, Gen. Taylor, GI-44, aqua, pint.. 95.00

"For Pike's Peak," GXI-22, aqua, pint, 7-3/4" h 60.50

"For Pike's Peak," reverse with Eagle, GXI-22, aqua, quart, 8-7/8" h... 82.50

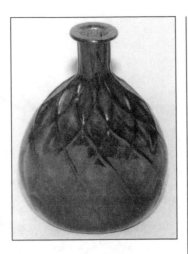

Dark-amber half-pint flask with quilted design, 5-1/2" h, $3,850.

"For Pike's Peak," reverse with Eagle and "Ceredo," GXI-36, aqua, minor roughens on lip, minor residue, pot stone, 6-1/2" h 49.50

"For Pike's Peak," GXI-41, aqua, pint, 7-1/2" h 55.00

Fraternal, "Union," GIV-40 variant, aquamarine, pint, 7-1/2" h 90.00

Hunter/Fisherman, GXIII-4, aqua, quart 125.00

Jenny Lind, GI-110, aqua, minor interior stain, lip chips, quart 412.50

Masonic, Eagle side with initials "JKB," GIV-3, greenish-blue, some sickness, pint, 7-3/8" h 412.50

Masonic, Eagle with "Ohio" and "Shepards," GIV-32, aqua, flared folded lip, interior ring, wear, broken blister, 6-3/8" h 385.00

Portrait, Benjamin Franklin, no inscription, GI-97, aqua, quart, 8-1/2" h 137.50

Portrait, Ulysses Grant, reverse has Eagle and "Union," GI-79, aqua, pint, 7-3/4" h 247.50

Portrait, Washington, "Fells Point," GI-2, light-green, small broken blister on bottom, quart, 8-1/4" h 247.50

Portrait, Washington, "The Father of His Country," Taylor on reverse, GI-45, aqua, quart 220.00

Portrait, Washington, Sheaf of Rye on reverse, GI-59, aqua, minor wear, half pint, 6-1/8" h 77.00

Shield and Clasped Hands, "FA & Co Union," GXII-42, aqua, minor residue in straw mark, pint, 6-1/4" h 104.50

Shield and Clasped Hands, "FA & Co Union," GZII-42, aqua, minor residue, half pint, 6-3/8" h 104.50

Sloop, 8-Point Star on reverse, GX-8, aqua, minor residue, half pint, 5-1/2" h............................. 71.50

"Success to the Railroad," GV-1, aqua, shallow flake on lip, pint, 6-7/8" h.................................. 192.50

"Success to the Railroad," GV-3, olive-amber, minor wear, pint, 7" h... 137.50

Sunburst, GVII-15a, olive-green, half pint, 6" h 660.00

Sunburst, GVIII-16, olive-green, half pint, 5-7/8" h 357.50

"Traveler's Companion," GXIV-7, aqua, iron pontil, broken blister, 6-1/4" h................................ 165.00

"Traveler's Companion" and "Ravenna Glass Co." with eight-Point Star, GXIV-3, pot stones, mold imperfection in neck, residue, pint, 7" h...... 192.50

Urn and Cornucopia, GIII-4, olive green, wear, pint, 6-3/4" h 220.00

Violin Scroll, eight-Point Star, GIX-37, aqua, pinpoints on lip, small pot stone, half pint, 6" h 93.50

Flow Blue

Background: Flow Blue is the term used for blue-and-white china that, when fired, produced a flowing or blurring of the blue. The flow can range from very slight to a heavy blur that renders the pattern almost unrecognizable.

Josiah Wedgwood is credited with producing the first Flow Blue, circa 1830 in the Staffordshire area of England. Many other potters followed, including Alcock, Davenport, Grindley, Johnson Brothers, Meakin, and New Wharf. Early Flow Blue, circa 1830s to 1870s, was usually made of ironstone. Later patterns, circa 1880s to 1900s, and modern patterns, after 1910, were usually made of more delicate semi-porcelain. Approximately 90 percent of all Flow Blue was made in England.

References: Susan and Al Bagdade, *Warman's English & Continental Pottery & Porcelain*, 3rd ed., Krause Publications, 1998; Mary F. Gaston, *Collector's Encyclopedia of Flow Blue China*, Collector Books, 1983 (1993 value update); Jeffrey B. Snyder, *Fascinating Flow Blue*, Schiffer Publishing, 1997; —, *Flow Blue: A Closer Look*, Schiffer Publishing, 2000; —, *Flow Blue: A Collector's Guide to Pattern, History, and Values*, Schiffer Publishing, 1992; —, *Historic Flow Blue*, Schiffer Publishing, 1994; Petra Williams, *Flow Blue China and Mulberry Ware: Similarity and Value Guide*, rev. ed., Fountain House East, 1993.

Collectors' Club: Flow Blue International Collectors Club, 1048 Llano, Pasadena, TX 77504.

Museum: The Margaret Woodbury Strong Museum, Rochester, NY.

Reproduction Alert: Flow blue reproductions have been made since the mid-1950s, but many of the patterns are sloppy, and the pieces exhibit an overall light-blue background.

Coffeepot, Shapoo pattern, octagonal, curved paneled spout, dome-shaped lid, pointed rosette finial, lid chip, nicked rim, 9-3/4" h 650.00

Fruit dish, Waldorf pattern, New Wharf Pottery, scalloped rim, 5-1/4" dia, set of three 65.00

Plate

Indian Jar pattern, plain rim, importer's mk, minor glaze flake, 9-3/8" dia, pr.............................110.00

Madras pattern, plain rim, minor glaze flake, two with small chips, 6-1/2" dia, set of six 130.00

Flow Blue plate with landscape scene, marked "Avon Ware," 9-1/4" dia, $75.

Flow Mulberry cup plate, 4-1/8" dia, $65.

Shapoo pattern, twelve-sided, John Wedgwood, two glaze flakes, 8-3/8" dia 80.00

Shapoo pattern, fourteen-sided, minor discoloring, 7-1/2" dia 40.00

Waldorf pattern, scalloped rim, 9-3/4" dia, set of six 340.00

Platter

Shapoo pattern, Wedgwood, rectangular, hairline, rim chip, glaze nicks, 15-3/4" x 12-1/4" 650.00

Chinese Basket pattern, C. James Mason & Co., basket and butterfly, oblong, 14" x 17-3/4" 357.50

Circassia pattern, oblong, J.&G. Alcock, two slight glaze chips, 13-5/8" x 10-3/4" 200.00

Lancaster pattern, oblong, scalloped rim, New Wharf Pottery, chip, 9-1/2" x 7" 100.00

Waldorf pattern, New Wharf Pottery, oblong, scalloped rim, minor glaze wear on rim, 10-1/2" x 7-5/8" 120.00

Waldorf pattern, New Wharf Pottery, oval, scalloped rim, minor annealing line on rim, 10-7/8" x 9", set of three 200.00

Soup plate, Waldorf pattern, New Wharf Pottery, scalloped rim, minor glaze flake, 9" dia, pr...............110.00

Vegetable bowl, open, Waldorf pattern, New Wharf Pottery, round, scalloped rim, slight nick, 9" dia 60.00

Vegetable tureen with lid, Argyle pattern, W.H. Grindley, scrolled handles on ends of base, scrolled finial, chips, lid doesn't seat properly, 4-3/4" h, 10-1/2" l....... 100.00

Waste bowl, Indian Jar pattern, 12-sided, footed, J.&T. Furnival, 3-1/2" h, 5-3/8" dia 130.00

Flow Mulberry

Background: Many of the same factories that produced Flow Blue china also produced Flow Mulberry, with some of the same patterns being used on both wares. The blackish purple or brownish purple mulberry designs were either hand-painted or transfer-printed. Made in the Staffordshire district of England between 1840 and 1870, Flow Mulberry was produced on sturdy ironstone bodies.

References: Petra Williams, *Flow Blue China and Mulberry Ware: Similarity and Value Guide*, rev. ed., Fountain House East, 1993; Ellen R. Hill, *Mulberry Ironstone: Flow Blue's Best Kept Little Secret*, self-published, 1993.

Bowl (serving), 4-1/2" h, 13" dia.......................... 250.00

Coffeepot with lid, Rose pattern, E. Challinor, unmkd, octagonal shape, scrolled handle, curved paneled spout, domed paneled lid, grapes finial, discoloring, lid chip, professional repair to handle and collar, 10" h.. 130.00

Cup and saucer, Rose pattern 80.00

Gravy tureen, landscape scene with body of water, with undertray, lid and ladle, 9" h, 8-1/2" w 810.00

Plate

Flora pattern, in-the-making glaze chip, 9-3/4" dia 130.00

Strawberry pattern, paneled, 8" dia 155.00

Platter

Vincennes pattern, octagonal, 10-1/4" x 13-1/2" 177.50

Pagoda pattern, 17" x 21"........................... 315.00

Teapot, Cyprus pattern, hexagonal-foot, nicks..... 465.00

Folk Art

Background: Folk art remains one area of collecting that doesn't have clearly defined boundaries. Some people confine folk art to non-academic, handmade objects. Others include manufactured material. When referring to artwork, the term encompasses everything from crude drawings by untalented children to works by academically trained artists that depict common people and scenery. The following listings illustrate the diversity of this category.

References: Wendy Lavitt, *Animals in American Folk Art*, Knopf, 1990; George H. Meyer, *American Folk Art Canes*, Sandringham Press, 1992; Donald J. Petersen, *Folk Art Fish Decoys*, Schiffer Publishing, 1996; Beatrix Rumford and Carolyn Weekly, *Treasures in American Folk Art from the Abby Aldrich Rockefeller Folk Art Center*, Little, Brown Co., 1989.

Periodical: *Folk Art Illustrated*, P.O. Box 906, Marietta, OH 45750.

Collectors' Club: Folk Art Society of America, P.O. Box 17041, Richmond, VA 23226.

Museums: Abby Aldrich Rockefeller Folk Art Center, Williamsburg, VA; Museum of American Folk Art, New York, NY; Museum of Early Southern Decorative Arts, Winston-Salem, NC.

Bird tree
    Four carved birds on potted tree, polychrome paint, 12-1/2" h 19,800.00
    Seven carved birds, six-branch tree, Luke W. Gottshall, Lancaster County Pa., dated 1982, 16-3/8" h 2,050.00
    Twenty carved birds, turned tree with turned limbs in black paint, limbs ending in semi-spherical decor in various colors, ball finial with owl on top, found in Vt., 66" h 1,595.00
Box, wooden, orig red and black floral decor, cutout double bird head crest, lift lid, minor edge damage, 6" h 1,430.00
Carving
    Bird, by Frank Texter, Mohns Hill Pa. (grandfather of Carl A. Moyer), curved multi-feather tail and comb, orange feet, legs and beak, gray body with black accents, red comb, red/gray/orange eyes, on green rectangular base, unsigned, 11-3/8" h, 16" l 4,400.00
    Geode, linear man's face with beard, attributed to Popeye Reed (purchased directly from Reed), 7-1/4" dia 275.00
    Hat, smoke-decor, mustard-painted carved walnut burl, stars around band and top, 19th C., minor wear, 4-1/2" h, 12-1/4" dia 920.00
    Tree, cherry orig finish, elaborate tree trunk with rope and anchor wrapped around the base, relief-carved initials with dates on cut limbs, dates range from 1840 to 1888 with one death date of 1918 added later, "Hope" on the anchor in relief, "God Bless Our House" on the rope, oblong well in the top with ivy carving surrounded by incised flower medallions and acorn drops at corners, age cracks, pieced restoration, 29" h 3,850.00
Ceramic figure, hand-formed, man in top hat, unglazed, slight pink color, firing lines, 8-1/2" h 110.00
Clock face (grandfather's), partial Glasgow signature, worn orig decor includes Scottish scene in arch with lady standing in a boat, man and dog on the shore, spandrels have different scenes for various nations including America, small areas of touchup, 20" h, 14" w 192.50
Desk set, carved, base with two glass inkwells with wooden acorn lids, drawer in the back, slanted pen rack, four wooden pens with acorn dangles, all sur-

faces highly carved, acorn dangles on base and "Emlek," 8" h, 7" w 178.00
Game wheel
    Decor with numbers, shapes and stars in red, blue, black and yellow, nail spoke with leather stopper, 23-1/4" dia 330.00
    Decor, red numbers and designs, yellow ground, 30" dia 110.00
Grouping, painted wood two-story house and carved and painted figures celebrating the 4th of July, includes band members and croquet players, 14 figures, house 10" h, base 14" sq 1,430.00
Hanging shelf, old yellow and greenish-yellow paint with black dot decor and trim, chamfered and arched top, one bowfront shelf, slender rounded base, "J.B. Copeland, Hapedale, Ohio" scratched into wet paint, 21" h, 8-1/2" w, shelf 7-1/2" d 1,017.50
Indian club, red and black grained, 18" h, pr 181.50
Painting
    Oil on tin, landscape with mill and stream, surface worn, modern frame, 20" h, 28" w 935.00
    Opaque watercolor on paper, "Apple Blossom," pink, white and green, ink label, frame in old gold repaint, stains, fold lines, 7-1/4" h, 5-1/4" w 55.00
    Pen and ink and watercolor on wove paper, primitive scene of two-story, half-timber house with fence, dog and trees with vintage, shades of green, red, blue, black and yellow, old decor frame in red and yellow, stains, edge damage, fold lines, 8-1/4" h, 10-3/8" w 2,530.00
    Watercolor on old ledger paper dated 1812, rooster, in red, green, yellow, blue and black, stains, wide pine frame, 5-1/2" h, 6-3/4" w 1,760.00

THE OTHER POPEYE

If you thought Popeye was some spinach-gulping sailor man, collectors of folk art and outsider art will set you straight. Ernest "Popeye" Reed was born in Jackson, Ohio, in 1919. The Buckeye State's most famous folk carver, Reed worked in both wood and stone, producing major pieces as well as souvenir items. Reed died in South Carolina in 1985.

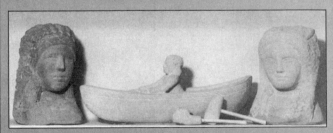

Popeye Reed limestone carvings: Busts of an Indian man and woman, marked "E. Reed 1976," 7-3/4" h, pair, $660; Indian in canoe, marked "E. Reed 1976 A.D.," 14" l, $6052; pipes, one with man's head, marked "E.R.," 2" l, one plain, 2-1/2" l (excluding stem), pair, $192.50.

Watercolor on paper, bird on branch with tulips, red, yellow and blue, teal border, inked name on front and "David Graybills AD 1832 Fir (sic) you" scratched out, light stains, edge damage, small holes, old walnut frame in alligatored dark-red paint, 5-3/4" h, 4-1/2" w 550.00

Watercolor on paper, flowers and heart, yellow roses and snowdrops in corners, heart formed from vining flowers in red, yellow, green and blue, "Forget me not" with verse, name and 1866, molded wooden frame, glued down, foxing, edge damage, 11" h, 12-1/4" w 110.00

Watercolor on paper, pr of lovebirds, urn of vining flowers, in red, green, yellow and orange, yellow repainted frame with smoked triangles, glued down with fold lines, edge damage, 5" h, 7-3/8" w 880.00

Watercolor, Hattie K. Brunner, Lancaster County, Pa., winter scene, covered bridge in foreground with horse-drawn sleigh, background with hills, trees, deer, framed, 11-3/8" h, 14-1/2" w 3,400.00

Watercolor, Hattie K. Brunner, Lancaster County, Pa., dated 1962, summer farm scene with barn, man feeding chickens, man on horseback, cow in meadow, flower garden, house, woman picking fruit, horse-drawn hay wagon, field and woods, etc., matted/framed, 10-1/2" h, 14-1/2" w 9,800.00

Papier-mâché and painted cloth fruit, old polychrome, 12 pcs 137.50

Print, woodblock, handcolored, two birds on branch, black with red and green, old frame, 9" h, 7" w 660.00

Rug, geometric, concentric circles in center, cross-flanked by Prince of Wales Feathers, quarter circles in each corner, shades of brown, gold, red, blue and green, small areas of loss and repairs, 36" x 65"... 1,725.00

Sculpture, limestone
    Cardinal, mkd "E. Reed 1976," 5-1/2" h........ 302.50
    Bust, Indian, mkd "E.R." (Popeye Reed), 9-1/2" h 275.00
    Bust, man with beard and long hair, 8-3/4" h 440.00
    Bust, woman with topknot, mkd "E. Reed," 8-1/4" h 385.00
    Indian in canoe, mkd "E. Reed 1976 A.D.," 5-1/2" h, 7-3/4" l 660.00

Oversized wooden dice, black and white, pair, $150.

Man with owl's head, wears fur loincloth and holds snake, mkd "E. Reed," attached to round limestone base, 13-3/4" h (excluding base)................ 1,155.00
Nude, full-figure woman with flowing hair, hand on one breast, signed "E. Reed, 1976 A.D.," 18-3/4" h 330.00
Owl, attributed to Popeye Reed (purchased directly from Reed), 6-3/4" h 192.50
Venus standing on seashell, nude, modestly covering herself, long hair, 16-5/8" h 1,650.00

Sculpture, sandstone
    Bookends, seated figures of Adam and Eve, mkd "E. Reed 1976 A.D.," 11" h, pr 495.00
    Bust, double-headed, two men, one with beard, mkd "E. Reed," 11-1/8" h 302.50
    Bust, Indian chief in headdress, "E. Reed," 13" h 660.00
    Bust, Indian man with headband and beaded necklace, 9-1/4" h 495.00
    Bust, Indian woman with headband, "E. Reed," glued break at one corner, 12" h 742.50
    Bust, man with long hair and beard, possibly Jesus, eyes painted-in white and black, incised "E. Reed," 11-7/8" h 440.00
    Bust, woman, "E. Reed," mkd in pencil "Indian Flat Head, 1982," 6-1/2" h 275.00
    Catfish, raised eyes, mouth and fins, attributed to Popeye Reed (purchased directly from Reed), 32-1/2" l 247.50
    Indian chief, seated, arms folded, wears headdress and fringed outfit with medal, mkd "E. Reed," 29" h, 10-3/4" w, 11-1/2" d 2,530.00
    Indian chief, seated, wears headdress and fringed clothing, braids and moccasins, attributed to Popeye Reed (purchased directly from Reed), shallow chip on back of headdress, 14-1/2" h, 4-1/4" w, 5" d 412.50
    Indian woman sitting cross-legged and holding a pot, mkd "E. Reed," base chips, 12-1/2" h 1,045.00
    Man wearing long hair and beard, carved lion on base, possible candlestick or lamp base, "E. Reed," 12-3/4" h 302.50
    Man's bust, bearded, "E. Reed," 7-3/4" h 385.00
    Owl and baby owl, "E. Reed," 10-1/2" h 357.50
    Two owls side by side, "E. Reed," 6-3/4" h........ 385.00
    Woman holding infant, full-figure, mkd "E. Reed," 15" h 1,155.00
    Two women standing back to back with lamb at their feet, 1 is nude and holds child, other wears long dress and holds sheaf of wheat, incised "E. Reed," 14-1/3" h 2,035.00

Stoneware
    Crock, six-gal, salt-glaze, freehand cobalt design of military figure with "Seymour" banner and words, "I am going up the Salt River. Where are you going, Frank?," political reference to Horatio Seymour and Frank Blair running against U.S. Grant in 1868, stains, wear 17,050.00
    Jug, two-gal., impressed "M.&T. Miller, Newport, Pa.," bust of man with a mustache, coat and string tie in cobalt slip 4,290.00
Straight razor, walnut, red finish on handle, gray on blade, mkd "WIK," 20" l 330.00

Folk art weathervane combining American flag with arm and hammer, sheet copper, weathered surface with gilt, later silver paint, 25-1/2" h, 65" l, $35,650. (Photo courtesy of Skinner Auctioneers & Appraisers of Antiques & Fine Arts, Boston and Bolton, Mass.)

Sun face, tin, full-bodied, painted in shades of cream, yellow and orange, black highlights, thirteen rays remain (one detached, two missing), imperfections, American, early 20th C., 22" dia 1,725.00

Table, carved legs each with trapped ball, intricate inlaid Parcheesi top with American flag in center block, 29" h, top 28" x 28".. 3,125.00

Watercolor and ink
  Pennsylvania-Dutch, two birds with hearts on wings, stylized flower, in red, yellow and black, minor paper damage, signed/dated 1825, 4" h, 6-1/4" w 2,860.00
  Pennsylvania-Dutch, rooster in red, yellow and black, signed/dated 1825, 4" h, 3-1/2" w............... 2,530.00
  Pennsylvania-Dutch, woman with parrot and stylized tulips, red green, yellow and black, initialed/dated 1825, small tear, 4" h, 3-1/4" w 5,500.00

Folk Pottery

Background: This category covers the broad realm of stoneware and pottery items that fall into the folk art genre. Numerous contemporary potters have revived the tradition of American folk pottery, and their works are often quite collectible.

Collecting Hint: The popularity of this form has led to contemporary folk potters who concentrate on quantity rather than quality. Face jugs and other forms seen in abundance at flea markets and other venues are not often worthy of consideration.

Collectors' Club: Southern Folk Pottery Collectors Society, 1828 N. Howard Mill Rd., Robbins, NC 27325-7477.

Bust, Marie Rogers, glossy brown with various drippings, clay teeth and eyes, brown pupils, incised eyebrows, eyelashes, mustache, goatee and chest hair, bowtie beneath chin, script signature, early 1980s, 12" h... 220.00

Chicken
  Edwin Meaders, pedestal style rooster, high-gloss dark-green glaze, white clay eyes, script signature, 15" h... 1,485.00
  Charles Moore, gray/cream salt glaze, incised neck, wing and tail feathers, script signature, dated 1987, 8-3/4" h, 8" l.................................... 192.50

Dog, Billy Ray Hussey, satin gloss black and green over buff poodle holding basket in mouth, red lead glaze, incised curling to mane and tail tip, incised weave to basket holding three flowers, incised eyes, pupils with eyelashes and claws, incised "BH," circa 1988, from Hussey's first two wood-fired kiln openings (after the second all items have sequential kiln numbers), 6-1/2" h, 5-1/4" l 1,210.00

Face jug
  Jerry Brown, black slip, clear glaze on eyes and teeth, bright blue pupils, incised mustache, eyebrows and eyelashes, indented cheeks, mkd "10-91 Jerry Brown Hamilton, AL" in script, c. 1991, 11-1/8" h 247.50
  Brown Pottery, pinched features, applied teeth, minor imperfections, 8" h......................... 2,860.00
  General Foster Cole, clear syrup color glaze, white clay teeth and eyes, brown inserted pupils, applied short curly incised mustache, eyebrows and chin, incised curly hair and beard, mkd "G.F. Cole 84" and "Cole Pottery, Cox Mill Rd., Sanford, N.C.," 1984, 10-1/2" h................................ 330.00
  General Foster Cole, clear syrup color glaze, white clay teeth and eyes, brown inserted pupils, incised mustache, eyelashes and eyebrows, incised curly hair and beard, mkd "G.F. Cole 85" and "Cole Pottery, Cox Mill Road, Sanford N.C.," 1985, 14-1/4" h... 880.00
  Burlon Craig, devil face, glossy crushed Coca-Cola bottle glass glaze, white clay eyes with two inserted pupils (unusual for period of production), one-pc eyebrow, spaced china teeth, pierced nostrils, horns with slight curl, mkd "B.B. Craig, Vale, N.C.," c. 1982-84, 11-5/8" h....................... 825.00
  Burlon Craig, double face jug, glossy crushed Coca-Cola glass glaze, one side shows man with mustache and goatee, other has clean-shaven man, both with china plate teeth, pierced nostrils, mkd "B.B. Craig, Vale, N.C.," c. 1985-87, 11" h 1,155.00
  Burlon Craig, face jug with applied snake, glossy crushed Coca-Cola glass glaze, one-pc eyebrow, china-plate teeth, pierced nostrils, snake has clay slip eyes and slit mouth and wiggles down back side, mkd "B.B. Craig, Vale, N.C.," c. 1985-87, 12" h 1,870.00
  Burlon Craig, glossy black-brown Albany slip, large ears, pop-eyed, one-pc eyebrow, china plate teeth unusually spaced, pierced nostrils, mkd "B.B Craig, Vale, N.C.," c. 1980-82, 6" h 247.50
  Burlon Craig, Swirlware face jug, crushed-glass gray/white swirl, double handles, one-pc eyebrow, pierced nostrils, china plate teeth, mkd "B.B.C., Henry N.C.," c. 1985-87, 12" h 1,760.00

Anna Pottery salt-glazed pig flask, "Good Old Bourbon in a Hog's --," $2,500.

Burlon Craig, weeping-eye face jug, high-gloss alkaline and crushed-glass glaze with blue and melted glass runs, two handles, contrasting opaque glass meltings with bright blue and white colors, one-pc eyebrow, pierced nostrils, china plate teeth, incised "B.B.C., Henry, N.C.," c. 1982-84, shallow chip to lower lip, 19" h 2,970.00

Crocker, "Michael A. Crocker & Melvin S. Crocker 1990," green ash glaze, large nose, individual teeth, 11-1/2" h 247.50

Charles Lisk, glossy opaque and olive glaze, incised one-pc eyebrow, white porcelain eyes and rounded teeth, punched pupils, mkd "Charles Lisk, Vale, NC," c. 1985-86, 9-1/8" h................... 467.50

Charles Lisk, Swirlware face jug, satin gloss brown/ white glaze, one-pc incised eyebrow, mustache and beard, impressionistic mouth with white teeth, mkd "Charles Lisk, Vale NC," c. 1986-87, 8-1/2" h 275.00

Mayappee Pottery, Almond, N.C., pinched features, applied eyes and teeth, imperfections, 3-3/4" h 220.00

Cleater Meaders, double devil face (one per side) with four candle sockets, glossy medium-olive alkaline glaze, both faces with clear clay teeth and eyes with brown pupils, incised eyelashes, pointy eyebrows and horns, script signature, dated 1988, 10-3/4" h.. 990.00

Cleater Meaders, glossy dark-olive streaked alkaline glaze, white clay teeth and eyes, dark-brown pupils, incised eyelashes, script signature, dated 1991, 7-1/8" h.. 143.00

Lanier Meaders, double devil face, high-gloss medium-olive glaze, outlandish horns, white teeth (one side only) and eyes with black pupils, indented eyelashes, applied eyebrows, semi-cord style handles, pointy nose, pierced nostrils, script signature, late 1970s-early 1980s, 8-1/8" h... 4,950.00

Lanier Meaders, glossy and mat dark-olive alkaline glaze, six rock teeth, hawk-billed nose, pierced nostrils, white eyes, black pupils, ears set low and far back from the face, script signature, late 1970s, 9-1/2" h 1,650.00

Lanier Meaders, green-brown glaze, eyes looking right, crooked smile, 10" h 715.00

Lanier Meaders, medium-olive alkaline glaze, unglazed white clay overbite teeth, eyes with dark-blue pupils, mkd "Lanier Meaders" in script, dated 1987, 8-1/4" h 880.00

Black-motif face jug marked "John Dollings, Oct. 1881, Ohio," white clay, Albany slip, hairlines, 10-3/4" h, $7,975. (Photo courtesy of Garth's Auctions, Delaware, Ohio)

Lanier Meaders, purple alkaline glaze, white clay teeth and eyes, dark-blue pupils, fat hawk-bill nose, arched eyebrows, pinch-center lip style, script signature, early 1980s, 11-1/2" h 1,100.00

Reggie Meaders, high-gloss olive alkaline glaze, small facial application, unglazed teeth and eyes with black pupils, incised "Reggie Meaders," mid-1980s, 9-3/4" h 412.50

Marie Rogers, glossy Albany slip with multicolor drippings, tongue sticking out, white teeth, blue pupils, incised beard and eyelashes, script and impressed marks, early 1980s, 9-1/8" h..........................143.00

Figural, Billy Ray Hussey, seated African-American holding face jug, black skin, blue bibbed overalls, white clay teeth and eyes, incised features, mkd "BH XVII My First Face Jug," 1991, 7" h...................... 1,100.00

Jug, "Samuel Mellvill, Always this full of good whiskey," dark ivory glaze, red glaze underneath, scratch decor of man in top hat, coat and breeches carrying a shovel, beside a dog and farm, heart with banner and "SM, JM, 1816," glaze flakes, handle crack, 7-1/8" h 3,850.00

Lion

Billy Ray Hussey, glossy buff and brown lead glaze, early style with short legs, larger curly mane and small cord-style tail, brown mane, tail tip and whiskers, pierced ears and nostrils, incised teeth, incised "Owens BH," c. 1978-79, 6-1/8" h, 6-1/2" l.......825.00

Billy Ray Hussey, glossy dark-brown and buff glaze, seated lion on base, incised eyes, nostrils, whiskers, mouth and claws, curling tail, incised "Owens BH," c. 1979, 7-3/8" h................. 1,045.00

Pig, standing, embossed "Monmouth, Ill.," white front half, brown back half, 7-1/2" l......................... 1,650.00

Food Molds

Background: Food molds were used in commercial settings as well as in the home. Pewter molds were generally the choice for businesses, and molds made of copper or pottery were popular in domestic kitchens. Both types are collected today, largely for their decorative nature.

Reference: Judene Divone, *Chocolate Moulds*, Oakton Hills Publications, 1987.

Museum: Wilbur's American Candy Museum, Lititz, PA.

Also See: Ice Cream Molds

Cast-iron
 Pig head, 9" dia 302.50
 Sheep, 14-1/2" l 110.00
Graniteware
 Cake mold, cobalt/white swirl, 7-1/2" dia 235.00
 Rabbit, blue/white, 3-3/4" l, 3" w 130.00
 Rabbit, gray, 3-5/8" l, 2-7/8" w 170.00
 Strawberry design, gray, 1-3/4" h, 5" l, 4" w 235.00
 Turk's head, blue/white swirl 115.00
Ironstone, pineapple, oval with flat bottom, rounded fluted sides, discolored, 2-3/4" h,
 4-1/4" x 5-1/2" 250.00
Maple sugar, carved wood
 Dolphin, two-pc, 2-1/4" h, 4" x 6-1/4" 130.00
 Heart motif 330.00
 Leaf and florets, paddle-shaped,
 2-3/4" x 7-7/8" 30.00
Pastry
 Wooden, carved, panel-shaped with oval handle having carved fish design on one side, 5/8" h,
 8-1/8" x 3" 55.00
 Wooden, carved, two sections with scalloped borders, designs of a bird and a flower, rectangular,
 3/4" h, 3-1/4" x 4" 75.00
 Wooden, carved, four sections, designs of a swan, flower, bunch of grapes and building with banner flying from top of roof, rectangular, 1/2" h,
 3" x 3-3/4" 45.00
 Wooden, carved, six sections, designs of house, horse, deer, tree, bird on branch and flower, rectangular, 3/4" h, 4" x 6-1/2" 110.00
Pudding, copper and tin, pineapple design in copper bottom, fluted arched tin sides, rectangular, 4" h,
 6-5/8" x 3-7/8" 90.00
Redware, Turk's head, scalloped and fluted, hairlines, small chips, 11" d 71.50
Stoneware, round, interior scalloped design, salt-glaze,
 10-7/8" dia 137.50

Yellowware, pudding mold
 Ear of corn, fluted designs on interior sides, discoloring, oval, 2-1/8" h, 5" x 7-3/8" 260.00
 Ear of corn, scalloped designs on interior sides, simple gallery-like foot, oval, 4-3/8" h,
 7-3/8" x 9-1/4" 170.00
 Pear, deep bowl shape, ribbed sides, dark-brown glaze, roughness on rim, hairline, round, 4" h, 7" dia 49.50
 Rose, oval, hairline, chips, 4-5/8" h,
 7-7/8" x 9" 290.00
 Sheath of wheat, minor rim chips, 3-1/4" h,
 7-5/8" l 110.00
Tin, fish pudding mold, minor rust, 2-3/4" h, 10" l,
 5-5/8" w 70.00
Wooden
 Bird's heads, carved, minor edge damage, worm holes, 11-3/4" l 55.00
 Birds in nests, worm holes, screw eyes in each end, two pcs, 1-5/8" h, 11-3/4" l.......................... 126.50
 Rice cake mold, carved, handle, old worn finish,
 10-1/4" l 27.50

Foot Warmers

Background: Foot warmers held hot coals and were placed on the floor at one's feet to ward off the winter chill. They were a common source of warmth in 19th-century America. These listings concentrate on the popular country form having a punched-tin case sandwiched between a wooden top and bottom with turned corner posts.

Collecting Hint: Look for examples with unusual patterns or with names punched in the tin.

Punched tin
 Circular design, mortised softwood frame, turned corner posts, 5-3/4" h, 9-1/8" w, 7-3/4" d 270.00
 Diamonds design, mortised wooden frame, turned corner posts, 5-3/4" h, 9" w, 7-3/4" d 220.00

Graniteware bundt cake mold, cobalt/white swirl, 7-1/2" dia, $235.

Foot warmer with heart-punched tins, $275.

Diamonds design, mortised wooden frame, turned corner posts, bail handle, traces of old red, minor split in bail, 5-3/4" h, 8" w, 9" d 143.00

Heart designs with Maltese cross on door, mortised birch frame, turned corner posts, punched solder repairs, 8-1/2" w, 7-3/4" d 302.50

Hearts in concentric circles, compass star, mortised wooden frame, turned corner posts, bail handle, coal pan, minor edge damage/rust, 5-3/4" h, 9" w, 7-3/4" d 275.00

Wooden, hardwood and pine, refinished, punched holes in case, sliding front panel, tin coal container, wire bail handle, 6-1/2" h, 10" w, 8-3/4" d........................ 209.00

Footstools

Background: In ancient Greece and Rome, footstools were used to help individuals mount the couches, which were relatively high. Over time, they were used as footrests. Footstools can range from simple utilitarian pieces to particularly elaborate examples.

Cherry, old finish, cutout feet mortised through top, edge wear, 7-1/4" h, 12-3/4" w, 7" d.......................... 192.50

Decor

Buildings, flowers and "E.H." stenciled on top in gold and black, alligatored red, yellow and green paint, scalloped apron and legs, two scalloped points missing on apron, 6-7/8" h, 14" w, 6" d 770.00

Cat painted on round top, three turned legs, 9" dia 330.00

Cherries and name, old repaint, pine, splayed hand-carved legs, edge wear, 8-1/2" h, 17" w, 8-3/4" d 110.00

Grain-decor

Black and red graining (orig), pine, cutout feet, scrolled aprons, chip carving, worn, 6" h, 14" w, 6" d 330.00

Black over earlier red paint, mortised, splayed bootjack ends, oval top, worn, 7" h.................... 220.00

Brown comb grain repaint, bootjack feet, scalloped trim, legs mortised through the top, 9" h, 17-5/8" w, 9-1/2" d 110.00

Painted

Black, turned splay legs, oak, worn, 7-3/4" h, 9" w, 6-1/2" d 77.00

Brown, hardwood, oblong top, narrow beveled edges, splayed turned and tapered legs mortised into top, wear, 8" h, 11-3/4" w, 6-1/4" d....... 350.00

Brown (old), gold stripes, poplar, splayed turned legs, worn paint, 9" h, 13-3/4" w, 9" d 275.00

Gray, oblong top with rounded ends, shaped plank legs with arched cutouts, legs mortised through top, wear, 6-7/8" h, 14" w, 6-3/8" d 550.00

Green, black and white striping, two tier, peaked top over canted footrest on each side, scrolled ends, 10" h, 14" w 440.00

Green crackled repaint, bootjack base, 9" h, 16" w, 8" d 55.00

Rolling pin, yellow paint, ring-turned legs, paint loss, 8-1/2" h, 19" l 143.75

Scrubbed top in orig finish, mortised construction, canted bootjack ends, serpentine piercing in top, walnut, 6-5/8" h, 16" w, 8-3/4" d 165.00

Twig art, upholstered top, halved branches around sides, four branch legs, X-stretcher, some soiling, 9-3/8" h, 15" w, 9-1/2" d 325.00

Walnut, canted bootjack legs mortised through oblong top, applied scalloped apron reinforced with nails/screw, top split, 6-1/2" h, 13-3/8" w, 6-1/2" d 90.00

Windsor, grain-painted, Maine, early 19th C., grain paint simulates mahogany over earlier red and green, rectangular top, chamfered edges, four splayed vase-and-ring turned legs, minor paint and height loss, 9" h, 11-1/2" w, 10" d, pr 2,875.00

Fountains

Background: Once found only in public places and large estates, fountains are found as elements in

18th-century Windsor foot stool, $2,500.

Fountain attributed to J.W. Fiske, 46-3/4" h, $2,875. (Photo courtesy of Skinner Auctioneers & Appraisers of Antiques & Fine Arts, Boston and Bolton, Mass.)

gardens and on lawns of many people who simply like their decorative appeal.

Note: All listings are cast iron.

Three-dolphin base, cherub in center of bowl, white paint, wear, rust, 45" h 2,200.00

Attributed to J.W. Fiske, base with cranes and cattails, molded circular platform, old white paint, 46-3/4" h, 26" dia 2,875.00

"Robert Wood & Co., Philadelphia," cast-leaf border, three-pc center section, three feet with applied leaves, lions' heads spout water on column, flared bowl in middle topped with full-figure cherub, mismatched, welded repairs, 63" h, 70" dia 4,125.00

Fountain figure, swan, cast iron, wings outstretched, neck stretched up and mouth open, white with black beak, on green cylindrical post, wear, late 19th C., 37-1/2" h, 17-1/2" dia 5,750.00

Frakturs

Background: Mainly of Pennsylvania Dutch origin, certain illuminated birth and baptismal certificates, marriage certificates, awards of merit, family registers, and other family documents are called fraktur because of their similarity to a 16th century German type-face of the same name. These hand-lettered folk art records generally incorporated bright watercolor borders, stylized birds, and heart motifs.

Museum: The Free Library of Philadelphia, PA.

Note: All listings are Pennsylvania German unless otherwise noted. Dates refer to the event commemorated by the fraktur.

Birth Record (Geburts und Taufschein)

1772, pen and ink and watercolor on wove paper, orange, black and brown, beveled frame with worn red graining, stains, fading, 7-5/8" h, 12-1/2" w 880.00

1804, Berks County, Pa., by Martin Brechall, watercolor on laid paper, red border topped with stylized tulips and other flowers in red, blue, brown and black, text in red and black, stains, paper damage, modern painted frame, 6" h, 8" w 715.00

1808, Northumberland County, Pa., circular sunburst in center with text surrounded by 4 circular sunbursts in each corner, floral designs, tulips in center of all four sides, orange, yellow, blue and brown, framed and matted, foxing, tears, minor paper loss, 13-1/8" h, 16-1/2" w 6,700.00

1812, Berks County, Pa., by Martin Brechall, printed text, verse and eagle, hand-done decor in pen and ink on laid paper, red, blue, and yellowish-gray watercolor, framed, stains, damage and color bleeding, 13-1/2" h, 9-1/4" w 385.00

1813, Noah Hampton County, labeled "F. Krebs," pen and ink and watercolor, printed format, heart motif, parrots, tulips and stars, orange, brown, green and yellow, framed, some damage, glue stains, 13" h, 15-1/2" w 1,100.00

1818, Union County Pa., by Francis Portzline, text in center, large circular design with bands of small hearts flanked by facing birds with small double entwined heart designs above and below text, sides flanked by large urns with tulips, brown and green, framed and matted, minor foxing, slight stains, minor border tears, 11-3/4" h, 18" w 10,000.00

1820, Berks County, Pa., printed by "Rotter, Reading," printed and handcolored, angels with cherub and birds, yellow, blue, orange, red and purple, unframed, stains, margin tears, 16" h, 13" w 192.50

1827, Lycoming County, Pa., by Henry Young, soldier on horseback, horse with red, yellow and blue saddle, blanket and bed roll, soldier dressed in red and brown striped pants, red coat with light-blue front and yellow epaulets, wearing helmet with large blue plume and blowing a yellow trumpet, below the figures are three lines of text, "Northumberland Troop. In Hepburn Township. Lycoming County, State of Pennsylvania," eight-point star in red, yellow and blue in each corner, period salmon-colored grain-painted frame, fold mark with some separation, foxing, water stains, frame damage, 10" h, 8" w 18,000.00

1831, Schuylkill County, Pa., printed by "Ruth, Rube and Young, Allentown," handcolored angels, birds, etc., in red, green, yellow and blue, framed, wear, fading, 19-1/2" h, 17-1/2" w 247.50

1833, printed by "D.P. Lange, Hannover, 1833," handcolored, angels, birds, etc., in red, blue and green, no information filled in, framed, paper damage, 14-3/4" h, 18-1/2" w 192.50

1838, Lebanon County, Pa., by Jacob Stiver, Lebanon, printed and handcolored, woodblock-printed flowers and leaves and eagle in black, red, yellow, blue and green, framed, stains, wear, 12-1/2" h, 15-1/4" w 495.00

1840, Centre County, Pa., signed "Daniel Diefenbach," printed and handcolored, red, yellow, green and blue, stains, worn edges, geometric inlaid frame, 8-1/4" h, 13" w 660.00

1849, Schuylkill County, Pa., printed by "J.T. Werner, Pottsville, Pa.," printed and handcolored, red and green, old reeded frame, stains, some damage, fold lines, 19" h, 16-1/4" w 302.50

1852, Berks County, Pa., printed in Reading, Pa., printed and handcolored, angels, cherub and birds in yellow, red, green and light-green, minor stains, bird's-eye veneer frame with damage, 19-3/4" h, 17-1/4" w 247.50

1859, attributed to Wayne County, Ohio, watercolor and pencil, angel wearing pink and light-orange dress, pink and green rose with hummingbird, blue lined paper, light stains, glued between mat, 16-3/4" h, 13-3/4" w 330.00

Birth and Baptism Record

1833, Mill Creek, Ohio, by Peter Kaufmann, printed and handcolored, "Certificate of Birth and Baptism," angels, cherubs and flowers, modern

Fraktur by Francis Portzline, 1818 birth record of Anna Borkhart, Union County, Pennsylvania, 11-3/4" x 18", $10,000. (Photo courtesy of Horst Auctioneers, Ephrata, Pa.)

painted frame, fold lines, minor stains, 19" h, 15" w... 605.00

1852, Center County, Pa., by Henry Young, small multi-point stars in orange, yellow and blue, 2 hand-drawn and colored figures of a man dressed in a black swallow-tailed coat with green pants and white/orange striped vest, handing a bouquet of flowers to a woman in a white dress having a floral print and lace collar, between the figures is a yellow tripod stand holding a vase with scrolled handles, green ground, minor tears and foxing, matted and framed, 11-3/4" h, 7-3/8" w........................ 8,500.00

Bookmark, heart design at bottom with alternating red and green sawtooth border, top corners with hearts and small red and green floral rosettes with black leaves, border of two black lines containing a sawtooth red line in the center flanked by green dots, framed, foxing, water stains, 5" h, 3" w 5,200.00

Bookplate

1829, pen and ink with red and yellow watercolor, bird on flower, verse, dark-yellow frame with smoke decor and black corner blocks, stains, edge damage, 6-1/2" h, 3-3/4" w 330.00

1884, Amish folk artist Barbara Ebersol, small heart in center outlined with yellow and orange scallops and containing small floral rosettes, dots and leaf motif in yellow, green and orange, "Dieses Buchein Gehoret Mir Lea Speicher" in black letters above heart, "Geschriben den 30 ten May 1884" below, all surrounded by blue and purple stripes with small diagonal corner brackets, 5-3/4" h, 3-5/8" w 425.00

Pen and ink and watercolor on wove paper, tulips and urn in red, green and brown, contemporary frame, glued down at corners, light stains, short tear, 5-1/8" h, 3-1/8" w 715.00

Certificate, watercolor and pen and ink, "For a Good Boy" in red, yellow eagle with branch, two stars, old curly maple frame, stains, tears, 6-1/2" h, 9-1/2" w 330.00

Fraktur by Henry Young, 1827 birth record showing soldier on horseback, water stains, 10" x 8", $18,000. (Photo courtesy of Horst Auctioneers, Ephrata, Pa.)

Contemporary, David Schoner, pen and ink and watercolor on textured paper, heart with tulip, damage and wear, framed, 8" h, 5" w 165.00

Family record

Holmes County, Ohio, pen and ink and watercolor, "The Record of Jacob & Maddalene Strome's family...," architectural motifs with arch, swags and urn finials, yellow, pink, green, brown, red and black, framed, stains, damage, color loss, 15" h, 13" w.. 770.00

Wayne County, Ohio, watercolor and pencil on paper, records 1857 marriage and subsequent births of eight children, angel at top, rose at bottom, green, faded yellow and brown, orig frame with ivory and yellow on dark brown, 15" h, 11-1/2" w.. 770.00

House blessing (haus segen), printed in Reading by John Ritter, printed and handcolored, cherubs, birds, fruit and grain in yellow, orange, blue and green, framed, stains, 16" h, 12" w 220.00

Miscellaneous

Pen and ink and watercolor, bird on scrolled leafy branch, butterfly in air, green and black, "18" in corner, border stripes in black, green and faded yellow, newer frame, wear, 3-1/8" h, 2-5/8" w 412.50

Pen and ink and watercolor, two birds on two stylized trees, two birds on ground under flowers, lettered "Louesa Fox, February 8th., 1849," blue, yellow, black, green and red, old ogee frame, tears, incomplete corners, 8" h, 9-3/4" w 275.00

Pen and ink and watercolor, heart in brown, yellow and blue, interior heart, flowers and foliage and "Maria Hoffert" in yellow, white, green and brown, minor stains, small amount of flaking, short edge tear, old frame, 6" h, 7-3/4" w 2,200.00

Watercolor, German Bible verse in red, green and yellow, floral border, translation on back mentions owner and 1843, worn gilt frame, glued down, stains, some damage, 6-3/4" h, 3-7/8" w 302.50

Tauf zedel, Pennsylvania German certificate, printed, handcolored, dated 1850, floral design in red, green, yellow and blue, old frame, minor stains, damage at fold lines, 9" h, 7" w 104.50

Frames

Background: The market for antique American picture frames is certainly in its infancy, having been virtually non-existent until the early 1980s. When determining the value of a particular frame, one must consider three constants—age, size, and rarity—and two variables—the desirability of the design and the condition of the surface.

A frame with the signature of the frame-maker or artist who crafted it is worth more than an example without identifying marks, but signed examples are increasingly difficult to find. When present, signatures are usually located on the back of a frame. Most frame-makers marked their work with a paper label, however. Unfortunately, many of those fragile identifiers have been peeled off or lost over the years.

Reference: Eli Wilner with Mervyn Kaufman, *Antique American Frames*, 2nd ed., Avon Books, 1999.

CDV wall frame

Walnut, divided for 12 photos (three rows of four), Victorian cross-corner frame, white porcelain tacks at corners of CDVs, shallow carved leaves

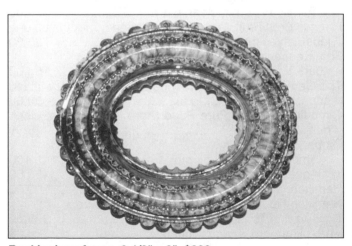

Rockingham frame, 9-1/2" x 8", $600.

at corners of frame, orig gilt liners and glass, with 12 CDVs 412.50

Walnut, divided for 15 (three rows of five), Victorian cross-corner frame, applied carved diamond-shaped blocks at corners of CDVs, shallow carved leaves at corners of frame, old gilt paint, one leaf missing, others chipped 110.00

Curly maple, good curl, 16-1/4" h, 16" w 385.00

Curly maple, pine beneath applied and boldly striped molding on the front and matching veneer on the sides, refinished, with replaced mirror glass, 26-3/8" h, 18-1/2" w 522.50

Folk art, applied wooden fragments, cross-corners, 15" h, 17-1/2" w 1,955.00

Grain-decor, pine, 17" h, 14" w 385.00

Horseshoe-form, white paint, gilt liner, 17-1/4" h, 13-1/2" w 95.00

Oak, two gesso borders in gold, 30" h, 25-1/2" w 132.50

Shell frame, 8-1/2" h, 6-1/2" w 65.00

Tramp art, divided for two photos, gold paint, minor damage, 13-1/2" h, 26-1/2" w 250.00

Walnut, shadowbox type, gilt liner, 14-1/2" h, 12" w 75.00

Wicker, orante, professionally stripped, one row of curls missing, 36" h, 32" w 1,125.00

Fraternal

Background: Benevolent and secret societies played an important part in America from the late 18th to the mid-20th centuries. Initially, the societies were formed to aid members and their families in times of distress, but by the late 19th century, they had evolved into important social clubs.

In the 1950s, with the advent of the civil rights movement, there was much concern regarding the secretiveness and the seemingly discriminatory practices of these groups. Membership in fraternal organizations, with the exception of the Masons, dropped significantly. Many local chapters closed and sold their lodge halls.

Museums: Iowa Masonic Library & Museum, Cedar Rapids, IA, www.gl-ia.org/museums.html; Masonic Grand Lodge Library & Museum of Texas, Waco, TX, www.gltexas.org; Museum of Our National Heritage, Lexington, MA, www.mnh.org.

Apron, white silk, blue border, yellow brocade, two tabs with metallic twists, decor with calipers, eye and "Solon 771" in gold metallic piping, "Peter Vogler Jun. 15. 1885" under flap, blue tassel braid ties, New York origin, 13" h, 14-1/2" w 55.00

Bible box, walnut and tiger maple, walnut case with diamond motif along sides, tiger maple edge molding and raised center panel on lid, hingeless lid recessed over base, square-nail construction, from a Masonic lodge, 4-1/4" h, 11-1/2" w, 8-1/2" d 250.00

Masonic panel painted on canvas, 50" sq, $920. (Photo courtesy of Skinner Auctioneers & Appraisers of Antiques & Fine Arts, Boston and Bolton, Mass.)

Flask, glass
    Eagle side with initials "JKB," GIV-3, greenish-blue, some sickness, pint, 7-3/8" h...................... 412.50
    Eagle with "Ohio" and "Shepards," GIV-32, aqua, flared folded lip, interior ring, wear, broken blister, 6-3/8" h.. 385.00
Panel, painted canvas, sun face surrounded by three intersecting triangles in white, dark green and black, uppermost points with black letters E.A.J.J.Y.A.O.A.H., surrounded by green serpent swallowing its tail, on red ground with black border, stains, fading, abrasions, 50" sq.. 920.00
Pitcher, transfer-decor, eye, compass and other Masonic symbols on front, sailing ship on reverse, spout missing, hairlines, 8" h.. 385.00

Fruit Jars

Background: Fruit jars are canning jars used to preserve food. Thomas W. Dyott, one of Philadelphia;'s earliest and most innovative glassmakers, was promoting his glass canning jars in 1829. John Landis Mason patented his screw-type canning jar on Nov. 30, 1858. There are thousands of different jars and a variety of colors, types of closure, sizes, and embossings.

Reference: Bill Schroeder, *1000 Fruit Jars Priced and Illustrated*, 5th ed., Collector Books, 1987 (1996 value update).

Periodical: *Fruit Jar Newsletter*, 364 Gregory Ave., West Orange, NJ 07052.

Collectors' Clubs: Ball Collectors Club, 22203 Doncaster, Riverview, MI 48192; Midwest Antique Fruit Jar & Bottle Club, P.O. Box 38, Flat Rock, IN 47234; Northwest Fruit Jar Collectors' Club, 12713 142nd Ave., Pulallup, WA 98374.

Note: In most cases, the date found on a jar refers to the patent date, not the age of the jar.

Acme Seal (script), clear, regular mouth, quart...... 50.00
Atlas E-Z Seal, green, pint.................................... 15.00
Atlas Mason's Patent
    Apple green, pint................................. 25.00
    Apple green, quart 35.00
    Light olive green, pint........................... 35.00
    Light olive green, quart......................... 25.00
Atlas Strong Shoulder Mason
    Apple green, quart 20.00
    Light cornflower blue, pint..................... 25.00
    Light olive green, pint........................... 40.00
    Light olive green, quart......................... 25.00
The Ball, Patent Appl'd For, aqua, quart 178.00
Ball Mason
    Apple green, quart 25.00
    Apple green, 1/2-gal 30.00
Ball Perfection, blue, no closure, pint.................. 100.00
Bosco Double Seat, clear, quart............................ 43.00
Boston Trade Mark Dagger Brand, with dagger, green, quart... 250.00
Brackett's Perfection Jar, aqua, lip chip, no closure, quart.. 325.00
A.E. Bray Fruit Jar, Pat Pend'g, with four-leaf clover, amber, no closure, quart................................. 750.00
Brighton, clear, 1/2-gal 145.00
The Canton Domestic Fruit Jar, clear, orig wire, quart.. 120.00
Commonwealth Fruit Jar, aqua, 1/2-gal 150.00
Commonwealth Fruit Jar, clear, quart 98.00
Erie Fruit Jar, with E in hexagon, light green, plain lid, quart.. 225.00
Everlasting Jar, light green, quart.......................... 30.00
F A & Co. (on base), iron pontil, aqua, no stopper, pint 350.00
The Family Fruit Jar, clear, pint........................... 995.00
Flaccus Bros Fruit Jar, with steer's head, milk glass, orig label, rayed insert, pint...................................... 725.00
Fruit Keeper, GCC Co. monogram, aqua, quart.. 50.00
The Gem on front, HGW monogram on reverse, whittled aqua, 1/2-gal 50.00
Gimball's Brothers Pure Food Store Philadelphia, clear, pint 48.00
Globe
    Amber, two lid chips, pint..................... 100
    Aqua, wide mouth, lip chip.......................... 155.00
Hamilton, clear, 1/2-gal 90.00
Hamilton No. 3 Glass Works, cornflower blue, 58 oz 995.00
Hero over a cross, aqua, quart............................. 38.00
The Hero, aqua, orig lid, 1/2-gal........................... 80.00

The Ideal Imperial, aqua, quart 35.00
Lafayette (script)
    Aqua, pint.. 300.00
    Clear, quart 190.00
Trademark Lightning Putnam (on base)
    Amber, 24 oz.. 135.00
    Aqua, tall quart... 100.00
Trademark Lightning on front, HWP on reverse, Putnam
    on base, aqua, quart..................................... 325.00
Trademark Lightning Registered U.S. Patent Office,
    cornflower blue, pint...................................... 125.00
Manufactured for J.T. Kinney, Trenton, N.J., aqua, lip
    flake, quart 250.00
Mason
    Green, quart.. 50.00
    Teal green, quart.. 45.00
Mason Fruit Jar (two lines), amber, pint 125.00
Mason Improved, two dots below Mason, apple green,
    quart 30.00
Mason's Improved, with CFJCo. logo, amber,
    1/2-gal 235.00
Mason's Improved Butter Jar, with CFJCo. logo, aqua,
    quart 250.00
Mason's Patent, teal, 1/2-gal.............................. 25.00
Mason's Patent, Nov. 30th 1858
    Amber, quart 325.00
    Apple green, quart 68.00
    Apple green, 1/2-gal 50.00
    Aqua marine, quart 520.00
    Aqua marine, 1/2-gal 420.00
Mason's Patent, Nov. 30th 1858, sun, moon and star on
    front, Ball on back, aqua, 1/2-gal 165.00
Mason's Patent, Nov 30th 1858, CFJCo logo
    Apple green, quart 55.00
    Light olive green, 1/2-gal 100.00
Mason's Patent, Nov. 30th 1858, with cross
    Aqua, lid unembossed, 1-gal 1,990.00
    Light apple green, quart.................................. 69.00
Mason's II Patent, Nov. 30th 1858, aqua,
    quart 35.00
Mason's III Patent, Nov. 30th 1858, aqua,
    quart 125.00
Mason's 13 Patent, Nov. 30th 1858, aqua,
    1/2-gal 65.00
Mason's 18 Patent, Nov. 30th 1858, aqua,
    quart 25.00
Mason's 20 Patent, Nov. 30th 1858, aqua,
    quart 30.00
Mason's 24 Patent, Nov. 30th 1858, aqua,
    quart 30.00
Mason's 401 Patent, Nov. 30th 1858, aqua,
    quart 275.00
Mason's Union, with shield, aqua, quart.............. 135.00
MGMCo monogram, clear, light embossing,
    1/2-gal 200.00
Michigan Mason, beaded neck seal, clear,
    pint 30.00
Peerless, aqua, quart... 198.00

Port Mason's, Patent Nov. 30th 1858, aqua,
    quart... 250.00
San Francisco Glass Works, aqua, two lip chips,
    1/2-gal 750.00
Sidney Trade Mark Dingo Fruit Jar, with dingo, light
    green, quart.. 490.00
C.F. Spencers Pat. 1868 Improved Jar, aqua, repro clo-
    sure, quart.. 395.00

WORTH PRESERVING

In a day when few people do their own can-ning, the market for fruit jars is extremely active. "I cannot stock good jars. They just go right out," said John Hathaway, owner of The Maine Idea in Bryant Pond, Maine. He specializes in fruit jars.

Hathaway used to stock 5,000 to 6,000 fruit jars, but increased demand and decreased availability have taken their toll on his inventory. Today he has about 2,000 to 3,000 on hand, and the best jars are getting harder to find, he noted.

What makes a fruit jar particularly valuable? Color is still king. Forget about the typical aqua color that was used for most jars. Collectors want rare colors. Ambers and red are in particu-lar demand, according to Hathaway.

Special thanks to John Hathaway, 3 Mills Road, Bryant Pond ME 04219-6320, (207) 665-2124, www.megalink.net/~meidea.

Magic Fruit Jar, Wm. McCully & Co., Pittsburgh Pa. Sole Proprietors, aqua, $900; Buckeye 4, aqua, $300.

Game Boards

Background: Before the advent of radio and television, entertainment took on a simpler form. Almost every house had at least a homemade checkerboard. Typically made of wood and often with a painted surface, checkerboards and other game boards have become highly popular with collectors.

Hints: Unusual color combinations and elaborate decorations bring the most interest. Look for examples that have gallery ends and/or compartments for storing the checkers.

Reproduction alert: The simple construction and painted designs have been easily recreated.

Decor, one side

Checkerboard, grain-decor, dark-red swirl and sponge decor, mustard ground, black checks, linear scroll decor, molded border, wear,
16-1/2" sq 1,955.00

Checkerboard, gray and brown squares,
10" x 13" 275.00

Checkerboard, green and yellow squares, salmon-red and black borders, 19" sq.................. 1,155.00

Checkerboard, red and mustard squares, back used as cutting board, 14" x 9-1/2" 165.00

Checkerboard, red and black squares,
18" x 27" 220.00

Grain-decorated checkerboard in dark-red swirl and sponge, mustard ground, one-sided, black checks, 16-1/2" sq, $1,955. (Photo courtesy of Skinner Auctioneers & Appraisers of Antiques & Fine Arts, Boston and Bolton, Mass.)

Checkerboard, red and black squares, rounded ends, chamfered edges, scribed checks painted black on red ground, wear,
25-1/2" x 13-1/2" 747.50

Checkerboard, red and black squares, white pinstripes, 14" sq.. 935.00

Checkerboard, red and black squares, white border, 14" sq 770.00

Checkerboard, red, black and white,
9" sq 357.50

Checkerboard, yellow and black squares, yellow ground, black border, wear, 16" x 19"......... 715.00

Checkerboard, yellow and black squares, red ends, 19" x 29" 467.50

Checkerboard, decorated, pine, orig black and red striping, stylized flowers in corners, yellow ground, lid slides off revealing pine board inlaid with walnut, with wooden checkers, found in Maine, 14" sq 7,150.00

Checkerboard, decor, pine, orig black paint, red and black squares, yellow border, applied gallery, 14-1/4" sq 1,595.00

Checkerboard, old pine cutting board, scribed checkerboard filled in with faded black marking ink, rounded ends, two wooden braces nailed to ends to stabilize age crack, worn, 18-1/8" x 19-3/4" 165.00

Checkerboard, pine, old black paint, red and yellow squares, earlier paint beneath, wear,
16-1/2" x 20".. 2,145.00

Checkerboard, pine, old worn brown, white and black paint, applied molded edge, hole for drawer, age cracks, edge damage, found in Maine,
15" sq 632.50

Checkerboard, pine, orig red and black paint, applied molded edge,
13-1/2" x 13-3/4"...................................... 1,760.00

Checkerboard, poplar, hardwood ends, old black, green and yellow paint over gray,
18-1/4" x 13-1/2"...................................... 1,540.00

Checkerboard, old dark-brown paint with green and yellow, 13" x 13-3/4" 1,870.00

Parcheesi board, red, yellow, blue, brown and white, 19" x 27" 880.00

Pine, old red, yellow and black decor, slide-lid compartment, wooden checkers, minor edge wear, 21" x 31-3/8" 4,400.00

Pine, orig light green paint with black and dark green, cross-shaped design, two-board, molded edge, wear, 26-1/4" x 27-1/4" 495.00

Poplar, old black and green paint, maroon striping and borders, wear, white paint shows beneath,
17" x 17-1/2"... 632.50

Poplar, old dark red and black paint, edge gallery with areas at both ends for checkers, relief-carved surface with raised squares, 13" w,
23-1/4" l 605.00

Softwood, orig black paint, red ground, checkerboard on one side with edge striping, all red on other side with black edge striping, dated "1880," 18-1/2" x 24-3/4" 2,695.00

Wooden, old black, green and red in worn repaint, gallery edge worn and damaged, 15-1/2" x 18-1/2" 302.50

Old worn yellow and dark-green, raised gallery edges, two-board, second game penciled on back, 18-1/4" x 28" 302.50

Dark mustard and white repaint over earlier salmon, gallery edges, two boards with nailed braces on back, age cracks, green paint splotches, 14" x 27" 247.50

Pine, one-board, orig painted decor, five circles in corners and center in salmon, blue and red, cross-shaped grid in blue, red and white, 16" sq 330.00

Old red over green repaint, black on reverse, rectangular, molded trim, age cracks, chips on rim, 18" x 28-1/2" 330.00

Decor, two sides

Checkerboard, black repaint (old), mustard and red checks, Parcheesi in green, red and yellow, applied molding, age cracks, 19-1/4" x 28-1/4" 770.00

Checkerboard, folding, black and white squares, red and black borders, backgammon board in green, red and white on other side 137.50

Checkerboard, old red and black repaint, other side with geometric design in black, white and red flourish, white line border around checkerboard, signed "H. Petty," 13" sq 715.00

Parcheesi game in shades of dark red, mustard and black paint on one side, backgammon in red, green and yellow on reverse, 19th C., minor wear, some edge roughness, 18" x 18-3/4" 2,070.00

Parcheesi game, multicolor with dark-green border on one side, checkerboard on dark-red ground on reverse, 19th C., paint wear, some rough edges 5,290.00

Folding

Checkerboard pattern, red ground, interior with backgammon and star motifs in shades of red, green, orange, yellow and black, white ground, paint wear, 14-1/2" x 17-1/4" (folds to 14-1/2" x 8-3/4") 345.00

Inlaid

Checkerboard, mixed woods, herringbone trim, decor borders include dog, pipe and cards, 24" sq 1,980.00

Checkerboard, mixed woods including ebony, mahogany, walnut and birch, checkerboard at center surrounded by sixteen miniature checkered panels, variegated band near edge, "Made by C.H. Klingberg" carved on back, moth damage to green wool backing, 22" sq 825.00

Checkerboard, pine, walnut inlay, diamonds on the border, other side has painted backgammon game in orig green, black and red, orig varnish, one small pc of inlay missing, 17" x 17-1/8" 715.00

Cribbage board, mahogany and beech, inlaid geometric designs on case and top, dovetailed drawer, 5" w, 15" l 275.00

Inlaid checkerboard, mixed woods, 24" sq, $1,980. (Photo courtesy of Cyr Auction Company, Gray, Maine)

Garden Furniture

Background: Benches, seats and tables for use outside fall under the umbrella term of garden furniture. Cast- and wrought-iron examples were popular because they were more durable than wooden furniture. Since they were exposed to the elements, it wasn't uncommon for owners to paint their garden furniture in order to hide the results of weathering.

Hint: Except in the case of unusual designs, values decrease rapidly for cast- and wrought-iron garden furniture that has cracks or breaks.

Bench, cast iron

Bird's-head arms, open geometric decor on seat, scrolled vining with flowers on back, scalloped crest, cabriole legs, scrolled feet, mkd "Kramer Bros., Dayton, Ohio," dark-green repaint, old repair on back, 33-1/2" h 990.00

Rococo detail, cabriole legs, scrolled feet, floral apron, openwork arms, back with geometric arches, scalloped crest, worn dark-green paint over earlier white, 36" h, 45-1/2" w 632.50

Twig and branch design, old blue repaint, 33" h, 35" w 1,430.00

Twig, branch and leaf design, layers of old paint, 32" h, 39" w 1,100.00

Chair, cast iron

Armchair, beveled sq feet, arched legs, round bars on seat, scrolled arms, urn and vintage designs on splat, scrolled rear posts, old dark green repaint, 28-1/4" h, pr 3,025.00

Cast-iron twig settee, 33" h, $1,540; cast-iron urn, 17-1/4" h, $385. (Photo courtesy of Garth's Auctions, Delaware, Ohio)

Armchair, openwork intertwining branches with leaves, arched arms and crest, dark-green repaint, welded restoration, 29" h 715.00

Side chair, tripod base, leaf legs and front apron, round seat with openwork geometric designs, back with vintage motif, black enamel finish over earlier colors, 31-1/2" h, pr 275.00

Side chair, cabriole legs, crosshatch casting on knees, round dished seat with scrolled openwork, horses and cherubs, balloon-shaped back with open petal design, dark-green repaint, 2 breaks in seat frame, 33-1/2" h 82.50

Garden seat, wooden, orig green paint, curving crest above arrow-back spindles, shaped arm supports, plank seat, square splayed legs with stretchers, 19th C., repairs, 32-1/2" h 1,725.00

Settee, cast iron
"John McLean, N.Y.," openwork vintage designs, cabriole legs, stretcher base, geometric patterns on seat, black repaint, repaired on back, 30-1/2" h, 43" w 220.00

Openwork detail, cabriole legs, scrolled feet, three medallions on seat, scrolled arms, scalloped back with Minerva-head crest, dark-green repaint, repaired break on 1 leg, 32-1/2" h, 44-1/4" w 990.00

Openwork intertwining branches with large leaves, dark-green repaint, 32" h, 38" w 880.00

Openwork intertwining branches with leaves, arched arms and back crest, dark-green repaint, 33" h 1,540.00

Garden Ornaments (see Lawn Ornaments)

Garden Urns (see Lawn Ornaments)

Gates

Background: Wrought-iron gates exhibit a simple rustic charm. Many have been reborn as decorative wall hangings, while others have been given new life in more contemporary garden settings. Except for the most unusual examples, breaks and other damage quickly reduces the value of a gate.

Hint: Keep security in mind. Decorative antique gates are a favorite target of thieves.

Note: All listings are wrought iron.

Double gate, overall scrollwork, top of each section curves down from sides, black paint, some rust, combined 51-3/4" h, 67-1/2" w 325.00

Double door with peaked top scroll and twist ornamentation, applied sheet-metal fleur-de-lis, 73-1/2" h, 25" w 1,430.00

Peaked top, scrollwork ornamentation throughout, 73-1/2" h, 38" w 1,760.00

Scroll detail, straight bars with arrow-point finials, "The Stewart Iron Works Co...Covington, KY" label, newer gray paint, 46" h, 50-1/4" w 192.50

Spear-like ornaments at top (2), some bent ornamentation, 41" h, 47" w 375.00

Cast-iron gate, "Edward R. Dolan" on banner over willow tree, doves and lambs, old black, green and white paint, 41" h, 29" w, $1,380. (Photo courtesy of Skinner Auctioneers & Appraisers of Antiques & Fine Arts, Boston and Bolton, Mass.)

Gaudy Ironstone charger with stick spatter floral design, border of rabbits and frogs, 12-1/2" diameter, $1,320.

ABC plate, hand-colored transfer design, 6-1/2" diameter, $135.

ABC plate, ironstone, transfer design of hen and chicks, 6-1/4" diameter, $120.

Flow Blue bowl, Oriental motif, W. Adams & Co., 10" diameter, $125.

Unsigned folk painting with cattle and sheep, 30" x 48", $2,000. (Photo courtesy of Davies Auctions, Lafayette, Ind.)

Portraits of a brother and sister, oil on canvas, 35" x 29", pair, $7,150. (Photos courtesy of Davies Auctions, Lafayette, Ind.)

Oil on board portraits of a husband and wife, attributed to Prior, old frames, 14" h, 10" w, pair, $14,300. (Photo courtesy of Garth's Auctions, Delaware, Ohio)

Pennsylvania German fraktur, pen and ink and watercolor on paper, "Maria Hoffert," 6" x 7-3/4", $2,200. (Photo courtesy of Garth's Auctions, Delaware, Ohio)

Bentwood child's drum with hand-painted flag and stars, $250.

Santa Claus candy container, electrified, holds feather tree with electric bulbs, $3,500.

Child's train, New York Central Railroad, lithographed paper on wood, $675.

German burlap-covered rocking horse, horsehair mane and tail, new rocker base, 30" h, 38-3/4" w, $440. (Photo courtesy of Garth's Auctions, Delaware, Ohio.

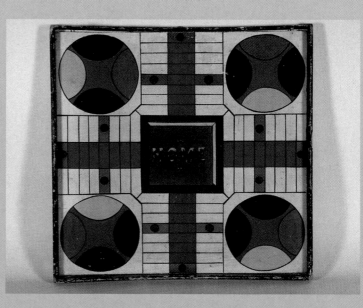

Painted Parcheesi game board, $17,250. (Photo courtesy of Skinner Auctioneers & Appraisers of Antiques & Fine Arts, Boston and Bolton, Mass.)

Cast-iron still bank, dog on pillow, original paint, 5-3/4" h, $425.

Automated goat nodder in real goat skin, glass eyes, $900.

Ohio sewer tile flat-head Spaniel, $1,750. (Photo courtesy of Jane Langol Antiques, Medina, Ohio)

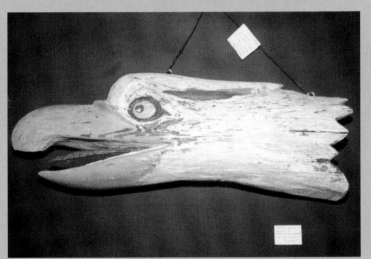

Carved eagle head, 24" long, possibly from a Maine lodge, $1,400. (Photo courtesy of Jane Langol Antiques, Medina, Ohio)

"Farm Wagon" in original green paint, $1,300.

Virginia walnut corner cupboard, carved lower doors simulate louvers, 88" h, 39" w, $5,500. (Photo courtesy of Davies Auctions, Lafayette, Ind.)

Walnut corner cupboard, $2,500.

Looks can be deceiving. This tiger maple Dutch cupboard was handmade in the late 1970s by D.L. Wendling, Boyertown, Pa., $6,600. (Photo courtesy of Davies Auctions, Lafayette, Ind.)

Mocha mugs, $300 each.

Emerald Ware cream can with graniteware lid, $1,900.

Keystone Egg and Cream Beater, metal top, $75.

Elm Wood Dairy butter mold, 9" x 10", $700.

Elgin National Coffee Mill, Woodruff & Edwards Co., 66" high, $1,050.

Sheraton tiger maple server, $12,100. (Photo courtesy of Davies Auctions, Lafayette, Ind.)

Federal chest of drawers, poplar with red graining on yellow ground, attributed to North Jackson, Ohio, 53-1/2" h, 40-3/4" w, $7,150. (Photo courtesy of Garth's Auctions, Delaware, Ohio)

Red flame-grained chest with black feet, 29-1/2", 24-3/4" w, $4,950; two-gallon ovoid jar with incised crane with fish, highlighted in blue, $3,410. (Photo courtesy of Garth's Auctions, Delaware, Ohio)

Painted Chippendale slant-front desk, maple and pine with old red surface, replaced brasses, $12,100; two pairs of English brass Queen Anne candlesticks, $440 per pair; miniature blanket chest in old green over black paint, initials in diamond, $1,210. (Photo courtesy of Garth's Auctions, Delaware, Ohio)

Pie safe in old red paint, $2,200.

Walnut stepback cupboard, Adams County, Ind., $6,050. (Photo courtesy of Davies Auctions, Lafayette, Ind.)

Tiger maple pie safe with Masonic tins, 45" h, 45" w, $3,500. (Photo courtesy of Davies Auctions, Lafayette, Ind.)

Buffalo Pottery pitcher, George Washington, Mt. Vernon on opposite side, 7-3/8" h, $250.

Blue-and-white Apricot pitcher, 8" h, $200.

Moss Rose ironstone wash bowl and pitcher, Alfred Meakin, $125.

Staffordshire tureen, "Alms House, Boston," J.&W. Ridgeway, hairlines and chip, 9-1/2" h, $3,300. (Photo courtesy of Garth's Auctions, Delaware, Ohio)

Unsigned advertising crock with chicken pecking corn, impressed "O. Vaupel, 11 Union Ave., Williamsburgh, N.Y.," restoration to cracks, $1,017.50. (Photo courtesy of Bruce and Vicki Waasdorp, Clarence, N.Y.)

"J.&E. Norton, Bennington, Vt." two-gallon jug with deer, tree and fence, restoration to stone pings, $6,600. (Photo courtesy of Bruce and Vicki Waasdorp, Clarence, N.Y.)

"Peoria Pottery" two-gallon crock with hard-to-find cobalt decoration, $5,000.

Columbian two-cup graniteware teapot, $850.

Rockingham-type pitcher, Rebekah at the Well, 8" h, $100.

Three-color coverlet, W. Minster, Allen Co., 1854, $400.

Coverlet, "Samuel Hicks, Chambersburg, Mon Co" (Montgomery County, Ohio), $1,000.

Four-color coverlet with eagle cornerblocks of Thomas Cranston, Switzerland County, Ind., $1,300.

Rag rug from the Welsh border, early 20th C., $450.

Country store sack holder with advertising, "Griffiths, Griffin & Hoxie, Utica, N.Y.," painted wood, $650.

Set of five painted egg crates with advertising, $1,650.

Painted wood gasoline sign, 20" x 31", $275.

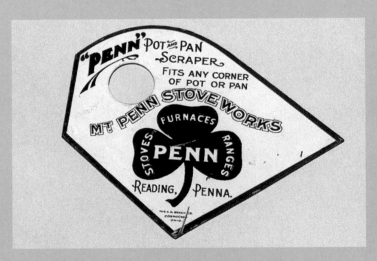

Mt. Penn Stove Works advertising pot scraper, $130.

O.B. Soap trade card, $25.

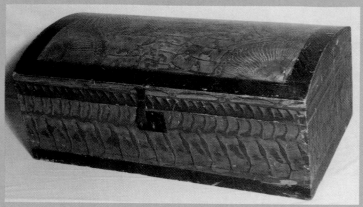

Trunk in original brown, green and black vinegar decoration, 12-3/8" h, 30-1/4" w, $1,650. (Photo courtesy of Garth's Auctions, Delaware, Ohio)

Small dovetailed box in old blue paint, interior divided for bottles, 7" h, 12-1/2" w, 6-1/2" d, $950.

Box in original red paint with decorations that include an eagle and banner, pheasants and cornucopia, and kissing birds, 4-3/4" h, 9" w, $12,100. (Photo courtesy of Garth's Auctions, Delaware, Ohio)

Dome-top box in original black paint with red and yellow floral decoration, brass bail handle and lock, 5" h, 10" w, $5,225. (Photo courtesy of Garth's Auctions, Delaware, Ohio)

Decorated box showing baskets of fruit, tulips and shells, 5-1/2" h, 10" w, $7,700. (Photo courtesy of Garth's Auctions, Delaware, Ohio)

Slide-lid box with a stylized floral design, 3-1/2" h, 7-1/4" w, $8,525. (Photo courtesy of Garth's Auctions, Delaware, Ohio)

Decorated slide-lid candle box, brown sponging and bands of green leaves, 4" h, 10-1/2" w, $5,775. (Photo courtesy of Garth's Auctions, Delaware, Ohio)

Kraut cutter with lollipop top, one scrolled ornament broken, 23-1/2" h, $150.

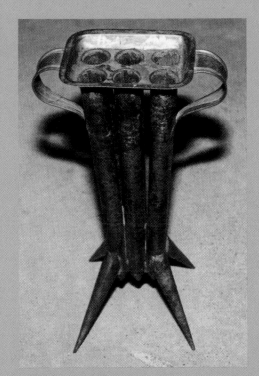

Six-tube tin candle mold with conical feet, $400.

Pewter 24-tube candle mold in wooden frame, "W. Humiston, Maker, Troy, N.Y., Warranted, Premium," $1,400.

Punched-tin squirrel cage, $500.

Round 12-tube tin candle mold, $500.

Cherry 48" S-rolltop desk, $2,700; cherry office chair, replaced vinyl seat and back, $200.

Pennsylvania decorated blanket chest, poplar with original black paint, lettered "Regina Jaeckelin 1805," $7,480; copper and zinc eagle weathervane with arrow, $3,850; Pennsylvania miniature painted blanket chest, original yellow paint and black feet, $5,225; kettle-shaped woven splint basket in old black paint, $825. (Photo courtesy of Garth's Auctions, Delaware, Ohio)

Ohio decorated grandfather's clock signed "L. Watson, Cincinnati," original reddish-brown vinegar-grained paint, $27,500. (Photo courtesy of Garth's Auctions, Delaware, Ohio)

Soap Hollow decorated blanket chest, original red paint, lettered "Jeremias Wever, 1859, Mf. by C.C.B.," $11,000; box in original black paint with geometric and floral design, pencil inscription "Douglas 1822, Massachusetts," $2,750; decorated dome-top box in old black repaint over earlier red, $495. (Photo courtesy of Garth's Auctions, Delaware, Ohio)

Hudson Valley rocking chair, $2,150.

Gaudy Dutch

Background: Gaudy Dutch is the name given to a particular type of English Staffordshire. Made specifically for the rural trade among the Pennsylvania Germans, most pieces featured flowers and bright splashes of red, green, and yellow. Gaudy Dutch was produced mainly between 1790 and 1825. Although the items had little appeal in England, they were enthusiastically accepted in Pennsylvania German communities because they were inexpensive and colorful.

References: Eleanor and Edward Fox, *Gaudy Dutch*, self-published, 1970; John A. Shuman III, *Collector's Encyclopedia of Gaudy Dutch & Welsh*, Collector Books, 1990 (1998 value update).

Collectors' Club: Gaudy Collector's Society, P.O. Box 274, Gates Mills, OH 44040.

Museums: Henry Ford Museum, Dearborn, MI; Philadelphia Museum of Art, PA; Reading Art Museum, PA.

Creamer, Double Rose pattern, 3-3/4" h 495.00

Cup and saucer, handleless

    Carnation pattern, imperfections 467.50
    Dahlia pattern 7,975.00
    Double Rose pattern 577.50
    Dove pattern, imperfections 495.00
    Grape pattern, minor imperfections 495.00
    Oyster pattern 467.50
    Single Rose pattern, imperfections 412.50
    Sunflower pattern, imperfections 715.00
    Urn pattern 550.00
    War Bonnet pattern, cup with hairlines, professional repairs 350.00

Plate

    Carnation pattern, 8-1/4" dia 935.00
    Carnation pattern, minor flakes, 10" dia 3,100.00
    Double Rose pattern, 7-1/2" dia 605.00
    Dove pattern, 7-1/2" dia 522.50
    Grape pattern, 9-1/2" dia 440.00
    No Name pattern, 8-3/4" dia 17,050.00
    Oyster pattern, 7-1/2" dia 577.50
    Oyster pattern, 10" dia 1,540.00
    Single Rose pattern, 3-1/4" dia 550.00

Gaudy Dutch: (from left) Dahlia pattern cup and saucer, $7,975; Butterfly pattern cup, saucer and plate, $1,650; No Name pattern plate, $17,050. (Photo courtesy of Alderfer's, Hatfield, Pa.)

    Single Rose pattern, 7-1/2" dia 495.00
    Single Rose pattern, 8" dia 440.00
    Single Rose pattern, 10" dia 2,400.00
    Sunflower pattern, imperfections, 9-3/4" dia 825.00
    Urn pattern, 8-3/8" dia 1,900.00
    Urn pattern, 10" dia 935.00
    War Bonnet pattern, 8" dia 605.00

Soup plate

    Double Rose pattern, 10" dia 1,760.00
    Single Rose pattern, 10" dia 1,485.00
    Zinnia pattern, mkd Riley, 10" dia 4,675.00

Sugar, covered

    Single Rose pattern, shell handles, restored, 5-1/2" h 550.00
    Sunflower pattern, shell handles, lid damage, 5-1/2" h 770.00

Teapot

    Single Rose pattern, spout chip, 6" h 1,210.00
    Single Rose pattern, spout restored, 5-1/2" h 1,045.00
    Urn pattern, 6-1/4" h 825.00
    War Bonnet pattern, with collar, spout chip, 7" h 4,400.00

Waste bowl, Sunflower pattern, 6-1/2" dia 495.00

Gaudy Ironstone

Background: Made in England around 1850, Gaudy Ironstone is a more heavy-bodied earthenware than the translucent Gaudy Welsh. The two types were decorated in similar patterns and colors.

Collectors' Club: Gaudy Collector's Society, P.O. Box 274, Gates Mills, OH 44040.

Museums: Henry Ford Museum, Dearborn, MI; Philadelphia Museum of Art, PA; Reading Art Museum, PA.

Bowl

    With shallow dish, leaves with red and green vining berries, "Wm. Adams & Co., Turnstall England," bowl 3-1/4" h, 6" dia, dish 1-1/4" h, 7-7/8" dia, pr 302.50
    Strawberry pattern, octagonal serving bowl, Flow Blue and copper luster, impressed "Elsmore Forster & Co.," 1-7/8" h, 7-5/8" w, 5-7/8" d 715.00

Charger, rabbit and frog border, floral-decor center in red and green, light crazing, 13" dia 1,100.00

Cream and sugar, Blackberry pattern, blue with yellow and orange enamel and luster, "E. Walley," fruit finial on lid, wear and small flakes, sugar has interior chip, 6-3/4" h 660.00

Cup and saucer, handleless, Blackberry pattern, blue with yellow and orange enamel and luster, "E. Walley," some variation, set of ten 1,375.00

Pitcher, Blackberry pattern, black, yellow, orange and luster, molded handle with branch and leaf design, unmarked, hairline in foot, black areas have some iridescence, 11-3/4" h 412.50

Gaudy Ironstone, Water Lily pattern pedestal fruit compote, 4-1/2" h, 13" l, $412.50.

Plate

    Bittersweet pattern, 12-sided, Flow Blue and copper luster underglaze, light stains, 8" dia 82.50

    Blackberry pattern, blue, polychrome and gold luster, "Walley," chip, 6-5/8" dia, pr 230.00

    Blackberry pattern, blue with yellow and orange enamel and luster, "E. Walley," some wear, 9-1/2" dia, set of seven 1,320.00

    Fern and Poppy pattern, molded rim, Flow Blue and copper luster, impressed English registry mark with "E. Walley Niagara Shape," one professionally repaired, others with worn edges, 8-5/8" dia, set of six 1,430.00

    Floral design in red, blue and green with stick spatter, black border of rabbits, frogs and trees with yellow and green enamel, 9-3/8" dia 467.50

    Floral vine design in red, rim with blue and green flowers, accented with gold luster, 12-sided, mkd Real Ironstone, discoloring, chip, two cracks, 9-1/8" dia 150.00

    Seeing Eye pattern, E. Walley, Niagara shape, 4-7/8" dia 300.00

    Stick spatter, cobalt flowers, cut sponge-decor stars in green, red floral border, minor flakes on edges, one with hairline, one badly damaged, 10" dia, set of eight 1,650.00

    Strawberry pattern, 12-sided, Flow Blue leaves, pink flowers, 10-1/4" dia 247.50

    Strawberry pattern, Flow Blue and copper luster leaves, paneled rim, one repaired, minor wear, flake, 9-1/2" dia, set of three 550.00

    Strawberry pattern, Flow Blue and copper luster leaves, paneled rim, flake, 8-5/8" dia, set of four 605.00

    Urn pattern in Flow Blue, pink and red flowers, copper luster highlights, stains, 8-1/2" dia 110.00

Platter, rabbits and frog in fenced field in brown transfer in center, yellow and green enamel, border with red, green and blue flowers in stick spatter, minor enamel wear on edge, oval, 10-1/4" x 14-1/2" 1,100.00

Soup plate, Blackberry pattern, blue with yellow and orange enamel and luster, "E. Walley," one impressed "Elsmore & Forster, Tunstall," 9-7/8" dia, set of three 605.00

Teapot, Strawberry pattern, paneled, Flow Blue and copper luster, minor flake on spout, glued finial, 9" h 1,375.00

Gaudy Welsh

Background: This translucent porcelain was first made in the Swansea area of England from 1830 to 1845. The designs and patterns resemble those of Gaudy Dutch, but the body texture and weight differ. One characteristic of Gaudy Welsh is the gold luster on top of the glaze.

References: John A. Shuman III, *Collector's Encyclopedia of Gaudy Dutch & Welsh*, Collector Books, 1990 (1998 value update).

Collectors' Club: Gaudy Collector's Society, P.O. Box 274, Gates Mills, OH 44040.

Child's creamer, Wagon Wheel pattern, paneled sides, squared handle, 3-1/8" h 70.00

Child's mug, Grape pattern, pink luster stripe, 2-1/2" h 140.00

Creamer

    Chinoiserie pattern, squat globular shape, ribbed base, hairline, 3-1/8" h 160.00

    Columbine pattern, globular body, scalloped edge, discoloring, 5-1/4" h 100.00

    Oyster pattern, footed ovoid body, scalloped top rim, 3-1/4" h 120.00

    Unidentified floral pattern, globular shape, flared foot, scalloped rim, six petaled red and blue flower, 3-1/8" h 170.00

Compote, ironstone, molded with floral design, blue, red and green with luster, minor wear, scratches, 4" h, 8-1/4" dia 357.50

Gaudy Welsh milk pitcher, 8-1/4" h, $250.

Pitcher, soft paste, molded rim and foot, vintage molded handle and spout, reds and greens with pink and copper luster, 6-1/8" h 220.00

Pitcher and bowl set, miniature, Grape pattern, various sizes, set of three 577.50

Plate, 12-sided, Dutch Rose pattern, stains, luster worn, 9-1/2" dia 99.00

Tea set, child's, Wagon Wheel pattern, eleven pcs including teapot, creamer, lidded sugar, two cups/saucers, two waste bowls, two plates, imperfections 522.50

Glass, Early

Background: This category focuses primarily on early American glass, a term that covers glass made in America from the colonial period through the mid-19th century. Early pressed glass and lacy glass made between 1827 and 1840 are included.

Prior to 1850, major glass-producing centers were located in Massachusetts (New England Glass Company and the Boston and Sandwich Glass Co.), South Jersey, Pennsylvania (Stiegel' Manheim factory and many Pittsburgh-area firms), and Ohio (several different companies in Kent, Mantua, and Zanesville).

References: George and Helen McKearin, *American Glass*, Crown, 1975; — *Two Hundred Years of American Blown Glass*, Doubleday, 1950; Kenneth Wilson, *American Glass 1760-1939*, 2 vols., Hudson Hills Press, 1994.

Periodical: *Antique Bottle & Glass Collector*, P.O. Box 187, East Greenville, PA 18041.

Collectors' Clubs: Early American Glass Traders, RD 5, Box 638, Milford, DE 19963; Early American Pattern Glass Society, P.O. Box 266, Colesburg, IA 52035; Glass Research Society of New Jersey, Wheaton Village, Millville, NJ 08332; National Early American Glass Club, P.O. Box 8489, Silver Spring, MD 20907.

Museums: Bennington Museum, Bennington, VT; Chrysler Museum, Norfolk, VA; Corning Museum of Glass, Corning, NY; Glass Museum, Dunkirk, IN; Sandwich Glass Museum, Sandwich, MA; Wheaton Historical Village Association Museum of Glass, Millville, NJ.

Ale glass, clear, Bull's Eye with Fleur-de-Lys, 6-1/4" h 650.00

Bell, cranberry, folded rim, clear handle with white looping, clear clapper, blown, 15-1/2" h 220.00

Bowl

- Amethyst, blown, folded rim, wear, 3-7/8" h, 6-1/4" dia 550.00
- Clear, blown, three-mold, GIII-4, 3-1/8" h, 5-1/2" dia 990.00

RECORD PRICE

Early pattern glass is gaining an increased following. One gem that sold in recent years was a Sandwich goblet, Vine pattern, clear with gilt highlights, that realized a record $16,500 at Green Valley Auctions, Inc.

- Clear, blown, three-mold, GII-22, wide rim, turned-over lip, 1-3/8" h, 6-1/4" dia 247.50
- Cobalt, blown, flared sides, rolled rim, kicked-up pontil base, 11-1/8" dia 880.00

Cake stand, clear, blown

- 6-1/4" dia to 8-3/4" dia, domed base, open air stem, applied collar around center, round top, graduated set of four 1,705.00
- 9" dia, 6-1/2" h, solid stem, plain circular foot, pontil 141.25
- 9-3/4" dia, 4-1/2" h, applied reverse baluster teardrop stem, domed circular foot with folded rim, pontil, mid-19th C. 423.75
- 12-/4" dia, 8" h, applied foot, decorative hollow stem 412.50

Candlestick, Boston and Sandwich Glass Co.

- Columnar, petal socket, canary, 1/2 of one petal missing, other chips, 9-1/4" h, pr 180.00
- Columnar, petal socket, clambroth with sand finish, c. 1850-65, chips, 9" h 60.00
- Dolphin, clambroth, petal socket, single-step base, c. 1845-70, 10" and 10-3/8" h, pr 900.00
- Hexagonal socket and base, clambroth, c. 1840-60, chip, roughness, 7-1/4" h 90.00
- Petal-and-loop design, clambroth, c. 1840-60, flake, crack, 7" h, pr 110.00
- Petal-and-loop design, yellow-tinged green, c. 1840-60, flake, chips, 6-3/4" h 140.00

Canister, covered

- 8-3/4" h, Pittsburgh glass, two applied rings on base, wafer finial, small interior broken blister 220.00
- 10" h, Pittsburgh glass, two pale-blue applied rings on base, one on lid rim, pale-blue wafer finial 220.00
- 10-1/4" h, 5-1/2" dia, blown, two applied rings on base, pressed finial, lid fits but slightly undersized 55.00
- 11-3/8" h, Pittsburgh glass, two applied cobalt rings on base, one on lid rim, cobalt wafer finial 660.00
- 11-5/8" h, Pittsburgh glass, two applied rings on base, wafer finial, slight amethyst tint, lid undersized 110.00

Celery

- Argus, clear, flake, chip, 10-1/2" h 100.00
- Bull's Eye with Fleur-de-Lys, clear, six-panel body, Boston & Sandwich Glass Co., c. 1850, 9-3/4" h 375.00
- Cable, clambroth, gilt-lined panels and band around foot, flake, 5-3/4" h 400.00

Clear, pillar mold, scalloped edge, baluster stem, minor scratches 8-7/8" h............................ 385.00

Clear, Pittsburgh, pillar mold, baluster stem, 9-1/8" h.. 220.00

Clear, Pittsburgh, pillar mold, round bases, 8 raised ribs ending in swirls on flared rim, 10" and 10-1/4" h, pr.. 522.50

Early Thumbprint, clear, 10-1/4" h 150.00

Emerald green, octagonal paneled base, paneled bowl, scalloped rim, roughness at base, 1 bruise at bottom of panel, 10" h 2,310.00

Frosted Leaf, clear, 9" h.................................. 90.00

Horn of Plenty, clear, 8-1/2" h 170.00

Christmas lights

Grape pattern, cobalt, Hearnwright mark....... 180.00

Tulip pattern, cobalt, Hearnwright mark......... 180.00

Tulip pattern, cornflower blue, Hearnwright mark.. 180.00

Diamond/harlequin pattern, emerald green 135.00

Christmas lights, Diamond pattern

Amethyst, horizontal rows of 16 diamonds, 2-7/8" h 141.25

Cobalt, horizontal rows of 16 diamonds, stains, 3-1/4" h 56.50

Cobalt, horizontal rows of 16 diamonds, 3-5/8" h 113.00

Emerald-green, horizontal rows of 16 diamonds, minor residue, 3-1/2" h 56.50

Emerald-green, horizontal rows of 13 diamonds, 3-1/2" h 84.75

Golden-amber, horizontal rows of 16 diamonds, stains, 3-1/4" h.. 56.50

Light-green with yellow tint, horizontal rows of 12 diamonds, 2-3/4" h 113.00

Medium-green, horizontal rows of 16 diamonds, stains, 2-3/4" h.................................. 28.25

Olive-amber, horizontal rows of 21 diamonds, pot stone, 3" h 28.25

Peacock-green, horizontal rows of 20 diamonds, 3" h.. 84.75

Red, horizontal rows of 14 diamonds, 3-1/2" h 113.00

Reddish-amber, horizontal rows of 13 diamonds, 3-1/2" h 56.50

Sapphire with cobalt streaking, horizontal rows of 15 diamonds, 3-1/4" h 84.75

Sapphire-blue, horizontal rows of 14 diamonds, 3" h 56.50

Violet-blue, horizontal rows of 20 diamonds, 3" h 56.50

Yellow-amber, horizontal rows of 16 diamonds, stains, 3-1/2" h.. 56.50

Compote, covered

Early Thumbprint pattern, clear, covered, ball form, 14-1/2" h.. 4,200.00

Baluster pedestal, folded rim, clear, blown, finial with regrinding and roughness, 12" h, 9-1/4" dia 467.50

Compote, open

Baroque, clear, blown, three-mold, knob stem, turned-in lip, amethystine tint, inverted variant of GV-24, imperfection in bottom of bowl, 4" h, 4" dia 385.00

Loop (Leaf) pattern, clambroth, attributed to Boston and Sandwich Glass Co., foot chip, bruise, small flakes, 7-1/2" h, 9" dia............................ 1,700.00

Clear, blown, pillar-molded, eight-rib bowl flaring at rim, applied tapering high stem and circular foot, probably Pittsburgh, mid-19th C., 10" h, 12" dia 1,469.00

Cobalt base, clear bowl, round foot and hexagonal stem with matching six panels on base of bowl, attributed to Central Glass Co., Wheeling W.Va., minor roughness on underside of foot, interior of bowl worn and scratched, 7-1/2" h, 9-1/4" dia..280.50

Creamer, blown, clear diamond pattern, applied cobalt threading around rim, applied handle, crimped end, 4-3/8" h 550.00

Cruet, blown pillar-molded, applied handle, pewter jigger top, 16 ribs, bulbous body, circular foot, probably Pittsburgh, mid-19th C., 7-1/2" h............................. 141.25

Cup plate, Lee/Rose #68, basket of flowers, clear with light touch of cloudiness, 3-11/16" dia............ 2,400.00

Decanter, clear, blown

Baroque, scrolled leaf design, three rings on neck, three-mold, straw mark imperfections, mismatched flat stopper chipped, 9-1/2" h........110.00

Club decanter, ball stopper, three-mold, GIII-5, minor residue, 11-1/2" h 220.00

GII-33, three-mold, with three rings on neck, mismatched ball stopper, some wear, annealing crack in second ring, 11" h 55.00

GIII-2, three-mold, mismatched ball stopper, minor sickness in bottom, 11" h............................ 137.50

GIII-5, three-mold, 10-1/4" h 110.00

GIII-5, three-mold, flat stopper not original, shallow flake at pontil, 7-1/8" h............................... 412.50

Greek Key design, matching stopper, three-mold, minor sickness, 14" h 49.50

Fire grenade

Harden's Hand Fire Extinguisher Grenade, violet blue, some residue, 6" h............................. 825.00

Imperial Fire Grenade, green, Prince of Wales feathers at top, sealed contents 535.00

Nutting, embossed "HSN," four diamond panels, amber, 7-1/2" h... 200.00

PSN, diamond shape, yellow, 7" h................. 430.00

Sinclair, cobalt, raised diamond pattern on back, space for label on front, no contents, crack at neck 170.00

Flip, clear, blown

GII-18, three-mold, amethystine tint, pot stone with star, 4-1/2" h...110.00

GII-25 variant, top ribs go left, three-mold, 5-7/8" 187.00

Polychrome enameled floral decor, probably German, 5-1/2" h... 452.00

Goblet, pressed glass, clear
  Argus, rim flake, 6-1/4" h 190.00
  Arched Leaf 160.00
  Bull's Eye and Diamond Point 180.00
  Comet 150.00
  Excelsior Plus 30.00
  Hawaiian Pineapple 160.00
  Lincoln Drape.. 190.00
  Magnet and Grape with Frosted Leaf and American
    Shield.. 350.00
  Scarab 130.00
Inkwell, olive amber, blown, 3-mold, GIII-29, some wear,
  1-1/2" h, 2-3/8" dia 165.00
Jar, storage, covered
  4" h and 5-1/4" h, clear, blown, pontil on bases, tin
    lids, 1 lid replaced, pr.............................. 935.00
  6-1/4" h, clear, blown, pontil on bases, tin lids, hole
    in 1 lid, pr. 605.00
  7-1/2" h and 8" h, clear, blown, pontil on bases, tin
    lids, pr. 495.00
  7-3/4" h and 8" h, clear, blown, tin lids, pr...... 385.00
  10-1/4" h and 11-1/2" h, clear, blown, tin lids, small
    area of residue, pr 275.00
  11-1/4" h, etched foliage bands, scrollwork and
    medallions with flowers, bands and buildings,
    applied etched ball finial 550.00
  12" h, clear, blown molded glass, tin lid,
    rim chip 209.00
Lamp, clear
  Horn of Plenty, fluid lamp, Boston & Sandwich Glass
    Co., c. 1845-70, 10" h.............................. 275.00
  Tulip font, hexagonal stem, round foot, pewter collar,
    minor chips, 9" h....................................... 137.50
Molasses jug
  Bellflower-SV, clear, ten-sided, blown-molded, flar-
    ing circular foot, 37 rays under base, tin hinged lid
    and collar, 5-1/2" h................................. 3,100.00
  Bellflower-SV, opalescent, orig Britannia hinged col-
    lar and lid, Boston and Sandwich Glass Co., c.
    1860, crack in applied handle,
    5-7/8" h 3,500.00
  Loop, opaque medium powder-blue, metal hinged
    lid, 6" h 1,700.00
Mug
  Etched bird and tulip in sun medallion, clear, blown,
    applied handle, 6" h 275.00
  Etched flower, clear, blown, 4-3/8" h.............. 247.50
  Etched flower and foliage, clear, blown, applied han-
    dle, 5-5/8" h 220.00
  White enamel floral decor, cobalt, blown, gilt rim,
    pontil, 4" h.. 90.00
Pan
  5-3/4" dia, 1-1/2" h, clear, blown, three-mold, GIII-
    20, minor wear.. 165.00
  7-7/8" dia, 1-7/8" h, clear, blown, three-mold, GIII-
    20, minor wear, ... 275.00
  6" dia, 1-1/2" h, clear, blown, three-mold, GIII-24,
    wear at kick-up 165.00

Pitcher
  Aqua, lily pad type foot, applied handle with crimped
    ends, blown, broken blisters, 5-3/4" h 1,870.00
  Cleat pattern, clear, 8-1/2" h.......................... 190.00
  Miniature, clear, blown, three-mold, applied handle,
    GIII-21, 2-7/8" h.. 203.50
  New England Pineapple, clear, 8" h 1,050.00
  New York Honeycomb, clear, 8-1/4" h 230.00
  Pillar molded, clear, blown, solid applied handle, pol-
    ished pontil, probably Pittsburgh, mid 19th C.,
    8-1/2" h 160.00
  Ribbed Palm, clear, 9" h 275.00
  South Jersey, deep amber, applied and tooled foot,
    bowl with four drawn fingers, applied handle,
    threaded neck, flared lip, base of handle chipped,
    stain, 7" h...110.00
Punch bowl, Early Thumbprint pattern, clear, 12" h, 14"
  dia 5,250.00
Rolling pin, free-blown, dark olive green with white spat-
  tering, rough pontil, 14" l, 1-3/4" greatest dia.... 100.00
Salt
  Boat, BT-4b, purple and blue, Boston and Sandwich
    Glass Co... 1,000.00
  Boat, BT-9, opalescent, Boston and Sandwich Glass
    Co... 600.00
  Chariot, CT-1, silvery mottled opaque blue, Boston
    and Sandwich Glass Co. 1,050.00
  Octagonal, alternating panels of diamonds and verti-
    cal ribs, blown-molded, chips, flakes, 1-3/4" h,
    2-1/2" dia 30.00
Spoon holder, cobalt, Bellflower-SV pattern, fewer than
  ten known to exist, 5-5/8" h........................... 7,000.00
Store jar
  6-1/4" h, 3" dia, clear, pushup pontil,
    tin lid 367.25
  6-1/4" h, 4-3/4" dia and 7-1/4" h, 5-5/8" dia, clear,
    pushup pontils, tin lids, pr......................... 310.75
Sugar and creamer, clear, Balloon pattern, flakes, sugar
  5-1/4" h 325.00
Target ball
  Man Shooting in Circle, pink amethyst, c. 1880s,
    2-5/8" dia 700.00
  Ribbed design, amber, mkd "G2".................. 182.50
  Van Cutsem, cobalt, crosshatch design......... 150.00
Tumbler
  Two red hearts flanked by floral sprigs in enamel
    polychrome, inscribed, "We two will be true," clear,
    blown, American or German, late 18th or early
    19th C., 3" h.. 536.75
  Copper wheel engraving of foliage and "I.F. Miller
    marr'd at Rudby Church Novr 16, 1784," probably
    Centennial, clear, blown, small interior broken blis-
    ter, 4-3/4" h 137.50
  Floral decor in enamel polychrome, opaque white,
    blown, American or German, late 18th or early
    19th C., 3-1/2" h 282.50
  Parrot in green and red enamel polychrome, addi-
    tional floral decor, clear, blown, American or Ger-
    man, late 18th or early 19th C., 3-3/4" h 678.00

HISTORIC TUMBLER

Not your typical piece of table glass, this 6-1/8" blown tumbler was made circa 1788-89 by John Frederick Amelung at the New Bremen Glass Manufactory, near present-day Frederick, Maryland. Having a grayish color, it is engraved "Federal" in a vine wreath.

The tumbler was made to commemorate the ratification of the Constitution in 1788. It sold at Skinner for $51,750.

John Frederick Amelung tumbler, $51,750. (Photo courtesy of Skinner Auctioneers & Appraisers of Antiques & Fine Arts, Boston and Bolton, Mass.)

Vase, clear, flint, Pittsburgh, wide applied foot, flared bowl with cut panels and sheaves, wear, scratches, 8-1/2" h.. 330.00
Whimsy, hat, clear, blown, three-mold, GIII-7, sickness in bottom, 2-1/8" h...110.00
Wine
    Bull's Eye with Diamond Point, clear, 4-1/2" h.. 375.00
    Cable, clear, 4-1/8" h 300.00
    Witch ball and stand, clear with white looping, attributed to Millville (N.J.) Glassworks, tiny pot stones, ball 5-3/8" dia, stand 8" h............................ 577.50

Graniteware

Background: Adhering single or multiple layers of enamel to metal items through the use of high temperatures resulted in a product with a glass-like finish that was referred to as graniteware. Although such pieces were advertised as quite durable, they do in fact chip rather easily. Pattern and color are extremely important when determining value.

References: Helen Greguire, *Collector's Encyclopedia of Granite Ware: Colors, Shapes and Values, Book I* (1990, 1994 value update), *Book II* (1993, 1998 value update), Collector Books; David T. Pikul and Ellen M. Plante, *Collectible Enameled Ware: American & European*, Schiffer Publishing, 1998.

Collectors' Club: National Graniteware Society, P.O. Box 9248, Cedar Rapids, IA 52409-9248.

Reproduction Alert: Contemporary makers of graniteware produce some of the same forms and colors as those used for vintage pieces. In addition, individual pieces of vintage graniteware have been reglazed in highly desirable patterns, including Red Swirl.

Ashtray, white-speckled, "Iron Clad Manufacturing Co., New York Pan-American Exposition 1901," central design of a child holding two matches and sitting atop a pipe, 5" dia 115.00
Bacon griddle, blue/white swirl, edge wear, chips, 18-1/4" l, 10" w... 235.00
Batter jug, gray, graniteware handle on the back side, tin lid with wooden finial, bail handle over top, orig tin lid to straight spout, 9" h 280.00
Berry bucket
    Blue/white swirl, graniteware lid, wire handle, lid knob reattached, lid chips, 4-1/2" h, 3-3/4" dia 295.00
    Brown mottled, tin lid, wooden knob, bail handle, 4-1/4" h, 6-1/4" dia... 85.00
    Brown/white swirl, graniteware lid, wire bail, 1" x 1-1/2" chip, two repaired holes in base, 7" h (including lid), 6-1/8" dia 275.00
    Cobalt/white swirl, graniteware lid, wire bail, knob chips, 7" h (including lid), 6-1/8" dia 275.00
    Columbian, blue/white base, black rim, graniteware lid with black knob, bail handle, chips, dents, 6" h, 6-1/4" dia 135.00
    Emerald Ware, graniteware lid, bail handle, crack around the lid's knob, 6-3/4" h, 6-1/4" dia 600.00
Biscuit cutter
    Blue/white swirl, black handle, considerable chipping along cutter edge, 2-1/4" dia............ 1,950.00
    Gray... 350.00
Bowl
    Emerald Ware, green/white swirl exterior, white interior, black rim, 3" h, 7" dia............................. 85.00
    Red/white swirl (orange color), black rim, white interior, minor chips, 4-1/8" h, 9-7/8" dia 350.00
Bread riser, cobalt/white swirl, tin lid, chips, 8-1/4" h (excluding lid), 17-1/2" dia 275.00
Bucket
    Black/white swirl 265.00
    Blue/white, straight sides flare to top, bail handle, 7-7/8" h, 10-1/2" dia..................................... 85.00
    Blue/white swirl, black rim, bail handle, minor dents, some loss to graniteware finish, about two gal 195.00
    Emerald Ware, green/white swirl exterior, white interior, black rim, bail handle, about two gal 275.00

Butter

Gray, oval carrier, black handle, metal wreath-type finial on lid, mkd "Granite Iron Ware," 9" l, 6-1/2" w 160.00

Gray, round covered butter, mottled cover exterior and bottom of base, plain blue-gray color to interior of cover and top of base, 7-3/4" dia 215.00

Gray, round, pewter finial, handles, edge trim and base, three pcs plus knife, 6-1/4" dia 305.00

Candlestick

Blue/white swirl, chamberstick, chips, rust, 2-1/4" h, 5-1/4" dia 135.00

Cobalt/white swirl, chamberstick, multiple chips, 2-1/2" h, 5-1/8" dia 150.00

Gray, chamberstick, 6-1/4" dia 95.00

Gray shell-shape, 5-1/4" l, 4" w 425.00

Catalog

Iron Clad Enameled Ware, softcover, 44 pgs, with price list, Pan American Special Offer, 7-3/8" x 4-1/2" 115.00

Lalance & Grosjean Mfg. Co., dated Feb 1892, hardcover, 419 pgs, binding detached, 6-1/4" x 5" 130.00

Checkerboard, red and black 120.00

Churn, blue/white swirl, black handles and rim, wooden lid and dasher, chips, 18" h 1,100.00

Coaster, Chrysolite, 1/2" h, 3-1/2" dia 190.00

Coffee biggin

Blue/white swirl, black handle, tin lid and biggin, chips, 5-1/8" h (base) 250.00

Brown/white swirl, gooseneck, tin lid and biggin, replaced wooden knob, rust on lid and biggin, one-cup 1,200.00

Cobalt/white swirl, gooseneck, tin lid and biggin, wire strainer, chip, one-cup 850.00

Gray, graniteware base with gooseneck spout, tin lid and biggin, one-cup 410.00

Red/white swirl, red handle, granite lid and biggin, chips, 12-1/2" h 155.00

Coffee boiler

Brown/white swirl, swirl handle, graniteware lid, chips to knob and edge of lid, 13-3/4" h 475.00

Chrysolite, green/white body, green handle, tin lid, wooden knob, 1 chip, 10" h (excluding lid) 325.00

Cobalt/white swirl, graniteware lid, wire bail, chips, 13" h 250.00

Cobalt/white swirl, blue handle, graniteware lid, Bakelite knob, slight rust, 12-1/2" h 300.00

Columbian, black handle and rim, graniteware lid, bail handle, lid chip, 13" h 525.00

Emerald Ware, graniteware base and lid, wire bail, chips, 12" h 550.00

Emerald Ware, graniteware lid, wire handle, chipped knob, 12" h 450.00

Coffeepot

Blue/white swirl, black handle and finial, 10-1/8" h 140.00

Chrysolite, lid reattached, 10-1/4" h 375.00

Emerald Ware, green/white body and lid, light chipping to knob and base , 9-1/2" h 475.00

Gray, bell-shaped, pewter lid, rim, handle, spout and base, 10-1/4" h 200.00

Gray, cast-iron handle, granite lid with wood finial, 1-cup, 5-1/4" h 260.00

Gray, gooseneck spout, pewter-decor engraved Victorian design, 9-3/4" h 150.00

Coffee server, gray, elaborate pewter lid, shoulder, handle and base in floral motif, base plug marked "Manning Bowman & Co., 400," 12-1/2" h 385.00

Colander

Emerald Ware, black rim/handles, wear, light rust, 4-7/8" h, 11" dia 325.00

Gray 35.00

Comb case

Gray, hanging, 5-3/4" h, 6-3/4" w 95.00

Gray, hanging, embossed "The Jewel" on back panel and "Comb Case" on comb holder, rust at grommets, 5-1/2" h, 7-3/4" w 150.00

Cream can

Blue, tin lid, base mkd with shield and rampant lion, chips, 7" h, 4-1/2" dia................................. 175.00

Blue/white swirl, tin lid, wire bail, 9-3/4" h, 6" dia 300.00

Blue/white swirl, Boston cream can, tin lid, bail handle, 7-1/2" high (excluding lid) 225.00

Chrysolite, green/white body, tin lid, wire bail, base chips, 6" h (excluding lid)............................ 400.00

Chrysolite, green/white body, tin lid, wire bail, 1 small chip, 8-1/2" h (excluding lid), 5-1/2" dia 950.00

Cobalt/white swirl, tin lid, wire bail, 6" h, 4" dia 500.00

Cobalt/white swirl, tin lid, wire bail, 7-1/2" h, 4-3/4" dia 450.00

Cobalt/white swirl, Boston cream can, tin lid, black side handle, 10" h, 6-1/4" dia, chips 110.00

Emerald Ware, green/white body, graniteware lid, bail handle, 9-1/4" h, 5" dia..................... 1,900.00

Emerald Ware, green/white body, tin lid, bail handle, 9-1/2" h, 6-1/8" dia 1,050.00

Gray, Boston cream can, tin lid, side handle, 4-7/8" h (excluding lid), 3-1/4" dia 305.00

Gray, tin lid, wire bail, 4-1/2" high, 3-1/4" dia 225.00

Emerald Ware graniteware cream can with tin lid, $1,050; Emerald Ware berry bucket with graniteware lid, $600.

Gray, tin lid, wire bail, partial paper label "Nesco Royal Granite Enameled Ware," 8" h (excluding lid) 155.00

Light-blue mottled, graniteware lid, strap and bail handles, inner rim chip, minor base chips, 10" h, 6" dia 95.00

Creamer, gray, pewter lid, shoulder, handle, waist ring and base, 6-1/2" h... 435.00

Cup, cobalt/white swirl, black rim, white letters "S.H.Co." (possibly Shapleigh Hardware Co.), white interior, small base chip, 1-7/8" h, 3-5/8" diameter 175.00

Dipper

Cobalt/white swirl, cocoa dipper, white bowl interior, black wooden handle, 14-1/2" l, bowl 4" dia 800.00

Columbian, Windsor style 345.00

Emerald Ware, green/white swirled bowl, black handle, 11" l, bowl 3-3/4" dia 130.00

Emerald Ware, Windsor style, green/white swirl bowl exterior, white interior, black handle and rim, 13-1/2" l, bowl 4-1/2" dia............................ 155.00

Gray, cocoa dipper...................................... 105.00

Gray, water dipper 40.00

Dustpan, gray mottled 35.00

Flask, gray, aluminum lid, 6-3/8" h 95.00

Food mold

Blue/white, rabbit design, 3-3/4" l, 3" w 130.00

Blue/white swirl, turk's head 115.00

Cobalt/white swirl, cake mold, 7-1/2" dia 235.00

Gray, rabbit design, 3-5/8" l, 2-7/8" w 170.00

Gray, strawberry design, 1-3/4" h, 5" l, 4" w.. 235.00

Frying pan

Blue/white swirl, black handle, white interior, 14-1/4" l, 7-7/8" dia 180.00

Columbian, black handle, blue/white base, white interior, 18-1/4" l, 10-5/8" dia 450.00

Funnel

Cobalt/white swirl, 6-1/4" h, 5-1/8" dia 415.00

Gray, witches' hat percolator funnel, 7-1/8" h.. 185.00

Green/white swirl, wear, 5" h, bowl 4" dia........ 95.00

Grater, gray, 13-1/2" h, 4-7/8" w 260.00

Kettle

Emerald Ware, graniteware lid, bail handle, 7" h, 7-3/4" dia 400.00

Emerald Ware, green/white, graniteware lid, wire bail, 5" h, 8-1/4" dia 375.00

Emerald Ware, Berlin kettle, green/white swirled base and lid, 5-1/2" h, 6-1/4" dia 225.00

Gray, child's, wire handle, 4" dia...................... 85.00

Lava, paper label 135.00

Lunch pail

Cobalt/white swirl, oval, cobalt lid, black rims, bail handle, 3 pcs 325.00

Gray, oval, bail handle, partial Nesco paper label, 10" h, 9" l, 7" w 225.00

Lunch set, gray, four stacking containers, graniteware lid, rusted metal clamp assembly, 13" h, 7-3/4" dia.. 375.00

Match safe, gray, double pockets, 5-1/8" h, 4-3/8" w... 225.00

Measure

Cobalt/white swirl, black handle, white interior, light wear/rust, 4-5/8" h 450.00

Gray, gill measure, partial paper label "Nesco Royal Granite Steelware," dated 1899, 2-7/8" h.. 200.00

Gray, gill measure, embossed "1/4 Qt. Liq'd".. 165.00

Gray, gill measure, embossed "1/8 Qt. Liq'd".. 500.00

Gray, seamless, "El-An-Ge Mottled Gray Ware" label, half-pint, 3-1/4" h................................ 85.00

Milk pan

Lava... 70.00

Red/white swirl, chips, 2-7/8" h, 12-1/4" dia 700.00

Miniature

Basin, cobalt/white, 4-1/4" dia 140.00

Bucket, gray, bail handle, 3" h, 3-1/4" dia 205.00

Bucket, light-blue, bail handle, 3-1/4" h, 3-3/8" dia 165.00

Colander, gray, 3-5/8" dia 425.00

Colander, gray body, black rim, 1-3/4" h, 3-7/8" dia (including handles) 800.00

Colander, light-blue, white interior, 1-1/2" h, 3" dia 230.00

Colander, light-blue, white interior, 1-1/8" h, 2-5/8" dia 345.00

Dustpan, blue mottled.................................... 105.00

Egg pan, gray, mkd "L&G Mfg. Co., Agate, Nickel-Steel-Ware," 7/8" h, 4-1/4" dia (including handles) 175.00

Funnel, witch's hat, confetti 305.00

Grater, light-blue 60.00

Potty, gray, mkd "L&G Mfg. Co.," slight handle chips, 1" h, 1-5/8" dia 3,000.00

Roaster, cobalt/white swirl, three-pc, black handles and rim, white graniteware insert, minor chips, 7-1/4" l, 3-7/8" w 1,800.00

Teapot, cobalt/white swirl, recessed graniteware lid, lid reattached, 4-3/4" h 185.00

Teapot, gray, straight-spout, tin lid, wooden knob, light rust, 4-1/4" h 475.00

Tub, gray, 2-1/2" h, 4-1/2" dia 525.00

Gray graniteware witch's hat percolator funnel, $185.

Utensil rack, light-blue, with skimmer, ladle and turner with white handles, rack 5-1/2" h, 3" w.. 700.00

Muffin pan

One-hole, cobalt/white swirl, white interior lettered "C.E.S.&Co., Terre Haute, Indiana," 3-3/8" dia 210.00

Six-hole, cobalt/white swirl............................. 175.00

Eight-hole, cobalt/white swirl (both sides), black trim, 14-1/2" l, 7-1/4" w 450.00

Eight-hole, gray, wire frame 60.00

Mug

Cobalt/white swirl, bulbous bottom, black handle and rim, 3-1/8" h 155.00

Green/white, child's mug 25.00

Mush mug, cobalt/white swirl 115.00

Pan

Angel food, lava 105.00

Baking, cobalt/white swirl, paper label "Genuine 'Delft,' Simmons Hardware Co. Inc., St. Louis, Mo.," near mint cond., interior 8" x 10", exterior 8-1/8" x 11-1/8" 800.00

Baking, Columbian, 9" x 11" 195.00

Bread loaf, cobalt/white swirl 75.00

Lady finger, gray, mkd "L&G Mfg Co., Agate, Nickel-Steel-Ware," 11-3/4" l, 6-1/4" w 145.00

Pie pan

Cobalt/white swirl... 65.00

Emerald Ware, green/white swirl exterior, white interior, 10" dia 90.00

Pitcher

Ice-lip, gray, paper label................................ 235.00

Water, blue/white swirl 215.00

Plate, dinner

Blue/white mottled 25.00

Cobalt/white swirl... 70.00

Emerald Ware, green/white swirl, dinner size 85.00

Roaster

Blue/white, black handles, 10-1/4" dia........... 170.00

Blue/white swirl, black trim, white interior, two-pc, minor chips, 17" l, 7" w 95.00

Cobalt/white swirl, granite lid and insert 165.00

Salt and pepper shakers, blue/white swirl, metal lids, 2-1/2" high, 1-5/8" dia, pr 900.00

Salt box, gray, hanging....................................... 350.00

Scoop

Blue/white swirl, thumb scoop 255.00

Gray, grocer's scoop, 12-1/4" l, 5-1/4" w 160.00

Gray, spice scoop, 5" l, 2-1/8" w 180.00

Gray, tea scoop, 9" l, 3-3/8" w 365.00

Gray, thumb scoop, 7" l, 3" w........................ 100.00

Gray, thumb scoop, 7-1/2" l 95.00

Gray, thumb scoop, 8" l, 4-1/4" w 105.00

Shaker, gray, with gray handle and punched-tin lid, 3-1/2" h, 3" dia 650.00

Slop jar, cobalt/white swirl, bail handle, chipped granite lid, 11" h 200.00

Gray graniteware shaker, $650.

Soap dish

Gray, hanging, covered, two pcs, lid with wooden finial, 6-1/4" h, 4-1/4" w............................... 130.00

Gray, hanging, shell-shape, partial paper label "French Gray Enamel Ware," 3" h, 5-3/4" w 120.00

Spittoon

Cobalt/white swirl, white interior, 4-1/4" h, 7-1/2" dia 300.00

Columbian, one-pc.. 275.00

Gray, lady's spit cup, 3" h, 4-1/4" dia 85.00

Spoon, gray, slotted graniteware bowl, turned wooden handle, 12-1/4" l... 300.00

Spoon rest, gray, horsehead shape, mottled front, plain gray back, three peg feet with rubber covers, 6-3/4" x 9".. 155.00

Stein, cobalt/white swirl, pewter handle, pewter and graniteware lid with white banner lettered "G. Pohl," white banner on body lettered "Fum Wohl," 5-5/8" h.. 265.00

Stew pot, end-of-day in red, orange, yellow and blue body and lid, black handle, brass tag on lid handle mkd "Juice Brand 12 Pints," 9-1/2" h, 19-1/2" long (including handle), 9" dia 95.00

Strainer, cobalt handle and rim, white interior, chips, 10-1/8" l, bowl 6-1/4" dia 400.00

Sugar bowl

Blue/white swirl, black handles, granite lid with black finial, 5-1/4" h... 155.00

Gray, pewter lid, rim, handles and waist ring, copper base, 7" h 200.00

Syrup

Blue/white swirl, metal lid, chips, 6" h............ 425.00

Cobalt/white swirl, cobalt handle, metal lid, 1 base chip, light tarnishing to lid, 7-1/4" h.......... 1,400.00

Gray, rust at edge of the lid, 6" h 195.00

Gray, pewter lid, shoulder, handle, waist ring and base, lid with woman's-head finial, 8-1/4" h 400.00

Teakettle, cobalt/white swirl, gooseneck, graniteware lid, bail handle, lid chips, 7-1/2" h, 12-1/2" l............ 215.00

Teapot

Chrysolite, gooseneck, Chrysolite handle and lid, chips, 8-5/8" h.. 300.00

Cobalt/white swirl, gooseneck, black handle, graniteware lid, replaced wooden knob, minor wear/rust, lid chip, 7" h 425.00

Cobalt/white swirl, gooseneck, graniteware lid, chips, 8-1/2" h.. 250.00

Gray, pewter lid, handle and shoulder ring, copper base, 5-1/4" h, 7-3/4" l 210.00

Gray, pewter lid, handle, spout, central ring and base, 8" h 120.00

Gray, pewter lid, shoulder, gooseneck spout and base, 10" h 225.00

Red/black swirl, end-of-day, gooseneck, recessed graniteware lid, tan interior, base mkd "Elite, Made in Czechoslovakia, Reg'd," chipped knob/spout, rusted rim, 5-3/4" h 95.00

Snow on the Mountain, green/white, gooseneck 95.00

Tea set, decor, three-pc, pewter trim, white graniteware body with handpainted heron designs under the glaze on front and back, pewter handles, shoulders, lid and bases, teapot 10" h, creamer 5" h 275.00

Tea steeper

Chrysolite, chips, rust, 5" h, 4-1/4" dia 410.00

Red/white swirl, black handle and rim, graniteware lid, minor base chips, rust on rim, lid chips, rusted-thru knob, 5-1/4" h, 4-1/2" dia 4,200.00

Tray

Blue/white swirl, white back, 17" x 13-1/2" 90.00

Gray, oval, pewter floral-decor rim and handles, impressed "Manning Bowman & Co.," 21" l (25" with handles), 17" w 2,000.00

Light-blue, oval, advertises "Stansky Steel Ware," white letters, pictures a teakettle and coffee boiler, 24-1/2" h, 19-3/4" w 400.00

White, child's tray, numbers one through ten and alphabet, three Sunbonnet Babies illustrations, 10" h, 15" l 105.00

Wash basin, Emerald Ware, green/white swirl exterior, base wear, 3-1/4" h, 11-3/4" dia 185.00

Wash pitcher and bowl

Blue/white swirl, pitcher with black handle, black rims, pitcher with some rust, pitcher 8-1/2" h, bowl 3-1/4" h, 11" dia 185.00

Cobalt/white swirl, black rims, pitcher 10" h, bowl 4-1/4" h, 14-1/2" dia 850.00

Iris swirl 400.00

Washtub

Cobalt/white swirl, black handles, white interior, minor chips, 6" h, 19-1/2" dia 105.00

Emerald Ware, green/white body, white interior, black rim, rust under rim, one inner chip, 5-1/2" h, 16" dia 225.00

Emerald Ware, green/white body, white interior, black rim and handles, minimal chips, 7" h, 17-1/2" x 14-1/2" oval 225.00

Waste jar, cobalt/white swirl, two handles, 8-1/2" h, 10-1/2" dia.. 275.00

Water cooler, cobalt/white swirl, graniteware lid, lettered "Filtres Epurateurs, Lutege, 15 Rue des Immeubles, Industriels, Paris," metal spigot, chips, 27" h.. 375.00

Grenfell

Background: The Grenfell mission in Labrador was known primarily for its production of hooked rugs, mostly depicting traditional Northern themes. Although rug hooking was a local art form prior to Dr. Wilfred Grenfell's arrival in 1892, he was responsible for promoting the work. Producing and selling the rugs filled the eight months each year that the fishing and fur-trapping society was locked in by ice.

Grenfell rugs have the tightest, finest hooking of any hooked rug. Their smooth surfaces give the rugs a needlepoint-like appearance.

Book cover, flourish design in blue and red, tan ground, red zigzag on blue border, labeled 880.00

Coasters, fowl decor, labeled, square, set of four..110.00

Coat, brown with green stripes at sleeves and waist, green piping on pocket flaps, embroidered flowers and leaves on pocket flaps and hood 330.00

Hooked rug, polar bear on ice flow with iceberg in distance, shades of gray and blue, shaded black and gray border, fabric loss on edges, stains, mounted on frame, 26" h, 30" w.. 431.25

Grenfell sailboat mat, soiling, $250.

Papier-mâché jack-o-lanterns with original inserts, pumpkin, $150; devil, $250.

Halloween

Background: Among holiday collectibles, Halloween is second only to Christmas. Early Halloween items have a distinctive look that appeal to many collectors.

References: Pamela Apkarian-Russell, *Collectible Halloween*, Schiffer Publishing, 1997; —, *Halloween: Collectible Decorations and Games*, Schiffer Publishing, 2000; —, *More Halloween Collectibles: Anthropomorphic Vegetables and Fruits of Halloween*, Schiffer Publishing, 1998.

Periodicals: *BooNews*, P.O. Box 143, Brookfield, IL 60513; *Trick or Treat Trader*, P.O. Box 499, Winchester, NH 03470.

Reproduction Alert: A variety of vintage items have been reproduced.

Figure, devil, composition, spring wire arms, leather hands, orange and green with brown horns, minor damage, 6-3/4" h.. 93.50
Lantern
    Cat, black cat on fence post, papier-mâché, paper insert, 7-5/8" h 192.50
    Devil, papier-mâché, orange, paper insert, 6-1/2" h 577.50
    Jack o' lantern, papier-mâché, orange, green base, paper insert, 5" h, 6-1/2" w 137.50
Noisemaker, devil, composition, wooden handle, roll-out tongue, paper cracked, body excellent, 11" h........ 192.50

Hearth Utensils (see Fireplace

Equipment)

High Chairs

Background: Used for centuries for confining and feeding little ones, these chairs have been made in a variety of forms.

Arrow-back high chair, old dark-green paint, probably Pennsylvania, c. 1800-20, 33" h, $372.50. (Photo courtesy of Skinner Auctioneers & Appraisers of Antiques & Fine Arts, Boston and Bolton, Mass.)

Arrowback, bamboo-turned legs, splayed base, well-shaped and incised seat, turned arms and supports, rabbit-ear posts, arched crest, mixed woods, light varnished finish, replaced footrest, 34" h 192.50
Ladderback, maple, refinished, tapered and turned legs, arms notched underneath with rolled hand holds, 3 arched slats, small turned finials, age cracks, chips on finial, replaced paper rush seat, 35" h 467.50
Painted
    Dark-brown, yellow striping, mid-19th C., three turned spindles, flared plank seat, slightly curved rectangular crest rail, turned posts, arms, stretchers and splayed legs 230.00
    Red, three-arrow back, splayed base with footrest, shaped seat, turned arms, worn paint, 32-1/2" h 467.50
    Red, old repaint with black and gold decor, four turned spindles, rounded-edge crestrail, turned legs and stretchers, 32" h 104.50
    Taupe, blue and red striping, turned legs, plank seat, horizontal splat, wear, 32" h 302.50
Windsor
    Firehouse, old black repaint, high ring-turned legs, turned front stretcher, shaped foot rest, D-shaped seat, small curved crest, damaged caning, 30" h 330.00
    Mahogany, circular top rail supported by ten turned baluster spindles with opening on one side for child's legs to fit through, round seat swivels on low turned pedestal, solid round footrest with concave surface over large turned drop finial, four turned splayed legs, turned X-stretcher base, top rail split in three places, worn finish, 30-3/8" h 850.00
    Rabbit-ear, four-spindle, dark-brown repaint, red line decor, bamboo turnings, round seat, turned arms, 36" h 467.50

Highboys

Background: Highboy is the American term for a chest of drawers mounted on a stand that is also fitted with drawers. The highboy was introduced in America around 1700 and was popular for the next century. This form has also been called a high chest.

References: Eileen and Richard Dubrow, *Styles of American Furniture 1860-1960*, Schiffer Publishing, 1997; Tim Forrest, *Bulfinch Anatomy of Antique Furniture*, Bulfinch Press, 1996; John T. Kirk, *American Furniture: Understanding Styles, Construction, and Quality*, Harry N. Abrams Publishers, 2000; Milo M. Naeve, *Identifying American Furniture*, W.W. Norton, 1998; Ellen T. Schroy, *Warman's American Furniture*, Krause Publications, 2001; Robert W. and Harriet Swedberg, *Collector's Encyclopedia of American Furniture*, Vol. 1 (1990, 1996 value update), Vol. 2 (1992, 1999 value update), Vol. 3 (1998), Collector Books; *Encyclopedia of American Oak Furniture*, Krause Publications, 2000.

Chippendale

    Cherry, nine-drawer, three short over two short over four graduated drawers, Pa., late 18th C., fluted corner columns, ogee feet, molded cornice, minor wood loss, cracked drawer edge, one foot broken, refinished, 66-3/8" h, 44-1/4" w, 22-1/2" d 6,500.00

    Curly maple, six-drawer, dovetailed case, ogee feet, scalloped returns, molded base, dovetailed drawers with molded edges, cove-molded cornice, refinished, replaced feet, restorations to drawers, 52-1/2" h, 39-1/2" w, 20-1/4" d 1,925.00

    Curly maple, six drawer (two over four), country Chippendale-style, probably early 20th C., varnished, scalloped base, brass pulls, applied escutcheons, two-board top, 48" h, 38-1/2" w, 18" d 1,430.00

    Maple with some curl, country style, six drawers, scalloped bracket feet, molded cornice, refinished, replaced brasses and escutcheons, backboards renailed and stained with small section added, cornice and feet replaced, 52-1/4" h, 38-1/2" w 2,475.00

    Walnut, bracket feet, dovetailed case, nine overlapping dovetailed drawers (three short over two short over four long), molded cornice, full dust shelves, old finish, replaced thistle brasses, small repair, edge damage, 58-5/8" h, 43" w, 24-3/8" d 4,400.00

    Walnut, ogee feet, molded base, dovetailed case, seven dovetailed overlapping drawers (two short over five long), cove-molded cornice, orig brass bails, replaced feet and molding, drawer restorations, 59" h, 39" w, 22" d 3,300.00

    Walnut and poplar, nine-drawer (three short over two short over four long), refinished, dovetailed case, bold ogee feet, fluted quarter columns,

Chippendale high chest, walnut and poplar, 69" h, 47" w, $1,870. (Photo courtesy of Garth's Auctions, Delaware, Ohio)

molded-edge drawers, molded cornice, full dust shelves, replacements including feet, top section of cornice, upper-left drawer and sections of beading, 69" h, 47" w, 24" d 1,870.00

Walnut with inlay, refinished, cabriole legs, small feet, shaped apron with scalloping, six drawers in top (three arched over three flat), three drawers in base, all with stringing, molded cornice arched to accommodate arched top drawers, top section old with some additions, base a later reconstruction, replaced brasses, 67-7/8" h, 41" w, 10-1/2" d 1,760.00

Hepplewhite

Walnut, six-drawer (two over four), refinished, inlaid, scrolled bracket feet, drawer with oval line and border inlay, old replaced eagle brasses, molded edge around top with banded inlay, edge repairs on drawers, 46" h, 37-1/2" w, 21-1/4" d 2,420.00

Queen Anne

Contemporary, curly maple, two-pc, cabriole legs, scalloped aprons, five long drawers in top, one long over three short drawers in base, molded edges, two drawers with relief-carved fans, cove-molded cornice, made by Roy McFadden, 63" h, 32" w, 16-1/2" d 2,530.00

Maple, Mass., c. 1750-80, five long graduated drawers over one long drawer over three short drawers, molded cornice, mid-molding to lower case, flat arched skirt, cabriole legs, pad feet, replaced brasses, old surface, imperfections, 71" h, 38-1/2" w, 19" d... 14,950.00

Maple, North Shore, Mass., mid-18th C., split top drawer over four drawers, base with one long drawer over three small drawers, center drawer is fan-carved, shaped skirt with scrolled drops, cabriole legs, high pad feet, cove-molded cornice,

replaced brasses, refinished, minor imperfections, 75" h, 38-1/2" w, 20-1/2" d 28,750.00

Maple, probably Conn., c. 1750-70, nine drawers, top with flat molded cornice above case of two short drawers over four graduated long drawers, set into lower section of three short drawers, cabriole legs, high pad feet, valanced skirt, orig brasses, old finish, 71" h, 38" w, 18-1/2" d 40,250.00

Maple and cherry with some curl, cabriole legs, scrolled apron, base with three dovetailed overlapping drawers, top case dovetailed with six dovetailed overlapping drawers, molded cornice, orig brasses, pieced repairs, legs ended out approximately 9", 62-3/4" h, 38-1/2" w, 17-3/4" d 3,575.00

Oak, dark-red finish, New England, eight drawers, top with two short over three long drawers, base with three drawers, scalloped apron, turned drops, molded waist, step-down cornice, replaced bat-wing brasses, restorations, 66" h, 37-1/2" w, 20" d 7,700.00

Walnut and maple, Mass., c. 1740-60, nine drawers, upper section with flat cornice above two short and three long drawers, lower case with one long over three short drawers, cabriole legs, pad feet on platforms, orig brasses, old surface, 70-3/4" h, 38" w, 20" d... 17,250.00

Sheraton, curly maple veneer and cherry, country style, eight drawers (three over five), turned feet, paneled ends, cove-molded cornice, some edge damage, refinished, replaced wooden knobs, replaced inlaid shield-shaped escutcheons, 67" h, 42-3/4" w, 21-1/2" d 4,345.00

Transitional

Chippendale to Hepplewhite, cherry, old mellow refinish, French feet with scalloped returns and molded trim around base, three short over five long graduated dovetailed drawers, dovetailed case, reeded quarter columns, cove-molded cornice, orig brasses, minor edge damage, 63-3/4" h, 42-1/2" w, 23" d 6,050.00

Hitching Posts

Background: Generally made of cast-iron, hitching posts ranged from plain to fanciful. They typically had a looped ring to which reins could be attached in order to keep a horse in place.

Reproduction Alert: Various forms have been reproduced.

Black boy holding lantern with green and white slag glass panels, square base, cast-iron, old green repaint, areas of rewelding at joints, 44" h........ 880.00

Horse-head, ring in mouth, round post, black paint, 57-1/4" h, pr 390.00

Jockey, left arm extended, right hand on hip, cast iron, "Champion Iron Fence Co., Kenton, Ohio," red, white and black repaint, 50-1/4" h 577.50

Homespun

Background: This 19th-century cloth, which was made at home or made from yarn spun at home, was characteristically rough and loosely woven. Designs tended to be plain. Manufactured versions are also included in this term.

Bed case
    Check, blue and white, initialed, 60" x 73" 475.00
    Check, blue and white, minor soiling,
      64" x 72" 325.00
    Check, blue and white, 58" x 67", with two matching bolster cases 275.00
    Check, red and white, five small sewn repairs, 58" x 62" 150.00
    Check, yellow-brown and natural, 58" x 66", with matching bolster case............................. 1,650.00
    Plaid, blue and white, 68" x 70", with matching bolster case with white fringe, initialed "WWK 1894," acquired at Lebanon County, Pa., farm auction 2,100.00
    Plaid, red and white, minor wear and soiling, 56" x 72" 75.00

Blanket, wool
    Check, black on natural, two-pc construction, wear, holes, 68" w, 76" l 330.00
    Natural, black pinstripe, holes, 56" sq.............. 93.50
    Navy blue and natural, two-pc construction, small holes, wear, 70" w, 84" l............................. 165.00
    Plaid, blue and tomato red, two-pc construction, small holes, repairs, 72" w, 78" l................. 192.50
    Plaid, medium blue and tomato red, two-pc construction, fringe on one end, 80" x 88"........ 522.50
    Plain, brown, woven, wear, soiling, seam separation, 72" x 82" 120.00

Bolster cover
    Blue and white, handsewn seams, some seams loose, 18" w, 55" l 137.50
    Blue and white, 19-1/2" x 60"........................... 99.00

Linen fabric, piece
    Check, brown and natural, 40" x 63" 725.00
    Check, brown and natural, hemmed ends, 38" x 64" 825.00
    Plaid, blue and white, minor soiling, 20" x 55" 150.00
    Plaid, blue and white, minor soiling, 40" x 84" 225.00
    Plaid, blue and white, minor stains, small sewn repair, 38" x 70" 100.00

Mattress cover, cotton, blue and white check, machine sewn, small holes, 68" x 73" 165.00

Show towel
    Dated 1806, embroidered diamonds, trees, urns of flowers, crowns and hearts in pink and blue, 6 embroidered line dividers beneath with triple fringed bottom, small holes, minor stains, 17-5/8" w, 61" l 192.50
    Dated "1848 with Seaver," hearts in stars, ladies in dresses, pots of flowers and birds, fringed bottom, stains, 15" w, 72" l 247.50

Red/white homespun pillow sham, $125.

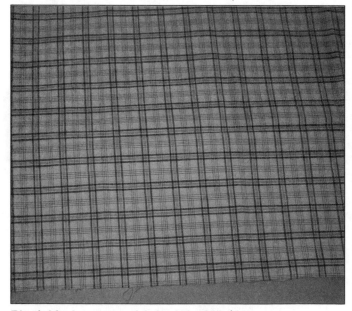

Blue/white homespun fabric, 40" x 84", $225.

Christopher Columbus ice cream mold, pewter, 5-1/2" h, $125.

Ice Cream Molds

Background: References to pewter ice cream molds date to the late 18th century, and the forms were used well into the 20th century to mold the popular dessert into a variety of shapes. Ice cream molds are often thick-walled to help maintain the cool temperatures needed.

The majority of pewter ice cream molds are individual serving molds. One quart of ice cream would yield eight to ten molded pieces. Banquet molds which held two to four pints of ice cream are relatively scarce.

Collectors' Club: The Ice Screamers, P.O. Box 465, Warrington, PA 18976.

Museum: Museum of Science and Industry, Finigran's Ice Cream Parlor, Chicago, IL.

Reproduction Alert: A variety of shapes have been reproduced.

Note: All listings are pewter unless otherwise noted.

Baby, mkd "E. & Co. N.Y. 1020," 4-3/4" h............... 49.50
Floral wreath, "E. & Co., 1142," 3-3/4" dia.............. 40.00
Flower, Britannia, 4-1/2" h...................................... 25.00
Heart, mkd "E. & Co. N.Y. 902," 4-1/8" h................ 38.50
Hen on nest, "Brevete," 2-1/2" h............................ 70.00
Santa Claus, 4-1/8" h 350.00
Santa Claus, full-figure, "E. & Co.," 4-5/8" h........ 247.50
Santa Claus, full-figure, hinges worn thin and are loose, 4-3/8" h.. 176.00

Inkwells

Background: Small receptacles designed to hold ink were a necessity in the days of quill pens and steel dip pens. Inkwells were most commonly made of glass and pottery, because the ink would not adversely affect those substances. Inkwells have become quite popular with collectors, who search for examples made of glass, bronze, pewter, pottery, and even wood. Particularly fascinating are the miniature wells designed for children's desks.

Reference: Veldon Badders, *Collector's Guide to Inkwells, Book I* (1995), *Book II* (1997), Collector

Books; William E. Covill, *Ink Bottles and Inkwells*, William S. Sullwold Publishing, 1971; Jean and Franklin Hunting, *The Collector's World of Inkwells*, Schiffer Publishing, 2000; Ray and Bevy Jaegers, *The Write Stuff: Collector's Guide to Inkwells, Fountain Pens, and Desk Accessories*, Krause Publications, 2000.

Collectors' Clubs: St. Louis Inkwell Collectors Society, Box 29396, St. Louis, MO 63126; The Society of Inkwell Collectors, 5136 Thomas Ave. S, Minneapolis, MN 55410, www.soic.com.

Glass, olive-amber, blown, three-mold, GIII-29, some wear, 1-1/2" h, 2-3/8" dia................................... 165.00
Treen, sponge-decor, brown and yellow, gilt stenciling, glass insert, "Manufactured by S. Silliman & Co...Conn.," wear to top, 2-1/2" h, 4-1/4"dia 192.50

Irons

Background: Cast-iron became the material of choice for irons during the second half of the 19th century. Before 1850, most irons had been engraved brass or hand-wrought.

Between 1850 and 1910, irons were heated in four ways: 1) a hot metal slug was inserted into the body, 2) coal or charcoal was placed in the body, 3) a liquid such as gas was fed from an external tank and burned in the body, and 4) the iron was placed on a stove top where it absorbed heat.

References: Dave Irons, *Irons by Irons*, self-published, 1994; —, *More Irons by Irons*, self-published, 1997; —, *Pressing Iron Patents*, self-published, 1994.

Periodical: *Iron Talk*, P.O. Box 68, Waelder, TX 78959.

Collectors' Clubs: Club of the Friends of Ancient Smoothing Irons, P.O. Box 215, Carlsbad, CA 92008; The Midwest Sad Iron Collectors Club, 24 Nob Hill Dr., St. Louis, MO 63138-4171.

Museums: Henry Ford Museum, Dearborn, MI; Shelburne Museum, Shelburne, VT; Sturbridge Village, Sturbridge, MA.

Miniature, fluting iron, cast iron, curved form with handle, 1-1/2" l... 400.00
Sad iron, arched scrollwork iron and wood handle with chicken catch, gold repaint, underside of lid mkd "AFG 3," worn old black paint on base, 8-1/4" l............ 88.00

Gray graniteware iron, $35.

Ironstone

Background: Charles Mason first patented ironstone in England in 1813. The dense, durable, white stoneware was named "Mason's Patent Ironstone China," even though the reference to china was misleading since the items were actually earthenware. Ironstone derives its name from the fact that iron slag was mixed with the clay used to produce dinnerware and the like. Manufactured throughout the 19th century, ironstone was available in plain white as well as decorated versions.

References: Ernie and Bev Dieringer, *White Ironstone China: Plate Identification Guide 1840-1890*, Schiffer Publishing, 2001; Dawn Stolzfus and Jeffrey B. Snyder, *White Ironstone: A Survey of its Many Forms*, Schiffer Publishing, 1997; Jean Wetherbee, *White Ironstone*, Antique Trader Books, 1996.

Collectors' Clubs: Mason's Ironstone Collectors' Club, 2011 E. Main St., Medford, OR 97504; White Ironstone China Assoc., P.O. Box 855, Fairport, NY 14450-0855, www.ironstonechina.org.

Pitcher, "Ashworth Bros., England," ribbed design, transfer decor of birds in flowering trees and foliage with polychrome enamel, 9-3/4" h 302.50

Plate
    "Feather," Wood and Challinor, green transfer, scalloped rim, accented in red and yellow polychrome, glaze flake, 9-3/8" dia 15.00
    "Florilla," purple transfer, urn of flowers, yellow, green, blue and red enamel, stains, 9-5/8" dia, set of six 137.50
    "Maltese Scroll," dark teal blue, foliage design, English registry mark, 10-5/8" dia, set of 4 .... 55.00

Platter
    Lakeside cabin with boaters, light-blue transfer, mkd "Cat, Albion," impressed "Turnbull, Stepney," 11-3/8" x 14-1/8" 121.00
    "Seine," purple transfer, oblong, J. Wedgwood, 13-1/2" x 10-3/8" 160.00

Sugar, "Medina," blue transfer, octagonal, scrolled acanthus handles, domed paneled lid with pointed finial, J.F.&Co., lid with minor discoloring, 8" h 200.00

Vegetable, open, "Aurora," purple transfer, rectangular, accented with yellow, blue and green, F. Morley & Co., 2-1/8" h, 10-7/8" x 8-1/2" 120.00

Waste bowl, "Garden Scenery," purple transfer, round, footed, paneled sides, Thomas, John and Joseph Mayer, unmkd, some discoloring, 3-1/4" h, 5-5/8" dia 50.00

White Ironstone

Children's dishes, tea set, Paneled Octagon pattern, 11 pcs, teapot with lid, creamer, sugar bowl with lid, four handleless cups/saucers, some damage including broken spout 550.00

Coffeepot, T.J.&J. Mayer, footed, octagonal, paneled sides, square handle, rounded lid, rosette-shaped finial, nicks and flakes, minor discoloring, 9" h 375.00

Creamer
    John Maddock & Sons, rectangular, paneled sides, rounded body, 5" h 20.00
    T.J.&J. Mayer, footed, octagonal, vertical paneled sides, square handle, slight nick, 6-1/4" h 220.00

Master salt, footed, round with rounded sides, slightly flared rim, unmkd, 1-7/8" h, 3" dia 75.00

Milk pitcher, James Edwards, octagonal, paneled sides, square handle, 1846 registry mark, Philadelphia importer's name, 8" h 475.00

Platter
    Henry Alcock & Co., plain, oval, some discoloring, minor glaze wear on rim, 20-1/2" x 15-1/2" 35.00
    "Wheat" pattern, Goddard & Co., oval, minor glaze flakes, 18-1/2" x 13-1/2" 70.00

Tureen
    Clements & Hanley, covered, round footed base, bowl with tapered sides, molded vine decor on bowl and lid, fruit finial, mismatched cracked ladle, hairline on lid, 11" h 110.00
    Meakin, Bros. & Co., oval, with lid, arched handles on end, arched finial, glaze nicks, 5-3/4" h, 8-1/2" x 5-1/4", with matching oval tray, molded scroll-like handles, minor discoloring, 8-1/2" x 6-1/8" 55.00

Vegetable, covered
    Elsmore & Forster, Ceres shape, Wheat pattern, oval, open arched handles, 1859 registry mark, 6-1/2" h, 12-1/2" l 170.00
    Henry Alcock & Co., footed, base with scrolled handles on ends, molded foliage motifs, rounded oval lid, fruit-finial, three glaze nicks, 7" h, 13-1/4" l 70.00
    J. Wedgwood, Fig pattern, oblong, footed, molded handles, pear-shaped finial, 1856 registry mark, 7-1/4" h, 13-3/8" l 150.00

Wash bowl and pitcher, T.&R. Boote, plain, ovoid water pitcher, arched handle, 12-1/8" h, round footed bowl, rounded flared sides, 4-3/4" h, 14" dia 110.00

DO NOT BLEACH

Don't do it! When it comes to cleaning ironstone, bleach is definitely not your friend. When ironstone is soaked in bleach, a chemical reaction occurs that can result in permanent damage. Although bleach may seem like a quick fix, it can eventually cause the glaze to flake off.

Kas

Background: A creation of the Dutch, the kas is simply a large cupboard that is generally paneled and most usually mounted on ball feet. Frequently found in the homes of the early Dutch settlers in New York and New Jersey, they were often painted with brightly colored designs.

Amish, grain-painted, orange-brown over tan graining, poplar, shaped bracket feet, paneled ends, two doors, beveled cornice, 93-1/4" h, 64" w, 20-1/4" d......... 990.00

Chippendale, walnut, Chester or Lancaster County, Pa., mid to late 18th C., two-door, cornice with dentil molding, each door with six raised panels, ornate brass escutcheons and wrought-iron bolts, doors flanked by vertical panels with three recessed panels, each side with three raised panels, base with two thumb-molded drawers with brass hardware, molded base, five bun feet are later additions (originally without feet), repairs, restoration, 88-1/4" h, 85" w, 30-1/4" d 12,000.00

Gumwood, paneled, attributed to Matthew Egerton (1738-1802), New Brunswick, N.J., cornice with dentil molding, frieze with blind fretwork, two shaped paneled doors with fluted paneled pilasters, lower case of three thumb-molded drawers, bracket base, replaced brasses, refinished, repairs............................ 5,175.00

Zoar, walnut, orig dark-brown alligatored finish, black-painted detail, two raised-panel doors, bracket feet, molded base, applied trim above doors, applied diamond below removable cornice with peaked front and relief fan design, minor cornice chips, small section of slide molding missing, 83" h, 56-1/2" w, 19" d 2,750.00

Kegs (See Barrels, Kegs, and Canteens)

Kettle Stands and Shelves

Background: Kettle stands and shelves were both types of iron trivets used for holding a hot kettle. They often had a turned wooden handle. Kettle stands were short, for use on a tabletop; kettle shelves had longer legs and were better suited for fireplace use.

Kettle shelf
   Black iron, pieced shelf, cabriole front legs, 13" h, 11" x 13" 165.00
   Wrought-iron, three penny feet, twisted iron cross member, ring top with smaller inner ring, 12" h 192.50
   Wrought-iron, cabriole front legs, curved front bar, 11-3/8" h, 17-1/2" w, 15-5/8" d....................110.00
   Wrought-iron and brass, cabriole legs, pierced top with bird decor, turned wooden handle, English, 10-1/4" h, 16-1/2" l................................... 275.00
   Reticulated brass top, wrought-iron base, turned wooden handle, 11" h, 14-1/2" l.................. 247.50

Kettle stand
   Wrought-iron framework, button feet, tall legs, brass top plate pierced at center, turned curly maple handle, repair where handle meets framework, 4-3/4" h, 15-3/8" w 110.00
   Wrought-iron and brass, high spider base, turned wooden handle, pierced brass top with compass stars and scalloping, hooks on 1 end for hanging, handle cracked, 7" h, 14-1/2" w, 9" d 55.00

Kettles

Background: Made of iron, brass, or copper, these pots or cauldrons were widely used for boiling liquid in the 18th and 19th centuries. Until the mid-19th century, copper and brass kettles were made by hammering and/or piecing sheet metal over a form. In 1852, inventor J.F. Flanders was awarded a patent (which he granted to Roys & Wilcox) for a method that used a lathe to spin the metal into shape.

Hint: Kettles are plentiful, with many imported from Europe and the Middle East. Except in cases of particularly rare examples, damaged ones should be avoided.

Brass
   6-1/8" h, 9-7/8" dia, mkd "H.W. Hayden," rounded bottom, flared sides, wing handle, wear 30.00
   6-1/2" h, 15-1/2" dia, slightly rounded bottom, stationary arched wrought-iron handle, wear 160.00
   8-1/2" h, 11-3/4" dia, rounded bottom, flared sides, illegible mark, swing handle, wear, minor dents... 45.00
   11" h, 15-7/8" dia, rounded bottom, flared sides, mark partially legible, swing handle, wear, minor rust 110.00

Brass kettle with iron handle, 20th C., 14-1/4" dia, $85.

Candy, copper
    6-1/2" h, 13" dia, dovetailed, wrought-steel handles, stamped label, polished 192.50
    7-1/2" h, 17-1/2" dia, dovetailed, round bottom, cast-iron handles 247.50
Cast iron, round, three tapered round feet, swing handle, mkd "OP&Co., 8," rust, 8" h, 10-3/4" dia 50.00
Copper
    7" h, dovetailed, wrought-iron handle, gooseneck side spout with flap, 7" h 49.50
    10-3/4" h, 15" dia, rounded bottom, dovetailed, iron loop-sided handle mounts, iron swing handle 220.00
    11" h, 15-7/8" dia, rounded bottom, dovetailed, flared sides, swing handle, wear, some rust 350.00
Gypsy
    Cast iron, 6-1/2" h, 5-3/4" dia, globular shape, three tapered half-round feet, flared rim, swing handle, cast-brass finial on lid 180.00
    Cast iron, 14-3/4" h, 18-1/2" dia, globular shape, two tapered triangular feet, wide flared collar, swing handle, black paint, some rust, collar chip 130.00

Kitchen Collectibles

Background: In early America, the kitchen was often the focal point of a family's environment. Many early kitchen utensils were hand-made and prized by their owners. These early examples, as well as later utilitarian kitchen items made of tin and other metals, are eagerly sought by many collectors of country.

References: E. Townsend Artman, *Toasters 1909-1960*, Schiffer Publishing, 1996; Kenneth L. Cope, *Kitchen Collectibles: An Identification Guide*, Astragal Press, 2000; Linda Fields, *Four & Twenty Blackbirds: A Pictorial Identification and Value Guide for Pie Birds*, self-published, 1998; Linda Campbell Franklin, *300 Years of Kitchen Collectibles*, 4th ed., Krause Publications, 1997; Helen Greguire, *Collector's Guide to Toasters and Accessories*, Collector Books, 1997; Frances Johnson, *Kitchen Antiques*, Schiffer Publishing, 1996; Barbara Mauzy, *The Complete Book of Kitchen Collecting*, Schiffer Publishing, 1997; David G. Smith and Chuck Wafford, *The Book of Griswold & Wagner*, Schiffer Publishing, 2000; Don Thornton, *Apple Parers*, Off Beat Books, 1997; —, *Beat This: The Eggbeater Chronicles*, Off Beat Books, 1994.

Periodicals: *Cast Iron Cookware News*, 28 Angela Ave., San Anselmo, CA 94960; *Kettles 'n Cookware*, Drawer B, Perrysburg, NY 14129; *Kitchen Antiques & Collectibles News*, 4645 Laurel Ridge Dr., Harrisburg, PA 17119; *Piebirds Unlimited*, 14 Harmony School Rd., Flemington, NJ 08822.

Collectors' Clubs: Griswold & Cast Iron Cookware Assoc., P.O. Drawer B, Perrysburg, NY 14129-

0301; Kollectors of Old Kitchen Stuff (KOOKS), 501 Market St., Mifflinburg, PA 17844 (send long self-addressed envelope for information); The National Reamer Collectors Association, 47 Midline Ct., Gaithersburg, MD 20878.

Museums: Corning Glass Museum, Corning, NY; Kern County Museum, Bakersfield, CA; Landis Valley Farm Museum, Lancaster, PA.

Also see: Utensils

Bottle opener, cast iron, parrot, orig polychrome paint, minor wear, labeled "John Wright, Copy 1947," 3-1/4" h 165.00
Butcher's block, round, 14" thick, two heavy round-turned legs painted light blue, replaced third leg, 29" h, 37" dia 400.00

Silver & Co.'s New Beater and Dessert Maker, cast-iron top, one-quart, $130.

Cherry seeder, cast iron, three splayed iron legs support frame holding seeder, turned wooden handle, 1863 patent date, 8-3/4" h... 60.00

Coffee roaster, sheet iron, rounded lid with tapered oven vent, interior cylinder, turned wooden handle, 10-3/4" h, 15-3/4" w, 6-3/8" d.. 170.00

Cutting board, curly maple, oval, handle with round head, refinished, 20" h, 7-1/2" w 192.50

Dipper, carved wood, Native American, oval bowl with notched rim, wide slightly curved flattened handle with carved motifs ending in arched loop, 12-3/4" l 160.00

Food chopper
  Handheld, iron blade with cutout heart, wooden handle, brass ferrule, 10-3/4" l 275.00
  Tabletop, square wooden block with hinged wrought-iron pivoting food chopper, blade 4-3/4" w, tapered iron collar, turned wooden handle, wear, 4-5/8" h, 10-1/8"x 13" 50.00

Food cutter, birch and poplar, orig red finish, "R.S. Morse, Dixfield," possibly Shaker, 12" h, 19-3/4" l.. 165.00

Fruit or lard press, Enterprise Mfg. Co., cylindrical, orig paint, four legs, small spout at bottom front, arched top with crank and gear mechanism, elongated wooden handle, wear 75.00

Grater, tin slant-front grating surface, wooden sides, 1 drawer, 7-1/2" h, 12" w, 6" d............................ 220.00

Herb grinder
  Cast iron, two-pc, iron disk blade with wooden handles, elongated oval slant-side trough, 6-3/4" h, 15" l 920.00
  With roller, iron, boat-shaped with feet, wooden handle, pitted, 5" h, 15-1/2" w........................... 341.00

Masher, curly maple, mushroom finials, one with round base with age crack, 9-1/2" h and 11-1/2" h, pr..... 137.50

Muffin tin, cast iron, hearts motif (eight) 110.00

Pastry board, carved-wood
  Rectangular, man with fish, English, 8" h, 4-1/2" w 49.00
  Rectangular, six-part, motifs of flower, cherries, butterfly, basket, swan and building, 6-3/8" h, 3-1/8" w 55.00
  Rectangular, eight-part, motifs include flowers, fruit, swan, fish and house, 9-1/2" h, 2-7/8" w 110.00
  Tombstone-shaped top, hole for hanging, made from two softwood boards secured by dovetailed battens, wear, 29-7/8" h, 15-1/4" w.................. 130.00

Pastry cutter, tin, set of twelve in round covered tin box 192.50

Pastry roller, wooden, carved floral designs, 4-3/4" l, wheel 2" dia.. 140.00

Peel
  Softwood, rounded end, tapered handle, wear, 8-1/2" w, 68" l.. 45.00
  Softwood, wide handle with arched oval cutout, mkd "J. Able," refinished, 39-1/2" l, 12-1/8" w 75.00
  Wooden, round plate, pierced handle end, 18th C., wear, 56-1/2" l... 373.75

Pie crimper
  Tin, 2-1/4" dia wheel, U-shaped bracket extends to round tubular handle with loop end, incised line decor around top of handle, 8-3/8" l 425.00

Wrought iron, 1-3/4" dia wheel, U-shaped iron bracket with tapered square shaft splays out at its bottom, with 1 side having a shell-shaped motif, the other with a round ray motif, simple punched decor on the crimper's bottom, late 18th/early 19th C., 5-1/2" l.. 700.00

Wrought iron, 2-1/8" dia wheel, U-shaped iron bracket with tapered square handle with chamfered edges, side of bracket with line decor, late 18th/early 19th C., 7-3/4" l.......................... 375.00

Pitcher pump, cast iron, "The Deming Co., Salem, Ohio," drive rod missing, 18" h 45.00

Pot scraper
  Aunt Hannah's Bread, "Baur's Pot and Pan Scraper Fits Any Corner of Pot or Pan, Always Look for this Label, It Guarantees Pure, Sweet, Wholesome Bread, Baur Bros. Co., The Cleanest Bakery in America, Pittsburgh, Pa.," litho tin, cond. 8-, 3" h, 3-3/8" w 1,155.00
  "King Midas Flour, The Highest Priced Flour in America, And Worth All It Costs," back view of child in bonnet, blue ground, litho tin, cond. 8, 2-7/8" h, 3-5/8" w.................................... 385.00

"Hunters New Lightning Sifter & Mixer, Size '000', Made Only By J.H. Day & Co., Cincinnati," original red and green paint, 23-1/4" h, $1,540. (Photo courtesy of Garth's Auctions, Delaware, Ohio)

"Sharples Tubular Cream Separator, The 1909 tubulars are better than ever, Foremost in dairy work, The only bottom-feed suspended bowl separator," woman with milk can by red separator, cond. 9+/8.25+ 308.00

Raisin seeder, Landers Frary & Clark, cast iron, C-shaped clamp, turned wooden handle, mkd "Pat. Nov. 24, 96, Wet The Raisins," 9-1/2" h 60.00

Shaking fork, wooden
Three-prong, 65" l 65.00
Three-prong, tapered round handle, mkd Henry Young, 50-1/8" l 170.00
Four-prong, child's, round handle, mkd "C. Musser," 25-5/8" l 270.00
Four-prong, mkd "D.K. Young," 65" l 95.00
Six-prong, slightly curved round handle, mkd "C. Musser," 71" l 170.00

Sifter, tabletop, orig red and green, white flourish decor, white and black line detail, double cast-iron gears and cranks with wooden handles, mkd "Hunters New Lightning Sifter & Mixer, Size '000,' Made Only By J.H. Day & Co., Cincinnati," 23-1/4" h 1,540.00

Spoon rack, architectural, ash, old red repaint, arched top with cornice and scalloped center section, scalloped base, three pierced racks for twelve spoons total, rosehead nails, 17-3/4" h, 8-3/4" w 660.00

Strainer, round brass dovetailed bowl with rounded pierced bottom, rolled rim, large applied iron hook on front of bowl below rim, applied iron handle, round turned tapering wooden handle with wide brass collar, 19-3/8" l, bowl 9-3/4" dia 90.00

Knife Boxes (see Cutlery Boxes and Trays)

Kraut Cutters

Background: Also known as cabbage cutters, slaw cutters, and slaw boards, these common kitchen tools of the 19th and early 20th centuries were used to cut cabbage for use in making sauerkraut. Small, commercial-made examples are common and are of minimal value. Industrial-size cutters are interesting because of their large size, but they generally have limited appeal. Instead, collectors look for homemade examples with interesting features, including shaped cutouts and hand-wrought hardware and blades.

Curly maple
19-1/2" l, curved crest with heart cutout, old worn finish, nail hole, age crack 495.00
25-1/2" l, 8" w, rounded top, old finish 330.00
Softwood, 18" l, 6-3/4" w, double arched top, single diagonal steel blade, applied molding at sides 55.00
Walnut
17-5/8" l, 4-7/8" w, rounded top with heart cutout, double diagonal iron blades, applied
molding 525.00

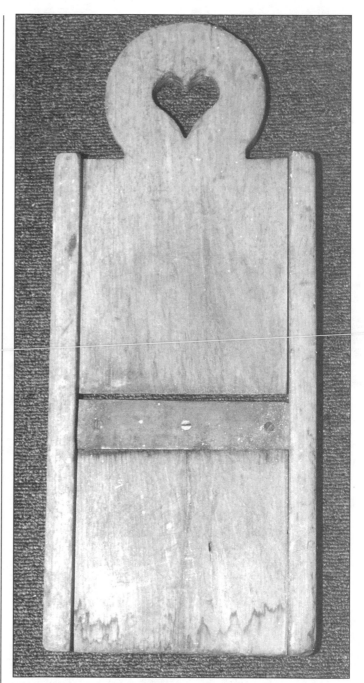

Kraut cutter with heart cutout, 16-1/2" h, $325.

20" l, 8" w, simple rectangular form 40.00
20-1/2" l, well-shaped crest with heart cutout, molded and chip-carved detail, old finish, age crack in crest, worn from use, ... 550.00
22" l, 7" w, well-shaped handle, chamfered edge, old patina 55.00
22-7/8" l, 7" w, rectangular, large pod-shaped top with large oval cutout handle, ... 60.00
23" l, 7-5/8" w, arched top with heart cutout, single iron blade, applied strips at sides, some surface rust 130.00

Lamps and Lighting

Background: Kerosene lamps were used from about 1860 until the advent of electric lighting. Metropolitan areas made the switch to electricity from about the turn of the century until 1920, and electrification of rural areas didn't occur until the 1930s and later. Because electric lighting was not particularly reliable, kerosene lamps were saved for emergencies, helping to ensure a plentiful supply today.

References: John Campbell, *Fire & Light in the Home Pre-1820*, Antique Collectors' Club, 1999; Nadja Maril, *Antique Lamp Buyer's Guide*, rev. and exp. 2nd ed., Schiffer Publishing, 1999; Denys Peter Myers, *Gaslighting in America*, Dover Publications, 1990; Catherine M. V. Thuro, *Oil Lamps*, Wallace-Homestead, 1976 (1992 value update); —, *Oil Lamps II*, Collector Books, 1983 (1994 value update).

Periodical: *Light Revival*, 35 W. Elm Ave., Quincy, MA 02170.

Collectors' Clubs: Aladdin Knights of the Mystic Light (Aladdin Lamps), 3935 Kelley Rd., Kevil, KY 42053, www.aladdinknights.org; Rushlight Club, 1657 The Fairway, Suite 196, Jenkintown, PA 19046.

Museums: Kerosene Lamp Museum, Winchester Center, CT; Pairpoint Lamp Museum, River Edge, NJ.

Reproduction Alert: Kerosene lamps have been reproduced.

Also see: Candlesticks, Lanterns

Angle lamp
  Single, tin, wall-mounted, The Angle Lamp Co., stenciled clear glass globular globe with bird and floral designs, white opaque conical-shaped shade, minor surface rust, 14-1/4" h, 13" w 160.00
  Double, copper-plated brass, The Angle Lamp Co., two clear globular-shaped globes, opaque glass conical-shaped shades, 18-1/2" h, 22" w 400.00
  Double, nickel-plated tin, hanging, The Angle Lamp Co., two clear globular-shaped globes, opaque glass conical-shaped shades, 18-1/4" h, 21" w 250.00
Astral, marble foot, prism band with clear cut prisms, frosted cut-to-clear Gothic arches and panels, prisms chipped, one missing, needs rewired, 19" h 55.00
Banquet, opaque violet-blue base, clambroth font, scalloped foot, ribbed tapered column and beaded-panel font, brass connector and collar, minor chips on base, 14-3/4" h.. 275.00
Betty lamp
  5-3/4" h, iron, hinged brass lid, with hanger 104.50
  5" h (excluding hanger), 5-3/8" l, sheet brass, double wick support, wrought-iron hanger, wire wick pick 55.00
  4" h, wrought iron, brass-plated top crest with engraved initials "R.R.R." 192.50
  12" h, wrought iron, old pitted finish, turned wooden stand, old worn black patina, with iron hanger 220.00
  16" h, wrought iron and copper, tripod base, round platform with copper disk mounted around the center column, adjustable crosspiece with candle socket on one side and betty lamp on other 357.50
Bull's-eye lamp, pewter, unmarked, well-developed foot and stem, drum-shaped font, mismatched whale oil burner, removable bull's-eye focusing lenses, weighted base, old repair, 10-1/2" h 605.00
Campaign torch, gimbal holder, weighted base on font, turned ash handle, small split in font, 30" h 55.00
Candelabra, wrought-iron, five sockets, tooled tripod base, 12-1/4" h...110.00

EVENING WORSHIP

During the 18th century, most services at meeting houses or churches were conducted during daylight hours. By the late 19th century, a number of meeting houses had been equipped with chandeliers whose many arms included candle cups with candles for light. This chandelier was purchased in 1947 by the First Church of Deerfield (Massachusetts) with funds provided by Henry N. Flynt and Helen Geier Flynt, founders of Historic Deerfield. Giltwood and iron, it was probably made in Italy during the late-18th or early-19th century. In an old surface and fitted with electric sockets and external wiring, the 39-1/2" chandelier sold at a Skinner auction for $19,550.

Giltwood and iron chandelier, $19,550. (Photo courtesy of Skinner Auctioneers & Appraisers of Antiques & Fine Arts, Boston and Bolton, Mass.)

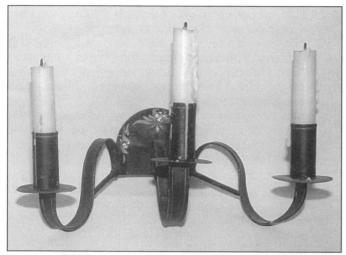

Tole-decorated triple-arm tin wall sconces, black and gold, 13" w, pair, $825.

Candle holder
    Adjustable candlestand, wrought iron, high spider base, penny feet, tapered center column, pan with socket on spring-loaded bracket, 60" h 770.00
    Adjustable, wrought iron, high spider base, penny feet, cross arm with two candle sockets, heart-shaped finial 550.00
    Adjustable, wrought iron, splint holder with conical candle socket, floor-standing, tripod base, penny feet, tapered center column, 40-1/2" h 605.00
    Adjustable, wrought iron, tripod base, penny feet, tapered center column with ring turnings, adjustable crosspiece with two sockets, 22-1/4" h.......... 770.00
    Alpine, wrought iron, high tapered feet (one scrolled), leaf-shaped platform base, scrollwork and turned column, spring-loaded candleholder, light pitting, 18-3/4" h................................. 154.00
    Table-mount, wrought iron, 26" h................... 440.00
Candle jack
    Wrought iron, one socket, turned column, 23" h 357.50
    Wrought iron, two sockets, spade-shaped hanger 357.50
Candle sconces
    Iron, three curved arms with candle cup and bobeche fitted into arrow-tipped wall brackets, American, 19th C., 14" h, 15" w, pr.......... 2,530.00
    Tin, three-candle, smoke-decor, crimped drip pans, oval reflector, 11" h, 15" w 495.00
    Tin, bulbous-top reflectors, crimped reflectors and drip pans, age but not period, 10" h 275.00
    Tin, mirrored, diamond shape, sections of glass form rayed pattern, round center section with reverse-painted scene of primitive bird and flowers, crimped tin candle socket, hairlines, wear to silvering, 11" h.. 495.00
    Tin, mirrored, round, pr 495.00
    Tin, mirrored, round, some age but not period, 9-1/4" dia, pr.. 385.00

    Tin, oval reflectors, crimped drip pans, some age, holes from electrification, 12" h 247.50
    Tin, oval reflectors, crimped edges, 12" h, pr... 385.00
    Tin, oval reflectors and drip pans crimped, some resoldering, old but not period, 8" h, pr.. 1,320.00
    Toleware, round mirrored back, single branch with round drip catcher and crimped rim, painted red, wear, 8" h, pr 2,450.00
Chandelier
    Candle, four arms, tin, crimped drip pans, 24-1/2" dia.. 1,155.00
    Candle, six arms, wooden turned column, dark gray-blue paint, bent wire-with-tin sockets and drip pans, reproduction, 26" h 357.50
    Candle, six candle cups, round flat band, suspended from linked metal rods, American, 19th C., wear, 26" drop 1,725.00
    Candle, ten arms, wood turned column, iron arms, crimped tin sockets, 21" h, 24" dia 1,650.00
    Candle, twelve arms, wooden turned posts, crimped tin sockets, 20th C., 24" h........................... 550.00
    Electric, candle motif, wood, turned column, smoke decor, red and green line detail, six iron branches, crimped tin pans, by David T. Smith, Morrow, Ohio, contemporary, 25" h, 30" dia............. 137.50
Cruise
    Double, wrought iron, twisted hanger, 5" h (excluding hanger) 132.50
    Wrought iron, square base, four shaped supports, center column of flat iron, candle socket mounted on one side, cruise lamp at top, arched handle, 15-1/2" h..110.00
Fluid (oil or Kerosene)
    5-1/4" h, clear, pressed lacy base, blown bulbous font with wafer, chips on base 137.50
    6-1/4" h, clear, pressed round stepped base, ribbed column and wafer attaching pear-shaped blown font, flakes, hairline 110.00
    6-3/8" h, clear, pressed base, tiered and paneled stem, bulbous blown font with two wafers, no burner, small chips on base........................ 137.50
    7-1/2" h, clear, pressed base with scalloped edge and interior ribbing, cut panels on font, pewter double-spout burner, flakes 137.50
    7-3/4" h, clear, pressed triangular base, paw feet, scrolled column and wafers attaching round blown font, roughness, hairline 357.50
    8-1/2" h, clear, pressed square-and-waterfall base, blown conical font, pewter collar mkd "A.C. Hobbs" (Boston glass engraver), possibly an uncut blank, small chips on base 220.00
    9-1/4" h, cobalt pressed base, clear font, round foot, octagonal stem, flared unpatterned font, brass collar, attributed to Central Glass Co., Wheeling, W.Va. 165.00
    9-1/4" h, cobalt pressed base, hexagonal base, paneled column, loop font, brass burner, straw marks, base reground 385.00

10-1/2" h, clear, pressed stepped base, wafer top attached to pear-shaped font, font has etched acorns and vintage pewter double-spout burner, flakes 137.50

10-3/4" h, clear, pressed stepped base, fluted columns topped with lions' heads, baskets of flowers between columns, pear-shaped blown font with wafers, brass collar, chips 165.00

12-1/8" h, marriage lamp, stepped milk glass base, tapered round column, brass collar, white clambroth center with well between two clambroth fonts with threaded brass collars, minor roughness 770.00

12-1/2" h, clambroth, stepped base, fluted column, stylized leaves, scalloped font, brass collar, flakes, chipped corner.......... 302.50

12-5/8" h, cut overlay, stepped milk glass base, brass collar, cobalt font with cut-to-clear panels and geometric designs, straw marks, flakes on base.......... 715.00

19-1/4" h, marriage lamp, Ripley, milk glass base, white clambroth fonts, cracked match compartment lid, 1 foot cracked, old burners with replaced chimneys 412.50

Gimbal pewter, unmarked, matching fluid burner, brass spouts, snuffer missing caps, dents, split at handle, 6-3/8" h.......... 126.50

Globe, gas light, blown glass, sapphire blue, 7-1/2" dia.......... 55.00

Hanging

Candle holder, wrought-iron, three sockets on twisted shaft with ring top, European, 12" h 275.00

Hall light, clear blown glass globe with floral cut design, embossed brass fittings, clear blown smoke bell, no burner, 28" h.......... 605.00

Star shape, six points, hexagonal pyramid sides, soldered-tin frame, 15" w.......... 220.00

Kettle lamp, wrought iron and brass, slightly domed round base, tapered column, U-shaped support, seamed reservoir, areas of pitting, 7-7/8" h 121.00

Lard lamp, tin, round saucer-shaped base with flared sides, tubular shaft with stamped banding, two ring handles on side, removable cylindrical font, minor rust, 9-1/2" h, 7-1/2" dia 325.00

Loom light

10-3/8" l, wrought iron, twisted hanger and hook, candle socket with overlapping seam.......... 110.00

15" l, wrought iron, twisted hanger, hook and candle socket with overlapping seam, light rust..... 165.00

Petticoat lamp, japanned tin, inverted conical base, acorn-shaped font, burner with two wick tubes, flaking, 4-3/4" h, 3" dia 160.00

Revere-type (conical punched tin, ring handle)

13-1/2" h, "N.A." in door, overall punched designs, some battering, repair.......... 302.50

14" h, 6" dia, overall punched designs, wear, rust.......... 330.00

16-1/2" h, 5-1/2" dia, overall punched designs, wear, rust.......... 320.00

Rush light

7-1/2" h, holder, wrought iron, twisted detail, curled counterweight, stepped wooden base scratch-carved "1804" on bottom, old edge damage.......... 412.50

7-1/2" h, holder, wrought iron, twisted stem and candle socket counterweight, penny feet 302.50

9-3/4" h, holder, wrought iron, twisted detail on stem, candle-socket counterweight, tripod base, stamped "FM".......... 247.50

Shade, hurricane, clear, blown, folded base rim, 19th C., 17-1/2" h 230.00

Sparking lamp, clear, well-detailed pressed base, blown bulbous font, chips on base, tin drop burner, 3-3/4" h 302.50

Student lamp

20-1/2" h, single, brass, adjustable, milk glass shade, polished and electrified but not drilled, dent on well 330.00

20-7/8" h, single, brass, round base, adjustable arm, "Cleveland Library Lamp," milk glass globe, clear chimney, never electrified 440.00

21" h, double, brass, round base, adjustable, "Bradley and Hubbard," light-green ribbed shades with milk glass interiors probably old replacements, finials replaced, electrified.......... 825.00

24" h, double, brass, round base, adjustable font and cross arm, arched handle, orig milk glass shades, clear chimneys, mkd "Post & Co.'s American Student Lamp, Cincinnati" 2,090.00

Taper jack

Brass, reticulated base with 3 hearts, cast handle, urn finial, with old wax taper, English, 5" h 770.00

Wrought-iron, square base, 4 legs with ball feet, center column with wide scissor blades held with screw, tooled lines on handle, with old wax taper, 8"h 522.50

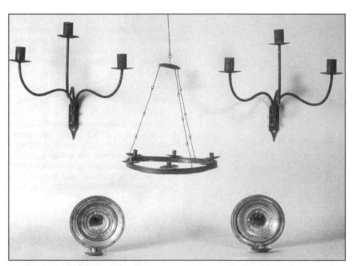

Iron three-arm candle sconces, 14" h, pair, $2,530; tin candle chandelier, $1,725; tin mirrored candle sconces, pair, $1,150. (Photo courtesy of Skinner Auctioneers & Appraisers of Antiques & Fine Arts, Boston and Bolton, Mass.)

Time lamp, pewter, unmarked, clear blown font, burner cover missing, wick support is present, 12-3/4" h.. 247.50

Tinder box
Tin, old dark finish, interior compartment with removable damper, lid fitted with candle socket, minor dent, 3-1/4" h 302.50
Tin, steel striker and damper, lid with candle socket, black paint, 3-7/8" h, 4-1/8" dia................... 412.50

Whale oil
Brass, turned round base and column, ball-shaped font, orig burner, dents, 8" h 27.50
Tin, circular pan base, large carrying ring, single burner, 8-1/2" h... 137.50

Lanterns

Background: A lantern is defined as an enclosed receptacle for a light, with the outside cover serving to transmit the light and also to protect it from drafts. Lanterns were not used to any great extent in America until early in the 18th century. Hexagonal, octagonal, and bell-shaped lanterns were among the most popular forms.

References: *Collectible Lanterns*, L-W Book Sales, 1997; Anthony Hobson, *Lanterns that Lit Our World*, Hiram Press, reprinted 1996; Neil S. Wood, *Collectible Dietz Lanterns*, L-W Book Sales, 1996.

FYI: "Dark lanterns" were introduced to America around 1800. Made with two tin cylinders, one fitting closely within the other, an opening in the inner cylinder allowed the light to shine through a bull's eye glass (magnifier) in the outer cylinder. A quick turn of the cylinder effectively shut off the light, hence the term "dark lantern."

Candle lantern, four glass panels with wire ring protectors, $175.

Barn
Tin, clear glass globe, wire handle, 14" h 220.00
Wooden, four glass panes, mortised frame, tin top, wire bail handle, one pane cracked, 10" h 275.00
Wooden, glass sides, corner posts mortised through top and base, tin candle socket, tin-lined air hole at top, wire hinges, latch and handle, minor edge damage, burned hole in top, 9-3/4" h (excluding handle) 522.50

Bull's eye, japanned tin, thick convex hinged lens, double burner, sliding blackout plate, double wire handles, belt clip, wear, 7-1/2" h....................................... 82.50

Footman's, wooden sides, base and lift-top lid in dark-green paint, handpainted red border designs and porcelain buttons, top has yellow stenciled label "H.B. Ost...Manufacturer, Angola, NY...," three sides with glass panes and wire guards, back with punched tin plate, floral felt panel under top, hook damage, minor wear, 6-1/4" h (excluding handle), 7-3/4" w, 5-1/4" d..220.00

Skater's
6-3/4" h (excluding handle), brass, clear glass globe, brass wire handle, minor dents 82.50
6-7/8" h (excluding bail handle), tin, clear pressed globe, "Perko Wonder Junior"....................... 71.50
6-7/8" h (excluding handle), 3-1/8" dia, brass, bell-shaped base, tin bottom, brass burner, clear globe, arched swing handle, minor dents 100.00
9-5/8" h (excluding handle), 4" dia, brass, bell-shaped base, tin bottom, brass burner, clear globe, tapering cylindrical threaded pierced top, arched swing handle, hole in bottom with rust, dent 130.00

Tin
9-1/2" h, clear globe, pear shape, removable round base, font with brass double-spout burner, wire handle and guards, mkd "Pat. Sep. 14. 78," some resoldering... 192.50
10" h, clear blown globe, traces of old dark japanning, light rust, font replaced with candle socket, ring handle... 385.00
10" h (excluding handle), clear blown globe, onion shape, star and diamond punching, removable base with tin font and brass collar, ring handle, old pitted finish 440.00
10" h (excluding ring handle), clear octagonal tapered glass globe, star and diamond piercing on tin top and base, replaced brass burner 330.00
11" h, clear blown globe, pear shape, orig brown japanning, pierced designs, removable font with whale oil burner, ring handle, probably New England Glass Co. 357.50
11" h (excluding ring handle), three clear glass sides, wire guards, star-punched top, mkd "Parker Patent, Boston, 1853".............................. 385.00
12-1/2" h (excluding handle), candle lantern, four glass panels with wire ring protectors, pyramid-shaped top with punched design, ring handle, sliding door, 1 old glass panel.......................... 165.00
19" h, 11" sq, three glass sides, one side hinged, black repaint, battered, one pc glass missing 192.50

Laundry Items

Background: Monday, wash day. Somewhere between pounding clothes against a rock along the creek and tossing them into a Maytag washer came the washboard. Rubbing clothes against the uneven surface of the washboard worked in the soap and forced out dirt. Most washboards had a galvanized metal scrubbing surface in a wooden frame; however, glass and pottery inserts were also made, with the latter being especially valuable. A number of other tools were also used to assist in early laundry duties.

Reproduction Alert: Washboards are still being made.

Fork, two tines, curly maple, minor damage to ends of
tines 104.50
Washboard
    Glass insert, wooden frame, National Washboard
      Co., No. 860 .... 30.00
    Graniteware, blue scrubbing surface, wooden frame,
      National Washboard Co., Soap Saver,   24" h,
      12-1/2" w 115.00
    Mother Hubbard, wooden rollers, one dowel
      cracked, 22-1/4" h, 12-1/4" w 105.00
    Redware in brown glaze, wooden frame, child size,
      top of backboard replaced, 13-3/8" h,
      6-5/8" w 577.50
    Wooden, carved heart handle, Pennsylvania Dutch,
      24" h, 7-1/2" w 200.00
    Wooden, heart cutout, worn, 24" h, 7" w 200.00
Wash stick, wooden, U-shaped bottom with oval cutout,
    shovel-shaped hand grip, refinished,
    30-1/2" l 65.00
Washtub, Shaker, round, blue paint, pine, staved and
    wooden rings, two extended handles with half-circle
    cutouts, 21-1/2" h, 27-1/2" dia........................ 2,185.00

Washboard with stoneware insert, Rockingham-type glaze, wooden frame, 22" h, 12" w, $605.

Lawn Ornaments, Garden Ornaments, and Urns

Background: Decorative ornaments were generally placed in the yards and gardens of 19th-century estates. Animals were the most common forms and were often close to life-size. Large examples were typically owned by the well-to-do, and they are relatively scarce today. Decorative garden urns, also the property of the rich, were often made of cast-iron. In addition to residential settings, urns were also commonly found in cemeteries.

Hint: Beware! Urns are a common target of thieves.

Ornaments
Cast Iron
    Deer (buck, doe and fawn), rectangular bases,
      minor resolder to fawn, fawn 36" h on 12" x 28"
      base, buck 62-3/4" h, doe 55-1/4" h, on bases 14"
      x 48", set... 6,820.00
    Dog, greyhound or whippet, one in old surface, one
      cleaned, 49" l... 6,050.00
    Lion, cast iron, recumbent lion figure, rectangular
      pedestal base, painted brown, wear, 19-1/2" h,
      13-1/2" w, 39" l, pr 6,325.00
    Rooster, crowing, rusted finish, 19" h 577.50
    Stag, cast iron, standing, possibly by J.W. Fiske,
      N.Y., late 19th C., painted brown, imperfections,
      62-1/4" h, 47" l, pr.................................... 6,900.00

Urns
Cast aluminum, round stepped base, openwork column
    and three egrets, relief scrollwork on bowl, scroll han-
    dles, old black paint, contemporary, 35-1/4" h,
    21" dia.. 467.50

Cast-iron garden urn with leaves design, two-piece, 44" h, $385. (Photo courtesy of Cyr Auction Company, Gray, Maine)

Cast iron

"J.W. Fiske, No. 21 & 23, Barclay St. N.Y., Patd June 1, 1875," cast foliage, woven detail, column and bowl with beaded detail, well and top edge with chased foliage, one-pc, new white paint, 18" h, 21-1/2" dia.. 660.00

"M.D. Jones Co.," square platform base, round tapering column, relief detail, double handled bowl with relief oval medallions, flared rim, dark-green repaint, enameled steel topiary bushes cemented into place, urn 20-1/2" h, pr 550.00

"Kramer Bros. Dayton" (one mkd), scrolled cast detail on base, fluted detail on wells, top edge scalloped, scrolled heart detail, two-pc construction, new white paint, one urn with added valve, 25" h, 22" dia, pr... 880.00

Walbridge & Co., Buffalo, N.Y., 19th C., tapered round form, boldly embellished with four scrolled handles, raised on baluster-shaped standard, flared square plinth, raised scrolled foliate decor on each side, three pcs, black paint, cracks, loss, wear, 58" h, 29-1/2" dia, pr 977.50

Scrolled detail around base, swallows in wells, tops have scrolled border with flowers beneath, three-pc construction, old worn white repaint, one with welded repair, 31-1/2" h, pr 550.00

Square base, round stepped column, bowl with shell-shaped base, double handles, flared rim with raised leaf detail, old dark-green repaint, handle design slightly different, one with chipped base, 28-1/2" h, 24" dia, pr.................................. 715.00

Square base, round stepped column, bowl with shell-shaped base, double handles, flared rim with raised leaf detail, relief shell design on bottom of bowl, old dark-green repaint, handle designs slightly different, one with chipped base, 14-1/2" h, 12-1/4" dia, pr 220.00

Square base, shell-shaped bottom in bowl, double ear handles, pitting, 10-1/2" h........................ 77.00

Square base, short round column under large bowl, relief cast leaves, two pcs, white paint, rust, 44" h 385.00

Square platform base, reeded column, radiating shell design in the bottom of the bowl, scalloped and flared rim, dark-green repaint, 17-1/4" h, 23" dia.. 385.00

Square platform base, relief-cast leaves, bowl with relief shell design on bottom, flared rim, scroll handles, pitting, one braised repair on rim, 12-1/4" h, 19-1/2" w, pr 275.00

White clay, three-part urn on plinth, base with relief moldings of herons in rushes, layers of white and red paint, damage, probably Ohio origin, 40" h, pr 770.00

Lightning Rods and Balls

Background: Lightning rods used on homes and other structures in rural America were often embellished with decorative glass ornaments. Although some were odd shapes, most were round with embossed star or swirl designs. Dark blue and amber were fairly common, but other rarer colors such as red can also be found.

Collectors' Club: Weather or Knot Antiques, 15832 S. CR 900 W., Wanatah, IN 46390.

Reference: Rod Krupka, *The Complete Book of Lightning Rod Balls with Prices*, (Rod Krupka, 2615 Echo Ln, Ortonville, MI 48462).

Classic round shape, amethyst, copper caps, 3-1/2" dia... 60.00

D&S

Blue milk glass, ten-sided, with short rod and stand.. 100.00

White milk glass, ten-sided, copper caps, 4" dia 85.00

Electra round, white milk glass, copper caps, 5-1/8" h, 4-1/8" dia.. 75.00

Hawkeye, blue milk glass, rounded top with starbursts, tapering bottom, copper caps, 5-1/8" h, 4-3/8" dia 175.00

Moon & Stars, white milk glass, copper caps, 5-1/8" h, 4-3/8" dia... 75.00

Ribbed grape

Blue milk glass, copper caps, 5-1/8" h, 4-3/8" dia 100.00

White milk glass, copper caps, 5-1/8" h, 4-3/8" dia 90.00

Round pleat (Barnett Ball), cobalt, copper caps, 5" h, 4-3/8" dia.. 175.00

White clay urns with heron design, three-piece, 40" h, pair, $770. (Photo courtesy of Garth's Auctions, Delaware, Ohio)

Sharp pleated, sun-colored amethyst (orig white milk glass), copper caps, 5" h, 4-1/2" dia 75.00

Shinn System, white milk glass, copper caps, 4-1/2" dia.. 32.00

Smooth round, sun-colored lavender (orig white milk glass), copper caps, 4-1/2" dia........................... 50.00

Linen Presses

Background: A cupboard with shelves (presses) for storing linens and clothing is called a linen press. This form usually has two blind (no glass) doors over three to five graduated drawers.

Chippendale, three-pc, with butler's desk, mahogany, dovetailed case, scalloped bracket feet with molded trim, four-drawer base with butler's desk having six drawers and nine pigeonholes, two doors in top section, figured panels and four interior drawers, refinished, replaced feet, small pieced repairs, 81-1/4" h, 49-1/4" w, 23" d... 3,300.00

Grain-decor

Brown over mustard old grain decor, two-pc but was orig one-pc, walnut and pine, bracket feet, scalloped front apron, two paneled doors with two interior shelves over two short drawers over two long drawers, wooden pulls, cove-molded cornice, small sections of cornice missing, 71" h, 47-3/4" w, 21" d 1,540.00

Brown over tan orig grain decor, one-pc, stepback, pine and poplar, dark-brown painted border detail simulates band inlay, two upper doors with inset panels over three drawers, shaped bracket feet and end aprons, ring pulls, blue-gray repainted interior, secret compartment, minor wear, attributed to Maine, 81-3/4" h, 49" w 4,400.00

Hepplewhite, three-pc, mahogany and figured mahogany veneer, ebony inlay, old finish, high French feet, scrolled apron, two doors with five-pullout interior shelves, base with two short over three long drawers, removable cornice with curved molding with inlay and ball finials, repairs to cornice, center finial missing, age crack to one door panel, attributed to New York, 88" h, 48-1/4" w, 22" d... 8,800.00

Luster Ware

Background: Lustered wares created to imitate copper, gold, silver, and other colors were first produced in the early 19th century in England. Copper, gold, and platinum oxides were applied to glazed objects that were then fired, resulting in a metallic effect. Various techniques included applying bands of luster decoration, painting luster designs, and coating entire objects.

Objects decorated in silver luster using the "resist" process are known as silver resist. Those parts of the objects to be left free from the luster

decoration were first coated with wax, which prevented the luster from adhering there.

Sunderland lustreware is a 19th-century English earthenware pottery that was made for everyday use. It is usually mauve with marbled decoration.

Copper luster

Bowl, footed, low pedestal base, beaded band around waist, concave sides, wide blue band with relief-molded shepherd tending sheep accented in green, red and black, 3-5/8" h, 5-5/8" dia.................... 85.00

Creamer, molded base, straight sides, dark-green band with relief decor of human figures accented in orange, green, purple and black, unmkd, 3-7/8" h... 50.00

Goblet, pedestal, round foot, bowl with tapering sides, 4-1/4" h.. 15.00

Miniature, creamer, ovoid shape, wide band of green around sides with copper luster band, 2-3/4" h.. 25.00

Mug, concave sides, molded foot, wide orange band, floral designs, three in-the-making flakes, 3" h... 30.00

Pitcher, globular shape, wide dark-blue band around neck, copper luster floral designs, 5-3/4" h....... 45.00

Water pitcher, ovoid, large curved spout with molded shell design, squared arched handle, round foot, English, early 19th C., 8-5/8" h...................... 45.00

Silver luster

Tea set, gadrooned and banded design, teapot, lidded sugar, creamer, waste bowl, imperfections 93.50

Pitcher, vining flowers decor in blue, flakes, some wear, 4-1/2" h 137.50

Silver resist, pitcher, silver luster with white resist floral medallions and highlights, ribbed body, beading, relief roses, small chip on spout, some wear, 6-3/4" h.. 165.00

Silver luster cup and saucer, $35.

Sunderland, pitcher

Pink luster, "West View of the Iron Bridge at Sunderland," handpainted transfers in yellow, green and red, two verses about a shipwreck and "To a Friend," base chips, rim roughness, 7-3/8" h...............495.00

Pink luster, "West View of the Iron Bridge at Sunderland," black transfer, handpainted in red, yellow and green, two verses of a friend, repairs, hairline, 7-1/8" h 220.00

Spindle-back mammy bench, original black paint, red and mustard designs, original baby gate, 48" l, $1,540.

Mammy Benches

Background: A 19th-century form, mammy benches were also known as rocking settees. The latter is an appropriate name, since it was actually a small settee with rockers. A removable gate allowed the piece be used as a cradle. Rod-back, arrow-back and fancy chair styles can be found.

Old black repaint, freehand and stenciled fruit and vining on crest, pineapple and leaves on seat protector, yellow flourishes on arm supports, legs and cross stretchers, repairs where legs meet rockers, 1 arm with pieced repairs, 30-1/2" h, 52" w 770.00

Windsor sack-back rocking bench, 31" h, 40" l 2,200.00

Mantelpieces

Background: The frame surrounding a fireplace is known as the mantelpiece. Made of wood, brick, stone or tile, the framework often incorporated a shelf and even sometimes a mirror.

Oak, two sections, fluted columns, mirror missing, 79" h, 62-1/2" w 330.00

Oak, turned columns, carved florals, 48" h, 60" w 825.00

Walnut, block front, gothic arch, egg-and-dart and dentil molding, scrolled supports with acanthus-leaf carvings, paneled columns, 62" h, 96-1/2" w 1,540.00

Match Holders and Match Safes

Background: As matches became increasingly popular after 1850, consumers needed a place to keep matches safe and easily accessible.

The first patent for a hanging match holder was issued in 1849. Match holders were used instead of the sliding cardboard boxes the matches were originally packaged in. Cast-iron and tin match holders were the most common types. Lithography methods developed during the late 19th century meant that tin match holders became the perfect medium for advertisers. By 1880, match holders were also being made of glass and china.

Pocket match safes, used for carrying matches in one's pocket, were introduced in the 1850s. They came in a variety of sizes and shapes and were made from a number of materials. Match safes served as a popular advertising medium from 1895 to 1910.

References: Denis B. Alsford, *Match Holders: 100 Years of Ingenuity*, Schiffer Publishing, 1994; W. Eugene Sanders Jr. and Christine C. Sanders, *Pocket Matchsafes: Reflections of Life & Art 1840-1920*, Schiffer Publishing, 1997; Audrey G. Sullivan, *History of Match Safes in the United States*, self-published, 1978.

Collectors' Club: International Match Safe Assoc., P.O. Box 791, Malaga, NJ 08328.

Reproduction Alert: Copycat, fantasy, and reproduction sterling silver match safes have been produced.

Advertising

Ceresota Flour, embossed die-cut tin, hanging, boy slicing bread, cond. 8+, 5-1/2" h 440.00

Columbia Flour, embossed die-cut tin, hanging, Miss Liberty dressed in American flag, bag of flour on basket, cond. 8, 5-1/2" h 1,155.00

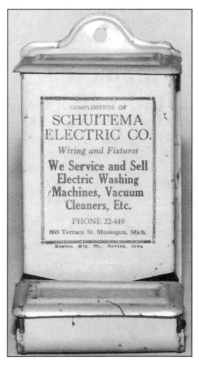

Tin wall-mount advertising match holder in light-blue paint, $50.

Dutch Boy Paints, embossed die-cut tin, hanging, trademark boy painting, cond. 8,
6-1/4" h 660.00

"Milwaukee Harvesting Machines, Always Reliable, Light Draft," hanging, litho tin, farmer holding basket with company logo, cond. 8.5+, 5-1/2" h,
3-3/4" w 742.50

Cast iron

Hanging, openwork scrolled back, two side-by-side urn-shaped holders, vertical oblong strike plate at bottom, 1867 patent date, minor rust, 7-1/2" h,
4-3/4" w 65.00

Hanging, oval pierced back with arched top, open rectangular holder at top with scrolled designs, striking plates on sides and bottom of holder, scrolled design and three small hooks below holder, 9-3/4" h, 3-5/8" w 135.00

Hanging, rectangular back with arched top, scrolled design, rectangular match compartment with hinged lid, strike plate across front, lid cast "C. Parker," 1869/1870 patent dates, 4-1/4" h,
5-3/4" w 160.00

Graniteware, gray, double pockets, 5-1/8" h,
4-3/8" w 225.00

Toleware, pedestal form, rounded weighted base, yellow feather-like design, dark-blue ground, inverted conical-shaped safe covered with sand on the exterior, interior tin compartment with removable tin lid, early/mid 19th C., 5-5/8" h, 2-7/8" dia.. 140.00

Wooden

Barrel-form, brown and tan sponge-painted,
2-1/8" h 115.00

Pedestal form with rounded foot, sides taper toward top, tin interior compartment, removable tin lid, mid-19th C., minor rust on lid, 5-3/8" h 85.00

Squirrel (full-bodied) and ear of corn, round base, ochre paint, traces of gilt, wear................... 460.00

Memorial and Mourning

Background: Pictures and special pieces of jewelry were two things 19th-century Americans kept to remember the dearly departed. Mourning jewelry typically contained pieces of the deceased's hair. The most desirable artwork are pictures from the early 19th century, usually depicting a cenotaph (a monument honoring a dead person whose remains lie elsewhere), bearing an inscription to a deceased person, with one or more female figures under a tree.

Bracelet, gold-filled clasp with fine scroll engraving, woven light brown hair in intricate design, one damaged, 7-3/8" l, pr.. 275.00

Brooches, gold filled or plated, beveled glass with woven hair, two dated 1834 and 1883, four enameled and two with engraved borders, one damaged, one missing its pin, one lens cracked, group of six 550.00

THE ART OF DEATH

We don't mark the passing of loved ones the way our forefathers did. One manner in which the dead were memorialized during the early 19th century was by creating a mourning picture. This great folk art example is from New England, and is backed up with documentation through a family record. The picture shows a young lady and a gentleman in mourning at a double classical memorial (cenotaph) inscribed, "In memory of Sally Fletcher wife of Peletiah Fletcher who departed this life Feb. 1st 1803, aged 33," and "In memory of Pelatiah Fletcher who departed this life May 7th 1811 aged 44." The willow trees are typical mourning motifs, and the detailed landscape with houses and boats gives the work added appeal. It sold at a Skinner auction with a watercolor-on-paper record of family births, marriages and deaths dating from 1767-1809.

Fletcher family memorial picture, 17" x 22-1/2", with a family record, $68,500. (Photo courtesy of Skinner Auctioneers & Appraisers of Antiques & Fine Arts, Boston and Bolton, Mass.)

Sampler

"To the Memory of W.H. Keely... This token was worked by Elizabeth Keely," strawberry border with willows and flowering trees above/below verse, two birds (one with a crest), c. 1844, minor edge damage, worn frame, 21-1/4" h, 18-1/4" w.........2,750.00

"HM Rowe 1775 The Dying Infant to His Mother...," inspirational verse, geometric floral border, English or American, fabric loss, toning, fading, 12-1/2" h, 16-3/4" w 690.00

Stickpin, lozenge-shape watercolor on ivory shows mourning figure at classical monument and urn, inscribed, "Be What Your Mother Was, and Claim The Skies," gold-plated mount, initialed, minor wear 258.75

Watercolor

Two women at memorial with urn and draped cloth, landscape ground with weeping willow, to "Mrs. Sarah S. Safford, 1810," framed, 17" h, 20" w...6,050.00

Hammond-Bradley family, Mass., unsigned, "Painted by Harriet M. Hammond about 1830, Miss Lois B. Batchelder, Teacher" in pencil on reverse, watercolor on paper, shows three classical memorials each inscribed with names and dates (1822-1829), landscape with trees, river, bridge, church and other buildings, minor foxing, stains, small tear, 17-1/2" h, 24-3/4" w....................................2,990.00

Mennonite

Background: This denomination of evangelical Protestant Christians traces its roots to the Anabaptist movement in Europe during the 16th century. Their name is derived from one of the group's leaders, Menno Simmons (1492-1559). Persecution eventually drove many members to the United States and Canada, where their numbers remain strongest today. Early Mennonites separated themselves from the world around them. Today, their doctrine includes Scriptural authority, plainness of dress, adult baptism, and restricting marriages to members of the group.

Bank, building-shape, cast aluminum, embossed "Kraybill (Pa.) Mennonite School," 3" h, 5" w, 3-1/2" d.......152.50

Blanket chest, grain-decor, orig red over yellow flame graining, poplar, turned feet, molded base, dovetailed case, 1-board top and sides, wrought-iron strap hinges, large interior till, bear-trap lock with key, attributed to Sonnenburg Mennonite Community, 27" h, 52-3/4" w, 22-3/4" d...2,310.00

Doll

Female, white and brown polyester body, green long sleeve dress, 16" h...60.50

Male, white fabric body, yellow cotton shirt, green pants, black suspenders, Jefferson County, Pa., early 20th C., 12-3/4" h...............................180.00

Pin cushion

Rectangular, patchwork diamond design, 3" x 7-1/2"...20.00

Square, embroidered flowers, floral print on back side, 7" sq..20.00

Square, embroidered flowers, 8" sq.................30.00

Quilt, pieced

Two-sided, Baskets design in red and white on one side, panels in mustard and red on the other, basket and leaf quilting, c. 1910-20...............1,375.00

Fans, 25 multicolor print fans on black and charcoal ground (five rows of five), Pa., c. 1900, 72" x 74"..455.00

LeMoyne Star variation, 20 blocks of eight-point star in pink and green on cream ground, green dividers between blocks with pink squares at intersecting points, red and blue printed borders, 75" x 85"...330.00

Mennonite quilt, LeMoyne Star variation, pink and green on cream ground, 75" x 85", $330. (Photo courtesy of Cyr Auction Company, Gray, Maine)

Pinwheels, red on black, green and gray ground, corners with added squares in orange flannel with printed blue, red plaid flannel back, heavy wool, wool flannel and twill, 78" x 80"..................357.50

Sawtooth Bars variation, green and watermelon calico, c. 1890, Pa., 82" x 90".........................760.00

Miniatures

Background: There's a certain fascination with anything particularly tiny. These small items are classified into three groups, depending on size: dollhouse, sample size, and child's size. Although all three are covered in separate categories in this book (Dollhouse, Salesman's Samples, Children's Furniture), this category serves as a catch-all for other small and interesting artifacts.

Reference: Herbert F. Schiffer and Peter B. Schiffer, *Miniature Antique Furniture: Doll House and Children's Furniture from the United States and Europe*, Schiffer Publishing, 1995.

Collectors' Club: National Assoc. of Miniature Enthusiasts, P.O. Box 69, Carmel, IN 46032.

Museum: Toy and Miniature Museum of Kansas City, MO.

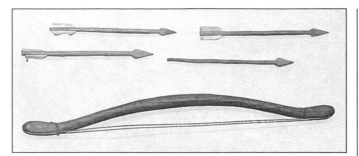

Miniature bow and four arrows, carved wood, bow 4-1/2" l, $100.

Basket, splint, tufted, 4-1/2" h, 4" dia 247.50
Basket, splint, two handles, 4" h, 6" dia 330.00
Bucket, 3-1/2" h.. 38.50
Ox yoke, wooden, traces of red paint, two bentwood collars missing pegs, 8-1/2" l.................................. 55.00
Porringer, pewter, "RG" crown handle, 2" dia....... 467.50
Shovel, carved wood, blue paint, wear, 23-1/2" l...... 165.00
Trunk, simulated black leather covering, brass nail-head trim, leather handle, interior lined with marbleized paper, maker's label "Theodore Kellogg No. 56 Hanover St., Boston," late 19th C., wear, damage, 4-1/4" h, 8" w, 5-1/2" d 143.75

Mirrors

Background: Practically unknown before the 17th century, mirrors are taken for granted today. The earliest American mirrors were in the Queen Anne style, made from about 1710 to 1765. Boston, New York, Philadelphia, Baltimore, and Charleston were important centers for mirror production during the 1700s. By the 19th century, however, production had spread widely.

Architectural, two-section
    Mahogany and mahogany veneer, old dark finish, reeded columns, corner blocks and molded cornice, worn glass, top glass with replaced reverse-painted scene of house, trees and fence, some molding replaced, repairs, 36-1/2" h, 19-3/4" w 330.00
    Pine, old refinishing, country style, reeded pilasters, cove-molded cornice, orig reverse-painted top section shows steamer "Ohio," pieced repairs at cornice 605.00
    Pine, old refinishing, reeded columns, reverse-painted castle with landscape, minor edge damage, flaking to painting and silvering, restored moldings, 21-3/4" h, 13" w............................ 220.00
Chippendale, scroll, hanging
    19-1/2" h, 12-1/4" w, cherry, old finish, mirror glass probably orig, repairs and restoration to ears and scroll work, worn silvering............................ 440.00
    20" h, 12" w, mahogany, Chippendale style, molded frame, worn silvering on glass, 20th C. 82.50
    20-1/4" h, 11-3/4" w, mahogany, Chippendale style, old alligatored varnish finish, 19th C........... 302.50

Chippendale scroll mirror, mahogany and veneer, English, 18th C., 40" h, $2,415. (Photo courtesy of Skinner Auctioneers & Appraisers of Antiques & Fine Arts, Boston and Bolton, Mass.)

    21-3/4" h, 12-3/4" w, mahogany and mahogany veneer, Chippendale style, refinished, silvering darkened, some age but not period............ 330.00
    24-1/2" h, 13-3/4" w, walnut, gilded composition, Prince of Wales feather in crest, refinished, 2 ears ended out, glass replaced 385.00
    24-5/8" h, 14-3/4" w, mahogany veneer on pine, glass with gilded liner, molded frame, ornate scrolled ears and crest, phoenix bird crest, veneer repairs, chips on inner liner, backboard replaced 385.00
    26" h, 14" w, mahogany, applied eagle in old regilding, molded frame, refinished, age cracks, 1 ear reglued, silvering worn 1,045.00
    36-1/2" h, 20" w, mahogany veneer on pine, scrolled framework, banded inlay, figured veneer on inner liner, refinished, restoration 412.50
    42" h, 23-1/4" w, mahogany veneer on pine, eagle and molded liner regilded, refinished, restoration 880.00
    45" h, 21" w, curly maple, good figure, Chippendale style, old finish, elaborate scrolls on crest, base and ears, one ear cracked and one small pc missing, worn silvering, early 20th C. 660.00
Courting
    Hardwood veneer, old refinishing, reverse-painted rose on white ground in crest, minor edge damage, worn silvering, 12-3/8" h, 7-3/4" w...... 715.00
    Molded rectangular frame, shaped crest enclosing reverse-painted glass panels, etched mirror glass with leaping stag, northern European, late 18th C., 18-1/2" h, 11-1/4" w 3,737.50
Dressing
    Cherry and curly maple, two drawers, turned posts, restoration, 27-1/2" h, 30" w, 11-3/4" d 357.50
    Sheraton, three drawers, shield-shaped mirror, inlaid, 25" h... 330.00

Empire, hanging, two-section

27" h, 13" w, half-turned pilaster frame in old black and gold paint, reverse-painted round scene of woman on stage, touchup repairs, old replaced mirror glass.. 192.50

31-3/4" h, 15-3/4" w, split columns and corner blocks, old black and gold repaint, old reverse painting on glass showing basket of fruit is probably orig but with over-painting on edges, mirror replaced..110.00

38-1/2" h, 22-3/4" w, architectural, turned half columns on sides/bottom, worn orig gilding, "James Todd, Looking Glasses, Portland (Maine)" paper label, top glass cracked............................. 550.00

Federal, hanging, two-section

22-1/2" h, 12" w, Federal style, black and gold half turnings, stamped tin rosettes, replacement reverse-painted ship "Constitution," flakes to silvering.. 495.00

34" h, 17-1/2" w, mahogany, carved, old dark finish, half-turned pilasters, leaf carvings, ring-turned dividers, reeding at base, applied carving and borders on crest, scalloped top, acorn drops.................. 275.00

40-1/4" h, 21-1/2" w, 2-tone gilding on half turnings, molded liner, gold painted rosettes in corners, reverse-painted glass of woman gathering flowers, gilt cornucopias in corners, paint in the border heavily crazed and flaking, few flakes in center, overall wear, mirror has worn silvering 770.00

41-5/8" h, 22-1/2" w, mahogany and mahogany veneer, orig dark finish, molded base, reeded stiles, cove-molded cornice, beveled mirror at bottom, orig painted scene on top shows lady by anchor on the shore with ships in the distance, crack in top corner, touchups, small sections of base molding missing, ... 220.00

42-1/2" h, 19" w, mahogany, Boston, c. 1820, molded cornice, frieze of applied scroll and flanking urns of flowers, tablet showing sailboat and cottages, flanked by half columns, old finish 1,150.00

Miscellaneous, hanging

Two-part, mahogany flame veneer frame, old alligatored finish, orig reverse-painted top section shows basket of fruit in red, yellow, green, black and white, orig mirror, back with partial label, flaking, 33-3/8" h, 18-1/4" w 192.50

Curly maple, frame and liner, 20th C., 17-1/2" h, 27-1/2" w 220.00

Curly maple, molded frame, good detail, old finish, 30-1/2" h, 20-3/4" w 1,705.00

Painted, orig mustard with brown vinegar sponging, mirror glass and back replaced, 16-1/4" h, 12-1/4" w 302.50

Tramp art frame, dark finish over varnish, stepped sawtooth border, stacked geometric designs, 15" h, 17-1/2" w 275.00

Walnut, scrolled crest, rectangular mirror within veneered molded surround, English or American, c. 1740, replaced glass, 21-1/2" h, 12" w 1,265.00

Queen Anne, hanging

Mahogany, molded frame, old finish, replaced mirror glass, 11-1/4" h, 10" w 550.00

Mahogany veneer on pine, old refinishing, scrolled crest, base and ears, molded frame, gilded liner, pierced and carved bird on crest, regilded, 34" h, 19" w... 1,320.00

Pine, orig black floral decor on red ground, molded frame, scalloped crest with orig backboard, typewritten provenance of owners 1826-1941, minor age crack, silvering worn, 21-1/2" h, 11-1/2" w 3,190.00

Pine, applied mahogany veneer, old refinish, two-section, lower section with beveled edge, applied veneer molded with a scalloped liner at top, top crest scalloped and scrolled, narrow piece of mirror glass missing, one corner glued, found in Hartford, Conn., 44" h, 17-1/2" w 2,200.00

Pine with mahogany veneer, raised molded frame, gilded liner, ornate scalloped crest with pierce-carved and gilded leaf design, old worn finish, veneer restoration, small chips, 45-1/2" h, 16-7/8" w 4950.00

Rosewood veneer on pine, old finish, scalloped base, scrolled ears and crest, carved shell at center, molded liner with gilding, two ears replaced with veneer repairs, regilded, 25-1/4" h, 16-3/8" w 495.00

Queen Anne mirror, walnut, English, early 18th C., 33-1/2" h, 14-1/2" w, $3,105. (Photo courtesy of Skinner Auctioneers & Appraisers of Antiques & Fine Arts, Boston and Bolton, Mass.)

Walnut, English, early 18th C., scrolled crest, shaped molded frame, scrolled bracket containing beveled mirror, minor imperfections, 33-1/2" h, 14-1/2" w 3,105.00

Walnut veneer, English, c. 1740-60, scrolled crest above rectangular molded frame, gilt liner, old refinish, minor imperfections, 39" h, 16-1/2" w 1,955.00

Shaving

Federal bowfront, mahogany veneer on pine, turned feet, facade with banded inlay, one dovetailed drawer, beaded edge posts, adjustable mirror, veneer damage, replaced pulls, glass cracked, 16" h, 14-1/4" w, 6-3/4" d 137.50

Mahogany veneer on pine, line inlay, bowfront case, turned feet, two drawers, adjustable mirror with turned posts, country style, repairs, replacements, 23-1/2" h, 18-1/2" w, 7-1/2" d...................... 137.50

Mustard paint, dark-red trim, carved and pierced frame with open scrollwork, small shaped shelf at top, two half-barrel-shaped holders flank arched mirror, lower comb tray, cracks, wear, 21-1/2" h, 10-1/2" w 402.50

Transitional, Hanging

Chippendale to Hepplewhite, mahogany veneer over pine, well-detailed scroll framework, inner liner with band inlay, refinished, replaced glass, bottom altered, old restorations, 41-1/2" h, 22" w... 467.50

Mocha

Background: Named for the similar markings found on mocha quartz, mocha-decorated cream-ware and yellowware was made by numerous Staffordshire potteries for export to North America. Produced from the late 18th century to the late 19th century, the mocha decorations were the result of a simple chemical reaction. Tobacco or hops was added to colored pigment of brown, black, blue, or green in order to give it an acid nature. When this acidic colorant was then applied to an alkaline ground color, the ensuing capillary action of the slip resulted in delicate mocha designs. In addition to feathery seaweed designs, mocha wares are also found with Cat's Eye and Earthworm patterns.

Collecting Hint: Marked pieces of mocha ware are extremely rare.

Bowl

Seaweed decor in blue, white band, blue stripes, footed, crazing, 6-1/2" h, 14" dia 467.50

Seaweed decor in black, brown band, white stripes, footed, 2-7/8" h, 4" dia 357.50

Seaweed decor in green, white band, brown stripes, spider in base, interior flaking, rim chip, 7" h, 14-3/4" dia 302.50

Mocha batter bowl, blue seaweed design, $650.

Creamer

Cat's Eye decor in black and white, rust band, tooled zigzag line around the rim, rounded form, repaired handle, crazed interior, 2-1/8" h............... 1,760.00

Marbleized decor in blue, brown and ochre, two blue stripes around neck, 4-1/4" h.................... 1,540.00

Seaweed decor in black, ochre band, black stripes, green beaded and quilted bands, impressed leaf handle, rim chips, handle crack, crow's feet, 4-1/2" h 1,320.00

Cup, banded, white band between brown stripes, yellow-ware body 275.00

Master salt, light-blue band, dark-brown stripes, footed, some discoloring, chip, 2" h, 3" dia 85.00

Mug

Earthworm decor in brown, white and light blue, light blue and gray bands, brown stripes, stains, crack, 3-1/8" h.. 385.00

Stripes, brown, blue and black on white ground, molded beaded band, handle with leaf ends, stains, crazing, crow's-foot hairline, 3-1/4" h.. 192.50

Stripes, green and brown, light-blue and burnt-orange bands with machine-tooled lines, tooled foliage bands, impressed leaf handle, repaired, damage, 4-7/8" h.. 715.00

Stripes (blue) and geometric band, black and white ground, applied ribbed handle with leaf ends, stains, minor damage, 2-3/4" h.................... 451.00

Wide white slip band extends down from lip, 3-1/2" h, 4" dia 450.00

Pepper pot

Earthworm decor in black and white, sand-colored band, brown stripes, chips, base damage, 4-3/8" h.. 385.00

Stripes, blue and tan, brown-check tooled bands, small flakes on base, lid rim with wear on finial, 4-1/4" h.. 1,210.00

Stripes, light-blue and black, chips, 4-1/2" h...110.00

Tooled brown lines (vertical), white ground, wear, 3-3/4" h.. 1,210.00

Pitcher
    Banded decor in blue and black, white ground, hair-
        lines, 4-1/2" h.. 165.00
    Banded decor in light-green, brown and tan, yellow-
        ware, machine tooling, molded leaf handle, wear,
        chips, hairlines, 6-3/4" h 1,980.00
    Cat's Eye decor in brown, blue and white, blue
        ground, green band, black stripes, badly
        cracked 907.50
    Cat's Eye (multiple) decor in blue and white, ivory
        ground, brown stripes, damage, stains,
        7-1/4" h 500.50
    Geometric and line decor in brown, pumpkin-color
        bands at top and bottom, pearlware, white
        ground, embossed leaf decor on handle and
        spout, minor chips and wear, interior glaze
        flakes, 7-7/8" h...1,320.00
    Seaweed decor in black, tan stripes, embossed blue
        bands at top and bottom, impressed leaves on
        handle, stains, crow's foot in bottom, crack,
        6-1/4" h 550.00
    Seaweed decor in black, taupe ground, blue band,
        black stripes, minor hairline, 6" h................ 440.00
Pitcher, earthworm decor
    Black and white, blue band, blue, tan and black
        stripes, impressed leaves on handle, damage,
        5-1/2" h 330.00
    Blue and black on brown band, black stripes, light-
        blue and green bands, molded leaf handle, chips,
        stains, cracks, 7-1/8" h 770.00
    Blue, brown and white, tan ground, white band,
        brown stripes, 5" h................................... 1,045.00
    Brown, blue and white (four designs), sage-green
        bands, blue stripes, molded leaf handle, repaired
        base, rim and spout, 6-3/8" h 440.00
    Dark-brown, tan and white, light-brown bands, dark-
        brown stripes, damage, repairs, 6" h.......... 385.00
    White, pale blue and brown, tan and dark-brown
        stripes on tan band, molded leaf ends on handle,
        professional repair to handle, 5" h.............. 660.00
Stein, checkered decor, ochre stripes, green bands,
    brown machine-tooled lines, pewter lid with engraved
    laurel wreath, name and 1816, stapled repairs to han-
    dle, 7-3/4" h.. 990.00
Waste Bowl
    Earthworm decor in blue, white and dark-brown,
        blue stripes, tan band, impressed leaves on han-
        dle, wear, stains, hairlines, chip, 3-1/8" h, 6-1/4"
        dia.. 357.50
    Marbleized band in blue, black, white and umber,
        incised line with green at rim, stains, cracks, 3" h,
        5-5/8" dia 495.00

Models

Background: Defined as a miniature representa-
tions of an item, models have always been fascinating. This category looks at a few examples
made during the 19th century.

**Painted wood mansion model, 57" h, 28" sq,
$4,025. (Photo courtesy of Skinner Auctioneers
& Appraisers of Antiques & Fine Arts, Boston
and Bolton, Mass.)**

Building, possibly a church, two-story with tall steepled
    entrance, wood and plywood, orig varnish and green
    and yellow paint, wire nails, some edge damage,
    37" h... 715.00
Mansion, painted wood, brick-painted Italianate-style
    building, central octagonal tower, "S" banner weath-
    ervane, blue bull's-eye lights, widow's walk above
    octagonal turret corners and circular palladian and
    gothic arched painted glass windows, four entrances,
    orig paint, some repairs, American, 19th C., 57" h,
    28" sq 4,025.00
Sailing ship, old white repaint, green and red striping,
    salmon-colored decor, painted canvas backdrop, pine
    case, needs restrung, 19-1/8" h, 23" w, 9" d.........385.00
Stagecoach, carved and painted, Bath and Rockland
    (Maine), black and yellow paint, turn of the century,
    reputedly made by John Creighton Sr., Thomaston,
    Maine, 24" h, 24" l... 3,025.00

Mortars and Pestles

Background: Commonly found in early pharma-
cies, mortars are bowls with shallow curved bottoms that were used with a pestle in order to grind

Burl mortar and pestle, $250.

Tiger maple violin with carved whale-bone fittings, patriotic decorations, 23-1/4" l, $2,070 (Photo courtesy of Skinner Auctioneers & Appraisers of Antiques & Fine Arts, Boston and Bolton, Mass.)

medicine or foods. They date to prehistoric times, when they were made of stone. Most 19th-century examples were made of wood.

Brass, engraved "H. Poppenberg," small edge splits, 3-3/4" h.. 55.00
Wooden
    Burl, footed mortar 6" h, pestle 9-1/4" l.......... 192.50
    Burl figure (traces), tooled rings, pestle with minor edge damage, 6" h, 5-1/2" dia 93.50
    Burl, old finish, turned detail, edge damage, age crack, mortar only, 6-1/2" h........................... 60.50
    Burl, tight figure, turned rings, edge chips, 7" h, 5-7/8" dia 165.00
    Curly maple, old varnish, turned, mortar only, 8" h 330.00
    Hardwood, old red paint, turned, minor age cracks, 7-1/4" h 275.00
    Painted, green mortar, unpainted pestle, mortar 8" h 220.00
    Poplar mortar, old red paint, 7-1/2" h............. 275.00

Mule Chests (see Chest over Drawers)

Musical Instruments

Background: The most popular antique instruments are violins, flutes, oboes, and other instruments associated with the classical music period of 1650 to 1900.

The collecting of musical instruments remains in its infancy, but it is a field that is growing. Investors and speculators have played a role since the 1930s, especially in the area of early stringed instruments.

Reference: Philip F. Gura and James F. Bollman, *America's Instrument: The Banjo in the 19th Century*, University of North Carolina Press, 1999.

Periodical: *Concertina & Squeezebox*, P.O. Box 6706, Ithaca, NY 14851.

Collectors' Clubs: American Musical Instrument Society, RD 3, Box 205-B, Franklin, PA 16323; Reed Organ Society, P.O. Box 901, Deansboro, NY 13328.

Museums: Miles Musical Museum, Eureka Springs, AR; Museum of the American Piano, New York, NY; Streitwieser Foundation Trumpet Museum, Pottstown, PA; University of Michigan Stearns Collection of Musical Instruments, Ann Arbor, MI; Yale University Collection of Musical Instruments, New Haven, CT.

Saxophone, tin, homemade, six keys made from small tin spoons, traces of gold paint, dents, one key broken off, late 19th/early 20th C., 25-1/2" l................. 260.00
Trumpet, Imperial Band Instrument Mfg. Co., Williamsport, Pa., silver-plated brass, orig leather-covered case, wear.. 45.00
Violin, Salzard, playing condition, with bow and case 99.00
Violin, tiger maple, carved whale-bone fittings, decor with red, white and blue patriotic symbols, grain-painted case, mid-19th C., imperfections, 23-1/4" l 2,070.00

Needlework

Background: Needlework is a general term for work produced by hand with a needle, just as the name implies. In particular, it refers to all kinds of handmade embroidery.

Adam and Eve with snake in apple tree, green, yellow, red and browns, on homespun, framed, small stain, some bleeding of colors, 8-3/8" h, 10" w............ 82.50
Church and federal house flanked by trees, fenced garden and duck pond, gentleman walking with dog, surrounded by floral meandering vine border, "By Anna Margaret Houghtaling aged 9 years 1835," American, unfinished, toning, fading, 16-1/2" sq............. 2,875.00

Needlework picture, signed and dated 1835, 16-1/2" sq, $2,875. (Photo courtesy of Skinner Auctioneers & Appraisers of Antiques & Fine Arts, Boston and Bolton, Mass.)

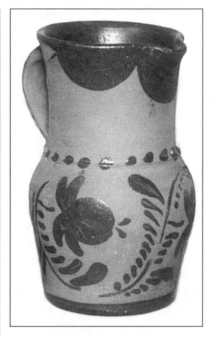

New Geneva pitcher, 6-1/8" h, $770. (Photo courtesy of Garth's Auctions, Delaware, Ohio)

Landscape, silk on silk, scene in shades of green, brown, yellow, white and black, old label mkd "The handiwork of Miss Chloe, a school teacher...born in Abington, now Rockland, Mass. in 1786," wear, tear in sky, 18-1/4" h, 20-1/4" w 385.00
Panel
    Two figures in wooded setting, wool in needlepoint and petit point, ogee bird's-eye maple frame with gilded liner, wear and damage, 30" h, 23-3/4" w...715.00
    Shepherd with flock and pots of flowers in green, tan and red, sailboat and trees in background, portion of house shown in upper-right corner with red and salmon checked roof, areas of restored moth damage, early reeded frame with wear, 22" h, 24-1/4" w 220.00
Sailing ship with American flag, on canvas-covered stretcher, in brown, yellow, red, tan and blue, contemporary frame, edge wear, some floss missing, 22" h, 35" w... 935.00
Verse, Greek key line in oval, "June 9th 1798 Daily Word, Rejoice, O ye nations…," black and ivory silk thread on homespun, framed, small holes, 6-1/2" sq.. 632.50

New Geneva Tanware

Background: Unlike the familiar cobalt-decorated stoneware of the second half of the 19th century, some items made in Greensboro and New Geneva, Pennsylvania, featured Albany slip (dark brown) decoration on a tan-colored body. Known today as tanware, examples typically exhibit brushed decorations, although stenciled pieces also exist. Flourishes and floral designs are the most common.

Flower pot, tulips with vining swags decor, ovoid, saucer base, applied ring handles, rim chips on undecorated side, hairlines, 8-1/2" h 1,100.00
Jug
    "M.C. Russell, Maysville, Ky." reverse stencil, rim flakes, 10-3/8" h.. 275.00
    "Little Brown Jug…S.T. Suit, Suitland, Md." reverse stencil, dated 1880, lip flakes, 6-1/2" h....... 275.00
Pitcher, floral decor
    5" h, with wavy line decor, rim flake............... 440.00
    6-1/8" h 770.00
    7" h, rim flakes 880.00
    8" h, 2 rim flakes 605.00
    9" h 715.00
    9-3/8" h, hairline.. 577.50
Pitcher, other
    Draping decor, rim chips, 6" h........................110.00
    Flourishes, rim chip, hairlines, 10-1/2" h........ 330.00
    Flourishes and lines decor, minor rim, roughness, 7-3/4" h... 440.00

Niddy Noddies

Background: A 19th-century hand reel for yarn, a niddy noddy typically consists of a turned wooden shaft with one crossarm on each end, set perpendicular to each other.

Round turned shaft with baluster turnings, mortised into slightly curved top and bottom, 18-7/8" l, 13" w.......75.00
Softwood, tapered shaft mortised through tapered and slightly curved ends, minor wear, 15" w, 18" l..........85.00

Walnut, carved, detailed chip-carved decor, initialed and dated 1798, small age splits, 14-1/4" w, 17-1/2" l.. 402.50

Wooden, block and turned shaft, crested ends, bentwood supports, pegged, scribe marks, 1 peg missing, 17-1/2" l, 12" w... 90.00

Noah's Arks

Background: Throughout most of the 18th century, Germany was the leading producer of carved wooden toys, sometimes with entire villages devoted to creating small figures. The villages of the Erzgebirge region were noted for their fine Noah's Arks, which were exported worldwide. So popular were they that, by 1911, the R. Bliss Manufacturing Co. of Pawtucket, Rhode Island, was importing Erzgebirge animals to include with its own arks. It is interesting to note that, for many children of the 18th and 19th centuries, Noah's arks were among the few toys they were permitted to play with on the Sabbath.

Two figures, 43 animals, miniature, white with red roof, black windows, wear, some damage, 2-1/2" h, 5-5/8" l.. 522.50

Thirteen animals, Converse, orig polychrome screened decor with label, some damage/repairs 385.00

Noah's ark with more than 30 pairs of animals, original box and packing material, $4,500.

Thirteen animals, insects and birds, four people, mkd "Wyn," orig polychrome paint, minor wear, 8" l.. 3,300.00

Painted, with carved-wood figures, 14" h, 22" l... 415.00

Paper litho scenes of animals and Noah around sides, comb-painted roof, 14 carved-wood animals, 6-1/4" h, 14" l... 405.00

Nutcrackers

Background: Considered the jaws of death for any defenseless nut, these devices come in two versions—one with a screw press, the other with a levered jaw. The jaw example, which worked like a pair of pliers, evolved into a number of fanciful designs. Most nutcrackers were made of cast-iron, but other materials were also used.

Reproduction Alert: Reproductions were made in a variety of forms.

Cast iron, rectangular base and cracker, cracker with tall tapered square handle, green paint, Potter Walnut Cracker Co., minor rust, 4-1/2" h, 3-1/4" w 55.00

Graniteware, white dog on black base, black tail and lower jar, graniteware over cast iron, 5-3/4" h, 10-1/2" l.. 115.00

Wooden

Crocodile, full-figure, Swiss or German, screw press in belly, 8" l 585.00

Dog's head, Black Forest style, glass eyes, levered jaw, mkd "Chalet Minerve & Chalet Suisse Egger & Bruger...," oval base, 3-1/2" h, 7" l.......... 520.00

Eagle's head, Swiss, glass eyes, levered beak, 6-1/2" l 310.00

Elephant's head, glass eyes, levered mouth, 10-1/2" l 650.00

Laughing Boy, German or Swiss, boy in hat and coat standing on round pedestal, screw press in boy's back, 9" h... 1,425.00

Man with umbrella, bearded, smoking a pipe, German, one foot reattached, 8-1/2" h 570.00

Walnut, Black Forest, bear, glass eyes, curved tail with lever that operates the mouth, 4-1/2" h, 8" l 165.00

Old Sleepy Eye

Background: A Sioux Indian chief inspired the name for Sleepy Eye, Minnesota, as well as its Sleepy Eye Milling Company. The mill was in business from 1883 to 1921, using the Indian's bust as its trademark. From 1899 through 1905, the Weir Pottery Co. in Monmouth, Illinois, produced the mill's first premiums—a Flemish butter crock, salt bowl, stein and vase—which were given away in sacks of flour. After the merger of seven potteries in 1906, the resulting Western Stoneware Co. produced the Sleepy Eye premiums until 1937.

In addition to the original four premiums, Sleepy Eye pottery and stoneware included five sizes of pitchers, along with various mugs, steins, sugar bowls, and tea tiles. Most were blue and white, but pieces were also made in brown, gold, and green. Non-ceramic items, including bakers' caps, lithographed barrel covers, beanies, fans, pillow tops, postcards, and trade cards were also used to advertise the company.

In 1952, Western Stoneware Co. produced 22- and 40-ounce steins with a redesigned Indian's head and a chestnut-brown glaze.

Reference: Jim Martin and Bette Cooper, *Monmouth-Western Stoneware*, Collector Books, 1998; Elinor Meugnoit, *Old Sleepy Eye*, self-published, 1979.

Collectors' Club: Old Sleepy Eye Collectors Club of America, P.O. Box 12, Monmouth, IL 61462, http://maplecity.com/~oseclub/index.htm

Reproduction Alert: Old Sleepy Eye items manufactured during the Western Stoneware period are being reproduced. Toothpick holders and salt-and-pepper shakers are also being made, although these items were never originally produced.

Old Sleepy Eye pitcher, blue and white, 5-1/4" h, $198.

Bowl, Flemish, rounded bottom, 4" h,
6-1/2" dia 355.00
Butter crock, Flemish, straight-sided, 5" h,
6-1/2" dia 375.00
Mug, 4-1/4" h 110.00
Pillow top, Chief Sleepy Eye before the Great Father,
known as the Monroe top, 1901 .... 500.00
Pitcher, blue and white
No.1, blue rim, 4-1/8" h 275.00
No. 1, plain rim, 4-1/8" h 180.00
No. 2, 5-1/4" h 275.00
No. 4, blue rim 410.00
Salt crock, hanging, blue and white, 5-1/2" h,
5-1/4" dia 1,650.00
Vase, cylindrical, rim chip 450.00
Vase, Flemish, cylindrical, 8-1/2" h 350.00

Paintings

Background: This category could fill several books by itself. Included here is a sampling of the artwork offered by several leading U.S. auction houses that specialize in country antiques and Americana.

Note: The following listings are grouped into six categories: Animals, Children (portraits), Miscellaneous, Portraits (adults), Scenic, and Still Life. Categories are further divided into sections devoted to signed works and unsigned works.

Animals, signed

Cat, Gaylord, oil on board, gray and white cat with bow in wooden travel crate, American, framed, surface grime, 9" h, 8-1/2" w.. 13,800.00

Cat, Alfred A. Brunel de Neuville, oil on board, three kittens, two on chair, one at dish of milk with insect in center, framed, 12" h, 9" w............................. 1,925.00

Horse, L. Pappe, dapple gray horse with landscape background, dated 5-11-14, black and white graphite drawing on heavy paper, framed, 24-1/4" h, 30-1/4" w 302.50

Animals, unsigned

Birds, pen and ink and watercolor on laid paper, "Gold Crest Wren" and "Sparrow Hawk" in natural habitat, penciled notes on back, matted and old frames, minor stains, pages were bound, 8-7/8" h, 7-3/8" w, pr 605.00

Cat, oil on artist board, gray tiger-striped cat wearing red bow, reclining in grass, framed, 13" h, 16" w...... 9,900.00

Painting of cat by Gaylord, oil on board, 9" h, 8-1/2" w, $13,800. (Photo courtesy of Skinner Auctioneers & Appraisers of Antiques & Fine Arts, Boston and Bolton, Mass.)

Cat, oil on canvas, white cat sitting on edge of wooden fence, tops of trees in background, oil on canvas... 3,300.00

Children, signed/attributed

Attributed to Zedekiah Belknap (American, 1781-1858), oil on canvas, child in blue dress, holds pet rabbit, unsigned, strip frame, scattered abrasions, minute losses, surface grime, 26" h, 22-1/2" w........ 47,150.00

George Henry Durrie (American, 1820-63), oil on canvas, two boys and their dog in a landscape, one boy holding a book, the other holding a whip, unsigned, identified on presentation plaque and label on reverse, framed, lined, retouched, 53" h, 41" w 17,250.00

Attributed to Aaron Dean Fletcher (American, 1817-1902), oil on canvas, boy holding a watch on a chain, framed, 29" h, 26" w, scattered punctures and tears, some repairs, flakes, losses........................ 23,000.00

Prior Hamblin School, oil on canvas, child holding a watch, unsigned, 19th C., framed, relined, retouched, 21-1/4" h, 17-1/4" w 18,400.00

In the manner of William Matthew Prior (American, 1806-1873), oil on board, child holding whip, unsigned, framed, scattered losses, 13-1/2" h, 10-1/4" w...............24,150.00

Children, unsigned

Boy

Oil on canvas, boy identified as Charles Tristam Chase, wearing blue outfit with white collar, holding hat and sitting beside table with pocket watch on top, red drapes, framed, 30" h, 24" w . 5,500.00

Oil on canvas, boy in blue outfit, holding hat, framed, lined, retouched, 22-1/2" h, 18" w............ 2,530.00

Oil on canvas, boy holding apple and knife, American, mid 18th C., framed, mounted on Masonite, retouched, 29-1/2" h, 25" w 2,990.00

Oil on canvas, boy holding dog on his lap, boy has brown hair, gray eyes and wears black jacket with wide-collared white shirt and yellow vest, red curtains in background, naïve but well done, framed, relined, restoration, 30" h, 25" w.............. 2,805.00

Watercolor on paper, boy with dog standing in a landscape, overlooking a harbor, grain-painted frame, toning, stains, scattered foxing, 8" h, 5-1/2" w 1,725.00

Child, miniature

Watercolor on ivory, child in white dress and bonnet, holding rattle, oval, framed, 2" h, 1-1/2" w.......546.00

Watercolor on paper, child in red dress and holding rattle, seated in a chair on a blue rug, old gilt frame, wear, stains, 4-3/4" h, 3-1/4" w 715.00

Watercolor on paper, child in red and black dress, oval, in black lacquered frame 4-3/4" h, 4-1/4" w 302.50

Girl

Oil on canvas, two girls, older in blue dress and holding something metal, younger in red dress and holding a pink rose, unframed, orig stretcher, small patch, areas of touchup, black tape over edges of canvas, 28" h, 24-1/8" w.......... 2,310.00

"Robert Young aged 52 years" and "Mrs. Robert Young aged 50 years," unsigned, identified and dated 1831 on reverse, oil on canvas, 26" x 21-3/4", pair, $1,955. (Photo courtesy of Skinner Auctioneers & Appraisers of Antiques & Fine Arts, Boston and Bolton, Mass.)

Oil on canvas, girl in blue-striped dress, holding straw hat filled with flowers, framed, lined, surface grime, 50" h, 36" w 5,750.00

Watercolor on paper, miniature, girl in dress with gray highlights and white lace collar, side view from the waist up, oval, rectangular frame 5-1/4" h, 4-3/4" w 880.00

Watercolor on paper, miniature, girl with brown hair, red dress with rose and red bead necklace, oval, in rectangular black lacquer frame, light stain, minor fading, frame 5-1/8" h, 4-1/4" w 715.00

Miscellaneous, signed

"Henry C. Curtis, 27 Congress Avenue," watercolor on paper, entitled "Fairy Hose, E. J. Loines, Foreman," scene of early hose car with man in top hat, stains, some paper damage, framed, 12" h, 16" w 440.00

Miscellaneous, unsigned

Pen and ink on paper, anniversary memorial, red and brown ink with penciled leaves and diamond detail, dated "June 10, 1884, ninety third anniversary, Miss Eleanor Bright, Born 1791, Married 1817 to Mr. Jacob Pealer," period frame, minor stains and fold lines, 28-1/2" h, 20" w 330.00

Watercolor

Birth commemorative, "Eliza Morrison, Born September 20th, 1805," red and green letters, red and green floral border inside red and yellow decor border, framed 1,650.00

Heart in Hand motif, four blue hands, each with a red heart, pointing to top, bottom and sides, framed 330.00

"N.Y. Central & Western Railway Co. 1892," shows locomotive pulling coal car, framed, 11" h, 18" w 220.00

Portraits, signed/attributed

Attributed to Prior, oil on board, husband and wife, both in black clothes, he with gold watch fob, she with gold necklace and earrings, old frames, minor paint flaking, one corner missing, 14" h, 10" w, pr 14,300.00

David Sheley, 1982, watercolor, man and woman, he wears black coat with yellow vest, she wears black dress with red belt and lace collar, bordered in light-green, yellow, red and white, old cut-down grained frames, contemporary, 10-3/4" h, 9-5/8" w, pr 220.00

Carl Weinedel (American, 1792-1845), watercolor on ivory, miniature, man in black coat, signed "Weinedel: 1837," gilded copper pendant case with hair compartment (empty) on reverse, 2-1/4" h, 2" w 920.00

Portraits, unsigned

Oil on board, man in black coat with wide lapels and high white collar, one edge of chair showing yellow and black decor, unframed, touchup, over-varnish, 12" h, 9-5/8" w 880.00

Oil on canvas

George Washington, early 19th C., wear, framed, 19" h, 14" w 1,925.00

Man with brown hair and beard in black coat, gray vest and white shirt with gold eyeglass chain, identified as John Kerr of Barrow, relined with patches and professional restoration, contemporary frame, 32-1/4" h, 25-5/8" w 1,430.00

Man and woman, 18th C., man in white wig wearing olive-green frock coat, white waist coat and red cape and holding a letter, woman in white wig wearing blue dress, silver jewelry and peach shawl, holding a rose, framed, rebacked on canvas and restored, 30" h, 24-3/4" w, pr 5,500.00

Woman with brown eyes and brown hair in ringlets, in black dress with white lace collar, cameo brooch and red paisley shawl, contemporary wooden frame, relined with possible touchup, crazed, 30" h, 25" w 770.00

Young man seated in red chair, black waist coat and frock coat with black tie, attributed to Indiana, framed, rebacked on canvas, restored, yellowed band of varnish on his forehead, 26-1/4" h, 22" w 1,430.00

Oil on wooden panel, man and woman, man in black coat and vest with white shirt and bowtie, woman in green dress with white bonnet and lace collar and wearing brooch and rings, said to be Harriet Williams, framed, illegible signatures, worn surface, old touchup repair, 12" h, 9-3/8" w, pr 1,320.00

Pencil, ink and watercolor on paper, similar profile portraits of man and woman, matching gutta percha frames, 4-1/8" sq, pr........................... 715.00

Pencil and watercolor drawings on paper, facing portraits of man and woman, matted, old frames, 6" h, 4" w, pr 1,430.00

Watercolor on ivory, miniature

    Man in blue double-breasted coat and white shirt with high collar, oval, in rectangular lacquered black frame 6-3/8" h, 5-3/4" w 385.00

    Officer, possibly George Washington, wearing blue coat with red lapels, gold epaulettes and star-shaped medal, white vest, oval, in rectangular lacquered black frame 5-1/2" h, 4-5/8" w 825.00

    Young man in blue frock coat with yellow waistcoat and white collar, oval, in black lacquered frame 5-1/2" h, 4-3/8" w 2,310.00

Watercolor and pencil on paper, husband and wife, man with brown hair and eyes, black coat, red plaid vest, blue neck scarf, woman with brown hair, blue eyes, blue dress, ivory bonnet, framed together, minor stains, each 6-1/2" h, 4" w, pr 1,430.00

Watercolor on paper, man in black coat, brown vest and black collar, identified and dated 1834, rosewood veneer frame, 9" h, 7-1/2" w 495.00

Watercolor on paper, miniature

    Man in black coat holding pin in hand, wooden frame with worn black and gold paint, 4-5/8" h, 3-1/2" w 220.00

    Man in a black coat or uniform, oval, framed, 5-1/2" h, 4-3/4" w 192.50

    Woman in blue dress with white bonnet and accessories, oval, brass frame with convex lens, wear, some damage, 4-1/2" h, 3-7/8" w 110.00

Woman in lace bonnet, green dress and black shawl, lacquered black frame, 5-1/8" h, 4-1/8" w 357.50

Woman in white and black dress, coral beads, elaborate hairdo, lacquered black frame, edge damage, diamond-shape, 4-1/4" sq 825.00

Scenic, signed

Hattie K. Brunner, country sale scene with Amish in horse-drawn buggy, barn, house and outbuildings, early furniture and quilts in yard, with 1976 letter from Brunner, framed, 10-1/2" h, 14-1/2" w 4,400.00

Alvan T. Fisher (American, 1792-1863), "Bishop's Farm, Hartford, Conn." nameplate, landscape with cattle in a stream, framed, rebacked on canvas, cleaned and restored, 30" h, 45" w 11,000.00

Hershburger, farm scene, Quincy Pa., primitive, cattle and fowl outside barn, inscribed "...painted by Major Hershburger, Fall of 1877" in pencil, initialed "WRH," oil on board, 12-3/4" h, 19" w 17,250.00

S.J. Prentiss, snowscene with cut trees and two men, boy, two oxen pulling sled, mountains in background, oil on canvas, framed, 14" h, 18" w 6,600.00

F.H. Shapleigh, 1874, New Hampshire town scene, houses and church, picket fence, dirt road, cattle, oil on canvas, 14" h, 24" w 8,125.00

Scenic, unsigned

Oil on artist board, landscape with trees, lake and boy fishing with dog nearby, repainted frame, 10" h, 13" w 330.00

Oil on board, "Pumpkins in the Cornfield, Autumn," American school, 19th or 20th C., framed, retouched, 18-1/2" h, 24-1/2" w 862.50

Oil on canvas

    Federal house with white fence and leafless trees, shadowbox frame, cleaned, some touchup repair, revarnished, 21" h, 32" w 935.00

    Kittery Shipyard, framed 2,475.00

    River scene with barns and houses in foreground surrounded by trees, mountains in background, refinished frame, one old repair, 15" h, 20" w.. 357.50

Watercolor on paper, ruins of Old Norwich Mill, Norwich, Conn., pencil inscription "To Jane A. Flagg from her school mate Sarah H. Burroughs," 19th C., framed, 13-1/4" h, 16" w... 1,265.00

Still life, signed

J.A. Woodside, fruit in ceramic openwork basket on table, oil on canvas, oval image..................... 7,150.00

Still life, unsigned

Oil on canvas, fish and creel, monogrammed, dated 1882, American, framed, lined, retouched, 13" h, 16" w 1,265.00

Pastel on paper, fruit on marble shelf, unframed, signature of "Mrs. Woodhouse" on reverse, minor abrasions, stains, 9-1/4" h, 12" w............................ 690.00

Pantry Boxes

Background: A bentwood box with a flat bottom and a flat removable lid is called a pantry box. This 19th-century form can be found in a rainbow of painted colors, as well as mellow natural finishes.

Reproduction Alert: Although reproductions have been made, the larger problem for today's collector is that vintage boxes have been repainted but represented as having original paint.

Note: All listings are for round boxes. The values listed illustrate a wide range of prices realized at major auction houses. An extremely high price may be indicative of an unusual shade of a particular color, or it may simply be the result of overzealous bidding.

4-1/4" dia, natural finish, carved lap 110.00
5-1/4" dia, blue paint 137.50
5-1/2" dia, red paint 82.50
6" dia, putty paint 110.00
6-1/2" dia, black paint 137.50
6-1/2" dia, blue paint 165.00
6-1/2" dia, traces of blue paint 71.50
6-1/2" dia, gray paint 110.00
6-1/2" dia, green paint 82.50
6-1/2" dia, green paint 110.00
6-1/2" dia, sage green paint 385.00
7" dia, green paint 660.00
7-1/8" dia, 2-7/8" h, old dark-green paint, two fingers, "Ginger" on lid, old chip on lid 660.00
7-1/2" dia, green paint 137.50
7-1/2" dia, pumpkin paint 110.00
7-1/2" dia, red paint 330.00
7-3/4" dia, blue paint 55.00
8-1/2" dia, 5-1/2" h, electric-blue paint, traces of green beneath rim, copper and steel tacks, bail handle, lid 770.00

8-1/2" dia, green paint 165.00
8-1/2" dia, sage green paint 357.50
8-3/4" dia, natural patina, brass tacks, small chip on base 137.50
8-3/4" dia, yellow paint 550.00
8-5/8" dia, orig dark-green paint, small chips 165.00
9" dia, 5" h, old cream-yellow paint, lap seam, bail handle, age crack in paper-covered bottom 467.50
9" dia, 5-1/2" h, orig deep-blue paint, wood-peg and steel-nail construction, bail handle, exterior split at handle 440.00
9-1/4" dia, blue paint, bail handle 330.00
9-1/2" dia, blue paint, bail handle 440.00
9-3/4" dia, blue paint 495.00
10" dia, black paint 66.00
10" dia, pumpkin paint, bail handle 82.50
10-1/4" dia, old dry red paint, stamped "M. Dunster," lid chips 247.50
10-3/4" dia, green paint, bail handle 154.00
11" dia, red paint 385.00
11-1/4" dia, gray paint 55.00
11-1/4" dia, gray paint, bail handle 247.50
11-1/2" dia, black paint, bail handle 82.50
11-1/2" dia, light-blue paint, bail handle 495.00
11-1/2" dia, green paint, bail handle 385.00
11-1/2" dia, 6-1/4" h, orig red paint, steel tacks, with lid, few late nails added near bottom 522.50
12" dia, 10-1/4" h, old green and red paint, large turned finial on lid 632.50
12" dia, mustard paint, bail handle 110.00
12" dia, natural finish, bail handle 93.50
12-1/4" dia, 6-1/4" h, old green paint, double staves, slightly mismatched top, minor split 440.00
Nested set of five, Thos. Annett, N. Jaffrey, N.H., natural finish, 5-1/2" dia to 9-3/4" dia 220.00

Paper Ephemera

Background: When used by collectors, the term ephemera generally refers to paper objects such as letterheads and bookplates that were intended to be used for a short time and then thrown away.

References: Ron Barlow and Ray Reynolds, *Insider's Guide to Old Books, Magazines, Newspapers, and Trade Catalogs*, Windmill Publishing, 1995; Gerard S. Petrone, *Cigar Box Labels: Portraits of Life, Mirrors of History*, Schiffer Publishing, 1998; Robert Reed, *Advertising Postcards*, Schiffer Publishing, 2001; —, *Paper Collectibles*, Wallace-Homestead, 1995; Gene Utz, *Collecting Paper*, Books Americana, 1993.

Periodicals: *Paper & Advertising Collector*, P.O. Box 500, Mount Joy, PA 17552; *Paper Collectors' Marketplace*, P.O. Box 128, Scandinavia, WI 54977.

Collectors' Clubs: Calendar Collector Society, American Resources, 18222 Flower Hill Way #299, Gaithersburg, MD 20879; Cigar Label Collectors

Pantry box in old blue paint, 18-1/4" dia, $1,200.

International, P.O. Box 66, Sharon Center, OH 44274; Citrus Label Society, 131 Miramonte Dr., Fullerton, CA 92365; Ephemera Society of America, P.O. Box 95, Cazenovia, NY 13035; The National Assoc. of Paper & Advertising Collectors, P.O. Box 500, Mount Joy, PA 17552; Society of Antique Label Collectors, P.O. Box 24811, Tampa, FL 33623.

FYI: You can blame Benjamin Franklin for a portion of your junk mail. He issued the first mail-order catalog in 1744, starting the trickle that would ultimately become a deluge of paper-bound advertising material. Catalogs were particularly useful for spreading information about innovations, fashion, and health care to those who lived in rural America.

Account book

John Ross (first husband of Betsy Ross), fifteen
entries, 1-1/2" h, 6" w 55.00

James Short, Newbury, Mass., 1743-96, leather-
bound, tears, stains, wear, 7-3/4" h,
12-1/4" w 230.00

Almanac, "American Anti-Slavery Almanac for 1840," woodcut print of free man standing on a whip, a mother and children burying their chains, wear, soiling, back missing corners, 7-1/2" h, 4-1/2" w............110.00

Bookplate, watercolor on lined paper, red and green checked lettering, border and geometric flowers, "29 November 1863 Barbara Lapp," worn grain-decor frame, glued down, few stains, 7-1/4" h,
5-1/4" w... 1,650.00

Exercise book, 88 pages, pen and ink math problems on both sides with calligraphic headings and some drawings, eleven in watercolor, name and dates 1831 to 1842, cardboard covers, wear, paper damage, 12-7/8" h, 8-1/2" w.. 275.00

Insurance policy, nautical

1772, for sloop named "Molly" sailing from Philadelphia to Boston, 16-1/2" x 12-1/2"................110.00

1791, for sloop named "Parrot" sailing from Philadelphia to Newbury, 16-1/2" x 12-1/2" 93.50

Land indenture, Pennsylvania

1763, Northern Liberties, splits 23" h,
24" w... 82.50

1764, Bucks County, signed by John Penn, sale of
1,000 acres, seal with some chipping, 15" h,
32" w... 220.00

1772, Lancaster County, 24-1/4" h,
29-5/8" w 330.00

Letter, concerning release of George Washington's slaves, Jan. 4, 1800, from John Butcher to Sarah Horner, Alexandria, Va., 1 page........................... 3,850.00

Sale bill, March 1893, printed in Bellefonte Pa., framed, folds, 10-3/8" h, 14-1/8" w................................. 35.00

Stock note

Free Society of Traders in Pa., 1683, society seal,
21-1/2" h, 7-1/2" w 742.50

Free Society of Traders in Pa., 1683, heavily damaged Society's seal, 21-1/2" h, 7-1/2" w 550.00

Salem Glass Works, unissued, pr.................. 275.00

The Deering Binder trade card, $35.

Tax log, Newbury, Mass., 1755, contains order by assessors of Newbury to Ambros Berry (Constable) to collect taxes due to the town and province, lists townspeople and amounts, tears, wear, 7-1/2" h, 9-1/2" w..115.00

Tray, papier-mâché, shows maiden holding gray graniteware milk pail and standing next to a cow, "Souvenir" in the upper-right corner and "To the Patrons of Granite Ironware" below the image, back mkd "Patent Granite Ironware, The Best Cooking Utensils Ever Made, Light, Wholesome, Durable, Easily Cleaned," tear, 10" h, 7" w...115.00

Pearlware

Background: Josiah Wedgwood introduced pearlware around 1780 and considered it to be an improvement on his earlier creamware. Although "pearlware" suggests an iridescent appearance, the term is actually a misnomer. Pearlware contains more white clay than creamware, and the addition of cobalt oxide to the glaze often results in pieces with a bluish-white cast.

Child's mug, Franklin's Maxims, "Keep thy shop and thy shop will keep thee," black transfer, red highlights, repairs to handle and rim, hairline, 2-1/2" h.........201.25

Child's plate, "Flowers That Never Fade, Attachment, Brothers & Sisters...," brother reading to his sister in front of house, black transfer, serpentine rim with wide black band, some discoloring, glaze nick, 5-1/8" dia.. 180.00

Coffeepot, Strawberry pattern, footed, oblong, arched scrolled handle with molded acanthus leaf, curved spout, strawberry and floral designs in red, yellow, purple and green polychrome, brown stripes, rounded oblong lid with molded twisted-rope border and strawberry finial, 6-1/4" h, 11-3/8" l............................ 250.00

Creamer

Figures seated at table, molded design, pink luster,
discoloring, chip, minor glaze flakes,
5" h 80.00

Leeds-type decor, blue and green, impressed leaf ends, rim wear, 3-5/8" h 110.00

Rose design, pink polychrome, auxiliary flowers and buds, red stripe, ovoid, gallery-like foot, chips, 3" h 50.00

Shell pattern, seaweed and floral designs, yellow, red, blue, green and black polychrome, red border, orange stripes, chips, 2-5/8" h, 3-1/8" dia 35.00

Strawberry pattern, footed, oblong, arched scrolled handle, accented in red, yellow, purple and green polychrome, brown stripes, minor discoloring, minor flaking, 4-3/8" h, 6" l 100.00

Strawberry pattern, footed, oblong, arched scrolled handle, accented in red, yellow, black, purple and green polychrome, blue stripes, some discoloring, small chip, minor glaze wear, 4-3/8" h, 4-7/8" l 160.00

Strawberry and King's Rose, line border, roses in pink, red, green, yellow and black, wear, stains 192.50

Cup and saucer, handleless

Gaudy Leeds floral decor in blue, yellow, green and two shades of ochre, small edge chips, hairline in saucer 82.50

King's Rose, red rose, red and yellow auxiliary flowers, yellow and green leaves, wide pink band with diamond and floret design, hairline, chips, discoloring, 2-3/8" h 65.00

Strawberry pattern, pink basket containing red and yellow strawberries, pink peony-like flower, blue and yellow auxiliary flowers, green leaves, yellow border, pink half-round sunbursts and swags of red and yellow strawberries with green leaves, red stripes, slight chips 200.00

Plate

Eagle, molded shell border, blue scalloped rim, eagle with shield on its breast, holds olive branch and thunderbolt of seven arrows, thirteen stars above, two nicks, two flakes, discoloring, 5-1/4" dia 1,100.00

Same design, chip, discoloring, 7-3/8" dia.. 1,000.00

Same design, green scalloped rim, 9-3/4" dia 2,400.00

King's Rose, pink rose, red and yellow auxiliary flowers, green and yellow leaves, pink border with diamond and floret design, red striping, minor rim flake, 9-3/4" dia 150.00

Peafowl, molded shell border, green scalloped rim, peafowl perched on green spatter tree with brown branches, minor discolor, 6-1/8" dia 900.00

Same design, minor discolor, 9-3/4" dia 2,100.00

Rose design, pink polychrome with green leaves, orange stripe, knife marks, 7-1/4" dia 35.00

Strawberry pattern, pink basket containing red and yellow strawberries, pink peony-like flower, blue and yellow auxiliary flowers and green leaves, border of yellow and pink half-round sunbursts and swags of red and yellow strawberries with

green leaves, red stripe, minor discoloring, polychrome flaking, hairline, 8-1/8" dia 80.00

Same design, minor discoloring, some polychrome faking, minor base flake, 9-7/8" dia 130.00

Strawberry and King's Rose, line border, roses in pink, red, yellow and black, wear, light stains, enamel flakes, pr 137.50

Platter, Gaudy blue and white floral decor, scalloped border, molded fish scale and feather design, minor wear, 13-3/8" l 1,540.00

Soup plate, Strawberry and King's Rose, line border, roses in pink, red, yellow and black 110.00

Sugar, covered

Gaudy Leeds-type decor, green and yellow flowers, blue stripes, blue beehive finial, small chips, hairline, bowl flange missing, 5" h 110.00

Leeds-type, yellow tulip, green and ochre flowers, octagonal, swan finial on lid, stains, crazing, 6" h, 5" w 1,485.00

Strawberry pattern, footed, oblong, molded strawberry and leaf motif in relief, horizontal molded twisted-rope bands, concave shoulder, accented in red, yellow and green polychrome, brown stripes, rounded lid, rosette finial, significant discoloring, 5-3/8" h, 6" l 140.00

Teapot

Child's, dome top, blue transfer, small flake on flange of lid, 5-1/8" h 495.00

Strawberry pattern, footed, oblong, arched scrolled handle, accented in red, yellow, purple and green, brown stripes, spout damaged, some discoloring, hairline, chips, flaking, 5-1/2" h, 9" l 250.00

White ground, brown stars and stripes, rough spout, 7-1/4" h 330.00

Vase, finger or tulip vase, blue feather edges, hand-painted designs, base chip, hairlines, 6-3/4" h, 7" w 495.00

Pease

Background: The Pease family worked in Ohio during the 19th century. They are known for their turned wooden containers, which were sometimes painted.

Covered jar

3-1/4" h, turnings on body, lid with urn finial, pencil inscription with name and 1863 date, age cracks 275.00

4" h, squat form, turned rings, urn finial, uneven worn finish, age cracks in body 467.50

4-1/2" h, turned rings, domed lid, tall urn finial 247.50

4-3/4" h, turned rings, urn finial, worn finish, lid slightly warped 220.00

5-1/8" h, turnings, flattened ball finial 330.00

5-1/4" h, squat form, turnings, urn finial 660.00

6-1/4" h, 5-1/4" dia, turned rings, urn finial, worn finish, short age crack in foot, small stain on lid 385.00

Pease covered jars, 6-1/2" h, $600; 5-1/2" h, $400.

6-1/4" h, 5-3/4" dia, turnings on body, lid with flattened ball finial, darker patina on lid 495.00
6-1/2" h, 5" dia, turned rings, urn finial, lightly worn patina 605.00
7" h, 6-1/2" dia, turnings on body, lid with sloping shoulders, urn finial, lightly worn patina, age cracks in bottom 495.00
7-1/4" h, 8" dia, footed base, stepped ring turnings on body, urn-shaped finial 935.00
8-1/2" h, 8" dia, maple, turned rings, tall urn finial, minor rim damage on body, glued chip on lid 495.00
Covered jar, with bail and wooden handle
  3-3/8" h, turnings on body, lid with flattened ball finial, age cracks, small stains 247.50
  3-3/8" h, turnings on body and lid, shiny varnish, ink inscription "From Oran...Sept. 29/89. Bought at the Detroit Exposition Sept. 25th 1889" 880.00
  4" h, high foot, turned rings on body, lid with elongated finial 385.00
  4-1/2" h, turnings on body, lid with flattened ball finial 605.00
  4-1/2" h, turnings on body, lid with high urn finial, age crack in lid 385.00
  6-3/4" h, 6-3/4" dia, ring turnings on body, flattened knob finial, slightly out of round, age cracks in body 330.00
  7-3/8" h, 6-1/2" dia, turned rings on body, lid with urn finial, small chip and age crack in lid 715.00
  8" h, 6-1/2" dia, ring turnings, urn finial, wire bail handle missing 456.50
  9" h, 10-1/2" dia, turnings on body, flattened finial, light stains 1,650.00
  9-1/2" h, 9" dia, turned rings, flattened urn finial, worn finish, areas of dark color, short age crack in foot, lid split and reglued 440.00
  9-3/4" h, 10" dia, turned foot, raised rings at shoulder, turned finial, glued cracks 495.00
Sewing caddy, three-part, metal rods for spools, paper label "D.M. Pease Manufacturer of American Hollow Ware, Spool Stands...Address orders to D.M. Pease, Concord, Lake Co., O.," worn finish, lid chips, 5-3/4" h 302.50

Peg Rails

Background: In its simplest form, a peg rail is a horizontal-hanging board with wooden pegs for hanging coats, hats or other articles of clothing.

25-1/2" l, 2-1/2" h, softwood, five curved mortised pegs, minor wood loss 80.00
59-1/2" l, pine, old dark worn finish, nine turned pegs, beaded edges 220.00
68-3/4" l, 1-5/8" h, blue repaint, seventeen turned pegs, mushroom ends, molded edges, iron tulip-shaped hangers recent additions................................. 300.00

Pewter

Background: Pewter is an alloy of tin and lead, and often contains traces of other metals as well. Most pewter items are utilitarian domestic ware, and much of it is plain. England was the primary source of pewter for the American colonies for nearly 150 years. Once the American Revolution ended the embargo on raw tin, a small American pewter industry developed and flourished until the Civil War.

Reference: Henry J. Kauffman, *The American Pewterer: His Techniques and His Products*, Astragal Press, 1994.

Collectors' Club: Pewter Collectors Club of America, 504 W. Lafayette St., West Chester, PA 19380-2210.

Basin
  8-3/4" dia, 2" h, "Richard Lee" touch, slightly raised rim, polished, minor wear and pitting.......... 577.50
  10" dia, 2-1/2" h, "Love" and "London" touches, hairline.. 150.00
  10" dia, unmarked, European, "H.K." engraved on rim 165.00
  11-3/4" dia, 2-7/8" h, crowned rose touch, English, battering, repair 302.50
  12" dia, "T.D" and eagle touch (Thomas Danforth III, Stepney, Conn., and Philadelphia, 1777-1818), incised ring around lower interior, flared rim, light pitting.. 1,155.00
  13" dia, 3-1/4" h, London partial touch, hammered booge, flared rim, areas of pitting............... 247.50
  13-1/8" dia, "A. Griswold" with eagle touch (Ashbil Griswold, Meriden, Conn., 1807-1815), wear, scratches 495.00
  13-1/4" dia, "Samuel Pierce" faint eagle touch (Greenfield, Mass., 1792-1830), edge damage, wear, dents, pitting 220.00
  Samuel Kilbourne partial eagle touch (Baltimore, 1814-1839), dents 467.50
Candlestick
  6" h, "R. Dunham" touch (Rufus Dunham, Westbrook, Maine, 1837-1861), edges battered 165.00
  6-1/4" h, unmarked, with bobeche, some battering, pr 247.50

ANOTHER LEGEND?

George Washington ate here! Such is the claim regarding this pewter plate. Marked "London" and having a monogram on the front, the 9-1/2" plate was engraved "One of a set of plates in the house of Walter Franklin, corner of Cherry Street and Franklin Square, New York City, when occupied by General George Washington in 1789 as his first Presidential Residence." Could this have really been a plate from which the Father of our Country supped? Or did the inscription amount to nothing more than just another cherry tree story?

Pewter plate with George Washington legend, 9-1/2" dia, $770. (Photo courtesy of Cyr Auction Company, Gray, Maine)

7-3/4" h, varying touches, Continental, scalloped base, baluster stem, pr 275.00

10" h, unmarked, American, baluster stems, domed bases, push ups, professional restoration, pr 330.00

10" h unmarked, stepped petal base, paneled baluster stem, paneled and scalloped socket, two-pc, short repaired split in base 110.00

Chalice, unmkd, wear, 5-1/8" h 55.00

Charger
13" dia, unmarked, scratch-engraved initials on back, polished, wear, scratches.................. 275.00
13-1/4" dia, "B.L." touch, wear, pitting............ 192.50
13-1/2" dia, English, touchmarks include "SE" and "..asson & Son London"............................. 352.00

13-1/2" dia, "London" with flower and crown touch, hammered booge, incised rim and bowl, edge restoration, dents... 275.00

14-1/2" dia, faint touch, very worn 165.00

15-3/8" dia, "G.N.K." and partial touch, rim slightly rolled... 330.00

18-1/4" dia, eagle and rose and crown touches, hammered booge, wear, pitting, splits........ 302.50

Chalice, "I. Trask" touch (Israel Trask, Beverly, Mass., 1807-1856), flared rim, stepped base, polished, minor wear, 5-3/4" h, pr... 1,045.00

Coffeepot
10" h, "Roswell Gleason" touch (Dorchester, Mass., 1822-1871), paneled design, scrolled wooden handle and finial 302.50

10-1/2" h, "T.B.M. Co." touch, footed base with fluting, domed lid with stepped rings, wooden finial, scrolled wooden handle, repairs, damage.. 220.00

11-1/4" h, "Boardman & Hart, N-York" touch, tooled lines around base and above/below spout, scrolled handle, domed lid, turned finial, spout restoration 357.50

11-1/4" h, unsigned, attributed to Henry Homan, Cincinnati, Ohio, 1847-1864, tooled floral decor with acanthus leaf spout, scroll handle, grape finial, minor dents... 165.00

12" h, "R. Dunham" embossed mark (Rufus Dunham, Westbrook, Maine, 1837-1861), ring-turned foot and body, black enameled scroll handle, domed lid, wooden disk finial, minor dent 467.50

12-1/4" h, "A. Porter" touch (Allan Porter, Westbrook, Maine, 1830-1840), gooseneck spout, bulbous body, handle and knob finial in black paint 412.50

13" h, "Roswell Gleason" signature (Dorchester, Mass., 1822-71), octagonal footed base, paneled sides, enameled scrolled handle and finial, base repair 165.00

Communion flagon, "Reed and Barton" touch, 11-1/4" h.. 220.00

Inkwell, English, wide flat base, blue glazed ceramic insert, polished, minor dents, 2-7/8" h, 8-7/8" dia... 121.00

Flagon
9-5/8" h, "Reed and Barton" stamped signature, tapered sides, tooled rings on body, scrolled handle, domed lid, pierced thumb lever, minor pitting on handle... 440.00

10-5/8" h, "Sheldon & Feltman, Albany" (Smith, Sheldon and James Feltman Jr., New York, 1847-1848), large stepdown foot with tooled rings, domed lid, scrolled handle, area of pitting on the base, dents.. 385.00

12-1/4" h, "I. Trask" embossed signature (Israel Trask, Beverly, Mass., 1807-1856), tapered sides, raised rings at top and bottom, scrolled handle with thumb rest, domed lid, turned knob finial 1,100.00

Lamp
Bull's-eye, unmarked, well-developed foot and stem, drum-shaped font, mismatched whale oil burner, removable bull's-eye focusing lenses, weighted base, old repair, 10-1/2" h 605.00

Camphene, unmarked, cone-shaped base, tooled rings, double burners, polished, 9-3/4" h, pr 357.50

Chamber, "H. Hopper" touch (Henry Hopper, New York City, 1842-1847), tooled lines, whale-oil burner, polished, 5" h................................ 192.50

Gimbal, unmarked, matching fluid burner, brass spouts, snuffer missing caps, dents, split at handle, 6-3/8" h 126.50

Time lamp, unmarked, clear blown font, burner cover missing, wick support is present, 12-3/4" h.. 247.50

Unmarked, brass collar, fluid burner with snuffers, 4-1/2" h..115.50

Unmarked, pedestal base, fluid burner, pitting, base uneven, soldered repair, 8" h...................... 137.50

Whale oil, unmkd, cone-shaped base, tooled rings, minor dent, one missing double burner, small split, 8" h, pr 55.00

Whale oil, unmkd, cone-shaped base, tooled rings, double burners, minor dents, 8" h, pr 247.50

Lighthouse coffeepot

7" h, "Morey & Ober Boston" touch (David B. Morey and R.H. Ober, 1852-1855), gooseneck spout, ear handle in partial black paint, polished, minor dent... 275.00

10-3/8" h, raised rings on body, beehive finial, wear.. 165.00

10-3/4" h, "F. Porter, Westbrook" and "No. 1" circular touch (Freeman Porter, Westbrook, Maine, 1835-1860s),....................................... 467.50

11" h, "J. Munson" signature (John Munson, Yalesville, Conn., 1846-52), round raised ring on base, enameled black scrolled handle, domed lid, wafer finial 605.00

11" h, "Sellew & Co., Cincinnati" touch, stepped base, paneled spout, scrolled ear handle, minor wear, bent wafer finial................................ 412.50

11-1/4" h, "Whitlock, Troy, N.Y." touch (John H. Whitlock, 1836-1844), some pitting, well-done repair 330.00

11-3/4" h, "E. Smith" stamp (Eben Smith, Beverly, Mass., 1813-1856), raised rings around top and bottom, engraved shield-shaped panels surrounded by flowers on either side, wood handle, scrolled top, worn black paint 467.50

Measures

Set of four (assembled), English, bellied, brass rims, half pint mkd "Gaskell & Chambers," gill, two half gills, battering, pitting, 2-1/4" to 3-3/4" h 357.50

Set of five (assembled), English, bellied, half pint, two gills, two quarter gills (one mkd "Gaskell & Chambers Birmingham"), polished, dents, soldered repair at handle of 1 gill, 2" to 3-5/8" h 247.50

Mug

4-1/2" h, Jacob Whitmore partial touch (Middletown, Conn., 1758-1790), polished, wear, possible handle repair... 4,015.00

6" h, "James Yates" touch, English, raised bands, polished, rim dent, one quart 165.00

Pewter baluster-form measures: (from left) English pint marked "C.M." on the lid, possibly for the Commonwealth of Massachusetts, c. 1725-75, $900; American quart, "Boardman & Hart, N. York," dated 1841, $5,000; American pint marked "CP" on the handle, Commonwealth of Pennsylvania, 18th C., $1,000.

Pitcher

Milk, "R Dunham" touch (Rufus Dunham, Westbrook, Maine), tooled rings on body, 7" h 715.00

Water, covered, "Boardman and Hart, N.York" touch, domed lid with stepped rings, lid somewhat battered, small holes, repairs, 9-3/4" h............ 385.00

Plate

Nathaniel Austin hallmarks and partial eagle touch (Charlestown, Mass., 1763-1800), battered, rim repair, 9-1/2" dia 220.00

Thomas Badger touch with eagle (Boston, 1787-1815), bottom of bowl pitted, wear, 8-1/2" dia 247.50

"B.B."" and eagle touch (Blakslee Barns, Philadelphia, 1812-1817), minor rim dents/wear, 7-3/4" dia 385.00

Frederick Bassett touches (New York City and Hartford, Conn., 1761-1800), polished, minor scratches, 8-3/8" dia.................................. 550.00

William Billings touch (Providence, R.I., 1791-1806), polished, scratches, 8-3/8" dia 440.00

"Carr," touchmark and "London," molded rim, wear, 7-3/4" dia 85.00

"T. Danforth, Phila" and "T.D." with eagle touch (Thomas Danforth III, Philadelphia, 1777-1818), 7-3/4" dia... 385.00

William Danforth eagle touch (Middleton, Conn., 1792-1820), wear, scratches, 8" dia 275.00

"S. E., London" (Samuel Ellis), English, scratch-engraved initials, wear, scratches, 7-3/4" dia 110.00

"S. Kilbourn" touch (Samuel Kilbourn, Baltimore, circa 1820), wear, scratches, 7-3/4" dia 275.00

""G. Lightner, Baltimore" and eagle touch, minor rim dents, 8-3/4" dia 357.50

"S. Stafford" and "Albany" touches (Spencer Stafford, Albany, N.Y., 1794-1830), hammered booge, polished, knife scratches, 8-7/8" dia 302.50

Porringer

2" dia, "RG" crown handle (probably Roswell Gleason, Dorchester, Mass., 1822-1871) 467.50

3-3/4" dia, "Richard Lee" touch, pierced floral handle, polished 1,182.50

4-1/8" dia, Samuel E. Hamlin Jr. touch (Providence, R.I., 1801-1856), pierced geometric handle, polished, minor pitting 495.00

5" dia, "TD & SB" touch, pierced crown handle, polished, minor pitting and scratches 440.00

5-1/8" dia, William Billings touch (Providence, R.I., 1791-1806), pierced floral handle, polished, minor pitting and scratches................................. 550.00

5-1/4" dia, 2" h, unmarked, attributed to Pa., solid curved handle with hole, polished, small rim split 440.00

Spittoon, unmkd, Josiah Danforth, Middletown Conn., two-pc, round with flat bottom on three feet, tapered sides, removable funnel-shaped top with rounded rim, pinholes in side and base, hole in rim, 3-1/2" h, 8-1/4" dia 85.00

Spoon, set of nine, assembled, small holes, 8-1/4" l 220.00

Soup plate, thistle touch, rim engraved "AS," English, 9-3/4" dia 137.50

Tall pot

"R. Gleason" touch (Roswell Gleason, Dorchester, Mass., 1822-1871), minor pitting 412.50

"Thomas & Townsend" partial touch, also "T.C." and lion, English, rim repair, 7-5/8" dia 82.50

Unmarked, American, 9-7/8" h........................ 385.00

Unmarked, American, tapered body, domed lid, scrolled pewter handle, light pitting, 11-1/4" h 368.50

Tankard, "T. Wildes, New York" touch, stepped base, tooled rings at middle of body, old replacement domed lid, scrolled pewter handle, 8-1/4" h 1,072.50

Teapot

4-1/2" h, "Vickers" touch, individual teapot, English, wooden handle and finial in black paint, spout slightly crooked.. 55.00

6" h, "B&V" with crowned "X," Irish, Queen Anne, wooden handle and wafer on finial, polished, wear, dents, handle and possibly spout repaired 495.00

6" h, "R. Dunham" touch (Rufus Dunham, Westbrook Maine), footed, curved spout, domed lid missing its finial, lip of spout bent 160.00

6-5/8" h, "Putnam" (James H. Putnam, Malden Mass.), footed, curved spout, domed lid with cast rosette finial, base damage and repair 85.00

6-3/4" h, Roswell Gleason touch (Dorchester, Mass., 1822-1871), pear-shaped, paneled spout, wood finial wafer split, flake on black-painted handle 825.00

6-3/4" h, "Smith & Co." touch 302.50

6-7/8" h, "Boardman & Hart, N-York" touch (Thomas Danforth Boardman and partner), round body, tooled lines, stepped lid, scrolled ear handle, wear, hinge repair, handle dented 192.50

7" h, "J.W. Cahill & Co." touch (1830s, location unknown), rounded body, tooled lines, handle and scalloped finial wafer painted black, polished 357.50

7" h, "A. Porter" touch (Allen Porter, Westbrook, Maine), tooled rings, scrolled handle, worn wafer finial on lid 302.50

7-1/4" h, "J.B. Woodbury" touch (Eastern Mass. or R.I., c. 1820-35), round body, stepped dome top, black pewter handle, polished, minor dents 165.00

7-1/2" h, "L. Boardman" partial touch (Luther Boardman, South Reading, Mass., 1836-1842), polished, black-repainted scroll handle, repairs 247.50

7-1/2" h, "Sellew & Co., Cincinnati" touch (1830-1860), gooseneck spout, ear handle, small dent 302.50

7-3/4" h, "Smith & Co." touch, minor damage, repair 137.50

8" h, "TD & SB" touch, pear-shaped, paneled spout, ivory finial wafer, polished 880.00

8-1/4" h, "A. Griswold" and eagle touch (Ashbil Griswold, Meriden, Conn., 1802-1842), domed lid, wooden wafer finial, paneled spout, small hole in handle, repaired hinge, splits in bottom, dents.. 247.50

8-1/4" h, "Sellew & Co., Cincinnati, 12," (1830-1860), damage, old base repair 302.50

9" h, "Dixon and Sons," English, footed, fluted body, domed lid, wooden handle, repairs, dents.. 165.00

9" h, "J.B. Grav..." partial touch (probably Joshua B. Graves, Middletown, Conn., circa 1850), footed, pewter scrolled handle, tooled lines around body, domed lid, minor dents 291.50

9" h, "J.D. Locke, New York" touch (J.D. Locke, New York City, 1835-1860) 412.50

11-1/2" h, "A. Griswold" and eagle touch (Ashbil Griswold, Meriden, Conn., 1802-1842), footed base with alternating tooled rings top to bottom, scrolled handle, domed lid, wafer finial, foot restored 302.50

"I. Trask" pear-shaped touch (Israel Trask, Beverly, Mass., 1807-1856), pitting, wear, old repair 715.00

Pie Safes

Background: Pie safes were designed as a place to keep food away from insects while still allowing for ample ventilation. Built largely during the second and third quarters of the 19th century, pie safes are cupboards with doors that have pierced-tin panels or, less frequently, wire screens. Many have tins or screens in the sides, also. Form varied greatly, with some examples standing on tall legs while others were designed for hanging. Some versions featured one long drawer or two short drawers, and regional differences are often noticeable.

Collecting Hint: Many pie safes were given a coat of paint in an attempt to hide the inexpensive softwoods that were so commonly used in their construction. Collectors prize those examples which retain their original painted surface. When in a natural finish, pie safes of walnut, cherry, tiger maple, and curly maple are especially prized.

Reproduction Alert: Contemporary child-size pie safes have become quite popular with the decorator market over the last 10 years. Unfortunately, some of those miniature pieces have entered the antiques market, where they have been marked as vintage.

Hanging
    Tin, punched stars and pinwheels, Bucks County, Pa., 32-1/2" h, 37" w, 19" d...................... 2,200.00
    Wooden, two-tin front (one per door), punched star and pinwheels in large circles, smaller hearts, green paint, 40" h, 33" w, 15-1/2" d 825.00

Standing
    Four-tin, old red paint, probably N.J., early 19th C., two hinged doors each with one long punched-tin panel with star and geometric patterns, long punched-tin panel on each end, panels framed in applied beaded moldings, front panels surrounded by reeding, reeded posts continue to turned feet, straight skirt, 46-1/4" h, 31-1/4" w............... 632.50
    Six-tin, painted, green over multiple layers, poplar and walnut, square corner posts, high feet, solid paneled ends, one drawer at top, two doors with three star-punched tins each, damage to tins, found in Missouri, 54" h, 38-1/2" w, 16-1/2" d.................... 440.00
    Six-tin, painted, old black, poplar, high feet, bootjack ends, two upper doors, each with three tins punched with diamonds surrounded by four stars, over one drawer over two paneled doors, light stains on side, 84-1/2" h, 41-3/4" w, 16" d............. 1,980.00

Six-tin pie safe in old black paint, 84-1/2" h, 41-3/4" w, $1,980. (Photo courtesy of Garth's Auctions, Delaware, Ohio)

Twelve-tin, painted, old black repaint, poplar, star and circle designs with urn behind center star, high square legs, two three-tin doors, three tins per side, one side tin deteriorating, door with small half-moon cutout where previous turnbuckle was, tins are backwards, 59" h, 41-1/2" w, 17" d.............2,090.00

Twelve-tin, walnut, mortised and pinned construction, square corner posts, high turned feet, three punched tins per door/side with pinwheel and quarter circles, molded cornice, tins in old gold repaint, some side tins damaged, 57" h, 44-1/4" w, 19-3/4" d 1,540.00

Painted, old green repaint, cherry, twelve punched tins on two front doors, large pinwheels and circles with hearts, pinwheels and birds on sides, turned feet, beaded edges around doors and two upper drawers, square nails and pegged, hardware old replacements, 64" h, 58" w, 24-1/2" d 4,675.00

Screened, old brown over mustard-yellow graining, two doors with screen inserts, Rockingham pulls, wooden turnbuckles, narrow screen panels in ends with applied moldings, ornate scalloped backsplash, one rear foot and shelf missing, 50-1/2" h, 61" w, 18" d...1,320.00

Screened, pine, N.J., early 19th C., one long drawer with two recessed panels, over two doors each with four screened sections, flanked by reeding, old refinish with some red color remaining, imperfections, 54" h, 44" w............................... 2,654.00

Pipe Boxes

Background: Distinguished by their tall, narrow shape, hanging pipe boxes were used during the 18th and 19th centuries for storing pipes.

Decor, shield, wreath and monogrammed "B" in green, red, blue and yellow, red ground, red and yellow outlines, pine, pierced and scrolled back, sides and front, one drawer, New England, early 19th C., 15" h.........2,875.00

Pine, hanging, pierced round hanger, one drawer, 19th C., restoration to base, replaced drawer, 20-1/4" h, 6" w, 4-1/8" d 230.00

Pipsqueaks

Background: Pipsqueaks got their name because of their small size and the noise that they made when a miniature bellows was compressed. These 19th-century penny toys delighted children and adults alike.

Bird in cage, papier-mâché, orig polychrome paint with fiber, wire, etc., bellows recovered and silent, 6-1/2" h 165.00

Elephant, papier-mâché, old polychrome paint worn, bellows recovered and silent, 2-7/8" h....................110.00

Hen, animated wings, wood, leather, papier-mâché and polychrome paint, bellows silent, some damage, 3" l 302.50

Rooster on spring legs, papier-mâché, orig polychrome paint with minor wear, edge damage, beak damaged

and touched up with black, bellows silent,
4-1/2" h.. 55.00
Rooster and chicken in coop, wooden, paper covering, faded felt on birds, bellows work but squeak is silent, wear, edge damage, 5-3/4" h, coop
6-1/2" x 4-1/4" 110.00
Stork on nest, papier-mâché, orig polychrome paint crazed, bellows squeak, 3-1/2" h 412.50

Porringers

Background: In American usage, the term porringer refers to a shallow silver bowl with a flat, pierced handle horizontal to the rim. When discussing English silver, the term is used for a wide-bodied, two-handled cup for serving hot drinks made of wine.

Cast iron, openwork handle, 5" dia, pr 137.50
Pewter
    William Billings touch (Providence, R.I., 1791-1806), pierced floral handle, polished, minor pitting and scratches, 5-1/8" dia.................................. 550.00
    "RG" crown handle (probably Roswell Gleason, Dorchester, Mass., 1822-1871), 2" dia 467.50
    Samuel E. Hamlin Jr. touch (Providence, R.I., 1801-1856), pierced geometric handle, polished, minor pitting, 4-1/8" dia... 495.00
    "Richard Lee" touch, pierced floral handle, polished, 3-3/4" dia 1,182.50
    "TD & SB" touch, pierced crown handle, polished, minor pitting and scratches, 5" dia 440.00
    Unmarked, attributed to Pa., solid curved handle with hole, polished, small rim split, 2" h,
5-1/4" dia 440.00

Portraits (see Paintings)

Prattware

Background: Prattware is a type of creamware decorated in high-fired colors including ochre, green, brown, and blue. The earliest examples were made in the late 18th century by William Pratt, a potter in the Staffordshire district of England. From 1810 to 1818, Felix and Robert Pratt, William's sons, ran their own firm, F.&R. Pratt, in Fenton, in the Staffordshire district. Potters in Yorkshire, Liverpool, Sunderland, Tyneside, and Scotland copied their products.

Output consisted of relief-molded jugs, transfer decorated tableware, commemorative pieces, and figures and figural groupings of people and animals. Most of the early items are unmarked.

Reference: John and Griselda Lewis, *Pratt Ware 1780-1840*, Antique Collectors' Club, 1984.

Child's plate, Franklin's proverb
    "Silks and Satins, Scarlets and Velvets Put Out The Kitchen Fire," pink transfer, octagonal, pink luster band, discoloring, minor glaze wear,
5-7/8" dia 100.00
    "Three Removes Are As Bad As A Fire, A Rolling Stone Gathers No Moss," green transfer, octagonal, molded floral rosettes accented with green polychrome or pink luster, pink luster band, minor discoloring and glaze wear, crack 100.00
Child's plate, motto
    "Benevolence is commendable in all persons, Begin to be good in time it cannot be too soon," blue transfer, molded floral designs in relief accented with blue, yellow and green polychrome, scalloped rim with pink luster band, chips, 5-3/8" dia.............50.00
    "He that by the plough would thrive, Himself must either hold or drive," blue transfer, molded floral design accented in red, blue, yellow and green polychrome, scalloped rim with pink luster band, small tight spider crack, 5-1/4" dia.............. 130.00
    "I never saw an oft removed tree, Nor yet an oft removed family, That throve so well as those that settled be," brown transfer, molded floral designs in relief accented in blue, red, green and yellow polychrome, scalloped rim with pink luster band, mkd J.K.K., crack, 5-3/8" dia 90.00
Child's plate, other
    "A Present For Elizabeth," two arched ribbons and floral designs, black transfer, molded florets, scalloped rim, 5-1/8" dia 260.00
    "Robinson Crusoe," black transfer, accented in red, yellow, green and blue polychrome, molded florets in relief accented in red, blue and green, minor discoloring, 6" dia 75.00
Creamer, molded scenes of children in hearts, blue, goldenrod and green enamel, wear on spout,
4-7/8" h 275.00

Prints and Lithographs

Background: Currier & Ives were among the leading makers of prints in the 19th century. Like many other companies of the time, they focused on urban, patriotic, and nostalgic scenes.

References: Karen Choppa, *Bessie Pease Gutmann: Over Fifty Years of Published Art*, Schiffer Publishing, 1998; Karen Choppa and Paul Humphrey, *Maud Humphrey*, Schiffer Publishing, 1993; Max Allen Collins and Drake Elvgren, *Elvgren: His Life & Art*, Collectors Press, 1998; Erwin Flacks, *Maxfield Parrish Identification & Price Guide*, 3rd ed., Collectors Press, 1998; Martin Gordon, ed., *Gordon's Print Price Annual*, Gordon and Lawrence Art Reference, published annually; Tina Skinner, *Harrison Fisher: Defining the American Beauty*, Schiffer Publishing, 1999; Kent Steine and Frederick B. Taraba, *J.C. Leyendecker Collection*, Collectors Press, 1996.

Periodicals: *Illustrator Collector's News*, P.O. Box 1958, Sequim, WA 98382; *Journal of the Print World*, 1008 Winona Rd., Meredith, NH 03253; *On*

Paper, 39 E. 78th St., #601, New York, NY 10021; *Print Collector's Newsletter*, 119 E. 79th St., New York, NY 10021.

Collectors' Clubs: American Antique Graphics Society, 5185 Windfall Rd., Medina OH 44256; American Historical Print Collectors Society, P.O. Box 201, Fairfield, CT 06430; Gutmann Collectors' Club, P.O. Box 4743, Lancaster, PA 17604.

Museums: American Museum of Natural History, New York, NY; John James Audubon State Park and Museum, Henderson, KY; Museum of the City of New York, NY.

Reproduction Alert: Reproductions of Maxfield Parrish prints are particularly common, but works by many other artists are also being copied. Shiny, crisp white paper is a sure indicator of newness. Early versions mellow with age and may even have acquired a light brown tone due to acids in the paper or from being framed against wood. Details that appear fuzzy and colors that separate into dots under magnification are both signs of later copies. But, since many early prints were copied soon after their introduction (particularly those attributed to Currier & Ives), reproductions can display the same aging characteristics as period pieces.

Note: Most descriptions include "sight" measurements—the size of that portion of the artwork that is visible within the frame. Sizes for the frames are not included.

Currier & Ives (handcolored)

American Autumn Fruits, old gilt frame, margins slightly trimmed, minor stains, 27-1/4" h, 33-1/2" w 935.00

American Express Train, margins trimmed slightly, minor soiling and stains, 25" h, 33" w 3,190.00

American Field Sports - Flushed, 1857, framed, retouched, 20-3/4" h, 27-1/2" w 1,725.00

Currier & Ives, *American Hunting Scenes - An Early Start*, 1863, 20-1/2" h, 28" w, $3,565. (Photo courtesy of Garth's Auctions, Delaware, Ohio)

American Hunting Scenes - An Early Start, 1863, framed, toning, margin stains, 20-1/2" h, 28" w 3,565.00

The Champion Pacer Johnson, toning, stains, foxing, 23-1/4" h, 30-1/4" w 345.00

The Deacon's Mare, framed, light water staining on bottom margin, 13-1/2" h, 17-1/2" w 247.50

E. Pluribus Unum, reclining man steadying gun with bare foot, framed, 13" h, 16-1/2" w 660.00

The First Bird of the Season, matted and framed, 13" h, 16-3/4" w 385.00

Fruit Piece, framed, 13" h, 16" w 137.50

Hudson River-Crow Nest, matted/framed, trimmed, minor edge damage, stains, 10-1/8" h, 13-3/4" w 192.50

James Polk, Eleventh President of the United States, period decor frame, light water stains, top margin worn, 14" h, 9-7/8" w 220.00

Jay Eye See, Record 2:10, cherry frame, stains, minor damage, edge repair, 13-3/8" h, 17-5/8" w 165.00

Lady Washington, period veneer frame with chips, slight stains, one small pc missing from margin 275.00

Landscape, Fruit and Flowers, framed, minor crease/tear, few scattered fox marks, 21-1/2" h, 28-1/2" w 2,185.00

Life in the Woods - Starting Out, 1860, framed, margin stains, pale foxing, 21-1/4" h, 28-1/2" w 1,840.00

Little Snowbird, framed and matted, minor stains, 15-11/16" h, 12-1/8" w 352.00

Longfellow, horse racing print, framed, stains, minor edge damage, 11-3/4" h 15-3/4" w 330.00

The Lovers Quarrel, period painted frame, foxing, 16" h, 11-3/4" w 75.00

The Lovers Reconciliation, dated 1846, period veneered frame, 14" h, 10" w 95.00

Lucy, period frame, foxing, tear, 14" h, 10" w 180.00

A Mansion of the Olden Time, framed, minor stains, paint on top margin, 13-1/4" h, 16-1/4" w 137.50

New England Winter Scene, framed, tears, toning, title trimmed from sheet and matted with image, 17" h, 24" w 1,035.00

Newport Beach, matted/framed, damage, some repair, 11" h, 15-1/2" w 165.00

The Old Mill-Dam, matted/framed, minor stains, edge damage, 11" h, 14" w 275.00

On A Strong Scent, matted/framed, 16" h, 10" w 385.00

Partridge Shooting, margins trimmed, old frame, 10" h, 14" w 275.00

The Pride of the Garden, period decor frame, stains in upper-right, 16-5/8" h, 13-1/2" w 110.00

The Roadside Mill, framed, 10" h, 14" w 192.50

The Star Spangled Banner, Lady Liberty with flag, period frame, foxing, 2 areas of touchup, 16-3/8" h, 12-1/4" w 165.00

A Summer Landscape, Haymaking, margins slightly trimmed, minor stains, tape repair, old gilt frame, 13" h, 17-1/4" w 357.50

View of Harpers Ferry, Va., rosewood veneer frame with gilded liner, good margins, minor corner damage 27" h, 30-1/2" w 550.00

View on the Harlem River, N.Y., framed, toning, 18-1/2" h, 22-1/2" w 750.00

Washington's Reception by the Ladies, period walnut frame with ink graining, minor margin tears, 14" h, 10" w 192.50

Winter Morning, Feeding the Chickens, framed, toning, unobtrusive stains, 17" h, 21-1/2" w............. 2,530.00

The Wonderful Maud S., Record of 2:10, old beveled walnut frame, 12" x 15-7/8".................. 440.00

N. Currier

General Z. Taylor, Rough and Ready, period frame in old red paint, light stains, 14-1/8" h, 10-1/8" d 302.50

William Henry Harrison, Ninth President of the United States, shows Harrison wearing a black suit and holding a top hat and cane while standing beneath a tree, period frame with veneer chips, 13-5/8" h, 10" w 71.50

Endicott & Co., sidewheeler *C. Vanderbilt*, color litho, framed, toning, scattered abrasions, 18-1/4" h, 34-1/2" w 1,035.00

W.W. Denslow, *Pennsylvania State College*, four small oval vignettes in corners show "Experimental Farm Buildings," "Vice President's Residence," "Barn" and "President's Residence," published by C.J. Corbin, Thos. Hunter, Philadelphia, framed/matted, 14-3/4" h, 19" w 1,100.00

Gould and Richter, pr of mallards and heron, hand-colored, both with Latin names, matted/framed, 21-3/4" h, 28" w 715.00

Haskell and Allen, *Almont, the Great Sire of Trotters*, hand-colored, framed, pale staining and foxing, 20-5/8" h, 26" w 287.50

Kellogg & Comstock

The Angler, girl reading letter to man fishing, grain-decor frame, margin tear, stains, fold line, 9-3/4" h, 14" w 137.50

Amelia, hand-colored, refinished curly maple frame with good figure, print 10" w, 14" h, frame 17-3/8" h, 13-3/8" w 330.00

The Fruit, light stains, walnut cross-corner frame, short margin tear, 10" h, 14" w 88.00

Wallace Nutting, *Washington Cherry Blossoms*, hand-colored, 6-5/8" x 4-1/2" 45.00

Other

The 9:45 a.m. Accommodation, Stratford, Connecticut, Edward Lamson Henry 1845-1919, train at depot, framed and matted, light stains, foxing and stains on mat, 21-1/2" h, 31-1/4" w............. 165.00

Found, print, howling collie standing in front of lost lamb, framed, 16" h, 20" w 82.50

Sacred to the Memory of the Illustrious G. Washington, round image of tomb and three mourners, "T. Clarke Sculp. 1801 Boston," molded frame with

E.B.&E.C. Kellogg lithograph, "Christ Blessing Little Children," 13-1/2" x 9-1/2", $100.

worn gold repaint, edge damage, 8-1/2" h, 8" w... 550.00

Scenes on the Ohio, Above and Below Cincinnati, 4 overlapping inset scenes of steamboats and views of cities, cross-corner frame with jigsaw crest, 17-3/4" h, 13-1/2" w 110.00

Botanical prints, Philips, hand-colored engravings of fruit, framed, stains, edge damage, 14" h, 9-7/8" w, set of 4 .... 357.50

Owl and other birds, "A. Wilson," framed, stains and minor damage, 14-1/4" h, 11-1/2" w, pr 110.00

Pull Toys

Background: As the name implies, these playthings were called pull toys because they were mounted on wheels and were designed to be pulled by a child. Horses mounted on wheeled platforms were common 19th-century variations.

Reference: *Collector's Digest Price Guide to Pull Toys*, L-W Book Sales, 1996.

Bear, Steiff, steel-tube base, white rubber wheels, worn brown fur, tan mohair muzzle, glass eyes, ear button, yellow tag, 1 wheel damaged, 18" h, 23" l 357.50

Camel, gold mohair, red felt saddle blanket, black button eyes, metal rod-and-spoke wheel base in worn bold paint, wear, 12-3/4" h, 17" l 495.00

Cat, seated kitten, papier-mâché, amber glass eyes, brown felt ribbon with added stars, white with traces of yellow, wooden base and wheels in faded red paint, minor wear, one ear damaged, 7" h, 9" l 220.00

Cow and calf, leather and papier-mâché on wooden platform with grain-painted surface, cast-metal wheels, calf standing under the neck of the mother, leather-covered, moveable head and hair tail on mother, 9" h, 14-1/2" l, 5-1/8" w 925.00

Goat (billy), wooden, tan felt and hide covering, green glass eyes, leather and cloth harness, orig white and black paint on base, metal spoke wheels, wooden handle with paper label advertising "Gimbel Brothers Pure Food Store, Philadelphia," wear, fur loss, horns missing, 10-3/4" h, 10-1/2" l 385.00

Horse

Burlap-covered, brown, orig red base with brown trim, cast-iron wheels, partial saddle and bridle, covering worn, missing 1 ear, 1 glass eye and 1 wheel, 28" h 357.50

Burlap-covered, brown, leather straps/stirrups/ears, mismatched base in orig gray and cream grain decor with red borders, German, 24" h, 24" l 110.00

Cloth-covered, brown, paper and felt tack, fur mane, horsehair tail, traces of red on wooden base, metal spoke wheels, wear, nose possibly repaired, 11-1/4" h, 10" l 192.50

Felt-covered, dapple gray, tack eyes, white leather mane, horsehair tail, tack eyes, trotting, wooden base, metal spoke wheels, worn black leatherized harness, 9-1/4" h, 10-5/8" l 330.00

Hide-covered, brown, on wooden platform, cast-iron wheels, 13" h, 13-1/2" l 247.50

Hide-covered, white, carved wooden head and hooves, scalloped pine base in old back repaint, ears and some saddle missing, replaced cast-iron wheels, 20-1/2" h, 19-1/2" l 220.00

Papier- mâché, 7-1/2" l 55.00

Papier-mâché, wooden legs, leather ears, fiber mane and tail, orig dapple gray paint, black harness and eyes, worn light-blue base, spoke wheels, wear, age cracks, 8-1/2" h, 8" l 192.50

Tin, running mare and foal, mare in traces of red with black saddle and bridle, worn green paint on base, metal spoke wheels, few loose seams and dents, 6-1/2" h, 8-1/2" l 440.00

Wooden, black-on-white smoke decor, shaped platform, cast-iron wheels, horsehair tail, missing its mane, saddle and one ear, worn paint, late leather bridle, 32" h, 35" l 220.00

Wooden, dapple gray paint, black fur mane, horsehair tail, base with salmon paint and black sponging, metal spoke wheels, prancing, repaired front leg, 11-1/4" h, 9-1/2" l 192.50

Wooden, white paint, wooden platform, cast-iron wheels, wear, 18" h, 18" l 357.50

Nodders

Donkey, wooden, white and gray felt covering, red and black paper-covered tack, glass eyes, metal wheels, wear, some damage, 8" h, 9-1/2" l 357.50

Sheep, composition, white wool coat, blue felt saddle cloth, tin wheels, minor wear, 5" l 1,100.00

Santa Claus on reindeer, Lou Schifferl, orig polychrome paint, signed "Schifferl," 14" h........ 1,045.00

Carved and painted wood horse, wooden platform, cast-iron wheels, $250.

Sheep

Composition on wooden base, natural wool on body, black paint on legs and face, leather ears, blue ribbon with bell, eyes missing and neck loose, coat worn, 8-1/2" h, 11" l 137.50

Tin, white paint, black feet, base with traces of dark-green paint, wear, 3" h, 4-1/4" l 385.00

Tin on wooden base, white paint, red painted ribbon, yellow bell, dark-green on tin base attached to wooden base, mkd "Made in Germany," wear, 5-3/4" h, 6" l 247.50

Punched Paper Pictures

Background: Although actually a type of Victorian needlework, the designs and inspirational mottoes of punched paper pictures have endeared them to country collectors. Similar to a paint-by-number, but utilizing thread instead of paint, they were created by following a pattern that indicated where to weave the threads in and out of the prepunched backing. Many of the designs illustrate Christian themes.

Centennial motif, eagle with banner, laurel wreath and "United We Stand…1776-1876" in shades of green, gray, ivory and lavender, cross-corner frame with applied leaves, back label "From W.R. Reid…Cleveland, O.," 13-5/8" h, 26" w 192.50

"Forget Me Not," red lettering, red and green flowering vines, cross-corner frame with damage, some yarn loss and water damage.................................... 127.50

"Give Us This Day Our Daily Bread," cream, orange and rust needlework, framed, 10-1/8" h, 22" w 160.00

"Heaven Is My Home," burgundy, pinks and light green, framed, 8-1/2" h, 21" w 155.00

"Nearer My God To Thee," cross-corner frame, 8-1/2" h, 21" w 105.00

"Ninety And Nine," dog overlooking hills, damaged cross-corner frame, minor water marks, foxing, broken glass, 13" h, 15" w 152.50

Puzzle Blocks and Related Toys

Background: Wooden blocks with lithographed-paper covers instantly created, not one puzzle, but six—one corresponding to each of the six sides of the cube. Puzzle blocks typically came in a wooden box with a lid. Examples produced during the last quarter of the 19th century are distinguished by the superior quality of the lithography. Production of these challenging playthings continued well into the 20th century.

Reproduction Alert: Reproductions exist and are often offered as originals, sometimes by unsuspecting sellers. These newer examples can be ferreted out because the lithography is generally poor.

Boxed set, 48 wooden blocks with hand-colored engraved coverings, makes six scenes of birds, some wear, box 11-1/2" x 15" 357.50

"Bird Slips," Peter G. Thompson, Cincinnati, boxed, lid shows parrot, slips of lithographed cardboard make turkey, hawk, duck, wren, pigeon, parrot, owl, jay, falcon, ostrich, eagle, guinea, peacock and crane, with cardboard letters to spell out the name of each bird, lacks two letters, one slip broken in half, box worn 60.00

"Flora, The Game of Flowers," wooden, hand-colored images, orig box with print of woman in garden, worn, stains, 6-1/4" sq 110.00

Pyrography

Background: Pyrography is the process of burning a picture or design into a wooden surface. Skilled artisans introduced the art form to America in the mid 1800s, but it became a hobby for the masses around the turn of the century, when several companies began offering items with designs stamped on them for burning. The Flemish Art Co. of New York was the largest producer of pyrography products, and the term Flemish Art has become synonymous with burnt wood pieces of that era. The hobby was most popular from 1890 to 1915.

Reference: Frank L. Hahn, *Collector's Guide to Burnt Wood Antiques*, Golden Era Publications, 1994.

Box, poinsettia and leaves on lid, basketweave design on sides, interior stained green with felt bottom, 4" h, 14-3/8" l, 10-1/2" w.. 30.00

Chair-table, floral and other decor, sides with 2 large oval cutouts, 47" h 495.00

Game board, triangle-design surface, owl on reverse, 11" x 14"... 104.50

Plate rack
    Fruit motif, 12" h, 42" l 220.00
    Water scene with stork, swans, cattails, etc., scalloped top, 52" l... 357.50

Table, pedestal, floral and geometric design, three scrolled legs, triangular base, 29" h, top 29" sq.. 330.00

Wastebasket, woman's bust and grapes decor, square, scalloped top, 14" h 71.50

The Brownie Blocks, litho-paper scenes by Palmer Cox, dated 1891, original box, $1,200.

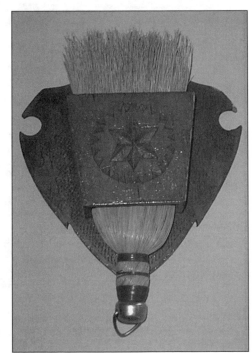

Pyrography whisk broom holder, 8-1/4" h, $60.

Quilt Patterns

Background: These templates were used to trace a design on the fabric to aid in stitch placement.

Note: All listings are tin unless otherwise noted.

Heart and scroll, large center heart motif surrounded by scrolling and surmounted by smaller heart, some rust, 8-1/8" h, 10-1/2" w 300.00

Parrot, perched on branch, punched design on head and wing, tin, minor rust, 5-1/4" h, 11" w 250.00

Star or radial, 6 points, small round hole in center, 4-1/2" dia 50.00

Quilts and Quilt Tops

Background: Quilting is a method of securing padding between two layers of fabric through the use of stitches worked in decorative patterns. Patchwork quilting was quite common in rural communities, where economical use of scraps of material was important. The simplest patchwork quilts consisted of geometric shapes in repeating patterns, but more elaborate designs became popular in the last half of the 19th century.

Appliqué quilts are similar to patchwork examples, but scraps of material were stitched onto a flat piece of fabric rather than being pieced with other scraps to form a block or design. Because the technique allowed greater freedom in creating designs, appliqué quilts are often more elaborate than patchwork examples.

Maryland appliqué album quilt, red, green, yellow and gold, 77" x 91", $4,950. (Photo courtesy of Garth's Auctions, Delaware, Ohio)

References: Anne Gilbert, *Instant Expert: Collecting Quilts*, Alliance Publishing, 1996; Deborah Harding, *Red & White: American Redwork Quilts and Patterns*, Rizzoli Publications, 2000; Patricia T. Herr, *Quilting Traditions*, Schiffer Publishing, 2000; Carter Houck, *Quilt Encyclopedia Illustrated*, Harry N. Abrams and the Museum of American Folk Art, 1991; Patsy and Myron Orlofsky, *Quilts in America*, Abbeville Press, 1992

Periodicals: *Quilt Journal*, 635 W. Main St., Louisville, KY 40202; *Vintage Quilt Newsletter*, 1305 Morphy St., Great Bend, KS 67530.

Collectors' Club: American Quilt Study Group, 660 Mission St., Suite 400, San Francisco, CA 94105-4007.

Museums: Colonial Williamsburg Foundation, Colonial Williamsburg, VA; Museum of the American Quilter's Society, Paducah, KY; National Museum of American History, Washington, DC; New England Quilt Museum, Lowell, MA.

Appliquéd

Block pattern of geometric feather and stylized tulip and foliated devices, inner sawtooth border, meandering tulip and vine outer border, red, green and yellow on white, stains, 87-1/2" sq 2,070.00

Bouquet of flowers tied with ribbon as central motif, early multicolor printed chintz, bordered by pieced and appliquéd chintz motifs, early 19th C. 3,000.00

Clover-shaped vining flowers, green and red calico, quilting with feather, stars and flowers, stains, 86" sq 247.50

Dresden Plate, multicolor prints, quilted border duplicating half Dresden Plate pattern, 73" x 82" 110.00

Eagle, triple sunburst design in center in yellow, red and light blue, each corner with eagle in red, yellow and blue, red sawtooth border, dark-green ground, Lancaster County, Pa., minor stain, 78" x 84" 2,600.00

Feather pinwheels (six), green with red centers, each surrounded by four red hearts, red vining border with green leaves, white ground, finely quilted, wear, stains, 62" x 79" 385.00

Floral medallions

72" x 88", stylized polka-dot flowers in slate-blue, teal, green and red, white ground, red binding 385.00

78" x 80", flowers with pollen, medium blue on red and white, well quilted, stains, minor wear 770.00

82" sq, pink calico and solid red, green and goldenrod, very worn frayed fabrics, damage, stains 220.00

87" x 107", red flowers with green and gold leaves, star blocks in green, gold and red, flying geese border in blue and red with dark-green borders, wear, frayed fabric, stains 247.50

90" x 94", red and yellow print flowers surrounded by green leaves, Princess Feather border, light fading, stains, wear 495.00

93" sq, nine medallions with tulips and stylized flowers in red, green and yellow calico, sawtooth border in red calico, well quilted, stains 1,760.00

95" x 100", nine medallions, vining border, green calico, solid red and goldenrod, wear, stains, green frayed in places 467.50

Flower and bud stylized design (four) and borders in red with green printed leaves, quilted with feather designs and leaves at center, green edge border, stains, overall wear, "Hannabell Benedict" added cloth label, 96" x 96-1/2" 605.00

Floral wreaths, red and yellow-green calico, appliquéd work alternates with trapunto work that includes pineapples, leaves and feathers, very worn, calico frayed, color loss, 92" sq.. 275.00

Hawaiian style, nine red foliage squares on white ground, stains, 84" sq 546.25

Oak Leaf Wreath (nine), red and green, yellow ground, green border, Lancaster County, Pa, 80" sq 1,400.00

Patriotic, red, white and blue stripes with Union Jacks, central motif of crown with leaf design and "Aloha," 73" x 74" 2090.00

Pinwheels (stylized, nine) in red and green calico on white, quilted with feather circles between pinwheels, minor stains, old label notes maker as Diana Wolf in the 1850s, 90" x 94" 1,265.00

Pots of flowers in red, beige and goldenrod, quilted with white on white pots of flowers between the appliqués, Pa. origin, wear, stains, colors somewhat faded, 70" x 78" 550.00

Princess Feather, eight-pointed star in red and gold surrounded by four large princess feather designs in red and gold, blue ground, Lancaster County, Pa., 82" x 84" 2,500.00

Rose motif, centered flower surrounded by four flowers, red and green, meandering vine and blossom border, white ground, stuffed, 82" x 84" 2,530.00

Stars (eight-point) surrounded by ragged-edge border surrounded by double line border, design in pink, navy blue, rust and green, nine plates with four smaller stars in red and green around the center plate, zigzag and scalloped borders in navy blue, ivory ground, quilted with hearts and leaves, stains, 86" x 90".......... 3,300.00

Tulip medallions, green, red and goldenrod, red border and binding, quilted with stylized scrolls and braided bands on border, minor stains, 78" x 80" 880.00

Tulip medallions (eight), four crossed tulips in pink and green, single tulip in each corner, white ground, 80" x 82" 770.00

Tulips and flowers in blue, yellow, violet and pink, blue border, white ground, stains, 80" x 84" 715.00

Tulips in pinwheel pattern, red and green, flowering tulip border, green binding, minor stains, 72" x 86" 880.00

Four Tulips variation, four patterns each with four yellow and red tulips crossed with four feather-like designs coming out of a blue center, white ground, 68" x 80" 385.00

Vintage, green and red, puffed grapes, leaf and vine border, princess feather and tulips quilting, red edging, orig pencil lines, minor stains, 92" x 94" 2,310.00

Washington centennial, fabric cutouts stitched on background, reds and browns, central motifs of George Washington, Benjamin Harrison, and Washington standing by his horse, "1789" and "1889" stitched above portraits, smaller scattered motifs included baseball and tennis players, animals and statehouses..........8,250.00

Appliqué and Pieced

Tree of Life center, with appliqués of birds, hearts and stars, late 18th or early 19th C., fabric loss, staining.. 1,265.00

Appliqué and Trapunto

Eight-Pointed Star variation (sixteen), vining border, green calico on white, trapunto work with flowers, foliage and pineapples, wear, areas of discoloration, color loss, 94" x 96" 990.00

Potted flowers with vines, green and red, white ground, trapunto in appliquéd pieces, minor restoration, 77" x 84" 1,045.00

Crazy

Multicolor, satin and velvet, embroidered flowers, animals and fishing frogs, 80" sq........................ 1,650.00

Multicolor fabric, colorful yarn stitching, wide burgundy border, yellow stitched stars and geometric shapes, wear, 78" x 80" 165.00

Multicolor prints, satin and black velvet, repeated design with circles and rays, wear, some fraying, 64" x 78".. 165.00

"Lillie F. Scholer," dated 1897, center medallion, triple border, feather stitching, striped back 660.00

Velvet, also corduroy and some felt, blues, purples, reds, browns, greens black and gray, "1923" stitched date, minor wear, 72" x 82" 247.50

Crib

Amish, pieced, black, magenta, burgundy and mauve, 17-1/2" x 18-1/4" 27.50

Irish Chain, blue and white print on white ground, machine and hand stitching, stains, mid 20th C., 33-1/2" x 52" 192.50

Log Cabin

19" x 24-3/4", multicolor plain and print fabric patches, early 20th C., wear, one square with damage 65.00

20" x 30", assorted cotton print patches, Centre County Pa., late 19th C., stains.................. 200.00

38" x 44", bright colors, black corner patches arranged in zigzag pattern,...................... 1,155.00

Princess Feather and Heart, four large yellow feathers emerging from cluster of four red hearts, small red heart separating each of the feathers, yellow sawtooth border, purple ground, Lancaster County, Pa., 33-1/2" sq.. 1,800.00

Star, one large star made of multicolor squares, surrounded by yellow and red, Lancaster County, Pa., 40" x 42" 1,750.00

Star design, diagonal bands of red and gold, alternating squares with blue, green, red or gold eight-point stars or squares fashioned from large red and gold triangles, Lancaster County, Pa., 38" sq 425.00

Doll

Flying Geese variation, cotton print, three rows of blue-and-white triangles, stripes in red, white and blue, Pa., 13" x 16" 1,000.00

Joseph's Coat, narrow stripes of yellow, gold, green, blue, red and purple, diagonal-stripe border in same colors, 9" x 9-1/2" 750.00

Yo-Yo, cotton, white with multicolor print designs, minor soiling, 11" x 15" 55.00

Pieced

Autumn Leaf variation, red leaves, white ground, light stains, 70" x 87" 605.00

Barn Raising, brown and blue prints, very good quilting, feather stitching, 82" x 85" 825.00

Bars, alternating stripes of yellow and blue, Amish, 84" x 94" 825.00

Basket, sawtooth border in navy polka dot and white, stains, 63" x 74" 550.00

Baskets motif (seven rows of seven baskets), blue and white, blue border, stains, minor damage, 72" x 75" 330.00

Baskets of flowers, red, yellow and peach, colors repeated in border, stains, some wear, 64" x 80" 192.50

Broken Dishes, triangles in alternating rows of red and blue, white ground, triple border of red, white and blue, 64" x 69" 467.50

Cherry Basket (six rows of five baskets, three rows face one direction, three face the other), pink calico, triangle border, on white, quilted diamonds, hearts and feathering, orig pencil marks, 85" x 90" 467.50

Country Wife, multicolor on red ground, 70" x 79" 440.00

Cross squares (30) in calico and other prints with green ground, gold blocks, pink border, cotton paisley backing, 83" x 97" 330.00

Diamond patch design, blue calico and white, white squares with quilted flowers, wear, stains, 83" x 84" 440.00

Diamond pattern, blue and white, diamond quilting, light stains, 69" x 85" 467.50

Double Irish Chain

    76" sq, pink calico on white, double borders, Pa. origin, minor stains 330.00

    80" sq, yellow and tomato-red calico, green ground, quilted with flower designs, back with bands of dark-red calico, wear, stains 247.50

    82" x 92", variant, hand stitched, pink and blue with multiple polychrome pattern patches, serrated pink and blue border, stains 495.00

Double T, quilt top, alternating brown, blue and gray shirt fabrics, 19th C 302.00

Fan motif, striped and checked cloth with some floral pieces, burgundy calico ground, multicolor cotton backing, hand-stitched, 67-1/4" x 68" 220.00

Flying Geese variation, red and white, hand-stitched except for binding, minor stains and edge wear, overall yellowing, 82" x 76" 357.50

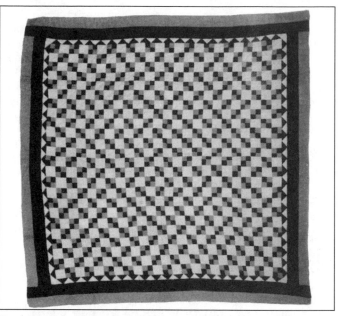

Four Patch quilt, Pennsylvania Amish, red and blue squares, yellow ground, sawtooth border in blue and yellow, blue and red outer borders, 80" x 82", $660. (Photo courtesy of Cyr Auction Company, Gray, Maine)

Four Patch

    72" x 82", multicolor squares, green ground, white inner border, green outer border 715.00

    80" x 82", red and blue squares, yellow ground, sawtooth border in blue and yellow, blue and red outer borders, Pennsylvania Amish 660.00

Geometric squares, multi-color, brown calico ground, white backing, pink floral print binding, stains, 64" x 84" 220.00

Goose Chase, indigo print and white, Pa. origin, minor wear and stains, 78" sq 660.00

Hour Glass or Bowtie variation, blue and white prints, Pa. origin, minor stains, 66" sq 110.00

Irish Chain

    84" sq, medium blue and mauve, initialed "KR," well-quilted with feather design borders, Pa. origin, minor stains 467.50

    92" x 93", variant, flowers and leaves border, blue and white, quilted with stars in feathered medallions, orig pencil marks, stains, minor damage 880.00

Joseph's Coat, alternating stripes of red, yellow, green, black, gold and shades of blue, diagonal-stripe border in same colors, Lancaster County, Pa., 84" x 86" 2,300.00

LeMoyne Star variation, 20 blocks of eight-point star in pink and green on cream ground, green dividers between blocks with pink squares at intersecting points, red and blue printed borders, Mennonite, 75" x 85" 330.00

Log Cabin

    71" x 80", assorted fabrics in various colors, machine-sewn red wool scalloped edge border with embroidered flowers, holes, some patches 935.00

76" x 80", multicolor pattern, black ground, multi-color borders, Berks County, Pa., minor wear.. 1,250.00

79" x 83", Barn Raising variation, earth tones and bright colors 825.00

80" x 82", Sunshine and Shadow variation, chevron border, reds, blues, greens, oranges and browns, plaid backing, hand and machine quilting 1,485.00

88" x 90", Sunshine and Shadow variation, assorted fabrics including wool, shades of black, gray, brown, blue and ivory, minor stains and wear.. 715.00

Lone Star

66" x 68", blue and white, white ground, blue border 330.00

72" x 80", multicolor star, white ground.......... 715.00

72" x 86", multicolor star with dominant pink color, white ground.. 385.00

77" sq, multicolor star, gold ground............. 1,045.00

80" x 82", multicolor, yellow ground, red and yellow borders, Lancaster County, Pa., minor stain 1,400.00

88" sq, blues, burgundy, pinks, green, goldenrod, etc., on white, light-blue border with pink diamonds, meandering feathering quilting................... 1,100.00

Monkey Wrench (30 plates), blue calico on white squares, blue border with white polka dots, light stains, 68" x 80" 467.50

Nine Patch

76" x 80", sawtooth border in yellow calico on red and white polka dot ground, red and white homespun backing, machine-sewn binding......... 550.00

69" sq, variation, triangles in blue and white, diagonal line quilting, stains, minor edge wear.... 165.00

87" sq, variation, red and yellow diamonds, green borders with red squares at intersecting points, wide red outer border 605.00

Nine Patch Irish Chain variation, red print and white, triple border of rose-and-pink and green, minor stains, 74-1/2" x 87-1/4" 345.00

Patriotic motif, white stars in blue squares at corners of 48 blocks with red and white striped borders, centers embroidered with state birds, 68" x 92" 660.00

Pine Tree (25 plates), green and white, very good quilting with meandering borders and round medallions, some color loss to greens, 80" sq.................. 1,705.00

Pinwheel

72" x 84", lavender and white, stains............. 357.50

78" x 80", red on black, green and gray ground, corners with added squares in orange flannel printed with blue, red plaid flannel back, heavy wool, wool flannel, twill, probably Mennonite 357.50

1000 Pyramids, multicolor calico, pink and green calico border, red and yellow calico back, minor stains, 80" sq 330.00

Rob Peter to Pay Paul, indigo blue print and white, 73" x 74".. 440.00

Rolling Stone

72" x 88", red, orange and white squares, black dividers with orange and white squares at intersecting points, white inner border, black outer border, some patches 495.00

84" x 86", red and yellow squares, white ground, yellow inner border, red trim.............................. 385.00

Sawtooth, alternating stripes in pink and black with sawtooth edge, Berks County, Pa., stains, 84" x 92".. 250.00

School House, red and white, scalloped border, 16 plates, minor wear, 71" x 72" 1,430.00

Snowflake, navy blue and white, quilted with diamonds, circles and stars, minor stains, wear, 64" x 70".. 715.00

Squares, multicolor, 70" x 80" 330.00

Stained Glass Window, solid and printed fabric, Berks County, Pa., minor fading, 70-1/2" x 71" 345.00

Star designs

66" x 78", pink calico on white squares on blue ground, brown calico binding, minor stains 550.00

82" x 86", central large star, smaller stars in corners and along sides, red, blue, yellow and yellow-green on white, wear, fading, stains 357.50

83" x 88", star border in pastel prints and lavender, lavender border 357.50

84" x 86", multiple stars in alternating diagonal stripes of red and gold, blue and red borders, Lancaster County, Pa., ... 2,300.00

Star designs, eight-point

70" x 86", made of red and white triangles (12 blocks), double border, quilted with princess feathering, spirals and flowers, orig pencil marks.. 660.00

72" sq, nine blocks, green, yellow and pink calico and red/green calico grid, white ground, pink binding, diamond and stripes quilting, light stains, some wear 385.00

76" sq, made of red and white diamonds, 49 blocks (seven rows of seven each), white ground, red zigzag border 495.00

Stripe, alternating stripes of blue-and-white, green, pink and orange-and-white, Berks County, Pa., stains, 82" x 88".. 250.00

Sunset over the Mountain, multicolored prints, black and white gingham and double-wide pink calico border, wear, stains, 65" x 84".................................... 330.00

Triple Irish Chain, red and white cotton, white on white fern quilting, signed "Jennie S. Boggs," 84" sq... 880.00

Tumbling blocks, alternating blocks of solid green and red, green, blue and brown print fabric, on pink and white floral print ground, Centre County Pa., late 19th C., 70" x 78"... 525.00

Yo-Yo, solid and print cotton patches, scalloped edges, Centre County Pa., early 20th C., 92" x 102".. 300.00

Wedding Ring, prints and solids, scalloped edge with blue binding, quilting in blue thread, overall wear and stains, 64" x 89" 330.00

Pieced and Appliquéd

Washington's Monument, green and red on white, appliquéd vining berries border, diagonal stripes on the border, small diamond pattern elsewhere, tiny stains, 81" x 84"... 2,035.00

Redware

Background: American colonists began making redware in the late 17th century, using the same clay as for bricks and roof tiles. Ready availability of the clay meant that items could be produced in large quantities to supplement the pewter and treenware already in use. The lead-glazed items retained their reddish color, hence the name redware, although various colors could be obtained by adding different metals to the glaze.

References: Susan and Al Bagdade, *Warman's American Pottery and Porcelain*, 2nd ed., Krause Publications, 2000; William C. Ketchum Jr., *American Redware*, Henry Holt and Company, 1991; Kevin McConnell, *Redware: America's Folk Art Pottery*, Schiffer Publishing, 1988.

Collecting Hint: Redware items were seldom marked by the maker.

Redware, Contemporary

Breininger Pottery

   Charger, flowers in green and brown, yellow slip ground, green flourish decor around edges, mkd, 14" dia 93.50

   Pie plate, strawberry plant in pot, sgraffito design in yellow slip with green leaves, mkd "Breininger Pottery, Robesonia, Pa. June 14, 1990. Humid," 10-1/4" dia 77.00

   Pie plate, Washington on horseback sgraffito image, "Patriots everywhere, unite!," feathered yellow slip with green highlights, coggled rim, mkd "Breininger Pottery, Robesonia, Pa. June 3, 1991. Sunny & hot," 10-1/4" dia 77.00

Redware ovoid storage jar, incised line on shoulder, lid missing, $125.

Pie plate, wavy lines in feathered yellow slip, green splotches, coggled rim, mkd "L. Breininger, Robesonia, Pa.," smaller mkd "July 2, 1992. Lovely day," larger mkd "7-14-91," 7" dia and 9" dia, pr 99.00

Foltz Pottery, bowl, tulip sgraffito decor in cobalt, dated 1980, 14-1/2" dia 137.50

Stahl Pottery (Powder Valley, Pa)

   Fish mold, mottled brown glaze, mkd, dated 1939, glaze imperfections, 3" h, 11" l 165.00

   Inkwell mkd "Stahl, 1953," 1-5/8" h, and jug, greenish mottled glaze, mkd "Made by T.S. Stahl, Aug. 18, 1951," 4-1/2" h, pr 110.00

   Jar, dark reddish-brown glaze, ovoid, shoulder handles, mkd "Made in Stahl Pottery by Thomas Stahl, April 16, 1936," chips, hairline, 3-3/4" h 82.50

   Jug, green glaze, braided handle, incised flower decor, unmkd, 5-1/2" h 495.00

   Pitcher, silvery-brown glaze, tooled shoulder, mkd "Made for Betty & Brace by Thomas Stahl, Sept. 14th, 1936," rim rough, 7" h 55.00

   Pitcher with lid, mottled moss-green glaze, impressed flower on handle, incised "Ruth A. Dreibelbis," mkd "Made by I.S. Stahl March 26, 1939, Ruth + Bill Newell, 11/30/41," imperfections, 6" h 110.00

   Rooster, greenish mottled glaze, mkd "R.R. Stahl, 11-4-50," 4-1/4" h 220.00

Unknown maker

   Plate, bird and foliage sgraffito decor, yellow slip ground with green sponging, mkd "1723 H.R." but probably mid-20th C., 13" dia 247.50

Redware, Vintage, Marked

John Bell

   Bank, jug-shaped, mottled brown and orange ground, ovoid, impressed "John Bell," 4" h 3,250.00

   Bowl, green-brown glaze, impressed "John Bell, Waynesboro" on bottom, 3" h, 7-5/8" dia 1,900.00

   Canning jar, orange glaze, cylindrical shape, impressed "J. Bell" on bottom, side repairs, chips, 5-5/8" h, 4-5/8" dia 425.00

   Crock, light greenish-brown glaze, slightly rounded sides, impressed "John Bell" below collar, cracks, 4-3/8" dia 270.00

   Flowerpot with attached saucer, green glaze, impressed "John Bell, Waynesboro, Pa." on side of pot, poorly repaired crack, 5" h, 5-5/8" dia 925.00

   Food mold, turk's head, mottled brown glaze, impressed "John Bell," hairlines, base chip, 3-3/4" h, 6-3/8" dia 275.00

   Jar, dark-brown glaze, ovoid, impressed "J. Bell" on shoulder, glaze wear, flaking, crack, 6-5/8" h, 6" dia 1,150.00

   Lady's spittoon, mottled green and brown glaze, handled, impressed "John Bell" on bottom, 3-1/2" h, 4" dia 850.00

Redware inkwell, Shenandoah Valley, Va., 5-1/4" h, 6-1/4" w, $522.50.

Solomon Bell, Strasburg Va., pitcher, mottled green, brown, yellow and orange ground, ovoid, stamped "S. Bell, Strasburg" on shoulder, chips, 6-1/8" h 3,850.00

Upton M. Bell, Waynesboro Pa., butter jar, dark green-ish-brown glaze, molded bands, arched twisted han-dles, impressed "Upton M. Bell, Waynesboro, Pa." on bottom, crack, one handle restored, 3-1/2" h, 5-1/2" dia.. 1,050.00

Christian Link, Berks County Pa. (1870-1900), jar, ovoid, dark-brown glaze, impressed "C. Link," lip chip, 3-5/8" h.. 55.00

Jacob Medinger, ovoid vase, two handles, mottled green and orange ground, coggled band around rim and shoulder, inscribed "Made By Jacob Medinger for Tho-mas L. Rhoads," 11" h.................................. 5,300.00

"Samuel Mellvill, Always this full of good whiskey," folk-decor jug, dark ivory glaze, red glaze underneath, scratch decor of man in top hat, coat and breeches carrying a shovel, beside a dog and farm, heart with banner and "SM, JM, 1816," glaze flakes, handle crack, 7-1/8" h.. 3,850.00

"Thomas & Bro." (Huntingdon Pa.), crock, one-gal, ovoid, impressed mark.................................... 130.00

"A. Wilcox, West Bloomfield," preserve jar with lid, brick red glaze, chips on finial of lid, pot stone near base, 9-3/4" h.. 412.50

Redware, Vintage, Unmarked

Bank, acorn form, painted brown, gold textured cap, 4-1/2" h.. 264.00

Bean pot with lid, one handle, orange-brown lead/manga-nese interior glaze, unglazed exterior, interior glaze flaking, chipped lid/finial, 5-1/8" h, 5-1/2" dia....... 375.00

Birdhouse, globular shape, flat bottom, knob finial, impressed scroll and rosette design in wide band, arched hole, sloping rim-like perch, Schofield Pa., late 19th C., chip on finial, 6-1/4" h, 5-1/2" dia......... 175.00

Bottle, fish shape, Moravian (N.C.), incised features, dark-brown glaze, some wear and flaking, 5" l... 4,100.00

Bowl
    7" dia, 3-1/4" h, dark-brown sponging on deep-orange ground, tooled band, rolled rim 440.00
    8" dia, cross and dots in yellow slip, wear, edge chip.. 302.50
    11" dia, spit decor 275.00
    11-1/2" dia, three rows of squiggle decor around rim in yellow slip, shallow, hairline, glaze flakes 2,645.00
    13-1/2" x 10-1/2", oval, mottled green and brown decor, lipped, surface damage, chips......... 137.50
    15-1/2" x 12-1/4", serving, three-line yellow slip decor in three sets of wavy lines, imperfections.......605.00

Chamber pot, Gonic glaze, incised line decor, N.H., 19th C., applied strap handle, glaze chips, 5-1/2" h 690.00

Canning jar, glazed with black splotches, tooled lines at shoulder, glaze flakes, edges rough, 10-5/8" h 385.00

Charger
    Four-line yellow slip decor in wavy lines with straight lines highlighted in green slip, coggled rim, old chips, wear, glued repair to rim, 11-3/4" dia 357.50
    Plain glaze, imperfections, 12-1/4" and 12-3/4" dia, pr... 440.00
    Yellow slip decor and green wavy lines, olive glaze, damage, glued repair, attributed to the Moravians, 14-1/2" dia 137.50

Dish
    2-line decor in yellow slip, minor wear, crazing, 7-1/2" dia 467.50
    Brown sponging on orange ground, minor chips, 4-3/8" dia 330.00
    Leaf decor in brown slip on amber ground, coggled rim, old chips, 5-1/2" dia 412.50
    Windmill stylized decor in green glaze, ochre splotches, mustard ground, tapered, attributed to Bucks County Pa., chips, 1" h, 3-5/8" dia... 431.25

Distlefink, molded, unglazed, old black patina, hanging hole, 6-1/4" l.. 55.00

Dog, reclining, dark-brown glaze, forlorn expression, on base, flakes, 3-1/8" h, 8-7/8" l.............................110.00

Flower pot, dark sponging, tooling, wear and chips, no saucer, 5-1/4" h and 5-5/8" h, pr 148.50

Food mold
    Spiraled flutes, scalloped rim, brown sponging on pinkish-amber ground, wear, slight hairline, 8" dia 137.50
    Straight flutes, dark sponged rim, deep orange ground, minor chips and wear, 4-3/8" dia 115.50

Jar

Dark-brown running glaze, ovoid, applied shoulder handles, chips, 10-1/2" h 495.00

Flower decor in yellow slip with touches of green, reddish-brown ground, tapered oval body, textured band around neck, hairline, chips, 8-7/8" h 5,175.00

Orange spots, dark-green and brown glaze, flared rim, embossed tin lid with shield and "Banner Jelly," glaze hairlines, 5-3/4" h 137.50

Mottled brown glaze, tooled lines, flared rim, handle, 5-1/8" h, 4-5/8" dia 330.00

Jug, ovoid

Brown splotches, Maine, chips, 7-1/2" h 632.50

Dark-brown glaze, black running spots around shoulder and strap handle, tooled foot and neck, old edge chips, 8" h 550.00

Running green, tan and brown glaze, rim chips, flakes, 10-3/4" h 1,320.00

Loaf pan

Three-line yellow slip decor, coggled edge, chips, hairlines, flaking, 3-1/4" h, 15-1/2" w, 11-1/2" d 220.00

Tree decor in yellow slip, also wavy lines, tapered sides, coggled rim, wear, glaze flakes, old restoration to rim, 2-1/2" h, 14" w, 10-1/4" d 6,600.00

Milk pan, unglazed exterior, flared rim, tapered sides, glazed interior with small brown running streaks, chips, found in Va., 9-1/2" h, 18" dia 247.50

Milk bowl

Brown glazed interior, molded rim, wear and flaking to interior, 3-3/4" h, 16-1/2" dia 110.00

Ovoid redware jug, 8" h, $550. (Photo courtesy of Garth's Auctions, Delaware, Ohio)

Daubs of brown glaze on orange ground, tooled band, wear, 5-1/2" h, 13" dia 715.00

Floral decor in yellow, green and brown slip, interior glaze, wear, chips, hairline, 2-3/4" h, 8-1/2" dia 192.50

Slip decor, piecrust edge, worn interior, hairline, 3-1/4" h, 12" dia 110.00

Miniature, jug, Schofield Pa., dark-brown lead and manganese glaze, globular shape, minor flake, 3-5/8" h 175.00

Mixing bowl, brown sponge decor around rim and in lines down the side, raised rim with tooled band, hairlines, in base, rim flakes, 4-3/4" h, 10-3/4" dia 302.50

Mug, bulbous shape, imperfections, 3-1/2" h, pr 302.50

Orange, painted orange, chips, paint wear, 3" h 300.00

Pie plate, two-line

Swag decor, yellow slip, imperfections, 11-1/2" dia 247.50

Wavy decor in yellow slip, shallow rim flakes, 7-1/2" dia 467.50

Pie plate, three-line decor in green slip, coggled rim, shallow rim chips, interior glaze wear, 11-3/4" dia 880.00

Pie plate, three-line, yellow slip

7" dia, coggled rim, minor chips 220.00

8-1/2" dia, wavy decor, wear, hairlines, ... 440.00

10-1/4" dia, coggled rim, wear, chips, some slip wear and flakes 412.50

11" dia, coggled rim, glaze and edge chips 715.00

11-3/8" dia coggled rim, edge chips, interior ear, hairline 412.50

Pie plate, four-line

8" dia, squiggled lines, yellow and green slip, imperfections 330.00

8" dia, yellow slip, wear, hairline 412.50

Pie plate, other

"ABC" in script over flourish, tooled rim, old black on back, chips, 11-1/4" dia 1,072.50

"ABC" in script over wavy line and flourish, flaking, hairline, 10-1/8" dia 825.00

Bird's-claw decor in three-line yellow slip, coggled rim, hairlines, rim chips, 9-1/2" dia 247.50

Crossed double wavy lines in yellow slip, slightly scooped bottom, 1-7/8" d, 9" dia 495.00

Flower in yellow slip, coggled rim, wear, 11" dia 385.00

Lines decor, short dark-brown sponged lines perpendicular to rim, flakes 165.00

Slip decor (no distinct pattern) in yellow, edge wear, flakes, 9" dia 330.00

Slip decor (no distinct pattern) in yellow, wear, hairlines, old chips, 9" dia 385.00

Undecorated, burnt-orange glaze, coggled rim wear, 10-1/2" dia 165.00

"W" monogram in sweeping yellow slip decor, coggled rim, chips, minor flaking, hairline, 9" dia 935.00

Wavy daubs in green, 7-1/8" dia.................... 605.00
Wavy lines in yellow slip, running brown, coggled edge, glaze wear, crazing, chips,
9-1/2" dia 165.00
Wavy lines and flourishes in yellow slip, minor flakes, 10-3/4" dia...................................... 715.00

Pitcher
Brown running glaze, 7-1/8" h 385.00
Dark-brown sponged vertical lines, with lid, rim flakes, 5-3/4" h... 660.00
Dark-brown sponging, ovoid, diagonal decor, slightly larger lid, edge chips at lip, 8" h 385.00
Green and light-brown, dark-brown splotches, ovoid, flared rim, edge chips, firing separation,
9-1/4" h 880.00
Green and orange spotted decor, 7-1/2" h 312.50
Green and red spotted decor, 5" h..................110.00
Green and yellow slip decor, tooled lines, applied ribbed strap handle, chips, 4-1/4" h........... 495.00
Mottled green, brown and ivory glaze, illegible mark, possibly Shenandoah Valley, wear, flakes,
7" h 2,035.00
Peach glaze with brown drip decor,
4-1/2" h.. 522.50
Red glaze with brown spots, 6-1/2" h 412.50

Plate
Three-line yellow slip decor, coggled rim, 3 shallow rim chips, hairline, 8-1/4" dia 495.00
Five wavy lines, yellow slip, wear, chips,
10" dia 275.00
Initials "S.B." in yellow slip decor, glaze wear, chips, 9-1/4" dia 460.00
Swag decor in faint yellow slip across two sides, coggled rim, medium-brown glaze, chips,
9" dia 220.00
Twist yellow slip decor, red-brown ground, textured rim, 9" dia 805.00

Preserve jar
Dark-brown splotches, minor edge damage,
10-1/2" h.. 550.00

Greenish-cream colored slip, reddish-tan mottled glaze, brown squiggles, applied handles, flared lip, gallery for lid, paper label from "George McKearin Collection of American Pottery," chips,
8" h...2,860.00
Roof tile, Zoar, tulip design, edge chips,
15-3/4" l, pr 55.00
Tray, three-line wavy yellow slip decor, four sets of lines, wear, chips, 13-1/2" x 9" 715.00
Washboard, child-size, brown glaze, wooden frame, top of backboard replaced, 13-3/8" h, 6-5/8" w....... 577.50
Whistle, red clay, mottled black glaze with specks,
2-1/2" h 385.00

Rocking Chairs

Background: As the name implies, a rocking chair is a chair that has rockers fitted to the legs. The rocking chair was an American invention of the 19th century. The style quickly became popular, and many were created by simply adding rockers to existing chairs.

FYI: The Boston rocking chair is a uniquely American creation. Introduced around 1840, it evolved from the popular Windsor chair and featured a wooden seat with a downward curve on the front part and an upward curve on the back part. Boston

Redware footed toothpick holder, impressed "W.W.C." (William W. Cline, Hartford City, Ind.), 2-1/2" h, $250.

Mule-ear arrow-back rocking chair, $100.

rockers were also characterized by high backs consisting of a series of vertical spindles topped by a flat crest rail.

Banister-back, blue repaint, rush seat, 39" h 440.00

Boston, painted, old yellow and gold repaint, stenciled basket of fruit on crest, restorations, 42" h........ 275.00

Child's, arrowback, worn orig decor, red with green and yellow trim, 19" h.. 247.50

Comb back, five arrow spindles, scrolled arms, rabbit ears, small comb crest, stretcher base, shaped rockers, shaped seat, refinished, pieced restorations, 36" h... 192.50

Grain-decor, orig red and black graining, yellow striping, gold stenciling of fruit, turned legs, S-curved seat, scrolled arms, spindle back, rockers worn, 39-1/2" h... 220.00

Ladderback, armed

Painted, old dark red-brown, three arched slats, turned legs and double stretchers, old woven splint seat with damage 75.00

Tapered and ring-turned front posts, mushroom arms, four slats, large turned finials on rear posts, old dark refinish, old replaced rush seat......110.00

Turned posts and arms, four arched slats, splint seat, maple (some curl) and hickory, attributed to Ohio, few splint breaks, 46-1/2" h............... 192.50

Vase-turned front posts, notched arms, four arched horizontal splats on back, turned finials on rear posts, shaped rockers, old refinish, replaced splint seat, one arm with old nailed repair, chip on runner, 46" h 302.50

Pressed-back, oak, embossed griffin seat, 37" h.. 121.00

Slat-back, armed, painted old salmon red, New England, late 18th C., three arched slats, turned stiles, scrolled arms, turned tapering supports and legs, double stretchers, 41" h... 460.00

Twig, heart-motif at top of back, simple chip-carved detail, old worn finish, 42-1/2" h......................... 495.00

Windsor

Bamboo armed rocker, refinished, nine-spindle, base with H stretcher and old added rockers, well-shaped D seat, old pieced repair in crest with screw added, 33-1/4" h............................... 192.50

Bow-back, New England, early 19th C., eight-spindle, shaped pommel seat, bamboo-turned legs, swelled H stretcher, old brown paint, rockers added mid 19th C., minor imperfections, 32" h 690.00

Stepdown bamboo arm rocker, seven-spindle back, old brown and black seat, painted line decor on crest, shaped runners, shield-shaped seat, slightly scrolled arms, "L. Clark, E. Pitt, 1839" signature in old paint beneath seat, restorations, 33-3/4" h...220.00

Windsor, comb-back

Armed, four arrow spindles, rectangular crest, scrolled arms, bamboo supports, shaped seat, splayed legs, orig yellow green foliate designs,

Windsor comb-back rocking chair, New England, early 19th C., 40-5/8" h, $230. (Photo courtesy of Skinner Auctioneers & Appraisers of Antiques & Fine Arts, Boston and Bolton, Mass.)

mottled brown and black ground, New England, c. 1830, imperfections, 38" h.......................... 632.00

Armed, curving rectangular crest, tapering spindles, incised seat, splayed bamboo-turned legs, off-white paint, gilt, New England, early 19th C., surface imperfections, 40-5/8" h...................... 230.00

Armed, bamboo-turned legs, scrolled arms, rabbit ear posts, stepdown crests, worn orig decor in black and brown with yellow freehand foliage, one spindle repaired, 45" h, 17" w..................... 770.00

Bamboo-turned, old dark-green (black) repaint, yellow striping, crest dated "1769," "C" on comb, shaped seat with gutter around border and traces of a scene in the center, found in Vermont, 44" h 770.00

Rocking Horses

Background: Cradles had been used for centuries, but it wasn't until the 19th century that anyone thought to apply rockers to other forms. Rocking horses quickly gained favor with children and adults, and by the middle of the 1800s, simple homemade examples had given way to commercially produced horses. The body of the horse was usually made of carved wood that was either painted or covered with cloth or horsehide. Generally, the tails were made of horsehair.

Around 1845, much to the delight of mothers who were tired of rockers that cut carpets and damaged hardwood floors, the platform rocker was introduced. Its stationary platform allowed the horse to move without affecting the surface beneath it.

Reference: Patricia Mullins, *The Rocking Horse: A History of Moving Toy Horses*, New Cavendish Books, 1992.

Platform rocker, horse
> Dapple gray (orig), base with white stencil on deep red ground, cracks in orig brown leather saddle, edge damage, 29-3/4" h, 35" w 715.00
> Orig gray and white smoke decor, worn red platform base, orig saddle and reins, areas of touchup, wear, 33-1/2" h, 44" l 550.00
> White horse, red base, horsehair tail, 28" h, 30" l 357.50

Platform rocker sleigh, child's, worn orig red paint, gold and white border, shaped rails with turned spindles, applied brass rosettes on sides, worn corduroy seat, horse head missing from front, footboard replaced, 19" h, 32" w, 16" d 302.50

Traditional rocker (full-figure horse)
> Burlap cover, brown, white horsehair mane and tail, cowhide ears, red bridle, goldenrod velvet saddle, glass eyes, German, new rocker base, one hoof split, 30" h, 38-3/4" w 440.00
> Decor, orig red-brown, black painted platform with American flag, red stripes and stars, fully carved, leather saddle, J.A. Yorst, Philadelphia, 1860-90, imperfections, 39-1/2" h, 73" w 1,725.00
> Decor, worn orig white paint with black sponging, rockers in old burgundy paint with bright-red line detail, primitive lake scene with sailboats on center panel, worn oil cloth saddle and leather straps, nailed repair on 1 runner, 29-1/2" h, 56" w 687.50
> Decor, worn orig white paint with smoke decor, rockers in red over white, unusual design with rocker on each foot, articulated front legs advance when the reins are pulled, small wooden wheels on rear rockers, velvet saddle blanket, leather and cloth straps, reins missing, replaced peg in leg, 30" h, 36" w 495.00
> Hide-covered, brass label "Nouvelles Galleries, Marseille," red rockers, small orig saddle, horsehair mane/tail, glass eyes, hide separating at seams, one rocker cracked, 25" h, 31" w 275.00
> Painted, horse is white with black rings, worn orig red rockers, white scrollwork on base, partial saddle, missing ear, bridle and tail, damage, 23" h, 45" l 660.00
> Painted, orig white, smoke decor, stenciled red base, orig cloth and velvet saddle, cast bit, glass eyes, stirrups missing, mounting bars replaced, some wear, 28" h, 36" l 880.00

> Painted, worn white and pink, pine, nailed repairs, 43-1/2" l 412.50

Rocking horse, painted, red rockers with light-green scrolling, olive-green carved horse head and neck in old repaint with traces of mane and ears, horse head attached to a wooden platform having a shaped wooden seat with wicker back, 24-1/2" h, 39" w, 20" d........275.00

Rockingham Pottery

Background: During the mid-1700s, a pottery was located on the English estate of the Marquis of Rockingham, but it wasn't until 1826 that the Rockingham name was formally adopted by the facility after receiving financial assistance from the Marquis' heirs. The factory produced much earthenware and stoneware, but is perhaps best known for its mottled, manganese brown lead glaze. The Rockingham glaze was used by numerous potteries in England and the United States, most notably Bennington Pottery in Vermont, and similar glazes were also used by several Midwestern potteries.

Reference: Mary Brewer, *Collector's Guide to Rockingham: The Enduring Ware*, Collector Books, 1996.

FYI: Rockingham glaze was used by more than 150 potteries between 1830 and 1900. Many of the potteries were located in the Mid-West, hence the increased availability of those items in that area.

Note: Although the following items were produced by a number of makers, they all exhibit the well-known dark brown Rockingham glaze.

Also See: Bennington & Bennington-Type Pottery for additional background.

Bank
> Bureau motif, five tiers of drawers flanked by rope-twist design, arched feet, coin slot on top, chip, 3-1/4" h, 3-1/8" w 150.00

Yellowware bowl with a Rockingham glaze and two brown stripes, footed base, 4-3/4" high, 10-1/4" dia, $100.

Chest of drawers motif, bowfront, 4 drawers flanked by rope-twist design, round feet, coin slot on top, 2-1/2" h, 2-3/4" w 250.00

Bottle, coachman figure, impressed "Lyman Fenton & Co., 1849, Bennington Vt.," chips, spider crack in base, 10" h 385.00

Bowl

7-1/4" dia, 3-1/4" h, mkd "168" on bottom 66.00

9" dia, 4" h, footed, four narrow white bands 132.00

9-1/2" dia, 2-1/2" h, flared sides 99.00

9-1/2" dia, 4" h, interior crazing 55.00

10-1/2" dia, 3" h, column and dot design around rim, impressed "195" on bottom, crazing, short hairlines 55.00

10-1/2" dia, 4-1/2" h, petal design impressed with dots, minor rim chip, glaze flakes 66.00

13" dia, 6" h, raised panel sides, rolled rim, hairlines, chips beneath table ring 99.00

Candleholder, bowl-shaped, single socket in center surrounded by outer ring, 2-1/4" h, 6-1/4" dia 180.00

Candlestick, round pedestal and shaft, in-the-making imperfection on socket, 8-1/2" h 632.50

Canister, covered

Molded handles, scalloped design on mismatched lid with finial repair, 8-1/2" h, 6-1/2" dia 49.50

Rib pattern, mkd "1849," rim nicks, 9-1/4" h 431.25

Creamer

Cow, chipped lid possibly mismatched, 5" h, 7" l 137.50

Plain design, flaring foot, pinhead glaze flake at rim, 3-3/4" h 66.00

Dog, seated Spaniel, freestanding front legs, base chip, 10-3/4" h 330.00

Flask, book form, pint, repaired corner, 6" h 316.25

Food mold, Turk's head

8-1/4" dia, 3-1/2" h, slightly swirled ribs 49.50

9" dia, 3-7/8" h, slightly swirled ribs 55.00

9-5/8" dia, 3-1/2" h, swirled ribs, minor roughness 71.50

Foot bath, lobed oval vessel, two handles, 8-3/4" h, 14-1/2" w, 19-1/2" l 3,737.50

Humidor, ovoid, round hole in front above foot, flared top, lid with two holes, inner rim chips, 6-1/4" h, 4-7/8" dia 110.00

Inkwell

Column-shaped, paneled sides, concave center surrounded by concave band with three small quill holes and three-molded stars, base chip, 3-1/8" h, 4" dia 200.00

Girl resting her head on a stump, her hat in front, running brown glaze, dark glaze spots on face and dress, 3-1/2" h, 4-1/2" w, 2-1/2" d 82.50

Shoe motif, rim chip, 5-1/2" l 247.50

Jardiniere, straight sides, arched handles, cracked, 5-3/4" h, 8" dia 130.00

Loving cup, applied scenes of men with lantern, dogs and man seated at table with pitcher, raised leaves around rim, burst glaze bubbles on interior and table ring, 7" h, 12" dia (at handles) 357.50

Marble, blue and light-brown mottled glaze, minor glaze flakes, 1-7/8" dia 110.00

Mug, sides flare toward rim, incised lines, minor flakes/nicks, 4" h 110.00

Pitcher

Bust of woman, small base chip, 9-5/8" h 110.00

Cranes in bulrushes, deer-head spout, acorns, oak leaves and ivy at side of neck, branch-shaped handle with entwined snake, spout chip, large handle chip with poor repair, mismatched lid, 9-5/8" h 65.00

Floral petals and relief columns, scrolled handle, short pedestal foot on flared base, 9-1/2" h 176.00

Flower basket, spout rough, 7-1/2" h 66.00

Hunting dogs and deer, hound handle, elaborate decor of grapes and vines around top half, attributed to American Pottery Co., Jersey City, 9-3/4" h 550.00

Medallion portraits of men smoking, woman taking snuff, chipped lid, 9-1/4" h 88.00

Peacock, rim rough, 8-1/2" h 82.50

Plain, bulbous base, flake on handle, 8-5/8" h 302.50

Plain, straight sides, squared handled, 7" h 66.00

Plain except swag design at shoulder, minor stone ping, surface roughness at base, 7" h 99.00

Stag and Eagle, hound handle, 9-3/4" h 192.50

Toby form, 6" h 110.00

Tulip pattern, 5" h 121.00

Platter

Octagonal, bubble-like design, minor firing flaw, 9-3/8" x 12-1/2" 715.00

Square, scalloped edges with embossed accents, glaze wear, 9" sq 88.00

Salt box, Peacock design, round lid, imperfections, 6" h 247.50

Soap dish, lidded, rectangular, rib pattern, domed lid with loop handle, strainer insert, hairline, chips, 4-3/4" h, 5-1/2" w, 4-1/2" d 546.25

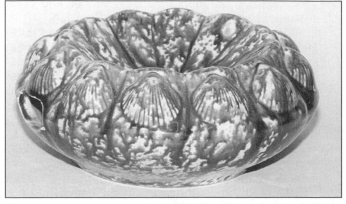

Spittoon with molded shell design, Rockingham glaze, $300.

Spittoon, paneled sides

    Scalloped rim, raised panels radiate from center opening, brown running glaze with blue-green spots on top, 9" dia.......................................110.00

    With medallions, verse on top "You should spit in this box sir," 4-1/2" h, 8" dia........................ 440.00

Teapot, yellow base, brown sponge decor,
5" h... 495.00

Tea tile, round, molded eagle surrounded by four urns, three small feet, 7-3/8" dia 550.00

Rolling Pins

Background: Little has changed in the evolution of the rolling pin since it became a kitchen staple in the 19th century. Although they have been produced from a variety of materials over the years (including wood, glass, metal, and marble), the design has remained essentially the same. Collectors look for unusual variations and for examples with exceptional wood, such as tiger maple.

H-shaped handle

    Double-handled, two round turned dowels form handles, top dowel has simple tapered baluster turning with suppressed ball-shaped elements in center, bottom dowel slightly tapered with incised line designs, handles mortised into side brackets which extend down to hold rolling pin, 5-7/8" h, 11" w.. 170.00

    Maple, round handle brackets at bottom with square tops, small squat ball-shaped finials, 6" h, 12" w.. 120.00

    Maple, ovoid-shaped handle brackets fitted with round horizontal dowel having tapered ring-turned handle, 5" h, 12-5/8" w 325.00

    Wooden, shaped brackets on ends, turned and tapered handle with simple ring turnings, round dowel below handle with line banding in center, wear, 14" w, 5-3/4" h....................................... 240.00

Traditional form, glass

    Free-blown, dark olive green with white spattering, rough pontil, 14" l, 1-3/4" greatest dia 100.00

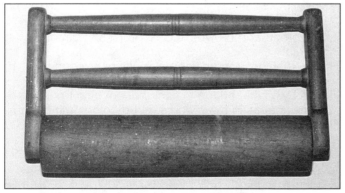

Rolling pin, double H-shaped handle, wooden, 7-1/2" h, 14" l, $225.

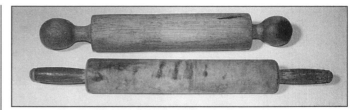

Maple rolling pins, top, $75; bottom, $30.

    Milk glass, maple handles, minor chips, 18" l 27.50

Traditional form, stoneware

    Blue and white, Colonial pattern................. 1,215.00

    Blue and white, Wildflower pattern 247.50

    Blue and white, Wildflower pattern, advertises "Compliments of C.N. Allen, Jr.," 8" l 435.00

    "C.R. Kelly, General Merchandise, Floyd, Iowa," rust-color bands, minor flake, 15" l 550.00

    Yellowware, turned maple handles, 15" l (excluding handles), 3" dia... 525.00

Traditional form, wood

    Attached mesh tin flour duster, 20-1/4" l........ 220.00

    Curly maple, pronounced curl, dark patina, 20" l 220.00

    Double, walnut and softwood, shaped brackets, simple ring turning, incised line designs 5-1/2" h, 10-1/4" l 370.00

    Split handle and body 27.50

    Turned ivory handles on brass pins, 1 handle with scrimshaw inscription "Bark Lorietta out of Bath, Maine," one handle damaged, other missing pinhead, 19-1/2" l 495.00

Rugs

Background: Rug styles and the techniques for making them have changed greatly over the years. Embroidered rugs date to the early 19th century. Braided rugs, made from strips of fabric that were braided and then sewn together to form a circular or oval shape, were popular from the 1820s to the 1850s. Hooked rugs, which were introduced about 1830 and came into vogue in the 1850s, were crafted from homemade designs, as well as from commercial patterns.

Reference: Joel and Kate Kopp, *American Hooked and Sewn Rugs: Folk Art Underfoot*, E.P. Dutton, 1975; Mildred Cole Peladeau, *Art Underfoot: The Story of Waldoboro Hooked Rugs*, American Textile History Museum, 1999; Jessie A. Turbayne, *Hooked Rug Treasury*, Schiffer Publishing, 1997.

Collectors' Club: RugNotes, 12700 Ardennes Ave., Rockville, MD 20851.

FYI: Hooked rugs often appeal to folk art collectors, who are attracted to examples with bold graphic designs, as well as pictorials with a folkish flair.

Hooked rug, red, blue and green, ochre ground, 31-1/2" x 55-1/2" w, $5,175. (Photo courtesy of Skinner Auctioneers & Appraisers of Antiques & Fine Arts, Boston and Bolton, Mass.)

Braided

Oval, wool, blues, grays, burgundy and tan,
5'8" x 9'3" 110.00

Hooked (rectangular unless noted)

Baby and dog, child in blue dress with shoe-button eyes, black dog, in pink and red circle, lettered "Baby" in multicolored and ochre rectangle surrounded by floral vine, lettered "Baby Dog" at the bottom on black ground, minor imperfections, one eye missing, 35" h, 44-1/2" w 2,530.00

Bow ties and checkerboard, burnt-orange, black and multicolor stripes, wear, some damage,
26" x 36"... 330.00

Bowl of stylized flowers, red, blue and green, ochre ground, meandering border of purple, cream, browns and ochre, mounted on a frame, minor imperfections, 31-1/2" h, 55-1/2" w 5,175.00

Checkerboard pattern, blocks of alternating stripes, multicolor, edge wear, 36" x 62"............................. 275.00

Chickens, brown hen and rooster, brown and white chicks, landscape ground, blue and tan borders, 25" h, 40" w 247.50

Collie, landscape ground, birds in air, border in stripes of red, blue and white, 30" h, 48" w 495.00

Diamond grid, multicolor stripes, wear,
23" x 68".. 247.50

Dog in black, brown and gray ground, c. 1910,
3' sq.. 1,650.00

Dog in brown, green and tan ground, band of green leaves inside maroon/black borders, repairs,
55" x 39".. 385.00

Dog, in quatrefoil flanked by cornucopias of flowers, shades of brown, cream, red, pink, green and black, ochre and brown ground, mounted on a frame, minor fading, 26" h, 39-1/2" w................................. 402.50

Dog and chickens, seated black-and-white dog watching black-and-white hens, chicks and ducks, tan ground, red highlights, 2 black borders, mounted on frame, minor imperfections, 28" h, 43-1/2" w 862.50

Floral
   Flowers in red, white and green, flanked by cow and horse on green and brown mottled ground, oval, wear, stains, 23-1/2" x 42-1/2"...................... 90.00
   Multicolor on beige, flanked by scenic view with house and trees, oval, minor wear,
   22" x 41" 325.00
   Multicolor, elliptical center panel on white ground, flowers in outer corners on dark ground,
   27" x 44" 247.50
   Red flowers and stars on white ground,
   24" x 36"..115.50
   Red roses and green leaves in large white diamond, outer corners with multicolor geometric design,
   30" x 48".. 220.00
   Roses, morning glories and tulips, green foliage on white ground, leaf border, dark-green edging, signed "Mrs. Josephine Shawver, St. Regis, 1950," 70" x 39"..110.00
   Silver, red and yellow flowers, moss-green ground, brown and black borders, edge wear, oval, 32-1/2" x 42-1/2".. 82.50
   Tulips, daffodils, lilies and iris, white central oval ground, gray border, 54" x 35".................... 357.50
Floral and confetti design, multicolor, white inner border, yellow outer border, 29" x 56" 907.50
Flowering tree in a pot flanked by leaping stags, black ground, horse at each corner, wide border of hit-or-miss geometric shapes, mounted on frame, minor imperfections, 41-1/2" h, 48" w 5,462.00
Geometric
   Fourteen squares, red, greens, blue and gray, some wear, 26" x 46"..110.00
   Twenty-eight squares (fourteen with medallion, fourteen striped), gray, salmon, black and multi-color, wear, 35" x 60".. 247.50
   One-hundred-twenty-eight squares (eight rows of sixteen), braided border, 82" x 42" 2,200.00
   Multicolor, dark and cream blocks with swirling colors, 7' 9" x 8' 5".. 3,630.00
   Multicolor, red and black border, 5" unraveled edge,
   31" x 55".. 440.00
   Multicolor, yellow and green border, wear, separation, 37" x 71" 247.50
Girl chasing goose, landscape ground, 27" h,
38" w.. 192.50
Four hens, tan ground, multicolor triangle border in red, tan, green and brown, "L.C.S." and "83," circular mat, 54" dia.. 715.00
Horse, running, impressionistic multicolor ground, 24" h,
34" w.. 192.50
House by a lake, bridge in background, pine trees, road, maple leaves in the corners, good colors, minor damage, 19" x 32"..110.00
Leaves, green leaves with brown and yellow vines, gray ground, brown border, 5' x 8'.......................... 357.50
Lion, reclining, among jungle flowers and trees, shades of brown, green, red, pink and yellow, red and multicolor striped border, minor imperfections, 30-1/2" h, 61" w 690.00

Lions, reclining adult and standing baby in tan, brown and pink, landscape ground with red and green plants and green and yellow trees, 34" h, 64" w.......... 550.00

Log Cabin pattern, multicolor in shades of yellow, browns, red, green, gray and black, repairs, c. 1900, 33" h, 65" w...................... 258.00

Logs and leaves, red, green, brown, gray and cream, old rebinding, 30" x 55"......................... 165.00

Middle Eastern design, central medallion in burgundy, ivory and maroon, blue ground, thin white line, maroon and black borders, minor wear and color loss, 76" x 37"...................... 165.00

Mosaic, multicolor, 26" x 92" 220.00

Mottled multicolor design, white border, 31" x 45"................................. 247.50

Oriental rug motif, blue, red, gray and cream, approx. 36" x 72"....................... 193.00

Two parrots on basket of flowers, also butterflies, bright colors, 33" h, 51" w 825.00

Two pigs, black, on green grass against blue and white sky, 20" h, 37" w................... 605.00

Poppies, red, green, brown and yellow, foliage scroll border, 22" x 37"................................110.00

Rooster, yarn hooked in red, various shades of brown, black highlights, oatmeal-colored ground, checkered border, mounted on a frame, 24" h, 41" w......... 1,495.00

Roses, burgundy and pink on cream ground, burgundy border, oval, 59" x 35-1/2" 82.50

Roses and other flowers, pink, tan, burgundy and brown in center surrounded by oval flower-and-leaf border, scrolls and leaves around the edge, dark-green ground, 44" x 66" 220.00

Tree of Life, flowers, leaves, etc., tree in rust, tan and gray on gray ground with maroon and black borders, flowers in blue, salmon, yellow, orange and tan, 58-1/2" x 37" 220.00

Tumbling Blocks, yellow, red and black, 24" x 35"......................... 247.50

Penny

Six-sided, tan, orange, blue, dark- and light-green circles on tan ground, staining, minor damage, 19-1/4" w, 33" l.................................. 220.00

Rag

Carpet, room-size, woven, seamless, wool, stripes of colored fabric, 8'4" w, 13' l............................. 1,320.00

Runner, stripes of red, green, white and black, 33" w, 120" l.. 220.00

Strip of Pennsylvania carpet, blues, black, gray, and purple, charcoal end binding, 32-1/4" x 90" 165.00

Shirred

Geometric, circles in center, octagonal border, multicolor, 38" x 40".................................. 258.50

Geometric, concentric circles in center, cross-flanked by Price of Wales Feathers, quarter circles in each corner, shades of brown, gold, red, blue and green, small areas of loss and repairs, 36" x 65" 1,725.00

Multicolored stripes, stains, 39-1/4" x 18-3/4" 71.50

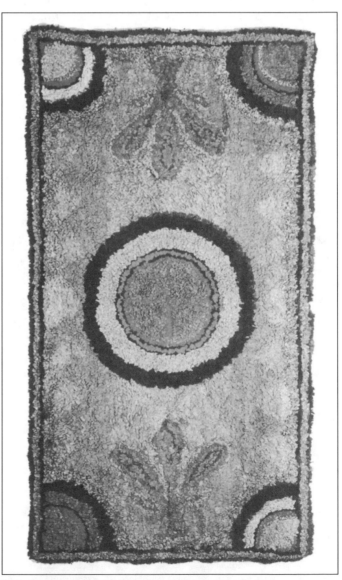

Shirred rug, shades of brown, gold, red, blue and green, small areas of loss and repairs, 36" x 65", $1,725. (Photo courtesy of Skinner Auctioneers & Appraisers of Antiques & Fine Arts, Boston and Bolton, Mass.)

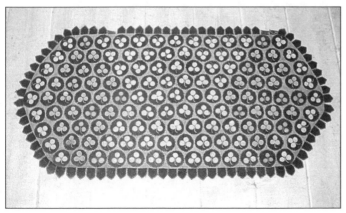

Penny rug, $295.

Rustic Furniture

Background: Necessity being the mother of invention, many pieces of rustic furniture were created by individuals who needed something and decided they could make it themselves from wood they harvested. Stick or twig furniture is a perfect example, although the production of it and other related furniture styles eventually spawned a cottage industry.

Hickory

Armchair, seven-spindle, splint seat, double stretchers, crackled white paint over earlier green, unmkd, surface imperfections, 38-3/4" h, pr 805.00

Armchairs, five with hoop design with orig woven splint back over solid seat and splayed legs, sixth armchair with rectangular back with orig woven splint back over solid seat and circular cutout under each arm, refinished, hoop chairs 34" h, rectangular chair 40" h, set of six 1,265.00

Bench, rectangular top, X-shaped supports with key-tenon detail, refinished, mkd Old Hickory, 18" h, 49" w, 14" d, pr 184.00

Desk, rectangular three-board top over three drawers, splayed slab sides with diamond cutouts, refinished, mkd Old Hickory, 30" h, 42" w, 20" d 161.00

Side table, rectangular top, lower shelf supported by vertical sides, shoe-foot base, refinished, unmkd, 24" h, 26" w, 14" d, pr 431.25

Stick furniture

Footstool, upholstered top, halved branches around sides, four branch legs, X-stretcher, some soiling, 9-3/8" h, 15" w, 9-1/2" d 325.00

Rocking chair, bentwood, shaped coiled arched back, bent arms, splint seat, arched and coiled seat supports, old worn paint, small repair, 41-1/2" h 920.00

Table, tripod base

Base with horseshoe-shaped stick decor, square top, mustard, silver and brown paint, 24" h, top 12-1/2" sq 71.50

Burl base in old brown paint, round top accented with split-log and stick trim, 29" h, top 18-1/2" dia 220.00

Stick base, heart-and-arch bent-stick decor, square top with stylized floral decor, green, silver and blue paint, 29-1/2" h, top 16-1/2" sq 165.00

Twig stand, $75.

Hickory high-back curved-arm rocking chair, $895.

Horse-drawn plow, "Blount True Blue Steel Plow, Evansville, Ind.," $2,500.

Salesman's Sample

Background: These working, scaled-down versions of full-size products were carried by salesmen as they called on prospective clients. They are especially prized by collectors for their relative scarcity and unique size.

Collecting Hint: Many items offered as salesman's samples are actually miniatures or children's items. As such, they are of lesser value than authentic salesman's samples.

Canoe, wooden ribbed interior, painted white with black line decor, with oars, 48" l 9,350.00
Spittoon, brass, bottom mkd "Cuspidors made by Ireland & Matthews Mfg. Co., Detroit, Mich.," three stress cracks, 2" h, 2-3/4" w at bottom 65.00
Wash basin, graniteware, Chrysolite.................... 195.00
Windmill, metal
  Paris-Dunn, one-blade................................... 330.00
  Samson.. 6,600.00
  Woodmanse.. 4,400.00

Salt Boxes

Background: Dating to the second half of the 19th century, these containers were made for storing table salt. They can be found in both hanging and tabletop versions.

Hanging, pine, layers of old worn green paint, cross-member crest and box with hinged lid, old repairs, 19" h.. 220.00
Hanging, softwood, oblong, arched back, sloping hinged lid, dovetailed, overlapping divided drawer, brass pulls, stained, wear, 16" h, 8-5/8" w, 9-3/8" d 475.00
Slant front, poplar, inlaid star on front with center circle in bird's-eye maple, dovetailed, applied base molding, scalloped crest, varnish worn off in areas, minor damage, 9-7/8" h, 8-1/2" w, 5-3/4" d 495.00

Samplers

Background: The earliest samplers were actually examples (samples) of a variety of stitches and patterns. Needleworkers referred to these instructional tools when practicing their skills, but the samples were rolled up and placed in storage when not in use. During the 18th century, samplers forsook much of their functional role, becoming more pictorial and decorative.

References: Elizabeth Kurella, *The Complete Guide to Vintage Textiles*, Krause Publications, 1999; Glee Krueger, *Gallery of American Samplers*, Bonanza Books, 1984; Jack L. Lindsey, *Worldly Goods: The Arts of Early Pennsylvania 1680-1758*, Antique Collectors' Club, 1999.

Museums: Cooper-Hewitt Museum, National Museum of Design, New York, NY; Smithsonian Institution, Washington, DC.

1694 sampler by Mary Ogleed, Adam and Eve motif, silk on homespun, framed, 10-1/2" x 11", $5,775. (Photo courtesy of Garth's Auctions, Delaware, Ohio)

Care: Samplers should not be exposed to direct sunlight, as it will cause the colored needlework to fade. Samplers should also be protected from direct sources of heat.

Also See: Needlework.

1762, "Anna Greffen her sampler in the twelfth year of her age," rows of alphabets (one in open needlework), heart and diamond, ivory and green, on linen, small hole, worn frame, 9-1/2" sq 770.00

1776, English, Adam and Eve band sampler, alphabets above three central panels depicting Adam and Eve, a crucifix, couple with pets, birds, crowns, animals, lower panels of geometric and meandering vines, fading, toning, stains, 35-1/2" h, 9-3/4" w 2,300.00

1789, "Sarah Starrs work done in her 13 year 1789," American or English, alphabet and geometric bands, inspirational verses, parrot flanked by urns of flowers, row of geometric tulips, cottage with trees, flora and fauna, animals and flowers, geometric vining floral border, fabric loss, stains, toning, 17-1/4" h 14-1/4" w 1,150.00

1795, "Nabey Bradley born December 23 in the year of our Lord 1785. This wrought in the 10 year...," Essex County, Mass., alphabets, inspirational verse, fruit tree, basket, bouquet of flowers with people, birds and animals in a landscape, geometric borders, toning, some thread loss, 15" h, 12-1/2" w 18,400.00

1795, "Betsy A ES Youngl," rows of alphabets and partial pictures, cross stitched, ivory, green, gold, brown and black, worn frame, 12-1/4" h, 8-1/2" w 770.00

18--, "Jane McClane her *sempler rought* (sic) in the year 18--," alphabets and numbers, blue, ivory and yellow, on linen homespun, framed, 17-3/4" h, 15-3/8" w 192.50

1804, Ann Hunter, map sampler, "The Map of England & Wales Worked by Ann Hunter in the Year 1804," red, green, yellow and black, silk on linen homespun, old gilt frame, minor edge damage, stains, tear, 24-1/2" h, 22" w 935.00

1805, "Ann Apps, aged 12, 1805," alphabets, verse surrounded by potted flowers, birds, hearts, pine trees, crowns and cats, zigzag border, framed, losses, 10-1/2" h, 9-3/8" w 862.50

1809, "Sarah Jubb Aged 9 Dec 4. 1809," inspirational verse, Solomon's Temple, panel with gentleman and lady, animals and flowers, geometric vining floral border, framed, toning, stains, fabric loss, 20" h, 18" w 690.00

1810, Anne Clarance, alphabets, flowers and verse, floral border, multicolor, silk on homespun, old frame, small holes, wear, rebacked on linen, 14-1/2" h, 14-1/4" w 605.00

1811, "Sarah Sutton her sampler marked in the year of our Lord 1811, Aged 9 years," alphabet panels above verse, floral border with birds, framed, toning, fading, 5-1/2" h, 19-1/2" w 345.00

1811, "Sarah Van Cleef, Her Sampler, Made July 20, 1811, Was Born April 9, 1800, Made Under The Care of Mary Bellamy," alphabets, house, trees and birds, vining border, framed 14,850.00

1809 sampler by Sarah Jubb, stains, fabric loss, 20" x 18", $690. (Photo courtesy of Skinner Auctioneers & Appraisers of Antiques & Fine Arts, Boston and Bolton, Mass.)

1814, "Ann Blenkin, May 21, 1814," Adam and Eve, angels, birds, baskets of flowers and verse, strawberry border, wool and silk on homespun, red and pink with olive white and brown, framed, some floss missing, wear, stains, 20" h, 6-1/2" w 715.00

1815, "Rebeckah Pilgrim finished this Sampler in the twelfth year of her age October 27 1815," American, alphabets and numbers, verses, framed, fading, stains, 11-3/4" h, 16" w 517.50

1816, "B.H.," flowers, birds, people, ducks and angels, vining floral border, shades of red, yellow, green, white, brown, black, etc., cotton, stains, wear, fading, missing floss, unframed, 22-3/4" sq 660.00

1817, Mary Ann Godfrey (N.H., 1802-1887), girl on edge of lake, floating basket of flowers, trees, sheep, alphabet and verse, elaborate floral border, green, blue, yellow, creams and black silk chenille and metallic threads and paper on linen, gesso frame with damage, 1 lamb unfinished, minor stains, sold with daguerreotype of Godfrey, 21-3/4" h, 20-1/4" w 22,550.00

1819, "Wrought by Cynthia Phelps, Aged 13 Years, Wilton, July 28 AD 1819," Essex County, Mass., alphabets, flowering shrubs, double sawtooth border, minor thread loss, toning, fading, 9-3/4" h, 16-1/4" w 1,265.00

1820, "Mary Barker Her Work in the MIDD Society School Aged 11 Years 1820," American, inspirational verses, trees, birds and flowers, geometric floral border, framed, toning, minor stains, 21-1/2" h, 13" w 1,150.00

1823 sampler by Martha Mary Miller, Newport, 17-1/4" sq, $1,955. (Photo courtesy of Skinner Auctioneers & Appraisers of Antiques & Fine Arts, Boston and Bolton, Mass.)

1822, "Amelia Gross, Aged 14, March 1822," alphabet, blue letters and numbers, vining floral border in gold and green, heart and vine dividers, old frame with chips, fading, 18-1/4" h, 10-1/4" w 385.00

1823, "Martha Mary Miller Newport August 25 1823," alphabet panels, inspirational verse, maker's ID in wreath, floral border, minor toning, 17-1/4" sq 1,955.00

1823, "Harriet Williams, Aged 10 Years, Orange, September 19, 1823" and "Trust in Providence," house with double chimneys, fence, tree, small building with several birds, alphabets and verse, floral border, blue, green, brown, yellow, black and white, silk on homespun, framed, stains, 18" h, 14-5/8" w 990.00

1824, "Steubenville Jefferson County Ohio," alphabet and verse, floral bocks in lower corners, serrated border, red, green, blue and yellow, on moss green homespun, modern frame, fading, minor stains, 11-3/4" h, 12-3/4" w 2,420.00

1826, "Lydia Freed, Her Work In The Year 1826," urns of flowers, green, yellow and pink, silk on loosely woven homespun, repainted frame, stains, 8-3/4" h, 10-5/8" w 495.00

1827, "Sarah Maria Child aged 9 1827," New England, alphabets, inspirational verse, baskets of fruit, wreaths of flowers, sawtooth border, toning, fading, minor stains, 19" h, 14" w 2,760.00

1829, "Rebecca Charlesworth, October 29th, 1829," American or English, alphabets, verse, berry and vine border, framed, losses, 10" h, 8-1/2" w 575.00

1829, Elizabeth Ester Gibb, alphabets in light-blue, gold, yellow and brown over verse "The hand of the diligent

maketh rich," vines in green, gold and mauve, contemporary frame, 12-1/4" h, 13-1/4" w 330.00

1829, "Eleanor Wilson, aged 8 years, April 9th, 1829, Xenia (Ohio)," alphabets, verse, Federal-style house, fence, tree, birds and urns of flowers, green, gold, yellow, white and tan, silk on homespun, framed, with copy of family history, 16-3/4" h, 17-3/4" w 7,700.00

183-, Elize Riddell, name of parents, flowers, house, birds, verse, vining floral border, silk on homespun, faded blue, green, red, white and black, old mahogany veneer frame, wear, some missing floss, 28-1/2" h, 24-1/2" w 1,760.00

1830, "Sarah Goodall worked this sampler in the eighth year of her age 1830" and "Nottingham Castle," flowers, birds with crowns and eagle, vining strawberry border, multicolor, silk on homespun, old frame, minor bleeding, wear with damage in 1 corner, 18-1/4" h, 15" w 1,650.00

1831, "Alice Bagott St. Peter's School June 16th 1831" and "Home in View," verse, cornucopias of flowers and weeping willow over tomb, gold, ivory, green and blue, possibly Cincinnati, Ohio, framed, small stabilized hole, 20-3/4" h, 21-3/4" w 1,815.00

1832, "Sarah T. Root, Pittsfield (Mass.), Aug. 23 1832, Aged 12 Years" in cartouche, baskets of flowers, alphabet panels and inspirational verse, wave border, toning, fading, 15" h, 17-1/4" w 1,495.00

1833, Charlotte and Cynthia Ann Hatfield (sisters), alphabets and numbers, birds, butterflies and flowers, ivory, blue, green and brown, family histories on the back of each, framed, 17" h, 8" w and 18" h, 9-1/2" w, pr... 3,520.00

1834, Mary Turner, English, alphabet panel above rows of flowers, verse flanked by birds above seminary-style building, fruit trees and animals, vining floral border, repairs, fading, 15-3/4" h, 12-3/4" w 1,260.00

1834, "Albina Thorntons Sampler, Finished June 1834," alphabets, house and fenced yard, flowers and animals, vining floral border, framed, minor fading, general toning, 16-5/8" sq 2,415.00

1835, "Catherine S. Tirrell, 7, Boston, September, 1835," alphabets, faded blue, olive and brown, silk on homespun, framed, minor wear, stains, 17-1/2" h, 10-1/2" w 605.00

1839, "Sara Ann Hunt Aged 12, 1839," animals including giraffes, rabbits, peacocks and deer, plants and verse, vining floral border, gold, brown and green, silk on homespun, rosewood veneer frame, 26" h, 24-1/2" w 5,280.00

1841, Elizabeth Abrey, verse, building, trees, birds, animals, butterflies and baskets of flowers, floral border, brown, green, cream and pink, modern frame, fading, small holes, 19-3/8" h, 15" w 2,420.00

1841, Harriet Perry, with instructress' name Huldah Cannon, verse, alphabet and baskets of flowers, vining floral border, green, blue, cream and brown, on homespun, framed, thread loss, stains, small holes, 17-1/4" h, 18-3/4" w 660.00

1843, Margaret, alphabets in blue, green and gold on tan, light stains, small hole, contemporary frame, 10-1/8" h, 13" w.................................... 357.50

1843, "Agnes Whitaker, aged 8," alphabets, baskets of fruit with flowering trees, birds and dog, small house at the bottom, green vine border, margin stains, old frame, 11-5/8" h, 11-1/8" w................................ 550.00

1844, "__ Thompson Clark," alphabets, verse, two houses, trees, flowers and birds, vining strawberry border, multicolor, wool on cotton, modern frame, stains, floss damage, missing stitches, 21-3/4" h, 19-1/2" w..715.00

1845, "Elizabeth Bennett, Her Work, Sept. 1845," baskets of flowers and birds with alphabets, stylized flowers and shades of brown, blue and green, silk on linen homespun, unframed, small areas of floss missing, light stains, holes in border, 12-1/4" h, 12" w.............. 880.00

1845, house, flowers, angels, birds, teapot, etc., several sets of initials, vining floral border, multicolor, wool on canvas, old frame backed by Dutch-American newspaper, wear, stains, canvas damage, missing floss, 25-3/4" h, 27" w.................................... 660.00

1846, "E.R. Bennett, March 1846," alphabets, green line and vine dividers across center, faded, worn backing, 16" h, 8" w.. 467.50

1849, "Mary Miller aged 8 years Febuary (sic) 27th...1849" and The Lord's Prayer, birds, lambs, tree, basket of flowers and alphabet, vining flower border, cross stitch in thread and yarn, red, ivory, green and yellow, on linen, grain-decor frame, stains, 21" h, 20-3/4" w.. 385.00

1852, Martha Jane Sterret, alphabet, verse, trees and pots of flowers, green-blue, olive and cream, homespun, framed, 21" h, 20-3/4" w....................... 1,540.00

1859, "Eliza Matthews, May 1859," American or English, alphabet and numbers, leafy vine border, framed, minor losses, 8" h, 4-1/8" w 373.75

1865, "Cawthorne, near Barnsley" and "God is love...," blue and green leaf border, silk and wool on loosely woven canvas, dated pen and ink presentation paper on back, unframed, wear, yarn missing, 17" h, 12-3/4" w 330.00

1867, "Ebth. Pashley, Mexbrough, 1867," English, stylized flowers, brick house, verse, birds, butterflies, Adam and Eve, lion and unicorn, vining floral border, multicolored, wool on loosely woven canvas, modern frame, wear, damage, stains, large hole, 29-1/2" h, 30-1/2" w 385.00

1868, "M.E. Hornick Aged 12 Years December 3, 1868," birds, baskets of berries, rows of alphabets, strawberry border, cross stitch in gold, lavender and pale green, framed, 17-1/4" h, 14-1/4" w 330.00

1882, "A.B. Minot," mammy and dancing black children, deer, elephant, fox, monkeys, cats and birds, on unstitched needlepoint canvas, 21" x 22".......... 1,100.00

"Abigail Baylies Born March 29 1788," alphabet and verse, 2 bluebirds at top, bottom shows house, animals and couple under weeping willow, borders of vining flowers, butterflies and birds, blue, green, yellow and brown, on homespun, framed, some fraying, stains, repairs, 19-1/8" h, 18-1/2" w 770.00

"Made by Mary Cassidy at the Sisters of Notre Dame," Cincinnati, Ohio, alphabets, convent at center, urns of flowers on sides, birds, vining border, green, gold and mauve, light stains, 16-1/4" h, 20-5/8" w........... 770.00

"Eleanor C. Chambers," alphabets, house and trees, vining floral border, silk on homespun, faded multicolor, modern frame, wear, small holes, some loss of floss, 17-1/4" h, 17-3/4" w 715.00

"Mary Ann Godlonton," alphabets and numbers, multicolor, silk on linen homespun, framed, wear, damage, 10-1/2" h, 16-1/2" w 357.50

"Mary Osborn worked this in the thirteenth year of her age," alphabets, numbers and verse, strawberry border, wear, holes, some stitched repairs, 18-1/4" h, 11-1/8" l 220.00

"Easter Ellen Rudd," Pa. origin, flowering trees, baskets of flowers, birds and house, polychrome yarn on loosely woven Berlin canvas, painted frame, minor damage, 21-3/4" h, 19-1/4" w 385.00

"Elizabeth Saunders," Welsh, large house surrounded by trees and birds, alphabet, strawberry border, with family history, contemporary frame, 16-3/4" h, 18-1/2" w... 1,210.00

"Mary Elizabeth Pearson Toddington, Jany," alphabet, fruit tree, birds and small animals, repainted frame, edge damage, 9-1/4" x 12-3/4" 247.50

"Catherine W. samplered," ABCs, house with fence, birds and trees, on homespun linen, grained frame with damage, 15-1/4" h, 12-1/4" w 1,045.00

"Catherine Walton, Born July 5, 1784, Wrought This Sampler," alphabets and geometric bands, bird on flowering tree, verse, geometric vining floral and sawtooth borders, unframed, toning, fading, small losses, 21" h, 21-1/2" w... 1,495.00

Adam and Eve

Alphabets, numbers, verse, angels flank tree with birds, urn of lowers, large house, early frame, stains, small holes, 16" h, 10" w.............. 1,045.00

Serpent and tree, house, ship, geese, other animals, verse and name, silk on linen, vining floral border, green, brown, gray, pink and black, framed, stains, some color bleeding, 19-1/4" h, 24" w........2,310.00

Alphabet, blue line border, vine divider, tan, red, teal and blue, silk on cotton homespun, unframed, small repairs, stains, frayed edges, 7-1/4" h, 10-1/2" w 165.00

Scales

Background: Prior to 1900, the simple balance scale was commonly used for measuring weights. Since then, scales have become more sophisticated in design and increasingly more accurate.

Reference: Bill and Jan Berning, *Scales*, Schiffer Publishing, 1999.

Collectors' Club: International Society of Antique Scale Collectors, 300 W. Adams, Suite 821, Chicago, IL 60606.

Balance, "V.W. Brinckerhoff, New York," cast iron, scroll designs on front and back of base, VWB monogram in

Encased balance scale, New England, 19th C., 18" h, 12-1/2" w, $1,265. (Photo courtesy of Skinner Auctioneers & Appraisers of Antiques & Fine Arts, Boston and Bolton, Mass.)

center, 2 6-1/4" dia brass pans, rust, minor pitting to iron, some corrosion to pans, 7-1/4" h, 14-3/4" w 85.00

Encased balance, New England, 19th C, brass pans suspended from painted tin arm, two paper-and-ink registers, glazed case of red grain-painted pine, one door at base, salmon interior, 18" h, 12-1/2" w 1,265.00

Hand-held

    Brass and iron, tole case, late 18th/early 19th C 49.50

    Brass and iron, uncased, late 18th/early 19th C 27.50

Hanging, wrought iron, brass trim above arm hooks, engraved initials and "1849," minor damage, 13" h, 19-3/4" w 55.00

Spring

    Fray's Improved Spring Balance, brass and iron, 48 lb, 14-3/8" l 30.00

    Penn Scale Mfg. Co., brass and iron, 100 lb., 17-1/2" l, wear 35.00

    Morton & Bremner, iron, brass face, 24 lb., 9-1/4" dia round tin pan, 11" l 35.00

Tabletop, Universal Family Scale, brass and iron, 24 lb., round brass dial, 1865 patent date, black with red and gold striping, floral decals on sides, round tray on top, wear, 8-3/4" h, 6-1/2" w, 9-1/4" d 40.00

Scherenschnitte

Background: Scherenschnitte is the art of decorative paper cutting. Unlike silhouettes, this form involves more elaborate full-sized scenes, including landscapes. In addition to pictures, the term also includes decorative elements that may be part of a larger work.

Birth record, latticework border with leaves and tulips on top and bottom, "Jannes Stratingh, Ge Boren Den 4 October, 1812," two other names, leaf dividers, early mahogany veneer frame, margin stains, 16-5/8" h, 21" w 1,320.00

Decorative tree and 4 birds, lined school paper on green backing, old carved frame with note "Pa. Dutch Cutout, Lancaster County," 4-3/4" h, 2-3/4" w 467.50

Secretaries

Background: Also referred to as a desk and bookcase, a secretary consists of a desk with drawers or doors beneath the writing surface and a bookcase on top. Personal papers were frequently stored in the cabinet portion. Around the turn of the 20th century, some secretaries were made with the bookcase section beside the desk rather than on top.

References: Eileen and Richard Dubrow, *Styles of American Furniture 1860-1960*, Schiffer Publishing, 1997; Tim Forrest, *Bulfinch Anatomy of Antique Furniture*, Bulfinch Press, 1996; John T. Kirk, *American Furniture: Understanding Styles, Construction, and Quality*, Harry N. Abrams Publishers, 2000; Milo M. Naeve, *Identifying American Furniture*, W.W. Norton, 1998; Ellen T. Schroy, *Warman's American Furniture*, Krause Publications, 2001; Robert W. and Harriet Swedberg, *Collector's Encyclopedia of American Furniture*, Vol. 1 (1990, 1996 value update), Vol. 2 (1992, 1999 value update), Vol. 3 (1998), Collector Books; —, *Encyclopedia of American Oak Furniture*, Krause Publications, 2000.

Also see: Desks

Chippendale, slant-front

    Cherry, dark varnish stain finish, dovetailed case, ogee feet and scalloped drop, four dovetailed drawers with replaced brasses, seven interior drawers with old brass pulls, center compartment with door and eight pigeonholes, bonnet top with reeded mullions, two interior shelves and replaced finials, cut-down top, bonnet top and feet are old replacements, lid repair, edge damage, 80" h, 38-1/2" w, 21" d 2,750.00

    Cherry, southeastern New England, c. 1780, top section with flat molded cornice, two cupboard doors with recessed panels set into lower section, slant lid with fitter interior, over four drawers, bracket feet, old brasses, refinished, restored, 82" h, 40-1/4" w, 18" d 2,760.00

    Country style, two-pc, butternut, old dark red finish, dovetailed bracket feet, dovetailed case, four dovetailed drawers with cockbeading, fitted interior of five drawers, one hidden drawer and eight pigeonholes, top has two doors with inset panels and scalloped crests over two drawers, H hinges on side of case (two replaced), nailed repairs to feet, brasses replaced, scrolled brackets on pigeonholes replaced, found in Vermont, 78-1/2" h, 37-1/4" w 11,550.00

Curly maple and bird's-eye maple, two-pc, bracket feet with scrolled returns, inlaid fan on front apron, paneled ends, two raised-panel doors over two drawers in top, base with desk over three drawers, canted cornice, reconstruction, 94" h, 43" w, 20" d 2,310.00

Federal secretary, mahogany flame birch and bird's-eye maple veneer, Spooner & Fitts, Athol, Mass., c. 1810, old replaced brasses, old refinish, 61" h, 39" w, $17,250. (Photo courtesy of Skinner Auctioneers & Appraisers of Antiques & Fine Arts, Boston and Bolton, Mass.)

Federal

    Cherry, New England, c. 1800-10, flat molded cornice over two doors with recessed panels, interior of four drawers and five valanced compartments, the projecting lower section with fold-out writing surface and case of three graduated drawers with incised beading, flaring French feet, inlaid shaped apron, replaced brasses, old finish, imperfections, 55" h, 42" w, 22" d 1,840.00

    Mahogany flame birch and bird's-eye maple veneer, Spooner & Fitts, Athol, Mass. (1808-1813), c. 1810, the upper portion having two doors with flame birch veneer ovals and patterned stringing over bird's-eye maple veneered drawers outlined in cross-banded mahogany veneer and patterned stringing, the lower portion having a foldout felt-lined writing surface above three drawers flanked by icicle inlays, cyma-curved skirt with central oval flame birch veneer drop, ring-turned tapering legs, small ball feet, old replaced brasses, old refinish, minor imperfections, 61" h, 39" w, 20-1/2" d 17,250.00

Sheraton, mahogany, two eight-pane doors over fold-over writing surface over three graduated drawers, upper doors with arched upper panes, interior with shelves, drawers and pigeonholes, broken-arch pediment, shaped apron, well-turned legs, 72" h, 39" w, 18" d 3,575.00

Painted, New England, early 19th C., cove-molded cornice over two blind doors over a lower case with a hinged lid opening to a desk interior over 2 blind doors, old dark-red paint outside, old mustard paint interior, imperfections, 84-1/2" h, 48" w, 14-3/8" d........................ 1,380.00

Servers

Background: Also called a serving table, a server is a plain side table used in the dining room for the service of meals.

Federal, mahogany and mahogany veneer, probably Boston, c. 1815-20, overhanging top with elliptical front, square corners, beaded edge, conforming case of three short cockbeaded drawers, beaded skirt, vase-and-ring turned reeded legs, turned feet, old finish, orig brass ring pulls, minor imperfections, 37" h, 48" w, 22" d 47,150.00

Queen Anne, curly maple, crackled finish, high tapered legs, shaped apron, one drawer, bat-wing brasses and lock escutcheon, two-board tray top, "David T. Smith, Morrow, Ohio" reproduction, 36" h, 28-1/2" w, 16-1/4" d 1,375.00

Settees

Background: A settee is a seat for two or more people, and has a back and arms. Very few upholstered settees were made in America until the Chippendale period, with production increasing during the Hepplewhite period and succeeding styles. The chief difference between an upholstered settee and a sofa is that the sofa is generally larger with an over-stuffed appearance.

Decorated

    Floral decor in white on green ground, yellow stripes, half-spindle back, shaped crest, plank seat... 935.00

    Rosewood-like painted ground, gold stenciled compotes of fruit and leafage, crest above triple back, scrolled arms, seat rail with scrolled drop pendants, tapering legs and stretchers, New York, c. 1815-25, old surface, 35-1/2" h, 76-3/4" l.....................920.00

Federal, painted

    Brown grain-painted surface with gilt decor, crest rails decor with anthemia, acanthus leaves and scrolled vines, five horizontal spindles separated by spherules joining five raked thumb-back stiles to the scrolled arms on faceted conical supports, painted rush seat, half-rounded seat rail, twelve vase-and-ring turned legs, square stretchers sep-

Windsor bamboo-turned settee, New England, c. 1810, old refinish, restored, 75-1/8" l, $5,175. (Photo courtesy of Skinner Auctioneers & Appraisers of Antiques & Fine Arts, Boston and Bolton, Mass.)

arated by spherules, probably Mass., c. 1815-25, 33-1/2" h, 76" w, 19-1/2" d 13,800.00

Orig brown paint with gilt and red highlighting, tablet crests above spindles with medallions and urn shapes, rush seat, arms with similar design elements, turned legs with medallions on front stretchers, painted, New England, c. 1810-20, imperfections, 33" h, 70" w, 16" d 2,070.00

Windsor

Bamboo-turned, ash, pine and maple, straight crest rail with bowed ends, twenty-five spindles, slightly scrolled arms, shaped seat, eight legs joined by stretchers, New England, c. 1810, old refinish, restored, 35-1/8" h, 75-1/8" l 5,175.00

Shaped back, six turned legs, turned stretchers, arms and spindles, 76" l 4,125.00

Bamboo-turned, maple and pine, New England, c. 1810, straight crest rail with bowed ends above three shaped panels and parallel rail, twenty-one spindles, four stiles, flanking arms, shaped seat, eight splayed legs joined by stretchers, old refinish, imperfections, 33" h, 78" l 3,220.00

Settles

Background: One of the earliest forms of seating for two more people, the settle usually had a high paneled back with paneled arms and sides. Generally, the seat was hinged to provide access to a chest-like area below the seat.

Child's, pine, old comb-grained repaint, mortised, rose-head nails, small worn feet, arched aprons, inset panels in base surrounded by molded trim, sideboards shaped for arms, lift-lid seat with compartment beneath, three inset panels in back, edge wear, one hinge damaged, 37-1/2" h, 36" w, 14" d 2,475.00

Decorated

Birds and fruit across back panels in red, blue, green and tan, yellow borders, orig paint, ring-turned legs and stretchers, plank seat, scrolled arms, three-section back, turned half spindles, scalloped crest, Pa. origin, wear, arm repairs, 35" h, 73" w, 24" d 1,210.00

Green vining and blue-and-white flowers on crest, old yellow repaint, eight-spindle back, turned legs, stretcher base, plank seat, shaped arms with scrolled ends and ring-turned supports, reglued joints, back stretcher broken, 31" h 660.00

Yellow angel wings and fruit on crest, orig freehand and stenciled decor, worn, stretcher base, turned front legs, plank seat, three-section back, single slats and half-turned spindles, scalloped crest, one end stretcher replaced, temporary wire supports added to base, crack at back corner of seat, 34-1/2" h, 70-1/2" w, 22-1/2" d 1,017.50

Miniature, old green repaint with gold and black floral decor and striping, turned legs, stretcher base, plank seat with rolled front edge, scrolled arms, slat back, scalloped crest with floral detail, arm repair, 16-3/8" h, 26" w, 10" d 935.00

Sewer Tile

Background: Also called sewer pipe, sewer tile was produced from about 1880 through the early 20th century. Draining tiles and sewer tiles were produced at the factories, but the workers often spent their spare time creating other items of utilitarian or whimsical nature. Although some molded pieces were made, much of the production was one-of-a-kind items. Pieces that are signed and/or dated are especially prized.

Ohio is recognized as the leading producer of sewer tile, but other states, including New York, Pennsylvania, and Indiana, all had a strong presence in the sewer tile market.

Alligator, Ohio, 15" l 440.00

Bank, dog, seated Spaniel, slot in back of head, round opening on bottom, minor glaze flakes, probably Tuscarawas County, Ohio, 10-1/2" h 220.00

Bust, Abraham Lincoln, shiny glaze, flowing black on jacket, incised eyes, minor edge damage, 7-1/8" h 110.00

Cat, seated, glaze with copper speckles, small chips, one front foot missing, 7" h 330.00

Chicken feeder, cylindrical, incised tree trunk decor, applied handle over top, opening on one side of base, 10-1/2" h 220.00

Crow on stump, initialed "E.J.E" on base, shallow chip on tail feathers, 9" h, 14" l 990.00

Dog, seated, Spaniel

5-1/2" h, minor edge chips 192.50

7" h, bottom incised "Chas. Domino, C.D.," molded, tooled, foot repair 192.50

7-1/2" h, base incised "E.J.E." (Tuscarawas County, Ohio) 330.00

8-1/4" h, incised detail up the back, over the head and down the front leg, incised collar and chain, deep-brownish red glaze, oval base, minor base chips 275.00

10" h, light-brown glaze, black eyes and collar, incised detail on open front legs, made by George Bagnell, Newcomerstown, Ohio, glued crack on front, base chips 1,540.00

Sewer tile frog doorstop, $100.

10-1/4" h, bottom incised "Superior, 10-15-70" (Superior Clay Corp, Tuscarawas County, Ohio), few firing separations, shallow chip on back of base 247.50
10-1/2" h, light-brown glaze 330.00
11-1/2" h, minor wear, few flakes 165.00
Fish plaque, probably Ohio, 10-1/2" l 357.50
Lion, reclining, rectangular base
Base, base initialed "EJE" (Tuscarawas County, Ohio, maker), 6" h, 8-3/4" l 550.00
Base with reeded edges, unglazed red clay, incised "4-22 34, W E, Wadsworth, O." 5-1/4" h, 8-3/8" w, 4-1/8" d 275.00
Owl, perched
On log, 20th C, 8-1/2" h 165.00
On tree stump, 12-3/4" h 550.00
Planter
Mortar shape, incised "Made by Donald Milby, June 16, 1958 at Perrless Clay," 9-1/2" h, 10" dia 82.50
Rectangular, raised feet and corners, mkd "Cambria Clay Products, Plackfork, Ohio," 1 foot restored, 12" h, 14-1/2" w, 10-1/4" d, pr 192.50
Triangular base, cast lion's heads and leaves, edge chips, cracks, 23" h 192.50
Planter, stump
17" h, 4 stumps rising from one base, chips, glued restoration 220.00
17" h, 10" dia, four branches 330.00
17-1/2" h, 10" dia, two branches with Minerva heads, edge damage, cement patch 110.00
19" h, 9-3/4" dia, hand-tooled bark, five molded and applied ducks (one resembles woodpecker), mkd "Milburn Larson Clay," damaged branches 467.50
24-1/2" h, 14-1/2" dia, molded and hand-tooled bark, incised "Margaret H. Dryden, Born Aug. 22, 1890, Died Nov. 23, 1942," minor edge damage 247.50
26" h, 9" dia, hand-tooled bark, three branches 220.00
28-3/4" h, 18" dia, hand-tooled bark, three branches, one damaged 385.00
Umbrella stand, tree trunk design, applied roses, chips on flowers, 25-1/2" h 330.00
Wall pocket, tree trunk design, small cut limbs, 9" h, 6-1/4" w 143.00

Sewing

Background: During the 19th century, sewing was a learned skill required of all girls. Even as late as the mid-20th century, sewing was a necessary activity for many American families, helping them stay clothed at a reasonable cost. All manner of objects have made the task of sewing simpler and more pleasant over the years.

References: Elizabeth Arbittier et al., *Collecting Figural Tape Measures*, Schiffer Publishing, 1995; Lori Hughes, *A Century of American Sewing Patterns 1860-1959*, C&B Press, 1998; Bridget McConnel, *The Story of Antique Needlework Tools*, Schiffer Publishing, 1999; Glenda Thomas, *Toy and Miniature Sewing Machines, Book I* (1995), *Book II* (1997), Collector Books.

Periodicals: *That Darn Newsletter*, 461 Brown Briar Circle, Horsham, PA 19044; *Thimbletter*, 93 Walnut Hill Rd., Newton Highlands, MA 02161.

Collectors' Clubs: International Sewing Machine Collectors Society, 551 Kelmore St., Moss Beach, CA 94038, http://ismacs.net; Thimble Collectors International, 8289 Northgate Dr., Rome, NY 13440-1941; ThimbleGuild, P.O. Box 381807, Duncanville, TX 75138-1807.

Museums: Antique Sewing Machine Museum, Oakland, CA; Museum of American History, Smithsonian Institution, Washington, DC; Shelburne Museum, Shelburne, VT.

Reproduction Alert: Reproductions of Victorian and Georgian sterling thimbles and needle cases are relatively common. Many are marked "Thailand."

Basket, coiled rye straw, round with flat bottom, slightly rounded flared sides having woven openwork band, interior lined with fabric with matching pincushion attached to rim, 4" section of rim missing to accommodate pincushion, 19th C, 3-1/2" h, 10-1/8" dia 130.00
Box
Carved and painted, three-tier rectangular box, carved and pierced scalloped border at top, glass beads, carved spire finials, pierced diamond and scallop motifs, drawer below, dark-blue, red and yellow, probably Pa., one carved spine missing, minor paint loss, 7" h, 7-1/2" w, 5-1/4" d 747.50

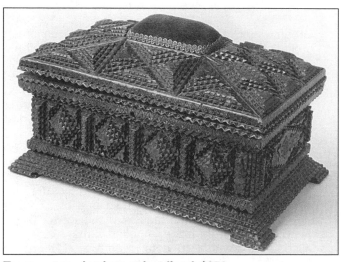

Tramp art sewing box, velvet-lined, $250.

Decor, floral and fruit bouquet stenciled in gilt and brown, floral vine border, mustard ground, brass escutcheon with raised shell motif, molded brass feet, fitted interior with lift-out tray, possibly Baltimore, early 19th C., 5-1/2" h, 10" w, 7-3/4" d 1,150.00

Decor, orig stenciling in flower and leaf design, green borders with silver and gold stars, red lines, smoke ground, pine, sliding lid, brass pull, pencil inscription "Mary Houghton Stowe who was born in Hubbardstone, Mass. in 1808," ball feet, Mass., minor wear, 4-1/4" h, 9" w, 6" d 5,225.00

Mahogany veneer with inlay, turned ball feet, two dovetailed drawers with string inlay, top of case with banded inlay and pincushion, back fitted with wooden thumb screw for clamping to a table's edge, replaced feet, veneer damage, 1 pull missing, with family provenance, 5-1/2" h, 4-1/2" w, 3" d 275.00

Shell art, fitted interior with mirror in lid 55.00

Step-down, hex symbols on end panels, old mustard repaint, red border, beveled base, two upper drawers, three lower drawers (two stacked beside one), velvet pincushion on top a later addition, holes in back and bottom panels, 6-1/2" h, 10-5/8" w, 10-1/2" d 220.00

Caddy

Maple and softwood, square base with one drawer, tapered round shaft holds octagonal holder for four spools, round stuffed pincushion in black fabric, 9-1/2" h, 4-1/4" w, 4-1/2" d 90.00

Walnut, curved sides, purple velvet stuffed pincushion, one drawer, with burl veneer face, turnip-shaped feet, bottom molding incomplete, 6-3/8" h, 8-1/2" w, 6" d 200.00

Chair, ladderback, hardwood, old red paint, short turned legs and stretcher, three slats, turned finials, replaced tape seat in blue and ecru, 31-3/4" h 170.50

Chest, miniature, grain decor, early repainted black over light bran with tan line detail, pine, scalloped bracket feet, aprons, applied base molding, two drawers at bottom, two small false drawers at top, hinged lid, divided interior painted red, glued repairs on feet, one foot ended out, 11-3/4" h, 10" w, 9-1/4" d 605.00

Clamp, hemming (all are American, 19th C)

American shield colored red and blue, carved ivory, carved ivory star thumbscrew, chip, 4-1/2" h 690.00

Decor with two contrasting ivory triangles and polka dots, carved ivory and baleen, turned wooden screw, age cracks, 5-3/4" h 632.50

Decor with three applied ivory diamond motifs, carved ivory and bone, chip-carved edge decor, iron screw, hairline, 4" w, 2-1/2" l 575.00

Dolphin motif, carved ivory and bone, ivory dolphin figure with baleen eyes, whalebone C-clamp and thumbscrew, minor age cracks, 8" h 2,990.00

Hand clenching a hook, bronze, bronze table clamp and thumbscrew, 3-3/4" h 575.00

Whale figure atop clamp, carved ivory, ivory disk thumbscrew, cracks 805.00

Clamp, sewing (all are American, 19th C)

Birdbath motif, carved ivory, carved and incised crested bird on oval platform, carved edge, pierced heart motif below, brass thumbscrew, cracks, 4-3/4" h 977.50

D-shaped, cast iron, heart-shaped thumbscrew, wear, 7" h 143.75

Hand, carved ivory, closed-fist handscrew, clamp body decor with incised leaf and stippled tulip motifs, heart-shaped metal thumbscrew, age cracks, 5-1/4" h 1,495.00

Horse head with studded brass eyes and wire-twist reins, carved ivory and horn, carved horn clip, clamp body decor with pierced star, heart-shaped thumbscrew, minor age cracks, 4-1/2" h 805.00

Screw top depicts man's head wearing Civil War period cap, carved ivory, teeth-shaped clamp, incised heart motif, ivory thumbscrew, age cracks 690.00

Clamp, spool and cutter version, ivory and abalone, turned ivory finials, two metal cutting blades flanked by two whalebone spool holders, diamond-shaped abalone inlay on carved ivory clamp, iron thumbscrew, cracks, 3-1/2" h 632.50

Flange sign, porcelain, "Ladies' Home Journal Patterns," white on red, cond. 8, 7-1/2" h, 18" w 385.00

Pincushion, cloth

Ball, cotton, hand-sewn pieced and sectioned fabric, red, yellow and browns, 2-1/2" dia 100.00

Ball, cotton, hand-sewn pieced printed fabric, alternating designs of triangular and square pieces of printed cotton in red, white, blue and green trimmed with yellow border, fabric loop, minor wear, 2-3/8" dia 650.00

Ball, wool, hand-sewn pieced fabric, alternating designs of small triangles and squares in red, brown, green and yellow, narrow white border, black and green fabric loop, some wear, 2-1/4" dia 500.00

Dog, brown and white floral print fabric, glass bead eyes, red stitched mouth and nose, brown fabric ears, minor wear and soiling, 4-1/8" h, 4-1/4" w 30.00

Dog, velvet, black and brown, stitched features, minor wear, 3-3/4" h, 4-1/2" l 250.00

Pincushion, ivory, carved

Round foot, pedestal base with barrel-like top, rounded red velvet cushions on either end, 1-5/8" h, 1-5/8" w 40.00

Vegetable ivory, round foot, pedestal base, scalloped edge, threaded shaft, flattened globular top in round green worn fabric, 3-5/8" h, base 1-1/4" dia 230.00

Pincushion box, wallpaper-covered, cylindrical, padded green silk covered top, cardboard sides, 19th C, wear, wallpaper loss, 2-1/2" h, 3" dia 460.00

Sewing bird

Cast metal, squared C-clamp, back of bird with velvet pincushion, 4-3/4" h, 3-3/4" l 250.00

Wrought iron and brass, squared C-clamp with brass vertical bar, iron bird, wing nut with heart cutout, 4" h, 3" l 370.00

Spool caddy

Cherry, metal posts, worn pincushion top, mkd "Hand turned by J.C.B. (Brown) Painesville, O. 1954, Cherry sewing box," (Brown acquired Pease's tools and equipment), 7" h 165.00

Wooden, turned, old dark repaint over earlier red, three tiers with wire pins, several pins missing, 10-1/4" h 247.50

Wooden, turned base, column and posts supporting two tiers for spools, dovetailed drawer in base, ivory pull, edge damage, finial missing, top tier split, 11-1/2" h, 6-1/4" dia............................ 275.00

Spool holder, rectangular with arched handle with hanging hole, fitted for twelve dowels (four rows of three dowels) for holding spools, painted green over red, three dowels missing, one broken, 10-7/8" h, 5-1/8" w.............. 240.00

Spool winder, carved ivory, American

6" h, 19th C 517.50

6-1/2" h, 19th C, triple spool holder with ivory finials, scored heart-shaped thumbscrew, age cracks 805.00

Stand, Sheraton

Two-drawer, mahogany and mahogany veneer, well-turned and tapered legs with ring-turned tops and biscuit corners, dovetailed drawers with beaded edges, turned pulls, top drawer with divided compartment, one-board top, old ink label with some provenance in drawer, refinished, 29" h, top 17-3/4" x 18" 1,980.00

Two-drawer, bird's-eye maple, drop-leaf, rope-carved and turned legs, dovetailed drawers with beaded edges, pull-out bag frame, refinished,

Paint-decorated folk art sewing stand, orange wash with yellow and black striping, name and "May 28, 1892," 13-1/2" h, 8-1/2" dia, $4,025. (Photo courtesy of Skinner Auctioneers & Appraisers of Antiques & Fine Arts, Boston and Bolton, Mass.)

replaced wooden pulls, age crack, 28-1/2" h, top 16-1/4" x 18-1/2", leaves 7-1/2".............. 1,265.00

Five-drawer, country style, drop-leaf, curly maple with bird's-eye veneer, refinished, turned legs, half-turned pilasters on front, two short over two short over one long dovetailed drawers, wooden pulls, drop leaf with scalloped corners on back side, two L brackets added under top, 30-1/3" h, 25-1/4" w, 16-1/2" d, leaf 11-3/4" 5,060.00

Yarn winder, harvest table model, 2-pc, old red paint on winder, black on base, pegged shoe feet, 21" h... 275.00

Shaker (Religious Sect)

Background: In 1774, Ann Lee founded the religious sect known as the Shakers, so named because of their tendency to shake during their lively prayer services. The first settlement was near Albany, New York, with nine other settlements established by 1880. Shaker workmanship mirrored the group's religious beliefs, resulting in items with clean lines and simple designs devoid of decoration. Examples of Shaker craftsmanship are prized among collectors.

References: Edward Deming Andrews and Faith Andrews, *Masterpieces of Shaker Furniture*, Dover Publications, 1999; Christian Becksvoort, *The Shaker Legacy: Perspectives on an Enduring Furniture Style*, The Tauton Press, 1998; John T. Kirk, *The Shaker World: Art, Life, Belief*, Harry N. Abrams, 1997; Charles R. Muller and Timothy D. Rieman, *The Shaker Chair*, Canal Press, 1984; June Sprigg and Jim Johnson, *Shaker Woodenware*, Berkshire House, 1991; Timothy D. Rieman and Jean M. Burks, *Complete Book of Shaker Furniture*, Harry N. Abrams, 1993.

Museums: Canterbury Shaker Village, Canterbury, NH; Hancock Shaker Village, Pittsfield, MA; Shaker Historical Museum, Cleveland, OH; Shaker Museum and Library, Old Chatham, NY; Shaker Museum at South Union, South Union, KY; Shaker Village of Pleasant Hill, Harrodsburg, KY.

FYI: In some cases it is possible to determine the Shaker community in which a chair was made by the design of the finials on the back posts. Additionally, Shaker chairs were designed to be light so they could be moved easily and hung on peg rails.

Basket

Berry, woven splint, large "AP" on sides in black paint, square with flat bottom, sides flare to rounded rim, iron tacks, 4" h, 3-3/4" dia 75.00

Cheese, woven splint, 23" dia 247.50

Splint, round, painted light green-blue, shaped looped handles, 5-1/2" h, 14-1/2" dia 2,990.00

Bed steps, old red paint, arched cutout feet 2,200.00
Bench, pine, natural brown finish, legs with arched cut-outs, aprons beveled along bottom edge, pencil inscription "Owned by Daniel Beal, Shaker of Enfield," signed "Mason Foley, 1954," wear 302.50
Bonnet box, cylindrical
  One-finger, gray paint, ash and pine, bail handle, lid repaired, 8-1/4" h, 10-1/4" dia 230.00
  One-finger, red paint, ash and pine, bail handle, age splits, losses at bottom, wear, 8" h, 10-1/2" dia 488.75
Box, oval, bentwood, lidded
  One-finger, 4-3/4" l, worn green paint, copper tacks, C. Hersey type 577.50
  One-finger, 6-1/4" l, 2-5/8" h, mustard paint with slightly darkened over-varnish, copper tacks, minor wear 220.00
  Two-finger, cleaned to old patina, copper tacks, minor damage, age cracks 275.00
  Two-finger, 5-1/4" l, 2-1/4" h, dark patina on lid, traces of red at fingers, copper tacks 275.00
  Two-finger, 5-1/2" l, 2" h, orig mustard paint, copper tacks, small split at tack in lid 4,070.00
  Two-finger, 5-7/8" l, worn varnish finish, copper tacks, edge damage 275.00
  Two-finger, 6-1/4" l, 2" h, chrome-yellow paint, maple and pine 2,645.00
  Two-finger, 9" l, cleaned to worn natural patina, copper tacks, edge damage 330.00
  Three-finger, 7-3/4" l, 2-7/8" h, scrubbed finish, copper tacks 330.00
  Three-finger, 11-3/8" l, 4-3/4" h, old finish, copper tacks 478.50
  Three-finger, 12" l, 9" w, 4-3/4" h, blue over green paint, wear 440.00
  Three-finger, 12" l, 4-3/4" h, green, maple and pine, cracks 862.50
  Four-finger, 8-5/8" l, 4-7/8" h, blue paint, splitting, wear 2,185.00
  Four-finger, 12-1/2" l, 9-1/2" w, 5-1/4" h, gray paint, wear 605.00
Brush, turned wooden handle, round head, 8" l 104.50
Bucket
  Child's, two-color wood, 4-1/2" h 192.50

Painted, dark-green, covered, stave and metal bands, bail handle, lid cracked, 15-1/2" h, 17" dia 920.00
Butter mold, rectanglar, two-pc, "Canterbury NH Shakers" in three lines, maple and brass, 6" w 1,955.00
Carrier, bentwood, two-finger
  Oval, blue paint, maple and pine, ash handle, 7-1/2" h, 11-1/4" l 1,035.00
  Round, copper tacks, two splits, 2-1/4" h (excluding bentwood handle), 5-1/4" dia 330.00
Chair
  No. 4 low-back dining chair, Mount Lebanon, N.Y., old dark-brown varnished stain, ball finials, two horizontal turned spindles, mkd with decal, 38" h 517.50
  Side chair, Watervliet, N.Y., c. 1850, maple stain, arched slats, taped seat, turned legs and double stretchers, rear tilters refinished, minor imperfections, 41" h................ 920.00
Churn, box-shaped on stand, blue paint, pine, turned handle at side, 38" h, 8" w, 19" l........................ 402.50
Clothing, Sister's robe, Canterbury, cobalt wool broadcloth, made by Hart & Shepard..................... 1,150.00
Cupboard, poplar, old light-gray paint, Mt. Lebanon N.Y., c. 1850-60, two drawers over two recessed-panel doors, arched base, 73" h, 36-3/4" w............ 2,760.00
Cupboard and case of drawers, Mt. Lebanon N.Y., c. 1830-40, thin molded cornice, door with recessed panels over three drawers, flat base, old brown paint, restored, 62-3/4" h, 24-3/4" w, 12" d 2,300.00

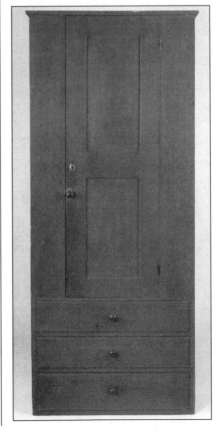

Shaker cupboard and case of drawers, Mt. Lebanon N.Y., c. 1830-40, old brown paint, restored, 62-3/4" h, 24-3/4" w, $2,300. (Photo courtesy of Skinner Auctioneers & Appraisers of

Desk on stand, maple and pine, Watervliet, N.Y., slant-lid, arched tapered skirt, drawer on one end, ink bottle drawer on other end, turned legs, 28-1/2" h.. 3,335.00

Duster, turned maple handle, one black, one natural, multicolor dyed woolen heads, 10" l, pr 86.25

Dustpan, sheet metal, turned handle with scribe lines and knob end, 7-3/8" w, 15-1/2" l 920.00

Foot bench, No. 0, Mount Lebanon, N.Y., c. 1875, maple, square top on slanted stool, turned legs, dark-brown varnish, decal, 6-1/2" h, 11-1/2" sq......... 230.00

Footstool, No. 1, Mount Lebanon, N.Y., maple, old brown stain, tape seat, turned stretchers and posts, mkd with label, 9-1/2" h, 12-3/4" w, 9-1/2" d..................... 488.75

Gathering box, pumpkin-color wash, iron handle, 18" l.. 7,015.00

Harness rack, 6 tapering pegs on rectangular board, orig blue paint, 4-1/2" h, 62" l................................. 1,150.00

Herb sieve, 60-mesh screen, initialed "D.H.," 11" dia 1,610.00

Pail, blue paint with black trim, turned maple, with ears, brass bail, brass disk with "43" on base, 8-1/2" dia... 1,380.00

Rocking chair
    No. 1, armed, Mount Lebanon, N.Y., old brown varnished stain, taped back and seat, acorn finials, double stretchers, mkd with decal, minor imperfections, 28" h.. 575.00
    No. 3, Mount Lebanon, N.Y., thin orig reddish-brown finish, small tapered finials, label on runner, replaced burgundy and white taped seat, 35-1/4" h 192.50
    No. 3, armed, Mount Lebanon, N.Y., old brown stain, taped backrest, acorn finials, decal, 33-1/2" h 488.75
    No. 5, armed, Mount Lebanon, N.Y., worn orig finish, stenciled label, old replacement woven tape seat and back in blue and ivory, 37-3/4" h.......... 715.00
    No. 7, Mount Lebanon, N.Y., old finish, acorn finials, taped back and seat, imperfections, 42" h 575.00
    Canterbury, N.H., c. 1840, early black paint, arched splats with beveled top edges, turned tapering arm supports, old taped seat, minor repairs, 45-1/4" h 2,185.00

Rug, shirred, concentric circles of blue, burgundy and polychrome, hole, 41-1/2" dia 137.50

Seed chest, Hancock Mass., six-drawer (three rows of two), cherry and pine, 33" h 2,587.50

Sewing box, oval, three-finger
    8-1/2" l, hardwood and pine, copper tacks, lid, swivel bentwood handle, interior lined with old blue brocade, two accessories, ... 275.00
    9-1/2" l, 3-1/2" w, swing handle, interior lined with blue silk, fitted with straw pin keep and needle book, a fabric pincushion, emery and wax block 690.00

Sewing desk, Canterbury N.H., c. 1860s, butternut and chestnut, gallery divided into thirds with door flanked by three drawers per side, base with four drawers on the

Shaker sewing desk, Canterbury N.H., c. 1860s, butternut and chestnut, refinished, 38-1/4" h, 29" w, $17,250. (Photo courtesy of Skinner Auctioneers & Appraisers of Antiques & Fine Arts, Boston and Bolton, Mass.)

right side, a sliding work surface over two recessed horizontal panels beside a door, left side with two horizontal recessed panels, turned tapering legs, refinished, 38-1/4" h, 29" w, 24" d..................................17,250.00

Spools, turned
    Triple-spool, 3-1/2" l (longest), set of three 2,070.00
    Yellow paint, 1-1/16" l (longest), set of four 3,450.00

Stand
    Tray-top, Canterbury, cherry and butternut, turned legs, top 17-3/4" x 28-3/8" 16,675.00
    Canterbury, cherry and birch, 1-drawer, turned legs, top 29" w, 19" d.................................. 40,250.00

Washtub, round, blue paint, pine, staved and wooden rings, two extended handles with half-circle cutouts, 21-1/2" h, 27-1/2" dia 2,185.00

Winder, tabletop, Hancock Mass., 19th C, contrasting light and dark wood tones, 12-1/2" l.................. 431.25

Work table, cherry and pine, New Lebanon, N.Y., overhanging pine top, breadboard ends, one drawer, turned tapering legs, leg boots, old surface, 30-3/4" h, 58" w, 27-3/4" d... 3,335.00

Shaving Mugs

Background: Shaving mugs were used to hold the soap, brush, and hot water used to prepare a beard for shaving. Personalized mugs were made exclusively for use in barbershops in the United States. Introduced shortly after the Civil War, they were still being made into the 1930s. Unlike shaving mugs used at home, these mugs typically had the owner's name in gilt. The mug was kept in a rack at the barbershop, and it was used only when the owner came in for a shave. Occupational shaving mugs, which have a hand-painted scene depicting the owner's line of work, are especially prized.

References: Ronald S. Barlow, *Vanishing American Barber Shop*, Windmill Publishing, 1993; Keith E. Estep, *The Best of Shaving Mugs*, Schiffer Publishing, 2001; —, *Shaving Mug and Barber Bottle Book*, Schiffer Publishing, 1995.

Collectors' Club: National Shaving Mug Collectors Assoc., 1608 Mineral Spring Rd., Reading, PA 19602-2229.

Museums: Atwater Kent History Museum, Philadelphia, PA; Barber Museum, Canal Winchester, OH; Lightner Museum, Saint Augustine, FL.

Note: All listings are hand-painted.

Farmer, Lancaster County, Pa., farmer plowing behind two horses, farmhouse in background, name above, Anchor Pottery logo and "G.B.S. Co." on base, cond. EXC, 3-1/2" h 1,540.00

Finish carpenter, man planing a board, name above, floral sprigs on sides, handle crack, 3-3/4" h 357.50

Fireman, men on horse-drawn hook and ladder wagon, considerable wear to gold lettering, "H&Co." stamp on base, 3-3/4" h 1,540.00

Grinding machine, name above, floral springs beside hand-cranked machine, pink ground, cond. EXC, 3-5/8" h 577.50

Hardware store, owner showing customer a saw, faint traces of gold lettering, "D&C"on base, 4" h 1,072.50.00

Patriotic, flying bald eagle with pole-mounted U.S. flag and sprig of green leaves with red berries clutched in its claws, gilt ribbon across flag with name, wear, 3-1/2" h 220.00

Preztel maker, baker with oversized pretzel, lettering and trim possibly redone, cond. EXC, 3-5/8" h 880.00

Shaving mug with artist's pallet and name "Schalk," $275.

Shelves

Background: Books come to mind when many people think of shelves. Yet, these simple utilitarian structures have been used to hold a variety of household items, from clocks to lighting devices.

Candle shelf, tin, square back with large stamped twelve-pointed star in center surrounded by stamped branding and having two small round holes in top corners, rolled top and sides of back, rectangular tray with low gallery rail across its front with rolled top edge and arched brackets on sides, some rust, 13-7/8" h, 3-5/8" w, 4" d 400.00

Clock shelf, painted
   Old putty repaint, hardwood, one-board back, molded trim, stepped molding, 30" h, 25" w, 6" d 55.00
   Worn orig green, hanging, scalloped shelf and support, rosehead nails, 17" h, 22" w, 7" d 165.00

Comb shelf, carved, two-tier, pine, old dark finish, relief scroll and foliage carvings, star and scrolls on lower pocket, rectangular shelf near top with pierced trim detail, 18-5/8" h, 10-5/8" w 137.50

Hanging
   Chip-carved, walnut, old tan repaint, half-round shelf, half-round back, porcelain buttons for decor, edge damage, hanging holes added, found in Wayne County, Ohio, 10-1/2" h, 17" w 302.50

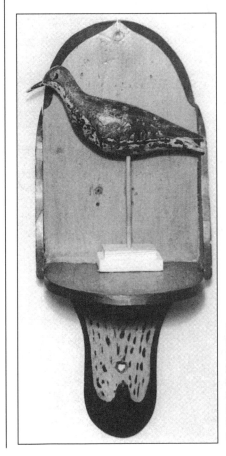

Folk art painted shelf marked "J.B. Copeland, Hapedale, Ohio," 21" h, 8-1/2" w, $1,017.50; plover shore bird, $192.50. (Photo courtesy of Garth's Auctions, Delaware, Ohio)

Curly maple, shaped side brackets support upper shelf and create wall pocket, matte finish a rich honey color, wire-nail construction, 8-1/4" h, 12-3/4" w, shelf 6-3/4" d 550.00

Folk art, old yellow and greenish-yellow paint with black dot decor and trim, chamfered and arched top, 1 bowfront shelf, slender rounded base, "J.B. Copeland, Hapedale, Ohio" scratched into wet paint, 21" h, 8-1/2" w, shelf 7-1/2" d 1,017.50

Pine, old dark finish, scrolled ends, 18-1/2" h, 23-1/4" w 385.00

Pine, worn finish, whale ends, found in Lancaster County, Pa., 30" h, 31" w, 10" d 660.00

Oak and walnut, orig dark finish, elaborate scroll-cut ends with scalloped edge, four graduated shelves, minor hairlines, 39" h, 24" w, 10-1/4" d 302.50

Stained, red, cutout ends, two shelves, scrolled crest, 18-1/2" h, 13-1/4" w, 6" d 467.50

Walnut, old refinish, interior fitted with three shelves, bottom shelf with molded plate rail, molded cornice at top, square nails, 33-1/2" h, 20" w, 9-1/4" d 302.50

Whale end, walnut, old finish, three shelves, dovetailed base with two drawers, 35-3/4" h, 24-1/8" w, 7-3/4" d 2,750.00

Hanging, painted

Old black, walnut, carved eagle with wings spread below shaped shelf, leaf borders, minor crack, 12-1/2" h, 9-3/4" w 275.00

Old worn black, oak, shaped ends, three shelves, 34-1/4" h, 29" w, 6-3/4" d 110.00

Old electric-blue repaint, scalloped end panels with compartment in the middle, notched ends on top shelf, square nails, 14" h, 26" w, 6-1/4" d 440.00

Old green, three shelves, turned supports, octagonal-shaped back, 22" h, 12" w 385.00

Old green in two shades, pine, scalloped ends and crests, shelf over three nailed drawers, 11-1/2" h, 12-1/4" w, 4" d 880.00

Old mustard, walnut, curved ends on top shelf, shorter lower shelf, backboard with scrolled sides, age cracks, old edge damage, 8-3/8" h, 18-3/4" w, 5" d 522.50

Old reddish-brown finish, poplar, country style, two drawers under top, end panels taper towards bottom, turned wooden pulls, 1 drawer chipped, 16" h, 19-1/4" w, 8" d 522.50

Shooting Gallery Figures

Background: Many a person has been coaxed to "step right up" and test their skill by shooting at arcade targets. Popular at fairs and carnivals during the 19th century, most shooting galleries featured cast-iron figures that are now eagerly sought by collectors.

Note: All figures are cast iron unless otherwise noted.

Cast-iron arcade shooting gallery, painted black, green, yellow, orange and red, purportedly from Coney Island, N.Y., 51-1/2" h, 48-1/2" w, $2,530.

Bird, 2-1/2" h, set of three 165.00

Bird in flight and donkey, bird 4-1/2" h on steel base, donkey 6" h excluding wooden base, pr 143.00

Birds and stars, bar with alternating pattern, eight targets, 4-1/4" h, 26" w 429.00

Rooster, mounted together, pr 275.00

Squirrel and duck, cast-iron squirrel with traces of red paint, 7-3/4" l, heavy sheet-steel duck, pitted from use, 6-1/2" l, no bases, pr 154.00

Sideboards

Background: A sideboard is a piece of furniture with drawers and cupboards for dishes, table linens, silver, and other dining needs. It is also called a buffet.

Empire

Cherry, solid curly maple facade, old refinish, three short drawers with rounded fronts over 1 long beveled-edge drawer stepped over two raised-panel doors, shaped cherry backsplash, turned front feet, tapered rear feet, turned pilasters (one loose), age cracks, burl chips, 60-1/2" h, 44" w, 23" d 1,705.00

Mahogany and mahogany veneer, old dark worn finish, paw feet with acanthus leaves at cuffs, central doors with relief-carved fan, four ionic columns across front with raised panel door at each end and drawer above, inset shelf and drawer above fan, minor veneer loss, feet worn, 47" h, 68" w, 24" d 2,310.00

Federal

    Mahogany, inlaid, Providence area, R.I., c. 1790-1825, rectangular top, crossbanded veneer, cockbeaded drawers flank central cupboard, two drawers on left, single deep drawer on right having stringing with ovolo corners, front legs outlined in stringing, cuff inlays, replaced brasses, old refinish, minor imperfections, 39" h, 50" w, 21-1/2" d 20,700.00

    Mahogany and mahogany veneer with inlay, turned and reeded legs, reeded stiles, four doors, one dovetailed drawer, inlay consists of banding and stringing with corner fans, veneer damage, age cracks, pieced repairs, 38" h, 71-1/2" w, 24" d 2,200.00

    Mahogany veneer, serpentine, Baltimore, Md., or Norfolk, Va., c. 1800, serpentine top with ovolo corners, conforming case with central drawer over two doors flanked by bottle drawers flanked by doors, stringing inlay, satinwood inlaid panels on tops of legs, lower sections with oval drops and stringing, inlaid cuffs, replaced brasses, old refinish, imperfections, 39" h, 80" w, 26-5/8" d 23,000.00

Sheraton

    Mahogany veneers, high turned feet with reeded columns, biscuit corners, dovetailed drawers at each end with cabinet beneath, center section has pullout butler's desk with six dovetailed drawers and pigeonholes, large drawer in base with bottle drawer on either side, pencil inscription with "1820," refinished, replaced brass pulls, small veneer loss, 41" h, 73-1/4" w, 22-3/4" d 3,850.00

Southern

    Yellow pine, old dark varnish, two doors, high turned feet in old black paint, mortised construction, molded base, picture-frame molding around top and sides of case, inset panels on ends, three inset panels (one horizontal over two vertical) on each door, two-board top, attributed to the Carolinas 3,630.00

Southern sideboard, yellow pine, attributed to the Carolinas, $3,630. (Photo courtesy of Garth's Auctions, Delaware, Ohio)

Silhouettes

Background: A profile or shadow outline of an object is referred to as a silhouette. Early examples were made by projecting a shadow on a sheet of white paper by the light of a candle and then filling in the resulting outline with black. The term also refers to a profile cut from a piece of black paper with scissors.

An impressed stamp marked "Peale" or "Peale Museum" identifies pieces made by members of the Peale family, which was well known for its silhouettes.

Museums: Essex Institute, Salem, MA; National Portrait Gallery, Washington, DC.

FYI: The name silhouette is taken from Etienne de Silhouette. As the French Minister of Finance, he enacted strict economic measures and proposed many unpopular forms of taxation. Driven out of office after only four months, his name became synonymous with anything extremely simple or plain.

Double, male and female

Hollow cut, black lacquered frames, with edge damage, minor stains, 6-1/8" h, 5-3/8" w, pr 247.50

Hollow cut, pen and ink details, eglomise glass with gilded frame, some damage, stains 5-1/2" h, 8-5/8" w 330.00

Hollow cut, woman with hair comb, penciled names of Sarah and Samuel Wilcox, woman possibly reversed in frame, some damage to man, stains, cracked frame, 5" h, 3-7/8" w 357.50

Lady and gentleman, reverse-painted glass, attributed to Henry Williams, Boston, embossed brass frames, oval, 6-3/4" h, 5-1/2" w, pr 880.00

Man in chair, bust of woman with bun, each 3/4 view, black paper, gilded detail, white ground, beveled maple frames with gilded liners, 7-1/4" h, 6" w, pr 440.00

Single, female

Black paper with gilded detail, white ground, red printed label "Cut with common scissors by Mr. Seville," pencil inscription with name and "1825," black lacquered frame with gilded liner, 4-5/8" h, 3-7/8" w 605.00

Black paper, stenciled label "Gallery of Cuttings, Cut by Master Hankes with Common Scissors," embossed brass on wood frame, 5-1/2" h, 4-1/4" w 495.00

Old paper label "Judith Sturn, First Wife of Phillip Tomy," black cloth backing over board, foxing, fold lines, fame with black foliage decor, 5-5/8" h, 5" w 330.00

Hollow cut

    Black ink hair and bodice, signed "Doyle," with 1808 newspaper ad for silhouettes by Wm. M.S. Doyle, worn gilt frame, creases, pinpoint holes, 5-3/8" h, 4" w.. 412.50

    Full-length, hair up, wearing fancy dress and carrying bouquet, traces of green watercolor at flowers, worn gilt frame, stains, 6-1/4" h, 4-3/8" w 247.50

Hair in a bun, laid paper with minor stains, black frame with oval opening, 5-3/8" h, 4" w 110.00

Ribbon at top of bonnet, black cloth backing, period mahogany frame, stains, tears, 4-3/8" h, 3-1/2" w 275.00

Wearing bonnet, black cloth backing, erased pencil inscription, old backing labeled "Mrs. Nichols Johnson," old black molded frame, 6-3/4" h, 5-1/2" w 247.50

With book, backed with woven fabric, black watercolor costume and embellishments, framed, minor toning, 3-3/4" h, 2-1/8" w 1,380.00

With hair comb, paper embossed with floral scrolls, curly maple frame, fold lines, minor stains, 6" h, 4-3/4" w 1,127.50

With hair comb, puff sleeve dress in ink wash, old glue stains, glued to backing board which is glued to underside of eglomise mat, flakes on mat, worn gilt frame, 7-1/4" h, 5-7/8" w 440.00

Young girl, cut and penciled detail, black cloth backing, minor damage, old pen and ink label on back, "Sally Tilton 5 years old, 1822," frame in black repaint, 5-1/4" h, 4-1/4" w 357.50

Young woman, black fabric backing, bodice is black printed, old molded walnut frame, stains, 6" h, 4-3/4" w 165.00

Young woman, possibly Peale Museum, black cloth backing, added oval mat, old black frame, 6-7/8" h, 5-1/4" w 192.50

Young woman, woman wearing bonnet and blue dress with puffy sleeve and holding flower sprig, watercolor, American, c. 1830-31, framed, minor creases, 3-5/8" h, 2" w............................. 4,887.50

Single, male

Black paper, back with stenciled label "Cut with Scissors by Master Hubard...," old gilded frame, 6-1/4" h, 5-1/4" w 302.50

Black paper on heavy stock, worn gilt frame, 5-5/8" h, 4-3/8" w 55.00

Full-length, ink, man has coat, ruffled sleeves and walking stick, slight discoloration to ink, black frame, gilt liner, 12" h, 9-5/8" w 110.00

Ink, blue and white watercolor highlights including striped vest and cap, early frame in old alligatored red, light stains, fold lines, edge damage, 4-5/8" h, 3-3/4" w 110.00

Ink on heavy paper, black on black-and-white detail, old black reeded frame with gilded liner, 6" h, 5-1/8" w 302.50

With hat, cut black paper, old but not orig backing paper labeled "Nicholas Johnson Jr. born 1760," back of silhouette paper labeled "Gallery of Cuttings, Cut by Master Hankes with Scissors," with pencil inscription "Nicholas Johnson Jr. N.P. 1810," ink smudges, oval ebonized frame with age crack 275.00

Young man with dark-blue kepi, pen and ink portrait, shiny white paper, penciled names "W. Becke, -- Dupre...11/4.56," framed, 5-5/8" h, 4-3/4" w 220.00

Young man with high collar, illegible penciled note on front, back note "By Mr. Chapman. This is the part from the hollow cut," oval frame, 4" h, 3-3/8" w 275.00

Hollow cut

Black cloth backing, faint "Peale Museum" mark, framed, 6-1/4" h, 5" w 357.50

Boy, good detail, shows hair and bow at neck, identified in old brown ink on front as "Robt. Watson," partial Peale embossed mark at bottom, black cloth backing, mahogany veneer frame with corner chips, margin stains, 5" h, 4" w 385.00

Embossed stamp "Museum" (possibly Peale's Museum), ink note, backed with black cloth, walnut frame, 7" h, 5" w 110.00

Profile head of gentleman topped by large crown and flanked by flowers and an "S" (two other letters missing), later pencil inscription, found in Lancaster County, Pa., stains, matted and framed, 7-1/4" h, 6-1/4" w 330.00

Young man, black ink detail, sawtooth cut oval borders, tin frame, 3-7/8" h, 3" w 440.00

Young man, black paper backing, faint embossed "Peale Museum" label, old frame with gold repaint, 5-3/4" h, 4-3/4" w 275.00

Young man, framed, slight stains, 5-5/8" h, 4-3/4" w 110.00

Watercolor, lady in black dress sitting side-saddle on gray horse, man standing in front of horse and wearing gold pants with black coat, faces in silhouette, some gold tinting, background fence with blue-gray flecks, period frame in old red paint, 7-7/8" h, 10" w...............1,100.00

Sleds

Background: What can compare to flying down a snowy hill at break-neck speed on a favorite sled? Sledding was one of the simple pleasures of winter during the 19th century.

Collectors look for vintage examples in original paint. Some show fanciful decorations or the owner's name.

Decor

"Chester" on seat, old yellow paint, black and red repaint, runners with beveled detail, age cracks, 14" h, 16" w, 34-1/2" l 605.00

Flowers in yellow and Indian head in black stencil, red ground, metal covered runners, Paris Mfg. Co., Paris, Ill., wear, 26" l 412.50

Horse on red ground, curved runners, 30" l 550.00

Medallion stenciled in yellow and white with small stars, old dark-blue repaint, gold scrolls, edge striping, curved iron runners, 8-3/4" h, 13-1/2" w, 29" l, ... 412.50

Poinsettia in red and yellow, dark-green paint over earlier blue, yellow stripe, pine, curved metal runners, three small holes, minor paint wear, light rust, doll-size, 17" l 550.00

Painted wooden sled, red and black with roses and "Flora Temple, 1877" in banner, paint restoration, 55-1/2" l, $1,955. (Photo courtesy of Skinner Auctioneers & Appraisers of Antiques & Fine Arts, Boston and Bolton, Mass.)

Roses and leaves with "F.C.W" and banner with "Flora Temple" and "1877" in shades of red, yellow and green, black ground, scrollwork and shaped sides, cast-iron runners, restoration, 6-1/4" h, 55-1/4" l 1,955.00

Painted
Old red repaint, black and yellow stripes, runners end in curved swan heads, edge damage, age cracks, 34" l 330.00

Orig green and brown, traces of yellow line decor, bentwood runners with cast gooseneck finials, worn, pieced repair, age crack, 36" l 275.00

Wooden, steam-bent frame, curved wooden runners braced with iron, refinished, 33" l, 12-1/4" w 200.00

Sleighs

Background: "Come on, it's lovely weather for a sleigh ride together with you..." Before the advent of motorized vehicles, horse-drawn sleighs were often the easiest way to get from one place to another over snowy roads. While few people today have room to display a full-size sleigh, smaller versions, such as children's sleighs and skating sleighs, attract considerable interest.

Albany cutter sleigh, mustard yellow, full-size 1,870.00

Child's, decor, black ground, red and gold lines and flourishes, 34" l 1,045.00

Skating sleigh, old repainted decor in blue with black and red borders, runners in red, black and yellow, gold finials, brown grained seat, scrolled and chamfered runners, iron and wood handle, composition eagle finial, carved lions' heads on front of sides, 30" h, 54" l, 26" d 1,100.00

Sofas

Background: The chief difference between a sofa and an upholstered settee is that the sofa is generally larger with an over-stuffed appearance.

Empire, lyre frame, mahogany and mahogany veneer, old finish, paw feet with applied and relief-carved cornucopia returns, arms with acanthus leaves and flow-

Federal sofa, mahogany veneer, Massachusetts, c. 1800, 76" l, $2,530. (Photo courtesy of Skinner Auctioneers & Appraisers of Antiques & Fine Arts, Boston and Bolton, Mass.)

ers, reeded crest with pineapple finials, reupholstered in gold velvet, 35" h, 77" w 1,430.00

Federal, mahogany veneer, square back, Mass., c. 1800, crest above reeded arms and arm supports over a maple inlaid rectangular die above reeded tapering legs, swelled and turned feet, square rear legs, old surface, imperfections, 33-1/2" h, 76" l 2,530.00

Mahogany inlaid, probably Boston or North Shore, Mass., c. 1800-10, arched crest, shaped sides, molded arms continue to vase-and-ring turned reeded posts, inlaid panels at legs and arm supports, bowed seat frame, turned feet, old finish, imperfections, 39" h, 80-1/2" w, 25" d 17,250.00

Sheraton, mahogany veneer, inlaid panels on crest and outer legs, 8 legs, veneer damage, 35" h, 74" l 2,750.00

Soft Paste

Background: Sometimes referred to as "artificial" porcelain, soft paste porcelain is distinguished from hard paste in that it contains little or no kaolin (china clay). Because soft paste porcelain usually vitrifies and becomes translucent during the first firing, the second firing process (the glaze-firing) takes place at a lower temperature. This results in a clearly discernible layer of glaze on the surface of the piece. Because the glaze was easily scratched and the finished product was not very durable, the production of soft paste porcelain was gradually abandoned.

FYI: Because bone china is fired at a similar temperature, it is usually classified as soft paste, even though it is 25% kaolin.

Creamer, verse in floral wreath, "Health to the sick, Honour to the brave, Success to the lover, And freedom to the slave," transfer decor, polychrome enameling, iridescent tan rim and border, uneven blue-tinted glaze, 3-1/8" h 137.50

Cup and saucer, handleless, floral design in green, blue and red, minor stains, pr 49.50

Pitcher

> Black transfer, "The Sailor's Farewell," "Forget Me Not" and verse, handpainted polychrome with worn apricot luster, 6-3/4" h 495.00

> Molded relief acanthus leaves around body, satyr heads on foot and base of spout, cornucopias on neck, dragon spout and handle, pale-blue glaze, worn gold luster, stains, hairline, minor flakes, 10-1/8" h 110.00

Plate, Queen's rose in pink, scalloped and molded rim, minor enamel wear, rim flake, 10" dia 165.00

Spatterware

Background: Named for the spattered decoration used to trim this hand-painted ceramic dinnerware, spatterware was popular in the early 19th century. Mainly imported from England, spatterware was available in a variety of colors, with central designs featuring birds, flowers, and houses. Most early spatter-decorated ware was not marked by the manufacturer.

Reference: Kevin McConnell, *Spongeware and Spatterware*, 2nd ed., Schiffer Publishing, 1999.

Museum: Henry Ford Museum, Dearborn, MI.

Reproduction Alert: Reproductions and contemporary examples are quite common. Cybis spatter, a line of spatterware produced in the 1940s by Polish artisan Boleslaw Cybis, has become quite collectible in its own right.

Note: The central motif is located in the center of the piece for flatware, on both sides of the piece for hollowware.

Bowl, Tulip, yellow spatter, design in red and green, hairlines, light stain, 2-1/2" h, 4-3/4" dia 2,310.00

Child's teapot, Peafowl, green foliage, numerous rim chips, 4" h 734.50

Green spatterware child's tea set, Peafowl, $6,000.

Child's tea set, fifteen pcs, cobalt blue bands, six teacups, six saucers, teapot, open sugar and creamer, cracks, damage 546.25

Coffeepot, Thistle, blue spatter, chips, hairline, reglued finial, 8" h 1,921.00

Creamer

> Fort, blue spatter, paneled, design in red, black, green and yellow, hairline in handle, small chips, 5-5/8" h 990.00

> Peafowl, red spatter, design in red, blue, green and black, 1" hairline, rim and table ring with roughness, 4-1/4" h 770.00

> Peafowl, red spatter, design in green, red, black and blue, paneled, minor glaze flakes on spout, 6" h 990.00

> Plain, yellow spatter, restored, 4-5/8" h 522.50

> Rose, rainbow spatter, blue and purple rose with red, green and black, chips, glued break on rim, 4-3/4" h 550.00

Cup, handleless

> Rooster, blue spatter, design in yellow, blue and red 1,100.00

> School house, blue spatter, design in red, blue and yellow, minor rim roughness 385.00

Cup and saucer, handleless

> Acorn, blue spatter, restoration to foot, small rim chip 1,582.00

> Adams Rose pattern, red and green rainbow spatter on sides of cup and interior of saucer 550.00

> Buds, blue and green spatter, design in red and green, four buds on saucer, three on cup, saucer mkd "Harvey," stains, minor flakes, hairline in saucer 110.00

> Cock's Comb, blue spatter, design in red, green and black 1,155.00

> Fort, blue spatter, small chip on foot, some discoloring 750.00

> Peafowl, blue spatter, design in green, yellow and red, cup stained 385.00

> Peafowl, blue spatter, mkd B&T, hairline, some discoloration 339.00

> Peafowl, green spatter, mkd B&T 1,808.00

> Peafowl, red spatter, hairlines 339.00

> Peafowl, red spatter, design in blue, green, black and red, saucer impressed "Adams," hairline in saucer, cup flaked 330.00

> Peafowl, red spatter, design in blue, yellow, black and green 825.00

> Peafowl on branch, blue spatter, design in blue, red, yellow and black, impressed "B. and T. Stoneware," pinpoint flakes on cup 715.00

> Peafowl on branch, red spatter, design in blue, yellow, black and green 880.00

> Peafowl on branch, red spatter, design in blue, green, yellow and black, minor staining 770.00

> Plain, blue spatter, sawtooth edge, minor flake on table ring 110.00

> Plain, purple spatter, minor glaze flake 400.00

> Plain, red spatter, decor varies slightly, chips on table ring of cup 55.00

Rainbow spatter, blue and red, red center on
saucer.. 192.50
Rainbow spatter, blue and red, minor rim roughness
on cup, saucer restored.............................. 440.00
Rainbow spatter, blue, red and green, small rim
flakes, miniature size.................................. 440.00
Rainbow spatter, purple and black, bruised saucer,
hairline in cup 467.50
Rose, blue and red rainbow spatter, design in red,
green and black, saucer mkd "Adams," minor rim
roughness on cup 605.00
Star, six-point, blue spatter, design in red, green and
dark yellow, impressed "R" 1,210.00
Stripes, blue and purple spatter..................... 385.00
Thistle, maroon spatter, design in red and green,
minor stains, hairline in cup, glaze hairline in
saucer.. 385.00
Thistle, yellow spatter, design in red, green and
black, rim flake on cup............................ 3,410.00
Thistle, yellow spatter 1,808.00

Cup plate
Boy on exercise horse, green spatter rim, brown
transfer design, 3-1/2" h 621.50
Boys playing leapfrog, red spatter rim, blue transfer
design, 3-1/2" dia.. 536.75
Fort, blue spatter, design in black, red and green,
paneled rim, edge wear, chips on table ring and
rim, 7-1/2" dia 165.00
Parrot, blue spatter paneled rim, design in red and
green, stains, painted-in rim chip,
4" dia 660.00
Peafowl, red spatter, mkd PW&Co, glaze flake, light
discoloration, 4-1/8" dia 678.00

Miniature
Cup, Peafowl (primitive), teal-green spatter, design
in red, blue, green and black, dark stains, wear,
hairlines 165.00
Cup and saucer, handleless, brown spatter, two
flakes 110.00
Cup and saucer, handleless, rainbow spatter, red
and green, mismatched, old staple repair to sau-
cer.. 55.00
Cup and saucer, handleless, Rose, blue spatter,
design in red, green and black, color variation
between cup and saucer, pinpoint
flakes 330.00
Saucer, Peafowl, red spatter rim, design in yellow,
blue and red, glaze hairline, 4-1/8" dia 110.00
Teapot, Peafowl on one side, House on other, green
spatter, four feet, minor roughness to lid,
4-1/4" h.. 605.00

Pitcher
Fort, blue spatter, acanthus leaf scrolls on handle,
repaired base, hairline, 10-5/8" h 440.00
Peafowl, blue spatter, design in green, yellow, black
and red, handle with molded leaf detail, minor
wear at table ring, glaze spider in base,
7-3/8" h... 3,630.00

Peafowl, blue spatter, paneled, design in red, yellow,
green and black, hairlines in base, wear, stains, 6-
1/4" h 742.50
Plain, blue spatter, hairline, 10" h 247.50
Pitcher and bowl, Adams Rose, blue spatter, design in red,
green and black, tall paneled pitcher, bowl with three
roses in line across interior on white panels, 1-1/2" blue
band around exterior of bowl, hairlines on pitcher, 12" h,
restoration on bowl, 4-1/2" h, 13-1/2" dia..........2,090.00

Plate
Acorn, blue spatter, twelve-sided, three brown
acorns with green caps and leaves, some discol-
oring, 9-1/4" dia 1,600.00
Adams Rose, blue bowknot spatter border, blue
stripe on rim, small rim chip, some discoloring, 8-
5/8" dia 200.00
Adams Rose, blue spatter, twelve-sided, minor
glaze wear on rim, 8-1/2" dia...................... 260.00
Adams Rose type, blue spatter,
8-1/4" dia 423.75
Bull's Eye, purple and black rainbow spatter, 8-1/4"
dia... 1,243.00
Cock's Comb, blue spatter, design in red and green,
wear, stains, small flakes, 8-1/2" dia 907.50
Cock's Comb, yellow spatter, design in red, green
and black, 8-1/2" dia............................... 3,080.00
Flower, red and green spatter rim, design in red,
green and black, stains, 8-1/2" dia 220.00
Fort, bright-blue spatter paneled rim, flake, hairline,
9-3/8" dia 165.00
Open Tulip, purple spatter, six-petal flower in blue,
red, green and black, twelve-sided, discolored,
crack, significant glaze wear on rim,
8-3/8" dia 270.00
Peafowl, blue spatter, minor glaze nicks on rim, 9"
dia.. 536.75
Peafowl, green spatter, 8" dia.................... 2,260.00
Peafowl, red spatter, design in blue, red, green and
black, impressed "Adams," cracked, wear, stains,
blue glaze worn on peafowl, 8-3/4" dia......... 55.00
Rainbow spatter, red, blue and green, red rose on
green foliage, scalloped rim, impressed "Adams,"
minor rim wear, 8" dia................................. 495.00
Rainbow spatter, red, blue and green borders, scalloped edge, impressed "Adams," stains, chip and
minor wear, 9-1/8" dia, pr 550.00
Rainbow spatter, red, blue and green scalloped rim,
9-1/2" dia 495.00
Peafowl, blue spatter, 8-1/4" dia.................... 412.50
Peafowl, blue spatter, design in light-blue, yellow
and red, feather edge, 8-1/2" dia................. 770.00
Peafowl, blue spatter, design in red, blue and green,
stains, 8-3/4" dia... 770.00
Peafowl, blue spatter, design in yellow, red, black
and green, minor glaze flakes on rim, yellow glaze
flaked on peafowl, oblong, 8-1/4" l,
6" w.. 2,035.00
Peafowl, green spatter, design in blue, yellow and
red, rim chip with professional repair,
6-7/8" dia 375.00

Peafowl, red spatter, design in light-blue, yellow, green and black, pinpoint flakes on rim, shallow chip on table ring, 9-1/4" dia........................ 715.00

Peafowl, red spatter, bird with green tail and black wavy lines, paneled rim, neck enamel missing, rim chip.. 275.00

Peafowl, red spatter, design in blue, green, yellow and black, pinpoint flakes on edge, peafowl body unglazed, 9" dia... 275.00

Peafowl, red spatter, design in blue, yellow, black and green, feathered edge, rim flakes, 8-1/4" dia.. 275.00

Profile Tulip, blue spatter, twelve-sided, light discoloration, 7-1/8" dia 395.50

Schoolhouse, blue spatter, twelve-sided, center with red schoolhouse with yellow roof over a black spatter ground with a green spatter tree at right, minor glaze wear and rim flakes, 8-1/2" dia 3,600.00

Schoolhouse, red spatter, center with all-red schoolhouse on brown and green spatter ground with spatter tree at right having brown trunk and green top, discolored, 5-1/8" dia........................ 4,600.00

Star, six-point, blue spatter, star in red, green and blue, 9-1/2" dia 1,072.50

Star, six-point, blue spatter, star in dark-blue, green and red in center of white multi-point star, 9-3/8" dia 935.00

Thistle, red spatter, design in red and green, molded feathered edge, three flakes, 8-1/4" dia 1,155.00

Tree, blue spatter, design in green and black, impressed "Best Goods," wear, stains, edge chips, old rim repairs, 9" dia................................. 165.00

Tulip, blue spatter rim, design in red, green and yellow, 7-1/4" dia... 825.00

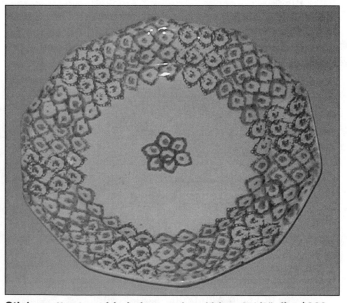

Stick spatter ten-sided plate, red and blue, 9-1/2" dia, $200.

Tulip, blue spatter, design in red, yellow and green, 8-7/8" dia 192.50

Tulip, red spatter, design in red and green, edge wear, stains, 10" dia 742.50

Platter, plain, blue spatter, octagonal, wear, stains, 15-3/4" l.. 330.00

Reproduction

Margaret E. Weaver, Akron, Pa., 33-pc set, service for twelve, schoolhouse decor, yellow spatter, includes coffeepot, gravy, twelve dinner plates, three oblong serving dishes, oval platter, water pitcher and thirteen cups/saucers, mkd "M.E.W.," purchased from maker in 1960s................. 385.00

Margaret E. Weaver, Akron, Pa., eight pcs, blue spatter Schoolhouse serving dish, red and yellow spatter Dahlia serving dish, three dinner plates (black spatter Rose, red spatter Peafowl, red spatter Acorn), yellow spatter toddy, blue spatter Peafowl waste bowl, acorn cup and saucer, mkd "M.E.W.," purchased from maker in 1960s....................302.50

Margaret E. Weaver, Akron, Pa., nine pcs, five dinner plates with red spatter and various floral decor, small Schoolhouse wash bowl and pitcher, 5-1/2" bowl in red, 9-1/2" Peafowl plate in plate in purple and one in brown, mkd "M.E.W.," purchased from maker in 1960s... 275.00

Sauce dish, Peafowl, blue spatter, 5" dia............. 375.00

Saucer

Schoolhouse, blue spatter, design in red, green and black, rim flake, wear, 6" dia........................ 770.00

Rainbow, green, yellow, red and brown spatter, green pinwheel center, very light discoloration, 4-5/8" dia 1,921.00

Star (eight-point), red spatter, design in blue, small kiln spot, 5-3/4" dia 110.00

Tulip, red spatter, design in red, green and black, chip on one table ring, 6" dia, pr................. 550.00

Stick spatter

Charger, foliage in Flow Blue with red and green sprig and flowers, minor edge wear, light crazing, 12-1/4" dia 165.00

Plate, blue rim with red stripes, red fruit with green leaves, bruise, rim flake, 9-1/8" dia 192.50

Plate, red border, leaves with flow blue stripes and flowers, 10" dia 275.00

Sugar, covered, blue, green and red designs, blue stripes, minor roughness on inside flange, 5" h, 5" dia.. 275.00

Sugar, covered

Adams Rose, blue spatter, design in dark-pink and green, paneled, scalloped handles, minor flakes, glued finial, 8-3/4" h.................................... 495.00

Adams Rose, red and green spatter, light lid discoloration, 4-1/4" h...................................... 3,503.00

Bull's Eye, purple and black rainbow spatter, light discoloration, 4" h 1,356.00

Fort, blue spatter, design in black, gray, red and green, chip and pinpoint flake on base, glazed-over flake with minor roughness on inside flange, 4-1/4" h.. 770.00

Fort, red spatter, design in red, black and green, stains, chips on foot of bowl, mismatched lid with damage and old repair, 4-1/8" h 357.50

Peafowl, blue spatter, design in red, yellow, black and green, paneled, domed lid, double handles mkd "P.W. and Co. Stoneware," 8-1/4" h 1,045.00

Peafowl, blue spatter, design in red, blue, yellow and black, chips, repair, 4" h 385.00

Peafowl, green spatter, design in red, blue and green, stains, professional repairs, 4" h, 4-7/8" dia 440.00

Plain, brown spatter, hairline, rim chips, 4-1/2" h 4-3/8" dia 82.50

Schoolhouse, green spatter, rim hairline, 4-1/2" h 2,475.00

Teapot

Peafowl, light-red spatter, design in green, red and blue, paneled, molded handle, stains, damage, 7-1/4" h 495.00

Peafowl, red spatter, design in red, blue, black and green, red ground, paneled body, domed lid, embossed "B" on base of pot, minor flakes, 9" h 2,420.00

Plain, blue spatter, paneled sides, minor hairline, flakes on spout, wear on finial, 9" h............ 330.00

Spice Boxes

Background: Spice boxes were used for the same purpose as spice chests—to hold valuable spices. The spice box did so in a different medium, however, often being made of tin. Spice boxes were popular in the 16th and 17th centuries, but most examples on today's market are from the second half of the 19th century.

Bentwood, round

"Rice," old reddish-brown paint, dark-yellow striping and label, edge damage, 5-5/8" dia............ 330.00

"Spices," contains eight matching canisters, orig varnish finish, tin edge bands, black stenciled labels, bottom mkd "Made in New Jersey," 9-1/4" dia 440.00

"Spices," stenciled labels on lid and base, eight labeled spice containers inside, tin band, slight bottom warp, 3-1/2" h, 9-3/8" dia 302.50

Toleware

Double slant lids, alligatored japanning with stenciled labels, handle, wear, one lid loose, 5-1/4" h, 9-1/2" w, 6-1/8" d 165.00

Round, hinged lid with hasp and brass bail handle, japanned with broad gold band around top, red and gold stripes, seven interior round canisters with removable lids stenciled with names of spices, each 2-1/2" dia, overall 3-1/2" h, 8-1/2" dia 95.00

Spice holder with nutmeg grater, two tiers of spice containers, japanned tin, $1,000.

Wooden

Walnut, old finish, chamfered sliding lid with hammer marks, dovetailed, four-part interior, 2-1/2" h, 7" w, 5" d 825.00

Walnut, slide-lid with raised center panel, three small finger notches, four interior compartments, dovetailed, 2-3/4" h, 9" w, 4-1/4" d 210.00

Wooden, hanging

Eleven-drawer, oak, impressed labels on drawer fronts, "Gibsonburg, Ohio" advertising on crest, white porcelain pulls, worn finish, 25" h, 10" w, 4-1/2" d 495.00

Eleven-drawer, poplar and oak, impressed black lettering, white porcelain knobs, attributed to the Pure Food and Spice Co., Cincinnati, Ohio, minor corner chips on two drawers, 23-1/2" h, 10" w, 4-1/2" d 247.50

Spice Chests or Cabinets

Background: A spice chest is a piece of furniture designed specifically for holding spices. Some examples resembled a chest of drawers mounted on a stand, except the upper section was fitted with doors that hid an interior fitted with many small drawers. The stand was generally fitted with a row of drawers. Examples were made to be free-standing, hang on a wall or do both.

Free-standing

Four-drawer, pine, old black repaint over earlier red and blue, one-board door with applied molding, turned feet, molded-edge base and top, drawers

Painted tin spice chest, $350.

with divided interior, edge damage, 11-7/8" h, 9-7/8" w, 6-3/8" d 2,200.00

Six-drawer, oak with bird's-eye maple drawer fronts, turned wooden knobs, square nails, 17-3/4" h, 14-1/2" w, 7-1/2" d 385.00

Six-drawer, pine and oak, refinished, nailed drawers with old ring pulls, mortised and pegged door with inset panel on front, rosehead nails on case, bottom and top moldings replaced, English, 15-3/4" h, 14-5/8" w, 9-1/2" d 330.00

Seven-drawer, Chippendale style, mahogany and mahogany veneer, old finish, bracket feet, molded base, door with arched tombstone panel, nailed drawers with brass ring pulls, arched pigeonhole at center of interior, reconstructed, 23" h, 17" w, 11-3/4" d 990.00

Ten-drawer (five rows of two), green case, red drawer fronts, 29-1/2" h, 15" w, 12-1/2" d 770.00

Twelve-drawer, orig red wash, gold lettering and trim, wire nails, brass ring pulls, one drawer with mouse damage, others with edge chips, 11-7/8" h, 15-3/4" w, 5-1/8" d 715.00

Fifteen-drawer (five graduated rows of three), black walnut, refinished, white porcelain pulls, molded base and cornice, Ohio origin, 14-3/4" h, 18-1/2" w, 7-1/8" d 715.00

Hanging

Six-drawer, oak, orig varnish, impressed labels, white porcelain knobs, arched crest, stamped advertising "Pure Food Co., Cincinnati, Ohio," 12-1/2" h, 8-1/4" w, 4-1/2" d 302.50

Eight-drawer (four rows of two), oak, old finish, turned pulls, molded and scalloped edge, "Spice Cabinet" on crest, old advertising on back for "May & Company, Dayton, Ohio," age cracks in back, 16-3/4" h, 10-3/4" w, 5-1/4" d 522.50

Eight-drawer, pine, old finish, molded-edge back, damage, some replaced knobs, wire nails, 17-1/2" h, 10" w, 5" d 220.00

Thirteen-drawer, cherry, old refinish, porcelain knobs, old edge damage, 20-1/4" h, 12" w, 4-1/2" d 275.00

Fifteen-drawer (five rows of three), mustard paint with sponge decor, pine, scalloped crest, wire nails, turned wooden knobs, drawers hide traces of bittersweet on front of cabinet, 18-1/2" h, 11" w, 4" d 2,200.00

Spinning Wheels

Background: The spinning wheel was an early kind of machine used for spinning raw wool, cotton, or flax into thread or yarn. A revolving wheel supported on a stand was driven by either a hand treadle or a foot treadle, with the wheel rotating a single spindle onto which the yarn was spun. Spinning was popular among women of all classes, and almost every farmhouse contained a spinning wheel.

Soxany-style, three baluster-turned legs, wheel with twelve turned spokes, adjustable flyer, turned vertical and horizontal distaff arms with replaced three-prong branch, Pa., late 18th or early 19th C 220.00

Soxany-style, three sausage-turned legs, turned wheel supports, wheel with twelve tapered spokes, adjustable maiden and flyer, turned distaff with replacement sides, bench stamped "S. Reiner," early 19th C, refinished, wheel 19-1/2" dia 425.00

Spittoons

Background: Also known as cuspidors, the stereotypical spittoon is the large brass vessel seen on the floor of the saloon in old Western movies. A receptacle for tobacco spittle, they were also made of ceramic and metals other than brass.

Reproduction Alert: Spittoons, especially brass examples, have been widely reproduced.

Cast iron, turtle form, copper shell and bowl, orig paint, mkd "Golden Novelty Co., Chicago, Ill.," 1901 patent date, 13-1/2" l 485.00

Graniteware

Cobalt/white swirl, white interior, 4-1/4" h, 7-1/2" dia 300.00

Columbian, one-pc 275.00

Gray, lady's spit cup, 3" h, 4-1/4" dia 85.00

Ironstone, warrior and lion transfer, copper luster 265.00

Blue/white swirl graniteware spittoon, two-piece, $100.

Pewter, bulbous body, flared rim, handle, unmarked, 4-3/4" h.. 82.50

Spongeware, circular sponged dabs around body, blue bands at rim and shoulder, 4-1/2" h 99.00

Staffordshire, Romantic, blue transfer, molded bas-ketweave pattern... 260.00

Stoneware

    Albany glaze, incised "L.J. Underwood. Barberton, Ohio. July 24, '09" and "L.J.U., 7-24-1909," 4-1/2" dia.. 93.50

    Blue and white, butterfly and shield pattern, 6" h, 7-1/2" dia 85.00

    Brown glaze, embossed vines 35.00

    Green and cream, stylized floral design 85.00

Spongeware

Background: Extensively produced in England and America, spongeware items were most commonly blue and white, but yellowware with mottled tans, browns, and greens was also popular. The design was achieved by sponging, spattering, or daubing on the color, and it was generally applied in an overall pattern.

References: William C. Ketchum Jr., *American Country Pottery: Yellowware and Spongeware*, Alfred A. Knopf, 1987; Kevin McConnell, *Spongeware and Spatterware*, 2nd ed., Schiffer Publishing, 1999.

Reproduction Alert: Reproductions and contemporary examples are quite common.

Note: All listings are blue-and-white, unless otherwise noted.

Baking dish, overall sponging, 3-1/2" h, 10-1/2" dia.. 154.00

Bank, pig, brown and green sponging, pierced eyes and coin slot, 3-1/2" h, 6" l 209.00

Bean pot, Uhl Pottery Co., no lid........................... 200.00

Bowl

    11-1/2" dia, green and brown sponging, glaze flakes 330.00

    12" dia, blue sponging above and below blue stripe 275.00

    12" dia, blue sponging overall........................ 412.50

Bowl, mixing

    9-1/4" dia, 4" h, scalloped panels on sides, glaze wear in bottom, rim hairline 165.00

    10" dia, 4-3/4" h, blue, heart panels, large glaze imperfection on interior.............................. 137.50

    12" dia, 5-1/2" h, molded arched panels........ 275.00

    13-1/4" dia, 6-1/2" h, column design, overall sponging with free-form white stripe in center...... 302.50

Butter crock

    "Butter" in oblong border, sponged band above and below, sponged lid, bail handle, lid cracked, 3-3/4" h, 5-3/4" dia...................................... 192.50

    "Butter"" framed with dark chicken-wire sponging, orig lid, two rim chips filled, 3-3/4" h 247.50

    Good Luck pattern, 5" h, 7-1/2" dia................ 225.00

    Simple sponging, 5" h, 7" dia........................ 150.00

Casserole, lid cracked, 3-1/2" h, 10-1/2" dia 125.00

Chamber pot with handle, overall sponging, 5-1/2" h, 10" dia 121.00

Custard, minor surface wear, hairline, 2-3/4" h 44.00

Honey pot, bulbous, matching lid, dark sponging, 4-1/2" h 247.50

Mug, black accent bands at rim and base, dark sponging, 4-1/2" h.. 209.00

Nappy, 3-1/4" h, 10" dia....................................... 247.50

Pitcher

    Bulbous form, double bands around top and base, sponged body, 9-3/4" h.............................. 632.50

    Lattice design, brown and green sponging, yellow body, rim chips, 9-1/4" h 88.00

    Miniature, brown and green chicken-wire sponging, 3" h 220.00

Girl and Dog pitcher, blue sponging, $1,500.

Bulbous pitcher, blue sponging, Uhl Pottery Co., $475.

Old Fashioned Garden Rose 852.00
Plain form, dark chain-link sponging, large interior rim chip, 9" h 302.50
Plain form with low flared waist, small spot missing glaze inside, 9" h 522.50
Straight sides, tapered at top, rim flake, 8-7/8" h 385.00
Wild Rose, roses highlighted in cobalt, upper and lower part of pitcher sponged, small surface chip, 9" h 412.50
Window Panes, glaze pop, hairline 185.00
Soap dish, 4-5/8" w, 3-1/4" d 110.00
Spittoon
    Blue bands, imperfections, 5" h, 7-1/2" dia 99.00
    Circular sponged dabs around body, blue bands at rim and shoulder, 4-1/2" h 99.00
Teapot, chips on lid and spout 700.00
Vase, embossed ribbon, dark sponging, rim chip, 7-1/2" h 110.00
Wash pitcher, bulbous base, three blue lines around body 302.50
Water filter, "The Allen Germ Proof Filter, Toledo, O.," 30-gal, two hairlines 2,200.00

Spool Cabinets

Background: Serving the dual purpose of promoting the manufacturer while containing the product, these store display cabinets are popular on today's market. The large, fancy cabinets were used to catch a customer's attention. Early versions were made of wood and often had glass inserts in the drawers. Eventually, manufacturers turned to less-expensive models made of lithographed tin. The wooden versions are in greater demand and realize higher prices.

Collecting Hint: Most spool cabinets were made of oak. Examples in cherry or walnut are more valuable.

Clark's Thread, "Clark's Mile-End Spool," wood, five drawers with reverse-painted glass fronts advertising product, paint loss to glass, minor scuffs to cabinet, 19" h, 30" w, 18-1/2" d 495.00

J.&P. Coats spool cabinet, $1,500.

Corticelli, "Corticelli Spool Silk, Always Reliable," wooden, hinged lift top, one drawer, tin insert sign showing silk worm, butterflies and cocoons, scattered light staining and wear to sign, cond. 7.5+, 4" h, 20-1/2" w, 14-1/2" d 1,430.00
"J&P Coats" over four drawers, wood, spool shape, plaster cord around sides, one slat missing, 22" h, 18" dia 1,045.00
J.P. Coats Spool Cotton, drum shape, four-drawer, 17" h, 22" w 2,090.00

Staffordshire Figures

Background: Porcelain figures were quite popular in 19th-century Britain, creating a demand for less-expensive imitations suitable for the mass market. Obligingly, most of the potters in Staffordshire, England began producing small figures and groupings that could be used as mantelpiece decorations. Pairs of dogs were the most popular and were turned out in large numbers, but depictions of royal figures, politicians, military heroes, and notorious villains were also made.

References: Adele Kenny, *Staffordshire Spaniels*, Schiffer Publishing, 1997; Griselda Lewis, *A Collector's History of English Pottery*, 5th ed., Antique Collectors' Club, 1999; Clive Mason Pope, *A-Z of Staffordshire Dogs*, Antique Collectors' Club, 1996.

Museums: American Antiquarian Society, Worcester, MA; The Detroit Museum of Arts, MI.

Reproduction Alert: Reproductions are plentiful. Collectors should exercise caution before investing. A small vent hole in the side of a figure or hidden amidst the decoration is usually indicative of early Staffordshire. A large vent hole in the base of a figurine will almost always mean the piece is a modern reproduction.

Collecting Hint: A pair of figures will always be worth more than twice the value of a single component of the set.

Boxers, "Heenan-Savers," one in yellow pants with blue belt, one in pink pants with orange belt, minor flakes on hair, 9-1/4" h.. 440.00
Cat, seated, brown and black spots, one with in-the-making imperfections, 3-3/4" h, pr 412.50
Dog
    Reclining, black, 5" h 115.50
    Reclining, white, about 6" l 165.00
    Sanded coat, white, black muzzle, yellow eyes, gilt collar with lock, 4-5/8" h, pr 412.50
Elephant under coleslaw tree, two shades of gray, pink and green blanket, minor enamel wear, one leg with in-the-making hairline, 5-3/4" h 550.00
"Eva & Uncle Tom," polychrome and gilt, crazing, repair, 8-1/2" h.. 192.50
Gentleman, 7-1/2" h.......................................110.00
Girl sitting on a goat, girl in cobalt dress and white hat with green plume, goat with mottled orange and black body and applied decor to simulate fur, twisted horns, copper luster highlights, oval base, 4-3/4" h.. 120.00
Lion, seated, with sheep, imperfections, 4-1/2" l... 1,045.00
Man and spaniel, man sitting on ground next to reclining dog, 4" h.. 220.00
Man and woman, 7-1/2" h 165.00
Man on horse with basket of fruit, polychrome decor, 9-1/2" h.. 302.50
Spaniel, sitting
    7" h, white body, black spots, ears, tail and muzzle, red collar with gold locket, pr 605.00
    9" h, black body 220.00

Staffordshire: castle (left), $110; Tom King on horseback, $247.50; castle watch hutch, $275; set of three dog figures, $192.50. (Photo courtesy of Cyr Auction Company, Gray, Maine)

10" h, white body, black spots, ears and tail, white body, orange muzzle, collar with gold locket, pr 385.00
White body, black spots, ears and tail, holds flower basket in mouth, pr.................................. 1,485.00
"Uncle Tom" with Eva on his shoulders, polychrome, crazing, 10-3/8" h.. 440.00
"Uncle Tom," with girl on knee, polychrome decor, 10-1/4" h 770.00
Woman, holding basket and flower bouquet, dog at her side, minor chips, hairlines, glaze wear, 11-3/4" h.. 230.00
Zebra
    Polychrome, repair, late, 5" h........................ 137.50
    Polychrome, wear and crazing, 8-3/4" h........ 495.00

Staffordshire Transferware

Background: The process of transfer-printing designs onto earthenware items was first developed in England during the mid-18th century. An engraved copper plate was inked and the design was then transferred to a sheet of tissue paper and affixed to the item. When transferware is examined closely, it is often possible to detect the seam left when prints did not fit exactly.

The technique was quickly hailed as an acceptable alternative to expensive hand-painted wares. Early examples were printed in dark blue, but light blue, green, red, pink, purple, black, and brown were quickly introduced. Romantic landscape scenes, historical views, animals, and flowers were among the most popular designs. American views continue to bring the highest prices on the U.S. market.

References: Jeffrey B. Snyder, *Historical Staffordshire: American Patriots and Views*, Schiffer Publishing, 1995; —, *Romantic Staffordshire Ceramics*, Schiffer Publishing, 1997.

Collectors' Club: The Transferware Collector's Club, 1500 E. College Way #541, Mount Vernon, WA 98273-5637, www.transcollectorsclub.org.

Museums: American Antiquarian Society, Worcester, MA; Cincinnati Art Museum, OH; Elverson Museum of Art, Syracuse, NY; Henry Ford Museum, Dearborn, MI; Metropolitan Museum of Art, New York, NY; The Henry Francis DuPont Winterthur Museum, Winterthur, DE.

Specialty Auction: Historical & Commemorative Wares Collector's Sales and Service, P.O. Box 4037, Middleton, RI 02842.

Note: All listings are dark-blue transfer unless otherwise noted.

ABC plate
    "For My Nephew" and "JLK," boys at play, pink transfer, molded ABCs in relief, mkd Staffordshire, 5-5/8" dia 150.00

"Franklin's Proverb" and "Keep Thy Shop and Thy Shop Will Keep Thee," black transfer, accented in green, blue, yellow and red polychrome, molded ABCs in relief, red stripe, two minor glaze flakes, 6-1/8" dia 150.00

"The New Pony," black transfer, accented in red, green and blue polychrome, molded ABCs in relief, pink stripe, discolored, 5-1/8" dia 110.00

Scottish hunters with dogs behind rocks, brown transfer, molded ABCs in relief, minor discoloring, 6-7/8" dia 80.00

"Trap Bat & Ball" and "GHI," children playing with ball and bat, pink transfer, molded ABCs in relief, Charles Allerton & Sons, crack, 5-7/8" dia 130.00

"The Walk," rider on horse, black transfer, accented in red, yellow and green polychrome, molded ABCs in relief, red stripe, minor discoloring, 6" dia 170.00

Bidet, Ridgeway's Beauties of America, medium-blue transfer, exterior scenes include the Charleston Exchange and Bank of Savannah, interior has Washington Capitol, heavily restored, 4-1/2" h, 18" l 990.00

Child's mug

Boys feeding animals, title illegible, black transfer, accents in red, yellow and green, some discoloring, two nicks, 2-1/2" h 85.00

"March, The jovial days of feasting past...," mother and child with begging dog, pink transfer, two in-the-making glaze flakes, slight nick on base, 2-1/2" h 160.00

"William" in beaded and grapevine frame, black transfer, slight rim nick, 2-1/2" h 180.00

Child's tea set, "Pet Goat," black transfer, ten pcs, teapot with lid, sugar bowl with lid, four cups and four saucers 525.00

Coffeepot, Lafayette at Franklin's tomb, scrolled handle, domed lid, glued spout repairs, in-the-making imperfection on lid, 13" h 3,300.00

Compote, "The Capitol, Washington," deep bowl with flared sides, Tams, Anderson & Tams, discoloring, rim chip with pieces glued in, crack, 4-3/4" h, 11" dia 1,850.00

Cup and saucer, handleless

"Franklin" (tomb), saucer mkd "E&G Phillips, Longport" 385.00

Home in the Woods, blue transfer, luster rim, impressed "Adams," minor wear, pinpoint flakes 220.00

Going to the Well, impressed "Clews," pinpoint flakes 137.50

Lafayette at Washington's Tomb, saucer impressed "Wood and Sons," eagle mark, hairline, rim repair on cup 440.00

Young couple in forest, impressed "Clews," minor wear 203.50

Cup plate

Customs House, Philadelphia, hairlines, repaired, 3-1/2" dia 275.00

"The Ethiopians," brown transfer, dancing black minstrels with banjo and drum, whites in horse-drawn carriage in background, pearlware body, c. 1850-60, 4" dia 264.00

"Landing of Lafayette," impressed "Wood," hairlines, 3-3/4" dia 137.50

"Octagon Church, Boston" (mismarked, shows scene of Staughton's Church, Philadelphia), white rim, hairline, 4-1/4" dia 220.00

"Staughton's Church, Philadelphia" (mismarked, shows Octagon Church, Boston), impressed "Stevenson," pinpoint flakes, 4-1/8" dia 412.50

"The Tyrants Foe," brown transfer, scalloped edge, text of 1st Amendment, border with U.S. shield-breasted eagles and two other quotes, c. 1830-40, two short hairlines, stains, 4" dia 550.00

Ladle, women and child by cottage, 7-1/2" l 605.00

Mug, "Eva Dressing Uncle Tom," black transfer, shows Eva placing flower wreath around Uncle Tom's neck with basket of flowers and fountain in background, gold band at lip and foot scroll, C handle, c. 1840-50, lip crack 198.00

Pepper pot, Landing of Lafayette, domed top, shallow chips and flakes on top, 4-5/8" h 2,750.00

Pitcher

"Am I Not a Man and a Brother," black transfer print around body, copper luster band at top, cream pitcher, African in chains on sea coast with ship in background on one side, pro-abolition poem entitled "The Negros" on other side, c. 1830, hairline, 4-1/2" h 2,090.00

"Landing of Gen. Lafayette," scrolled handle, scalloped rim, stains, 6-1/4" h 1,760.00

New York Insane Asylum and City Hall, Clews, minor stains and wear, bottom crazed, 9" h 1,100.00

"States" border, James and Ralph Clews, 1819-36, English castle view, repairs to handle, 10-1/2" h 1,150.00

"The Tyrants Foe, The Peoples Friend," light-blue transfer, milk pitcher, Miss Liberty standing at printing press and African American kneeling at

"Eva Dressing Uncle Tom" Staffordshire mug, black transfer, crack, $198. (Photo courtesy of Cowan's Historic Americana)

her feet, other side with text of 1st Amendment, c. 1840, hairline, minor chips on table ring, small hole in bottom 1,320.00

Plaque, portrait of bearded man, "Salisbury" banner, blue, green and amber, face and beard repainted, chip, 12-1/4" h, 9" w 55.00

Plate

"America and Independence," states border, two-story building with curved drive, impressed "Clews," 8" dia 330.00

Building with colonnade, three people and swans in foreground, floral border, unmkd, 9-7/8" dia 192.50

Cadmus, shell border, impressed "E. Wood & Sons," 10-1/8" dia 495.00

"Catskill Mountain House," scene with flying American flag and cat border, Wood & Son, 9" dia 132.00

"Commodore MacDonnough's Victory," shell border, impressed "Enoch Wood & Sons, Burslem," minor wear, knife scratches, 8-3/8" dia.................. 357.50

Cupid and Psyche, floral border, scalloped edge, impressed "Adams Warranted Staffordshire," slight scratches, 9" dia................................ 275.00

Eagle and shield, blue transfer, "E Pluribus Unum" banner, geometric border, mkd "R. Hammersley" and "Gem," stains, minor edge wear, two flaked, two with hairlines, 8-5/8" dia, set of 11 .... 495.00

"East View of LaGrange, The Residence of Marquis Lafayette," impressed "Enoch Woods and Son," 9-1/2" dia 220.00

"The Effects of American Slavery Whipped for Wanting to Live a Christian Life," black transfer, scene of African whipping white kneeling at cotton bale, pearlware body, embossed floral lip, 7-1/2" dia 660.00

"Eva Dressing Uncle Tom," light-blue transfer, shows Eva placing flower wreath around Uncle Tom's neck, pearlware body, embossed lip of Chinamen and trees, one chip underside of lip, 7-1/2" dia 385.00

"Faulkbourn Hall," medium-blue transfer, floral border, shallow scallops, impressed "A. Stevenson Warranted Staffordshire," 10" dia 192.50

Floral decor with beehive, Stevenson & Williams, minor wear, 10" dia...................................... 99.00

Hunters (two) with hounds and game, minor wear, 9" dia... 220.00

"Landing of Gen. Lafayette," impressed "Clews," 8-7/8" dia 385.00

"Landing of Gen. Lafayette," impressed "Clews," minor knife scratches, wear, 10" dia........... 440.00

"Lovejoy, The First Martyr of American Liberty at Alton Nov. 7, 1837," light-blue transfer, scalloped edge, central quote from 1st Amendment, rim with eagles and transfer of Miss Liberty at printing press with slave at her feet, commemorates the murder of Elijah Lovejoy, the publisher of the Alton Ill. abolition newspaper, The Observer, circa 1845, 10-1/2" dia 935.00

Men fishing and houses on hillsides decor, trees border, impressed "Clews," 10" dia 165.00

"Millennium," pink transfer, scalloped rim, unmkd Ralph Stevenson & Son, minor glaze wear, 6-1/4" dia.. 130.00

Oriental scene, wear, scratches, 10-1/2" dia 93.50

"Peace and Plenty," man in toga with basket of fruit, basket of flowers in border, impressed "Clews Warranted Staffordshire," hairline, 7-3/4" dia 82.50

"Peace and Plenty," man in toga with basket of fruit, flowers and fruit border, impressed "Clews Warranted Staffordshire," minor knife scratches, 10-1/4" dia 330.00

"Plains Hill Surrey," R. Halls, 10" dia............. 247.50

"Sancho and the Priest and the Barber," floral border, unmkd Clews, minor wear, 7-5/8" dia 137.50

"Table Rock, Niagara," impressed "E. Wood and Sons," 10-1/8" dia..................................... 495.00

"Transylvania University, Lexington," wear, kiln damage, 9-1/8" dia 302.50

"Winter View of Pittsfield, Mass.," floral and medallion border, scalloped edge, impressed "Clews Warranted Staffordshire," chips, hairline, 8" dia 110.00

Platter

Boats, children and tower with spire, English scene, floral border, impressed "Davenport," hairline, wear, 11-1/2" w, 14-1/2" l........................... 385.00

Cows and horses in pasture, floral and vintage border, mkd "Clews Warranted Staffordshire," minor scratches, 11-3/4" w, 13-3/4" l 990.00

Deer and park, vintage border, scalloped rim, impressed "Adams Warranted Staffordshire," minor wear, 13-1/2" w, 15-1/2" l.............. 1,100.00

"Detroit," rare dark-blue version, minor wear, scratches, small area of professional repair on back edge of rim, 18-1/2" l....................... 3,025.00

Eagle and shield, "E Pluribus Unum" banner, geometric border, English registry mark with "R. Hammersley" and "Gem," stains, edge wear, 10" w, 13-1/2" l 302.50

Eagle with shield, blue transfer in center, blue spattered scalloped edge, stains, four hairlines, 10-1/2" w, 14" l... 220.00

Fruit, oblong central panel with melon, peaches, pears and foliage, light-blue flower and leaf border, wear, 14-3/4" w, 18-7/8" l..................... 770.00

"Harper's Ferry," red transfer, scalloped rim, eagle signature on back, 15-3/8" l........................ 440.00

"Landing of Gen. Lafayette," floral border, impressed "Clews Warranted Staffordshire," minor wear, knife scratches, 11-1/2" w, 15-1/4" l......... 1,100.00

"Landing of Gen. Lafayette," impressed "Clews Warranted Staffordshire," slight scratches, 14-1/4" w, 19" l 2,970.00

Man herding cattle, flower and foliage border, scalloped edge, wear, 15-1/8" w, 17-1/2" l........ 990.00

Oriental design of two people on hill with house, palm trees and palm border, blue and white, scalloped rim, stains and glaze underneath, oval, 19-1/2" x 14-3/4" 275.00

"Palestine," harbor scene, willow trees and pagodas, scalloped rim, geometric foliage border, mkd "R. Stevenson," knife scratches, 15-1/4" w, 19-1/4" l 522.50

"State House Boston," scalloped eagle border, old stapled repairs, edge chip, 11-3/4" w, 14-1/4" l 247.50

Street scene, people, horse and buggies, tree border, impressed "Adams" and blue eagle mark, 12" w, 15-1/4" l 605.00

Saucer
City Hall, New York by Stubbs, medium-blue transfer, minor wear, rim chip, 6-1/4" dia 71.50
Lafayette at Franklin's Tomb, Wood & Sons, 5-3/4" dia 247.50

Soup bowl
"Boston State House," unmkd Enoch Wood & Sons, 10" dia 230.00
Baltimore & Ohio Railroad, E. Wood & Sons, minor scratches, 10-1/4" dia 805.00

Soup plate
"Fair Mount near Philadelphia," medium-blue transfer, pinpoint flakes, short scratched, crow's-foot crack, 9-7/8" dia.. 275.00
"Vue de Chateau de Coucy," vintage border, shallow scalloped rim, impressed "E. Wood & Sons, Burslem".. 165.00

Sugar, covered, "Landing of Gen. Lafayette," chips on rim and lid, 6-1/4" h 605.00

Teapot
Bird and nest, unmkd, minor enamel flakes to spout, mismatched chipped lid, 7-1/2" h, 10-1/2" l 220.00

Staffordshire teapot, octagonal, 11" h, $250.

"Sower," pink transfer, oval, footed, arched dolphin-shaped handle, curved spout, oval lid with flower finial, unmkd William Adams, chips, glaze wear, discoloring, hairline, 7-1/4" h, 11-1/4" l 250.00

Toddy plate
Girl playing harp, medium-blue transfer, 4-3/4" dia 104.50
House in the woods, impressed "Wood," 5-3/4" dia 137.50
"Panoramic Scenery, R.S.W.," wear, glaze imperfections, 5-1/4" dia.. 165.00
"Scudder's American Museum," white rim, impressed "Stevenson," hairline, pinpoint rim flakes, 5" dia... 165.00

Tureen
"Alms House, Boston," J.&W. Ridgeway, two hairlines in base, chip on inside edge of lid, 9-1/2" h, 12-3/4" l 3,300.00
"Dix Cove on the Gold Coast Africa," Enoch Wood & Sons, Burslem, 1819-46, with cover, interior stains, 11" h, 15" w 4,877.50
"Landing of General LaFayette," James and Ralph Clews, Cobridge, 1819-36, with cover and ladle, damage, 10" h, 16" w 5,175.00

Under tray
English castle, pearlware, blue transfer, reticulated rim, chips and surface flakes, 10-1/4" l....... 440.00
"Pass in the Catskill Mountains," E. Wood and Sons, minor scratches and edge roughness, oval, 8" l 440.00
Seashells, fruit border, molded oak branches at handles, impressed "Joseph Stubbs, Longport," handles rough, 11" w, 15" l 1,320.00

Vegetable dish, covered, "Peace and Plenty," James and Ralph Clews, Cobridge, 1819-36, minute chip under handle, 6-1/2" h, 12-1/2" w 1,725.00

Vegetable dish, open
Polar bears, blue transfer, impressed "Enoch Wood" mark, edge wear, 11-5/8" l.......................... 990.00
"State House," medium-blue transfer, eagle and floral scroll border, footed, glued repairs, 5" h, 11-5/8" w, 9-5/8" d 440.00
Tappen Zee from Greensburg, N.Y., impressed "W. Wood and Sons," rectangular, 8" l.............. 935.00
Windsor castle with men fishing in foreground, foliage and scroll border, impressed "Clews Warranted Staffordshire," wear, staining, 2-3/4" h, 12-1/2" l, 10-1/4" w 412.50

Wash bowl, English country scene with houses, cows, man on horseback and city in distance, blue transfer, floral border on rim, band of flowers on exterior, hairline, 5" h, 12-3/8" dia...110.00

Wash bowl and pitcher, Aladdin pattern, light blue transfer, basketweave edging, bowl 13" dia, pitcher 11" h... 220.00

Waste bowl, floral sprays and urns with eagles and shields, interior shows Oriental building, minor roughness, 3" h, 5-1/2" dia.. 385.00

Stands

Background: Stand is a rather comprehensive term used to describe almost any kind of furniture used to support something. Among the almost endless variety produced were stands for candelabra, urns, teapots, chests, cabinets, and even wigs.

References: Eileen and Richard Dubrow, *Styles of American Furniture 1860-1960*, Schiffer Publishing, 1997; Tim Forrest, *Bulfinch Anatomy of Antique Furniture*, Bulfinch Press, 1996; John T. Kirk, *American Furniture: Understanding Styles, Construction, and Quality*, Harry N. Abrams Publishers, 2000; Milo M. Naeve, *Identifying American Furniture*, W.W. Norton, 1998; Ellen T. Schroy, *Warman's American Furniture*, Krause Publications, 2001; Robert W. and Harriet Swedberg, *Collector's Encyclopedia of American Furniture*, Vol. 1 (1990, 1996 value update), Vol. 2 (1992, 1999 value update), Vol. 3 (1998), Collector Books.

Also see: Candle Stands, Crock Stands

Chippendale

    Cherry, worn orig finish, tripod base, snake feet, turned column, two-board round top, wrought-iron support on base, column restorations, 26-1/2" h, 17-1/2" dia 1,540.00

    Country style, walnut, varnished, splayed legs with beaded corners and aprons, drawer hidden in apron, two-board pin top, reconstruction, 28" h, top 24" x 19-3/4".. 495.00

    Tilt-top, mahogany, old surface, serpentine top mkd "I. Young," turned tapering pedestal, three cabriole legs, pad feet, Boston or coastal Essex County, Mass., c. 1775-1800, imperfections, 29-1/2" h, top 21-3/4" x 22" 2,185.00

Classical, one-drawer, tiger maple, New England, c. 1830, overhanging square top, conforming base, ring-turned and swelled legs, ball feet, old refinish, imperfections, 29" h, top 20" x 19" 2,070.00

Country style, maple and pine, refinished, splayed legs, ring turnings, molded edge along bottom of apron, one-board pine top, minor age cracks, legs repegged, one foot chipped, 29-3/4" h 440.00

Country style, one-drawer

    Cherry, turned legs, stretcher base/shelf, two-board top, 28-1/4" h, 23-1/2" w, 23-1/4" d.............. 440.0

    Drop-leaf, grain decor, orig red grain decor on base, flame decor on top, two leaves and drawer front in old repaint, turned legs, minor wear, 29" h, 15-3/4" w, 16-3/4" d, 7-3/4" leaves.......................... 522.50

    Grain-decor, orig red flame graining, poplar, turned legs, one-board top, surface damage to top, 27" h, top 19-3/4" x 20".. 302.50

    Painted, old black and dark-brown over light brown repaint, pine, high legs, drawer with divided interior, oblong top with shaped sides, edge wear, 30" h, 20-3/4" w, 14-3/4" d 825.00

Tiger maple Classical stand, New England, c. 1830, old refinish, 29" h, top 20" x 19", $2,070. (Photo courtesy of Skinner Auctioneers & Appraisers of Antiques & Fine Arts, Boston and Bolton, Mass.)

Country style, two-drawer

    Cherry and curly maple, turned legs, paneled ends, dovetailed drawers, upper drawer with rounded front, one-board top, age cracks, refinished, 29-1/2" h, 20-1/2" w, 17-3/4" d 605.00

    Curly maple, boldly turned legs, paneled sides, applied S scrolls on either side of drawers, replaced two-board top, 29-1/4" h, top 19" w, 18-3/4" d 660.00

Federal, one-drawer

    Mahogany, probably New England, c. 1800-10, rectangular overhanging top, drawer with scratch beading, straight skirt, tapering legs, refinished, 27-3/4" h, top 16-3/4" x 16" 1,265.00

    Mahogany and bird's-eye maple veneer, Mass., early 19th C., square top with ovolo corners, veneered drawer, ring-turned tapering legs, ball feet, old refinish on top, orig dark stained base, old brass pull, minor imperfections, 27-3/4" h, top 15-1/4" x 15"... 2,760.00

Hepplewhite, one-drawer

    Birch and chestnut, country-style, old varnish finish, square tapered legs, drawer with divided interior, two-board top, top reattached crooked and possibly replaced, 28-1/2" h 19-1/4" w, 21" d..............522.50

    Cherry, square tapered legs, one-board top, pegged, refinished, replaced brass pull, top 18-3/4" w, 24-1/4" d 715.00

    Cherry, square tapered legs, one-board top with ovolo corners, edge beading on drawer, old refinishing, replaced brass pull, 27" h, 17-3/4" w, 17-1/2" d.. 1,072.50

Cherry, tapered legs, pegged construction, dovetailed drawer with brass pull, three-board top with beaded border, some border missing, 27-3/4" h, top 17-3/4" w, 17-3/8" d 715.00

Cherry, country style, refinished, square tapered legs, replaced two-board top, drawer repaired, replaced brass, 27-1/2" h, 17-3/4" w, 19-3/4" d 302.50

Hardwood, old dark worn finish, country style, square tapered legs, mortised and pinned apron, 1-board top with cut ovolo corners, top reattached with large-head nails, 26" h, 18" sq 1,100.00

Mahogany and walnut, curly ash veneer drawer front, square tapered legs, drawer with beaded frame, refinished, replaced 1-board mahogany top, replaced wood pull, 29-3/4" h, top 19-1/2" w, 17-1/2" d 302.50

Painted, old red stain, pine, square tapering legs, square overhanging top, New England, early 19th C., 27-3/4" h, top 18-3/4" w, 20-1/4" d 2,300.00

Painted, pine, old red paint, slight splay to beaded and tapered legs, aprons beaded to top and bottom, mortise and pin construction, insect damage under one-board top, minor repair to one leg, 29-3/4" h, 19-1/2" w, 19-1/4" d 330.00

Hepplewhite, two-drawer, grain-decor in red and black, square tapering legs, 29-1/2" h, top 18" x 16" 825.00

Other

One-drawer, cherry, orig brown sponged vinegar graining, gold striping, old brown overvarnish, decal designs on drawer, turned legs, two-board top, porcelain pull, Pennsylvania origin, 30" h, 23-1/2" w, 22" d 2,200.00

One-drawer cherry stand, $400.

One-drawer, figured maple, square tapering legs, 28" h, top 18" sq 1,540.00

Amish, one-drawer, oak, old varnish, turned legs, scalloped front apron, one-board top slightly warped, found in Winesburg, Ohio, 27-1/2" h, top 19-1/2" x 20-1/4" 935.00

Dish-top, walnut, possibly Mid-Atlantic states, c. 1790, circular molded top, vase-and-ring turned pedestal, tripod cabriole legs, old refinish, minor imperfections, 27-1/2" h, 15-3/4" dia 1,380.00

Folk-carved, one-drawer, cherry, orig finish over-varnished, ring-turned legs, applied half-turnings flank drawer with carved basket and leaves, carved pull, pegged two-board top, one peg missing, 29-1/2" h, top 19-1/2" sq 1,760.00

Sheraton, one-drawer

Cherry, turned and rope-twist carved legs, two-board top, wooden pull, refinished, 27-3/4" h, top 19-1/2" x 18-1/2" 742.50

Cherry and curly maple, delicate turned legs, dovetailed drawer with solid curly maple front, clear Sandwich glass pull, one-board top with minor warp, 29-1/8" h, 18" w, 17-1/2" d 935.00

Country style, cherry, curly maple drawer front, orig finish with varnish overcoat, turned and chamfered octagonal legs, one-board top, wooden pull on dovetailed drawer, 28-1/2" h, 19-1/2" w, 19-3/4" d 467.50

Country style, curly maple, turned legs, dovetailed drawer, opalescent Sandwich glass knob, one-board top, good figure, refinished, chips on turnings, 30" h, top 18-1/2" x 21" 2,090.00

Country style, curly maple and cherry, well-turned legs, dovetailed drawer, two-board top, replaced wooden pull, 29-1/2" h, top 20" x 19-3/4" 660.00

Country style, painted, pine, old red paint, bamboo-turned legs, peg-and-ball foot, dovetailed drawer, replaced wood knob, minor edge wear, 29" h, 16-1/2" sq 605.00

Tiger maple, turned legs, 28" h, top 21-1/2" x 17" 1,210.00

Sheraton, two-drawer

Birch, delicate turned legs, dovetailed drawers with rounded edges, refinished, replaced one-board top with added band inlay, leg repair, replaced brasses, 28-1/2" h, 18-1/4" w, 18" d 247.50

Birch and bird's-eye veneer, turned legs with incised rings and reverse urns at top and bottom, dovetailed drawers with veneered panels and mahogany band inlay, inlaid diamond-shaped escutcheon, thin one-board top with slight warp, refinished, chips on band inlay, 28" h, top 20" x 15-1/4" 1,210.00

Cherry and maple with well-figured mahogany veneer facade, well-turned legs with some figure, dovetailed drawers, two-board top, restored break in leg, veneer repairs, replaced brasses, 30" h, 20-1/4" w, 17-1/2" d 220.00

Cherry and mahogany veneer, old finish, turned legs, serpentine case with conforming drawers having applied beading, one-board figured cherry top, clear lacy pulls, one pull chipped, minor age cracks to reattached top, lock removed, veneer damage, 28" h, top 20" x 20-1/2" 1,100.00

Country style, birch and maple, old reddish-brown surface, turned legs, dovetailed drawers, turned wooden pulls, height loss, minor pieced repairs, 26" h, 18-1/4" w, 18-1/2" w 440.00

Country style, cherry, old finish and over-varnish, well-turned legs, dovetailed drawers, glass pulls, 2-board top, 29-1/2" h, 20" w, 19-3/4" d 605.00

Country style, cherry, turned legs, dovetailed drawers, mahogany veneer fronts with beading, two-board top, replaced hinges, 28-1/2" h, 19-1/4" w, 22" d, 9-1/4" leaves 467.50

Country style, cherry, bird's-eye maple veneer drawer fronts, turned legs, Rockingham knobs, veneer damage, 28-5/8" h, 18-5/8" w, 18-1/4" d 467.50

Curly maple and cherry, country style, ring-turned legs, drawers with incised borders, refinished, one-board top with age cracks, 28-1/2" h, top 18" sq. 1,210.00

Curly maple and poplar, old refinishing, ring-turned legs, dovetailed drawer, old replaced brass pull, loose two-board top, 28-1/2" h, top 22" x 21-3/4" 495.00

Drop-leaf, mahogany, rope-twist legs, flame-veneer drawer fronts, one-board top, shaped leaves, few hairlines in legs, 29" h, 16" w, 17" d 880.00

Sheraton, four-drawer, country style, cherry, figured mahogany veneer facade, turned and ring reeded legs and posts, dovetailed drawers, one-board top, poplar secondary wood, mid-19th C., refinished, 29" h, 17-1/2" sq. 660.00

Sheraton, drop-leaf, one-drawer, cherry with tiger maple drawer front, turned legs, shaped leaves, 28" h, top 24" x 14-1/2" (leaves down) 990.00

Sheraton, drop-leaf, two-drawer

Maple, some figure, turned legs, dovetailed drawers with shaped fronts, carved hand slot under roll of lower drawer, refinished, replaced pulls on upper drawer, replaced top, 29" h, top 18-1/4" x 20-3/4", leaves 10-1/2" 605.00

Mahogany and mahogany veneer, refinished, turned feet with rope-carved legs, case with rounded corners, replaced brass pulls and drawer bottoms, veneer repairs, 28" h, 19" w, 15-1/2" d 495.00

Walnut, turned and tapered legs, one-board top, refinished, replaced brass pulls, 29" h, top 16-1/2" x 18", 8-1/4" leaves..................................... 412.50

Steiff

Background: In the late 19th century, Margarete Steiff created a line of soft animals that would revolutionize the toy industry. Over the years, the German firm of Steiff produced a wide range of soft toy animals, all of which are extremely desirable today.

Steiff animals are especially noted for their attention to detail and their superb quality.

References: Dee Hockenberry, *Steiff Bears and Other Playthings Past and Present*, Schiffer Publishing, 2000; Margaret Fox Mandel, *Teddy Bears and Steiff Animals*, 1st series (1984, 1997 value update), 2nd series (1987, 1996 value update), Collector Books.

Collectors' Clubs: Steiff Club USA, 31 E. 28th St., 9th Floor, New York, NY 10016, www.steiff-club.com; Steiff Collectors Club, 5001 Monroe St., Toledo, OH 43623, www.toystorenet.com.

Reproduction Alert: Steiff fakes have been produced, and the company has even released its own line of limited-edition replicas of earlier designs. Check for signs of deliberate distressing, and treat crudely made, inaccurately modeled examples with suspicion.

In some cases, the round, metal Steiff button has been attached to other antique stuffed animals. Remember that mohair plush was used for old Steiff animals, and the trimmings were usually made of velvet or felt.

Bear pull toy

Brass-spoke wheels, medium-brown mohair, black bead eyes, ear button, part of Museum Collection, orig box with damage, 5-1/4" h, 6-1/2" l...... 137.50

Steel-tube base, white rubber wheels, worn brown fur, tan mohair muzzle, glass eyes, ear button, yellow tag, 1 wheel damaged, 18" h, 23" l 357.50

Black cat

6-1/2" h, script button in ear, cond. 9.25+ 176.00

8-1/4" h, script button in ear, cond. 9.25+ 187.00

14" h, script button in ear, cond. 9.25+ 413.50

Cat pull toy, gray-striped, light-green glass eyes, ear button, ribbon and bell, minor wear, one wheel crooked, 6-1/2" h, 10" l 1,210.00

Camel, ivory wool, gold velvet legs and face, pale brown eyes, 13" h 110.00

Chimpanzee, "Jocko" name tag, seated, brown mohair, white chin, felt face, feet and hands, jointed, orange glass eyes, ear button, 7-1/2" h 137.50

Donkey, "Grissy" name tag, gray, brown and white fur, black mane, c. 1960s, ear button...................... 99.00

Elephant, glass eyes (one missing), fragment of purple blanket on back, wear, soiling, 6-1/2" h, 9-1/2" l.. 150.00

Giraffe, ivory mohair, orange spots, blue glass eyes, ear button, 13-1/4" h 55.00

Lion

Cub, mohair, growler, green glass eyes, one ear pulling away, 13" l... 55.00

"Leo" name tag, tan and brown mohair, darker brown mane and tail, embroidered nose, mouth and paws, orange glass eyes, 15" l (excluding tail) 220.00

Mountain goat, ivory mohair, light-brown felt horns, green glass eyes, ear button, 9-1/4" h, 7-1/2" l 165.00

Parrot, red, blue, yellow and green mohair, rubber beak, green glass eyes, wing button, 9-1/8" h 110.00

Poodle, "Snobby" name tag, gray-tan mohair, black button nose, brown glass eyes, jointed head and legs, ear button, 8-1/2" h, 8" l 82.50

Ram, white and black mohair, felt horns and ears, green glass eyes, button missing, 8-1/4" h, 9" l 220.00

Rhino, "Nosy" name tag, brown velvet, gray details, felt ears and horn, ear button, 13" l 104.50

Shetland pony, "Sheddy" name tag, white and brown with yellow mane and tail, brown glass eyes, ear button, 9-1/2" h 192.50

Squirrel
   Ivory mohair, tufts on ears, velvet nut, embroidered nose and paws, dark glass eyes, ear button, 7-1/2" h 137.50
   "Perri, Copyright Walt Disney Productions" tag, ivory and brown mohair, felt paws, velvet nut, dark glass eyes, ear button, minor wear, 5-1/2" h 192.50

Steer, Holstein with black and white plush, felt ears, orange glass eyes, 10" h, 15-1/2" l 220.00

Teddy bear, light-brown mohair, velvet paw pads, black bead eyes, embroidered nose, ear button, 9" l 165.00

Turtle, "Slo" name tag, tan over pale-yellow mohair, felt claws, rubber shell, dark-blue glass eyes, ear button, 7-1/4" l 55.00

Walrus, "Paddy" name tag, brown spotted mohair, blue glass eyes, white rubber tusks, 5" h 55.00

Stone Fruit

Background: Made of ceramic and often life-size, stone fruit was a purely decorative 19th-century ornamentation. Their popularity was revived again during the second half of the 20th century. Later examples have little value compared to vintage stone fruit.

Eight pcs, painted, various types 330.00

Ten pcs, orig polychrome paint, two apples, two pears, peach, orange, lemon, banana, fig and grapes, minor wear 522.50

Fifteen pcs, three ripe figs, two green figs, two apples, two strawberries, two peaches, orange, lemon, grapes and banana, orig polychrome paint worn, some damage 385.00

Stoneware

Background: When the highest temperature of the only firing process for stoneware has been reached, salt is thrown into the kiln. As it vaporizes, the sodium reacts with the silica in the stoneware body to form a thin, hard glass-like glaze on the piece. Pieces which exhibit slightly pitted surfaces are referred to as having an "orange peel" glaze. Stoneware items are impervious to liquid and extremely durable, making them ideal for food preparation and storage. The most desirable pieces are those with unusual cobalt decorations.

References: Georgeanna H. Greer, *American Stonewares: The Art and Craft of Utilitarian Potters*, Schiffer Publishing, 1999; Kathryn McNerney, *Blue & White Stoneware*, Collector Books, 1996; Terry Taylor and Terry & Kay Lawrence, *Collector's Encyclopedia of Salt Glaze Stoneware*, Collector Books, 1997.

Collectors' Clubs: American Stoneware Association, 208 Crescent Ct., Mars, PA 16066-3308; American Stoneware Collectors Society, P.O. Box 281, Bay Head, NJ 08742; Blue & White Pottery Club, 224 12th St., N.W., Cedar Rapids, IA 52405; Collectors of Illinois Pottery & Stoneware, 308 N. Jackson St., Clinton, IL 61727; Red Wing Collectors Society, Inc., P.O. Box 14, Galesburg, IL 61401; Southern Folk Pottery Collectors Society, 1828 N. Howard Mill Rd., Robbins, NC 27325-7477; Uhl Collectors' Society, 80 Tidewater Rd., Hagerstown, IN 47346.

Museums: Bennington Museum, VT; Brooklyn Museum, NY; DAR Museum, Washington, DC; Henry Ford Museum, Dearborn, MI; Henry Francis DuPont Winterthur Museum, DE; Museum of Ceramics at East Liverpool, OH; Shelburne Museum, VT.

Specialty Auction: Bruce and Vicki Waasdorp, P.O. Box 434, Clarence, NY 14031.

Note: All marks are impressed unless otherwise noted.

Also See: New Geneva

THE GOOD STUFF

"Good stoneware is bringing good money." That's how Bruce Waasdorp sums up the marketplace for decorated stoneware.

Competition remains keen for the most artistic examples, whether it's a piece of stoneware decorated with florals, animals, or birds. The only decline he's seen recently is prices for middle-line pieces of blue-and-gray molded pottery and Rockingham items.

"The best things sell for the best money," says Waasdorp, who specializes in decorated stoneware. "People are looking for decorative items and have the money to spend, and stoneware fits that bill."

Batter jug, marked

"Cowden & Wilcox, Harrisburg," salt-glazed, flowers and brushed detail, tin lid, bubbles in cobalt, edge chips, 9" h.................................. 962.50

"Cowden & Wilcox, Harrisburg," two-gal, salt-glazed, two flowers on each side of spout, back with double flowers, spout chips, hairlines, 11" h.. 1,210.00

"E.W. Farrington & Co., Elmira, N.Y.," six-qt, salt-glazed, brushed cobalt flower, restoration to chips, long hairline 467.50

Batter jug, unmarked

Cobalt flower decor, salt-glazed, restoration, bail and lid missing, 11-1/2" h........................... 302.50

Cobalt oak leaf decor, salt-glazed, orig bail and lid... 577.50

Whites Utica, running bird decor, three-qt, minor chip, glaze spider.................................... 1,017.50

Bottle, marked

"G.R. Gage," salt-glazed, cobalt accent, 9-3/4" h.. 176.00

"G.F. Hewett," cobalt accent, sloping shoulder, chips, 10-1/4" h... 27.50

"John Howell," salt-glazed, cobalt accent, 9-1/2" h.. 66.00

Salt-glaze figural bottle marked "G.R. Gage," cobalt highlights, minor chip, 9-3/4" h, $1,320. (Photo courtesy of Bruce and Vicki Waasdorp)

"Newton & Co. California Beer, Patd. Oct. 29, 1872," light-mustard glaze, 10" h.......................... 165.00

"J.P. Plummer 1853," salt-glazed, cobalt accent, stone ping, 9-1/4" h................................ 165.00

"A. Reynolds," salt-glazed, cobalt accent, chips, 10" h.. 66.00

"Smith & Snow, White Root...," salt-glazed, cobalt accent, five-line mark, dated 1873, 9-1/2" h... 209.00

Bottle, unmarked

"A" in brushed cobalt, salt-glazed, 10" h........ 412.50

Floral decor, salt-glazed, one-qt, discolored, 8-1/2" h... 176.00

Undecor, twelve-sided, base chip, 10-1/4" h.. 22.00

Bowl, 6-gal, salt-glazed, medium-brown glaze, flat bottom, flared sides, incised "6" on rim, 7" h, 18-3/4" dia.. 1,500.00

Butter crock

"Butter" in oval, blue sponging, 9" dia........... 275.00

"R.C.R., Phila.," Richard C. Remney, Philadelphia, salt-glazed, straight sides with freehand cobalt flourishes around lip and shoulder, inner rim chip, 4-1/4" h, 7-1/4" dia.................................... 825.00

Cake, "Frank B. Norton, Worcester, Mass.," 1-1/2-gal, salt-glazed, dotted floral decor.......................... 302.50

Cake, unmarked, salt-glazed

Cobalt floral and line decor, glued cracks, two-gal.. 412.50

Swag decor all around, glued crack.............. 275.00

Canning jar, marked

"Hamilton & Jones, Greensboro, Pa.," salt-glazed, cobalt stencil, minor chips, 8-1/2" h............ 132.00

"Mason Fruit Jar, Union Stoneware Co., Red Wing, Minn.," one-quart, bristol glaze, black ink-stamp mark 165.00

"Mason Fruit Jar, Union Stoneware Co., Red Wing, Minn.," 1/2-gal, bristol glaze, blue ink-stamp mark 220.00

"T.F. Reppert, Greensboro, Pa.," salt-glazed, cobalt stencil, tree-like design, minor chips, 10" h... 192.50

"Williams and Reppert, Greensboro, Pa.," salt-glazed, cobalt stencil, 10" h...................... 137.50

Canning jar, unmarked, salt-glazed

Three brushed stripes on front, short hairline, chips, 8-1/8" h... 192.50

Four brushed stripes on front, minor chips, 1/2-gal, 8" h.. 209.00

Brushed stripes at top and bottom, four diagonal stripes in center, 1/2-gal, 8" h.................... 247.50

Conical, four brushed cobalt stripes on front, minor rim chips, 12" h 440.00

Chicken waterer, "Wade & Henry, Phila.," salt-glazed, brushed cobalt flourishes, hooded-type opening, ear handles, chips, 8" h....................................... 3,630.00

Churn, marked

"Clark & Bros., Cannelton, Ind.," six-gal, salt-glazed 225.00

BUYER BEWARE

Oh deer! That's what collectors are saying about reproduction pieces of folk-decorated stoneware. One known example is a preserve jar impressed, "Whites Utica," and showing a leaping stag with a fence and pine tree in the background. It takes a bit of detective work, but the piece can easily be proven a fake. The body of the jar has crudely applied ears and is poorly potted from white clay. The color of the cobalt is too bright, the jar lacks a recessed rim for the lid, and the base is glazed, unlike legitimate pieces of Whites Utica.

Knowledgeable collectors need only glance at such an item to determine it's not all it appears. However, such pieces aren't made to fool the experts. Instead, the intent is to make a quick profit off of unsuspecting (and often unknowledgeable) buyers.

How do you protect yourself from buying a bogus piece? Begin by learning all you can about the type of stoneware you like. Personally examining as many items as possible is the best education there is. The greater the number of pieces you handle, the better acquainted you'll be with the look, feel and weight of legitimate items.

For information on this and other pieces of reproduction stoneware, see Bruce and Vicki Waasdorp's Internet site at www.antiques-stoneware.com.

"W.H. Crisco" (William Henry Crisco), two-gal, salt-glazed, grooved handles, flared collar, orig lid, late 19th or early 20th C., three chips, nicks 660.00
"Fort Edward Stoneware Co., Fort Edward, N.Y.," three-gal, salt-glazed, diagonal plume, inner rim chip 577.50
"Homell & ___, Manufacturers of Stoneware, Tuscarawas Co., Ohio," six-gal, salt-glazed, cobalt script, with wooden lid and dasher 660.00
Red Wing (unmarked), trademark double birch leaves, two-gal, bristol glaze 302.50
"W. Roberts, Binghamton, N.Y.," six-gal, salt-glazed, cobalt freehand vine and floral design, professional restoration to entire right side........... 797.50
Uhl Pottery Co., Acorn Wares ink stamp, two-gal, bristol glaze 150.00
Churn, unmarked
Four-gal, salt glaze, brushed cobalt budding flowers with decor lines, wooden lid and dasher....................... 247.50
Four-gal, salt glaze, overall brushed decor of vines, leaves, flowers and dots, western Pa., glued crack....................... 577.50

Five-gal, salt glaze, brushed cobalt "5" surrounded by three squiggled daubs, light stains, small pot stones, Ohio origin 192.50
Five-gal, salt glaze, cobalt stencil of two roses beneath round wreath with "5," hairline 192.50
Six-gal, salt-glaze, brushed cobalt leaves flaking "6" surrounded by squiggled daubs and scroll with dots, wooden lid and dasher, probably Ohio origin 495.00
Cooler
"A. Lambright, Newport, Ohio," salt-glazed, ovoid, cobalt freehand mark, double flowers on opposite side, two handles with impressed line decor, hairline, 21" h.. 1,980.00
Niagara Falls motif, unmkd Whites Utica, design in green, cobalt and brown highlights on embossed design on front, cobalt on embossed floral design on back, lid missing, cracked, 13" h 1,650.00
Unmkd, salt-glazed, ovoid, brushed cobalt branch with leaves, double handles, tapering top, probably Ohio origin, minor rim flakes, in-the-making base chip, 19-1/2" h................................... 880.00
Crock or storage jar, marked
"Ballard & Brothers, Burlington, Vt.," 1-1/2-gal, salt-glazed, dotted double flowers, large in-the-making base chip on back, cracks, glaze flake 176.00
"Jas. Benjamin Stoneware Depot, Cincinnati, O.," two-gal, salt-glazed, cobalt stencil, crack 77.00
"Boston," attributed to Frederick Carpenter, two-gal, salt-glazed, ovoid, dark-brown ochre accents at base and shoulder, rim chips................... 1,072.50
"S.B. Bosworth, Hartford, Conn.," two-gal, salt-glazed, dotted geometric decor 132.00
"C.W. Braun, Buffalo, N.Y.," three-gal, salt-glazed, cobalt wheat sheaths decor, hairline, chip... 852.50
"C.W. Braun, Buffalo, N.Y.," four-gal, salt-glazed, cobalt stylized dotted flower decor, stone ping.. 302.50

"W.H. Farrar & Co., Geddes, N.Y." one-gal. salt-glaze cream pot, pinwheel flower and tornado in cobalt, minor chip, $1,540. (Photo courtesy of Bruce and Vicki Waasdorp)

"C.W. Braun, Buffalo, N.Y.," six-gal, salt-glazed, cobalt sunflower decor, crack 247.50

"Brewer & Halm, Havana," two-gal, salt-glazed, cobalt freehand dotted flower and leaf decor, chips, stains.. 385.00

"Brown Brothers, Huntington, L.I.," two-gal, salt-glazed, cobalt freehand double tulip decor, professional restoration to lug handles (replaced), long crack.. 165.00

"J.F. Bryant & Co., Utica," one-gal, salt-glazed, ovoid, cobalt brushed plume decor, impressed mark... 412.50

"J. Burger Jr., Rochester, N.Y.," six-gal, salt-glazed, large ribbed flower, large glaze flake 385.00

"John Burger, Rochester," two-gal, flower decor, with lid, hairline 797.50

"Burger & Co., Rochester, N.Y.," three-gal, salt-glazed, wreath variation.............................. 412.50

"Burger & Lang, Rochester, N.Y.," two-gal, salt-glazed, wreath decor, chips, hairlines......... 165.00

"N. Clark & Co., Lyons," three-gal, salt-glazed, ovoid, brushed cobalt flower, chips............. 275.00

"F.H. Cowden, Harrisburg," two-gal, salt-glazed, cobalt stencil of geometric decor, cobalt at handles, chips.. 192.50

"Cowden & Wilcox, Harrisburg, Pa.," three-gal, salt-glazed, ovoid, floral decor 522.50

Dave the Slave, five-gal, alkaline glaze, ovoid, two handles, c. 1820s-30s, unsigned but with slash marks indicative of the potter................... 3,080.00

"Moody Dustin, Jeffersonville, IA" (Jeffersonville, Ind.), one-gal, salt-glazed........................... 450.00

"E.&S.B., New Brighton, Pa.," six-gal, salt-glazed, cobalt stencil, chips 140.00

"Excelsior Works, Isaac Hewitt Jr., Rices Landing, Pa.," three-gal, salt-glazed, cobalt stencil with tulip, minor chips...................................... 660.00

"W.H. Farrar, Geddes," three-gal, salt-glazed, cobalt bird and flower decor, dots, squiggles and filled body on bird, hairlines 1,925.00

"J. Fisher, Lyons," two-gal, bee-sting design, chips at ear 198.00

"J. Fisher & Co., Lyons, N.Y.," two-gal, salt-glazed, brushed tulip.. 220.00

"Hamilton & Jones, Greensboro, Pa.," two-gal, salt-glazed, cobalt stencil with floral motif, freehand stripes.. 280.50

"Hamilton & Jones, Greensboro, Pa.," two-gal, salt-glazed, cobalt stencil with shield motif, freehand, stripes, U-shaped hairline in base, small chips... 275.00

"Hamilton & Jones, Greensboro, Pa.," three-gal, salt-glazed, cobalt stencil and freehand stripes, chipped double handles.............................. 522.50

"Hamilton & Jones, Greensboro, Pa.," salt-glazed, cobalt stenciled name, brushed lines at top and bottom, hairline, 10" h................................. 165.00

"James Hamilton, Greensboro, Pa.," salt-glazed, cobalt stencil around fan decor, brushed freehand lines top and bottom, hairlines, 9-3/4" h........ 220.00

"L.B. Dilliner, New Geneva, Pa." salt-glaze crock, 6-1/2" h, $250.

"James Hamilton & Co., Greensboro, Pa." three-gal, salt-glazed, cobalt stencil and freehand stripes, double handles, minor stains, chips 385.00

"Jas. Hamilton & Co., Greensboro, Pa.," salt-glazed, cobalt stencil, name in meandering border of leaves, sides taper to base, 8-1/8" h 302.50

"T. Harrington, Lyons," three-gal, salt-glazed, triple floral decor, with lid, restored chip 742.50

"Harris Bros., Brownsville, Ohio," 20-gal, cobalt mark, shallow chips on handles 192.50

"S. Hart, Fulton," two-gal, salt-glazed, stylized cobalt floral design and large "2," restored hairline, chips 176.00

"Haxstun & Co., Fort Edward, N.Y.," two-gal, singing long-tail bird on dotted plume, rim chip, few stains 687.50

"Haxstun & Co., Fort Edward, N.Y.," three-gal, large bird on twig, few stains, long inner surface chip.. 385.00

"Higgins & Co., Cleveland," three-gal, salt-glazed, brushed cobalt tulip, hairlines, rim chips 440.00

"Hormell & Smith" (Paris, Ohio), two-gal, salt-glazed, name in freehand cobalt script 550.00

"D.F. Huggins" (Parke County, Ind.), one-gal, salt-glazed, ovoid 400.00

"N.G. Humill, Newport, Ohio," salt-glazed, name in freehand cobalt, hairlines, 9-1/2" h............. 192.50

"George Husher" (Brazil, Ind.), three-gal, salt-glazed... 225.00

"George Husher" (Brazil, Ind.), three-gal, salt-glazed, chips 175.00

"Jordon," two-gal, salt-glazed, cobalt starburst decor, orig lid 1,650.00

"Jordon," two-gal, salt-glazed, ovoid, cobalt brushed double flowers, professional restoration to chips, crack... 357.50

"J.B. Leathers, Mt. Eagle, Pa.," four-gal, salt-glazed, ovoid, freehand cobalt floral decor, with replaced stoneware lid 1,100.00

"Lewis & Cady, Fairfax, Vt.," three-gal, plume decor, stone pings, hairline..................................... 330.00

"Lyons," one-gal, salt-glazed, brushed flower, crack.. 132.00

"Lyons," two-gal, salt-glazed, brushed tulip, chip... 165.00

"J. Martin," two-gal, salt-glazed, ovoid........... 225.00

"I.M. Mead, Mogadore, Ohio," 1-1/2-gal, salt-glazed, ovoid.. 176.00

"I.M. Mead, Portage Co., Ohio," three-gal, salt-glazed, brushed cobalt on name and double handles, rim chips.................................... 275.00

"E.H. Merrill," salt-glazed, ovoid, chips on flared rim, 10" h 110.00

"P. Mugler and Co., Buffalo, N.Y.," three-gal, brushed cobalt flower, hairlines 467.50

"Neff Bros. Manufacturers, Taylorsville, O.," five-gal, salt-glazed, cobalt stencil 165.00

"New York Stoneware Co., Fort Edwards, N.Y.," one-gal, salt-glazed, ovoid, tornado decor, rim chip.. 302.50

"New York Stoneware Co., Fort Edwards, N.Y.," three-gal, salt-glazed, large bird on plume, orig lid, cinnamon clay.. 577.50

"E.&L.P. Norton, Bennington, Vt.," one-gal, salt-glazed, plume decor, short hairline............. 176.00

"E.&L.P. Norton, Bennington, Vt.," two-gal, salt-glazed, floral decor, with lid, restored rim chip.. 412.50

"E.&L.P. Norton, Bennington, Vt.," four-gal, salt-glazed, dotted floral spray, two full-length glued cracks 99.00

"F.B. Norton & Co., Worcester, Mass.," four-gal, salt-glazed, parrot on plume, hairlines 577.50

"J.&E. Norton, Bennington, Vt.," two-gal, salt-glazed, dotted floral decor, minor rim chip 605.00

"J.&E. Norton, Bennington, Vt.," two-gal, salt-glazed, floral spray, minor stone ping...................... 742.50

"J.&E. Norton, Bennington, Vt.," three-gal, salt-glazed, compote of flowers, minor glaze flaking 880.00

"J.&E. Norton, Bennington, Vt.," three-gal, salt-glazed, thistle decor, orig lid, glued freeze crack on back, glaze crazing............................... 412.50

"T.A. Packer," salt-glazed, ovoid, brushed cobalt tulip, hairlines, 12-1/2" h 302.50

"T.A. Packer," salt-glazed, brushed cobalt tulip, 13-1/2" h 1,100.00

"Penn Yan" (Penn Yan Pottery, Yates County, N.Y., 1840), salt-glazed, cobalt brushed floral decor, cobalt at handles, 8" h 385.00

"J.S. Perry" (Ind.), three-gal, salt-glazed, rim chip.. 300.00

"Jas. Peterson, Hopewell, Muskingham Co. O.," three-gal, salt-glazed, cobalt stencil, applied handles, stains.. 577.50

"S.L. Pewtress, Fairhaven, Conn.," one-gal, salt-glazed, leaf design, hairline....................... 176.00

"S.L. Pewtress, Fairhaven, Conn.," four-gal, salt-glazed, elaborate parrot.......................... 1,870.00

"Red Wing Union Stoneware Co., Red Wing, Minn.," twenty-gal, bristol glaze, small wing, ink-stamp mark, bail handles missing 192.50

"H.F. Reinhardt, Vale, N.C.," five-gal, olive alkaline glaze, lug handles, c. 1937-early 1940s, shallow chip 1,155.00

"R.C.R., Phila." (Richard C. Remney, Philadelphia), salt-glazed, freehand cobalt flourishes around lip and shoulder, chip, hairline, 8-5/8" h, 5-1/2" dia 1,150.00

"Remney 1882," one-qt, salt-glazed, Star of David decor, two restored cracks, 6-3/4" h 1,870.00

"T.F. Reppert, Eagle Pottery, Greensboro, Pa," sixteen-gal, salt-glazed, cobalt stencil with eagle, scrolls and name, cobalt freehand additions, hairlines, chips, stabilized crack in base........... 715.00

"M.M. Reynolds" (Ind.), one-gal, salt-glazed, cracks 200.00

"Sipe, Nichols & Co., Williamsport, Pa.," 1-1/2-gal, salt-glazed, freehand cobalt leaf 250.00

"H.C. Smith, Alex, D.C.," two-gal, salt-glazed, ovoid, vines and flowers decor, ear chips, hairline.. 852.50

"C.C. Thorp, Mogadore, Ohio," six-gal, salt-glazed, ovoid, freehand cobalt tulip, cracks 220.00

"Troy, N.Y. Pottery," two-gal, salt-glazed, bird on twig, with lid, small stone ping 275.00

"Uhl Pottery Co.," bristol glaze, one-gal, Acorn Wares ink stamp.. 35.00

"Union Stoneware Co., Red Wing, Minn.," twenty-gal, bristol glaze, four birch leaves, ink stamp mark 286.00

"West Troy Pottery, N.Y.," four-gal, salt-glazed, cobalt freehand decor of reclining dog, flying birds and tree, professional restoration to glaze flakes, one handle, crack and rim chip 907.50

"N.A. White & Son, Utica, N.Y.," one-gal, cobalt floral decor 632.50

"Whites Utica," one-gal, running bird decor in cobalt... 962.50

"Whites Utica," four-gal, fantail running bird decor in cobalt, short hairline, rim chip..................... 495.00

Crock or storage jar, unmarked

Three stripes on front, 1/2-gal, salt-glazed, ovoid, two chips 143.00

Eagle decor, five-gal, salt-glazed, cobalt stencil, cracks, chips... 247.50

Floral decor, five-gal, salt-glazed, hairlines 1,045.00

Plume decor repeated four times, one-qt, salt-glazed, minor clay separation..................... 121.00

Star decor, three-gal, salt-glazed, freehand cobalt design, top slightly tapered........................ 302.50

Cup, Albany slip, sgraffito decor, "Mr. Isaac Stevens" in scrollwork cartouche, chips, 3-1/2" h 275.00

Jug, marked

"S.H. Addington," two-gal, salt-glazed, ovoid, brushed cobalt flower decor, some design fry 687.50

"Bennace & Sutherland, Springfield, Portage, Ohio," two-gal, salt-glazed, ovoid, brushed cobalt highlights, handle damage 93.50

"John Burger, Rochester," two-gal, salt-glazed, poppy decor.................... 440.00

"Clark & Co., Rochester," three-gal, salt-glazed, ovoid, brushed cobalt flower and "3," handle missing... 198.00

"Clark & Fox, Athens, N.Y.," one-gal, salt-glazed, ovoid, cobalt brushed flower, stone pings... 550.00

"N. Clark & Co., Lyons," two-gal, salt-glazed, ovoid, brushed cobalt plume and "2"..................... 467.50

"Commeraw's Stoneware, Commeraw's Corlears Hook New York," two-gal, salt-glazed, ovoid, incised clamshell design in blue accent, impressed six-line mark, professional restoration to freeze line, stone ping in front 1,925.00

"F.H. Cowden, Harrisburg, Pa.," two-gal, salt-glazed, ovoid, brushed cobalt floral decor, chip, discoloring... 160.00

"F.H. Cowden, Harrisburg, Pa.," two-gal, salt-glazed, cobalt stenciled snowflake design, small chip 600.00

"Cowden & Wilcox," one-gal, salt-glazed, freehand cobalt flower with petals and scrolled leaves, chip 450.00

"M. Crafts, Whately," one-gal, salt-glazed, beehive form, pinwheel decor, stone pings, hairlines 121.00

"A.P. Donaghho, Parkersburg, W.Va.," two-gal, salt-glazed, beehive shape, stenciled "2" in circle motif above name, minor spout chips.................. 247.50

"DS" (Daniel Seagle), one-gal, olive alkaline glaze, ovoid, late 1840s-1867 .... 4,400.00

"Edmunds & Co.," three-gal, beehive shape, cobalt vine and flower decor 176.00

"1913 Last Christmas" pre-Prohibition advertising jug, pint, $220.

"W.H. Farrar & Co., Geddes, N.Y.," two-gal, salt-glazed, beehive shape, bird on double-flowered branch, body filled with lines and cobalt, minor design fry, restored full-length crack on back... 1,705.00

"J. Fenton," salt-glazed, ovoid, cobalt fish, 12" h 1,870.00

"Fort Edwards Pottery Co.," two-gal, salt-glazed, beehive shape, dotted stylized caterpillar decor, stains, design fry 825.00

"Gillig Bros., 273 Washington St., Buffalo, N.Y.," salt-glazed, mark in cobalt quill work, 11" h 220.00

"Hamilton & Jones, Greensboro," two-gal, salt-glazed, ovoid, cobalt stencil and freehand decor, minor chips on neck 302.50

"T. Harrington, Lyons," four-gal, salt-glazed, ovoid, brushed leaf, stains 247.50

"S. Hart, Fulton," two-gal, salt-glazed, beehive shape, cobalt flower design, minor stains 165.00

"W. Hart, Ogdensburg," two-gal, salt-glazed, beehive shape, cobalt dotted cross design 962.50

"Haxstun, Fort Edward," two-gal, chicken pecking corn, restored handle, hairline through design... 770.00

"JFS" (John Franklin Seagle), one-gal, dark-olive alkaline glaze, ovoid, third quarter of 19th C., old shallow nick 1,210.00

"Johnston Warner & Co...Philadelphia," beehive, machine-tooled bands, two-tone blue and gray, blue-washed label, drilled, short hairline, 10-1/4" h... 330.00

"Jordan," two-gal, salt-glazed, cobalt starburst decor, orig lid 1,650.00

"Jordan," two-gal, salt-glazed, cobalt wreath decor around freehand "2," minor chip 660.00

"W. A. Lewis, Galesville, N.Y.," two-gal, salt-glazed, beehive shape, cobalt freehand floral decor 742.50

""Lewis & Cady, Fairfax, Vt.," four-gal, salt-glazed, beehive, brushed cobalt floral design with spiral leaves, chips, worn cobalt 302.50

"Lyman & Clark, Gardiner," two-gal, salt-glazed, ovoid, gallonage number and accent stripe in ochre, spout chips, deep stone ping on back... 742.50

"Lyons," two-gal, salt-glazed, ovoid, flower decor, wide spout, stains................................... 357.50

"J. Maxfield, Milwaukee," two-gal, salt-glazed, ovoid, brushed cobalt floral decor, rim chips, stains 495.00

"J. McBurney, Jordan," two-gal, salt-glazed, beehive shape, brushed cobalt flower, restored chip... 632.50

"I.M. Mead, Mogadore, Ohio," two-gal, salt-glazed, ovoid, brushed cobalt tulip, minor flake 935.00

"I.M. Mead & Co.," two-gal, salt-glazed, ovoid, stains 247.50

"C.J. Merrill" (Akron, Ohio), two-gal, salt-glazed, ovoid, brushed cobalt at name and handle, minor rim flakes 220.00

"H.&G. Nash, Utica," one-gal, salt-glazed, ovoid, cobalt brushed flower decor, stone ping 220.00

"New York Stoneware Co., Fort Edwards, N.Y.," one-gal, salt-glazed, bird on branch decor, minor spout chips 605.00

"Norton & Fenton E., Bennington, Vt.," one-gal, salt-glazed, ovoid, brushed ochre accent, minor chips, stone pings 302.50

"F.B. Norton Co., Worcester, Mass.," two-gal, salt-glazed, cloverleaf decor, minor stains 275.00

"J.&E. Norton, Bennington, Vt.," one-gal, salt-glazed, bird decor, in-the-making base chip, spout wear 385.00

"J.&E. Norton, Bennington, Vt.," one-gal, salt-glazed, bird on stump, glaze pitting, chips 440.00

"J.&E. Norton, Bennington, Vt.," one-gal, salt-glazed, bird on twig, drilled hole for lamp ... 467.50

"J.&E. Norton, Bennington, Vt.," two-gal, salt-glazed, floral decor, hairlines 357.50

"Julius Norton, Bennington, Vt.," three-gal, salt-glazed, beehive form, triple floral decor, stains, in-the-making clay separation at base 165.00

"Ottman Bros., Fort Edward, N.Y.," two-gal, salt-glazed, fat bird on plume decor, stone ping 935.00

"S. Purdy" (Tuscarawas County, Ohio), three-gal, salt-glazed, ovoid 550.00

"S. Purdy," one-gal, salt-glazed, ovoid 632.50

"A.&J.H. Rhoads, Middlebury, Ohio," salt-glazed, ovoid, brushed cobalt double tulip, small flakes, 11-1/4" h 1,292.50

Collin Rhodes (unsigned but identifiable), three-gal, alkaline glaze with black, olive and gold streaks, ovoid, flower in freehand slip, top of flower is sideways "3" (gallonage), c. 1840s-50s, shallow chip 11,000.00

Collin Rhodes (unsigned but identifiable), alkaline glaze in khaki-olive, ovoid, sunflower in freehand slip, c. 1850s, three shallow rim chips, 8-5/8" h 8,525.00

Collin Rhodes (unsigned but identifiable), merchant's jug, one-gal, alkaline glaze in khaki-green, ovoid, "M.L. Brown & Co., Columbia S.C. 20" in freehand slip, "1" in medallion (gallonage), c. 1850s, chips 7,975.00

"I. Seymour and Co., Troy," one-gal, salt-glazed, ovoid, incised and cobalt accented antlers and grapes design 1,815.00

"W.J. Seymour, Troy Factory," two-gal, salt-glazed, beehive shape, cobalt stylized dotted design, minor age spiders 330.00

"P.H. Smith," three-gal, salt-glazed, ovoid, freehand cobalt floral decor, small hole drilled below decor 357.50

"G. Unser, Jeffersonville, Ind.," three-gal, salt-glazed 200.00

"C.W. Weaver, Stoneware Depot, Cincinnati, O.," two-gal, salt-glazed, cobalt stencil, handle cracked, small chips 110.00

"J.W. Weaver," two-gal, salt-glazed, ovoid, brushed cobalt tulips 550.00

"Westhafer and Lambright, 1865," six-gal, salt-glazed, beehive, double handles, brushed cobalt on mark and handles, brushed cobalt flower on other side resembles face 935.00

"West Troy, N.Y. Lottery," salt-glazed, freehand pecking chicken in cobalt quill work, 11-1/2" h 1,650.00

"Whites Utica," two-gal, brushed flower decor in cobalt, ovoid, stains 330.00

"Whites Utica," two-gal, brushed flower decor in cobalt, cylinder form, chips, stains 110.00

"F. Wunderlich, New Albany, Ind.," one-gal scratch jug, Albany glaze 100.00

Jug, miniature

"Compliments of Ed H. Westhoff, Waterloo, IA" (unmarked Red Wing), 1/8-pint, Bristol glaze, ink-stamp mark, bail handle missing, 2-3/4" h 770.00

"Detrick, Tippecanoe City, Ohio," white, blue ink stamp, beehive shape, 3-1/4" h 275.00

Motto jug, "Rye on Toast!...Detrick Distilling Co., Dayton, Ohio," brown over white, beehive shape, 4-1/2" h 143.00

Motto jug, "While We Live, Let's Live, Detrick Distilling Co., Dayton, O.," paper label on back, brown over white, beehive shape, 4-1/2" h 247.50

"Old Continental Whiskey," brown over white, acorn ink stamp, beehive shape, 3" h 55.00

Jug, unmarked

Albany slip, beehive shape, running black glaze, Southern origin, chipped lip, 19-1/4" h 82.50

Bee-sting decor, three-gal, salt-glazed, beehive shape, handle cracked 247.50

Tulip decor, three-gal, salt-glazed, brushed cobalt design, minor crazing 550.00

Pig, keg-type, salt-glazed, freehand cobalt decor, three feet, 8" h, 10" l 880.00

"J.&E. Norton, Bennington, Vt." four-gal. salt-glaze jug with stylized floral decoration in cobalt, chip, $1,045. (Photo courtesy of Bruce and Vicki Waasdorp)

Pitcher
Thomas Chandler, alkaline glaze, freehand brown and black slip loop and swag decor under collar and around shoulder, impressed "Flint Ware," c. 1845, professionally restored handle and 1/3 of rim, 10" h 14,850.00
"Frank B. Norton, Worcester, Mass.," salt-glazed, freehand cobalt leaf decor, flared rim, 10-1/2" h 687.50
"Williams & Reppert, Greensboro, Pa." two-gal, salt-glazed, cobalt stencil and freehand design, wear, hairlines, 13" h.. 935.00
Unmarked, Albany slip, incised line at shoulder, 9-1/4" h 27.50
Unmarked, salt-glazed, ovoid base, cobalt leaf decor, spout chips, stains, 10-1/2" h........... 605.00
Unmarked, salt-glazed, ovoid base, incised line at center of body, flared rim, stains, roughness, 10-1/2" h 99.00
Sieve, Albany slip, handle, raised lip, minor chips, 11" h... 165.00
Spittoon, salt-glazed, swag decor, minor chips, 4-1/2" h, 9" dia.. 247.50
Washboard
Dark glaze, wooden frame, 24" h, 12" w........ 605.00
Yellow and Rockingham glaze, wooden frame, 22" h, 12" w 605.00

Stools

Background: Defined as a seat without arms or a back and mounted on legs, stools could be square, round, rectangular, and, occasionally, triangular.

Natural finish, turned legs, box stretcher, top with heart cutout, 18" h.. 550.00
Red stain, poplar and hardwood, turned legs, round one-board top, 16" h.. 192.50
Sheraton, curly maple, old finish, turned ball feet, tapered legs, double stretchers, bentwood seat frame, rush seat, 16-1/4" h, 15" w, 11-1/2" d............. 1,980.00
Windsor, old black paint, three vase-and-ring turned splayed legs with stretchers, triangular top recovered in hooked rug fragment, 13" h........................... 550.00

Sheraton curly maple stool, rush seat, 16-1/4" h, $1,980. (Photo courtesy of Garth's Auctions, Delaware, Ohio)

Stoves

Background: Cast-iron stoves have long been used to heat homes and businesses, and they were often a favorite gathering place.

Collectors' Club: Antique Stove Assoc., 5515 Almeda Rd., Houston, TX 77004-7443.

Note: All listings are cast iron unless otherwise noted.

Fireplace inset stove, bowfront base, three feet, cast details, pillars on either side with acanthus leaves, brass rosettes and finials, mkd "James Wilson, New York," spider-web design on back, 38-1/2" h, 37-1/4" w, 25-1/2" d 1,180.00
Parlor, "Campbell, Ellisson and Co., Cincinnati, Ohio," three scrolled feet, shell insert in base, bowfront with four sliding doors, scrolled pilasters, "The Violet #4" on top with "1856," 27-1/2" h, base 28" w, 23" d..495.00
"Small and Smyser, York, Pa.," paneled sides, leaf detail, geometric designs on corners, doors on three sides with wrought-iron levers, semi-circular front tray, openwork base, 37" h, 38" w, 14" d 715.00

String Holders

Background: The string holder developed as a useful tool to assist the merchant or manufacturer who needed tangle-free string or twine to tie packages. The early holders were made of cast-iron, with some patents dating to the 1860s. Among the variations to evolve were the hanging lithographed-tin examples with advertising.

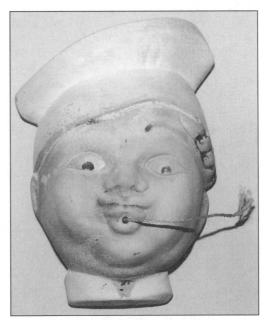

Chalkware chef string holder, 7-1/8" h, $45.

When string holders moved into households, lighter and more attractive forms developed, many made of chalkware. The string holder remained a useful kitchen element until the early 1950s.

Countertop

   Beehive, cast iron, embossed advertising for Walker's Soaps, crackling wear and darkening to early good finish 742.50

   Dome, clear etched glass, cobalt band around rim and base, engraved flowers, mid-19th C., minor chips 172.50

   Kettle shape, cast iron, embossed "S.S.S. For The Blood," missing handles, 4-1/2" h, 5" dia 110.00

Hanging

   "Buy King Midas, The Highest Priced Flour in America, Worth All It Costs," scattered scuffing and rust, cond. 7.5, 19-3/4" h, 15" w 2,200.00

Sugar Buckets

Background: Used to store sugar, these buckets typically had a wooden lid and are often found with a wooden handle and staves. The buckets were often painted and many have been repainted over the years. Examples in original paint are of greater value.

Reproduction Alert: Sugar buckets have been reproduced.

Painted

   Blue repaint over lighter blue, impressed "So. Hingham, Mass.," wooden staves, worn paint, 10" h, 9-1/4" dia 1,265.00

   Light-blue, stave constructed, no lid, handle missing, 13" h, 13-1/2" dia 165.00

   Old gray, partial "Apple Butter 1883, 1889" label, staves, bentwood handle, wear, 14" h 440.00

   Green, stave-constructed, steel tacks, with lid, traces of paint on handle, 13" h 440.00

   Green, wooden staves, impressed "C. Wilson & Son, So. Hingham, Mass.," bentwood swivel handle, 15" h, 14" dia 605.00

   Moss rose, finger seam bands, 8" h, 7-1/2" dia 550.00

   Olive-green, bail handle, wooden staves, steel tacks, with lid, worn paint, 6-7/8" h 522.50

   Red paint, bail handle, stenciled "Sugar," 14" h, 12-1/2" dia 440.00

   Tan, bentwood staves, copper tacks, bentwood handle, lid worn and has glued separation, two-board base, 14" h 275.00

   Yellow (pale) repaint over ivory, wood staves, single finger bands, copper tacks, lid stamped "Wilder P. Clark," paint worn, glued split, 9-3/4" h, 10-1/8" dia 330.00

Varnish finish

   6-1/4" h, 6-1/4" dia, wooden staves, possibly Shaker, split lid 38.50

   11-3/4" h, 11-7/8" dia, wooden staves.............. 55.00

Sugar Chests

Background: Often called a Kentucky sugar chest, this 19th-century American furniture form features a small chest on legs. The hinged top opens to reveal two compartments—one for white sugar and one for brown. A drawer was often incorporated into the area beneath the compartment. Sugar chests were especially prevalent in the southern United States.

Cherry

   Two drawers, paneled sides, turned tapered legs, divided interior, 35" h, 35-1/2" w, 16-1/2" d 6,050.00

   Refinished, French feet, scalloped base with banded inlay, dovetailed case, slant lid, interior divider missing, replaced pullout supports, foot facings replaced, other pieced repairs on case, slight burn damage to top, Kentucky origin, 30" h, 30-3/4" w, 14-1/4" d 1,870.00

   With poplar, orig dark-brown finish, dovetailed case with divided dovetailed drawer at bottom, upper compartment divided with lift-out lid and two tin canisters, brass bail handles on sides, interior locks, edge damage, warp on front with screws added, age cracks, front escutcheon plates missing, 11-3/4" h, 19-1/4" w, 11" d 1,210.00

   With poplar, refinished, small turned feet, pegged, five drawers (two over two over one), paneled ends, two-board top with molded trim, restorations including old alterations to drawers, replaced wooden pulls, found in Kentucky, 29-3/4" h, 37-1/4" w, 15-3/4" d 2,420.00

Cherry Kentucky sugar chest, original finish, $12,500.

Sugar nippers on iron base, $675.

Sugar Nippers

Background: Sugar nippers were used for cutting sugar, which at one time came in cones. Most nippers were imported from England in the late 18th century and throughout most of the 19th century. Hand-held examples resemble a pair of scissors with flattened, rounded ends. Less common were tabletop models, which were typically mounted on a wooden base.

Cast iron, circular engraving at pivot point, chip in blade, spring missing, polished, 10-1/2" l 93.50

Cast iron, scalloped and linear engraving at pivot point, minor rust, catch missing, 9-1/2" l 49.50

Steel, box hinge with simple incised line designs, crescent-shaped blades, some rust, 8-1/4" l............ 100.00

Swifts

Background: A swift is an adjustable wooden reel for winding yarn.

Brass and steel, brass pin cup, steel slats, shaft and clamp, tied with red silk ribbons, minor corrosion, lacks two silk ribbon ties, 22-1/2" h, 25-1/2" dia......... 488.75

Double swift, wooden, carved spire-topped swift with star and flower inlay, slats decorated with intricately carved fine motifs with red and green wax inlay and tied with silk ribbons in red and white, shaft with carved polyhedron, red and black wax inlaid crescent moons, names Durham and A. Dyer, clamp decor with wood inlay star and inlaid wax flower motifs, minor wear, some replaced ribbons, 31-1/2" h, 19" dia 2,070.00

Ivory, bone and wood, turned ivory cup above whalebone shaft and expanding slats, natural mahogany barrel-shaped clamp, turned ivory thumbscrew, America, 19th C., minor wear and cracks, 17" h, 16" dia..........1,840.00

Whale bone, decor with ribbon bows, carved and incised clamp and finial with red and black sealing wax decor, paint and ribbon losses, 22-1/2" h 1,035.00

Wooden, decor, red-painted cup with flowers at center, green and black shaft with natural-wood expanding slats, turned wooden clamp painted yellow with red and blue flowers, minor wear, 22-1/2" h............ 575.00

Tables

History: It can be argued that tables are the most essential piece of furniture. Generally thought of as a place for serving and eating food, they can also be used for playing games, working, reading, and sewing, in addition to serving a purely ornamental function.

References: Eileen and Richard Dubrow, *Styles of American Furniture 1860-1960*, Schiffer Publishing, 1997; Tim Forrest, *Bulfinch Anatomy of Antique Furniture*, Bulfinch Press, 1996; John T. Kirk, *American Furniture: Understanding Styles, Construction, and Quality*, Harry N. Abrams Publishers, 2000; Milo M. Naeve, *Identifying American Furniture*, W.W. Norton, 1998; Ellen T. Schroy, *Warman's American Furniture*, Krause Publications, 2001; Robert W. and Harriet Swedberg, *Collector's Encyclopedia of American Furniture*, Vol. 1 (1990, 1996 value update), Vol. 2 (1992, 1999 value update), Vol. 3 (1998), Collector Books; —, *Encyclopedia of American Oak Furniture*, Krause Publications, 2000.

Banquet
  Hepplewhite, three sections, cherry, old finish, square tapered legs, ovolo-shaped top and conforming apron, center section with drop leaves and swing legs, pristine condition, 28-3/4" h, 48" w, opens to 105" l 13,200.00
  Sheraton, country style, two sections, cherry, old refinishing, turned and reeded legs, D-shaped apron and conforming top, figured veneer on apron, brace removed from beneath leaves, with one extra leaf, 19" leaves, 18-3/4" w, 45-3/4" l.....................1,870.00

Baroque, gateleg, maple, Mass., c. 1720-80, hinged leaves flank single drawer, vase-and-ring turned legs and stretchers, turned shaped feet, refinished, imperfections, 25" h, top 45" x 47-1/2" (leaves up)...................19,550.00

Card table, Chippendale
  Birch, probably N.H., c. 1790, overhanging rectangular folding top, straight skirt, one drawer, molded straight legs, old finish, 27-1/8" h, top 35" x 16-1/2" 4,025.00
  Mahogany, attributed to Newport, R.I., tapered and molded square legs, fretwork brackets, dovetailed secret drawer behind swing leg, old dark finish, age cracks, two brackets missing, 27-3/4" h, 16" w, 32" d, opens to 32"............................. 4,620.00
  Mahogany, probably coastal northern Mass., c. 1780, folding overhanging top with molded edge, serpentine front and ends with conforming base, fan-carved apron, square molded legs, old finish, minor imperfections, 28-1/4" h, top 35-1/4" x 17-3/4" 18,400.00

Card table, Empire, mahogany and flame veneer, old dark finish, platform base, carved paw feet, brass casters, scrolled leaf returns, ring-and-urn turned column with carved acanthus leaves, two-section folding top, veneer repairs, column repaired, 29-3/4" h, 36" w, 17-1/2" d 1,045.00

Card table, Federal
  Mahogany, Boston, c. 1810, folding top with serpentine front, half-serpentine sides, ovolo corners, conforming skirt centering a shaped bird's-eye maple panel bordered by stringing in a mitred rectangle, flanked by satinwood panels bordered by stringing and cross-banding, repeated on the sides, lower edge of skirt with lunette inlay, inlaid half-engaged vase-and-ring turned reeded tapering legs, old refinish, imperfections, 30-1/4" h, 36" w, 18-1/2" d............................. 19,550.00
  Mahogany, North Shore Mass., c. 1800, top with elliptical front and ovolo corners, veneered skirt with central tiger-maple panel outlined with cross-banded mahogany veneer and tiger maple banding, which also outlines the skirt and the tops of the ring-turned tapering legs, the rear legs topped by fluting, old refinish, 29" h, top 36" x 17-1/4" 9,200.00
  Mahogany, Salem, Mass., c. 1800, folding top with rounded ends, elliptical front, square corners, string-incised edge, conforming skirt of three bird's-eye maple panels with mahogany cross-banded borders, four square tapering legs with inlaid panels and stringing, banded cuffs, refinished, imperfections 4,887.50
  Mahogany and mahogany veneer, Salem MA, c. 1790-1800, folding top with elliptical front and squared ends, dart-stringing inlay, conforming skirt, centering veneered oval reserve, tapering square legs, old refinish, imperfections, 29" h, top 35-3/4" x 15-1/2"....................................... 5,175.00

Maple butterfly table, New England, 18th C., refinished, 25-1/4" h, 36" w, $19,550. (Photo courtesy of Skinner Auctioneers & Appraisers of Antiques & Fine Arts, Boston and Bolton, Mass.)

Mahogany veneer, Salem Mass., c. 1800, ovolo-shaped top, paneled frieze centering an inlaid oval reserve with ribbed bowl of flowers and leaves on black ground, skirt outlined in inlay, double tapering legs topped by inlaid ovals and outlined in stringing above the cuff inlays, orig finish, minor imperfections, 29" h, top 35-3/4" x 17-1/2" 51,750.00

Card table, Hepplewhite

Cherry, square legs, fretwork brackets, one mkd "J.G. 1804," each roughly 28" h, top 32" x 16-1/2", pr...7,150.00

Country style, mahogany, tapered legs, one dovetailed and cockbeaded drawer, orig brass pulls, string inlay on cuffs and sides, refinished, restoration, legs repegged, 29-3/4" h, 32-1/4" w, 16-3/4" d 412.50

Mahogany, line inlay on square tapering legs, oval line inlay on skirt, shaped top, 29-1/2" h, 34-1/2" w 2,475.00

Card table, Sheraton

Cherry and flame veneer, refinished, five turned and tapered legs with reeding and fluted bands, raised front apron, flame veneer, ovolo corners, pieced restorations along hinge rail, 29-3/4" h, 35" w, 18-7/8" d..2,860.00

Mahogany, tapering reeded legs, scalloped top, sea and shell inlay, 30" h, closed top 37" x 19" 3,850.00

Cricket, pine, two-board round top, stretcher base, age cracks, putty repair under top, 28-1/2" h, 25-3/4" dia..550.00

Dining

Federal, mahogany, New England, c. 1790-1800, rectangular drop-leaf top, tapering legs, two legs swing to support the leaves, straight skirt, crossbanded and string inlaid edge, cuff-inlaid legs, orig finish, 28-1/2" h, top 47" x 17" 2,990.00

Queen Anne, Santo Domingo, mahogany, R.I., c. 1750-60, rectangular overhanging drop-leaf top, cabriole legs, pad feet on platforms, shaped apron, old finish, minor imperfections, 28-1/2" h, 47-3/4" w, 16-1/2" d 10,925.00

Queen Anne, Newport, R.I., c. 1750, square drop leaves, four block-turned tapering legs, pad feet on platforms, two legs swing to support the leaves, cutout apron, old finish, minor imperfections, 27-1/2" h, top 47" x 48"............................6,900.00

Dressing

Classical, faux, New England, c. 1820, scrolled backboard, chamfered top, conforming base, 1 long drawer, ring-turned tapering legs, all-over red fanciful graining, old brass, 32-1/2" h, top 29-1/4" x 14" 575.00

Decor, red and black paint, yellow stripes and stencils, turned legs, shaped splashback, Maine origin, 33" h, top 31" x 15"....................................412.50

Federal, decor, orig striping and fruit and foliage stencil, old yellow ground, olive-green and gold highlights, backsplash above two small indented drawers over long drawer, turned and decor front

Federal dressing table, fruit and foliage stencil, Newburyport, Mass., c. 1820-30, 40-1/2" h, 35-3/4" w, 17-1/2" d, $4,600. (Photo courtesy of Skinner Auctioneers & Appraisers of Antiques & Fine Arts, Boston and Bolton, Mass.)

legs, ball feet, orig brasses, Newburyport, Mass., c. 1820-30, minor surface imperfections, 40-1/2" h, 35-3/4" w, 17-1/2" d 4,600.00

Federal, cherry, inlaid, New England, c. 1815-20, rectangular top, ovolo corners, two thumbmolded short drawers, mahogany crossbanded borders, straight cockbeaded skirt with crossbanded edge, ring-turned reeded tapering legs, replaced brasses, refinished, minor imperfections, 29-3/4" h, top 33-3/4" x 21".................................2,875.00

Grain-decor, orig black and gold graining to simulate rosewood, shaped splashboard over two small drawers and 1 long drawer, ring-turned tapering legs, labeled "J.G. Briggs, Charlestown, New Hampshire," 1830-33, minor imperfections, 39" h, 36-3/8" w, 16" d 920.00

Queen Anne, cherry, coastal Mass., N.H. or Maine, c. 1750-80, thumb-molded top overhangs one long over three short drawers with cockbeaded surrounds, lower-center drawer is fan-carved, cyma-curved skirt, cabriole legs with spurs and arris knees, high pad feet, orig brasses, old refinish, imperfections, 30" h, 33" w, 20" d............29,900.00

Queen Anne, walnut, Mass., c. 1730-50, molded-edge top, notched front corners, one long drawer over three short drawers, fan carving on center drawer, skirt with flat-headed arches, cabriole legs, pad feet, replaced brasses, old surface, minor repairs, 28-1/2" h, top 34-1/2" x 19-1/2" 28,750.00

Sheraton, country style, cherry, turned legs and feet, shelf with arched cutout, one dovetailed drawer with turned pulls, three-board top, scalloped and dovetailed gallery, refinished, glued restorations, top reset, 34-1/2" h, 30" w, 16" d 550.00

Sheraton, country style, grained decor, maple and pine, old red grained paint, turned legs, tapered feet, one nailed drawer, orig turned wooden pulls, beveled edges on top, scrolled backsplash stenciled "Eliza Knowlton," 33" h, 30" w, 14-7/8" d.................. 495.00

Sheraton, grain-decor, red and black, yellow striping, stenciled floral decor on shaped backsplash with rosettes, one drawer, turned tapering legs, wear, 34" h, 32" w, 15" d............................ 440.00

Sheraton, pine, one drawer on top, one drawer in base, turned legs, short backsplash, 36" h, top 36" x 18" 275.00

Sheraton-style, hardwood and poplar, old yellow repaint, brown and black striping, turned legs, two short drawers stepped over one long drawer, scrolled crest, 39" h, 34" w, 17" d 330.00

Sheraton-style, mahogany, curly maple veneer drawer front, turned and reeded legs, arched aprons, cast-brass pulls, two-board top with biscuit corners, late 19th or early 20th C. with reconstruction, refinished, 29-1/2" h. 36-1/2" w, 19-1/4" d 770.00

Drop leaf

Chippendale, refinished cherry and walnut, claw-and-ball feet, cabriole legs, replaced one-board top and leaves with square butt joints, ends with scalloped aprons and replaced drops, 27-3/4" h, 48" w, 15-3/4" d, leaves 15-3/4"................... 935.00

Country style, poplar, turned legs, ball feet, two-board top, two-board leaves, refinished, reconstruction, 29-1/4" h, 36" w, 19" d, leaves 13".. 137.50

Drop leaf, Federal

Mahogany, rectangular leaves, straight cockbeaded skirts, reeded tapering legs, turned feet, on casters, refinished, minor repairs, 29-1/4" h, 46-3/4" w, 20-3/4" d 1,495.00

Maple, R.I., early 19th C., square drop leaves, straight skirt, square tapering legs, old color on scrubbed top, Spanish brown stained base, imperfections, 26-1/2" h, top 48-3/4" x 17" 3,737.50

Tiger maple, circular, New England, c. 1800-10, oval overhanging drop leaf top, four square tapering legs, straight apron, old refinish, 28-1/2" h, top 41-1/4" x 41-1/2" 2,645.00

Tiger maple, New England, c. 1820, rectangular overhanging top with rounded corners, straight skirt, baluster and ring-turned legs, tapering feet, old refinish, imperfections, 29-1/2" h, top 47" x 44" 1,150.00

Drop leaf, Hepplewhite

Cherry, old dark finish, six tapered legs, one-board top and leaves, minor age crack, 28-5/8" h, 45" w, 16" d, leaves 20".. 990.00

Country style, pine, old brown graining, square tapered legs, dovetailed drawer, round top when leaves extended, worm holes, wear, touchups to paint, 19th C., found in Maine, 29-1/4" h, 40-3/4" w, leaves 10-3/4" 1,320.00

Mahogany, bird's-eye maple veneer drawer fronts, tapered legs with line inlay and banded cuffs, dovetailed drawers at either end, old rosette shaped brasses and bail pulls, figured one-board top and leaves with double line inlay, refinished, restorations, 27-1/2" h, 44" w, 18-7/8" d, leaves 9-1/2" 1,100.00

Mahogany, refinished, tapered legs, band inlay along bottom of aprons and tops of legs, one-board top, stabilized age crack, pieced repairs, 27-7/8" h, 41-1/2" w, 15" d, leaves 15-3/4" 715.00

Drop leaf, Queen Anne

Birch, old dark finish on base, refinished top, cabriole legs, duck feet, scrolled apron, swing legs support drop leaf, one-board top, rounded one-board leaves, repairs, old restoration, 28-3/4" h, 41-1/2" w, 14" d, leaves 15-1/2" 1,815.00

Cherry and pine, orig dark-red finish, stretcher base, button feet, turned legs, one-board top, sliding supports for leaves, age cracks in top, country style, 28-1/2" h, top 16-1/2" x 36" 22,000.00

Maple, old dark refinishing, scalloped apron on ends, cabriole legs, duck feet, restoration, 27-1/4" h, 42" w, 13-1/2" d, leaves 14"................. 2,970.00

Maple, southeastern New England, c. 1740-60, oval overhanging drop leaf, straight skirt, block-turned tapering legs, pad feet, two legs swing to support

Queen Anne maple drop-leaf table, southeastern New England, c. 1740-60, refinished, 26" h, top 38-1/4" x 30-1/2" (leaves up), $6,325. (Photo courtesy of Skinner Auctioneers & Appraisers of Antiques & Fine Arts, Boston and Bolton, Mass.)

the top, refinished, minor imperfections, 26" h, top 38-1/4" x 30-1/2" (leaves up) 6,325.00

Maple and pine, scrubbed top, old dark finish on base, cabriole legs, duck feet, scalloped apron, leaves and one-board top are old replacements, feet drilled for castors, glued repair to one foot, 28" h, 48" w, 15-3/4" d, leaves 15-1/4" 880.00

Painted, old dark red repaint, hardwood, cabriole legs, duck feet, scalloped apron, old replaced top, leaves with rounded corners, base sized down at some time, repairs, 27" h, 47-3/4" w, 18-1/2" d, leaves 13-3/4" 1,045.00

Walnut, Pa. origin, c. 1740-60, oval overhanging top, cabriole legs, carved trifid feet, shaped skirt, 30" h, top 47-1/2" x 58" 12,650.00

Drop leaf, Sheraton

Country style, cherry, turned legs, one-board top and leaves, refinished, 28-1/2" h, 17-1/2" w, 36" l, leaves 13" 880.00

Country style, curly maple, turned legs, two-board top, one-board leaves, refinished, underside of leaves scored to remove warp, some damage and repair to rule joints, 27-3/4" h, 19" w, 42" l, leaves 15" 825.00

Country style, curly maple, turned legs, two-board top, one-board leaves cut into three sections and pegged, refinished, chipped foot, age cracks, 28-3/4" h, 47-1/2" w, 18-1/4" d 880.00

Curly maple top and end aprons, six turned cherry legs, one-board top and leaves with age cracks, some warp, refinished top, 29" h, 48" w, 19-3/4" d, leaves 18" 715.00

Mahogany, old dark finish on base, scrubbed finish on top, turned legs, one-board top and leaves, one swing leg with pinned repair, age cracks in leaves, 29-1/2" h, 42" w, 18-1/2" d, leaves 19-1/2" 385.00

Sheraton style, curly maple, six turned legs, one-board top and leaves, excellent figure, 20th C., top 21-1/8" x 48", leaves 22" 1,980.00

Tiger maple, turned legs, short drop leaves with rounded corners, 28-1/2" h, top 36" sq (open) 3,850.00

Tiger maple, New England, c. 1820s, rounded leaves, straight skirts, ring-turned legs, turned feet, old refinish, minor imperfections, 30" h, 40-3/4" w, 18-1/4" d 1,150.00

Tiger maple, New England, early 19th C., one drawer, scrubbed top, leaves with rounded corners, square tapering legs, old color on scrubbed top, base painted red, replaced pull, imperfections, 27-1/4" h, top 40" x 36-1/2" (open) 1,725.00

Farm

Painted, yellow, three drawers, turned legs, wear, 30-1/2" h, top 72" x 30" 990.00

Pine five-board top in mellow refinish, birch base in old red surface, turned legs, shaped side aprons, straight ends, Maine origin, chip on top, 29-1/4" h, 53-3/4" w, 41-3/4" d 1,650.00

Poplar and chestnut, old gray wash, scrubbed top, removable sawbuck legs with chamfered corners, three-board top with chamfered edge, Ohio origin, 29" h, 29-1/2" w, 34" d 1,210.00

Game

Empire, cherry and mahogany veneer, refinished, swivel top, turned legs, square columns, flame-grain veneer on apron, brass casters, two-section top with slight warp, minor veneer chips, 29" h, 33-3/4" w, 16-1/2" d 302.50

Regency, mahogany and figured mahogany veneer, old refinishing, four saber legs with brass caps and casters beneath octagonal plinth, turned column, two-section flip top with shaped corners, some veneer missing, replaced top has some warp, 29-1/4" h, 36" w, 17" d 605.00

Gateleg, tiger maple, turned legs, rounded leaves, 29-1/2" h, top 47" x 19" (with leaves down) ... 3,740.00

Harvest

Curly maple with maple base, refinished, turned legs, feet and stretcher base, pegged construction, drop leaf, one drawer, replaced top and leaves with bold curl and breadboard ends, feet ended out, supports and drawer added, 28-1/2" h, 73-1/2" l, 24-1/4" d, leaves 11-1/4" 3,190.00

Painted, early olive-green base, ring-turned tapering legs, scrubbed top with leaves, New England, late 18th or early 19th c., 20-1/2" h, 102-3/4" w, 18-1/4" d 11,500.00

Painted, old red wash, ash, turned legs, three-board top with empty nail holes, added supports, 31-1/2" h, 93-3/4" w, 26" d 660.00

Sheraton, country style, cherry and pine, old finish, turned legs with ring-turned tops, one-board top and leaves, stains, age cracks, base restoration, 29" h, 90" w, 18-3/4" d, leaves 9-1/2" 2,640.00

Hutch

Curly maple with bold figure, old refinish, cutout feet, two-board top, square nails, slight warp, old restoration and reconstruction to base, 29" h, 60" x 39-1/2" 1,925.00

Natural finish, oval top, shoe feet, scalloped apron, arched bootjack ends, 29" h, top 37" x 42" 4,950.00

Painted, old worn green repaint, pine, mortised base, bootjack ends, two-board seat, three-board top, chips, age cracks, 28" h, top 72" x 35" 3,300.00

Pine, birch and poplar, traces of old red finish, scrubbed two-board top, breadboard ends, mortise and pinned base, shoe feet, dovetailed drawer, age cracks in top, found in Vermont, 28-3/4" h, top 41-3/4" x 37-3/4" 4,180.00

Ice cream

Cast iron, "Paris" signature around the base, tripod base, relief shell and acanthus leaf designs, spiral column with reeding near top, dark-green repaint, 22" round gray marble top, 27" h.................110.00

Miscellaneous

Folk art, carved legs each with trapped ball, intricate inlaid Parcheesi top with American flag in center block, 29" h, top 28" x 28" 3,125.00

Pine, one-drawer, primitive, tapered legs with beaded edges, galleried shelf, drawer, one-board top with rounded corners, reconstruction, 24-1/2" h, 28" w, 21" d............................. 440.00

Pyrography, floral and geometric design, three scrolled legs, triangular pedestal base, square top, 29" h, top 29" sq 330.00

Parlor, oak, square top with scalloped edge, twist-turned legs, turned feet, stretcher shelf, 29" h, 24" sq................................. 99.00

Pedestal

Oak, quartersawn, round top, round pedestal with ring-turned top and reeded bottom, carved paw feet, 54" dia 440.00

Oak, round top, square split pedestal, squared legs, late Mission style, 48" dia 275.00

Pembroke

Mahogany and mahogany veneer, tapered legs with line inlay and banded cuffs on outer sides, drawer with bowed front, matching bowed apron on other end, old replacement brass pull, replaced two-board top and one-board leaves, restorations, 28" h, 31" w, 21-1/8" d 715.00

Transitional, Chippendale to Hepplewhite, walnut, drop leaves, dark refinish, X-stretcher base, molded and tapered legs, end aprons with beaded edges, dovetailed drawer with lock, two-board top, old replaced eagle brass, restorations, top 35-1/4" w, 18" d, leaves 9-3/4"................................ 880.00

X-stretcher base with pierced design, square reeded legs, shaped leaves, 28" h, top 34" x 19" (with leaves dropped)...................................... 3,125.00

Pembroke, Chippendale

Cherry, X stretcher base, square legs with chamfer and beading, two-board top, beaded apron, dovetailed drawer, 28" h, top 21-1/2" x 35-1/2", leaves 7-3/4" 3,190.00

Mahogany, 28" h, top 46" x 35" (open) 715.00

Mahogany, old finish, square molded legs with inside chamfer, cross stretcher, one dovetailed drawer with cockbeading, orig brass bail, two steel angle braces added, minor stains, 28-3/4" h, 31-3/4" w, 20-1/4" d, leaves 10-3/4" 3,575.00

Mahogany, New England, c. 1760-90, serpentine top, similarly shaped leaves, straight skirt with beaded edges, molded square legs, shaped medial platform, old refinish, imperfections, 28-1/2" h, top 30-1/2" x 30" 6,325.00

Pembroke, Federal

Mahogany veneer, New York, c. 1815, rectangular top, shaped drop leaves, two drawers (one working, one faux), cockbeaded skirt, turned and reeded legs on casters, old refinish, replaced brasses, minor imperfections, 29" h, top 22-1/4" x 34" 3,105.00

Federal Pembroke table, mahogany veneer, New York, early 19th C., old refinish, replaced brass, 28-1/8" h, top 22-1/2" x 36", $1,380. (Photo courtesy of Skinner Auctioneers & Appraisers of Antiques & Fine Arts, Boston and Bolton, Mass.)

Mahogany veneer, New York, early 19th C., shaped leaves, drawer at each end (one working, one faux), reeded tapering legs, feet on balls, old refinish, replaced brass, 28-1/8" h, top 22-1/2" x 36" 1,380.00

Pembroke, Hepplewhite

Bowed end, inlaid legs and drawer, rounded leaves, 28" h, top 38" x 32"................................. 3,025.00

Walnut, pegged, tapered legs, one dovetailed drawer, one-board top and leaves with notched and rounded corners, refinished, replaced oval brasses, restoration to top, 28-1/2" h, top 36" x 17", leaves 12-3/4" 797.50

Pembroke, Sheraton

Country style, cherry, old finish, turned legs, one drawer, one-board top and leaves, replaced knob, 30" h, 36" w, 18-1/2" d, leaves 13" 440.00

Mahogany and mahogany flame veneer, refinished top, old finish on base, turned and reeded legs, aprons with line inlay, drawer with beaded trim, false front on other end, one-board top, shaped leaves, replaced brasses with some age, break in one rule joint, minor restoration to other, leaves reshaped, attributed to Newburyport, Mass., 28-1/2" h, 30-1/2" w, 19" d, leaves 9-3/8" 2,090.00

Sawbuck

Poplar and pine with stained finish, center support board mounted flat for a shelf, two-board top is 1-5/8" thick, reconstruction using some old boards, steel L braces added for support, 29-5/8" h, 72" w, 21" d 440.00

Stained base in orig red, darkened top, New England, late 18th or early 19th C., top overhangs a trough, square tapered legs, minor imperfections, 28" h, top 34-1/2" x 23-5/8"........... 2,645.00

Sawbuck, painted

Old blue-gray repaint on base, pine, one-board scrubbed top, base with removable board that makes a small bin, age cracks, water damage to feet, 28" h, 36-1/2" w, 25-1/2" d 2,420.00

Blue-green paint over old red stain, pine, New England, 19th C., rectangular top, braces over cross-form legs with stretchers at bottom, encloses V-form trough, imperfections, 30-1/2" h, top 42" x 25-1/2" 805.00

Green, simple construction, 28" h, top 20" x 16" 275.00

Red base, scrubbed top, 28" h, top 40" x 26" 770.00

Sawbuck, pine

Old dark-brown finish, traces of red paint, rosehead nails, separation to tongue-and-groove two-board top, age cracks, minor wear, putty repair on 1 leg, 27" h, 72" l, 42" w 1,650.00

Nut-brown refinishing, one-board top, breadboard ends, molded edges, cross stretcher with beaded edges, old replacement base, pieced repairs, 26-1/2" h 40-1/2" w, 19-1/2" d 550.00

Traces of old red, board across the center base creates a well for storage, square nails, refinished, replaced top, nailed repair at corner, 34" h, 28" w, 13" d 467.50

Sorting, painted, pine, New England, 19th C., rectangular tray top, one drawer, square tapered legs, straight skirt, white paint over earlier green, 28-1/2" h, top 21-1/4" x 15-3/4" 690.00

Stretcher-base, New England, 18th C., maple and pine, top with breadboard ends, one drawer, block-and-baluster turned legs, square stretchers, old color, repairs to 2 feet, 26-7/8" h, top 31-1/2" x 22-3/4" 2,070.00

Tavern

Baroque, maple and pine, New England, mid-18th C., rectangular overhanging breadboard top, straight skirt, block-and-vase ring-turned legs, box stretchers, ring-turned feet, old red washed surface, repairs, 37" h, 52" w, 30" d 1,840.00

Chippendale, country style, pine, old nut-brown finish, stretcher base, square slightly splayed legs with molded corners, mortised and pegged apron with edge bead, 2-board top with breadboard ends, repair to beading on 1 apron, old replaced top, 28" h, 31" w, 21-3/4" d 715.00

Country style, hardwood and pine, old dark worn finish, turned legs, mortised and pinned stretcher base and apron, one dovetailed drawer, two-board top with breadboard ends, wear, feet worn down, top has narrow strip added between boards, 23-3/4" h, 38" w, 28-1/2" d 825.00

Country style, painted, pine and maple, greenish-black repaint on base, old finish on top, turned ball feet, molded stretcher base, splayed legs, molded apron with pegged construction, oval 1-board top with age cracks and repairs, cleats replaced, attributed to New Hampshire, 25-3/8" h, top 17-1/2 x 24-1/2" 2,750.00

Maple, New England, c. 1730-40, oval top, splayed block-and-vase ring-turned legs, turned feet, double-bead apron, box stretchers, old refinish, 27" h, top 33-3/4" x 25-1/2" 13,800.00

Maple, poplar and pine, stretcher base, high turned feet, turned posts, pegged construction, one-board top, single leaf, scalloped corners, refinished, replaced hinges, loose top, age crack, feet ended out, 29" h, 39-1/2" w, 23-1/2" d 1,320.00

Maple and birch, New England, old worn red finish, one-board pine top in scrubbed finish, breadboard ends, dovetailed drawer, beaded edge, brass pull, turned legs, button feet, stretcher base, age cracks, square nails added to top, 25" h, 22-1/2" w, 18-1/2" d 4,675.00

Maple and pine, New England, mid-18th C., red base, scrubbed rectangular top with breadboard ends, one drawer, block-and-vase ring-turned legs, box stretcher, minor imperfections, 27" h, top 42" x 24" 7,475.00

Miniature, walnut, pinned top, one drawer, deep aprons, block and turned legs, ball feet, box stretcher base, stretchers with molded top edges, refinished, 19" h, top 29" x 20-3/8" 7,800.00

Pine, old worn dark finish, shoe feet, shaped and pierced ends, chamfered cross brackets, two-board top an old replacement, alterations, wedge pins missing, 33" h, 72" w, 35" d 1,320.00

William and Mary, probably New England, mid-18th C., black paint, birch and pine, oval overhanging top, splayed vase-and-ring turned legs, turned feet, straight apron, box stretcher, imperfections, 17" h, top 24" x 33" 8,050.00

Windsor, ash or oak base, pine top, old nut-brown finish, turned legs, turned and plain spindle stretchers, apron comprised of two spindles and two slats mortised and pinned to legs, three-board top attached at top of legs, age cracks, restoration, 26-1/2" h, 37-1/2" w, 26-3/8" d 1,320.00

Tavern, painted

Black base with gold details, scrubbed top, square legs with turnings, turned feet, box stretcher, 27" h, top 26" x 17" 19,800.00

Red base, natural two-board top, breadboard ends, square tapering legs, 27-1/2" h, top 42" x 32" 825.00

Red base, scrubbed top with breadboard ends, one-drawer, turned legs, button feet, 28" h, top 48" x 27" 2,200.00

Red base, scrubbed top with breadboard ends, box stretcher, 25-1/2" h, top 38" x 23" 1,650.00

Red base, scrubbed top with breadboard ends, square legs with some well-defined turnings, box stretcher, 26" h, top 30" x 21" 2,750.00

Tavern, Queen Anne

Maple, brown over earlier red, turned legs, button feet, two-board top with molded edge and notched corners, dovetailed drawer, replaced brass, top reset, back edge ended out, glue blocks replaced, 25-7/8" h, 30-1/2" w, 19" d 1,925.00

Maple, refinished, areas of burgundy repaint, turned legs, duck feet, oval two-board top, repegged, insect damage, brace added beneath top, one foot ended out, others repaired, pieced repair in top, 26-1/4" h, 35-1/4" w, 27" d...................... 715.00

Tavern, Queen Anne, country style

Painted, pine, old worn red, turned tapered legs, worn button feet, one-board top with molded and cut corners, top possibly reattached, 27" h, 30-1/2" w, 23" d..................................... 1,100.00

Pine and hardwood, refinished, turned legs, molded stretcher, oval two-board top, made up out of old parts, 25-3/4" h, 29-1/2" w, 21-1/4" d.......... 495.00

Pine and maple, worn button feet, mortise-and-peg, stretcher base, ring-turned legs, molded-edge aprons, dovetailed drawer with early peg pull, refinished, two glued breaks, putty repairs in top, 27" h, 39" w, 26" d 2,640.00

Maple, old red base, top cleaned to old finish, turned tapered legs, duck feet, mortised and pinned apron, two-board top with notched corners, stains, minor age crack, 27-1/2" h, 36" w, 26-1/2" d........ 5,500.00

Maple, old red paint, molded stretcher base, turned and splayed legs, molded edge around bottom of apron, two-board oval top painted underneath with later yellow inside the aprons, refinished, age cracks in one leg, feet shortened, 24" h, 32" w, 24" d...3,850.00

Maple base, pine one-board top, old refinish, stretcher base, ball feet, turned legs, one drawer with pine front and turned wooden pull, top with breadboard ends, feet ended out, age cracks in top, 27-1/2" h, 41-1/4" w, 22-1/2" d.......... 1,760.00

Birch, cherry and pine tea table, New England, late 18th C., stationary top, old refinish, 26-1/2" h, top 30-1/2" x 23", $2,070. (Photo courtesy of Skinner Auctioneers & Appraisers of Antiques & Fine Arts, Boston and Bolton, Mass.)

Tea table, fixed

Birch, cherry and pine, New England, late 18th C., overhanging porringer top, square beaded legs, straight beaded skirt, old refinish, imperfections, 26-1/2" h, top 30-1/2" x 23" 2,070.00

Cherry, birdcage support, New England, 18th C., circular top, swelled and ring-turned pedestal, cabriole legs, pad feet, refinished, imperfections, 28-1/2" h, 35-1/2" dia............................. 1,265.00

Chippendale style, 3-tier, mahogany, tripod base, padded snake feet, urn-turned base, molded dish tops, spiral urn support columns, 19th C., repairs, hairline in column, 44-1/2" h 385.00

Queen Anne, painted maple, R.I., c. 1750, rectangular top, shaped skirt, cylindrical tapering legs, pad feet, brown stain, imperfections, 28" h, top 25" x 33" 4,485.00

Tea table, tilt-top

George II, mahogany, round flame-grain one-board top, arched tripod base, padded snake legs, baluster-turned column, orig brass latch, top warped, restorations, 28" h, 30" dia 715.00

Maple, probably Conn., c. 1760-80, circular top, birdcage support, cylindrical ring-turned post, tripod cabriole legs, base with carved knees, pad feet, old refinish, 28" h, 29" dia................ 2,070.00

Tiger maple, probably New England, late 18th C., circular molded top, vase-and-ring turned support, tripod cabriole legs, arris pad feet, old refinish, imperfections, 25" h, 25" dia.................... 5,060.00

Tea table, tilt-top, Chippendale

Cherry, New England, c. 1780, square tilt top diagonally placed on vase-and-ring turned post, tripod cabriole legs, pad feet on platforms, minor imperfections, 30" h, top 28" x 31-1/2" 1,265.00

Mahogany, southern New England, c. 1780, circular top, birdcage support, vase-and-ring turned post ending in tripod cabriole legs, ball-and-claw feet, old refinish, imperfections, 29" h, 34-3/4" dia 2,070.00

Mahogany, tripod base, padded snake feet, urn column, round two-board top, refinished, replaced cleats, restoration, 27-3/4" h, 28-1/4" dia 660.00

Mahogany, Virginia, mid- to late-18th C., molded dish top, birdcage support, vase-and-ring turned pedestal with carved swag, tassel and flower designs, cabriole legs with palm-like leaf carvings on knees, ball-and-claw feet, minor repairs, 27-3/4" h, 33" dia 35,000.00

Mahogany base, pine three-board round top, old alligatored varnish finish, tripod base, snake feet, turned column with scalloping on bottom edge, 30" h, 35" dia 1,210.00

Maple, padded snake feet, turned column, birdcage support, round three-board top, dishtop molded edge, refinished, restoration, 30-1/2" h, 35-5/8" dia 990.00

Walnut, snake feet, turned column, birdcage support, replaced round top with molded edge, one foot repaired, 28-1/2" h, 32-3/8" dia............ 715.00

Windsor, turned splayed base in red stain, scrubbed top, breadboard ends, pine, New England, early 19th C., 26-1/2" h, 29-1/2" w, 20-1/4" d 2,415.00

Work

Bird's-eye maple, tiger maple and cherry, possibly Pa., c. 1825, rectangular top, two drawers, straight skirt, vase-and-ring turned tapering legs, old refinish, 29" h, 21-1/2" w, 19" d 1,610.00

Chippendale, country style, maple, birch and pine, orig red finish, stretcher base, beaded corners on legs, apron and stretchers, dovetailed drawer with brass pull, scrubbed 1-board top, breadboard ends, attributed to Maine, age cracks, 26" h, 50-1/4" w, 29-3/4" d 3,300.00

Chippendale, country style, pine, old green paint, yellow striping on dovetailed drawer and legs, pegged two-board scrubbed top, attributed to Vermont, 27-3/4" h, top 35-7/8" x 23-3/8" 2,475.00

Federal, birch, inlaid, Portsmouth, N.H., c. 1800-10, overhanging serpentine top, one drawer with bird's-eye maple veneer and mahogany crossbanded border, medial shelf with scalloped edge, square tapering legs, orig brass pull, old refinish, imperfections, 29" h, top 16-1/4" x 15-1/2" 2,645.00

Work, Hepplewhite, country style

Birch and pine, one drawer, cleaned down to old red wash, pegged construction, square nails, tapered legs, replaced wooden pull, one-board top, chips, areas of touchup, 29" h, 41-3/4" w, 27-1/8" d 550.00

Birch base and pine top with breadboard ends, one drawer, tapered legs, legs mortised and pegged, drawer restorations, old replacement top, 28-1/2" h, 43" w, 26-3/4" d 440.00

Cherry, old finish, tapered legs, pegged construction, 1" thick two-board top, one peg missing, splits in one leg, 28" h, 36" w, 24" d 412.50

Drop leaf, birch and poplar, cleaned down to old red painted finish, square tapered legs, mortised and pinned apron, two dovetailed drawers with edge beading, removable one-board top and leaf, age crack, leg wear, red touched up, 28" h, 43" w, 29-1/4" d, leaf 9" 3,135.00

Painted, orig red, pine and poplar, tapered square legs, dovetailed drawer, two-board top, orig brass pull dented, 29-3/4" h, top 36" x 31" 880.00

Pine, tapered legs, pegged, drawer, two-board top, refinished, reconstruction, 28" h, top 41-1/2" x 25-1/2" 770.00

Walnut, refinished, tapered legs, pegged, two drawers, two-board top, age cracks, screws added, glued repair to drawer, 28-3/4" h, 47" w, 32" d 440.00

Work, painted

Blue, one drawer, square legs, wear, damage to drawer, 29" h, top 29" x 18" 495.00

Old dark green repaint on base, dark finish on top, pine, country-style, one-drawer, tapered legs, pegged, two-board top with age cracks, slight warp, 28-1/2" h, top 46-1/2" x 27-1/4" 605.00

Red base, scrubbed top, turned legs, 31" h, top 72" x 30" 770.00

Work, pine

Old dark-brown patina, turned legs and feet, mortised and pinned H stretcher and apron, old replacement two-board top with breadboard ends, castors added, 28-1/2" h, 57-1/2" w, 37-1/2" d 385.00

Old worn brown paint over red, Pa. origin, turned legs, two dovetailed drawers, wooden pulls, removable three-board top with replaced pegs, leg chips, age cracks, 30-1/2" h, 54" w, 36" d.....................1,760.00

Pine-top, three-drawer (narrow drawers flank wider drawer), square legs, 28" h, top 50" x 35" 1,760.00

Work, Sheraton, country style

Hardwood and poplar, pine top, old red paint, turned legs, mortised and pinned apron, two dovetailed drawers with beaded edges, orig brasses, removable two-board top with orig turned pins, Pa. origin, pristine orig cond., 30-1/4" h, 33" w, 55" d 7,150.00

Walnut, old dark over-varnish, stacked ring turnings at top of legs, pegged, two-board top, small molding added, few later nails and glue blocks, 28" h, top 31" x 25-1/4" 495.00

Walnut, orig finish, turned and chamfered octagonal legs, two dovetailed drawers, three-board removable top, 30" h, 48" w, 33-3/4" d 1,320.00

Tall Chests

History: Developed around the middle of the 18th century, the tall chest is also referred to as a high chest of drawers. Typically, it was configured with a single row of two or three small drawers above a group of five or six graduated long drawers. All of its drawers contained in one section is the feature that distinguishes a tall chest of drawers from a chest-on-chest

Chippendale

Cherry and maple, probably Conn., 18th C., flat molded cornice, central fan-carved short drawer flanked by two sets of small drawers above six graduated long drawers, tall bracket feet, oval brass pulls, old finish, minor restoration, added casters, 62-3/4" h, 37" w, 18" d 46,000.00

Cherry and pine, N.H. or Mass., five thumb-molded graduated drawers, bracket feet, centered drop pendant, flat molded cornice, old finish, minor imperfections, 48-1/4" h, 36" w, 18-1/2" d 4,600.00

Maple, Conn., c. 1760-80, seven drawers, tray top molded cornice, two short over five long drawers, tall bracket feet, centered drop pendant, orig brasses, old refinish, 58" h, 36" w, 16-1/2" d 9,200.00

Painted, old red-brown, six graduated drawers, bracket base with center drop, molded cornice, 57" h, 40" w, 19" d 8,800.00

Chippendale tall chest, old red-brown paint, 57" h, 40" w, $8,800. (Photo courtesy of Cyr Auction Company, Gray, Maine)

Tiger maple, five graduated drawers, bracket base, cove-molded top, brass pulls and escutcheons, old finish, 50" h, 37" w, 18" d 3,575.00

Walnut, Pa., c. 1800, eight drawers (three short over five long graduated), cockbeading, quarter columns, ogee bracket feet, molded cornice, 65-1/4" h, 42" w, 20-1/2" d 6,875.00

Maple, New England, late 18th/early 19th C., six thumb-molded graduated drawers, molded bracket base, cove-molded cornice, orig brass pulls, refinished, imperfections 5,462.50

Tiger maple, New England, 18th C., seven graduated drawers, flared cornice, orig brasses, old refinish, on new base, 59-1/4" h, 36" w, 19" d 8,625.00

Tea Caddies

History: A tea caddy is a small box or case for holding tea. Typically constructed of wood, caddies were also made of brass, pewter, silver, porcelain, and tortoise shell. Designed to hold both black tea and green tea, the interior was either partitioned and lead-lined or fitted with canisters for the two types of tea. Because tea was originally an expensive commodity, most caddies were fitted with a lock and key.

Pear-shaped fruitwood tea caddy, England, 18th C., 5-3/4" h, $4,312.50. (Photo courtesy of Skinner Auctioneers & Appraisers of Antiques & Fine Arts, Boston and Bolton, Mass.)

Box shape

English, fruitwood, inlaid shells on front and top, sawtooth band inlay around base, divided interior, with mahogany lids and turned bone pulls, refinished, edge damage, 4-1/2" h, 7" w, 4-7/8" d 522.50

Mahogany, dovetailed base and lid, gold stenciled swags around top edge, interior lined with worn gray paper, brass bail handle, escutcheon missing, worn finish, scratches, 6-1/4" h, 6-3/8" w, 6-1/2" d 275.00

Mahogany, rope-banded edge inlay, stepped lid, brass bail handle, small patch on lid, dividers missing, 5-3/8" h, 9-1/2" w, 5-1/2" d 412.50

Pear shape

Maple, varnished, worn foil lining, finial glued, lock latch replaced, 6-1/2" h 2,750.00

Wooden, worn finish, traces of foil lining, top latch removed and patched, 7" h 770.00

Teddy Bears

History: The first American teddy bear was produced by the New York-based Ideal Novelty & Toy Co., which was established around 1906. The jointed mohair bear known as "Teddy's bear" was supposedly modeled after a cartoon showing Theodore Roosevelt in the act of sparing a small bear cub while hunting. Examples by American companies Ideal, Knickerbocker, and Gund are quite collectible, as are teddies produced by the German maker, Steiff, a name virtually synonymous with teddy bears.

References: Jurgen and Marianne Cieslik, *Teddy Bear Encyclopedia*, Hobby House Press, 1998; Dee Hockenberry, *Steiff Bears and Other Playthings Past and Present*, Schiffer Publishing, 2000; Constance King, *The Century of the Teddy Bear*, Antique Collectors' Club, 1999; Margaret Fox Mandel, *Teddy Bears and Steiff Animals*, 1st series

(1984, 1997 value update), 2nd series (1987, 1996 value update), Collector Books; Ken Yenke, *Bing Bears and Toys*, Schiffer Publishing, 2000; —, *Teddy Bear Treasury*, Collector Books, 1999.

Periodicals: *National Doll & Teddy Bear Collector*, P.O. Box 4032, Portland, OR97208; *Teddy Bear & Friends*, 741 Miller Dr., SE, Suite D2, Harrisburg, PA 20175, www.cowls.com/maglist.html; *Teddy Bear Review*, 170 5th Ave., 12th Floor, New York, NY 10010.

Collectors' Clubs: Good Bears of the World, P.O. Box 13097, Toledo, OH 43613; My Favorite Bear: Collectors Club for Classic Winnie the Pooh, 468 W. Alpine #10, Upland, CA 91786; Teddy Bear Boosters Club, 19750 SW Peavine Mountain Rd., McMinnville, OR 97128.

Collecting Hint: Teddy bears come in all shapes, sizes, and colors, with the most desirable being marked examples from well-known makers. But, since many bears were not marked, knowledge of distinct characteristics of notable makers is beneficial when attempting to determine a manufacturer. Consideration should be given to the shape of the bear, the proportions of its limbs, the shape of the head, the size and position of the ears, the composition of the eyes, the type of stuffing used, and the size, shape, and type of material used for the paws. All can provide invaluable clues as to maker and age.

Brown, straw-filled, 14" h...................................... 302.50
Jointed
    Brown mohair, black bead eyes, small hump on back, stitched repairs, 11" h.......................... 27.50
    Brown mohair, humpback, some repair around pads, worn, about 20" 302.50
    Blond mohair, brown glass eyes, worn, wool pads replaced, 14" h 126.50
    Gold mohair (long), American, growler works at times, 1920s, 21" h.................................. 975.00
    Tan mohair (long), Farnell, English, 1920s, paw repaired, 15" h 2,200.00
    Tan mohair (long), possibly Farnell, English, 1920s, replaced eyes, 18" h.................................... 890.00
Perfume container, probably Schucco, worn gold mohair, 5" h 247.50

Telephones

History: Early telephones, especially wall-mount examples in wooden cases, have gained quite a following because of their uniquely country look.

Collecting Hint: Except when buying from a seller who specializes in antique telephones, expect to have a phone professionally restored in order to return it to working order.

Oak wall telephone, $250.

Candlestick
    Black, 1908 patent date.................................. 99.00
    A.T.&T. #337, black, 12" h.............................110.00
    Kellogg, chrome head, black metal body....... 121.00
Ringer box
    Oak, two bells, Chicago Telephone & Supply 33.00
    Oak, ten bells (five sets of two), Kellogg, 24" h, 8" w... 55.00
Wall, oak
    "The Elliott Telephone Co., Indianapolis," small box with two bells suspended over larger box with slant-front writing surface 450.00
    Kellogg, rectangular box, two bells over one-pc receiver and speaker.................................... 77.00
    Western Electric, sloping writing surface, 26-3/8" h, 9-1/2" w 250.00
    Rectangular box, two bells over adjustable mouthpiece over sloping writing surface, hand-held ear-piece at left, crank at right, mounted on backboard with arched crest, restoration, 24" h, 8" w 247.50
    Rectangular box, two bells over short-neck mouthpiece over sloping writing surface, hand-held ear-piece at left, 19" h, 7" w 88.00
    Square box, desk phone receiver hangs from left side, crank on right side, two silver bells on front 55.00

Textiles

History: Textiles is the generic term for cloth or fabric items, especially anything woven or knitted. Antique textiles that have survived are usually those that were considered the "best"" by their original owners, since these were the objects that were used and stored carefully by the housewife.

Textiles are collected for many reasons—to study fabrics, to understand the elegance of a historical period, for decorative purposes, or to use as originally intended.

References: Dilys E. Blum, *The Fine Art of Textiles: The Collection of the Philadelphia Museum of Art*, Philadelphia Museum of Art, 1997; Debra S. Bonito, *Graced by Lace: A Guide for Collectors of Antique Linen and Lace*, Schiffer Publishing, 2001; Frances Johnson, *Collecting Household Linens*, Schiffer Publishing, 1997; —, *Collecting More Household Linens*, Schiffer Publishing, 1997; Elizabeth Kurella, *The Complete Guide to Vintage Textiles*, Krause Publications, 1999.

Collectors' Clubs: International Old Lacers, P.O. Box 481223, Denver, CO 80248; Lace & Linen Collectors, P.O. Box 222, Plainwell, MI 49080.

Also See: Coverlets, Homespun, Quilts

Bedspread, Candlewick
  White-on-white, cotton, pots of flowers design, tied lace fringe, handsewn bindings and seams, minor stains, old patch, 86" x 96" 55.00
  Woven, three-pc, dated and initialed "1824 PT," center with vase and floral design surrounded by scrolled leaves and flowers, stains, fabric losses, 104" x 84" 460.00

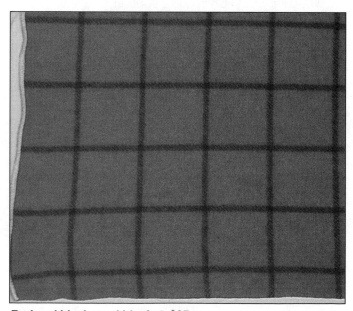

Red and black wool blanket, $95.

Blanket
  Chief Joseph pattern, cotton, dark blue, red, yellow and green 82.50
  Check pattern in blue and white, woven, wool, early 19th C., minor moth damage, 74" x 96" 500.00
  Plaid design in tomato red, navy blue and green, woven, two-pc, wear, small holes, 68" x 80" 220.00
Fabric, blue-and-white resist dyed, floral design, early 19th C., minor wear, slight stain, 16-1/2" x 14-1/2" 240.00
Handkerchief
  Continental political satire, printed cotton, red, blue and brown on tan ground, minor fabric losses, 26" x 28-1/2" 258.75
  Death of George Washington, central oval shows Washington on his deathbed attended by physicians and Mrs. Washington, surrounded by six reserves of printed tributes, dark-brown print, white ground, printed cotton, framed, fabric loss, stains, repairs, 18-1/4" h, 20-1/2" w 1,092.50
  "The Love of Truth, Mark the Boy" (George Washington and the cherry tree), printed cotton, minor stains, small holes, short tear, framed, 12-3/4" sq 385.00
Handkerchief, child's
  "The House That Jack Built" with cats, dog, rooster, man, woman, etc., printed linen, black ink, old frame, stains, small holes, 13-1/2" h, 15-1/2" w 467.50
  Punch and Judy, blackish-purple ink on cream ground, printed cotton, matted and framed, stains, minor damage, 13-1/8" h, 15-1/8" w 165.00
Historical
  Centennial, silk with brown printed images of Washington with America in a chariot pulled by leopards, Franklin with Lady Liberty, cherubs, the Liberty Tree, etc., stains, stitched repairs, framed, 33" h, 35-5/8" w 247.50
  Printed cotton, oval portrait of George Washington with crossed flags, eagle, flowers and fruit, colors in blue, green, tan and brown, framed, brown specks, minor fading, small holes, 16" h, 27" w 330.00
  Printed silk with bust of George Washington in medallion with crossed flags, bugles, oak leaves and acorns, eagle and "First in War, First in Peace...," border shows ship battle, black, olive-green, mustard and red, framed, minor stains, 24-3/4" h, 29-1/2" w 1,430.00
Lap robe, velvet and silk, embroidered, "1885 CLH," pieced in Windmill Blades variant, center with embroidered flora and fauna, border with padded silk roses and chenille embroidered leaves, pieced scalloped edge with silk embroidered fans and tassels, decorative embroidery throughout, minor losses, 56" x 58-1/2" 4,312.00
Mat
  Appliqued, large red heart surrounded by 4 smaller hearts, red border, white ground, 14" dia 220.00

Hooked, rooster against green ground, red border inside border with yellow ovals (eggs?), 15" dia 330.00

Penny, elongated hexagonal, beige, 3 colorful hexagonal medallions bordered by olive-green, blue petal border, 20" x 59-1/2" 316.25

Pillow, "Lottie Anderson's," wool needlework of insects, animals, children, flowers, plants, American flag, etc., 23" x 18" 715.00

Pocket, printed cotton, oval floral sprig pattern in red, blue and tan, black ground, red and black tape loomed belt, American, second quarter 19th C., minor fading, 9-1/4" h, 7-3/4" w, belt 31-1/2" l 373.75

Stumpwork pillow, one with red and white peacock perched on a pink flowering branch with green leaves, black velvet ground, one with two birds, variegated red and variegated pale-yellow, perched on a green branch tending a nest with three eggs, black cotton ground, both with variegated green loop fringe, repairs, wear, 12" sq, pr 1,725.00

Tablecloth

Cotton, work of Mary Nisly, Lancaster County Pa., signed and dated 1843, hand-woven geometric design with 2-1/2" w drawn work floral design panel running thru the cloth's center with small linen panels on either end embroidered in red cotton thread with stylized flower, facing birds, crowns and heart designs, fringed on all sides, minor soiling, 56" x 66" 2,600.00

Linen, eyelet rose pattern, embroidered vining leaves, minor stains, 90" x 106" 55.00

Linen, gray (two-tone) and natural woven with chain and lattice design and ivy leaves, 82" x 116" 121.00

Linen, white-on-white cutout and embroidery, floral and vintage design, scalloped edge, 72" x 113" 220.00

Table rug, black wool, appliquéd floral work in tan, white, light green and pink, scroll and leaf border, scalloped trim, stitched to a stretcher with black covering for hanging, restorations, 25-1/2" h, 40" w 522.50

Theorems

History: A theorem is a painting created with a stencil. Popular during the first half of the 19th century, theorems were most often done with watercolors on either velvet or paper; however, they have also been found on silk and wood.

Collecting Hint: Few theorem velvet paintings were signed.

Note: All listings are watercolor.

On paper

Bird

Beside nest with eggs, foliage and cherries, shades of green, brown, red and blue, signed in pencil "L. Lewis," old frame with red and yellow sponged repaint, 5-3/4" h, 7" w 357.50

On branch of small tree, brown, blue, black, yellow, red and green, minor fly specks and stains, old red and black sponged frame, 9" h, 7" w 330.00

Floral

Flowers in blue bowl, framed, toning, creases, abrasions, 15-1/4" h, 19-1/4" w....................... 4,312.50

Flowers in vase, blue, pink green, yellow and brown, old gilt frame, minor stains, 10" h, 15" w 1,650.00

Flowers in vase, pink and red roses, buds and carnations, also bird and bee, signed "Eliza A. Horan, May 1st, 1848," framed, fold lines, tears, top corners glued down, 15-3/8" h, 12-3/8" w........ 302.50

Flowers in vase, pink, yellow and blue, green foliage, brown vase, oval format, framed, minor toning, stains, 12-1/2" h, 10" w 488.50

Rose (pink) and blue columbine, stenciled and freehand painting, ink verse "...a token of friendship," signed "Miss Valentine," raised rose and morning glory border, worn gilt frame, stains, minor edge damage, 10" h, 8" w 192.50

Roses, columbine and bluebells, old faded colors, stains, old frame, 12" h, 9" w 302.50

Tulips and other flowers, peacock feather, dragonflies, shells and lady bug, in yellow, blue, green, white, brown and tan, period frame with walnut veneer and gilt liner with touchup, light water stains, foxing in margins, minor damage at corners, 17-3/8" h, 18-3/4" w 1,760.00

Fruit

In basket, framed, stains, 10" h, 14" w 1,100.00

In blue bowl, painted frame, toning, minor stain, crease, 7-1/2" h, 9-1/4" w 7,475.00

Watercolor on velvet theorem, fruit in bowls and a basket, 24-1/2" x 21", $12,650. (Photo courtesy of Skinner Auctioneers & Appraisers of Antiques & Fine Arts, Boston and Bolton, Mass.)

On velvet

Floral

Bouquet, red, blue, green and rust, framed, minor foxing, fabric abrasions, 18-3/4" h, 14-1/4" w 460.00

Magnolia and lilies with foliage in blue, burgundy, teal, green, repainted frame, stains, 12-7/8" h, 14-3/8" w 522.50

Rose in reds, pink, green and white, damaged old gilt frame, 15-3/4" sq 137.50

Fruit

Green, yellow and dark blue, framed, foxing, fabric abrasions, 7" h, 9-1/2" w 920.00

In bowls and a basket, framed, minor stains, toning, 24-1/2" h, 21" w 12,650.00

Peaches, pears, melon, grapes, cherries and strawberries, basket with double handles, grass below, period gilt frame, background stained, 17-3/4" h, 20-1/4" w 2,090.00

Signed "Wm. Rank" (William Rank, 20th-C. Pa. folk painter), red grained frame, 17-1/4" h, 19-1/2" w 440.00

Spilling from overturned Canton fruit bowl on marble table, red, blue, green, brown and yellow, wear, minor age stains, old frame, 18-1/2" h, 22-1/2" w 2,860.00

Strawberry tree, signed Wm. Rank (William Rank, 20th-C. Pa. folk painter), old molded frame, 14" h, 11-1/2" w 302.50

With foliage, green, blue, yellow and brown, with vintage note "Taken from frame by Carlton P. Crittenden at Fredonburg, 1862," unframed, wear, minor stains, damage to selvage, 16" h, 20-1/4" w 3,630.00

With flowers and bird, signed "W. Rank" (William Rank, 20th-C. Pa. folk artist), orig grained frame, 20-1/2" h, 21-1/2" w 522.50

Tinware

History: Edward and William Pattison settled in Berlin, Conn., in 1738, becoming America's first tinsmiths. Before that time, the pieces of tinware used in the Colonies were expensive imports. In 1749, the English parliament passed a law that prohibited the establishment of rolling and plating mills in the Colonies. Of necessity, the Pattison brothers imported sheets of tinplate from Wales, the only producer of tinplate for export. It wasn't until the discovery of tin near Goshen, Conn., in 1829 that tinplate was produced in America.

Almost every small town and hamlet had its own tinsmith, tinner, or whitesmith. They used patterns to cut out the pieces, then hammered and shaped them and soldered the parts. If a piece was to be used with heat, a copper bottom was added because tin has a low melting point.

Heart-shaped tin sieve, 14-1/2" x 13-1/2", $632.50.

The industrial revolution ushered in machine-made, mass-produced tinware, and, by the late 19th century, the handmade era had ended.

References: Marilyn E. Dragowick, ed., *Metalwares Price Guide*, Antique Trader Books, 1995; John Player, *Origins and Craft of Antique Tin & Tole*, Norwood Publishing, 1995.

Periodical: *Let's Talk Tin Newsletter*, 1 S. Beaver Ln., Greenville, SC 29605.

Museum: Cooper-Hewitt Museum, New York, NY.

Also See: Toleware.

Candle shelf, square back with large stamped twelve-pointed star in center surrounded by stamped branding and having two small round holes in top corners, rolled top and side edges of back, rectangular tray with low gallery rail across its front with rolled top edge and arched brackets on sides, some rust, 13-7/8" h, 3-5/8" w, 4" d 400.00

Chamberstick, unusual curved handle doubles as hanger for conical snuffer, 9" l 605.00

Coffeepot

Gooseneck, flared gallery foot inverted conical shaped top, stamped banding, arched C handle, rounded hinged lid with double row of stamped dots and small cross finial, lid hinge broken, minor surface rust, 10-1/2" h 325.00

Gooseneck, flared gallery foot, inverted conical top, stamped banding, arched tapered ribbon handle with handle brace, rounded hinged lid, wooden turned finial, 10" h 250.00

Punched heart and floral motif, V-shaped spout, 10" h 550.00

Cream pail, stamped banding around sides, arched bail handle, early solder repair, 8-3/4" h, 5-3/8" dia 60.00

Downspout, flared crimped half-round rim, funnel-shaped body, decor with cutout ten-point star, American, 19th C., 13-1/2" x 9-1/2" 287.50

Lunch kettle, hinged lid, two hinged brass handles, mkd "Champion," 1917 patent date, interior with removable tray and insulated container, minor rust, 5-7/8" h, 9-3/4" w, 6-1/4" d 75.00

Sieve, punched tin, heart shape
4-1/2" l, 3-5/8" h, three feet, strap hanger, minor rust 302.50
6" l, 3-1/4" h, three feet, wire loop hanger 192.50
14-1/2" l, 13-1/2" w, old black patina, three punched circles with compass stars in bottom, 3 feet, ring hanger 632.50

Tray, painted village scene, "Concord 1839," copper-painted rim with flowers, 15" x 18-1/2" 192.50

Wall pocket, shaped back with large arched top having crimped rim and large round hole for hanging, arched top flanked by two small circular elements, full-width rectangular pocket at bottom with tapering front, some rust, 7-5/8" h, 5-1/8" w, 1-3/8" d 200.00

Whale oil lamp, circular pan base, large carrying ring, single burner, 8-1/2" h 137.50

Tobacco Cutters

History: Merchants used tobacco cutters to cut bulk tobacco into desired sizes for their customers. After advances in processing and packaging rendered them obsolete, these gadgets became nothing more than oddities.

Browns Mule, R.J.R. Tobacco Co., by Enterprise Mfg. Co., 7" h, 19" l 75.00

Champion Knife Co., by Enterprise Mfg. Co., 1885 patent date, cast iron, orig paint, 7" h, 19" l 135.00

The Dominion Tobacco Co., Montreal, Canada, by Brunhoff Mfg. Co., Cincinnati, cast iron, 6" h, 16" l 120.00

Gateway Grocery Co., Wholesale Grocer, LaCrosse, Wis., 1914 patent date, cast iron, 8-1/2" h, 15-1/2" l 152.50

Griswold, cast iron, 7" h, 19" l 95.00

Horse motif, wooden bellows-shaped base, ring-turned handle, carved tulip, blade is a cutout horse silhouette with engraved face, bridle, mane and tail, loose ferrule, worm holes, 7" h, 13-1/2" l 660.00

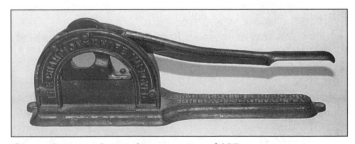

Champion cast-iron tobacco cutter, $135.

King George Navy Tobacco, by Enterprise Mfg. Co., 1885 patent date, cast iron, orig paint, 19" l 100.00

Little Imp, Brighton three, cast iron, 7" h, 10-1/2" l... 95.00

Lorillard's Climax Red Tin Tag Tobacco, by Reading Hardware Co., 1880 patent date, cast iron, 6-1/2" h, 17" l... 80.00

Rex, S.C.W.W.Co., St. Louis, cast iron 80.00

Superb, cast iron, 7" h, 17" l................................. 45.00

Uncle John/Chew Uncle John, S.W. Venable Tobacco Co., by Enterprise Mfg. Co., 1885 patent date, cast iron, blade welded, paint loss, pitting, 18-1/2" l 115.00

Toleware

History: Toleware refers to tinplated sheet iron covered with black asphaltum and painted with brightly colored flowers. Large quantities of toleware were produced in Pennsylvania in the 18th and 19th centuries. Several styles of decorating techniques were used, including painting, japanning, and stenciling. Designs were created by both professionals and itinerants.

Reference: John Player, *Origins and Craft of Antique Tin & Tole*, Norwood Publishing, 1995.

Bank, bank building form, yellow stencil design and "Bank," wear, damage, 3-1/4" h, 1-3/4" w 49.50

Box
Dome-top, orig black paint, mustard trim, red and green floral border, Chippendale brass handle, paint loss, 7" h, 9-1/2" w, 5" d 302.50
Dome-top, worn golden japanning yellow swags on lid, white band with red and black on front, hasp damage, 2-3/4" h, 4" w, 2-3/4" d 203.50

Candle sconce, round mirrored back, single branch with round drip catcher and crimped rim, painted red, wear, 8" h, pr 2,450.00

Candlestick, pushup type, domed square base, orig yellow on worn brown japanning, 6" h 165.00

Coffeepot
Conical shape, floral design in red, yellow, green, cream and black, yellow band, japanned ground, tapered stick spout, arched handle, scrolled finial on front of lid, wear, 8-5/8" h 375.00
Floral decor, bright red and yellow flowers, light-green panels with a circle of yellow brush marks on either side, yellow leaves around the base and domed lid, turned brass finial, japanned finish, repair at bend of gooseneck spout, 11" h 1,210.00
Lighthouse form, fruit and leaves in a diamond formation in shades of orange, yellow and green, black ground, hooked spout, early 19th C., wear, small hole, 10-1/4" h 862.50

Creamer, floral decor, red and yellow, black ground, 4-1/2" h 385.00

Document box, dome-top
Two birds and leafy branches of fruit on lid, sides with band of leaves in orange, green, yellow and

Toleware dome-top document box, decoration of birds and fruit, late 18th/early 19th C., attributed to Mercy North, Flycreek, N.Y., 7-1/4" h, 9-5/8" w, $1,150. (Photo courtesy of Skinner Auctioneers & Appraisers of Antiques & Fine Arts, Boston and Bolton, Mass.)

white, black ground, late 18th and early 19th C., attributed to Mercy North, Flycreek N.Y., wear, 7-1/4" h, 9-5/8" w, 6-1/2" d 1,150.00

Floral decor in red and green on white band across front, black ground, 6" h, 9" w, 5" d 165.00

Floral decor in red and green, yellow flourishes, ring handle, 4-1/2" h, 9 w, 5" d 550.00

Flowers and fruit in red, yellow and green, black ground, early 19th C., wear, small dents, 6-1/2" h, 10" w, 4-3/4" d 402.50

Orig japanning, yellow leaves on lid and front, wire handle, worn (mostly on lid), 3-1/4" h, 6-1/2" l 55.00

Rectangular, red plums, green and yellow leaves, yellow stripes, black ground, 3-1/2" h, 6-3/8" w, 3" d 100.00

Stenciled lattice on lid, flowers on front in green and white, brown japanned ground, lock and hasp, wire bail handle, wear, 6-3/8" h, 9" w, 5-3/8" d 60.50

Document box, flat-top, floral decor in red and green, white band, yellow flourishes, wear, 4-1/2" h, 10" w, 6" d 165.00

Match safe, pedestal form, rounded weighted base, yellow feather-like design, dark-blue ground, exterior of inverted conical-shaped safe covered with sand, interior tin compartment with removable tin lid, early/mid 19th C., 5-5/8" h, 2-7/8" dia 140.00

Spice box

Double slant lids, alligatored japanning with stenciled labels, handle, wear, one lid loose, 5-1/4" h, 9-1/2" w, 6-1/8" d 165.00

"Wh. Cinnamon," rectangular flat top, sloped front, rounded front edge, front of bin slightly rounded, painted black, gold band, yellow and red stripes,

stenciled scrolled design and label, significant paint flaking, 10" h, 8-1/2" w, 9" d 120.00

Tea caddy, floral decor, black with yellow stripes, repainted red and green flowers, dents, chipped paint, 7" h 192.50

Teapot, lighthouse form, floral decor

10" h 660.00

Decor in yellow and red, wear, 11" h 935.00

Tray, rectangular

Floral decor, flat bottom, flared sides, rounded ends, floral design on ends, diamond design on sides, cream and yellow stripes, wear, significant paint loss to interior, 2-5/8" h, 13-1/4" w, 8-1/2" d 55.00

Floral decor, rounded corners, 28" w, 21" d 605.00

Fruit decor, flared rounded ends, red and green daubs, yellow stripe, ends have white edge with red and green fruit, wear, 14" w, 8" d 385.00

Peacock on flowers, floral border, rounded corners, 20" w, 15" d 550.00

Traveling lantern

Collapsible with mica panels, brown with yellow stenciling, "Minor's Patent, Jan 24th 1865," minor wear, 5-1/8" h 385.00

Japanned, gold decor, mica inserts, 1865 patent date, wear, 5-1/8" h, 3" w, 3-7/8" d 220.00

Toolboxes and Carriers

History: Think about it—how many things are created just to hold the objects that created them? Toolboxes and carriers are often made with the very tools they will later hold. These utilitarian boxes served as storage areas for tools that were not in use, in addition to providing a measure of portability.

Box

Curly maple, one drawer in base, molded surround, lift lid, removable nail carrier, lid with applied quatrefoil panel, good figure, 10" h, 19-3/4" w, 9-1/2" d 825.00

Oak, lid with raised shaped panel inlaid with date 1876, front with oval brass escutcheon surrounded by four small inlaid hearts flanked by three inlaid stars, ends with large cast-iron bail handles with iron back plates surrounded by inlaid star and circular motifs, applied molding around base, interior of lid with hinged compartment inlaid with 4 small hearts flanked by stars, shields in corners, five interior drawers, stained finish, 17-1/4" h, 34-1/4" w, 18-1/2" d 400.00

Pine, narrow tongue-and-groove boards, old varnish finish, brass hardware, lock with key, 24-1/2" l 60.50

Carrier

Painted softwood, old blue, two compartments, splayed sides, center cutout handle, saw blade holders, built-in chisel box, 25-1/2" w, 15-1/2" d 522.50

Sheet metal, embossed leaf design, four compartments in top, wrought-bail handle, pitted areas on base, 15" h, 14-1/4" w, 10-1/2" d 275.00

Wooden, four-part, canted sides, crossed dividers, cutout handle, wire nails, worn black stain, edge damage, 4-1/2" h, 13" sq 93.50

Toys

History: The toy industry in America began in earnest in the 1830s. The development of both the railway system and the canal system at that time meant that it was possible to mass produce items and then effectively distribute them. Manufacturers responded by creating a wide range of hand-painted tinplate toys. By the 1880s, cast-iron was being used to produce large quantities of banks and toys, a phenomenon almost entirely confined to America. Another change in materials was seen around the turn of the century, when steel was used for friction toys. Later, it would be used to create an impressive array of pressed-steel cars and trucks. By the 1920s and 1930s, lithographed tinplate had become the material of choice.

References: Ronald S. Barlow, ed., *The Great American Antique Toy Bazaar 1879-1945: 5,000 Old Engravings from Original Trade Catalogs*, Windmill Publishing, 1998; Sharon and Bob Huxford, *Schroeder's Collectible Toys Price Guide, Antique to Modern*, 5th ed., Collector Books, 1999; Charles M. Jacobs, *Kenton Cast Iron Toys*, Schiffer Publishing, 1996; Elizabeth Stephan, ed., *O'Brien's Collecting Toys*, 9th ed., Krause Publications, 1999.

Periodicals: *Antique Toy World*, P.O. Box 34509, Chicago, IL 60634; *Toy Collector & Price Guide*, 700 E. State St., Iola, WI 54990; *Toy Collector Marketplace*, 1550 Territorial Rd., Benton Harbor, MI; *Toy Trader*, P.O. Box 1050, Dubuque, IA 52004; *US Toy Collector Magazine*, P.O. Box 4244, Missoula, MT 59806.

Collectors' Clubs: The Antique Toy Collectors of America, c/o Carter, Ledyard & Milburn, Two Wall Street, 13th Floor, New York, NY 10005; Cast Iron Toy Collectors of America, 1340 Market St., Long Beach, CA 90805; Toy Collector Club of America, 4515 20th Ave. SW, Cedar Rapids, IA 52404.

Museums: Eugene Field House & Toy Museum, St. Louis, MO; Evanston Historical Society, Evanston, IL; Hobby City Doll & Toy Museum, Anaheim, CA; Margaret Woodbury Strong Museum, Durham, CT; Smithsonian Institution, Washington, DC; Toy and Miniature Museum of Kansas City, MO; Toy Museum of Atlanta, GA; Washington Dolls' House and Toy Museum, Washington, DC.

Cast-iron Contractor's Dump Wagon, no driver, $275.

FYI: Francis, Field & Francis, also known as the Philadelphia Tin Toy Manufactory, was the first American manufacturer of tin toys. The company was in business from 1838 to the 1870s.

Also See: Pull Toys

Animals

Cat, sitting, cloth over hard frame, pulling mechanism between legs opens its mouth and activates squeaker, 8" h 385.00

Cow, papier-mâché and wood, two in white and gray paint with paper harness, one brown and white, mkd Germany, minor wear, 3-1/2" l and 2-7/8" l, set of three 55.00

Donkey, musical windup, wooden, gray felt, brown leatherized riding tack, amber glass eyes, fur mane, tail activates music box, wear, 7" h, 8" l 165.00

Giraffe, leather over wood, glass eyes, black painted features, glued leg, 8" h 27.50

Rabbit, fur-covered, papier-mâché face, crude wooden legs, on a rocker, ears flip 176.00

Sheep, composition, white wool coat, leather ears, white paint, pink satin ribbon, minor wear, 6" h, 5-3/4" l 110.00

Sheep, composition, white wool coat, long tail, white paint, red paper collar, brass bell, 4-3/4" h, 5" l 110.00

Sheep, composition, wood and wool, blue and pink ribbon, mkd Germany, 3" l and 3-1/4" l, pr 82.50

Sheep, composition, wood and wool, with ribbon, four mkd Germany, 2-1/4" to 2-1/2" l, set of 5 .... 154.00

Sheep, windup, white flocked coat, glass eyes, bell, tails revolve when wound up, some damage, one not working, 4" h, 4-1/2" l, set of 5 .... 220.00

Blocks, wooden

Letters and animals, set of twenty, pine, 1-1/2" h, 1-1/4" w, 1/2" d... 88.00

Polychrome numbers, relief-cut letters, set of 33, pine, wear, 1-3/4" h.................................... 275.00

Polychrome numbers, birds and animals, relief-cut letters, set of 44, pine, wear, 1" h 192.50

Cannon, cast iron, gold with red wheels, 4" h, 7-1/4" l... 120.00

Circus wagon
  Dayton circus wagon, tin body and wheels, cast-iron driver, wooden animal platform, cardboard animals, friction-driven, old repaint, cond. 8-................ 188.00
  Overland circus band wagon, two horses with outriders, driver, six band members and wagon, cast iron, polychrome paint, unmkd Kenton, wear, 15-3/4" l 715.00
  Overland circus wagon, two horses with outriders, driver, polar bear in wagon, cast iron, polychrome paint, unmkd Kenton, minor wear, 14" l 357.50
Drum
  Brass-plated with blue enamel and lacquered finish, relief stars all around, wooden hoops with stenciled designs, few small areas of rust, with sticks, 8" h, 10" dia 385.00
  Wooden, American flags and stars decor around sides, bentwood hoops on top and bottom, woven string and leather, old lacquer finish, small hole in bottom, 6" h, 6-7/8" dia 341.00
Hay wagon, wooden, spoke wheels, horse fork, dark-blue paint, yellow stripes, wear, 22-1/2" l 110.00
Horse and wagon, German, cast-iron horse, worn palomino paint, articulated legs, tin wagon with wood bottom and metal spoke wheels, alligatored red and green paint, yellow scrolls, legs damaged, 7" h, 18" l 192.50
Iron, metal sad iron, arched wooden handle damaged 33.00
Marbles
  Clay, lot of 275, various sizes 247.50
  Sulphide, chicken, 1-1/4" dia 90.00
  Sulphide, horse rearing, 1-1/2" dia 250.00
  Sulphide, lion, 2" 154.00
  Sulphide, lion (broken in the making), 2" 99.00
  Sulphide, sheep, 1-5/8" dia.............................. 80.00
  Sulphide, spaniel standing, 1-3/8" dia 270.00
Rabbit, dressed in woman's clothes and scrubbing wash on washboard, composition, jointed body, 4-1/8" h.. 575.00
Stove
  Eclipse, cast iron, silver paint, floral scrollwork decor, shelves and accessories including teapot and coal hod, 16-1/2" h, 13-1/2" w, 8-1/2" d 715.00

Painted wood floor train, black, red and dark-green ground, four pieces, 54-3/8" l, $6,900. (Photo courtesy of Skinner Auctioneers & Appraisers of Antiques & Fine Arts, Boston and Bolton, Mass.)

Little Fanny, Philadelphia Stove Works, cast iron, minor break, surface pitting, 7" h (excluding stovepipe), 7" w, 17" d... 270.00
Rival, J.E. Stevens Co., nickel-plated cast iron, 1895 patent date, 15-1/2" h, 7-1/2" w 935.00
Royal, cast iron, with frying pan, pot, anvil and top warmer lifter, missing shelf and warmer lid.. 550.00
Stuffed
  Cat, tiger stripes, 11" l................................ 192.50
  Cat and rabbit, printed cloth, tabby in black, tan and gray, rabbit in black, white and light green, mid-20th C., fading, 14" and 13-3/4" h 49.50
Sulky with woman driver and horse, cast iron, red sulky with gold accents and silver wheels, driver blue with brown hair, black horse, paint wear, 11-1/8" l 350.00
Tin
  Black man, flat, articulated limbs, some age but not early 19th C., 9-1/2" h................................110.00
  Hen on nest, place marble in chicken's head, press down and it lays an egg, worn, 6-3/4" h 82.50
Tin, windup
  Clowns, Schuco, felt costumes, drummer, violinist (minus violin) and acrobat with costumed mouse, all work, 4-1/2" h, set 137.50
  Li'l Abner and his Dogpatch Band, Unique Art, minor wear, works but needs adjusted, 8-3/4" l 302.50
Tractor, cast iron, Arcade, green iron wheels, red body, 2-7/8" h, 4-5/8" l 130.00
Train
  Locomotive, floor train, painted metal, 14" l 137.50
  Locomotive, friction, painted metal, 13" l 440.00
Wagon, pine, "Express" black stencil, tin wheels, new screws, glued crack in undercarriage, 13-1/2" l 247.50
Windmill, metal, Ohio Art, orig box, cond. 8+, assembles to 15" h.. 66.00
Wooden, dancing Black man, worn old red and black paint, one leg replaced, base with edge damage, 16-1/2" h 181.50

Trade Signs

History: Trade signs served as a symbol of the services or goods offered by early American businesses. Typically made of wood or metal, they depicted the object handled by a particular establishment, such as a pair of eyeglasses for an optometrist. The figural representation was particularly important during the 18th and 19th centuries, when many people couldn't read.

Barber pole, turned wood, painted
  34" h, red, white and gold, ball-shaped ends... 880.00
  40" h, blue and white stripes, acorn-shaped ends.. 3,850.00

Boot trade sign, cast zinc painted golden-brown, 22-1/2" h, $1,380. (Photo courtesy of Skinner Auctioneers & Appraisers of Antiques & Fine Arts, Boston and Bolton, Mass.)

76" h, red and white repaint, filled age cracks and chips on base, tin cover on top 550.00

7' h, red, white and blue design, ball top, worn paint 1,650.00

Boot

Cast zinc, wrought-iron angle bracket, painted golden-brown, American, 19th C., paint loss, 22-1/2" h 1,380.00

Pine, worn patina and "Repair" in red, heel and back edge restored, 20th C., 34" h 467.50

White repaint, black detail over earlier gilding, contemporary steel stand, age cracks, 25-1/2" h 385.00

Cigar, turned wood, "Papa's Best" in red letters on brown ground, late 19th C., paint losses, 37" l 402.50

Drugstore, painted wood, molded frame on rectangular sign, ochre colored raised lettering, dark-blue ground, minor wear, 19" h, 72" l 2,300.00

Fish, copper, gilded, full-bodied fish painted "Tackle," orig forged hinges, with provenance from orig owners, 25" l 9,900.00

Hand axe, painted zinc, 21" h, 9" w 431.25

Mortar and pestle, sheet zinc, 3-D, old worn gilt paint with traces of black, contemporary stand, dents, 36" h 770.00

Optometrist, cast iron and zinc, double-sided, polychrome decor with "Glass Fitted" arched above/below eye on one lens, "Eyes Tested" above/below eye on other lens, late 19th C., wear, old touchups to paint, 11-1/2" h, 26-1/4" l 4,312.50

Pawn broker, wrought-iron bracket with scrolled decor and twisted flame atop, three copper balls approximately 14" dia, brass fittings, worn black paint, 61" h, 50" w 1,595.00

Pocket watch, cast and sheet zinc, traces of gilt and Roman numerals, 19-1/2" h 357.50

Rifle, carved wood with gesso, old repaint, resembles Henry rifle, wrought-iron hangers, old repair at trigger guard, 70" l 935.00

Shoe

Wooden, high heel with bow on front, laminated, yellow, blue and salmon paint, worn and weathered, early 20th C., 25" l 2,365.00

Wooden, similar to Dutch shoe, white paint, 8" h, 22-1/2" l 275.00

Straight razor, carved wood

Blade painted "Razors Ground" in black on gray ground, black handle, wear, 14-1/2" h, 31" l 862.50

Painted black and white, wear, scratches, 43-1/4" l 920.00

Trammels (see Fireplace Equipment)

Tramp Art

History: Tramp art derives its name from the fact that many of the artists who created the chip-carved wooden items were itinerants. Cigar boxes and fruit and vegetable crates were common sources for the wood that was edge-carved and layered to create a unique 3-D effect. Popular from 1875 until the 1930s, examples include everything from banks to boxes and frames to lamps.

Tramp art mirrored cabinet, 24" h, 17" w, $935. (Photo courtesy of Cyr Auction Company, Gray, Maine)

Collected as folk art, most of the work was attributed to anonymous makers. A premium is placed on the more whimsical artistic forms, pieces in original painted surfaces, or pieces verified to be from an identified maker.

References: Michael Cornish and Clifford Wallach, *They Call It Tramp Art*, Columbia University Press, 1996; Helaine Fendelman and Jonathan Taylor, *Tramp Art: A Folk Art Phenomenon*, Stewart, Tabori & Chang, 1999; Clifford A. Wallach and Michael Cornish, *Tramp Art: One Notch at a Time*, Wallach-Irons Publishing, 1998.

Cabinet
 Hanging, mirrored door and fall-front compartment on shaped plaque with razor holder, comb box and pincushion, carved marquetry, five-point stars, circles and hex signs, loss to comb holder, 45" h, 23" w............ 825.00
 Medicine, mirrored door and drawer over shelf and comb box, scalloped crest rail, step-down chip carving, 24" h, 10-1/2" w............ 220.00
 Mirrored, 24" h, 17" w, 9" d 935.00
Comb box, hanging, arched scalloped back with layered notch-carved rosette in center accented with small round white porcelain knobs, front of open box slopes forward and has scalloped top edge, double dart-shaped ornament on front, dark-red paint, 10-1/8" h, 8-3/4" w............110.00
Doll dresser, three drawers, old white repaint, gold trim, worn, age cracks, 21-1/2" h, 15-1/2" w, 8-3/4" d............ 357.50
Dresser box, old finish, raised diamond designs, applied embossed decor, velvet-lined interior with lift-out divided tray, mirror in lid, brass paw feet, name on front, acorns and medallion on lid, lion pulls on ends, "1893" on back, edge chips, one small pc missing, 6-1/4" h, 10" w, 6-1/2" d 357.50
Frame
 10-1/2" h, 8" w, old varnish finish, X design in corners, one small pc missing 165.00
 12-1/2" h, 10-1/8" w, applied notch-carved molding with hearts and Xs around sides, stained finish............110.00
 14-3/4" h, 14-1/2" w, five layers of notch-carved strips of wood, two tiers with top tier having a single frame for a postcard-size picture with three frames below with equal openings 155.00
 18-1/2" h, 15-3/8" w, projecting corners, two small pcs missing............ 150.00
 23" h, 21" w, gold and silver repaint on inner liners and outer border, dark orig finish in-between, graduated strips of wood stacked and chip-carved, minor wear, holds 8" x 10" picture 495.00
 44" h, 28" w, tapered pine plinth with carved interlocking sections of wood, arched crest, applied relief stars on either side, finials, few broken points, one finial missing 440.00

Jewelry box
 6" h, 14" w, 8-1/4" d, hinged lid, four square layered notch-carved feet, one back foot missing 140.00
 4-1/4" h, 11" w, 6-3/4" d, hinged lid, layered sides, round ornament on front faced with mother-of-pearl, lid with four notch-carved hearts....... 270.00
 6-1/2" h, 12-1/4" l, paint-decor, four ball feet, sides and front with scalloped molding with floral decor in center of panel, one end with applied diamond design in corners, opposite end with applied hearts, front with applied clubs, top of lid with applied tapered ribbed molding to form a rayed motif surmounted by ball-shaped finial in center, brown ground accented in black, wear....... 150.00
Mirror, frame with dark finish over varnish, stepped sawtooth border, stacked geometric designs, 15" h, 17-1/2" w............ 275.00
Sewing stand, dark orig finish, four molded legs, applied sawtooth trim, shelf in base, well at top with handles on each side, large rectangular pincushions on front and back, lid missing, 27" h, 18-1/4" w, 13-1/4" d........412.50
Side table, projecting square top and medial shelf, square legs, applied multi-layer shape and chip-carved decor, old varnish finish, 26" h, top 16" x 15-1/2" 690.00

Treenware

History: Small, utilitarian household items made from treen (another term for wood) are referred to as treenware. Although most examples were made of maple, other woods such as ash, oak, pine, pear, apple, and walnut were also used. A wide range of objects was made, including bowls, spoons, spice boxes, mortars and pestles, drinking vessels, snuff boxes, and even nutmeg graters.

Bowl
 4" dia, 3-1/4" h, round tapered foot, rounded sides, dark-brown paint, cracks, rim broken and glued............ 30.00
 5" dia, 2-3/8" h, covered, green paint, flat base, straight sides, rounded shoulder, slightly rounded lid, oblong finial, age cracks 30.00
 7" dia, 3-1/4" h, covered, flat base, rounded sides, squat shape, rounded lid with oblong finial, black over earlier red paint, crack............ 160.00
 9-1/2" x 10-1/4" (excluding handles), 3-1/2" h, oval, rounded bottom, flattened flared handle........130.00
Canister, round, painted, reeded band, lid with knob-shaped finial, black and red ground, wide band of foliage motifs, top split in half with early repair, cracked body, chip, paint wear, 6-1/2" h, 5-1/2" dia........ 230.00
Charger, turned with decor rings on both sides, slightly oval, 19-3/4" x 21"............ 192.50
Churn, red paint, 14-1/2" h............ 385.00
Cup, vinegar grained, 3-1/2" h, 3" dia 715.00
Egg cup holder, fruitwood, sun-bleached finished, ebonized trim, turned base, three bun feet, incised rings, six-cup, turned column with turned spoon rack, ball fin-

ial, glued repair on spoon rack, with 6 coin silver spoons, 12-1/2" h... 247.50

Ink sander, green paint, turned, pr 220.00

Inkwell, sponge-decor, brown and yellow, gilt stenciling, glass insert, "Manufactured by S. Silliman & Co...Conn.," wear to top, 2-1/2" h, 4-1/4"dia........ 192.50

Jar, decorated

 3-1/4" h, 3-1/2" dia, sponge-decor, green and yellow, turned bands at top and bottom of base, age cracks 1,815.00

 5" h, 4-5/8" dia, red tulips and green leaves, footed base, lid with conical finial, yellow over-varnish flaking 110.00

 6-1/4" h, 6-1/2" dia, grain-decor, brown graining over yellow, yellow and black sponged tree or feather design, covered, wear, age cracks 1,430.00

 7-1/2" h, 6-5/8" dia, sponge-decor, reddish brown with yellow sponging and dots, flared foot, conical finial 1,072.50

 8" h, 6" dia, grain-decor, brown graining, yellow sponged tree or feather design, covered, wear, edge damage, age cracks 385.00

 12" h, 9-1/4" dia, orig reddish-brown vinegar sponge decor over yellow, poplar, footed base, raised ring around the top, domed lid with turned finial, minor grain separation on interior of lid, base cracks...3,850.00

 12-1/4" h, 13-1/4" dia, red vinegar decor over yellow ground, raised rings around base and top, slightly domed lid, turned finial 5,280.00

Match holder, barrel-form, brown and tan sponge-painted, 2-1/8" h..115.00

Noggin, scrubbed finish, possibly Indian, 12" h... 357.50

Pitcher, carved, salmon paint, 7" h....................... 275.00

Plate, curly maple, old finish, incised rings around the top and under the rim, 9-1/8" dia...................... 467.50

Sander, barrel-shape, top is bowl-shaped with pierced star design, sides with reeded bands, minor chips, 3-3/8" h, 2-3/8" dia 35.00

Spice container, decorated, orig reddish-brown vinegar decor over mustard, "Spice" in gold, turned foot and rim, raised ring around center, glued crack, rim chips, possibly missing its lid, 4" h, 7" dia 192.50

Storage container, turned, with cover, bulbous form, brown stain, bail handle, 19th C., 8" h, 9" dia..1,035.00

Trenchers

History: Trenchers began as a wooden board or plate on which meat was served or cut. During the 19th century the form evolved into an oblong bowl shaped like a small trough. Many trenchers were painted.

Collecting Hint: When buying trenchers, examine the paint carefully. Repainted trenchers are less valuable than those in original paint.

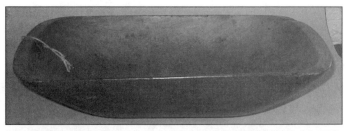

Trencher in old blue paint, repaired crack, 5" h, 20" l, 14-1/2" w, $400.

15" l, 9" w, 3" h, green paint 440.00

17" l, 10-1/2" w, 4" h, oblong, yellow paint 495.00

18" l, 10" w, red paint 577.50

19-1/4" l, 12-3/4" w, oblong, walnut, refinished, wear 150.00

20-3/8" l, 12-1/8" w, 5-1/8" h, oblong, rounded ends, flat bottom 850.00

22-1/2" l, 13-3/8" w, 4-1/2" h, oblong, old red painted exterior and rim, hand-hewn, age crack, chip 440.00

23-1/2" l, 11-1/2" w, softwood.............................110.00

24" l, 16" w, 5" h, oblong, blue paint..................... 440.00

Trivets

History: Although trivets today are often thought of as small, tabletop items used to hold an iron, pan or teakettle, the form actually began as a metal stand for a kettle in the hearth. Most trivets have three feet. Cast-iron trivets were mass-produced beginning in the 1850s. Prior to that, trivets were hand made of brass, copper, and wrought-iron.

Brass

 Heart motif, smaller heart at handle with larger heart in body, one-pc casting, three feet, 9-5/8" l 137.50

 Spade motif, hearts and diamond cutouts, 10" 110.00

Cast iron

 Fleur-de-lis with trefoil cutout, three feet, 10" l 27.50

 Horseshoe shape, "1886" cast in center, round turned knob-shaped finial with iron collar, handle cracks, 3/4" h, 9" w, 4-3/8" d........................ 45.00

 Shield shape, bust of George Washington, oval handle with scrolled ends, three round tapered legs, minor rust, 1-5/8" h, 9-1/4" l........................... 25.00

Wrought iron

 Round, splayed tripod base, penny feet, two grate hooks, long shaped handle, medallion finial, 11-1/2" h, 21-1/4" w 165.00

 Shield shape, open center with cross motif, handle with heart finial, three round legs with pad feet, minor rust, 1-1/2" h, 9" l............................. 360.00

Wrought iron, heart motif

 7-1/4" l, diamond center, three riveted feet 143.00

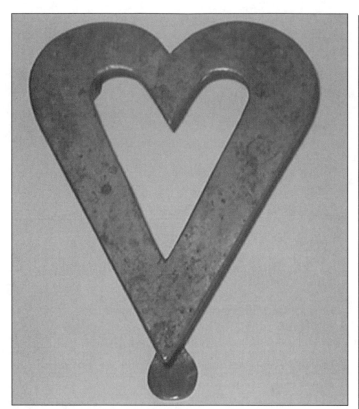

Iron heart-shaped trivet marked "T. Loose," penny feet, 5" l, $100.

7-3/4" l, penny feet with some damage.......... 302.50
7-3/4" l, 2" h, three round tapered legs, some
    rust.. 85.00
13-1/2" l, 5-1/8" h, footed, round outer shelf, inner
    heart shelf, tapered handle with hole at center,
    pointed end, pitted..................................... 143.00
Wrought iron and brass, tripod base, cabriole legs, urn-
    turned column, turned wooden handle with cast-brass
    insert, single bird spit fitted above the handle, old dark
    finish, light pitting, 19-1/2" h............................. 660.00

Trunks

History: Trunks typically have a clasp and were used to store or transport personal possessions. Normally "trunk" refers to the ribbed flat- or domed-top models of the second half of the 19th century.

Reference: Roseann Ettinger, *Trunks, Traveling Bags and Satchels*, Schiffer Publishing, 1998.
Dome-top
    Grain-decor, orig salmon graining highlighted with
        yellow striping simulating inlaid stringing, New
        England, late 19th C., orig hardware, 11-1/4" h,
        26-3/4" w, 13-1/2" d.............................. 1,150.00
    Miniature, stylized floral decor in orig mustard,
        green, orange, black, white and blue polychrome,
        bottom and interior of lid in light-green, small open

TREASURE WITHIN

Great folk art is turning up in the most unexpected places these days.

This canvas-covered storage trunk had whimsical pen-and-ink lettering and wonderful illustrations on the interior. It was lettered "Ephraim Warren, Chelmsford County Middlesex, State, Massachusetts, Ward No. 5, March 6th 1810, AE, 17." The lid also had a tale of "The Hermit," "On A Sudden Arose A Violent Storm" and "The Old Man and His Ass."

Partial newspapers, including a Middlesex Gazette of Concord, Mass., dated Aug. 22, 1817, lined the trunk, while a newspaper clipping from The Boston Globe, June 15, 1926, related the story of the trunk.

With stains and the lid unattached, the trunk soared past its pre-sale estimate of $1,000-$1,500, selling for $23,000. at a Skinner auction.

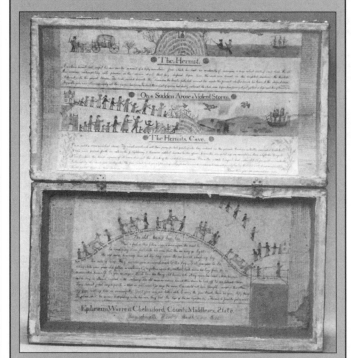

Folk-decorated trunk, $23,000. (Photo courtesy of Skinner Auctioneers & Appraisers of Antiques & Fine Arts, Boston and Bolton, Mass.)

till, old dark putty filler near hinges on lid, wire
    nails, 5-1/2" h, 8-5/8" w, 5-1/8" d................ 742.50
Painted, old red, foliage decor in black and yellow,
    poplar, wear, age cracks, incomplete hasp,
    24-1/2" l... 715.00
Paint-decor, orig brown, green and black vinegar
    decor, black border covers line of period sponging
    repaint, basswood, 12-3/8" h, 30-1/4" w,
    15-3/4" w.. 1,650.00

Leather-bound
 Black leather worn, decorative brass studs, engraved plaque with initials, wrought-iron lock with hasp and brass escutcheon, 11-1/2" h, 24" w, 14" d 467.50
 Black leather with tooled line decor, padded seat top, brass tacks around lid and on front and sides in swags and diamonds with initials "G.T.,"" cloth-lined interior, wear, leather damage, 16" h, 30-1/4" w, 15-1/4" d.. 330.00
Leather-covered, camphor wood, brass-bound edges, brass tack decor, brass bail handles at ends, areas of binding missing, leather damage, 13-3/4" h, 30-1/2" w, 15-1/4" d... 220.00
Miniature, simulated black leather covering, brass nail-head trim, leather handle, interior lined with marble-ized paper, maker's label "Theodore Kellogg No. 56 Hanover St., Boston," late 19th C., wear, damage, 4-1/4" h, 8" w, 5-1/2" d 143.75

Tubs

History: Wide and low, these bucket-like vessels are often the size of half of a barrel. They were originally formed with wooden staves, a round bottom, and hoops.

Cedar Ware (Andover Mass., 19th C.)
 4-1/4" h, 5-7/8" dia, alternating light and dark wood, staves, two metal scrolled handles, metal bands, turned lid and knob, paper label remnant, wear, loose band, repair.. 143.75
 5" h, 5-1/4" dia, alternating light and dark wood, staves, extended cutout handles, metal bands, wear, loose band 115.00

Shaker washtub in blue paint, 21-1/2" h, 27-1/2" dia, $2,185. (Photo courtesy of Skinner Auctioneers & Appraisers of Antiques & Fine Arts, Boston and Bolton, Mass.)

 5-1/4" h, 6-1/4" dia, alternating light and dark wood, staves, extended cutout handles, metal bands, oval paper label, wear, loose band 172.50
Wooden, painted
 Blue-green, cream interior, two overlapping staves, two pierced handles above the rim, 8" h, 10" dia 2,970.00
 Green, 6" h, 10" dia 137.50
 Stave-constructed, D-shape cutout handles, metal and lapped wooden band, wear, bands loose, 8-3/4" h, 12" dia.. 258.75

Utensil Racks

History: Because cooks preferred to keep tasting-spoons, ladles, and other utensils within arm's reach, they often hung them near the kitchen stove. By the 1850s, special utensil racks had been created, and they eventually incorporated a trough at the bottom to catch any errant drippings. Initially made of wood or wrought-iron, utensil racks were eventually formed out of enameled iron and stamped sheet aluminum.

Softwood, carved crest with scroll designs flanking a central petaled flower with two leaf clusters, two tiers of wrought-iron hooks (four hooks over six), band of small arches along bottom edge, cyma-curved ends, 16-5/8" h, 26-1/8" w 220.00

Wrought iron, ram's-horn detail at center and top of centered vertical arm, double ram's-horn detail at each end of horizontal arm, 14-1/2" h, 28" w 1,980.00

Utensils

History: Kitchen instruments typically reflect the materials of their day. Most early metal utensils were blacksmith-made. The Pennsylvania Dutch made wrought-iron kitchen items beginning in the early 18th century. Wooden utensils could be carved when metal examples weren't available or affordable. As brass, copper, and tin came into use, kitchen utensils were also made from those materials.

Also See: Kitchen Collectibles, Wrought Iron.

Dipper, copper bowl with flared sides, wrought-iron handle, "John F. Stratton, New York," 22-1/2" l 357.50

Dipper and skimmer, brass bowls, wrought-iron handles, mkd "F.B.S. Canton, O.," bowls dented, 5-1/4" dia bowl, 15" handle, pr 148.50

Dough scraper, wrought iron, twisted curved handle 55.00

Flesh fork, wrought iron, two tines

    16-3/4" l, flattened handle with hook end, heart stamped with "H" in circle flanked by letters "P" and "C" and clusters of punched dots........... 55.00

    17-1/4" l, tapered flattened handle with rounded end, mkd "W. Priar"... 75.00

    17-3/8" l, incised lines, large hook with scrolled tip 40.00

Fork and knife

    Bone-handled, steel, three tines, shaped knife blades, brass rivets, mkd "Lamson & Goodnow Mfg. Co.," set of 24 (twelve of each)........... 180.00

    Bone-handled, steel, "Riverside Knife Co.," set of 24 (twelve of each) 180.00

    Bone-handled, steel, decor pewter inlay, knife blades marked with "K" in diamond, set of 24 (12 of each).. 220.00

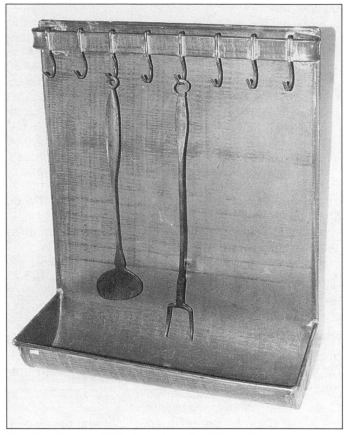

Tin utensil rack, $400; iron utensils, $85 each.

    Ebony slab handle, knife mkd "Landers, Frary and Clark,"" cleaned, age cracks, set of eight (four of each) 110.00

    Steel, black handles, four tines, mkd "Landers Frary & Clark, Aetna Works," set of sixteen (eight of each) 70.00

Ladle

    Brass bowl, iron handle fitted with later maple handle, side of handle split and repaired, bowl 9-1/8" dia, 38-5/8" l 160.00

    Brass bowl, wrought-iron handle with rounded section below flattened section inlaid with square and rectangular pieces of brass, closed hook on end, 19th C., some pitting, bowl 4-1/2" dia, 20-3/4" l 120.00

    Butchering ladle, wrought iron and brass, mkd "J. Schmidt 1847," one ladle and one strainer ladle, tapered flattened handle with loop end, one with early repair, 21" l, pr 575.00

    Copper bowl, wrought-iron handle with flattened sections above/below rounded section, hook end, some rust, bowl 5-1/2" dia, 19-1/2" l............. 45.00

    Curly maple, curved handle, 13-1/4" l............ 330.00

    Oyster ladle, wrought iron, 4-1/4" shallow bowl, slightly curved tapering flattened handle with hook end, dated 1860, 12-3/4" l 270.00

    Wooden, carved fluting on ends of handle, 7-3/4" l 99.00

Meat fork
Wrought iron, mkd "Anna Jacobs," two curved tines, tapering flattened handle with 4-3/4" round section and hook end, 13-1/4" l 85.00

Wrought iron, mkd "J. Schmidt," two curved tines, tapering flattened handle with hook, wear, rust, 17-1/2" l 125.00

Wrought iron, mkd "J. Schmidt, 1847," two curved tines, tapering flattened handle with loop, stamped, 18-1/2" l 325.00

Set, wrought iron, long rounded section at bottom with wide tapered flattened section at top ending in rounded end with hook having small scrolled tip, 17-3/8" ladle with 5" dia bowl, 17-1/8" strainer ladle with 5" dia bowl, 15-1/2" meat fork with two tines, 15-1/4" spatula with bell-shaped blade, set of four........ 170.00

Skimmer, pierced brass bowl, wrought-iron handle, 19th C., 18-1/2" l 99.00

Skimmer and spoon, wrought-iron, eye-hook handles, skimmer with brass bowl, 5-1/2" dia, 10-1/2" handle, spoon with simple tooling, 2-1/2" dia, 13-1/2" handle, pr 137.50

Spatula
Carved horn, Pennsylvania-German motifs, blade with pierced six-lobe radial design in circle with scrolled stem, curved scrolled and pierced handle with small heart cutout at end, small chips, 11-7/8" l... 450.00

Wrought iron, keyhole design, 10-1/2" and 16-1/2" l, pr 137.50

Wrought iron, rounded front edge, rounded top, handle and blade made from one pc of iron, incised lines/dots, loop end with scrolled tip, minor wear/rust, 10-1/4" l, blade 3-3/8" w 210.00

Wrought iron, wide square blade tapers at back to form handle with rounded section, handle tapers to flattened top with large tapered hook, 23-1/2" l, blade 5-1/8" w.. 60.00

Spoon
Gray, slotted graniteware bowl, turned wooden handle, 12-1/4" l 300.00

Wooden, carved, pierced handle with hook, shallow bowl, age crack, 8" l 550.00

Tasting ladle
Brass bowl, wrought-iron handle with tapered hook, "F.B.S. Canton, O.," 1886 patent date, wear, significant rust, bowl 3" dia, 14-1/4" l 170.00

Brass bowl, wrought-iron handle with stylized flower design, hook end, mkd "PR," minor dents, bowl 2-1/4" dia, 11-1/4" l 375.00

Wrought iron, handle flares out at top, loop with scrolled tip, incised crescent-and-dot design, minor wear/pitting, bowl 2-5/8" dia, 15-1/4" l 100.00

Wrought iron and brass, mkd "J. Schmidt 1849," tapered flattened handle with loop end, slight crack in rim of brass bowl at handle, 14-3/4" l 325.00

Wagons and Carts, Children's

History: Wagons and carts were everyday modes of transportation during the 19th century. Taking the "like father, like son" approach to life, scaled-down versions were made for the use and enjoyment of children.

Cart

Painted, old green repaint, decal of eagle and shield on wooden plank seat, spoke wheels with rubber tires, handle pumps forward and backward for motion, paint worn, 23-1/2" h, 39" w, 16-1/2" d........................ 165.00

Painted, red, wooden including wheels, 22" l......... 60.50

Yellow pine, old finish, two-seater, steel-spoke wheels, small cast-iron wheels on front, seat backs flip, 36" h, 65" l, 21-1/2" d 330.00

Wagon

"Express" wagon, wooden bed and undercarriage, wooden wheels with metal rims, made to be pulled by dog or other small animal, with yoke, wagon backboard missing, 10-3/8" h, 22-1/2" l, 13-5/8" w................ 320.00

Folk art, walnut and pine, orig olive paint, wooden disk wheels held by later nail pins, tombstone-shaped windows and doors, arched roof, 9-1/2" h, 24" w 192.50

Goat wagon, green paint, wooden wheels
    15" h, 18" w, 26" l (excluding tongue) 250.00
    Wheels with iron rims, 32" h, 30" w, 56" l (excluding tongue) 495.00

Child's wagon with advertising, "Spring Coaster, OVB, Our Very Best," wooden with original mustard paint, metal spokes and wheels, $750.

Wardrobes

History: Because most early homes did not have closets, wardrobes were created to provide the necessary space for storing clothes. Usually designed with a shelf at the top, a hanging rod, and one or two drawers in the base, wardrobes were intended primarily for hanging clothing, rather than simply storing it folded. Bedrooms were usually located in the upper level of the house, and it was difficult to maneuver the large, bulky wardrobe into position there. Furniture makers solved this problem by creating knock-downs—collapsible pieces of furniture that were much easier to transport.

FYI: The term "wardrobe" was not commonly used until the latter half of the 18th century, when it was popularized by George Hepplewhite, noted English cabinetmaker and designer.

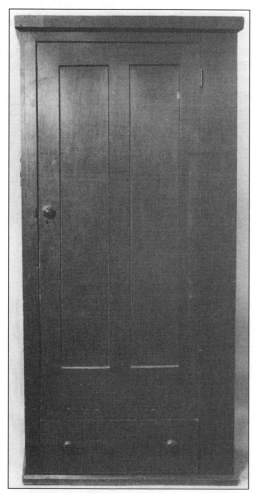

Wardrobe in old brown repaint, poplar and pine, Rockingham knob, age crack, 83-1/2" h, 39-3/4" w, $522.50. (Photo courtesy of Garth's Auctions, Delaware, Ohio)

Corner, painted, red, country style, walnut and poplar, high shaped feet, one door with inset panel and beaded edge, turned wooden pull, pegged and square nails, paint removed from framework of door, cove-molded cornice with edge damage and corner restoration, damage to feet, areas of touchup, 81" h, 42" w, 23" d 3,025.00

Grain-decor, orig brown over mustard flame and comb decor, maple and pine, two-pc, top with two paneled doors, open interior with pegs, scalloped base with two dovetailed drawers, turned wooden pulls, chamfered corners on case, inset panels on sides of top and bottom, molded cornice, 20th C. with some age, 80" h, 35" w, 16" d.. 1,595.00

Knockdown, grain-decor, brown over mustard grained repaint, poplar, country-style, two doors with inset panels and molded surrounds, dovetailed case, molded base and cornice, four interior shelves and peg rack, 80" h, 59" w, 17" d.. 440.00

Painted

Old brown repaint, poplar and pine, door with two vertical inset panels and Rockingham knob over drawer with wooden pulls, interior fitted with fourteen small cast-iron hooks and replaced shelf, molded base, age crack in door, 83-1/2" h, 39-3/4" w, 19" d 522.50

Mustard repaint, country style, poplar, bracket feet, one dovetailed drawer with old brass pulls, two doors with square- and tombstone-shaped raised panels, cove-molded cornice, replaced escutcheons, repaired breaks in feet, 67" h, 45" w, 20" d 2,750.00

Pine, Canadian, mortise and peg construction, bracket feet with scalloped returns, molded edge on base, 2 doors with 3 panels each, molded edges, rat tail hinges, raised panels in ends, step-down cornice, refinished, feet and small section of cornice replaced, 76" h, 50" w, 18" d... 1,870.00

Washboards (see Laundry Items)

Washstands

History: Created during the second half of the 18th century, a washstand was a small piece of bedroom furniture used to hold a washbasin. One form, the commode, was an enclosed, cupboard-type washstand, usually including one or more drawers or doors.

Corner stand, Hepplewhite, mahogany, cutout opening, three lower drawers, arches splashback with candle stand, 40" h, 18" d.. 770.00

Federal

Painted, yellow with dark-green decor and graining, shaped backsplash behind cutout for bowl, lower drawer, turned feet, 37" h, 18" w, 16" d 715.00

Stained, New England, early 19th C., flaring scrolled splashboard above solid board, straight

Federal washstand, New England, early 19th C., 35" h, 20-1/2" w, $460. (Photo courtesy of Skinner Auctioneers & Appraisers of Antiques & Fine Arts, Boston and Bolton, Mass.)

skirt, turned supports, one lower drawer, ring-turned tapering legs, orig pull, lightly cleaned old surface, minor imperfections, 35" h, 20-1/2" w, 13-3/4" d 460.00

Hepplewhite, country style, cherry, square tapered legs, bottom shelf with one dovetailed drawer, top with cutout for bowl and two accessories, worn refinish, edge wear/damage, 28-1/2" h, 16" w, 16-1/4" d......... 302.50

Pine, orig red and black decor, turned feet, one dovetailed drawer, walnut knobs, bowfront top shelf with cutout for bowl, dovetailed and scalloped gallery, signed in pencil "Glen Sheet, Congress," 37" h, 19-1/4" w, 16" d 990.00

Sheraton, cherry, one drawer, turned legs, shaped shelf, dovetailed gallery with shaped sides, orig brass pulls, refinished, restorations, 32-1/2" h, 22-1/8" w, 17-1/4" d 522.50

Sheraton, country style, 1 drawer

Cherry, refinished, turned feet and legs, lower shelf, replaced brass pulls, replaced scalloped backsplash, drawer veneer painted, 34-1/4" h, 34-3/4" w, 18-7/8" d... 330.00

Sheraton country-style curly maple washstand, refinished, 33" h, 20" w, $3,410. (Photo courtesy of Garth's Auctions, Delaware, Ohio)

Curly maple, excellent figure, high ring-turned legs, dovetailed drawer in base, pressed glass knob, turned and tapered supports, top with cutout for washbowl, scalloped dovetailed gallery, refinished, 33" h, 20" w, 17" d 3,410.00

Pine, old red paint over earlier mustard, turned legs, button feet, compartment in base, overlapping dovetailed drawer, turned supports, one-board top, hairline in one leg, chips in feet, 31" h, 20" w, 18-1/2" d 385.00

Smoke decor, cream colored ground, green stripes, one drawer, turned legs and feet, cutout for bowl, scroll-cut back and side splashes, minor edge wear, 28-1/2" h, 18-3/4" w, 16" d 770.00

Walnut

One drawer under top, scalloped back above top over one drawer, top flanked by turned towel bars, block and turned legs, turned feet, stretcher shelf, 32" h, 27" w, 17" d 165.00

Commode-style, one long drawer at top, two short drawers beside door, raised burl panels on drawers, doors and backsplash, reeded stiles, molded-edge top, 39" h, 29" w, 16" d 297.00

Watch Hutch

History: A watch hutch was a small case used to hold a pocketwatch. Because the watch was still visible through an opening in the case or from behind a glass pane, the stand, in essence, became a miniature clock.

Eagle (gilded cast-iron) and Rococo design, white marble base, 7" h 137.50

Hanging, pine, worn orig bittersweet paint, one-pane door, shaped crest, square nail and screw construction, beveled base and top, 12" h, 7-1/2" w, 5-5/8" d 1,320.00

Mahogany, scalloped shaped top, chip-carved decor with diamond, heart and snowflake motifs, minor wear, loss to backboard, 6-1/2" h, 2-1/4" w, 1-1/2" d .. 747.50

Watt Pottery

History: Owned and operated by the Watt family, Watt Pottery was incorporated in 1922. Occupying the old Burley Pottery site in Crooksville, Ohio, the company's early years were devoted to manufacturing utilitarian stoneware. In 1935, the pottery dropped its crocks and churns in order to produce more modern ovenwares, and in 1949 the company began hand-decorating its products. The simple patterns and bright colors of the designs contrasted nicely with the creamy clay, resulting in a uniquely country look.

References: Sue and Dave Morris, *Watt Pottery*, Collector Books, 1998; Dennis Thompson and W. Bryce Watt, *Watt Pottery*, Schiffer Publishing, 1994.

Collectors' Clubs: Watt Collectors Association, P.O. Box 1995, Iowa City, IA 52244; Watt Pottery Collectors USA, P.O. Box 26067, Fairview Park, OH 44126.

Reproduction Alert: Using clay that is close in color to that of the original pieces, Four Rivers Stoneware in Hazel, Kentucky, has reproduced

Casserole, Apple pattern, $125.

Watt Pottery. These contemporary pieces are marked, but examples have been found with the marks ground off.

Original Watt items have also been used to create molds that can then be used for producing reproductions that include the impressed marks found on the authentic pieces.

FYI: Most pieces of Watt ware are well-marked, with large marks that often cover the bottom of the piece. The impressed phrases "Watt" and "Oven Ware U.S.A." are generally included with one or more concentric rings, although early marks consist of a script "Watt" without the rings. Additionally, most pieces have an impressed mold number for easy identification.

Bowl, Apple pattern, #7, two-leaf variation,
  wear 55.00
Bowl, advertising, Apple pattern
    #5, "Kinnards Dairy, Estherville, Iowa,"
      wear.. 49.50
    #6, "1958 Becker Hardware, Janesville,
      Iowa"... 44.00
    #6, "Bremer Oil Co." with Phillips 66 logo 55.00
    #63, "Anamosa Farmers Creamery," wear 49.50
    "Whittemore Co-op Elevator" with Phillips 66 logo,
      9" dia 66.00
Pie plate, advertising
    Apple pattern, #33, "To A Good Cook, Frederika Co-
      op Creamery".. 99.00
    Autumn Foliage pattern, #33, "B&B Co-op Oil,
      Waverly, IA" 66.00
Pitcher
    Apple pattern, #16, 6-1/2" h............................ 99.00
    Starflower pattern, #17, 8" h 143.00
Pitcher, advertising, Apple pattern
    #15, "B&B Co-op Oil, Waverly, IA,"
      5-1/2" h... 66.00

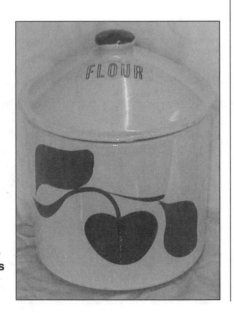

Flour canister, Apple pattern, lid with chips and cracks, 8-1/2" h, $250.

#15, "Davison Hardware, Frederika, IA,"
    5-1/2" h 66.00
#15, "Fecht's Service Station, Allison, Iowa," chip,
    5-1/2" h 44.00
#15, "Kalona Creamery, Arch Haberman, Old Fash-
    ioned Ice Cream," 5-1/2" h 55.00
#15, "Lange's D-X Trucking, LaPorte City, IA,"
    flakes, 5-1/2" h... 49.50
#15, "Fern Creamery Co.," 5-1/2" h 132.00
#16, "Baker Lumber Co." 77.00
Spaghetti bowl, Apple pattern, #39, two-leaf variation,
  two cracks 77.00

Weathervanes

History: In addition to being decorative, weather vanes filled a more functional role by enabling farmers to determine wind direction from a distance. Although agriculture no longer dominates the American workforce, weathervanes are still extremely desirable. Examples in animal form are the most popular with collectors, and cows and horses are particularly common since farmers sometimes used vanes that mirrored the livestock they raised. Chickens, pigs, sheep, and eagles can also be found, but vanes portraying unusual animals such as beaver and wolverines are much harder to find.

The earliest examples were found on late 17th-century structures in the Boston area. The vanes were handcrafted of wood, copper, or tin. By the last half of the 19th century, weather vanes adorned farms and houses throughout the nation, and mass-produced vanes of cast-iron, copper, and sheet metal were sold through mail-order catalogs and at country stores.

References: Robert Bishop and Patricia Coblentz, *Gallery of American Weathervanes and Whirligigs*, E.P. Dutton, 1981.

Reproduction Alert: Reproductions of early weathervanes are being expertly aged and then sold as originals.

Collecting Hint: Because they were popular targets for hunters and gun-toting boys, many old weathervanes are riddled with bullet holes. Filled holes generally can be detected with a black light.
Arrow
    Copper, ball finial, dents, 13" h, 25" l 345.00
    Copper, feathered tail, verdigris patina with traces of
      gilt, slight bend, 17-1/2" h, 42-1/4" l 2,070.00
    Sheet and cast copper, old green patina, decorative
      arrow atop sphere, old repairs, modern base, 36"
      h, 32" l 1,375.00
Arrow and banner, zinc, cutout scalloped banner with
  weathered gilt surface, 13" h, 68" l 2,070.00

Molded and painted William Tell weathervane, bow missing, 32" h, $18,400. (Photo courtesy of Skinner Auctioneers & Appraisers of Antiques & Fine Arts, Boston and Bolton, Mass.)

Banner

    Bronze, six stylized C scrolls within riveted strap-work frame, solder repairs, lacks arrow, 20-5/8" h, 49-1/2" l 747.50

    Copper, pierced "ECL," with directionals and pole, traces of gilt, repairs, imperfections, banner 29-1/2" h, 72" l, overall 12' h 575.00

    Copper, pierced "K," traces of gilt, post split and separated, break in one cone finial, bullet hole, late 19th C., 19" h, 37-1/2" l 1,725.00

    Copper, pierced "Smith" at center, scrollwork decor, some verdigris patina, traces of gilt, some loss, solder repairs, 24-5/8" h, 37" l 1,840.00

    Wooden carved arrow point, swallow-tail end, old white paint, wear, paint loss, stains, 39" h, 60-1/4" l 1,380.00

    Zinc and wrought iron, three-part finial composed of banner and arrow motif, four arched slender iron rods ending with four flower blossoms, on baluster-form standard, wear, 54-1/2" h 690.00

Car, open roadster, carved and painted wood and copper, with copper driver, 12" h, 23" l 6,900.00

Cow

    Copper, full-bodied heifer, gilt surface, weathered, minor imperfections, late 19th C., 21" h, 33" l 13,800.00

    Copper, gilt, numerous bullet holes, 17" h, 29" l 2,640.00

    Tin, 10" h, 14" l 93.50

Eagle

    Copper, hollow-bodied, embossed detail, old green patina, old repairs, remounted on wooden base, 20" h, 23" wingspan 880.00

    Copper, on sphere, full-bodied, spread wings, 36" h, 72" w 7,700.00

    Copper and zinc, later worn gilt surface, hollow body, solid zinc head, minor edge damage, modern base, 15-1/2" h, 18-1/2" wingspan 385.00

Eagle with arrow

    Copper, zinc head, traces of gilt, perched on ball with wings spread, arrow directional, resoldering at seams, patina removed at one time, dents, on wooden base, 23-1/2" h 605.00

    Copper and cast zinc, old gilding, green patina, hollow body, modern stand, 16" h, 17" wingspan 2,310.00

    Sheet iron, black repaint, landing eagle with wings spread, arrow beneath with separate pole and directionals, welded repair, 59" h 605.00

Fish, flat sheet metal, applied fins, green glass eyes, gilt finish, gilt loss, glass eye cracked, 13-3/4" h, 16" l 1,035.00

Flag directional, tin, embossed, coned base, fluted ball at center, pierced star and crescent moon finial, few bends, small hole in base, pitted, 31-3/4" h 605.00

Horse, prancing

    Cast aluminum, over arrow, on copper holder, bullet holes, small size 49.50

    Sheet iron, repainted dapple gray mane, tail and hooves, orig mounting bar, old pitting, few bullet holes, 26-1/2" h, 32" w 715.00

    Tin, with arrow, small hole in head, minor seam splits, St. Louis origin, 6" h, 9" l 93.50

Horse, running, copper

    Black Hawk, verdigris surface, minor dents, 17-1/2" h, 25" l 3,220.00

    Black Hawk, flattened full body, verdigris patina, traces of gilt, seam splits, dents, some solder repairs, 18-1/2" h, 25-3/4" l 4,025.00

    Copper and zinc, rubbed gilt surface, minor gilt loss, 18-1/2" h, 24" l 2,185.00

    Gilt copper, molded, late 19th C., with directionals, dents, gilt loss, seam separation, 15-1/4" h, 24-1/2" l 2,530.00

THERE SHE BLOWS!

Sometimes it's the top-dollar lots that attract all the attention. However, there are certainly plenty of interesting items of a more affordable nature. Consider the example of a horse with a history. That's what you could call one particular tin leaping-horse weathervane from a barn in Oakham, Mass. It reputedly came off the structure during the hurricane of 1938. The piece was made from two sheets of tin riveted together and painted black. Measuring 22-1/2" high and 35-1/2" long, the horse was missing one foreleg and had dents. It sold at a Skinner's auction for $546.25.

Gold paint, traces of green patina under old gilding, 19-1/2" h, 31-1/2" l 1,430.00

Old dark patina, cast-iron directionals with old gold paint on letters, part of the "N" broken, one ear missing, tail broken/glued, modern wooden stand, 15-1/2" h, 29-1/2" w 550.00

With zinc head, 16" h, 26" l 2,585.00

With zinc head, bobbed tail, 23" h, 38" l 3,630.00

With zinc head, Ethan Allen, flattened full-body, loss of bottom of forefoot, crease on tail, 10-1/2" h, 16-1/2" l 2,415.00

Worn gilding over earlier patina, applied zinc ears, contemporary steel base, restorations, 17" h, 31-1/4" w 2,530.00

Horse, running, sheet metal

Arc-welded, with directionals, rod and stand, found in Canton, Ohio, pitted, repairs, 26" l 275.00

Holes, wear, 16" h, 28" l 220.00

No tail, wear, 16" h, 30" l 110.00

Horse running, tin

Full-bodied, on arrow, 24" l 825.00

Stamped, black paint, one side retaining some orig gold, one leg with open seam, wear, 10-1/2" h, 14" l 160.00

Horse running, wooden, painted mustard, carved details, Vermont origin, age cracks, metal braces, 27-1/2" h, 60" l 6,050.00

Horse running, zinc, old oxidized patina, hollow body, hollow tin rod with rust damage, on stand, from barn in Berlin Center, Ohio, 22" h, 31" w 2,420.00

Horse, running, with rider, copper

Bob-tailed horse, full-bodied, 19th C., regilded, 18" h, 31-1/2" l 4,600.00

Full-bodied, Cushing & White, 19th C., old ochre paint, traces of gilt, impressed maker's tag on rod, minor seam splits, 16" h, 26-3/4" l 13,800.00

Horse, standing, sheet metal, large tail to vane, 26" l 110.00

Horse and sulky, with jockey, running, copper

Attributed to Cushing & White, full-bodied, gilt, old ochre paint, minor paint loss, 16" h, 26" l 8,050.00

Full-bodied, 21" h, 38" l 4,950.00

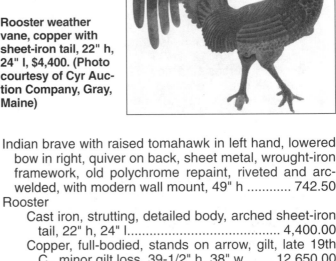

Rooster weather vane, copper with sheet-iron tail, 22" h, 24" l, $4,400. (Photo courtesy of Cyr Auction Company, Gray, Maine)

Copper full-bodied rooster weathervane, gilt, 39-1/2" h, 38" w, $12,650. (Photo courtesy of Skinner Auctioneers & Appraisers of Antiques & Fine Arts, Boston and Bolton, Mass.)

Indian brave with raised tomahawk in left hand, lowered bow in right, quiver on back, sheet metal, wrought-iron framework, old polychrome repaint, riveted and arc-welded, with modern wall mount, 49" h 742.50

Rooster

Cast iron, strutting, detailed body, arched sheet-iron tail, 22" h, 24" l 4,400.00

Copper, full-bodied, stands on arrow, gilt, late 19th C., minor gilt loss, 39-1/2" h, 38" w 12,650.00

Copper, full-bodied, stands on arrow, traces of gilt, late 19th C., split front foot, creased comb, 21" h, 24" l 4,312.50

Metal, cast in two sections, one side a later recast in white metal, sheet metal tail feathers in old multi-color paint, one leg resoldered, 59" cast-iron directions with welded repair, 24" h, 26" w 715.00

Sheet iron, silhouette of simple design with four-feather tail, reinforced with riveted iron strapwork, 36-1/2" h, 27-1/2" l 977.50

Sheet metal, alligatored brown repaint, hollow body, raised wings and eyes, tail feathers cut from one pc with cutouts and embossing, on later wooden base, one bullet hole and bent feather, 22-1/2" h, 18-1/4" w 2,640.00

Zinc, hollow body, embossed detail, traces of polychrome paint, early 20th C., on domed wooden base, from Henry Ford home in Sand Harbor, Mich., 23-1/4" h 1,100.00

Sailing ship, gilt-copper and iron, from Gloucester, Mass., late 19th C., gilt loss, imperfections, one directional missing, 32" h, 25" w 2,300.00

Soldier, sheet metal, man standing at attention, wearing kepi and frock jacket, holding rifle in front, pierced eyes and mustache, hand-wrought brackets on back, rust, 35" h 1,320.00

Wheelbarrows

History: Used for moving small loads, wheelbarrows typically have one front wheel and two back legs, as well as two handles that extend behind the bucket or platform.

Adult's

Wooden, green paint, metal wheel, 27" h, 62" l 225.00

Child's
> Painted, old dark blue repaint, white striping, interior and wheel in orange, handles chamfered, screws and later nails added, age cracks, break along one side, 11-1/2" h, 38" w, 12-1/4" d 434.50
>
> Stenciled gold horse on each side, orig black over red paint, cross stretcher on rear legs, small section of wheel with orig gold over-paint, square nails, some later nails added, minor edge damage, 11-1/2" h, 12" w, 38" l 412.50
>
> Stenciled horses and flowers, dark-green exterior, red interior, wheels and handle tops, paint loss, 13" h, 46" l 575.00

Whirligigs

History: A variation of the weathervane, whirligigs indicate wind direction and velocity. Often constructed by the unskilled, they were generally made of wood and metal and exhibited a rather primitive appearance. Flat, paddle-like arms are characteristic of single-figure whirligigs, but multi-figure examples are usually driven by a propeller that moves a series of gears or rods. Three-dimensional figures are commonly found on 19th-century whirligigs, but silhouette figures are generally indicative of 20th-century construction.

Reference: Robert Bishop and Patricia Coblentz, *Gallery of American Weathervanes and Whirligigs*, E.P. Dutton, 1981.

Carved and painted wood whirligig, man with paddle arms, 22" h, $7,150. (Photo courtesy of Cyr Auction Company, Gray, Maine)

Indian in canoe, wooden, carved and painted, paddle arms, 14" h, 18" l 440.00

Man, light-blue outfit, blue hat, rubber arms, composition, looks like weathered wood, contemporary, 24-1/2" h 605.00

Man sawing logs, cut tin, wooden base, old worn gold, red, green and black paint, directional in green and black, propeller in green and orange, 32-3/4" l 137.50

Man, wooden, carved and painted, red jacket, blue pants, black boots, brown hat, painted paddle arms, 22" h 7,150.00

Patriotic motif, black man with hat pumping water for woman in polka-dot bandana and with washboard, wooden, propellers in red, white and blue with stars on the ends, white stars along the base, compass stars on the directional, glued age cracks in directional, other minor age cracks, wear, weathering, 26-1/2" l 1,072.50

Pot-bellied man, large hooked nose and pointed chin, wears black top hat and shoes with curled toes, face painted red and white, tin, wind-activated arm baffles, mounted on rod on wooden base, white and red paint shows under black on body, wear, age cracks, arms damaged and one replaced, 11-3/4" h (excluding base) 3,300.00

Roosters, two facing each other, on tower made resembling an oil derrick, wooden, red, green and black paint, 62" h 110.00

Sawmill motif, wooden, two men running boards thru saw, under wooden roof, tail mkd "Old Tiamciw (?)1860 Saw Mill," said to be from Vermont c. 1939, 13" h, 32" l 715.00

White Clay

History: Lighter than stoneware or sewer tile, white earthenware was sometimes used to make some of the same decorative objects found in stoneware and sewer tile. Many pieces were given an Albany glaze, so they would resemble their courser-clay counterparts.

Cat, seated, free-standing forelegs, oval base with rope-twist design, running brown glaze, wear, flakes, 11-1/4" h, 10-1/4" l 935.00

Dog, seated, hollow-molded, mottled green glaze, black painted eyes and whiskers, two chips on underside, 6" h 27.50

Dog, seated, spaniel
> Dark-brown glaze, two smaller white dogs on base resemble bull terriers, one with damaged tail, 7" h, 7-1/8" l 1,540.00
>
> Dark-brown glaze, top of oval base mkd "Souvenir 1877 F.M. King Co. 1897," bottom mkd "Galesburg Pottery Co.," minor wear, 7-5/8" h, 7-1/4" l 825.00
>
> Dark glaze, minor glaze flake, 7-7/8" h 55.00
>
> Light-brown glaze with heavy streaks, large paws on stepped base, 8-3/4" h, 8-1/2" l 440.00

White Ironstone (see Ironstone)

Whites Utica

History: Decorated molded stoneware was added to the production of the Whites family pottery in Utica, N.Y., during the late 19th century. Hugo Bilhardt, a German designer, was hired in 1894 to produce molded stoneware in the German tradition. Referred to in advertisements as "Flemish stone ware," production ranged from match safes to punch bowls, and many pieces were souvenirs.

Collecting Hint: Most items are highlighted in blue. Look for additional colors, which boost the value of an item.

Note: All items in this category are molded wares in a salt glaze with cobalt highlights.

Batter pail, oak leaf and vine embossed design, four qt 330.00
Bean pot, "Boston Baked Beans," children eating, minor clay separation near handle, 9-1/2" dia at handle 440.00
Bottle (jug-form)
    "James E. Pepper Est. 1780 Lexington Ky. Geo. H. Smith Distributor, Utica N.Y.," rose design, restored handle, 7-1/2" h 440.00
    "White Rose Rye Whiskey, P.J. Bowlin Liquor Co., St. Paul, Minn.," rose bouquet, 7-1/2" h 440.00

Globe-shaped bank, "World's Fair, My expenses to Chicago, Pat. applied for," train on track, from 1893 Chicago World's Fair, 4-1/2" h, $3,740. (Photo courtesy Bruce and Vicki Waasdorp, Clarence, N.Y.)

Butter crock, "J.B. Shattuck's Creamery, Cherry Creek N.Y.," and "This package manufactured by the Central N.Y. Pottery Utica N.Y.," extensive chipping, hairlines, flakes, 7" h 495.00
Cream pot, cobalt dotted horse-head decor, some cobalt loss, full-length glued crack on back, one-gal 5,050.00
Humidor, hunting dog, orig lid, minor clay separation, 6-1/2" h 176.00
Jar
    Two-gal, leaf decor, minor stains 330.00
    Three-gal, running bird decor, design fry, restored stone ping 247.50
    Novelty, "L.A. Delicatesse, A Confection in Cheese," lid replaced, 4" h 88.00
Match safe
    Plain, tooled pattern, minor surface roughness, mold mark #1, 3" h 44.00
    "American Brew Co., Rochester, N.Y.," eagle inside badge, small impact fracture on rim, 2-3/4" h 220.00
    "Crystal Spring Brewing Co., Syracuse N.Y.," three cobalt bands, tooled design, 5" h 742.50
    "Westcott & Parker, Dealers in Coal & Wood, Utica, N.Y.," 3" h 275.00
Mug
    "25 Bezirks Turnfest West New York, Syracuse N.Y. 1894" and "C.N.Y. Pottery, Utica N.Y.," hairline, 5" h 302.50.00
    "Bayle's St. Louis, Pretzels Are The Best," 4" h 577.50
    Bismarck face mug, short hairline, 4" h 440.00
    "Compliments of Crystal Spring Co., Syracuse N.Y., Crystal Lager," two women filling jug, 4-3/4" h 275.00
    "Iroquois Brewing Co., Buffalo, N.Y.," Indian logo, 5" h 187.00
    "Jos. Schlitz Brewing Co., Milwaukee," Schlitz logo, German verse on opposite side, hairlines, 5" h 198.00
    "Pan American Exposition 1901 Buffalo N.Y. USA," tree-bark form, base mkd "Whites Pottery, Utica N.Y.," 4" h 275.00
    "World's Fair Chicago 1893," hairlines, 4-3/4" h 522.50
Mug, handled
    "Pan American Exposition 1901, Buffalo, NY USA," standing buffalo on opposite side, base mkd "Whites Pottery Utica, N.Y.," 7" h 357.50
    Same as previous, with tavern scene on opposite side, 6-1/2" h 357.50
Pitcher
    Children pulling a log, blue, green and brown accents, pewter lid, surface wear at spout, crazing, 5-1/2" h 495.00
    Daffodil design, chips, 6-1/4" h 44.00
    Gen. Steuben profile on 1 side, fife and drum motif on other, bark-like ground, chips, 7-1/2" h 77.00
    Paul Revere, bark-form handle, chips, 6-3/4" h 247.50

Steins (from left): Washington crossing the Delaware, some glaze loss, 13" h, $440; man toasting/children toasting, four-color, green, brown, white and blue, 15" h, $687.50; couple reading/German verse, three-color, blue, brown and green, unusual large size, 15-1/2" h, $1,017.50; man toasting/children toasting, hairline, 14-3/4" h, $467.50. (Photo courtesy Bruce and Vicki Waasdorp, Clarence, N.Y.)

Stein

Couple drinking at table on front in dark-green, brown and blue, vine design on back in blue, mold mark #6, hairline restored, 10-1/2" h 550.00

"Empire Theatre, Wed. Eve. March 30th, 100th Performance, The Conquerors," elves design, children at play around bulbous base, mold mark #39 .... 522.50

George Washington bust on front, German verse on back, gargoyle handle, mold mark #44, 8" h 330.00

Nathan Hale bust on front, German verse on back, gargoyle handle, mold mark #43, 8" h 302.50

Pond scene with ducks, birds and swans on front, tavern scene on back, mold mark #6, two short clay separation lines, no lid, 10" h 577.50

"The Prince of Pilsen," couple dancing, "Here's to the heart that beats for me" verse on back, 9" h 247.50

Tavern scene on front, German verse on back, gargoyle handle, mold mark #43, 7" h 110.00

Tavern scene (medieval), vine design on back, brown and blue, mold mark #7, 13" h 467.50

Tavern scene (medieval), vine/acorn design on back, brown and blue, mold mark #7, 13-1/2" h 357.50

Woman playing tuba on front, vines and acorn on back, blue and brown, mold mark #5, 12-1/2" h 357.50

Water cooler, Niagara Falls on front, floral design on back, green, brown and blue, lid missing, cracked, 13" h 1,650.00

Windmill Weights

History: Manufactured primarily during a 50-year period starting around 1875, windmill weights served as either counterbalance or governor weights on windmills. Counterbalance weights, primarily figural, were used on vaneless windmills to counterbalance the weight of the windmill's wheels. Examples include bulls, horses, squirrels, arrows, and stars. Governor or regulator weights tended to be non-figural.

Reference: T. Lindsay, *A Field Guide to American Windmills*, The University of Oklahoma Press, 1985.

Reproduction Alert: Reproductions are relatively commonplace. Collectors should be particularly leery of examples that exhibit new paint and/or new rust.

Collecting Hint: Windmill manufacturers and the farms that utilized their product were located almost exclusively in the Midwest. Therefore, the majority of weights offered at local auctions and farm sales will be found in Kansas, Nebraska, Minnesota, and the Dakotas.

Note: All listings are cast iron unless otherwise noted.

Ball

Fairbury Vaneless No. 1 counterbalance weight for 10' wheel, "Add 25 LBS" 100.00

Fairbury Vaneless No. 1 counterbalance weight, 67 lbs, 8" dia 190.00

Perkins 10' open wheel counterbalance weight, No. 10K27, 11-1/2" dia 190.00

Battleship, for 12' Baker wheel, 28-1/4" l 2,500.00

Bell, governor weight, for Ozark 12' wheel, 6-3/8" h 675.00

Buffalo, A56, 10-7/8" h, 16-1/8" 4,150.00

Bull

Fairbury, plain, orig base, for 10' wheel, 55 lbs 575.00

"Fairbury," orig base, for 12' wheel, 18" h, 24-3/4" w 2,875.00

"Fairbury, Neb.," orig base, for 10' wheel, 18" h, 24-3/4" w 950.00

Simpson, Hanchett Improved, full-bodied, 13" h, 15" w 2,000.00

Crescent

Dempster (Mill Mfg. Co.), 417, small ear, points up, 2-1/2" thick 120.00

Dempster, A417, fat ear, points down, 2-5/8" thick 100.00

Dempster, B417, fat ear, points up, 3-3/8" thick 135.00

Dempster, C417, large right-hand ear, points up, 4-7/8" thick 280.00

Dempster, C417 small ear, points up, 4-7/8" thick 250.00

Eclipse, A12, points down, 2-1/2" thick 325.00

Eclipse, A13, left-hand ear with parts number below, 2-1/2" thick 135.00

Eclipse, A13, LM Co. foundry mark, points up, 2-1/2" thick 195.00

Eclipse, A13, points up, right-hand ear, large block letters, 2-3/8" thick 150.00

Eclipse, A13, points up, short left-hand ear, 2-1/2" thick 175.00

Eclipse, AA13, points up, right-hand ear, small parts number, 2-1/8" thick 120.00

Eclipse, AA13, points up short left-hand ear, 2-1/8" thick 330.00

Eclipse, B13, BF foundry mark, points up, 3-1/4" thick 170.00

Eclipse, B13, mismarked example of A13, 2-5/8" thick 440.00

Eclipse, B13, points up, large left-hand ear, 3-3/8" thick 125.00

Eclipse, B13, points up, short left-hand ear, 3-1/4" thick 120.00

Eclipse, B13, points down, 3-3/4" thick 270.00

Eclipse, B13, points up, right-hand ear, large letters, 3-3/8" thick 150.00

Eclipse, C13, points up, large left-hand ear, 5-1/8" thick 220.00

Eclipse, C13, points up, short left-hand ear, 5" thick 320.00

Eclipse, 13, for Crescent Jr. 8-1/2', points up, 2" thick 180.00

Eclipse, no parts number, points down, 3-1/4" thick 280.00

Flint & Walling, Leader, A13L, 2-1/2" thick 280.00

Flint & Walling, Leader, B13L, 3-3/8" thick 200.00

Flint & Walling, Leader, C13L, 5-1/8" thick 425.00

Standard, no part number, for 10' wheel, 2-1/2" thick 275.00

Standard, A 13, steel-strap ear, 2-1/2" thick 450.00

Standard, AA13, steel-strap ear, 1-7/8" thick 400.00

Standard, B13, cast-iron ear, 3-1/2" thick 525.00

Standard, B13, steel-strap ear, 3-3/8" thick 375.00

Standard, C13, steel-strap ear, 4-1/4" thick 675.00

Success, B13, for 12' wheel, 3-1/2" thick 575.00

Unidentified maker, debossed A13, points up, left-hand ear, 19 lbs, 2-1/2" thick 330.00

Hildreth Iron Works

"Hildreth Iron Works Success, Hastings, Neb." counter balance, D17, 8-1/2" dia 370.00

Same as previous, no part number, 8-5/8" dia 275.00

"Fairbanks Morse" vaneless type V counterbalance weight, 10-1/2" dia, 5-7/8" d 675.00

Football shape, cement, 17-1/8" w 125.00

Horse (Dempster Mill Mfg. Co.)

No. 3 and 4, short-tail horse, 22" h, 17-1/2" w 500.00

No. 14, short-tail horse, 22" h, 17-1/" w 575.00

No. 58, long-tail horse, 18-1/2" h, 17-3/4" w 1,025.00

Horseshoe, Holdrege Mfg. Co., 12-1/2" h, 8-3/4" w 2,150.00

Model E

P249-B13, raised letters, 8-1/8" dia 1,075.00

S262, raised letters, 8" dia 325.00

O-shape, Breyer Bros. Whiting and Co., for Ozark 12' wheel, largest variety, 13-3/4" h, 19" w 2,600.00

Plattner Yale, oval

215, closed top, 7-1/2" h, 17-1/4" w 500.00

B26, 5-3/4" h, 11-1/2" w 275.00

B75, 6" h, 11-1/4" w 325.00

B215, open top, 8" h, 17-1/4" w 525.00

Rooster

Elgin, Barnacle Eye, 18-1/2" h, 18-1/4" w 4,600.00

Elgin, Large Hummer, 17-1/2" h, 16-3/4" w 2,800.00

Elgin, Large U-Base Rooster, 19-1/4" h, 18" w 2,200.00

Elgin, Model E Hummer, Long Stem, 13-1/2" h, 10" w 750.00

Elgin, Mogul Rooster, on repro base, 22-3/4" h, 20-3/4" w 4,500.00

Elgin, No. 2, for 10' wheel, 15-1/2" h, 16-5/8" w 1,575.00

Elgin, No. 2, for 12' wheel, 17-1/2" h, 21-3/4" w 5,800.00

Elgin, Rainbow Tail, 18-1/4" h, 18-3/8" w 4,000.00

Elgin, Short Stem rooster on Model F ball 1,175.00

Elgin, Short Stem rooster on large Model F ball, for 12' wheel, repaired, 22" h 925.00

Elgin, Short Stem rooster on Model L ball, 19" h 825.00

Elgin, Small U-Base Rooster, 15-7/8" h, 16-1/2" w 975.00

Elgin, Smaller A20, 17-1/2" h, 20-1/2" w 4,900.00

Shield, Dempster Mill Co., Capital Vaneless, 10-1/2" h, 8-1/4" w 850.00

Spear (Challenge Co., Batavia IL)

Model 1913, 14-1/4" h, 30" w 800.00

Model 1719, 14-1/4" h, 30" w 750.00

Model 1719, rare hook version, 14-1/4" h, 30" w 1,875.00

Squirrel, Elgin, 17-1/2" h, 13-3/8" w 4,900.00

Stover, B13, raised letters, 7" dia, 2-3/4" d 360.00

Star, Flint and Walling

Full-bodied star, C24, 10" w, 2-3/4" thick 2,300.00

Raised star on round base, B13, 7-5/8" dia, 3-3/4" thick 750.00

Raised star on round base, no parts number, 7-5/8" dia, 2-5/8" thick 470.00

Star, U.S. Wind Engine & Pump Co., H37, 15" h 3,400.00

W- shape, Althouse Wheeler Co.
  For Raymond 10' wheel, 9" h, 16-5/8" w........ 250.00
  For Raymond 12' wheel, short version, 9-1/4" h,
    17-1/4" w 575.00
  For Raymond 12' wheel, tall version, 10" h,
    17-1/4" w 725.00
  For Raymond 14' wheel, 60 lbs, 9-1/4" h,
    19-1/2" w 2,300.00
  For Raymond 16' wheel, 118 lbs, 10-7/8" h,
    19-1/2" w 6,025.00

Wood Carvings

History: Largely recognized for their folk art characteristics, wood carvings range from well-executed items made by professional carvers to crudely crafted pieces by unskilled makers.

Among the noted American woodcarvers was John Bellamy (1836-194). He was often commissioned by the U.S. government to carve figureheads, ship decorations, and patriotic symbols. He is especially noted for his eagle carvings, including numerous examples of the regal bird carrying an American flag in its beak or talons.

Angel, head and wings, white paint, glass eyes, 12" h,
  30" l 2,475.00
Bird on ball, spread wings, 28" h 220.00
Black Uncle Sam, red-and-white striped pants, red vest,
  dark jacket with white stars, stained hands and face,
  old alligatored varnish has yellowed, missing cane,
  11" h 5,775.00
Bust, man, minor age cracks, 14" h 192.50
Cat, worn paint, detailed facial features,
  15" h 550.00
Cricket, rectangular shaped top, four turned legs, light-
  blue paint, 19th C., wear, imperfections, 6-1/8" h,
  6-1/4" w, 11-5/8" l 201.25
Eagle, spread-wing
  Clenching three arrows in talons, gold paint, gilt
    highlights, 19th C., wear, 12-1/2" h,
    19-1/4" w 2,300.00
  Gilt, "E Pluribus Unum" banner in red, white and
    blue in beak, 45" w 550.00
  On limb or perch, gilt, 38" l 1,870.00
  Pine, worn gilding, red beak, some age, 10-3/8" h,
    18-3/4" w 440.00
  Sitting on rock, laminated, contemporary, attributed
    to Earnest Brumbergh, 11" h, 32-1/2" l 302.50
Eagle, with banner
  Attributed to John Hales Bellamy (American, 1836-
    1914), carved and painted pine, banner motto
    "Dum Vivimus Vivamus," eagle with breast shield,
    8-1/4" h, 25-1/2" l 23,000.00
  "Live and Let Live," talons hold shield of stars and
    stripes, late 18th or early 19th C., minor restora-
    tion, 23" h, 74" w 6,900.00
Farmer and wife loading hay wagon pulled by ox,
  impressed "Andre Dube, St. Jean-Port Joli," chip on
  woman's hat, 9" h, 22" l 660.00

Horse wood carving in old red paint with real horsehair tail, 12" h, 13" l, $8,800. (Photo courtesy of Cyr Auction Company, Gray, Maine)

Hobo with knapsack and patched clothes, incised "P. Arpin," stamped "Paul Arpin Inc., Phillipsburg, Que. Ch 8-3161, Made in Canada," 15" h 220.00
Horse
  Horse head, mahogany, old dark worn finish, chip-
    carved detail, possibly some sort of architectural
    element, 20th C., wear and damage,
    32" l, pr 220.00
  Prancing, bobbed tail, old black paint, newer base,
    7" h 880.00
  Running stallion, orig buckskin-colored paint, age
    cracks, ears and one leg missing, one leg
    repaired, driftwood base 6-3/4" h, 11" l 110.00
  Standing, old red paint, horsehair tail, 12" h,
    13" l 8,800.00
Plaque
  Eagle in relief with shield and olive branches, four
    brass tacks for eye, traces of gold paint on eagle
    and shield, good patina, old edge damage, tack
    holes, 9-1/2" h, 10-5/8" w 385.00
  Eagle, spread-wing, gold paint, 20th C., glued
    repairs, 19-1/2" h, 17-1/2" w 275.00
  Fruit on shield, walnut, 13" h, 11" w 77.00
  Patriotic shield and furled American flags, blue ban-
    ner "Our Country and Our Liberty," motto "Let The
    Flag of Freedom Wave Over Our Country For
    Ever," molded edge panels bordered by silver and
    gold stars on black ground, fading, paint and
    minor wood losses, 16" h, 40-1/2" w 6,325.00
Rooster
  Antiqued polychrome paint, 20th C.,
    14-1/2" l 110.00

Patriotic carved plaque, "Our Country and Our Liberty," paint-decorated,16" h, 40-1/2" w, $6,325. (Photo courtesy of Skinner Auctioneers & Appraisers of Antiques & Fine Arts, Boston and Bolton, Mass.)

Old finish, good details, carved initials "C.S." (Carl Snavely, 20th-century Pa. carver), 7" h 313.50

Polychrome paint, minor loss to tail, 22-1/2" h 1,375.00

Red, brown and yellow alligatored paint, on twig stand, 5-1/2" h 275.00

Wrought Iron

History: The term wrought is applied to metals beaten or shaped with a hammer or other tool. At very high temperatures, wrought iron is extremely malleable and can be rolled or hammered into virtually any shape.

Bar, possibly for utensils, two hooks, three brass knobs with escutcheons, iron has primitively engraved tulips, some wear, 21-3/4" l 550.00

Bird spit and broiler, penny feet, adjustable rack in base, six prongs, pull handle, 19-3/4" h, 11" w, 11-3/4" d 192.50

Bird roaster, tripod base, penny feet, tapered column, turned finial, adjustable bell-shaped bracket, 23-1/2" h 396.00

Broiler
 Rotary, medallion finial on handle, worn penny feet, 24-1/4" l 220.00
 Rotary, twisted detail and wavy lines, circular top, 12" dia, 27" l 165.00
 Stationary, platform with fifteen scrolled sections that join at turned handle, three short feet, pitting, 31" l, 19" w 522.50

Calipers (double), ring finial, mkd "J.R.," pitted, 17-1/2" l 110.00

Candle stand, tripod base, penny feet, square column with chamfered corners, adjustable cross bracket, two sockets with small scrolled hooks on the bottom, 21-7/8" h 660.00

Door handle, thumb latch, serpentine or vining ends, with mismatched bar, 13-1/2" l 577.50

Figure, patriot on horse, 12" h, 12" l 522.50

Fire carrier, scrolled finial at end of handle, rectangular tray for coals with sliding cover, scrolled finger loop, 24-1/4" l 550.00

Fire-starting strikes, some tooling, group of six 302.50

Flesh fork
 Two tines, incised lines, large hook with scrolled tip, 17-3/8" l 40.00
 Two tines, tapered flattened handle with rounded end, mkd "W. Priar," 17-1/4" l 75.00

Frying pan
 "W. Foster," round pan, flared sides, tapered iron handle ending in large loop, late 19th C., pitting and rust, 1-1/2" h, 8-3/8" dia, 19" l 130.00
 "Whitfield," No. 5, flaring sides, long flattened diagonal handle with beveled edges ending in a loop, substantial pitting, significant rust, 2" h, 11" dia, 24-5/8" l 110.00
 Unmkd, flaring sides, flattened handle with beveled edges ending in large loop, black paint, late 19th C., minor rust, 2-1/4" h, 10-7/8" dia, 40-1/2" l 170.00

Kettle shelf, three penny feet, twisted iron cross-member, ring top with smaller inner ring, 12" h 192.50

Lark spit, hanging, four cast-lead faces around top, five hooks for birds, incomplete brass wire wrap, 17-1/4" h 302.50

Peel
 45-1/2" l 55.00
 Ram's head finial, 41" l, pr 192.50
 Ram's-horn finial, tapered square-to-round handle, 36-1/2" l 165.00

Scraper, wide oblong blade with rounded top, long round handle with flattened end having scrolled heart motif, 19th C., 6-1/4" w, 45-1/4" l 375.00

Shutter dogs, square mounting plates, square shaft extending out from center, large diamond-shaped end with pod-shaped top and scrolled bottoms, painted gray, late 18th or early 19th C., 5-1/2" h, 3-7/8" l, 1-3/4" w 35.00

Skewer pins (four) and hanger 220.00

Sickle, tapered crescent-shaped blade, turned wooden handle, illegible mark, 18-1/2" w, 21" l 20.00

Spatula
 One mkd Krider, one with heart handle, 12-3/4" l, group of three 220.00
 Wrought-iron and brass, 12" to 18" l, group of 4 .... 192.50

Trivet, heart motif, footed, round outer shelf, inner heart shelf, tapered handle with hole at center, pointed end, pitted 143.00

Utensils, four tasters (three with brass bowls, one with copper bowl) and skimmer with brass bowl, three mkd "T. Loose" (20th century Pa. metalsmith), group of five 275.00

Wafer iron, oblong irons with incised shield surmounted by crown with bird and "1773," flanked by floral designs, tapered square handles with one ending in loop, minor rust, 9-1/8" x 5-1/8", 42" l 475.00

Yellowware

History: This type of utilitarian pottery has been produced in the United States and England since the early 19th century. Because yellowware was quite durable, it became the kitchen pottery of choice, replacing the more fragile redware. Color may range from pumpkin orange to deep yellow to pale cream, and most of the pieces are unmarked. Horizontal bands in white, brown, blue, or a combination thereof were the most common type of decoration.

References: William C. Ketchum Jr., *American Country Pottery: Yellowware and Spongeware*, Alfred A. Knopf, 1987; Joan Leibowitz, *Yellow Ware*, Schiffer Publishing, 1985 (1993 value update); Lisa S. McAllister, *Collector's Guide to Yellow Ware*, Collector Books, 1997; Lisa S. McAllister and John L. Michael, *Collecting Yellow Ware*, Collector Books, 1993.

Museums: Bennington Museum, VT; Henry Ford Museum, Dearborn, MI; Museum of Ceramics, East Liverpool, OH.

Also See: Mocha.

Beater jar, three white stripes, base chip,.
5-3/4" h.. 170.00
Bowl, molded foot, two white bands flanked by light-blue stripes, two slight chips on foot, 2-7/8" h,
4-1/8" dia... 425.00
Bowl, mixing
    Four bands of brown slip, 2-3/8" h,
      4-1/4" dia 110.00

Yellowware advertising beater jar, black ink, two raised brown stripes, 20th C., 4-3/8" h, $80.

Mixing bowl, yellowware with stripes in brown and white slip, 10-1/2" dia, $150.

Blue seaweed decor in white band around center, brown line borders, spider in base, flaking on interior, rim chip, 7" h, 14-3/4" dia 330.00
Green seaweed decor in cream-colored band around center, brown line borders, rolled rim and foot, rim hairline, glaze flakes in bottom of the bowl, 5-1/4" h, 11-5/8" dia........................ 385.00
Nesting set of five, thick white stripe between thin white stripes 275.00
Set of four, assembled, graduated sizes, thick table rings and rims, brown and white bands, slight color variation, two with hairlines, 8", 9-1/2", 10", 12" dia 247.50
Butter crock, white band and stripes, lid not orig, chips, 4-3/4" h, 7" dia 210.00
Chamber pot
    Seaweed decor, white band, ribbed handle,
      7" dia 330.00
    Seaweed decor in blue, white band, chips on base ring, hairline, 5-1/2" h, 9-1/8" w 110.00
Cup, seaweed decor in blue, white band, brown stripes, repaired handle, 3" h.. 110.00
Dog, octagonal base with incised crosshatch work, detailed face, base mkd "Geo. Diehl, Jul. 9th 1870," minor glaze flakes on base, yellow with brown running glaze, 7-5/8" h.. 4,400.00
Container, earthworm decor, white and brown stripes, flared base and rim, hairlines, chips, 4-5/8" h, 6-5/8" dia 440.00
Dish, rectangular, canted sides, 2-1/4" h, 11" l,
8" w 270.00
Hen on nest, oval base, scalloped rim, wide brown band around base, early 20th C., 2-1/4" h,
2-1/2" l... 280.00
Inkstand, bust of man in center accented with gold luster, flanked by removable covered inkwell and covered sander, small round lids with beaded band and oval wreath-like handles, oval tray, English, 19th C., 4" h, 5-1/2" w... 475.00
Jug, shoulder jug, blue sponging, one-gal 522.50
Match holder, lion motif, two chips to the holder, 5-7/8" h, oval base 7-7/8" x 4-7/8"................................. 280.00

Barrel-form yellow-ware wax-seal canning jar, one-quart, $140.

Miniature, chamber pot
  "Wild Water Sport, Pan American 1901" in freehand brown slip under the glaze, white band, in-the-making rim chip, 2" h 220.00
  White band, 2-1/4" h 100.00
Nappie, 4 embossed lines, minor in-the-making imperfection, 3-1/2" h, 14" dia 110.00
Pie plate, stains, 12" dia 198.00
Pudding mold
  Ear of corn, fluted designs around interior sides, discoloring, oval, 2-1/8" h, 5" x 7-3/8" 260.00
  Ear of corn, scalloped designs on interior sides, simple gallery-like foot, oval, 4-3/8" h, 7-3/8" x 9-1/4"
  .... 170.00
  Pear, deep bowl shape, round, ribbed sides, dark-brown glaze, roughness on rim, hairline, 4" h, 7" dia 49.50
  Rose, hairline, chips, oval, 4-5/8" h,
  7-7/8" x 9" 290.00
  Sheath of wheat, minor rim chips, 3-1/4" h,
  7-5/8" l 110.00
Rolling pin, turned maple handles, 15" l (excluding handles), 3" dia 525.00

Zoar

History: Among the separatist movements in the United States were the Zoarites. About 200 German Protestant peasants separated from the state church of Germany and settled in Zoar, Ohio, in 1817. The settlement was named after the Biblical town to which Lot fled, seeking refuge from Sodom. A seven-pointed star of Bethlehem was chosen as their emblem, and the acorn was their symbol of strength. The communistic religious society disbanded in 1898.

Baby buggy, earlier red and brown repaint, white line decor, wooden-spoke wheels, wooden undercarriage, turned spindles on sides, oil cloth folding hood with damage and restoration, 36" h, 42-1/2" l 990.00

Bookplates, watercolor, set of three, religious portraits with cutout flowers and stems, two of women with pin-prick detail, labeled "S. Catharina," "Ecce Homo" and "Imaculata Maria," framed, wear, stains, minor damage, blued between mat and backboard, 8-5/8" h, 6-5/8" w, set 440.00

Bowl, wooden, almond shape, dark patina, leather thong hanger, attributed to Zoar, 4-1/2" h, 12-5/8" x 20-1/4" 495.00

Cupboard, cherry, dovetailed case, molded base and cornice, one dovetailed drawer, door with raised panel and diamond design, wrought-iron rat-tail hinges with leaf finials, old refinish, missing feet, small base chip, lip damage on drawer, 36" h, 26-3/4" w, 14-1/4" d 3,575.00

Kas, walnut, orig dark-brown alligatored finish, black-painted detail, two raised-panel doors, bracket feet, molded base, applied trim above doors, applied diamond below removable cornice with peaked front and relief fan design, minor cornice chips, small section of side molding missing, 83" h, 56-1/2" w, 19" d 2,750.00

Roof tile, redware, tulip design, edge chips, 15-3/4" l, pr 55.00

Religious allegory, opaque gouache on paper, three interlocking circles with numbered divisions and initials, pale-blue ground, top with lamb, center shows Crucifixion and Adam and Eve, bottom has soldiers guarding the tomb, center circle has border of white roses, matted, bird's-eye maple frame, 18-5/8" h, 16-3/8" w 2,200.00

Watercolor on paper, allegorical scene in strong polychrome colors, floral swags and garlands surrounding oval with clouds and light rays around a heart with a colonnade and hill strewn with broken weapons, below is a panel with cherub's face and wings and German inscription, mahogany flame-grain veneer frame, minor stains, paper folded under at top and bottom, Zoar, Ohio, 12-1/4" h, 7-7/8" w 2,750.00

Miscellaneous

Bathtub, galvanized tin and wood, rectangular dovetailed case, zinc-lined tub with drain and place for spigots, wooden rim around top on end and both sides, designed to fit into corner of room, wear, small section of top rim missing, 60-3/8" l, 26-1/2" w 150.00

Black collectibles, chromolith cardboard black butlers, four with wooden stands, 7-3/4" h, set of nine 82.50

Book, non-fiction, *History of the Horn-Book* by Andrew W. Tuer, 1897, with three examples of writing 605.00

Bottle chest, Chippendale, mahogany, lower drawer, brass handles 7,150.00

Bread plate, earthenware, New England, relief decor of dog, ferns and flowers, minor flakes, 13-1/4" x 11" 825.00

Brush, black and light tan horsehair bristles spell "J.Q. Adams," curly maple veneer, backing has worn black stain, early campaign giveaway, edge damage, 10-1/2" l 825.00

Buggy, full-size, horse-drawn, one-seat open style, fully restored, 8'5" l, 5' w 1,100.00

Carousel figure, horse, attributed to C.W. Parker, running stance, good carved detail, restored and old polychrome repaint, edge damage, age cracks, steel reinforcing bars on legs, on modern stand and base with wheels, 57" l 660.00

Celestial globe on stand, mahogany, old finish, "J. Wilson & Sons, 1826, Albany St., N.Y.," cast-brass paw feet with castors, tapered saber legs, relief acanthus leaf carving on knees, carved petal-and-leaf column, reeded supports, molded ring at top with worn paper

zodiac label, red paint around outer ring, small cracks in globe, 35" h 11,275.00

Charger, faience, green bird in center, blue rim with green vine and red berries on border, 11" dia 77.00

Diorama of sailing ship, wood, putty, string and paint, blue homespun flag with white star, 19" h, 24" w 275.00

Hanging game rack, old red repaint, scalloped backboard, nine wrought-iron hooks, one scallop chipped, 9" h, 32-1/2" w 247.50

Horn tumbler, straight sides flaring toward top, 2-1/4" h, top 2" dia 35.00

Hourglass, poplar, orig teal, black and gold paint, turned supports, 8-5/8" h 935.00

Ice box, painted, red and tan, softwood, cutout bracket feet, metal lining, 24" h, 23" w, 18" d 412.50

Marble lamb, white, sleeping lamb with plant, two corners missing, 3-1/4" h, 7-1/2" w, 5-1/4" d 275.00

Noisemaker, wooden, lyre-shaped body, turned wood handle, two cogged wheels that click across wooden tongues to produce noise, typically used at political rallies, c. 1850-70 .... 143.00

Pen holder, softwood, from school at Waddle, Pa., rectangular board having 36 diagonal pen slots (four rows of nine), wear, ink stains, 1-3/4" h, 14" l, 5-1/2" w 45.00

Pipe case, velvet-covered box with hooked designs applied on top and sides, interior lined with satin and fitted for a pipe, wear, fading, 3-1/2" h, 7" w, 4-1/2" d 27.50

Shoemaker's tin boot patterns (tops and bottoms), mkd "S.C. Shive ... Bloomsburg, Pa.," 1847 patent date, adjustable with brass wing nut, wear, mid-19th C., pr 70.00

Smoothing board, painted and carved, orig green, red and black paint, molded edge with compass stars and chip carving, relief-carved hearts within top star, "KA.D., 1833," carved animal handle in old reddish-brown paint, old replacement head, 24" l 605.00

Birdhouse made of stones, rounded base, asbestos-shingle roof, $65.

"Instantaneous Ice Cream Freezer," 1890 patent date, $400.

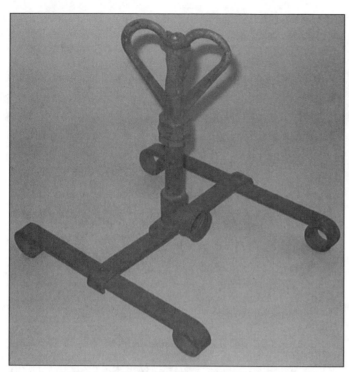

Lawn sprinkler with heart-shaped head, H-base, metal, 9-3/4" h, $150.

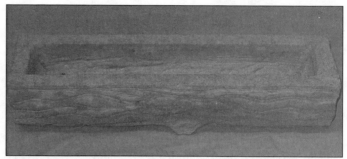

Carved-limestone planter, tree-form, 18-3/4" l, $125.

Spencerian drawing, Eagle in flight, signature card in corner in black and colored ink with glitter, "J.W. Hough, The Automatic Penman, Plain, Ohio," framed, 18" h, 23-1/4" w...110.00

Squirrel cage, painted, peaked building with chimney, cylindrical rotating cage, painted blue, red and yellow, 23" h, 27" w, 12" d..517.50

Starting cannon, late 19th C., bronze barrel, wood and steel-banded carriage, one hub pin missing, barrel 14-3/4" l, overall 27" l....................................2,760.00

Stencils, brass, one set with A-Z plus period and ampersand, 2-3/4" h, 2-1/2" w; one set with A-Z plus ampersand, 4-1/4" h, 4" w, minor wear, two sets..........60.00

Tape loom, hardwood, old slate-blue paint, red decor with initials and "1817," heart cutout in curved crest, 14-1/2" h, 9-1/2" w...2,970.00

Tinsel picture, vase of flowers in polychrome, black ground, shadowbox frame, 21" h, 17" w........... 440.00

Velocipede, child's horse and sulky, orig black and gold paint on horses, red with black on sulky, stenciled "Joy Ponies" on seat, cast-iron legs, metal-spoke wheels with worn rubber, pedal action, old cloth reins, minor wear, one rein torn, wooden handle bar replaced, 23" h, 16" w, 48" l..2,530.00

Wall bracket, gilt carved wood, oval shelf with beaded trim on carved eagle perched on rocks, American, 19th C., 16" h, 11-1/2" w, 8-3/4" d..................2,185.00

Wall pocket, wooden, dry red paint, small open compartment in base, tombstone-shaped back, applied mirror, carved candle sockets, 16-1/2" h, 9" w............. 275.00

Watering can, brass, Perry Son & Co., oval, straight sides, bands of stamped ribbing, flat top, hinged lid, arched handle, tapered tubular bent spout, 12-1/2" h, 15-1/2" l, 6" w... 75.00

Wax busts of George and Martha Washington, polychrome, framed, damage, George is loose in frame, 6-1/2" h, 5-1/2" w, pr...110.00

Whieldon platter, brown tortoise shell glaze, octagonal, oval well, raised rim, scratches, restoration, 12-1/4" x 16-3/4" 275.00

More References Guides You Can Depend On

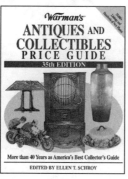

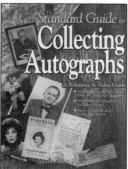

Reference Guides for Collectors